FUNDAMENTALS OF PRETRIAL LITIGATION

Third Edition

By

Roger S. Haydock
Professor of Law, William Mitchell College of Law
Member, Minnesota and Federal Bars

David F. Herr
Partner, Maslon Edelman Borman & Brand
Adjunct Professor of Law, William Mitchell College of Law

Jeffrey W. Stempel
Professor of Law, Brooklyn Law School
Member, Minnesota and Federal Bars

AMERICAN CASEBOOK SERIES®

WEST GROUP
ST. PAUL, MINN., 1994

610 Opperman Drive
P.O. Box 64526
St. Paul, MN 55164–0526
1–800–328–9352

Library of Congress Cataloging-in-Publication Data
Haydock, Roger S.
Fundamentals of pretrial litigation / by Roger S. Haydock, David F. Herr, Jeffrey W. Stempel. — 3rd ed.
p. cm. — (American casebook series)
Includes index.
ISBN 0–314–04079–X
1. Pre-trial procedure—United States. I. Herr, David F. II. Stempel, Jeffrey W. III. Title. IV. Series.
KF8900.H433 1994
347.73 ' 72—dc20
[347.30772] 94–25387
CIP

ISBN 0–314–04079–X

TEXT IS PRINTED ON 10% POST CONSUMER RECYCLED PAPER

2nd Reprint–1999

To
Marni, Marci and Jeffrey

To
Mary Kay, Ehrland and Alec

and

To
Ann, Ryan, Shanen and Reed

*

Preface

The adventure of pretrial litigation resembles most life experiences. There will be times of success, failure, joy, sorrow, excitement, weariness, confidence, fear, laughter, depression, and mirth. You will face another client!, continuing investigations?, more pleadings (phooey), endless discovery (sigh), countless motions (#$%¢&) and satisfying settlements (ahhh). This book has been designed to provide you with the knowledge, procedures, tactics, and skills to guide you through these thrills of victory and agonies of defeat.

The civil litigation process includes both pretrial procedures and trial itself. The amount of time a litigator spends in trial is minimal. The amount of time a litigator spends on pretrial matters is enormous. Pretrial litigation is the heart and soul of litigation practice and constitutes the vast universe of how most litigators spend their professional life: breathing and thinking investigation, pleading, discovery, motions, hearings, negotiations, strategies, tactics, rules, cases, procedures, research, and the law.

The conceptual and pragmatic considerations addressed in this book provide an overview and an inner view of the dynamics of the pretrial litigation process. This book is based upon the authors' experiences as practitioners and professors, the contributions of colleagues and commentators, common sense, and the law. What law? The Federal Rules of Civil Procedure and federal court decisions mixed with representative state law form the primary focus of this book. There often is, in actuality, little difference between federal rules, statutes, decisions, and the respective laws of many states. Similarity also exists between federal and state practice even in those states that have not modeled their laws after federal practice. Admittedly the courthouses are blocks or cities apart and the captions are different, but many litigation strategies and tactics are the same in both systems.

Following the amendments to the Federal Rules of Civil Procedure in 1993, much greater variation exists in federal court rules. The 1993 amendments allow individual districts to "opt out" of the rule changes or to modify the rules as they determine is best. The result is that about half of the federal districts are either not following some of the rules or are considering not following them. The new rules are discussed in this edition, but with the understanding that in some districts the changes of the new rules are just experiments being conducted in other districts, and that do not affect the local practice.

The litigation process represents one method to resolve disputes. This method needs to be placed in perspective. The end result of litigation—a trial—resolves a small percentage of disputes. Negotiated settlements resolve many, many, many more disputes. Other dispute resolving procedures—notably arbitration, conciliation, and mediation—can be more efficient and less costly than litigation. These alternative approaches to dispute resolution are covered at the end of this book. This placement does not reflect any bias in favor of or prejudice against any of these remedies, but merely reflects that this book covers the primary means our society relies upon to resolve civil disputes: the pretrial litigation process.

This process involves a sequence of events that typically occur in a reasonably patterned order. The Table of Contents of this book outlines that pattern, although this outlined sequence will not always occur in this order. A motion may be interposed instead of a pleading; discovery may follow the submission of motions. You should not presume—now having reread the Contents—that the real world reflects this precise sequence. Much of the litigation process will proceed in a set pattern: pleadings will follow research and investigation; discovery will precede motions; negotiation settlement discussions will likely resolve the case. But it should come as no surprise to you that facets of the litigation process will be as out of "order" as other facets of your life.

This book covers all facets of the pretrial litigation process. Chapter 1 presents an overview of the litigation process, including planning. Chapter 2 covers legal research and factual investigation. Chapter 3 explains pleadings. Chapter 4 addresses motions, pleadings and jurisdiction. Chapter 5 introduces the scope of discovery (and, where followed, disclosure) followed by Chapters 6, 7, 8, and 9 that deal respectively with depositions, interrogatories, requests for production and physical examinations, and requests for admissions. Chapter 10 describes the enforcement of discovery rights. Chapter 11 introduces motion practice. Chapter 12 covers a variety of pretrial motions relating to the merits. Chapter 13 explains motion presentations. Chapter 14 explains portions of settlement negotiations. Chapter 15 concludes this book with a discussion of pretrial conferences and orders. Chapter 16, which was omitted, explained how litigators, with the assistance of either the divine or the devil, created this whole process and continue to revel in its functions.

Analyzing and deciphering these chapters should explain the whys and wherefores and dos and don'ts of litigation practice. But learning about litigation also requires direct involvement in the practice of analyzing problems, planning a case, conducting an investigation, drafting pleadings, engaging in discovery, presenting motions, and resolving a dispute. These skills can be developed and refined by completing the problems and exercises that appear throughout the book.

There are two types of problems. Short, self-contained problems appear at the ends of each chapter and present a concise problem scenario. Case files of various lengths appear at the end of the book and provide factual settings for some of the exercise assignments in the chapters. In particular, the adventures of Case File A, *Hot Dog Enterprises v. Tri-Chem, Inc.*, provide a rich factual and legal background from which a number of exercises (either included in this book or created by the instructor) can result. Relevant substantive laws appear in legal memoranda included in each case file. These memos provide the basic law necessary to conduct the litigation exercises. Other or additional laws from another jurisdiction may also be applied, if necessary.

Some of the problems, particularly the discovery exercises, may require the inclusion of detailed information that does not appear in the problem or case file. Confidential information may be available through supplemental materials from your instructor. Further, you and your opponent may add such facts if it is reasonable that an attorney, witness, or client would know of such facts and would remember them. These added details must be consistent with the facts given and cannot distort or exaggerate the situations.

Fact situations have been designed and selected that mimic typical and common cases civil litigators face. Alternative fact scenarios have been provided that raise the same or similar issues in different contexts. This variety allows the reader or the instructor the option to exclude problems and exercises from coverage in a class or program.

Forms, examples, sample pleadings, discovery documents, and motions are included throughout the text and files. A caveat needs to be added to your use of these forms. They provide illustrative examples. They are not written in stone. We offer them as visual illustrations of what the litigation process looks like and to assist you in drafting your own documents. They are not perfect examples of what should be done in every case. Nor are they comprehensive. Readily available sources provide more forms than any reasonable litigator needs. These sources include West's Federal Forms, Moore's Federal Forms, and state court form books. Some of these proposed forms are unduly verbose, others needlessly formalistic. Sample documents should not be blindly copied unless the form applies directly to the specifics of the particular case involved. The examples in this book or any book need to be modified and adapted for use in each individual case.

Each chapter also contains cross-references to sources of more complete and detailed information. This does not mean that this book does not contain absolutely *everything* you need to know about litigation. Some of you, in your lonelier moments, may wish to peruse other litigation materials and articles and you can do so at your leisure. Two appendices appear at the end. Appendix A includes a set of instructions for the preparation of deponents. This "brochure" can be read by prospective deponents to better prepare them for depositions. Appendix B contains the case files previously described.

Dashes of humor appear throughout this book. These occasional comments may seem out of place to some of you, irrelevant to others, and even humorous to still others. We only encourage the last response. Sometimes we take ourselves and the practice of law too seriously (just think of law school exams and the bar examination) and an occasional guffaw, moan, or titter helps put things in perspective.

We now begin this book with the hope that you have or will discover the excitement and adventure that accompanies litigation practice. If you don't believe us, return this book (easy now). If you do, read on.

Correspondence may be sent to the authors at:

Professor Roger S. Haydock
William Mitchell College of Law
875 Summit Avenue
Saint Paul, Minnesota 55105-3030

David F. Herr, Esq.
Maslon Edelman Borman & Brand
3300 Norwest Tower
90 South Sixth Street
Minneapolis, Minnesota 55402-4140

Professor Jeffrey W. Stempel
Brooklyn Law School
250 Joralemon Street
Brooklyn, New York 11201

R.S.H.
D.F.H.
J.W.S.

May 1994

Acknowledgements

Many persons made this book a reality. No three authors write a book without the substantial support, comfort, and assistance of each other and others. Those whom we love and who love us deserve public recognition for their special place in our lives. Roger thanks Cherie, Marni, Marci, Jeffrey, Sil, Sue, and Joyce. David thanks his family, his friends, his partners, and his colleagues. Jeffrey also thanks his family and friends, especially Ann.

Several students spent many hours working with us. Research assistants, editors, and cite checkers include: Mike "No problem" Miller, Sonja "I'll work late" Peterson, Hazel "This is funny?" Hanley, Nancy "You mean what?" Quattlebaum, Kay "I can get it" Tuveson, Tim "This is ethical?" Strom, Janey "Breaktime" Gohl, Carol "Another break?" Eckersen, Deborah "I have time" Hoch, Diane "Let me edit" Dube, and Mark "Index card" Thompson.

Alberta Dowlin, Annette Friedley, Jacque Krigbaum, Lynn Bourasa, Dawn Christensen, Betty Wade, Lynnette Shanahan, and Marthanne Juvland typed, corrected, and re-typed countless drafts and helped with many of the tasks necessary to place a final manuscript into our editors' hands.

Professors John Sonsteng, Michael Steenson, William Danforth, Melvin Goldberg, Marcia Gelpe, Geoffrey C. Hazard, E. Donald Elliot, and Guido Calabresi provided invaluable assistance in the form of inspiration, ideas, criticism, and encouragement. We thank West Publishing for publishing this book. We are also indebted to Little, Brown & Company for their permission to reprint at length from our earlier books, *Discovery Practice, Discovery: Theory, Practice and Problems,* and *Motion Practice*. Those works form a substantial foundation for this book and we gratefully acknowledge the contributions made by Little, Brown and its editorial staff. We are particularly indebted to William Mitchell College of Law for the continuous and substantial support throughout this project, and to all the lawyers of Maslon Edelman Borman & Brand, and to Donald Horton and Judith Langevin, whose support and forbearance are appreciated by each of us.

The judges before whom we have appeared and for whom we have clerked have taught us much about how litigation is and should be conducted. Judges Raymond Broderick, Jonathan Lebedoff, Harold Kalina, and Susanne Sedgwick, and Judge, then Chief Justice, Douglas Amdahl have been valuable and lasting mentors and examples of how the judicial system is supposed to work.

Peter Knapp, Cindy Jesson, Stephen Patrick Doyle, Richard Corky Wharton, Ann Juergens, Eric Janus, Renee Anderson, Teri Killen, and

Julie Antonson provided us with additional ideas and encouragement for this edition.

The lawyers at Maslon Edelman Borman & Brand have provided wonderful examples of excellent lawyering and their support and forbearance is appreciated. Lynnette Shanahan and Patricia Porter provided valuable assistance.

Thanks to Dean (now Judge) David Trager, Richard Allan, Margaret Berger, Richard Farrell, Maryellen Fullerton, Ann McGinley, Jennifer Rosato, and Liz Schneider of Brooklyn Law School. Special thanks to Brooklyn clinical professors (a/k/a real lawyers) Stacy Caplow, Mary Jo Eyster, Minna Kotkin, Kathleen Sullivan, and Carrie Teitcher. Jeff's colleagues on the Committee on Federal Courts of the Association of the Bar of the City of New York have provided frequent, useful (and real-life) suggestions that have benefited this book.

Aaron Dean, Shawn Raiter, Millicent Calinog, Margaret Kane, and Michael Rowley, Ana-Maria Galeano, Mark Kornfield, Nancy London and Terri Pandolfi served as very able research assistants.

We are grateful for the widespread acceptance the first and second editions received. We were in 1985, and are in 1994, convinced that the teaching and learning of how the civil litigation process works before trial is immensely important. We are glad to see law school curriculums increasingly focus on this area. We hope this book proves memorable, enjoyable, and useful.

We further acknowledge you—who will be reading and using this book—and your decision to attend law school and to enter practice. We have written the text, problems, and exercises for you, for the clients you will represent, and for the system you serve.

Summary of Contents

*

Table of Contents

FUNDAMENTALS OF PRETRIAL LITIGATION

Third Edition

*

PART ONE
PREPARATION FOR LITIGATION

*

CHAPTER 1
LITIGATION PLANNING

Our mission is to explore the intergalactic world of Justus.

—Aboard the Starship *Enterprise*

§ 1.1 ELEMENTS OF PLANNING

§ 1.1.1 Introduction

Pretrial Litigation Practice resembles most life experiences. There will be times of success, failure, joy, weariness, excitement, fear, laughter, depression, and mirth. This book has been designed to provide you with the theories, knowledge, rules, procedures, cases, statutes, strategies, tactics, techniques, and approaches to guide you through these professional experiences.

You will learn how to analyze a case, plan and implement discovery, and present and defend motions. You will learn what to do, when to do it, where to do it, and why to do it. You will learn how to litigate effectively, efficiently, and economically.

This book explains civil litigation practice in federal and state court systems. The Federal Rules and federal court decisions mixed with representative state law of civil procedure form the primary focus of this text. There exists significant differences between federal procedural rules and state procedural rules. There also exist many similarities between federal litigation practice and state litigation practice, even in those states that have not modeled their rules after the federal rules. This book will explore common strategies and tactics, as well as dissimilar practices, in both federal and state forums.

These materials analyze and present approaches used by successful litigators. Attorneys learn from each other and adopt strategies that work for other lawyers. This text presents common approaches to litigation practices.

Each chapter describes alternative strategies and tactics. The decisions litigators make—from the drafting of the pleadings to the planning of discovery and motions—are based on analytical legal reasoning and incisive judgments. Both the theory and practice of why and how litigators effectively think and reason are analyzed. This book will assist you in making well-reasoned litigation decisions.

The psychological and emotional dimensions involved in pretrial practice are also explored throughout this book. The adversary process can become overly adversarial. The information presented in this text will significantly increase your confidence level necessary to litigate a case well.

Litigators make mistakes in every case, and problems commonly occur during pretrial practice. One of the keys to success is to not let the mistakes and problems overwhelm you. Many problems can be anticipated and many mistakes eliminated by preparation and an understanding of available solutions explained in this book.

Ethical issues arise during pretrial practice. A major premise of this book is that litigators must hold themselves to high ethical standards. An understanding of professional rules and values assists you in identifying ethical concerns and resolving problems.

The legal profession is a helping profession. Litigators, like all lawyers, have the privilege and responsibility to help their clients. This humanistic view of advocacy shapes and influences the work of the litigator. The situations and problems printed in this book involve and affect the lives of clients, lawyers, and other people. You need to bring to life what you read so you can partially experience this human dimension of litigation.

The litigation system represents one way to resolve disputes. This method needs to be placed in perspective. The end result of litigation—a trial—resolves a small percentage of disputes. Negotiated settlements resolve many, many, many more disputes. Other dispute resolving procedures—most notably mediation and arbitration—can be more efficient and less costly than litigation. These alternative approaches to dispute resolution are presented throughout this book and need to be kept in mind as viable and effective ways to resolve disputes.

§ 1.1.2 The Litigation Process

This book covers the primary means our society relies upon to resolve civil disputes: the pretrial litigation process. This process involves a sequence of events that typically occur in a reasonably patterned order. The table of contents of this book outlines that pattern. Much of the litigation process proceeds in a sequence: pleadings follow research and investigation; discovery precedes dispositive motions; settlement discussions may then resolve the case. This sequence does not always, or even often, occur in this order. You should not presume—now having reread the table of contents—that the real world always reflects this precise pattern. What should come as no surprise to you is that facets of the litigation process are as out of "order" as other facets of your life.

As you read and digest these materials you will become knowledgeable, informed, surprised, curious, pleased, and shocked. Not everything in the practical and theoretical world of litigation will conform to your experience and expectations and your notions of the legal profession, the adversary process, and our system of justice. This book presents a variety of alternative approaches, strategies, tactics, and techniques based upon rules of law and ethics that are employed in the real world. We present both the ways things are and the way things could or should be. Your task, in part, is to make these ways coalesce.

There is no one way to "practice" litigation. Those of you still questing for dogma and natural law should reconsider your vocation and avocation. The bulk of litigation decisions involve judgmental and strategic decisions about which road to take: to the right or to the left or on the road less traveled. Yes, there are some mechanical black and white rules (you have to serve a complaint with a summons). Sure there are some commonly accepted tactical approaches (do not wear a clown outfit to court). But litigation practice requires the lawyer repeatedly to exercise discretion and make decisions based upon professional opinion and judgment.

This chapter focuses on this phenomenon and the various objective and subjective factors that underlie the litigation decision making process. We need to understand the dynamics and nuances that shape and influence the process before we take a conceptual and pragmatic trip through the litigation planning world. Various factors influence litigation decisions. The law school notion that the legally correct answer to a bluebook exam question is also the best answer to a client's situation needs to be placed in perspective. The theoretical impact of applicable legal precedents is only one aspect of litigation. The following sections describe the more common influences that affect litigation decisions: the law and the facts, the role of the litigator, the adversary system, the client, and games.

§ 1.1.3 The Law and the Facts

Knowledge of the Law. You knew before your first law school class that knowledge of the law is of paramount importance in representing a client. But not all legal minds have been created equal. Over estimating our legal knowledge or the unassailability of our litigation positions is perhaps the greatest danger. The willingness to admit doubt (at least to our allies) and a commitment to thorough legal research are indicia of a strong legal mind, not a weak one.

Standards of Excellence. Differences of opinion among judges and lawyers regarding the competency of lawyers reflect different professional standards. What is superior work for one lawyer is unacceptable to a judge. What is superlative work from one attorney's perspective is average work from the view of another litigator. There is more uniformity of opinion regarding incompetent work because of the development of malpractice standards and ethical guidelines. What is or is not excellent work depends more upon internal standards of excellence developed by individual lawyers.

Accountability for Excellence. All lawyers have their own internal set of professional and personal standards which guide their conduct. Unfortunately, these standards are not sufficient and external restraints may be necessary to prompt some lawyers to do their very best. Current external restraints establish minimal legal competency standards and do not establish high standards of excellence, allowing for sloppy lawyering in some cases.

Perceptions of Excellence. Lawyers do not wake up one morning and either in unison or individually say: "Well, today I feel like doing less than excellent work. In fact, I may try to scrape along as close to the line of minimal competency as possible." We believe that we at least do good work and try to do very good (if not excellent) work. Our perceptions of quality may affect the way we gauge the quality of our work, and our perceptions will be affected by our ability to engage in rationalization.

Litigation Rationalizations. All too often rationalizing becomes a substitute for thinking, analyzing, and doing what should be thought, analyzed, and done. Rationalization can become as much a part of the litigation process as it is part of everyday life. Have you ever tried to go a whole day without one solid rationalization? This phenomenon allows litigators to accept less than excellent work as acceptable work.

Familiarity With the Facts. Probably at that treasured moment in your professional training when you discovered the importance of the law you realized that a lawyer needs to know the facts in order to properly do his or her professional thing. The difficulty in becoming familiar with litigation facts is that the facts are not presented in a nice, neat package as they are in an appellate decision. A litigator has to collect and discover them, to create and interpret them, and to make sense out of information that is in disarray. This can be as difficult as finding a fact in the National Enquirer.

§ 1.1.4 The Role of the Litigator

Extra-Legal Considerations. The success or failure of a litigation effort depends upon applicable legal precedents and extra-legal factors. The litigator must not only be a lawyer but must also be a counselor, a motivator, a negotiator, and a host of other characters at different stages. The ability of a litigator to be more than just a lawyer will influence whether a case is won or lost. This phenomenon explains why some law graduates from the bottom half of the class own more condos than some top ten percent grads.

Various Roles. Lawyers view their roles in the litigation process differently. The same attorney will often view his or her role differently at various stages of a case. One attorney may focus on championing the client's cause; another may be concerned with obtaining a fair and just result for the client and the other side; still another wants to make as much money as possible in legal fees. These and other viewpoints influence how the litigation proceeds.

Litigation Role Models. To our knowledge all litigators did or do have a mother and father, although that is sometimes hard to believe. From their birth through law school and into practice lawyers model their litigation efforts after others. These role models may be a pedigree or a mixture of professionals who have influenced their professional life. Colleagues, opposing lawyers, judges, professors, and others shape how a litigator thinks. Role modeling can be an effective way of cloning effective litigators, assuming the role models are effective litigators. A reason why some lawyers do some curious things during litigation is because they have seen it done that way before by someone they consider effective. It is critical that litigators review the reasons for why they do things so that they do not unconsciously adopt poor techniques.

Litigator Personalities. The personality of litigators will shape their view of the role of the litigator. An attorney with a naturally aggressive personality may be that much more aggressive in the already competitive world of litigation. A lawyer with a naturally cooperative approach may be more conciliatory during litigation. The predisposition of a lawyer may help at some stages and be a hindrance at others. A litigator needs to remain aware of his or her dominant personality characteristics and control or use them effectively.

Cooperative Approaches. Modern litigation practice encourages lawyers to be friends. The tenor and purpose of the current rules openly promote, support, cajole and push attorneys into establishing a cooperative relationship. New federal rules and some state court rules often mandate that the attorneys actually talk to each other about bartering discovery information or compromising motion relief. These approaches are the clear preference of those who ordain litigation regulations and of the majority of lawyers who implement them.

Informal Exchange and Resolutions. In many cases it takes only a 7–digit number or the cost of a postage stamp to obtain basic factual information or to resolve a procedural dispute with an opposing lawyer. The approach taken by the litigators will determine the usefulness and success of informal telephone and letter communications.

The Litigator as Moralist. Ethical standards vary among lawyers. There are some guidelines to suggest what litigators can or should do or not do. But not many guidelines. Further, many of the ethical standards are broad prescriptions which when applied to a situation provide little ethical relief. It is up to litigators to decide what levels of litigation morality will guide their practice. Those decisions cut across a range of legally moral behavior. The situational ethical litigator may be more "flexible" than a fundamentalist litigator. Some litigators will not even consider a popular litigation approach they perceive to be questionable.

Watching Sunday morning television may or may not assist us in fashioning ethical standards.

§ 1.1.5 The Adversary System

Lawyer Control. The present litigation system places the initiation, use, and response to pleadings, discovery, and motions largely in the control of the lawyers. Litigators can do what they want, within reason and within the parameters of the applicable procedural law. Judges are there primarily to enforce discovery methods and to resolve motions if the attorneys are unable to conciliate their differences by mutual stipulation.

Stipulation Power. Litigators have in many situations unfettered discretion to modify, change, alter, tinker with, or transubstantiate many rules of procedure, by themselves, without resort to a court order or an oracle.[1] Litigators need only agree and their stipulation becomes the governing regulation. Judges encourage the use of this power.

Cooperative Approach. Recent revisions to federal and state rules of civil procedure require and encourage lawyers to disclose information, to attempt to resolve problems and disputes on their own, and to make reasonable efforts to cooperate with each other. These changes reflect a recognition that the prior litigation rules wasted money, caused unnecessary delays, and allowed abuses to flourish. Modern rules of civil procedure are attempting to return the litigation system to what it was supposed to be: an efficient, economic, and effective way for parties to have their dispute resolved.

Judicial Assistance. Recent changes in rules of procedure have also attempted to change the role of judges in pretrial proceedings. "Meet and confer" rules require lawyers to discuss pleading issues, agree on discovery requests and responses, and resolve motion disputes. These rules also require or encourage attorneys to submit to judges mutually agreeable schedules regarding discovery and motions. Judges now clearly have the responsibility and ability to assist attorneys early in a case and issue scheduling and conference orders. To facilitate the progress of a case.

The Litigator as Law Maker. Not all law is made by justices or legislators. Lawyers "make" law when they decide not to do something. A litigator's actions (serving a pleading, a discovery request, or a motion) will be controlled, in part, by the external restraints of the governing law. A litigator may refrain from action based on interpretation of the governing law. This internal interpretation makes the litigator a lawmaker for purposes of that one decision and case. The litigator who says, "This cannot be done because the law prohibits it" in effect has become a judge who has decided that issue in the case. That decision may be the correct and proper one but it is the litigator and not an

§ 1.1

1. *See, e.g.,* Fed.R.Civ.P. 29, discussed in § 5.11, *infra.*

actual judge who has resolved the matter. Differences in interpretation by different litigators of the status of the governing law explain, in part, why some litigators will not act in some situations and others will.

Litigation Theory. Every legal rule, case, and statute has its own theories supporting its existence or reasoning. A litigator must be aware of the philosophy that underlies the litigation process in order to properly interpret and apply the law. An attorney must understand why the rules exist, how the caselaw developed, and how the statutes evolved in addition to knowing how the law applies. A litigator must be a legal philosopher as well as a legal scientist and artist.

Judicial Differences. Anyone who knows of two federal or state judges who have an identical approach to the litigation process should first call the authors (collect) and then call Ripley's Believe It or Not. Different judges, even in the same district or county, have varying approaches to litigation requests. How they view the role of litigation within the adversary system affects their decisions.

The Adversary System. "One that contends with, opposes, or resists: the enemy." That is a dictionary adversary. The nature and extent of that contention, opposition, and resistance will vary from attorney to attorney and from case to case. Nonetheless the litigation process (which encourages some cooperation) often occurs in the midst of a battle within a war (with "enemies" in some cases). Resolving that confrontation can be achieved with the ease of putting a parallelogram peg into a hexagonal hole.

Partisan Differences. Attorneys on opposite sides of the case are partisan and naturally tend to interpret the law differently. This is due in large measure to the demonstrable truth that statutes, cases, and rules can be read from left to right and can be interpreted from right to left, particularly when applied to cases involving two or more varied stories.

Varying Factual Stories. "He was rollerskating at least 63 miles an hour." "No, it was a she, and she was skateboarding about 24.5 kilometers per minute." Differing accounts, varying perspectives, conflicting interests, slanted perceptions, defective memories, and different people result in varying stories. Having different lawyers representing divergent viewpoints inevitably leads to differing views regarding what happened and what should be done.

§ 1.1.6 The Client

The Best Interests of the Client. What the client wants, what the client needs, and what interests the client has: these and other factors influence the progress of a case. The client's choice of available legal options affects what an attorney can or cannot do during litigation.

Client Financial Resources. Economic restraints affect most litigation decisions. Whether a client can afford to pay the costs and fees of litigation often determine what approach the attorney may take. Attorneys with clients can dream about litigation strategies. But only attorneys with clients with sufficient money and resources can litigate. Litigation can be expensive, precluding pursuit of perfectly valid and correct legal strategies. A client may forgo a deposition or motion because of a lack of funds. Part of the task of the litigator is to conduct the litigation within the financial means of the client.

The reverse financial problem may arise when a client has extensive financial resources and the other party does not. Part of the litigation strategy may be to take advantage of this economic superiority and force the poorer party into further poverty. The ethical considerations involved in this tactic are addressed later in the book.

Client Participation. The extent to which a client participates in the litigation process may affect decisions made. Clients know what is best for them and what they can or cannot afford, usually. Litigators know what litigation tactics and techniques will be the most effective, usually. The extent to which a client participates during litigation depends upon the litigator's approach to client counseling and the type of case. Lawyers vary in their approach to client counseling. Some cases will be more appropriate for constant client involvement.

The Stake. What is the case worth? How important are the issues? What value do the client and attorney place on the case? How effective are the available remedies? Does the potential recovery or remedy justify a litigation decision?

Time. Sometimes there is insufficient time to conduct timely litigation. Remedies may be beyond reach, discovery may be unavailable, and motions may need to be delayed, because of varying timing considerations. Litigators cannot control time; if we could then we would be certain that cosmic forces are on our side and not on the side of the allegedly better-paid corporate lawyers.

§ 1.1.7 What, a Game?

Playing Games. A tactic used by some lawyers with alarming skill, gaming is designed to undercut the purpose and effectiveness of litigation by playing games with the process. Sometimes it is totally ignoring litigation correspondence; other times it is the inane assertion of laughable claims or frivolous defenses; other times it is incomplete or self-serving responses to discovery requests; and still other times it is the misuse of motions and hearings. Subgames include "Name that Claim," in which a defense lawyer must guess what the allegations of the complaint allege; "Wallpapering," in which a truckload of discovery requests or responses are delivered to the opposing lawyer in sufficient quantity to wallpaper a skyscraper; and "Motion Feud," in which law firms vie for prizes for being the most obnoxious, noxious, and just oxious.

Changing the Rules of the Game. Recent changes in federal and state rules of procedure are changing the rules of these games. New procedural rules explicitly prohibit abusive discovery of games and specifically regulate lawyer conduct further reducing the opportunities for lawyers to be gamers. Further, rule changes empower judges with the authority to enforce sanctions against lawyers who play games. These efforts and a growing recognition by lawyers, judges, and the public that our litigation system should be free of game playing reduces the frequency of these games.

"Oh, My Goodness." Many cases have a bit of information that if disclosed to the other side causes the disclosing lawyer to say silently, "Oh, my goodness." This harmful information weakens the case for the disclosing lawyer and it would be better if the other side and the world did not know this information. No one said life was going to be perfect, or even fair. The creative litigator places this information in perspective by reducing its harmful nature or by drawing from it reasonable and helpful inferences.

Lawyer Inaction. Sometimes lawyers don't do something because they don't know what to do or how to do it. This inaction results from a lack of even moderate competence, or a lack of sufficient confidence, or a lack of adequate experience. What we know or don't know about litigation practice clearly influences our approach to litigation. We all want to avoid the knots in our stomach, the weakening of our knees, the sweat in our palms, the shudder of our body, the quivering of our voice, and the whisper in our ear: "What have you just done? Why didn't you go to dental school?" The same afflictions that ravage lawyers ravage law students. None of us talks about this phenomenon often enough during lunch (unless it happens to someone else we don't like all that much) or about what effect it has on a case, and there is precious little in the legal literature. We all know that we should be naturally afraid of snakes and spiders. Many of us have a difficult time admitting we are afraid of the legal unknown. But we have all experienced this phenomenon and know the toll it has taken and takes on our judgments. Lawyers are able to reduce the impact of these fears through experience and charging fees. Law students are able to overcome these feelings by outpreparing the other side, by relying on their natural interest and enthusiasm to carry them through, and by resorting to the power generated by the competitive genes that initially caused them to enter law school.

§ 1.2 LITIGATION PLANNING

The process of making litigation judgments is another way of saying that the lawyer must "think like a litigator." This process of "thinking like a lawyer" may be more than just a convenient rationalization for law school or a preoccupation with law professors. Many effective litigators think in a systematic way. It is this systematic way that we want to explore in the remainder of this chapter.

It appears that successful litigators are also effective planners and creative problem solvers and understand how to analyze situations. It also helps, of course, if they have all the law and the facts on their side. There is usually little litigators can do to change the law (unless they can create jurisdictional firmament) or the facts (whatever happened to rent-a-witness?) but litigators can improve their abilities to plan, problem solve, analyze and reason.

Litigators must plan in order to be effective. Litigation is difficult enough without doing it in a haphazard and disorganized manner. Litigation planning consists of an organized, structured approach to case preparation. The factors that need to be considered in planning litigation include:

- Assessing the client's needs and interests.
- Identifying potential claims and defenses.
- Researching the elements of claims and defenses.
- Reviewing possible sources of information.
- Planning informal discovery approaches.
- Determining what information should be affirmatively disclosed to other parties and what information must be disclosed voluntarily under applicable rules.
- Planning document production requests, depositions, interrogatories, request for admissions, physical/mental examinations, and other discovery requests.
- Reviewing available litigation strategies, tactics, and techniques.
- Determining what procedural remedies and relief may be sought during litigation.
- Planning motions seeking such relief.
- Creating a time table for pleadings, discovery, motions, and other discovery phases.

This process needs to be reviewed and updated periodically as a case progresses. It is critical to develop an overall strategic plan initially in the case even if it will be significantly revised as the case progresses. A litigator's judgment about strategies and tactics needs to be based on an overall view of the case and not merely on reactions to individual or isolated situations.

A thorough planning process consists of a number of factors:

ASSESSING NEEDS

Determining What the Client Wants and Realistic Legal Remedies. A client may seek legal advice for any number of purposes. A litigation remedy may or may not be appropriate. Just like the surgeon may be eager to spend more time in the operating room, the litigator may be inclined to spend more time in the courtroom. What the client wants and what the client needs must be determined in order to decide what is legally available. Not all client problems may be resolvable through a legal remedy. The first stage of planning is deciding who wants what and what is available. Mediation may trump litigation.

ASSESSING APPLICABLE LAW

Reviewing the Law. The applicable law significantly affects the planning process. The law supporting a claim or defense is found wherever laws are found: in statutes, case law, constitutional provisions, and rules and regulations. A litigator needs to thoroughly research the substantive law of a jurisdiction to determine what law applies.

Creating the Law. A litigator faced with a situation for which no current legal doctrine provides a remedy may need to create a legal theory or remedy. The litigator may have to develop a good faith argument expanding existing law. Sometimes this process occurs in an evolutionary way in small increments. Occasionally, it occurs in a revolutionary way with a big bang.

ASSESSING FACTS

Gathering Facts. The process of gathering information for litigation occupies much of a litigator's time. Supportive facts need to be sought; corroborative information needs to be documented; documents need to be preserved; impeachment material needs to be identified.

Creating Facts. A litigation planner must not only collect facts but may also need to "create" facts during the investigation and discovery process. During the gathering of information, the litigator can shape and mold the information that is collected. These opportunities allow the litigator to create a set of facts that support the client's position and contradict the opponent's claims or defenses.

Identifying the Legal and Factual Issues. The gathering of the facts and the assessment of the law permits the litigator to identify the factual and legal issues relevant to the case. If the issues are multiple they need to be narrowed to those most relevant. Sometimes the distinction between legal and factual issues becomes blurred and often an issue may be stated in terms of legal and factual propositions.

ASSESSING AVAILABLE THEORIES

Developing a Legal Theory. A case without a legal theory is like a lawyer with no real sense of humor. Both will eventually lose. A legal theory consists of the elements of a claim or defense supported by the facts of the case. Legal theories are based on existing law or a good faith argument extending, modifying, or attempting to change existing law. Many legal theories are well recognized and accepted, such as a breach of contract theory for failure to perform an obligation under a written contract. Other legal theories may be proposed by an attorney to advance a claim or defense that expands existing law, such as a breach of an implied covenant of good faith and fair dealing in an oral employment contract.

Selecting Theories. At the beginning of the case a number of alternative claims and defenses may appear to be applicable. As the case develops, the legal theories supporting these claims and defenses need to be reviewed to determine their continuing usefulness and applicability. A litigator should attempt to reduce legal theories to the fewest possible, unless a case by its nature involves numerous legitimate theories. The assertion of too many claims and defenses may confuse the judge and jury, as well as the attorneys and cause them much misunderstanding and grief.

Composing a Theory. Words and phrases need to be chosen which portray the theory in the fairest description that is possible. An effective theory of the case should be phrased so that it is understandable, persuasive, comprehensive, and compelling. An effectively phrased theory is expressed in a theme that consists of simple, declarative sentences.

Maintaining an Objective Viewpoint. It is easy for the litigator as a partisan in the adversary process to view issues and theories from a slanted, or biased perspective. It is important for the litigator to maintain a balanced and objective perspective in assessing a case.

Weighing Strengths and Weaknesses. Every case has its strong points and weak points. We recognize that reality every morning when we view ourselves in the mirror. Thorough planning requires a complete assessment of the strengths and weaknesses of both sides of a case.

DEVELOPING THE PLAN

Composing a Tentative Plan. At some point, lawyers need a tentative plan. Sports litigators call them game plans; religious litigators call them God's plan. Whatever name or process employed, whether reduced to writing or emblazoned in the mind, this plan should delineate how the litigator anticipates obtaining what the client needs.

Revising the Plan. Little in the litigation process is static. One component affects another. The discovery of one fact may strengthen or weaken the applicability of a legal proposition. A recent judicial opinion may force a change in the results available to a client. The planning process requires the litigator to constantly and continually reassess its various components.

Seeking Planning Advice. An effective technique to assist with the planning process is to describe a proposed plan to a colleague. If the colleague laughs at the suggested approach, you may want to reconsider your position. If the colleague looks extraordinarily perplexed you may want to update your resume. If the colleague seems to understand your explanation or offers alternative ideas you may be on the right track.

Considering the Case From Other Perspectives. An effective way to plan is to review the proposed plan from the perspective of the opposing lawyer. What are the best theories, issues, and arguments of the other side? How do these factors affect the plan? Have they been taken into consideration? A similar technique is to view the plan from the perspective of the judge. Does the plan make legal sense? Are the most persuasive arguments advanced? What theories or issues have been overlooked?

MAKING PREDICTIONS

Making Predictions. Deciding what to do requires a litigator to predict the future. It helps to be naturally clairvoyant, but law school and law practice provide lawyers with extra sensory legal abilities. The accuracy and reliability of the litigator's abilities to predict what the other side, opposing lawyer, and judge will do affects the likelihood of planning success.

Predicting Time. Planning a case includes a prediction regarding how the case will proceed and how much time it will take. These reasonable estimates need to be made early on in the case in order to counsel a client initially regarding alternatives and to prepare an overall litigation plan. A litigator needs to make a reasonable estimate regarding the number of hours each of the major facets of the case may take. For example:

Factual Legal Investigation	12 hours
Drafting and Responding to Pleadings	8 hours
Discovery Requests, Disclosure, and Responses	45 hours
Motion Documents, Briefs, and Hearings	35 hours
Pretrial Preparation	30 hours
Trial	15 hours

Predicting Costs. A litigator also needs to determine how much the case may cost a client. The attorney can provide the client with a reasonable financial prediction and explain that unanticipated events may decrease or increase the estimate. The major financial cost for a client is attorney's fees. To provide a client with an estimate, an attorney who is being paid an hourly fee can multiply the estimated number of hours the case may take times the hourly fee. An attorney being paid on a contingency fee will need to subtract from the potential recovery the fees and costs. Another source of expenses includes litigation costs. These costs commonly include filing fees, service fees, deposition court reporter fees and transcript costs, and expert witness expenses.

Courts establish the amount of the filing fees which range from $30 to over $100 for the commencement of a law suit including the filing of pleadings. Ordinarily, there is no additional fee for filing discovery and motion documents after the initial filing fee. The amount of the service fee depends upon the type of process used. The federal rules and many states rules encourage the use of mail service, substantially reducing service costs. A plaintiff in a federal case who attempts to use mail service significantly reduces service costs. A defendant in a federal case who accepts service by mail receives an extra 30 days to answer the complaint and avoids having to pay personal service costs. Personal service costs include mileage and a fee or hourly rate established by law enforcement offices or private process servers who serve such documents.

The cost of court reporters for depositions varies widely. Reporters typically charge an hourly rate for their appearance at a deposition and a charge per page for each page of deposition transcript prepared. For example, a court reporter may charge $85 to attend a half day deposition and a $1.50 per deposition transcript page.

Expert witness fees may vary widely in amount. The type of expert, how many experts there are in an area, the expert's years of experience, and other factors determine the market rate for an expert witness. Most experts charge an hourly rate for their assistance, with some charging a set fee, and others charging a combination of a set fee and an hourly rate. The cost of an expert may range from as little as a hundred to several thousand dollars in a case.

IMPLEMENTING THE PLAN

Preparing a Litigation File. The organization of a case includes the creation of a file. The divisions or folders of a file typically consist of the following:

- A client folder, including information, the written fee retainer, and letters.
- A correspondence folder, including letters to and from opposing counsel, affidavits of service, and cover letters to the court.
- A chronological index, including a listing of all pleadings and discovery and motion documents in the order in which they were served, received, or filed.
- A pleading folder, including—surprise—all pleadings.
- An investigation folder, including memos and notes of investigative efforts.
- A disclosure folder, including information which a party must disclose or wishes to disclose to the other side without the need for discovery request.
- A discovery folder, including interrogatories, answers to interrogatories, requests for production of documents, deposition notices, requests for admissions, and responses to requests for admissions.
- A document folder, including copies of the documents made available to the other side.
- A document production folder, including a copy of all documents received from the other side.
- An "other" documents folder, including all other relevant documents.

- Deposition summaries, including a summary outline and digest of each deposition transcript. (The transcripts, because of their bulk, are usually retained in a separate division).
- A motion folder, including all motions, affidavits, briefs, and other supporting documents.
- An order folder, including all court orders issued in a case.
- A research folder, including all legal research conducted in a case and draft memos.
- A notes/ideas folder, including notes about the theory of the case and other miscellaneous materials.
- A settlement folder, including copies of demands, offers, offers of judgment, and ideas regarding settlement.
- A celebration folder, including restaurant reviews about where to eat during the litigation and travel brochures on where to go after the victory.

There are, of course, other ways to organize a file. For example all pleadings, discovery, and motion documents can be retained in chronological order in sequential files. Whatever system is used depends upon the attorney's organizational preference.

Organizing the Law Firm. Life can be difficult for the organizationally impaired. Every law firm needs to conduct litigation in an organized way. One-person law firms need not spend much time in meetings no one else attends. Multiple-lawyer law firms may employ a team approach to litigation with team members having specific responsibilities for particular tasks and meeting periodically to reassess the case and review each other's work.

Catching Up on Your Sleep. This planning process sounds like it could get exhausting.

These components have not been presented in any special sequence. Which comes first is something akin to the turkey and egg question. The process begins during the initial client interview and continues throughout litigation. As the case progresses, informal analysis becomes more formal. The goal remains the same throughout this process: What are the most favorable legal doctrines supported by the most persuasive facts that meet the client's goals?

§ 1.3 CREATIVE PLANNING

Litigators face many problems and need to be adept at resolving them. Creativity is one of the keys to the kingdom of effective problem solving. It is easy to say "be creative," it is another thing to provide specific suggestions on how to be creative. Creative approaches are readily recognizable and obvious after the fact. You need only look at a Disney cartoon or watch a Spielberg film to recognize creativity. Much of the creative process stems from innate talent. Some lawyers are naturally more creative than others. If you are not terribly creative then it makes ultimate sense to practice with someone who is. Otherwise, you can make yourself more creative by mimicking what it appears that creative individuals do and think. The following suggestions parallel some creative thinking patterns that creative individuals follow.

Brainstorm. Allowing the imagination to run wild may produce some creative ideas. This process can be difficult, especially in a group, because of fear that a proposed idea as well as its originator will be considered bizarre, naive, or just plain wacko. It often requires courage and the willingness to be laughed at to discover a truly creative solution. Brainstorm ideas should not be evaluated until brainstorming has been exhausted.

Broaden the Problem or Issue. Focusing on the specifics and details of a problem may reduce the vision necessary to see beyond the problem. Defining the problem or redefining the issues in broader terms may produce an innovative idea. The decision to bring a Rule 12 motion to dismiss may overlook the alternative of delaying such a motion and later bringing a summary judgment motion instead.

Narrow the Focus of the Inquiry. Considering broad and far ranging alternatives may result in abstract or unrealistic solutions. In some situations narrowing a broad inquiry is as effective as broadening a narrow inquiry in other situations.

Recognize the Significance of Not–so–Obvious Notions. Any litigator can recognize the obvious solutions. Discovering the less than obvious poses a challenge. It takes no great shakes to serve requests for admissions in a case. It does take some ingenuity to consider serving requests for admissions with a pleading to force the other side into admitting or denying certain information early in the process and then subsequently consider serving interrogatories requiring the other party to explain some of the requests for admissions denied.

Modify Assumptions and Positions. Doing something based solely on habit can squelch creative impulses. Reviewing assumptions and reexamining positions can liberate creative insights.

Formulate New Courses of Action. Set patterns and established systems may result in efficient procedures but also restrict alternative courses of action. For example, discovery schedules should be tailored to specific exigencies of a case.

Be Flexible. A proposed solution to a problem may initially appear appropriate but may need to be reexamined when implemented. The litigator needs to be flexible. The degree of flexibility is usually in direct proportion to the degree of rigidity supporting the initial solution. There is a time to be firm and persistent, even stubborn, but not during creative thinking.

Alter the Goals of the Litigation. Often a reasonable and workable solution cannot be achieved because what the client or attorney wants is not reasonable or workable. These goals may need to be reviewed to determine if the ends sought can or cannot be reached by any conceivable means.

Visualize the Problem. Sometimes the litigator gets caught up with concepts or words and loses the overall perspective of a problem. Viewing the problem in images may trigger new responses. How to approach a witness or present complex evidence may come easier if the litigator visualizes talking to the witness or handling the evidence.

Believe in Your Own Ideas. It is possible that you have thought of an idea previously unthought of by any other human or lawyer. It is much more likely, however, that you have only reinvented a small part of the wheel and that some other attorney has thought of the same idea in some other case, which may have been settled or unpublished. This realization—that this idea has been thought of and probably used before—may make it easier for you to seriously consider it and implement it.

Take a Break. Thinking too long and hard may block the development of fresh ideas. That's why most of us did not attend all our law school classes. Taking a break from thinking about the problem may later result in an idea when the litigator returns to analyze the problem.

Seek Advice. A third person may be able to offer fresh insights. Sometimes the litigator gets too close or involved in a problem and loses perspective. A colleague or friend may be a source to resolve a dilemma.

§ 1.4 FACTUAL ANALYSIS AND DEVELOPMENT

The process of obtaining information requires an understanding of the various types of information involved in litigation. The evidentiary concepts of direct evidence (I saw Bowie knife the plaintiff) and circumstantial evidence (I saw Bowie holding a knife standing over the body of the plaintiff) constitute two broad categories. Other sub-categories exist which provide a conceptual framework necessary to properly analyze the facts of a case. These sub-categories include:

INFORMATION

Existing Information About an Event. The initial information a litigator learns about a situation usually includes information which explains the details of the event. This information exists and the task of the litigator is to document and develop it.

Affirmative Information. Obviously, information that supports the story of a client must be discovered.

Negative Information. Less obviously, perhaps, information that negates the story of a client must also be sought. The primary reasons are twofold. First, it is necessary for the lawyer to know everything that happened; and second, it is essential that a lawyer learn the weaknesses of a case.

Potential Information About an Event. The initial stages of litigation also involve the development of information that may exist. The task of the lawyer is to discover what might have happened, what might have caused what happened, and other what might haves.

Information Supportive of the Opponent's Story. A complete investigation includes learning as much as possible about the supportive information available to the opponent.

Rebuttal Information. Information that disproves, contradicts, denies, clarifies, or negates the position of the other side also needs to be uncovered.

Non–Information. What did not occur, what someone did not say or do, what was not written down, these and other types of non-existent information will help prove or disprove a fact.

TYPE OF INFORMATION

Corroborative Information. A litigator needs to know the various sources of information. There may be more than one eyewitness to an event; a document may contain duplicate information. Corroborative sources strengthen both the quantity and quality of the information.

Before and After Information. What happened before and after an event often supports or negates a story. The event itself is only one aspect of the overall story. It is critical for a litigator to learn the events that precede and follow the main event.

Explanatory Information. Why something happened or why someone said or did something also comprises essential information. The factors that caused an event or the motives that influenced a person must be investigated.

Inferential Information. Some information will initially appear worthless because it has no direct impact proving or disproving an event. Information from which inferences may be drawn may tend to prove or disprove an event and can be linked with other information to form a supportive conclusion.

Opinion Information. The opinions of lay persons are commonly present in most every case. The opinions of experts are necessary in many cases. These opinions, often inseparably intertwined with the facts, need to be reviewed in the same way facts are assessed.

Information About Emotions and Feelings. What a person emotes or feels often reveals something of value in a case. These responses, whether normal or extreme, may lead to useful factual information.

WEIGHING THE INFORMATION

Credibility and Authenticity Information. Why a person should be believed or why a document is what it purports to be needs to be assessed. These factors are discussed later in this section.

The search for this information is an ongoing process throughout litigation. In the initial stages, the elements of legal claims and defenses are converted to factual terms. As the case progresses, alternative factual hypotheses are explored. At the trial, a story is presented. The evidence presented at trial should not unduly influence the development of the facts of a case. Whether information is admissable or inadmissable or is based on personal knowledge or is hearsay becomes critical at time of the trial. Information may then be admissable because it is proper opinion evidence or because there exists a rule permitting hearsay statements. The persuasive value of information and the weight it will have in a trial are important factors in developing a case but should not inhibit the development and analysis of facts.

§ 1.5 CREDIBILITY ANALYSIS

The manner in which the information is made available to a fact finder is often as important as the content of that information. Factors that influence the weight afforded a story, witness, or document include:

THE STORY

Is it Plausible? A story has to be reasonable. If facets of the story sound or appear unreasonable it loses its persuasive impact. A plaintiff who claims to have been rear-ended by a car driven by the defendant will tell a plausible story unless the plaintiff claims the driver was the Abominable Snowperson.

Is it Consistent? Is the story internally consistent? Does the story of the witness make chronological sense? The plaintiff who claims she was driving to Katmandu from Peoria when the accident occurred may not spin a credible story. Is the story externally consistent? Does corroborating evidence support the story? Unless the plaintiff can produce the Snowperson's drivers license, with a photograph, victory may be out of reach.

Is There Sufficient Detail? A story must contain those details a reasonable person would have perceived and remembered. The lack of sufficient details will reduce the believability of a story. The plaintiff who does not know whether the Snowperson wore sunglasses, or a fake fur, or snowmobile boots, has missed some critical details.

THE WITNESS

What is the Source of Knowledge? Does the witness have personal knowledge? First hand information? Did the witnesses learn what happened from another source? Did someone else tell them? Did they read it?

What did the Witness Perceive? Were the circumstances such that it is reasonable for the witness to have seen or heard what is claimed? What was the physical setting like? What was the witness doing?

What was the Physical/Mental Condition of the Witness? Was the witness alert? Attentive? Distracted? What?

What does the Witness Recall? Does the witness recall what a reasonable person would remember? Does the witness only recall helpful information and forget harmful information?

How Does the Witness Communicate? How does the witness sound? Credible? What is the demeanor of the witness? Incredible?

What Motivation Does the Witness Have? Why was the witness at the event? Why will they testify?

Does the Witness have Any Bias or Prejudice? Does the witness favor one party? Why? Does the witness dislike one party? Why?

What is the Status of the Witness? Is the witness likely to be believed by a jury of peers or by a judge?

Has the Witness Made Any Prior Inconsistent Statements or Omissions? Did the witness give a previous statement that contains information different from their present statement?

THE DOCUMENT

Is the Document Authentic? Can it be properly identified? Is it self-authenticating? Can the Snowperson write?

Is it Reasonable for the Document to Exist? Should it have been created? Is it a logical part of the event? Is there some reason why it may have been manufactured?

Is it an Original or a Duplicate? Where is the original? Is it an accurate duplicate?

These and other factors influence the value of various sorts of information. It is not enough in analyzing the facts of a case to determine their content. One must also focus on their source, credibility, and authenticity.

§ 1.6 LEGAL ANALYSIS AND REASONING

Analysis simply means reflecting on the information at hand, determining its significance, and using this understanding to decide what to do. Analysis is the process of using current information and informed predictions to plan for the future. Legal analysis requires the litigator to analyze the applicable law, available facts, needs and economic resources of the client, time limitations, strategic advantages and disadvantages and then make a professional judgment.

Well it's not quite that simple. The litigator first has to complete law school and pass the bar exam to earn the privilege of engaging in pure legal analysis . . . for money, that is.

Legal reasoning presumes an understanding of the implications of legal logic. The deductive, and less common, form of legal syllogism argues for example: that friends are biased, that witness *O* is a friend, and that therefore witness *O* is biased. The inductive and much more common form of legal reasoning argues that witness *O* as a friend is biased. Much of the litigation process involves the development of evidence through inductive analysis.

Deductive reasoning culminates in a rather conclusive and often incontrovertible position. Inductive reasoning does not lead to such certainty and remains subject to varying interpretations and inferences. Witness *O* may be a distant and not a close friend; witness *O* may recall events that only a reliable eyewitness knows; witness *O* may appear very credible while testifying.

The litigator who opposes the position asserted by inductive evidence has four options:

(1) the fact can be flatly denied (witness *O* is not a friend);

(2) contradictory information may be introduced (witness *O* spit at the alleged friend);

(3) additional facts can be offered (witness *O* is also a friend of the opposing party); and

(4) reasonable inferences can be explained away (the bias is not sufficient to influence witness *O* to lie).

These choices narrow the focus of legal analysis and reasoning.

There is nothing magically precise about the analysis and reasoning applicable to litigation practice. Litigation thinking, planning, reasoning, and analysis do not follow a set format. Common sense, life experiences, instinct, emotions, feelings, and attitudes also influence what a litigator does or says.

This does not mean that effective litigators are born and not made. Legal "intuition" is less a product of genes than it is a derivation of judgment derived from experiences with similar situations. These situations may be personally experienced, observed, read about, or thought about. The more a litigator directly or indirectly "experiences" litigation approaches and techniques from whatever source, the more effective and efficient a litigator can analyze and reason.

Litigators will be responsible for many cases at the same time. Most law students find challenge in juggling four or five courses each semester. Imagine the task of a litigator who may be supervising 5, 25, or 75 cases. These cases will not all demand action at the same time but many can demand nearly simultaneous action.

Litigation can be a complex, complicated process, as distinguished from a merely complicated process, but other lawsuits are rather simple. Litigators must learn how to plan to keep the simple simple and prevent the complicated from becoming overly complex.

There is no "recipe" for how any given litigation problem must be addressed. You should understand by now that the role of a litigator is not to copy what others have done but to exercise individual and informed judgment in making a decision. Planning, problem solving, analyzing, and reasoning aid in making those decisions. The remainder of this book will explain the legal research, fact investigation, discovery, motions, and settlement information that must be mastered to become an effective litigator. And you thought professional life after law school was a cinch.

§ 1.7 CLIENT INTERVIEWING AND COUNSELING

Detailed analysis of client interviewing and counseling extends beyond the scope of these materials. There are some aspects of interviewing and counseling a litigation client, however, that deserve special emphasis in a book on pretrial litigation.

Clear and Understandable Explanations. The litigation process is complex and chock full of procedures and tactics that make little sense to a lay person. A litigator must continually be certain that what he or she explains to a client is understood by the client. For example, clients may say "no" when a lawyer asks whether they were served with a "summons and complaint" and then later in the interview mention they received some papers they thought might be legal something-or-others. It is better for the lawyer to be overly simplistic than to presume the client knows the meaning of a legal term, while being careful not to insult a client.

More Than One Version. Whatever facts the client relates will 99% of the time be challenged or contradicted in part by someone or something else. A dispute is often caused by a disagreement over what happened. The differences may not involve major facts but will typically involve specific details and reasonable inferences. Many clients believe that their version is and must be the correct version. The task of the lawyer is not to agree that the client is correct but to prepare and present a favorable version of the facts that gain appropriate relief.

Lawyer's Attitude Toward Client. The legal counselor needs to remain aware of any conscious or unconscious attitudes toward a client that may affect representation. For example, some lawyers in representing an experienced business person are much more deferential to that client's opinion than to the opinion of an inexperienced client. The assumption that the business person knows best, whereas the lay person probably does not, may or may not be accurate. Similarly people who are financially better off or who occupy a position of authority may appear to be more credible and believable than others. An assessment is frequently based upon inappropriate stereotypes. Litigators must review their decisions to determine to what extent they may be based on improper and inappropriate attitudes.

Predicting Results. A litigator must provide the client with some information about the prospects of litigation. The degrees of prediction include: (1) the very likely, (2) the most likely, (3) the probably likely, (4) the possible, (5) the unlikely and (6) the very unlikely. These gradations do not lend themselves to exact percentages, and modified predictions will be appropriate in many cases.

Explaining Advantages and Disadvantages. Advice provided to a litigant is usually described in terms of the advantages and disadvantages of alternative remedies, approaches, and tactics. The client retains the litigator not only to litigate but for informed explanations of the strengths and weaknesses of alternatives.

Exploring Alternatives. Lawyers must consider alternatives to resolving the problem through litigation. Dispute resolution methods, including mediation or arbitration, may provide a more efficient and economical way to resolve disputes. *See* § 1.8.

Consequences to the Client. Litigation approaches and tactics have several effects on the client, including financial, psychological, business, and social consequences. The lawyer needs to discuss these consequences with the client. Often this type of discussion and the client's reaction will resolve or dictate what alternative approach or strategy should be implemented.

Psychological Impact on a Litigant. Being a litigant is a frightening and unnerving experience to many clients but they often underestimate or ignore the psychological price they will have to pay as a litigant.

Rendering Premature Advice. There are cases in which it is obvious that the client has no valid claims or defenses. Not many cases however, allow a lawyer to provide complete legal advice to a potential litigant during the initial client interview. The client's legal rights need to be researched and facts need to be investigated before the lawyer can meaningfully evaluate the client's case and available relief.

The Trial and Appeal. An explanation of the entire legal process including the trial and appeal process may provide a distorted view to the client—who may misunderstand the possibilities. Clients need to understand the realistic possibilities of delay and cost, as well as settlement. These clients need to understand that more than 90% of civil cases are resolved short of trial.

Assessing the Client as a Witness. One factor which affects the evaluation of a case is the ability of a client to be a credible witness at trial. This is, indeed, an important factor but should not be overly emphasized at the early stages of a case. The other lawyer may not be aware of the credibility problems of a client, even after a deposition of that client. The story of a less than credible witness may be butressed by other witnesses and documents. The initial assessment of a case should balance the credibility of a witness with other sources of corroboration.

Goals of Initial Interview. The goals of an initial client interview vary and may include: obtaining the client's story and information about documents and other witnesses; reassuring the client that the lawyer will represent the client's best interests; establishing a sound attorney-client relationship; explaining fees; describing necessary legal research and fact investigation; predicting costs and timing; and suggesting future steps.

Multiple Interviews. More than one interview may be necessary to discuss with the client what the research and investigation has revealed and what alternatives the client has. A firm decision by the client to litigate or not must await this second or third conference.

The Extent of Client Participation. Litigators differ on their approach to client counseling. Some lawyers will want to control all decisions; other counselors prefer to have the client make major decisions; and still others divide control within this range of counseling approaches. Clients also differ in their degree of participation. Some clients, especially business clients, want to be a dominant part of the decision-making process. Other clients prefer to be dependent upon the attorney.

It is best to involve the client as much as possible in all major decisions and in other appropriate decisions. The client retains the lawyer and pays for such services. Ultimately, only clients can really know what is best for them.

§ 1.8 DISPUTE RESOLUTION METHODS

Alternative methods to resolve disputes need to be considered prior to as well as during litigation. Another way of resolving a client's problem instead of litigation may well be a more efficient, economic, and effective way of meeting the client's needs and interests. This section will describe dispute resolution methods available before litigation or at the early stages of litigation. Additional methods may be available at later stages of litigation, particularly after discovery has been completed and motions have been resolved, which are discussed in chapter 14.

Common methods to resolve disputes prior to or instead of litigation are settlement, mediation, arbitration, and a variety of specialized approaches.

Settlement. Disputes may be resolved before or during litigation by the parties mutually agreeing to settle the case. The parties and their attorneys solve these disputes on their own initiative and on their own terms. The threat of litigation or actual litigation is a major motivating force behind the settlement ultimately reached, and settlement discussions frequently focus on what would happen if a lawsuit was filed or brought to trial. Settlement documents used by parties to end the litigation are explained in § 14.5.

Mediation. Mediation involves disputing parties voluntarily resolving their differences with the assistance of a mediator who facilitates the reaching of an agreement by the parties. Participants in a mediation include the parties, their attorneys or representatives, and the mediator. A mediator is a neutral, impartial person who serves various roles. A mediator can clarify what the parties want and why, focus on their needs and interests, remain a source of trust and confidence for the parties, diffuse hostilities and reduce the adverse impact of emotions and feelings, and suggest alternative and creative ways to reach an accord.

Mediation is a voluntary, non-binding, confidential process. Mediation differs from arbitration in that no person issues a decision that is involuntarily binding upon the parties. Mediation may take only a couple of hours, several hours, or a number of days, depending upon the complexity of the issues and the position of the parties. The costs of mediation include the mediator's fees and an administrative fee.

Arbitration. Arbitration involves the submission of a dispute to a neutral arbitrator who makes a decision following a hearing. There are three routes to arbitration: through a pre-dispute agreement, a post-dispute agreement, or court-mandated arbitration. In pre-dispute arbitration, the parties agree in a contract to submit future disputes to arbitration. In post-dispute arbitration, the parties submit an existing dispute to arbitration. In court-mandated arbitrations, a judge orders the parties to arbitrate the dispute at some point during litigation.

Many arbitrations involve hearings, with the parties presenting evidence through witnesses and documents. Others proceed by parties submitting documents to the arbitrator. Arbitration proceedings are less formal than trials. Arbitrators are generally not required to follow strict rules of procedure or evidence. Many cases are completed in half a day, with others not taking more than a full day. The costs of an arbitration include the arbitrator's fees and administrative expenses incurred by the arbitration organization selected by the parties to administer the arbitration.

An arbitrator usually decides a case by issuing a written arbitration award following the arbitration hearing. The award issued by the arbitrator is the final decision in binding arbitration. There is usually no appeal of a binding arbitration award.

Arbitration awards are legally binding and enforceable in all fifty states and in the federal courts. An arbitration award is as effective as a judgment entered after a judicial trial. All state laws and the federal laws allow a party to "confirm" an arbitration award to a judgment. A party simply has to follow applicable procedures in the court which has proper jurisdiction, and the confirmed award becomes an enforceable judgment.

Med–Arb. Med-arb proceedings combine both mediation and arbitration. Parties attempt to mediate the dispute first, and, if mediation fails, then arbitrate the dispute. The neutral who mediates the dispute with the parties may also be the arbitrator, or different individuals can split the roles. The mediation process may not resolve the entire dispute, but may resolve some of the issues, with arbitration resolving the remaining issues.

Early Neutral Evaluation. This method is a proceeding in which the attorneys present a summary of the dispute to a neutral evaluator in the presence of the parties. This presentation occurs soon after the case is filed and before discovery begins. The neutral provides a candid assessment of the strengths and weaknesses of the case and provides an impartial evaluation on the issues of liability and damages. If the parties are unable to settle the case based upon this assessment and evaluation, the neutral expert can assist in narrowing the disputed issues and suggest guidelines for proceeding with discovery and motions. Early neutral evaluation is a relatively new method which a number of state courts and federal district have adopted in lieu of using mediation and arbitration at the early stages of a case.

Attorneys need to consider these methods to resolve disputes before initiating a law suit on behalf of their clients. Litigation can be and often is the best way for disputes to be resolved, but it should be used in those situations where other more efficient, less costly, and equally effective methods have been considered and rejected.

§ 1.8.1 Mediation Criteria

This section list factors which need to be reviewed in determining at an early stage of the case whether or not mediation is a useful way to resolve the dispute. Whether or not a case can or should be mediated depends on multiple factors. The following list details some of those considerations.

REASONS TO MEDIATE

Time Considerations. Mediation may be able to create an agreement or resolve a problem faster than other methods.

Cost Considerations. A mediated agreement may make or save the parties money. The substantial costs of litigation and attorney's fees can also be avoided in the mediation process.

Party Preferences. One party may prefer or be eager to engage in mediation and should do so. Another party may also want, need or prefer to mediate the situation or problem. Lawyers or representatives may inform parties of the option to mediate and encourage and assist them.

The Effect of No Agreement. Parties may lose an opportunity to create a relationship or produce a profit if no agreement is reached. Mediation may allow the parties to get together and mutually gain.

Relief Sought. A jury verdict, a judge's order or an arbitration award may not provide the relief a party wants. A mediated settlement may be the only way parties can have their needs met.

Problems Initiating or Sustaining Negotiation Discussions. Parties may have difficulties initiating negotiation discussions. Neither side may want to suggest negotiation talks or negotiation efforts may have failed. Mediation may be the best way for the parties to start or continue this process.

Substantially Different Perspectives. There may be substantial gaps between the positions asserted by the opposing sides. These differences may be so significant that the skills of a mediator are necessary to reduce these differences of perceptions.

The Relationship Between the Parties. Opposing parties may have or hope to have, a continuing relationship after the litigation terminates. Mediation may offer the parties a better opportunity to maintain or create a relationship often not possible with litigation.

Complex Problems, Issues or Solutions. Some matters may be very difficult, time-consuming, and expensive to litigate or otherwise resolve. Mediation may provide a much more efficient and economic way to resolve problems.

The Need for Confidentiality. The process and results of mediation are more private and much less public than litigation or other efforts. Parties who want matters to remain confidential may prefer to mediate.

The Effect of Obtaining a Judgment. It may be best for a party to avoid the adverse effect of a judicial determination or judgment in a case. Mediation can avoid the permanent effect of a judgment and its precedential value for similar future cases.

REASONS NOT TO MEDIATE

The following factors suggest that mediation may not be useful and also need to be considered:

Substantial Party Resistance. A party may be so opposed to mediation that it would be useless to mediate. Mediation requires the cooperation of a party to engage in serious and good faith discussions.

Unavailability of Significant Participants. In a multi-party case involving significant persons not interested or available or in a situation involving insurance coverage with the insurance company refusing to participate, mediation efforts may be unsuccessful because those who are affected are not involved.

Non-negotiable Positions. If a party takes an intractable position regarding a critical mediation issue and states that nothing will change that position, mediation may not be successful. However, simply stating an unyielding position does not necessarily reflect an inflexible position. A party may only be "posturing" and may change a position when faced with "reality."

Sabotaging the Mediation. Usually, the parties want a mediation to succeed. There may be occasional situations when a party approaches a mediation with no intent or hope the mediation will succeed. This party may attempt to sabotage the mediation process. It makes little sense to attempt to mediate with a party who has this attitude.

Financially Destitute Party. Mediations which involve the payment of money or distribution of assets between parties may be unsuccessful if a party does not have the ability to make the necessary payments or distribution. The goal of some mediations may not be necessarily to collect payment but only to establish liability and have a party admit a debt. Mediation may expedite the achievement of this goal.

Necessary Information. Mediation scheduled before investigation or discovery is completed may need to be postponed and re-scheduled if one or both parties need to obtain or exchange information to be able to evaluate all the issues in the case. Oftentimes, early mediation assists in resolving discovery disputes and helps the parties exchange needed information.

§ 1.8.2 Arbitration Criteria

This section itemizes factors which help determine whether or not the parties should submit a dispute to arbitration instead of litigation. Whether or not a case can or should be arbitrated depends upon multiple factors. The following list details some of these considerations.

REASONS TO ARBITRATE

Willingness of Parties. Parties who are open to the arbitration process obviously will be the best candidates for arbitration.

Efficient Procedures. Arbitration avoids the use of strict procedural and evidential rules, legal technicalities, and delaying tactics. Discovery is often unavailable. The hearing is usually scheduled quickly or within a very reasonable amount of time.

Expertise of Arbitrator. An arbitrator may be selected who is an independent expert regarding the issues to be arbitrated and who is well equipped to resolve the dispute fairly and quickly.

Reduction of Adversarial Atmosphere. The arbitration process helps promote the development and continuation of good relations, reducing the adversarial posture of the parties, permitting them to work together during and after the resolution of the dispute. The simplicity of the arbitration process, compared to litigation, also helps reduce animosity and tension between the parties caused by lengthy and more complex litigation.

Privacy. The private nature of arbitration proceedings results in a confidential process.

Finality. The decision of an arbitrator in a binding arbitration procedure is final. The award will only be successfully attacked directly or on appeal in a few instances.

Overall Efficiency. The arbitration process ordinarily saves the parties substantial time and money and significantly reduces attorney's fees, although it may be that the parties may find this advantage much more advantageous than attorneys.

REASONS NOT TO ARBITRATE

Arbitration has limitations and may not be an effective way for the parties to resolve disputes. The following factors need to be considered to determine whether arbitration will be effective:

Need for Discovery. If the parties need to obtain essential information from each other in order to prepare and present a case, litigation may be preferred over arbitration. The use of interrogatories, depositions, and requests for production of documents are not typically allowed in arbitrations, unless by agreement of the parties or pursuant to the rules of the arbitration organization.

Need for a Jury Verdict. One or both parties may prefer that a dispute be resolved by a jury of peers from the community rather than one or more expert arbitrators. The nature of the case, especially the type and amount of damages in issue, may suggest a jury is much more preferable than an arbitrator.

Public Proceeding. Trials are public proceedings and verdicts by the jury and decisions by the judge are likewise public. A party may not want a hearing or a result to remain confidential.

Appealability. Parties may want to be able to appeal from a jury verdict or a judge's decision. Appeals are a matter of right in litigation, and much less likely to be available from an arbitration award.

Written Opinion. Litigation concludes with some form of a written document: either a jury verdict, a judge's order and memorandum, or an appellate opinion. These documents usually explain the reasoning why one party won and the other lost. Parties who prefer such written decisions may prefer litigation over arbitration.

§ 1.8.3 Selecting the Best Method

Reviewing these and additional considerations help the parties and their attorneys determine whether negotiation, mediation, arbitration, litigation, or another dispute resolution method will be the most effective remedy. In some cases, it may seem that no method will be effective. In these situations the attorneys may want to consider some, er, rather unusual methods such as dueling or letting bygones be bygones.

§ 1.9 ETHICS

Before you explore the rules and problems, you need to understand the importance and placement of ethics in this book. There are no special rules of ethics or professional responsibility which apply solely to pretrial proceedings. There are, however, certain aspects of frequently used pretrial procedures which present recurring ethical questions for attorneys. The following chapters discuss some of these recurring problems and the malpractice risks inherent in violations of the professional rules of ethical conduct.

Although popular mythology suggests that a profession is both self-regulating and ethical, both the public and the legal profession have long acted as though the lawyer's ethical compass was drawn from within, the sum total of the attorney's education, training, formative years, role models, and all sorts of other unquantifiable things. This myth may be at least partially true. In legal ethics, or any ethics, one undoubtedly meets many situations that are unique and outside the strict text of "by-the-book" responses. In these situations, ethical counsel, whether in pretrial practice or any other area of practice, must respond after extrapolating or interpolating from the fixed ethical rules of the profession. But today there exists more fixed and well-defined ethical rules than 20 years ago. During that time, the Code of Professional Responsibility and the Model Rules of Professional Conduct have been promulgated, the ABA and state bar associations have begun to provide interpretative guidance to these rules through ethics committee opinions, and courts have taken a more active role in policing the bar, applying the standards of the code, 18 U.S.C.A. § 1927, Rule 11, and the common law to impose sanctions on counsel who breach their ethical duties.

The major ethical rules based on the Model Rules of Professional Conduct that apply to litigators include:

Abide by Client's Decisions

Model Rule 1.2 states:

> A lawyer shall abide by a client's decision regarding the objectives of representation ... and shall consult with a client as to the means by which they are to be pursued.

The trial lawyer has an obligation to discuss with the client the objectives of the case and litigation strategies and tactics that are to be pursued, as discussed in section 1.1.6. After these consultations, the attorney then implements the decisions.

Confidentiality

The information a client provides a lawyer and the advice a lawyer renders is confidential and may not be revealed unless a client consents, or a specific situation allows or requires disclosure. See Model Rule 1.6.

Conflict of Interest

A lawyer may not represent a client if the representation will compromise or be compromised by the lawyer's representation of another client. A client, after being fully informed by the attorney, may knowingly and intelligently agree to be represented by the attorney in spite of the conflict of interest. See Model Rule 1.7.

Disclosing Controlling Authority

Model Rule 3.3(a) states:

> A lawyer shall not knowingly ... fail to disclose to the tribunal legal authority in the controlling jurisdiction known to the lawyer to be directly adverse to the position of the client and not disclosed by opposing counsel.

A lawyer must disclose controlling authority—supporting or adverse—but is not obligated to disclose legal authority if it is not controlling. Precedent that is not binding in a jurisdiction, such as cases from another forum, need not be disclosed. Such precedents may be relied upon to argue by analogy that a judge should adopt this authority from another jurisdiction, which requires the opposing party to argue against the application of the law even though it is not controlling.

Evidence

Model Rule 3.4(a) states:

> A lawyer may not unlawfully obstruct another party's access to evidence or alter, destroy or conceal a document or material having potential evidentiary value.

The obviously unconscionable conduct is obviously unconscionable and should not even require a rule to prevent it.

Expediting Litigation

An attorney must make reasonable efforts to expedite litigation, consistent with a legitimate interest of the client, and not delay proceedings for improper reasons. It is ethically inappropriate for an attorney to engage in expensive and extensive discovery and motion practices if these strategies are not employed to promote a client's case. It is also unethical for an attorney to employ delay tactics which are used for the primary purpose of wasting resources or unreasonably extending the litigation. See Model Rule 3.4.

Complying With Rulings

> Model Rule 3.4(c) states: a lawyer shall not . . . knowingly disobey an obligation under the rules of the tribunal except for an open refusal based on an assertion that no available obligation exists.

The rulings and orders of a judge must be complied with by an attorney except in extraordinary and unusual situations in which an attorney is willing to accept the consequences of a contempt citation for disobeying a judge.

Influencing a Court Official

A lawyer is prohibited from influencing a judge or a court official regarding a case and may not communicate ex parte with such persons regarding a specific case. A litigator may obtain information from court officers about general procedural matters but cannot contact such individuals in an attempt to influence them.

Good Faith

Model Rule 3.5 states:

> A lawyer shall not bring or defend a proceeding, or assert or controvert an issue therein unless there is a basis for doing so that is not frivolous, which includes a good faith argument for an extension, modification, or reversal of existing law.

Federal Rule of Civil Procedure 11 and related state rules contain a similar standard. These rules prohibit an attorney from presenting a claim or defense unless to the best of that attorney's knowledge, information, and belief, formed after reasonable investigation and research, it is well grounded in fact and is warranted by existing law or a good faith argument for the development of new law. This standard represents an objective standard of conduct as distinguished from a subjective belief. An attorney who personally believes that a claim or defense is valid does not meet the standard. The attorney must have an objective basis in law and fact to support a claim or defense. It is no longer sufficient for an attorney to have a "pure heart" in asserting a claim or defense. The rules require an attorney have a "good legal head" and factual and legal support for a claim or defense.

The discussion of these and other ethical issues in this book does not supplant the course in professional ethics, nor does it contain a complete listing of the ethical considerations which may affect pretrial civil litigation practices. And you thought we would have all the answers for you.

§ 1.10 LITIGATION REFORM

Changes in the rules and procedures governing litigation occur constantly. Some of these revisions are intended to clarify and modernize existing practice. Other changes constitute evolutionary improvements in litigation system. Still other revisions are efforts to revolutionize litigation practice. A litigator needs always to remain informed about these ongoing changes. While many changes are prospective and only apply to future cases, some revisions apply to existing cases. It is always better to know what the applicable rules are instead of having opposing counsel remind you of the changes or, even worse, have the judge chide you about how your professional life is passing you by.

Each year changes occur to federal and state rules of procedure. It is critical that a litigator have the most current version of the rules and double check to determine whether any revised or supplementary rules exist. It is also critical that a litigator check other sources. A source of change, which may not appear in a rule book, occurs when a court issues an opinion changing present practice. Federal and state court judges may also vary the rules by adopting local rules or standing orders which apply to all cases in a district or county or to specific types of cases. The federal rules permit judges to change some procedural rules applicable in their district, and some states allow state court judges to adopt local rules which supplement the state rules of civil procedure. It is not enough to rely on a rule book, you also have to do continuing legal research.

Changes may occur to any of the rules applicable in the litigation system. As you read this, changes are being proposed in a variety of procedural rules, especially regarding discovery. Federal and state court advisory committees have especially focused on pleading, discovery, and motion practice and make continuing efforts to ensure that these procedures are as efficient and effective as possible. Change as Heraclitus said, endures.

Discovery has been reformed, at least in federal cases. The 1993 revisions to the Federal Rules of Civil Procedure have dramatically changed the nature and scope of discovery. These significant changes include:

- A party must affirmatively disclose specific information about witnesses, documents, and insurance agreements at the initial stages of litigation.
- Parties must also affirmatively disclose expert reports and information about experts during the litigation.
- Pretrial disclosures now require parties to affirmatively disclose specific information about witnesses and documents.
- Parties must meet and confer shortly after litigation begins to discuss discovery issues and to attempt to mutually agree to a discovery plan.
- Discovery requests, including interrogatories, document productions, and depositions, may not be served or scheduled until after the parties have met to establish a discovery plan.
- Parties may create their own discovery process and vary the rules, with few limitations, to allow discovery requests and responses that meet the needs of the case.
- Judges through a scheduling order can impose a discovery plan on parties when they cannot agree and can otherwise assist the parties in developing an efficient and economic discovery program.
- Judges may also through standing orders and local rules change some of the federal rules of civil procedure applicable to discovery by imposing different rules or excluding certain types of cases from coverage under the revised federal rules.
- The revised rules attempt to place greater burdens on the attorneys to develop specific discovery plans and provide judges with the power to review discovery plans and control discovery abuses.
- Parties in asserting objections during depositions must be more specific and may only instruct witnesses not to answer in limited situations.
- Parties in objecting to interrogatories, document production requests, and requests for admissions must be specific and must timely respond to requests which are not objectionable.
- Sanctions have been revised to provide greater incentive for parties to comply with discovery rules and court orders.
- Rule 11 no longer applies to discovery requests and responses.

The enactment of revised rules have been heralded by some and condemned by others. Significant numbers of judges, practitioners, law professors, and commentators, strongly supported these revisions. Other judges, practitioners, law professors, and commentators with equal fervor have opposed these revisions.

Are these changes evolutionary in nature, and will they reform discovery and reduce discovery abuses? Or, are these radical, untested changes which will cause more litigation involving discovery problems and increase the costs and delays of litigation? Time will tell, along with the attitudes displayed by litigation participants and the approaches litigators and judges take toward the new rules. Many federal courts have "opted out" of the changes, either permanently or until further study.

PRACTICE PROBLEMS

This book presents you with a variety of problems and exercises to help you develop your litigation skills. Problems appear at the end of this and the following chapters which reflect the broad range of litigation practice. Many problems are based on the activities of Hot Dog Enterprises (HDE) and the lives of its top management. The disputes arise from the business operated by HDE, from the personal lives of its CEO, Pat LaBelle, and its Chairperson of the Board, Casey Pozdak, and from events involving companies and individuals who have contact with HDE and its personnel.

The problems presented throughout the text involve both continuing disputes and new disputes. One continuing problem that appears in each chapter involves a dispute between HDE and Tri–Chem, a corporation which manufactured and supplied a bonding additive known as Bond–Mor to the mortar used in the construction of some of HDE's restaurant buildings. This problem allows you to track the development of a major case through the litigation process. Every chapter also includes other problems, some continuing and some new. The new disputes raise issues germane to the subject matter of the chapter in which they appear. Additional case files appear at the end of the book and provide further fact patterns for chapter problems.

You will act as the lawyer representing the various parties in the problems. You will engage in diverse lawyering skills ranging from analysis to preparation to performance. We integrate these problems into this text to provide you with a richer educational experience and to prepare you better for the practice of law.

The problems and cases usually take place in the mythical jurisdiction of the State of Summit, County of West, City of Mitchell. This jurisdiction has adopted the Federal Rules of Civil Procedure and the Federal Rules of Evidence, has enacted applicable federal statutes, and has issued judicial opinions that reflect prevailing federal decisions. Further explanation regarding the problems appears in the Preface.

The following paragraphs describe Hot Dog Enterprises and facts about Tri–Chem and Bond–Mor. Further information including memoranda, letters, and promotional correspondence is available in Case A of Appendix C.

HOT DOG ENTERPRISES

Hot Dog Enterprises is a corporation which operates hot dog dining establishments throughout the country. HDE is incorporated in Delaware, has its corporate headquarters in Minnesota and its hot dog manufacturing plant in Texas, and owns hot dog stands and restaurants and operates franchises in every state.

HDE had its beginnings in a hot dog stand in Chicago, Illinois. Casey Pozdak and Pat LaBelle started a small hot dog stand on the Southwest side of Chicago in 1969. Their business grew over the years to its current status. HDE owns and operates more than 100 hot dog dining establishments consisting of hot dog stands and fast food drive-in and sit-down restaurants.

Approximately 50 franchisees operate another 50 restaurants. HDE owns about 25 buildings and parcels of property. In 15 of these locations it operates its own restaurants and in the other 10 it rents space to its franchisees. HDE markets itself nationally and locally through television, radio, magazine, newspaper, and other advertisements. HDE sponsors marathons and motorcycle races and donates generously to various charitable organizations and educational institutions.

Pat LaBelle is the Chief Executive Officer of HDE, and Casey Pozdak is Chairperson of the Board. Approximately 120 employees work in its corporate headquarters, which includes offices for its management, accounting, marketing, sales, and legal staff. HDE employs about 240 people at its manufacturing plant which produces its famous hot dogs based on a trade secret recipe. More than 1000 employees work at HDE dining establishments throughout the country. The managers of these restaurants and the managers of the franchise restaurants attend "hot dog school" at HDE corporate headquarters to learn the HDE way to serve and sell hot dogs.

TRI–CHEM CORPORATION

Tri–Chem Corporation is a company which develops, manufactures, distributes, and sells chemical additives and products for consumer and commercial use. Tri–Chem is incorporated in New York, has its corporate headquarters in California, and has research facilities, manufacturing plants, distribution centers, and sales offices in Massachusetts, Georgia, Arkansas, Michigan, Colorado, Arizona, Montana, and Oregon. Tri–Chem sells its products in every state and is a parent corporation to a number of wholly-owned subsidiaries involved in related products and also unrelated businesses including the media and communications field.

Tri–Chem developed, manufactured, and sells throughout the country a mortar additive for use in brick masonry and other types of buildings, known under the trade name Bond–Mor. Tri–Chem also provides technical advice and services to contractors, engineers, and architects who use Bond–Mor in the construction of brick masonry and other buildings. Between 1984 and 1988, the Tri–Chem Corporation sold Bond–Mor for use in the original construction of HDE's restaurant buildings in Kansas and Ohio.

Chapter Questions

1. In addition to those factors described in Section 1.1, what other factors, objective or subjective, influence litigation decisions?

2. How can an attorney maintain high standards of excellence in practice when faced with the difficulties discussed in Section 1.1.3?

3. What additional suggestions do you have regarding how a lawyer maintains a proper role as a litigator in addition to the comments made in Section 1.1.4?

4. What aspects of the adversary system discussed in Section 1.1.5 need to be reformed to make a litigator more effective? More efficient?

5. How may a client influence the progress of a case in addition to those factors described in Section 1.1.6?

6. Hot Dog Enterprises decides to hire a law firm to handle its litigation including its plaintiff and defense work. HDE interviews you, the managing partner of a medium sized firm in your community. What presentation would you make to HDE to obtain its legal business?

   (a) HDE asks what kind of a litigator are you. How would you respond?

   (b) HDE asks what interests and needs you think HDE ought to preserve and protect in litigation. What would you say in response?

7. You apply for an attorney's position in the litigation department of Tri–Chem Corporation. The General Counsel of Tri–Chem interviews you as a finalist for the position. What presentation would you make to the General Counsel to obtain the job?

   (a) General Counsel asks what kind of litigator are you. How would you respond?

(b) General Counsel asks what interests and needs you ought to protect in representing Tri–Chem. What would you say in response?

8. Congratulations! Hot Dog Enterprises retains your law firm. You learn that HDE is violating a number of federal and state environmental laws at its manufacturing plant and is also discharging employees at its headquarters in a way that may violate employment laws. What do you do?

9. You decide private practice is not for you. Tri–Chem thinks the world of you, and you accept its offer to be Director of Litigation. You learn that Tri–Chem has a policy prohibiting its attorneys from doing pro bono work. You want to do pro bono work. What do you do?

10. What reaction do you have to the "games" and problems discussed in Section 1.1.7? Why do lawyers play these and other games? How else may lawyers overcome "afflictions" that reduce their effectiveness?

11. Section 1.2 outlines a planning process for litigation. What other components of the planning process can you add?

12. Creative problem solving can be readily recognized after the fact. What creative solutions do you know or have you heard that have resolved legal or analogous problems?

13. Section 1.4 lists categories of information. What other categories can you add?

14. Section 1.5 explains some factors that influence the plausibility of a story, the credibility of a witness, and the authenticity of a document. What other factors can you add?

15. Hot Dog Enterprises claims that the Bond–Mor mortar additive manufactured and sold by Tri–Chem has caused damage to four of its restaurant buildings and that it will cost approximately $500,000 to repair the damage. Tri–Chem denies liability and claims that poor design and maintenance caused the problems.

(a) You represent HDE. Would you suggest that instead of litigation the dispute be submitted to mediation? To binding arbitration? To settlement negotiations between the parties? Why? Is any one method likely to be more effective than another?

(b) You represent Tri–Chem. Would you suggest that instead of litigation the dispute be submitted to mediation? To binding arbitration? To settlement negotiations between the parties? Why? Is any one method likely to be more effective than another?

16. Hot Dog Enterprises fires its sales manager for poor performance. The manager, who is a 55 year old woman, claims

the firing was discriminatory on the basis of gender and age and was also a breach of contract.

(a) You represent HDE. Would you suggest that instead of litigation the dispute be submitted to mediation? To binding arbitration? To settlement negotiations between the parties? Why? Is any one method likely to be more effective than another?

(b) You represent the sales manager. Would you suggest that instead of litigation the dispute be submitted to mediation? To binding arbitration? To settlement negotiations between the parties? Why? Is any one method likely to be more effective than another?

17. Compare the similarities and differences between the rules and practice of federal court with the rules and practice of a state chosen by you or your instructor regarding:

A. Pleadings

B. Discovery

C. Motions

D. Alternative Dispute Resolution

E. Other Pretrial Litigation Matters

CHAPTER 2
INVESTIGATION

The Lord God called the man and said to him, "Where are you?" . . . Then the Lord God said to the woman, "Why have you done this?"

God's First Investigation
Genesis 3:8–13

§ 2.1 INTRODUCTION

The litigation process begins for the lawyer when a client retains the lawyer or when a retained client notifies the lawyer. Many cases fall within the realm of the litigator's experience and expertise. Other cases fall beyond a lawyer's abilities. A litigator in these situations needs to convert capabilities into abilities or refer the case to someone who already has the abilities. A few moments spent discussing a case with someone who knows more, even if it costs $100 an hour or a racquetball loss, will not only bring the litigator up to speed but may save substantial time and efforts during later stages of the case.

Lawyers often plunge mistakenly into the initial "urgent" litigation task without gauging the depth. Clients and attorneys both tend to want action and results. Initially serving a summons and complaint may provide psychic satisfaction that may prove superficial or shortlived. Before commencing litigation, counsel should first review the considerations advanced in this chapter to properly prepare for a case. A plaintiff's lawyer should take the time necessary to conduct fully appropriate legal research and to complete essential factual investigations. This procedure applies to defense counsel as well even though time may be abbreviated.

Some cases provide little time for systematic preparation. Legal research and fact investigation are essential to all litigation settings and must be done in a streamlined, sometimes frantic, manner. The client who seeks an immediate temporary restraining order or who first visits a lawyer two hours before the statute of limitations runs presents severe time constraints. In these situations lawyers will need to adopt efficient litigation strategies rather than ignore the need to conduct necessary legal and factual inquiries. Extensions of time may be available to provide defense lawyers time to do research and investigation.

Whatever occurs, counsel should place on the calender important litigation dates and events. The applicable statute of limitations, the availability of witnesses, the timing needs of a client, and the court docket, all need to be reviewed prior to action.

§ 2.2 LEGAL INVESTIGATION

Not all wrongs are rightable. Some have legal consequences, others do not. When the client spins a tale of woe, counsel must soon determine whether these facts, assuming as true the client's story, make for a right to legal relief. Defense counsel needs to make nearly the same judgment shortly after receiving the complaint. Similar evaluations must occur throughout the case as discovery disputes and motions arise. Knowing the potential legal consequences, counsel can choose the appropriate strategy (*e.g.*, a motion to dismiss, a hard-hitting discovery campaign, negotiation, or capitulation).

Normally, some rudimentary legal research should follow basic fact-gathering but precede extensive fact investigation. At the risk of duplicating your first-year legal writing course (and not doing as well), we briefly review research sources and approaches. At the outset, defense lawyers have an edge. They don't have to check out every possible legal issue. They only need to check out the legal issues raised by the claimant. Occasionally, a bright and industrious judge will spot and apply a legal ground for relief missed by plaintiff's lawyer. That's rare. In addition, even this mythical Solomon must give the defendant an opportunity to respond to the legal issue raised *sua sponte,* preserving defense counsel's edge in avoiding legal research. Where counterclaims or cross-claims are contemplated, defense counsel shares the plaintiff's burden to research and not miss applicable law.

Planning Research. How legal research should be conducted depends upon what the researcher knows and doesn't know and what is available. The knowledge or lack of knowledge by the researcher determines the scope of the initial research and how general or specific the research needs to be. Whether research needs to be conducted in a law library (which prohibits eating and drinking), whether a few books can be perused, or whether a computer can be utilized to search for the law depends upon what is the most efficient and economic way of researching the law.

Index Research. Lawyers depend first upon their own knowledge to raise possible legal grounds for relief. Thereafter, they should brainstorm with colleagues. After that comes basic, boring index research studying potentially applicable statutes and the common law digests.

Although it may not be the height of the profession's creativity, this task can test the lawyer or clerk's mettle. Will the answer be under "strict liability," "products liability," "torts," "negligence," "punch presses," "master and servant," or some other index category? Learning the language of the local reference source gnomes can make a big difference in the speed and accuracy of early legal research. The local annotated statutes and case digests are usually the best places to begin introductory legal research.

Practice Books. Another preliminary and instructive source includes practice books written for a specialized area of the law and bound looseleaf publications that cover the legal waterfront of an area of the law. These books not only provide citations but also provide textual explanations of basic and sophisticated legal analyses, at times a welcome source of information. It beats embarrassing yourself by asking a colleague who pauses and after feigning a puzzled look says "What was your class rank?" The danger in reviewing these specialized materials early on in the legal research process is that the researcher may ignore or miss other potentially applicable areas of the law.

Encyclopedias. A search through the index to legal periodicals or other applicable indexes may provide additional and broader sources. Legal encyclopedias such as *Corpus Juris Secundum* and single-subject treatises such as Prosser on Torts can provide both a general understanding and overview of the potentially applicable law as well as doctrinal analysis and reference to more narrowly focused and detailed sources.

Treatises. If the lawyer already has the big picture of the law governing the particular question but desires more specific information or case citations to support what the lawyer already knows to be the truth, multi-volume treatises with annual supplements usually are most useful. In the pretrial litigation field, Wright & Miller [1] and Moore [2] on federal practice and Weinstein on Evidence [3] are particularly authoritative. Shorter treatises dealing with civil procedure issues may provide faster, simpler answers to initial questions.[4] Other books focusing on the procedural and practical aspects of pretrial litigation may be useful as well.[5] These books may be especially useful because of the increased role that pretrial proceedings, rather than trials, have in most civil cases.[6]

§ 2.2

1. Charles A. Wright & Arthur R. Miller, Federal Practice and Procedure (various dates) (36 vols.).

2. James W. Moore, Moore's Federal Practice (1994) (31 vols.).

3. Jack Weinstein & Margaret Berger, Evidence (1975).

4. *See, e.g.,* Fleming James & Geoffrey Hazard, Civil Procedure (2d ed. 1977); Milton D. Green, Civil Procedure (1972).

5. *See* David F. Herr, Roger S. Haydock & Jeffrey W. Stempel, Motion Practice (2d ed. 1991); Roger S. Haydock & David F. Herr, Discovery Practice (2d ed. 1988). These books not only cover everything a litigator needs to know but also make wonderful gifts for anyone.

6. *See* Roger S. Haydock, Negotiation Practice (1984); Louis Brown & Edward Dauer, Planning By Lawyers (1978).

Legal Periodicals. Although less pragmatically focused and often given to faddishness (*e.g.*, a symposium on the Law of Kumquats), law review articles may be useful both for assembling information and providing reflections on a legal issue. Lawyers' magazines are mercifully much shorter and usually more practical—especially magazines for litigators (no, not the ones about guns or famous battles).

Cases and Statutes. Consultation of these various sources should produce some general rules of doctrine and promising case citations. Yes, one really should read the cases at this point rather than taking the annotated summary at face value. These cases will cite other cases, many of which should also be reviewed. The most, important cases, pro and con, should be Shepardized to determine whether they remain good law or have been interpreted further. If leading cases from other jurisdictions are found, West's Practice Digest and Key Number system will facilitate finding similar cases in the applicable jurisdiction. These cases can be traced further through Shepardizing, and so on. In using traditional legal sources, counsel may wish to concentrate on the thing involved in the case (*e.g.*, a punch press), the act complained of (*e.g.*, assault and battery), the persons involved (*e.g.*, minors, or landlord and tenant), the place in question (*e.g.*, public lands), or some combination of these components.[7]

Computerized Research. Research with the aid of a computer can be used at any time during the research process. In some cases, the computer may be the most effective way to begin the research. In most cases, computerized legal research can be best used after traditional sources have been reviewed. If the subject matter of the case is clearly defined, relatively rare, and closely related to the legal issues of the case, the computer may be made to order for the project. For example, a search for cases involving claims against a tenant for excrement damage to an apartment's carpeting will probably net only a handful of cases with one or two simple search commands to the computer. In 10 minutes counsel has located the applicable precedent. In other fact situations, *e.g.*, a rear-end automobile collision producing whiplash, all but the most scalpel-like search commands will produce a mountain of cases too voluminous to read. Legal doctrines present the same problem. Only relatively clear cut doctrines using the same terminology throughout jurisdictions will produce the short list of relevant cases desired by counsel.

The computer can help to convince the client or senior partner that there really isn't a case in any jurisdiction discussing whether a circus promoter may obtain specific performance of a contract with a singing camel. Computers are also ideal for finding the case known only by name or subject matter through a conversation and recent cases not yet published in printed reporters. Computers can also quickly find the cite to the official report of the slip opinion read about in a trade publication and can be a wonderfully efficient way to Shepardize cases.

7. *See* Marjorie D. Rombauer, Legal Problem Solving (3d ed. 1978).

Specialized Research. The research sources and techniques listed above suffice for most legal questions faced by a practicing attorney. However, specialized areas require resort to specialized research tools. Complex questions of statutory interpretation can be aided by examination of legislative history, to which U.S. Code Congressional and Administrative News is the most convenient conduit and a guide to more detailed research. Administrative litigation makes knowledge and use of the Code of Federal Regulations, the Federal Register, Administrative Law Judge Decisions, Agency Board of Appeals Reports, informal rulings (such as Internal Revenue Service letter rulings published in the Cumulative Bulletin), and looseleaf reporters essential. Law review articles (yes, some do serve a practical purpose) and annotated cases contained in American Law Reporters (A.L.R.) may be helpful, or may be mere tangential overkill, depending on the problem.

§ 2.3 DETERMINING THE APPLICABLE LAW

In researching the law, one should be sure to get to know the right law. Normally, this is obvious and reflexive. Most litigation involves parties within the same state or subject to the same federal laws. The typical case does not require any choice of law analysis. Where a case does admit of some choice of law issue, most often either the choice of law is clear or the differences between the choices are inconsequential. Occasionally, however, the case requires consideration of choice of the applicable law. This should occur early in the case analysis to avoid wasted effort or taking an unwarranted position.

State Litigation. State courts usually apply the law of the forum unless the law of another state applies. See, you too could have written some of this book. The strong preference of most state courts is to apply the law of the forum state unless there exists some clear reason why the law of another state should apply. Under contract law, the state law where the contract was executed usually applies, but the law of another jurisdiction may apply if one or both parties have significant relationships in that state. Under tort law, the state law where the incident occurred typically applies, but the law of another jurisdiction may apply if significant contacts exist in that state. Cases which involve facts occurring in multiple states may present a complex choice of law question, the resolution of which extends far beyond the parameters of this book and the care of the authors. Section 4.5.2 explains the concepts of minimum contacts. Other authoritative sources provide answers to such questions for those with either an insatiable curiosity or a client with fee paying abilities.[1]

Federal Litigation. Federal courts rely on federal law most of the time, not an odd result considering that federal statutes, decisions,

§ 2.3

1. *See, e.g.,* Restatement (Second) of Conflicts of Laws (1971): Russell J. Weintraub, Commentary on the Conflict of Laws (1971); Robert Leflar, American Conflicts Law (1968); Albert A. Ehrenzweig, Treatise on the Conflict of Laws (1962).

regulations, and the Constitution comprise the usual basis for federal court jurisdiction. However, federal jurisdiction may also be based on diversity of citizenship involving state law claims between citizens of different states. In these cases based on state law claims, which comprise 25 percent of federal case filings and half the cases tried, the federal court must apply the most appropriate state law.[2] In selecting the applicable law, the federal court applies the choice of law principles of the forum state,[3] as discussed in the previous paragraph.

Generally, all states now provide for the weighing of the contacts of the various states with the claims presented and parties involved in the litigation [4] and often the governmental interests of each state as well [5] in choosing the applicable law. Although federal courts are reputedly not as prone to apply forum law as state courts, both courts tend to favor local law.

The applicable law in a federal diversity cases involves both state and federal law. Federal courts apply state law to the substantive issues and federal law to the procedural aspects of the case. They also apply any other applicable federal law intended to override state law concerning the subject matter of the case.[6] In determining whether state law is substantive, the court must decide whether its application would significantly affect the outcome of the case.[7] Generally, state rules regarding the existence of a cause of action, liability, and the measure of damages, are substantive and outcome determinative. Rules regarding pleadings, motions, pretrial practice, case management, and admissibility of evidence are procedural. Some, such as the right to a jury trial, are both procedural and implicate a strong federal policy interest or law such as the seventh amendment. Statutes of limitation, although obviously important to case outcomes, are usually viewed as procedural. If you can sue in a jurisdiction with a long limitations period, you get the benefit of the extra time even if the case has little relation to that forum. Because of the ultimate impact any procedural rule may have on the ultimate result in a case, the rules and precedent regarding the substantive/procedural distinction under *Erie Railroad Co. v. Tompkins* [8] are complex and sometimes apparently inconsistent. (If you do not recall the *Erie* doctrine you may want to check your passing grade in Civil Procedure or the professor's resume.)

2. *Erie Railroad Co. v. Tompkins,* 304 U.S. 64, 58 S.Ct. 817, 82 L.Ed. 1188 (1938).

3. *Klaxon Co. v. Stentor Electric Manufacturing Co.,* 313 U.S. 487, 61 S.Ct. 1020, 85 L.Ed. 1477 (1941).

4. *See* Restatement (Second) of Conflict of Laws § 6 (1971).

5. *See, e.g., Melville v. American Home Assurance Co.,* 584 F.2d 1306 (3d Cir.1978).

6. *Hanna v. Plumer,* 380 U.S. 460, 85 S.Ct. 1136, 14 L.Ed.2d 8 (1965).

7. *See Byrd v. Blue Ridge Rural Electric Cooperative, Inc.,* 356 U.S. 525, 78 S.Ct. 893, 2 L.Ed.2d 953 (1958); *Guaranty Trust Co. v. York,* 326 U.S. 99, 65 S.Ct. 1464, 89 L.Ed. 2079 (1945).

8. 304 U.S. 64, 58 S.Ct. 817, 82 L.Ed. 1188 (1938). For further information on *Erie*, see Charles A. Wright & Arthur R. Miller, Federal Practice and Procedure § 1208 (2d ed. 1990; Supp. 1994) (deals with pleading of diversity jurisdiction); John Cound, et al., Civil Procedure 277–325 (3d ed. 1980); Henry J. Friendly, In Praise of *Erie*—And of the New Federal Common Law, 39 N.Y.U.L.Rev. 383 (1964).

Applicable Law. A litigator making a vertical (federal-state) election of judicial forum usually does not influence the substantive law applied. Whether a state law claim is decided in a federal court or in a state court, the same state law will apply. Whether a federal claim is decided in a state court or a federal court, the same federal law will apply. However, horizontal (state-state) forum selection may well determine the substantive law, because different forums will apply different substantive law because these forums apply different choice of law factors. Further, the procedural law of a case may influence its progress and outcome, and a litigator who has an option of more than one forum must determine the influence of the various procedural laws. Section 3.2.2 details these and other considerations involved in selecting the most appropriate judicial forum.

§ 2.4 FACT INVESTIGATION

§ 2.4.1 Introduction

A fact source is anything that provides, describes, or explains facts helpful to the litigation. The most common fact sources include people, documents, records, physical objects, and scientific data. Much of the information obtainable by investigation methods will also be obtainable pursuant to discovery requests and subpoenas. Chapters 4 through 9 discuss these formal methods. This Chapter covers pre-discovery fact investigation.

There are several investigative approaches used to obtain information from or about people and events. These approaches include: searches for documentary or physical evidence, interviewing, and obtaining witness statements.

The success of a case depends upon preliminary factual investigation as much as any other facet of litigation practice. Perceptions and memories of witnesses are invariably incomplete and filtered. Interview techniques employed may easily affect the information obtained. Identifying and locating documents can be an elusive project. Informal investigation substantially increases the chances of success. Prior to litigation, counsel must depend upon the cooperation of witnesses, the professional skills and ingenuity of the investigation, and such devices as the Freedom of Information Act.[1] Many investigatory tasks can be and should be done by non-lawyers. However, litigators still need to understand investigation techniques to evaluate and direct the litigation.

§ 2.4.2 The Investigation Process

The legal and practical ramifications of an investigation affect the determination of whether and how an investigation should proceed. Before and during an investigation, the litigator must review and consider the various facets of the investigation process. These questions include:

§ 2.4

1. *See* 5 U.S.C.A. § 552.

- When should an investigation begin? (§ 2.5.3)
- Who should conduct the investigation? (§ 2.5.4)
- What sources of information are available? (§ 2.5.5)
- What physical evidence is available? (§ 2.5.6)
- Who should be interviewed? (§ 2.5.7)
- Why should a witness be interviewed? (§ 2.5.8)
- How can a witness be located? (§ 2.5.9)
- What types of interviews are there? (§ 2.5.10)
- What types of witnesses are there? (§ 2.5.11)
- Why should a witness talk? (§ 2.5.12)
- How can the cooperation of a witness be obtained? (§ 2.5.13)
- What types of questions should be asked? (§ 2.5.14)
- What topics should be covered? (§ 2.5.15)
- How should the interview be conducted? (§§ 2.5.16 & .17)
- What should be included in a file memo? (§ 2.5.18)
- Should a witness statement be obtained? (§§ 2.5.19 & .20)
- Should the interview be recorded? (§ 2.5.21)
- Who should be provided a witness statement? (§ 2.5.22)
- Can a witness be paid? (§ 2.5.23)
- What advice can be provided a witness? (§ 2.5.25)

The resolution of these questions has a profound (is there any other) impact upon the development of a case. Who conducts an investigation and under whose authority may ultimately determine whether the information obtained is privileged.[2] The existence and location of individuals who have information about a case and whose identity is obtained through investigatory efforts may be discoverable even if those individuals have unfavorable information.[3] A signed witness statement may be discoverable in some jurisdictions where an unsigned statement would not be discoverable.[4]

§ 2.4.3 Timing of Investigations

The best time to begin an investigation is when the investigation begins. But you knew that before you started law school. A litigator should review several factors that influence the determination of when an investigation should be initiated.

Type of Case. Certain cases lend themselves to early investigation. An auto accident case usually prompts the lawyer to immediately conduct an investigation including obtaining photographs, preserving poten-

2. *See* Section 5.7.
3. *See* Section 5.7.2.
4. *See* Section 5.7.2.

tial evidence, and contacting eyewitnesses. A commercial contract case usually can be factually developed through formal discovery and depositions without the need for immediate informal investigation. The facts of each case ultimately determine the timing of an investigation.

Legal Issues. The nature of the legal claims and defenses also affect factual investigations. Cases that involve simple and straightforward legal matters often proceed without factual investigation. Cases that involve complex claims or complicated defenses often proceed with attempts to dismiss, clarify, or narrow the issues before conducting extensive investigation.

Initial Client Contact. The point at which the client contacts a lawyer also influences the need to begin immediate investigative efforts. If the events creating the claims or defenses are completed before the initial client contact then a complete investigation may commence. If the events are still evolving when the client contacts the attorney, then an investigation may await completion of the events, unless it is advisable to begin collecting information immediately.

Sources to Be Investigated. The source of the factual information further affects the beginning of the investigation. The search for documentary information that is not subject to change or loss may be delayed until later in the investigation process. The search for accurate and reliable information from a witness should begin as soon after an event as possible to avoid loss of memory.

There are other advantages to the early interview of a witness. Interviewing a witness before the other side does increases the probability that the story will be fresh, will reduce the chance that the witness will have developed a bias or prejudice, and may develop an interest on the part of the witness toward the party who conducts the first interview. A neutral witness may not consider the first interview as much a bother as subsequent interviews and may be susceptible to suggestions made by the first investigator. An adverse witness, particularly an unsophisticated witness, may provide information or give a statement that may harm the adversary later. Further, an unfriendly witness may not yet have developed enough hostility to refuse to be interviewed. A potential party who has not yet retained an attorney will still be able to be interviewed because DR7–104(A)(1) of the Code of Professional Responsibility bars such contact only if an attorney has been retained.

Delaying Investigation. Delaying factual inquiries may prevent potential opposing parties from becoming aware of possible litigation and conducting themselves in a way which favors their interests. Parties made aware of the legal consequences of their conduct may immediately begin to act differently to avoid potential liability. Postponing an informal interview may be appropriate in favor of a deposition. Delaying factual investigation may also permit necessary legal research. The pursuit of legal research before the pursuit of facts may provide new insights and perspectives that make initial factual investigation more effective and efficient.

§ 2.4.4 *Investigative Personnel*

There are a number of individuals who can and should conduct a factual investigation. The litigating attorney, an associate attorney, a paralegal, a law clerk, the client, a law firm investigator, and a private investigator are all possible candidates.

It is proper and legal for a law firm to hire a full time investigator or to retain a private investigator for a specific task.[5] Most states require investigators to be licensed. These statutes establish qualifications, create a board to review complaints, and establish grounds for revocation or suspension.[6] For example, it is improper for an investigator to solicit business for a lawyer, to impersonate a law officer or government official, or to commit dishonest or fraudulent acts(?).[7] Information obtained by an investigator may be privileged and only communicable to a client.[8]

Who should do what depends upon their availability, their knowledge of the case, their qualifications and abilities, and what needs to be done.

Knowledge of Case. Before conducting an investigation an investigator needs to know information relevant to the investigation. Exactly what an investigator needs to know will depend upon the type and scope of the investigation. The more extensive the investigation to be conducted, the more an investigator needs to know about the entire case. The more narrow or limited the scope of the investigation, the less an investigator needs to understand.

Whoever is selected to investigate facts must be qualified and have the abilities to effectively conduct the investigation. Obviously simple investigative tasks, *e.g.*, going to a governmental office and obtaining public documents requires neither a Holmes nor Mason. Not as obvious is that the interview of any witness, however favorable or cooperative, demands special knowledge and abilities. Whether an attorney, or a paralegal, or an experienced investigator should investigate depends upon an analysis of the preceding factors. An attorney will usually be more knowledgeable about a case; a paralegal will usually cost less; and an experienced investigator may be the most effective and efficient. The degree of difficulty required for the investigation, along with the availability of an individual, will determine who will do what.

Some investigations should not be conducted by the attorney as this may result in the attorney becoming a witness at the trial. DR 5–102 of the Code of Professional Responsibility and Rule 3.7 of the Model Rules for Professional Conduct strongly discourage attorneys from testifying in

5. *In re Moore,* 8 Ill.2d 373, 134 N.E.2d 324 (1956).

6. *See, e.g.* Minn.Stat.Ann. § 326.331.

7. *See, e.g. Bryant v. Private Investigators' Licensing Board,* 92 Nev. 278, 549 P.2d 327 (1976); *Commonwealth v. Gregg,* 262 Pa.Super. 364, 396 A.2d 797 (1979); *Sterling Secret Service, Inc. v. Michigan Department of State Police,* 20 Mich.App. 502, 174 N.W.2d 298 (1969); *People v. Corey,* 21 Cal.3d 738, 147 Cal.Rptr. 639, 581 P.2d 644 (1978).

8. *See, e.g.,* Nev.Rev.Stat. 648.200.

a case, lest the jurors have to evaluate the credibility of the lawyer as a witness as well as an advocate. In situations where the investigator may become a witness, for example, to provide impeachment testimony, a non-lawyer should conduct that part of the investigation. Use of non-lawyers also frees the lawyer to concentrate on the overall case management.

§ 2.4.5 Sources of Information

Most sources of information are apparent from the nature of the case. Individuals with information are often known by a client. The location of many documents are apparent from the circumstances. The following list details common sources of information available in many cases.

Motor Vehicle/Department of Transportation	Vehicle Registration/Ownership, Driver's license information, Auto license information
Secretary of State	Status of Corporations/Business licenses
Public Utilities	Names and addresses
Telephone Directory	Phone numbers and addresses
City Directories	Name, address, employment, family
Cross–Reference Directory	Address or telephone number
Business/Professional Directories	Employment information
Government Offices	Marriages, births, deaths, wills, divorces, military information
Post Office	Address
Court Records	Litigation information and criminal record
Departments of Taxation	Real estate information/Income information
Property Departments	Real estate information
Credit Bureaus	Names, addresses, debts
Police Records	Criminal Violations
Employers	General information
Banks/Financial Institutions	Credit information/Financial condition
Retail Stores	Credit and personal information
Housing Departments	Building permits
Newspapers	Past and present information
Libraries	You name it
Department of Education/Schools	Educational information

Some of this information may be unobtainable because of internal regulations by a source or because the law has declared some information private and confidential. Other basic information about a witness can be easily obtained from a number of these sources. For example:

City and county directories provide an alphabetical list of the name, address, marital status, and occupation of each resident and the name, address, office personnel, and nature of business of firms and corporations. These directories list people who have unlisted telephone numbers or who may not appear in the local telephone directory.

The Post Office will supply a forwarding address upon receiving an address correction request (assuming the last address is known) and a small fee.

The state agency that licenses drivers will usually make available the current address of a driver. The agency will need the name of the person along with some other information, such as date of birth.

Real estate records maintained by the local government office will provide information about a person's property assets.

It may be advisable or necessary in some situations to contact a source by letter or phone to schedule an appointment to obtain information. Scheduling an interview may prevent a wasted trip and may allow a source to gather some information. On the other hand, providing notice may prepare a source when it would be better if the contact was a surprise.

Another consideration relating to information sources is to determine the order of seeking information. Who should be contacted first? Who should be interviewed next? What documents should be gathered when? Counsel must answer these and other questions before an investigation begins.

§ 2.4.6 Tangible Objects and Physical Evidence

Cases will usually involve some form of tangible objects or physical evidence that need to be investigated or preserved. Categories of such information include:

> Documents including statements, contract letters, records, computer discs, and other writings and forms of writings;
>
> Photographs, slides, movies, videotapes, x-rays;
>
> Diagrams, maps, charts, models;
>
> Laboratory or medical tests and results;
>
> Objects or articles involved in the event; and
>
> Physical surroundings and the location of an event.

An investigator may only need to collect and catalogue some of these objects, such as documents, and may need to create or supervise other exhibits, such as photographs. Typical tasks include the collection and copying of exhibits, sending and reviewing of documents, taking of photographs and drawing of diagrams, visiting of a scene, and testing of an object and related tasks.

§ 2.4.7 *Purposes of Interviews*

Documentary evidence is particularly useful and persuasive in a case. Witnesses may be mistaken or confused, but a document speaks for itself, especially if an opponent's document provides helpful information. Usually, documents will be available from friendly or neutral sources. An unfriendly source, *e.g.*, a potentially adverse party, will not often cooperate in voluntarily disclosing the smoking paper. Friendly sources usually cooperate. Neutral witnesses may balk at first, but after being reminded that the documents can be subpoenaed may mellow. Custodians of privileged documents (like medical and hospital records) may not be able to disclose such information without a written release. Governmental sources may disclose through the Federal Freedom of Information Act and related state law statutes.

An investigative technique that involves the creation of evidence is photographing, filming, or videotaping an adverse witness or party. In a personal injury case, for example, the defendant or potential defendant may film the plaintiff to prove what the plaintiff can do or looks like to reduce claims of injury and damages. Surveillance films may be taken after litigation has begun and close to the trial date. There is nothing unethical per se in the creation of these films, even though done surreptitiously. The tactical use of the information will depend upon its results. If the plaintiff, a supposed paraplegic, is filmed playing playground basketball then the film should be used and later sold to Francis Ford Coppolla. Film showing a real paraplegic who looks depressed 60% of the time should be left on the editing room floor. Jurors usually resent invasions of privacy unless the film portrays the party as a malingerer or liar.

§ 2.4.8 *Who Should Be Interviewed and Why?*

All persons should be interviewed who have information whether helpful or harmful. Witness interviews serve several purposes, including:

1. Learning everything the witness knows about an entire event or part of an event.

2. Seeking limited and specific information about a particular event.

3. Obtaining admissions from the witness and committing the witness to an established story.

4. Leading the witness and suggesting what happened in an attempt to have the witness agree with favorable facts and disagree with unfavorable facts.

5. Obtaining information useful to impeach the witness or to reduce credibility.

6. Uncovering information the other side already knows.

§ 2.4.9 Locating Witnesses

Many individuals with information about a case will be known to the client, obvious from the circumstances, or identifiable through investigation. Known individuals may know of unknown witnesses. A canvas of people who might have seen or heard something may produce additional witnesses. Searching through sources listed in Section 2.5.5 may likewise produce witness leads.

In some cases, witnesses will avoid being contacted or may disappear. It may be necessary in these situations to retain an experienced investigator or "skip tracer" to locate difficult to find witnesses. Traditional methods to locate witnesses may be unsuccessful, prompting the use of subterfuge or pretexts to find a witness. Often individuals, such as relatives, friends or employers, who know the whereabouts of a prospective witness will not disclose the location of the witness if they know why the witness is being sought. In these circumstances the investigator will either assume another identity or advise the person that the witness is being sought for another reason. For example, the investigator may identify himself or herself as a prospective employer seeking to offer the missing witness a lucrative job. Or the investigator may pretend to be a florist and ask for the address of the witness so that the flowers can be delivered. Or the investigator may claim to owe the witness money or to be an old school friend. These pretexts and other subterfuges may be necessary because they may be the only successful method to locate a recalcitrant witness.

Those of you bothered by these tactics, particularly if directly used by an attorney, may also be bothered by tactics presented in the following section. The ethical issues inherent in these tactics will be discussed in that section. Hold on to your convictions and concerns until then.

§ 2.4.10 Types of Witness Interviews

There are three types of witness interviews.

1. *The Overt Interview.* The witness knows the true identity of the interviewer and the purpose of the interview. This is by far the most common type of interview in litigation.

2. *The Discreet Interview.* The witness knows the identity of the interviewer but does not know the true purpose for the interview. The interviewer may either not explain the real purpose of the interview or may pretend that the information will be used for some purpose unrelated to litigation.

3. *The Covert Interview.* The witness does not know either the true identity nor the real purpose of the interview. The interviewer employs tactics similar to the skip tracer tactics explained in the previous section.

Legal investigators should always conduct or try to conduct an overt interview. Neither the Code of Professional Responsibility nor the Rules for Professional Conduct provide any specific guidance regarding the ethical nature of discreet or covert interview techniques. The occasions when a discreet or covert interview is necessary should be reserved for those situations when the witness will not talk if they know the identity of the interviewer or the purpose of the interview. This is far easier said than done. It is difficult to anticipate whether a witness will balk at being interviewed and a discreet or covert interview is necessary. Obviously, it will be too late to use those approaches if the witness refuses to cooperate after learning the interviewer's goal.

The legal investigator should not rely upon pretext or subterfuge except in situations when an honest and straightforward approach will not be effective. The first instinct of a legal investigation should be to apply investigative techniques which persuade a reluctant witness to talk. The second instinct should be to try those techniques again. Only then should a legal investigator consider using questionable methods to obtain information.

Tactical reasons also militate against using lies and falsehoods to obtain information. How facts are obtained may taint their value in the litigation. Jurors may consider pretexts and subterfuge improper and view the lawyer who authorized or used such tactics as less credible. These methods are possibly more acceptable in criminal cases where certain crimes could not be successfully prosecuted without the use of informants or surreptitious surveillance. Fortunately, legitimate and honest investigative approaches usually are effective in civil cases.

Many lawyers find pretext and subterfuge techniques sleazy and ethically improper. Other lawyers believe they are legitimate investigative tools. The techniques appear to be unseemly, and they do not project an image of an honest and fair profession. However, these questionable techniques may prove necessary in some cases if a lawyer is to obtain essential information and if a lawyer is to fulfill the obligation to represent client interests zealously. As you know from agency law, the ethical dilemma does not disappear by having an independent investigator conduct the investigation.

§ 2.4.11 Types of Witnesses

Witnesses may be favorable or unfavorable, cooperative or uncooperative, neutral or biased, impartial or prejudiced. A witness may begin as cooperative and become uncooperative. A witness may have both helpful and harmful information. The approach taken towards a favorable, cooperative witness may be far different than the approach taken toward an unfavorable, uncooperative witness. The anticipated information and the expected reaction of the witness needs to be analyzed in preparing for a witness interview.

Friendly Witness Interviews. These interviews, though usually easy to conduct, involve some aspects that may be troublesome. The investigator must be careful that the witness does not provide slanted or biased information, that the witness does not withhold unfavorable information, and that the cooperative attitude of the witness does not reduce the credibility of the witness.

Neutral Witness Interviews. These interviews may be easy or difficult to conduct depending upon the reaction of the witness. It is very difficult to provide specific suggestions for these witnesses because of the numerous possible responses.

Unfriendly Witness Interviews. These witnesses usually make it difficult for an interviewer to obtain useful or helpful information. Commonly effective tactics to employ with these witnesses are: (1) attempting to obtain information in as least harmful an explanation as possible and (2) establishing the factual or other basis for the unfriendly attitude and prejudice.

Favorable Information Interview. It is usually best to record favorable information obtained from a witness. This procedure preserves the favorable nature of the facts.

Unfavorable Information. It may not be best to record unfavorable information. There may be no need to preserve such facts. The other side will benefit more from such information and the witness may later change the story reducing the unfavorable impact.

§ 2.4.12 ***Reasons to Talk***

Witnesses will usually be willing to be interviewed if they have a reason to talk. Cooperative witnesses will have their own reasons to provide information. Neutral or uncooperative witnesses may need to be provided a reason by the interviewer. A reasonable explanation by the interviewer of the vital need of the information usually prompts most witnesses to provide some information. This direct explanation may not persuade all witnesses and an interviewer needs to consider employing additional techniques. The following examples include alternative explanations which may convince a witness of the wisdom of talking now instead of later.

> If you tell me what you know now it will help resolve the matter without any further involvement on your part.
>
> This will only take a few minutes of your time now and save you time later.

These explanations point out to the witness the convenience of providing information now.

> If you were in my client's position you would want someone like yourself to help, wouldn't you?
>
> We all have some responsibility to help others and this will be your way of helping my client.

These reasons play to the sense of responsibility a witness may have.

> You need not tell me what you know but you can confirm or deny what I know so that I can make sure it is accurate. I will tell you what I know and you can confirm or correct it, O.K.?

This approach may induce the witness to begin giving yes or no responses followed by some narrative information.

> You may want to tell me some things, at least that relate to you, because some of this information directly involves you and what you said and did. Let me ask you a few questions to clarify your involvement.

This technique attempts to gain information by suggesting that it is in the best interests of the witness to answer some questions.

> You may change your mind and want to talk if you knew what some people have said about you. Ms. Parker told me you were drunk that night and slapped her.

This approach may prompt some witnesses to become defensive or emotional and talk to protect themselves.

> If you decide not to talk to me now you will have to talk to me later. You will be subpoenaed and will have to appear at some inconvenient time and place to talk. Let's talk now to avoid that.

This approach may result in the witness talking, but it may also backfire with the witness becoming irritated over the threat.

§ 2.4.13 ***Obtaining and Maintaining Witness Cooperation***

An interviewer can significantly increase the cooperation provided by a witness by following specific interviewing approaches. An effective interviewer will:

Select the Appropriate Time, Place, and Circumstances for an Interview. The interview should not occur at a time of major inconvenience for the witness. A time should be selected when the witness will have sufficient time to talk. The location of an interview should be selected that provides sufficient privacy, avoids distractions, contributes to a comfortable environment, and otherwise is appropriate for the interview.

Consider the Effect of the Presence of Others. Try to interview a witness separately to avoid the influence caused by others present. If there is more than one witness present this may take more time but may produce more independent recollections. If a witness is with a spouse, relative, friend, or group it may be tactically difficult to talk with them individually. When someone else is present the interviewer should concentrate on obtaining information from the witness while attempting to reduce whatever influence others may have.

Create and Maintain a Comfortable Atmosphere. Effective eye contact, appropriate body language, supportive facial expressions, appropriate physical distance, and other nonverbal behavior should be employed to establish a comfortable environment for the witness to talk.

Empathize With and Respect the Witness. It can be uncomfortable, inconvenient, and difficult for a witness to be interviewed. An interviewer who treats the witness with respect and who appears to care about the witness may be more favorably received by that witness.

Listen and Identify With the Witness. Listening provides the interviewer with the opportunity to identify with any positions or interests mentioned by the witness. The interviewer should listen not only for facts but also for matters which relate to the personal interests of the witness. Inquiries into these areas may make the witness more comfortable and willing to disclose more information.

Personalize the Client. Witnesses may be more inclined to talk if they perceive themselves as helping someone who deserves their assistance. Descriptions of the client that portray an individual who needs help creates such an image.

Be Polite and Courteous While Being Persistent. It is obvious that an impolite and rude interviewer will obtain no interview. It is difficult to remain polite and courteous with witnesses who may themselves be impolite and rude. The professional investigator needs to remain calm and persist in continuing the interview.

Reinforce Responses and Behavior by the Witness. Witnesses who are continually encouraged to talk during an interview will provide additional information.

Remain Aware of Resistance and Defensiveness. An interviewer can prevent a witness from becoming defensive or refusing to talk by remaining cognizant of questions or answers that may trigger such a response. The timing of inquiries often determines whether a witness will respond. Certain questions asked early in the interview may not be answered, but may be answered if asked later after an interviewer establishes a relationship with the witness.

§ 2.4.14 Interview Questions

A variety of interview questions may be employed by an interviewer to obtain information. The type and timing of a question will depend upon the kind of information sought and the purpose for asking the question. Investigation questions are identical or similar to questions used during client interviews, depositions, and direct and cross-examinations and are not unique to the investigative process.

Narrative Questions. Broad, open-ended questions usually lead to narrative responses by the interviewee. "What happened?" and "What did you see?" questions are designed to allow the witness to generally describe events.

Specific Questions. Narrow, closed-ended questions seek specific information. "Where was Mr. Prince standing?" and "What was the license number?" are designed to obtain detailed facts.

Probing Questions. Witnesses may not reveal everything they know. Persistent follow up questions or unanswered questions reasked later may result in a witness providing the missing information.

Yes/No Questions. These questions which seek a yes or no response verify or confirm affirmative or negative facts. Examples are "Did you see Ms. Hamilton sign the contract?" and "Were you at your office at 3:30 P.M.?" These questions differ from leading questions in that they do not suggest the answer.

Leading Questions. Questions which suggest the answer may be asked to suggest answers and validate or invalidate certain facts. "You weren't speeding through the intersection, were you?" and "You did leave your keys in the car, right?" are examples.

Opinion Questions. Information disclosing opinions in addition to facts will be helpful to an investigation. Opinion and factual information often overlap, *e.g.*, "Why do you think he did that?" and "About how far away was she?"

Attitude Questions. These questions may result in useful information. Examples include: "Did you like him when he did that?" and "How did you feel then?"

Memory Aid Questions. Witnesses may not initially remember some fact or may only recall a portion of an event. By asking certain questions the interviewer may assist the witness in recalling the forgotten. For example, retrospective questions which place the witness back at the time, place, and circumstances of the situation may help. "What time of the day did it happen?; Who else was present?; Where were you roller blading?" are examples.

§ 2.4.15 *Interview Topics*

The preparation for every interview requires the investigator to decide what topics need to be covered. The particular facts of each case will influence what is asked but a review of generic topics assists in determining what to cover.

- Identity of witness, including the name, address, phone number, employment, and other personal information.
- Who, what, where, when, why and how inquiries.
- Documents and physical objects.
- Favorable information.
- What the witness does not know.
- Hearsay and gossip.
- Corroborating or contradictory information.
- Prior interviews or written statements.

The interview should be thorough. Detailed information should be sought. For example, when a witness is asked to describe a person, the witness may describe the person's sex, race, apparent age, height, weight, and perhaps some additional details. Numerous specific questions may reveal substantially more information, such as the person's:

Hair	Color of Clothes	Speech
Eyes	Fabric/Texture	Scars
Ears	Articles Carried	Tattoos
Shape of Face	Glasses	Physical Posture
Complexion	Smoking	Walking Gait
Build	Jewelry	Right/Left Handed
Facial Hair	Condition of Teeth	Physical Handicaps

The interviewer should conclude the interview by asking if the witness knows anything else. Occasionally a witness will offer some information not covered during the interview. The investigator should also leave a card or name and phone number with the witness so the witness can later contact the investigator if something is omitted or subsequently learned.

A common alternative tactic is to conduct two interviews of a witness. The first interview is designed to determine what the interviewee knows or does not know. The second interview will follow if the information the witness knows should be preserved. The investigator during the first interview may conduct a narrative interview. The investigator during the second interview may solicit or suggest certain information through direct and cross-examination techniques and preserve the information provided by the witness. These multiple interviews avoid the problem of having the investigator make a spontaneous decision of how to ultimately approach a witness and preserve information.

§ 2.4.16 Interview Techniques

The three most common interviewing techniques are: the narrative approach, direct examination, and cross-examination. These techniques may be and usually are mixed during any one interview. The narrative approach has the witness relate in story form what the witness knows. Direct examination involves the use of specific questions and elicits new information, clarifies previous information, and adds details. Cross-examination resembles the approach taken during depositions to resolve conflicting information, complete and pursue evasive answers, draw inferences, test the perception and memory of the witness, evaluate the credibility of the witness, and search for impeachment areas.

§ 2.4.17 Slanting the Interview Responses

Investigators may attempt to influence the responses a witness gives during an interview. This approach recognizes that witnesses may not have seen or heard everything, may have forgotten some things, or may be mistaken regarding their perceptions. An investigator may assist a witness in accurately remembering and correctly reciting information. This approach also provides an opportunity for misuse if an investigator tries to force the witness to provide false information or unknown facts.

This latter approach is clearly unethical and illegal. The former approach may or may not be appropriate or effective.

Techniques that investigators employ to influence witnesses are subtle and indirect and include:

- *Word Choice.* The selection of certain words may create a more helpful and persuasive witness story and statement. The suggestion or inclusion of adjectives and impact words may strengthen a witness' version. For example, adding "very" to modify the word fast will make an obvious difference; and substituting "slapped" for "hit" or "screamed" for "yelled" may make a slight difference. Investigators may select certain words or phrases and attempt to have the witness adopt them.
- *Leading Questions.* As mentioned previously these questions which suggest the answer may have the witness agreeing with the suggested answer.
- *Filling in Details.* A witness may forget some detail and the interviewer may tell the witness what happened so that the witness will include that information in his or her story or statement.
- *Other Versions.* Before interviewing a witness about part or all of a story the investigator may tell the witness what other witnesses have said to influence the interviewee. For example, the investigator may say: "Three witnesses have told me the light was green, what color did you see?" This technique uses peer pressure to influence the witness.
- *Disagreeing With the Answers.* After a witness relates some information the interviewer may explain why the information is inaccurate, implausible, or mistaken in an attempt to change the mind of the witness.
- *Composing the Story for the Witness.* After an interview, the investigator may draft a witness statement. In composing the story the investigator may state the information in as favorable a light as possible for the client.

§ 2.4.18 *Maintaining a Record of the Interview*

Information obtained from a client interview that is not recorded may be difficult to use, corroborate, or contradict. The information may be useful for planning purposes, but unless it is preserved, it may be difficult to recreate later. The three primary ways to corroborate or contradict an oral statement are: (1) another witness who is present, (2) interview notes, and (3) a recording. The first two means are fraught with deficiencies because the issue focuses on the credibility of the investigator as well as the witness. The recording option is the most common and effective.

An investigator who needs to make a record of the interview for future reference may select from three main techniques.

1. A file memo.

2. A written statement.

3. A contemporaneous recording.

File Memo. A file memo of an interview may contain several parts:

1. A summary of the information obtained. If no written statement or recording is made the file memo will typically include this information.

2. A description of the demeanor, characteristics, and credibility of the witness and the importance and implication of the information for trial. If the witness may testify in the case the interviewer will include impressions of the witness as a trial witness.

3. Additional relevant comments produced in the interview.

All memos should be drafted under the direction and supervision of the litigator. The content and comprehensiveness of the memo should reflect the needs of the litigation. Whatever the reasons for the memo—to assist with a preliminary analysis of the case, to be a source for references, to summarize information, or to preserve information for later use—influence the content of the file memo.

These file memos usually are not discoverable either because they are trial preparation materials or include attorney mental impressions, both components comprising "work product." File memos will be trial preparation materials as defined by Fed.R.Civ.P. 26(b)(3) and related state rules if they are conducted in anticipation of or during litigation, are created for litigation purposes, and are completed by or under the supervision of the litigator. Section 4.7 discusses in detail this transformation and the exceptions which justify the disclosure of these memos in certain cases.

Part of a file memo may be discoverable and part non-discoverable. Portions of investigative memos may be excised with the opposing party gaining access to the discoverable portions. A section of a memo that contains facts provided by a witness may be discoverable as a source of information; a portion of a memo that includes comments by the investigator will be non-discoverable as trial preparation materials or protected mental impressions. A memo that contains a summary of the facts may be made non-discoverable if the drafter mixes the facts with mental impressions and weaves comments by the investigator throughout the memo. These distinctions and alternative approaches need to be considered by the drafter.

Usually, it is best that the memos not be automatically discoverable by the opposing party. It is better for the litigator to have the option to disclose or not disclose a memo rather than be compelled by the rules. A litigator can voluntarily disclose a memo to the other side if it contains information the litigator wants the opposition to have.

A litigator may have to disclose documents containing facts as required by Federal Rule 26(a). This rule, and similar state rules, require the identification and disclosure of documents that contain certain information. Section 5.7 describes the nature of these documents in detail.

§ 2.4.19 Written Statements

The precise components of a written statement depend upon its purpose or purposes. An example of a witness statement appears on page 701. Witness statements typically include the following components:

1. *The Identity of the Witness.* The name and address or other identifying information should be included. This information may serve two purposes: to identify the person making the statement and to provide information for locating the witness later.

2. *Statements in the First Person.* Usually a witness statement will be written as "I" statements, as if the witness was telling the story. This will make the story more accurate and reliable and avoid the problems of describing an event in the third person.

3. *The Witness' Own Language and Expressions.* The statement should be written employing the words and method of expressions the witness used. The statement should read as if the witness provided the information not the investigator.

4. *Clear and Understandable Language.* The information contained in the statement should not be ambiguous or confusing unless that approach serves the interests of the client.

5. *Objective Information.* Usually the information should be stated in as objective a manner as possible, unless a slanted version serves the purpose of the interview.

6. *Opinion Information.* In addition to including acts in the statement, the addition of helpful opinions and conclusions by the witness may strengthen the impact of the statement.

7. *Edited Information.* Favorable information can be emphasized. Unfavorable information can be subordinated. Inconsequential information can be added to bolster the witness' perception and memory.

8. *Negative Information.* What the witness does not know about all or part of an event should be presented.

9. *Inadmissable Evidence.* Whether or not a statement should include information that would be inadmissable at trial depends upon the reasons for including the inadmissable evidence.

10. *Concluding Remarks.* The last sentence should include a statement that the witness has read the statement and that the statement is true and complete. Additional statements may be added, for example, that the witness voluntarily made the statement.

11. *Some Witnesses' Statements May Contain Form Information Including:* a title, persons present, date and beginning time, location where statement is made, and date and ending time. An occasional statement may also include a preamble which specifies some of the conditions for taking the statement to prevent the witness from later reneging, such as:

> My name is Oscar the Grouch and I live on Sesame Street. I agree to be interviewed by Kermit the Frog who is investigating this case for Ms. Piggy. I voluntarily make the following statement of my own free will which concerns my garbage can. I want to tell all the facts I know. I will not withhold any information. I agree to tell the truth. I understand this statement may be used in some form of public hearing or trial.

This form may be revised and included at the end of the statement as part of the closing remarks.

§ 2.4.20 Witness Statement Mechanics

Various factors compose the mechanical aspects of witness statements.

Timing. A witness statement may be composed during or immediately after an interview has been completed or may be composed at a later date. Completing the statement in the presence of the interviewee is the most efficient and economic procedure. Completing the statement later requires the investigator to meet with the witness again which permits some event to occur in the interim which may cause the witness to change the story. The advantage of not composing a statement during the initial interview is that the investigator can draft a more careful, favorable, and selective statement at a later date having had time to reflect on what the witness knows.

Format. Witness statements are typically handwritten or typewritten documents either by the witness or, more commonly, by the investigator. The investigator in drafting the statement is able to control its structure, the words used, the facts omitted, and related tactics. Statements may be typed or word processed if such equipment is available at the time of the interview or if the statement is composed at a time after the interview. Which format should be employed depends upon various factors, including the purpose for the statement and the information obtained.

Affidavit. A witness statement may also be composed as a sworn affidavit. The statement would begin with an affidavit preface and include a notary inscription signed by a notary who witnesses the signature of the witness. The form resembles any affidavit, an example of which appears on page 477. The value in using a sworn statement instead of an unsworn statement is the witness may take the matter more seriously, the oath will influence the witness to be sure to tell the truth, and the impeachment impact will be increased because of the inclusion of the oath. The disadvantage of an affidavit is the witness may be overly cautious or reluctant to talk under oath.

Review. After the statement has been drafted the witness should read it for accuracy and completeness. This procedure is necessary to conform to the concluding sentence which states that the witness has read the statement. This procedure is also necessary to correct any mistakes. Some investigators in drafting a statement intentionally include one or more errors which the witness discovers or which are pointed out to the witness after the witness finishes reading the statement. The witness will then correct and initial the corrections. These corrections are evidence the witness did read the statement, the other uncorrected information must be accurate, and the investigator did not make up the statement.

Adopting the Statement. There are a variety of ways in which a witness may adopt a statement. The witness who hand writes the statement, who initials each page, and who signs it clearly vouches for the statement. Some witnesses refuse to write, initial each page, or sign a statement. An investigator may be able to obtain the approval of the witness by suggesting alternative procedures. Some witnesses will agree to initial the last page of the statement; others will be comfortable signing a postscript after the statement which states they read the statement and that it is true and complete; others will agree to sign a postscript written by the investigator that the investigator read the statement to the witness and that the witness agrees it is true and complete; and still others may balk at signing anything no matter how creative or persistent the investigator may be.

§ 2.4.21 ***Recording the Statement***

Recording the interview may be preferable to composing a witness statement. The two most common forms of recording are audio recordings and court reporter statements. Audio recordings may be made with a tape recorder operated by the investigator or someone else. Statements may also be recorded by video camera.

A court reporter statement is a transcript prepared by a court reporter who accompanies an investigator and who contemporaneously records the interview with a steno machine or notepad. The court reporter statement may be taken under an oath administered to the witness by the notary public reporter. Many investigators prefer to use a court reporter who uses a pen to record the interview because the steno machine is too obtrusive. Some investigators dislike sworn statements because the oath will, as noted previously, disturb some witnesses. An example of the first page of a sworn statement appears on the adjacent page. Some court reporters use a tape recorder as a back up device to assure accuracy.

In most states it is permissible to electronically record a face to face interview without the knowledge or consent of the interviewee. It is permissible in all states to electronically record a face to face or telephone interview if both the interviewer and interviewee consent. It is permissible under the regulations of the Federal Communications Commission to record a telephone interview as long as one party consents.[9]

WITNESS STATEMENT UNDER OATH FORM

STATEMENT OF JANE EVERS

Stenographic report of statement of Jane Evers taken at [Outer Temple Inn], commencing at about the hour of 10:00 a.m. on [*day and date*], 19__.

PRESENT:

Brook Swane, Attorney-at-Law [or Investigator]

Jane Evers, Witness

Gene Ortiz, Reporter and Notary Public

Jane Evers, being first duly sworn by Gene Ortiz, a notary public, was interrogated by Brook Swane and stated as follows:

Q. Your name is Jane Evers?

A. Yes.

Q. You understand this statement is being [reported] [recorded]?

A. Yes.

Q. Ms. Evers, I am Brook Swane and I am going to be asking you some questions about an accident....

Swane: Well, I think that is all. Thank you very much.

(Statement concluded at 10:45 a.m.)

The alternative methods have advantages and disadvantages. These forms of recording are efficient and preserve the exact words of the witness. An audio recording also captures the voice inflections and sounds of the witness. A tape recorder or camera may make some witnesses uncomfortable causing them to decline to be interviewed. Electronics recordings may result in poor quality recordings if other people interject or comment when the recorder is on or if mechanical difficulties occur. A court reporter statement may cost a substantial amount of money to pay for the reporter's time during the interview and for transcribing the interview.

The frequency with which these methods are used depends upon the resources available and the issues at stake. Insurance claims agents investigating a minor case may conduct a tape recorded interview over the telephone and if investigating a major case may conduct a face to face recorded interview. Telephone interviews do not permit the investigator to positively identify the witness or properly evaluate credibility or appearance. Some lawyers traditionally prefer court reporter statements if the issues merit such a method and if the client can afford such an expense.

9. *See* 18 U.S.C.A. § 2511 and regulations promulgated thereunder.

§ 2.4.22 Copies of Witness Statements

Section 5.7.2 discusses the discoverability of witness statements by a party or by the witness under the rules of civil procedure. It may be advisable for an investigator to voluntarily give a copy of a statement to a witness immediately after the interview so that the witness can provide that statement to subsequent investigators and avoid making a second, and different, statement. This tactic is particularly applicable if the witness has favorable information. It may be inadvisable to provide a copy of a statement to a witness if the opposing side may prematurely obtain access to such information. A tactical decision may be unnecessary, because many states have statutes requiring anyone obtaining a written or recorded statement to provide the witness with a copy upon request.

§ 2.4.23 Payments to Witnesses

The general rules concerning payments to witnesses are: (1) the only expenses that may be reimbursed a lay witness include reasonable costs of travel and compensation for loss of time, (2) a lay witness cannot receive any money for being interviewed or for testifying, and (3) expert witnesses may be paid for their professional services. Jurisdictions usually codify or modify these general rules and may further restrict the scope of permissible compensation or the amount. DR 7–109(c) of the Code of Professional Responsibility and Rule 3–4(b) of the Model Rules of Professional Conduct clearly prohibit the payment to a lay witness for information or testimony and permit the payment or advance of "expenses reasonably incurred by a witness in attending or testifying" and "reasonable compensation ... for loss of time." Tactical considerations also influence the payment of compensation, even if legitimate, to witnesses. A witness who receives substantial reimbursement may appear to a fact finder to be biased in favor of the party who paid the money. This effect may preclude a litigator from paying a witness.

Some witnesses may expect to receive reimbursement for their time spent being interviewed. Individuals who may often be eyewitnesses, such as police and highway patrol officers, anticipate or request payment for their time. Unless a witness requests payment or unless the local practice requires the tender of expenses it is advisable not to offer to pay a witness. The amount that is authorized is usually so low that it will be an insufficient incentive to encourage the witness to cooperate and any larger payment may be illegal or unethical and will surely be a tactical mistake appearing to be an improper influence.

Other witnesses may expect and demand to be paid for providing information to an investigator about the location of a witness, document, or other source of information. Payment in these situations does not appear to run afoul of the ethical standards because the money does not pay for facts or testimony but only pays for source information. In some cases this distinction may be blurred rendering payment inappropriate. For example, if a witness provides both factual information and location information then it would be improper to pay that witness because of the mix of information. Criminal investigators will be able to pay informants but civil litigators may not, notwithstanding what Rockford and Lacey role model on television.

§ 2.4.24 Carrying Lethal Weapons

Are you kidding? Did you really think we took this topic seriously? Leave the weapons to Barney Fife.[10]

§ 2.4.25 Advising Witnesses

An attorney cannot render legal advice to a witness unless the attorney represents the witness. Neither can an attorney cause an investigator to provide legal advice.[11] The most tempting advice to give a witness is not to talk to anyone else about the case. But it is unethical and a tactical error to tell a witness to refuse to talk. It is clearly improper and a conflict of interest for an attorney to provide legal advice to a non-client witness. It is also a tactical mistake allowing the other side to later argue that the litigator had something to hide and had to rely on withholding information in an attempt to win.

Some witnesses may ask during or after the interview whether they should talk to anyone else. An investigator in this situation may be able to carefully explain the consequences to a witness of talking or not talking to the other side without providing legal advice. There may be a fine line between answering a witness' question and providing legal advice. The difference may be that the investigator cannot suggest or tell the witness what to do and should expressly tell the witness this when answering a question seeking advice. If a witness statement has been obtained the witness may be able to provide a copy of the statement to the other side instead of being interviewed. Or if no statement is preserved, the witness may talk with the other side but not give a witness statement.

§ 2.4.26 Use of Experts in Investigation

In many cases it is desirable or even necessary to obtain expert assistance in the beginning stages of an investigation. This assistance may take the form of an investigator with expertise in a specific type of investigation. For example, if a case involves potential issues relating to the cause of a fire, it may be imperative to hire an experienced arson or fire cause and origin investigator. Early expert assistance may be obtained not to conduct an investigation, however, but rather to assist in guiding the attorney's investigation. In the same example, an accoun-

10. Trivia Question: Who played Barney Fife in what show?

11. *See State ex rel. State Bar of Wis. v. Keller,* 16 Wis.2d 377, 114 N.W.2d 796 (1962), *vacated* 374 U.S. 102, 83 S.Ct. 1686, 10 L.Ed.2d 1026 (1963), *on remand* 21 Wis.2d 100, 123 N.W.2d 905 (1963), *cert. denied* 377 U.S. 964, 84 S.Ct. 1643, 12 L.Ed.2d 734 (1964).

tant might provide valuable assistance to the lawyer in evaluating the case and determining what evidence of damages needs to be preserved.

In any case that is likely to involve complicated technical issues, it is of tremendous value for the lawyer to obtain expert assistance early. Often this assistance allows the investigator to preserve facts which, without expert assistance, the attorney would not know. In product liability actions most attorneys would have the presence of mind to secure and preserve the product involved in causing the injury. There may be other conditions which bear on the question of the product's defectiveness or causal relation to the loss which in many cases even an astute lawyer would not realize are important. An expert may be able to provide invaluable guidance to the attorney.

The involvement of an expert early in the investigation is an important decision. Often the expert retained at the beginning of the case will be the most logical expert to use at trial. It is therefore important to consider the expert as a potential witness. Even if it is known that the witness will not be available, suited or invited to testify at trial, it may be worthwhile to retain the expert for consultation. It is often more cost-effective, however, to retain an expert for the initial investigation who at least shows some promise of being a suitable trial witness. One use of the initial expert in an investigation is to assist in identifying and retaining other experts who may be needed. Even if the first expert will not be able to testify as an expert, that person may be a great value in locating a trial witness.

Expert witnesses may be located by a wide variety of means. One is to contact other attorneys. As always, it may be possible to obtain in a short phone call to a colleague what would take days to locate by other means. Moreover, the information to be learned from another attorney will normally include valuable information which would not be available elsewhere (*e.g.*, is the witness plaintiff or defense-oriented?, how does the witness appear on the witness stand?, or how reliable is the witness in meeting obligations to attorneys and deadlines?). An attorney friend may be a valuable guide to an expert's reputation in the community. If an expert is known to have opinions available to anyone willing to pay the fee, it may be counter-productive to retain the expert if settlement is desired, because the opposing attorney will just laugh at the expert's involvement in the case.

Professional associations may be helpful in locating an expert in the specific area needed. Many law firms maintain records of experts who have either been used by the firm or by the firm's adversaries and these records may be useful as well. Local colleges and universities also are potential sources of information. Many attorneys have found well-qualified experts through reference aids in a local public library. Much of the initial work in identifying potential organizations, contacting local members, and canvassing those members to determine their expertise and their interest in consulting may be done by paralegal assistants. Interviewing and retaining the expert should normally be done by the attorney because of the need to develop a close working relationship with the attorney and the need for the attorney's judgment about the expert's qualifications, demeanor, and potential value to the case.

PRACTICE PROBLEMS

ADDITIONAL BOND–MOR INFORMATION

Ordinary cement mortar lacks sufficient adhesive strength to permit construction of a single width brick wall without reinforcement. Tri–Chem developed a family of Zetes Latex products which provides mortar with the strain and adhesion to Tri–Chem prefabricated brick panels and walls to allow their use without reinforcement. Zetes Latex is described as a polymer or copolymer with vinylidene chloride as the primary non-aqueous component. Bond–Mor contains approximately 70% by-weight of vinylidene chloride and 30% of vinyl chloride.

Chloride is highly corrosive to steel. Steel embedded in cement mortar is normally resistant to or passified against corrosion because the mortar itself is highly alkaline. Alkalines effectively neutralize ordinary rust and corrosion. Zetes Latex additives, Bond–Mor in particular, contain chlorides, including a small amount of free chloride ions in hydrochloric acid that is highly corrosive to steel. The highly alkaline cement in mortar and concrete continuously reacts with the Bond–Mor additive to strip additional chloride ions from the vinylidene chloride component of Bond–Mor. Water and heat, among other things, will cause and accelerate the stripping process resulting in excessive corrosion.

Prestressed concrete is susceptible to corrosion problems when very low levels of chlorides are present. The American Concrete Institute (ACI) established a 0.06% limit for chloride by-weight of cement. Bond–Mor and other Zetes Latex additives typically release 36 to 50 times the 0.06% chloride standard when mixed with concrete or mortar.

The American Bonding Institute (ABI) and the Structural Products Institute (SPI) have recommended against the use of calcium chloride. Under standard masonry practices, significantly fewer disruptive chloride ions are emitted than were found in Bond–Mor systems containing metals. For example, SPI, in its suggested practices for construction, recommended that "calcium chloride or admixtures containing it shall not be used in mortar or grout in which reinforcement, metal ties or anchors are to be embedded."

The presence of the chloride ions work to corrode steel. The free chloride ions initially present in Bond–Mor, plus those continuously coming into being due to stripping, corrode steel embedded in or adjacent to the Bond–Mor mortar, including steel coated with zinc (i.e. galvanized) or cadmium. Rust generated from the corrosion of steel and the by-products related to the corrosion of zinc occupy more space than is occupied by the metal itself prior to corrosion. This creates expansive forces on the surrounding mortar and brick. Cracks result that deteriorate and weaken the masonry.

Bond–Mor was test-marketed in 1983. And from that time to the present it has been marketed nationally to the construction, masonry, and architectural industries. In March 1985, bricks fell from HDE's Ohio building. After the bricks fell, HDE was told to cordon off the area beneath and to post warning signs so that customers will not walk near nor touch the bricks. Tri–Chem investigated this problem, made repairs to the walls, and removed the fallen bricks.

Chapter Questions

Attitudes Toward Clients

Consider the positive, neutral, and negative attitudes an attorney may have toward representing:

1. Hot Dog Enterprises (Chapter 1, p. 34–35).
2. Tri–Chem (Chapter 1, p. 35).
3. Martha Giacone in *Giacone v. City of Mitchell* (Case D).
4. The Danforths in *Northern Motor Homes v. Danforth* (Case J).
5. Northern Motor Homes in *Northern Motor Homes v. Danforth* (Case J).

Client Participation

What degree of participation should the following client have regarding (A) the initiation of litigation, (B) the taking of a deposition and the progress of other discovery requests, (C) the bringing of motions, and (D) the settlement of the case:

6. Hot Dog Enterprises (Chapter 1, p. 35).
7. Tri–Chem (Chapter 1, p. 35).
8. Mack and Meg Luger in *Luger v. Shade* (Case H).
9. Juanita Vasquez in *Vasquez v. Hot Dog Enterprises* (Case F).

Client Counseling

Counsel the following client including (A) seriousness of the case, (B) alternative solutions, (C) advantages and disadvantages of these alternatives, (D) the consequences to the client, (E) the litigation process, (F) a prediction of the outcome of the case, (G) the extent of the client's participation, (H) attorney fees and expenses, (I) and any other information and advice:

10. Hot Dog Enterprises (Chapter 1, p. 35).

11. Tri–Chem (Chapter 1, p. 35).

12. Mack and Meg Luger in *Luger v. Shade* (Case H).

13. Juanita Vasquez in *Vasquez v. Hot Dog Enterprises,* (Case F).

Counseling Problems

14. Assume in *Giacone v. City of Mitchell* (Case D), Martha Giacone comes to your law office before her water is shut off and tells you: "The City has threatened to turn my water off. It was my mistake not doing something about this before. I should know better. I know the law favors the City, and there is nothing you can do for me. Do you know where I can get some extra money to pay off the water bill?" How would you respond?

15. Assume in *Giacone v. City of Mitchell* (Case D), Martha Giacone comes to you for legal assistance before her water is shut off by the City. She asks you: "Can they turn my water off? If they can, what can you do for me?" How would you answer her questions?

16. Assume in *Pozdak v. Summit Insurance Company* (Case B), Pozdak retains you to represent him after the fire. During the course of your initial interview with him he says to you: "I'm not really sure how valuable some of my work was. I think it's worth a lot of money, but I don't know. I figure at least we have to really inflate the value of the personal property so that I can get as much money as I can from the insurance company. What do you think?" How would you respond?

17. Assume in *Vasquez v. Hot Dog Enterprises* (Case F), Juanita Vasquez has retained you. During your initial interview with her she says: "I really want to sue HDE and Wankle and everyone else involved who was trying to get me. I want to teach them a lesson they won't forget. I want them to suffer the way they made me suffer." How would you respond?

18. Assume in *Vasquez v. Hot Dog Enterprises* (Case F), Juanita Vasquez retains you. Before you explain the status of the law to her and her available remedies, she says: "I am really confident about winning. A friend of mine was in a similar situation and her lawyer was able to get her a lot of money. It seems pretty obvious to me that HDE violated the law, and any judge or jury is sure to agree with me. Right?" How would you respond?

19. Assume in *Vasquez v. Hot Dog Enterprises* (Case F), Dan Wankle retains you to defend him. During the course of the

initial interview he says: "I don't know what to do. The more I think about it the more confused I get. I just don't know. You're the expert—I'm paying you. Tell me what to do. What would you do if you were in my shoes?" How would you respond?

20. Assume in *Vasquez v. Hot Dog Enterprises* (Case F), Dan Wankle retains you to defend him. After you explain the law and procedures to him, he says: "Well I may have said and did some inappropriate things, but it will be my word against hers. Who will know what really happened? My memory may not be really clear about some things. Why should I say anything that will hurt me or my case. Right?" How would you respond?

Lawyer Representation

21. In *Vasquez v. Hot Dog Enterprises* (Case F), assume Vasquez sues Hot Dog Enterprises and Dan Wankle. Should these defendants retain separate counsel? Outline the reasons for and against separate counsel.

22. In *Luger v. Shade* (Case H), assume the Lugers sue Sam Shade and the Develco Corporation. Should these defendants retain separate counsel? Outline the reasons for and against separate counsel.

Legal Research

What legal research efforts would you conduct representing:

23. Hot Dog Enterprises in *Vasquez v. Hot Dog Enterprises* (Case F). (Chapter 1, p. 35).

24. Tri–Chem in HDE's action (Chapter 1, p. 35).

25. Mack and Meg Luger in *Luger v. Shade* (Case H).

26. Juanita Vasquez in *Vasquez v. Hot Dog Enterprises* (Case F).

27. Hot Dog Enterprises in its potential lawsuit against Tri–Chem (Chapter 1).

Judicial Forum

What factors need to be reviewed to determine in what judicial forum the following case should be brought:

28. Mack and Meg Luger versus defendants in *Luger v. Shade* (Case H).

29. Juanita Vasquez versus defendants in *Vasquez v. Hot Dog Enterprises* (Case F).

Investigation

Assume no lawsuit has been started and the other side has not retained an attorney. Plan how you would investigate the following case and consider:

(a) When should the investigation begin?

(b) Who should investigate?

(c) What sources of information are available?

(d) What physical evidence is available?

(e) What experts should be contacted?

(f) Who should be interviewed and why?

30. You represent Hot Dog Enterprises in its potential lawsuit against Tri–Chem (Chapter 1).

31. You represent Tri–Chem in defense of the potential litigation involving Bond–Mor (Chapter 1).

32. You represent the family of Mariko Miyamoto in *Miyamoto v. Snow Cat* (Case C).

33. You represent the Summit Insurance Company in *Pozdak v. Summit Insurance Company* (Case B).

Witnesses

Assume no lawsuit has been started and the witness is not represented by an attorney. For the following case determine:

(a) What witnesses would you interview?

(b) How would you approach each witness?

(c) How would you maintain the cooperation of the witness during the interview?

(d) How would you conduct the interview?

(e) What types of questions would you ask?

(f) What topics would you cover?

34. You represent Hot Dog Enterprises in its potential lawsuit against Tri–Chem (Chapter 1).

35. You represent Tri–Chem in defense of the potential litigation involving Bond–Mor (Chapter 1).

36. You represent the family of Mariko Miyamoto in *Miyamoto v. Snow Cat* (Case C).

37. You represent Juanita Vasquez in *Vasquez v. Hot Dog Enterprises* (Case F).

Witness Interviews

Assume no lawsuit has been started and the witness is not represented by an attorney. For the following case:

(a) Decide how you would contact the witness to obtain an interview.

(b) Interview the witness.

(c) Outline what should be included in a post interview file memo.

(d) Draft a file memo.

(e) Should the information be recorded? How?

(f) Outline the topics to be covered in a witness statement.

(g) Draft a witness statement.

(h) Outline the topics for an audio recording.

(i) Obtain a tape recorder and conduct an interview.

(j) The witness has refused to talk. Provide some reasons why the witness should consent to an interview.

(k) You hope to obtain as much favorable information as possible. What words or phrases will you suggest the witness adopt? What techniques may be effective to influence the witness to provide favorable information?

(*l*) The witness refuses to talk unless you pay some money. What can you do? What should you do?

(m) The witness asks for a copy of the witness statement. What do you do?

(n) The witness asks whether it is okay to talk to other investigators. How do you respond?

38. You represent Hot Dog Enterprises in its potential lawsuit against Tri–Chem (Chapter 1).

39. You represent Tri–Chem in defense of the potential litigation involving Bond–Mor (Chapter 1).

40. You represent Martha Giacone and plan to interview Kay Olsheski in *Giacone v. City of Mitchell* (Case D).

41. You represent Juanita Vasquez and plan to interview Robert Clune and co-workers in *Vasquez v. Hot Dog Enterprises* (Case F).

Critiquing Witness Statements

42. Critique the witness statements of Byron Cascades and Alma Weymurth in *Miyamoto v. Snow Cat* (Case C).

Case Planning

Prepare an overall litigation plan by planning:

(a) The pleadings

(b) Anticipated disclosures by the other party

(c) Anticipated discovery

(d) Anticipated motions

(e) Anticipated negotiations

43. You represent Hot Dog Enterprises in its potential lawsuit against Tri–Chem (Chapter 1).

44. You represent Tri–Chem in defense of the potential litigation involving Bond–Mor (Chapter 1).

45. You represent Summit Insurance in *Pozdak v. Summit Insurance Company* (Case B).

46. You represent the family of Mariko Miyamoto in *Miyamoto v. Snow Cat* (Case C).

47. You represent Martha Giacone in *Giacone v. City of Mitchell* (Case D).

48. You represent the Mitchell Computer Club in *Mitchell Computer Club v. Rainbow Computer Company* (Case E).

49. You represent Juanita Vasquez in *Vasquez v. Hot Dog Enterprises* (Case F).

PART TWO
PLEADING

*

CHAPTER 3
PLEADING THE CASE

The wisdom of Solomon, accentuated by the legal lore of Coke and Mansfield, could not devise a judgment which this complaint would support.

Huston, J.
Wilson v. Thompson

§ 3.1 PRELIMINARIES TO PLEADING

Lawyers often speak as though the litigation process begins with drafting the complaint (or, perhaps, being retained by the client and then drafting the complaint). This results, one hopes, not from ignorance but because they have already mastered the preliminaries to pleading and integrated them into litigation decision making. Law students and new lawyers must normally act more self-consciously regarding these doctrinal and strategic concerns: subject matter jurisdiction; personal jurisdiction; and venue. Even experienced lawyers must pay careful attention to these matters. For example, in *The Buffalo Creek Disaster,*[1] which describes a major tort action, the author describes both extensive preliminary investigation and analysis regarding available forums as well as the interrelation between substantive law and pleading strategy.[2]

Jurisdiction and venue are doctrinal in that they have developed largely through reasonably complex case law rather than through appli-

§ 3.1

1. Gerald M. Stern, The Buffalo Creek Disaster (1976).

2. In a nutshell, Stern, attorney for persons injured in the massive Buffalo Creek flood of 1972, sought to obtain federal court jurisdiction (largely out of fears that the state court judges were too sympathetic to the defendant coal company, which built the dam that failed, causing the flood). By naming the out-of-state parent company but not the in-state subsidiary, plaintiffs successfully established diversity jurisdiction in federal court. *See id.* at 70–90.

cation of clear statutes or civil rules. These issues also often raise concerns rooted in the U.S. Constitution such as the parameters of federal judicial power and due process. They are strategic in that their resolution often has major implications for the litigation, *e.g.:* state vs. federal court; particular forum state; opposing parties named; claims pleaded. This section provides a brief overview of the doctrines and considerations involved. Attorneys facing these issues ordinarily should consult a secondary source focused upon the substantive law of civil procedure as well as controlling case law in the jurisdictions under consideration for the lawsuit.[3]

§ 3.1.1 Subject Matter Jurisdiction

Subject matter jurisdiction is the power of a court to hear and decide a case—power over the dispute. Courts derive this authority from constitutional provisions and legislative enactments. To properly process a lawsuit, a court must have proper subject matter jurisdiction.

Ordinarily, this is not a problem in state court, as state courts are usually considered courts of general jurisdiction: they will hear and decide any legally cognizable dispute. State courts often have divisions with more particular and circumscribed authority, *e.g.:* small claims court; housing court; probate court; family court. The respective confines of each court's authority must be ascertained and observed by counsel in order to avoid dismissal without prejudice.[4] Although a claimant may be "bounced" out of a particular state court, some forum in the state judicial system ordinarily will hear the case if it states a recognized legal claim and if the defendant is subject to the personal jurisdiction of the court—that's why they're called courts of general jurisdiction.

By contrast, federal courts are courts of limited jurisdiction—they may hear and decide only "cases and controversies" coming within their authority conferred by Article III of the Constitution and federal statutes. Normally, this requires that the claim "arise" under federal law (federal question jurisdiction) or that the dispute involve opposing parties from different states (diversity jurisdiction).

§ 3.1.1(a) Diversity Jurisdiction

Diversity jurisdiction, codified at 28 U.S.C.A. § 1332, requires that plaintiff and defendants be citizens of different states *and* that the matter in controversy exceed the sum or value of $50,000, not counting any interest claimed on the amount at issue or any court costs or counsel fees claimed by the plaintiff. The federal court determines its subject

3. For a good listing of the major civil procedure treatises, *see* § 2.3, *supra* regarding legal research.

4. After dismissal without prejudice, the claimant may bring the matter in another, more appropriate forum. The dismissal does not operate as an adjudication on the merits of the dispute and the rules of preclusion (*see* § 3.2.6, *infra*) do not apply. By contrast, a dismissal with prejudice is a final adjudication on the merits and the case may not be brought again.

matter jurisdiction by examining the face of plaintiff's complaint. If the complaint as drafted claims breach through nonperformance of a contract with $50,000 face value, the jurisdictional amount has not been met. However, if the dispute involves a less rigorously quantifiable amount, such as pain and suffering from an automobile accident or lost business revenues from construction delays, courts generally find the jurisdictional amount satisfied if the plaintiff has pleaded in good faith and the court can not say with certainty that a jury would award less than $50,000 to a successful plaintiff. Multiple claims that individually fall below the jurisdictional amount usually can not be aggregated by more than one party to satisfy the statutory minimum.

"Citizenship" within the meaning of 28 U.S.C.A. § 1332 is a term of art. It does not refer to patriotism or civic virtue. Rather, it means "domicile," a concept also encountered in trusts and estates law and conflict of laws courses. A person's domicile is the political jurisdiction that serves as a permanent home. We are all born not only with parents but domiciles as well. However, unlike parents, domiciles are subject to change simply by moving and expressing through intent and conduct a desire to treat the new domicile as a permanent home.

A person has only one domicile, usually his or her home. It connotes something more than residence. The expectation is that, wherever we roam, we intend to return to our respective domiciles (sort of like Lassie or homing pigeons). For example, a college student attending school in a state different than his domicile of birth or upbringing (*i.e.,* Mom and Dad's house) is generally presumed to retain the former domicile but this presumption can be rebutted by evidence that the student has moved to the new state "permanently" (*i.e.,* for the foreseeable future) with intent to remain.

Ever since Chief Justice John Marshall's opinion in *Strawbridge v. Curtiss,*[5] 28 U.S.C.A. § 1332 has been interpreted to require complete diversity: all the plaintiffs *and* all the defendants must be from different states. If even one of several defendants is a citizen of the same state as even one of several plaintiffs, there is no complete diversity and the court lacks diversity jurisdiction. Limited partnerships, partnerships, and unincorporated associations lack complete diversity if even a single member is a citizen of the same state as an opponent. *See C.T. Carden v. Arkoma Assoc.,* 494 U.S. 185, 110 S.Ct. 1015, 108 L.Ed.2d 157 (1990).

Pursuant to 28 U.S.C.A. § 1332(c)(1), corporations are considered citizens both of the state where incorporated and the state where the corporation has its principal place of business. Courts vary in their

5. 7 U.S. (3 Cranch) 267, 2 L.Ed. 435 (1806). Most interpreters regard *Strawbridge* as a decision interpreting the diversity statute rather than the limits of Article III of the Constitution. Consequently, Congress could amend the statute to confer subject matter jurisdiction where the complaint reveals only minimal diversity (at least one plaintiff and at least one defendant from different states). Congress has shown no interest in so amending § 1332 but has provided for jurisdiction by minimal diversity in interpleader actions brought under 28 U.S.C.A. § 1335. *See* § 3.10, *infra,* regarding intervention and interpleader.

preference regarding whether the corporation's principal place of business is its main office (the "nerve center") or its principal production facility, with the modern trend favoring the nerve center test.

Where diversity jurisdiction exists, the court possesses ancillary jurisdiction to hear and decide claims between the parties that would not, standing alone, meet the criteria for federal jurisdiction. Ancillary jurisdiction also permits federal courts to adjudicate third-party claims even if the third-party defendant is not diverse from the third-party plaintiff. However, if the necessary diverse parties are dismissed from the case, ancillary jurisdiction is not sufficiently broad to permit the court to decide claims remaining between the remaining nondiverse parties.[6]

§ 3.1.1(b) Federal Question Jurisdiction

Unlike, diversity jurisdiction, which is party-centered (*i.e.,* litigants from different states can raise legal issues with no implications for federal substantive law), federal question jurisdiction is claim-centered. Federal question jurisdiction exists only when the plaintiff's claim arises under federal law. Courts determine the existence of federal question jurisdiction by examining the face of plaintiff's complaint but will disregard surplusage or material that is not part of a "well-pleaded" complaint.[7] Federal question jurisdiction does not exist even where federal law provides the basis for a defense or the criteria for resolving an issue in the case. The court will not be influenced by a complaint that anticipates invocation of federal law in the answer or other responses to the complaint.[8] Rather, federal law must create the cause of action.[9]

However, in addition to general federal question jurisdiction under 28 U.S.C.A. § 1331, several statutes provide for federal jurisdiction over specific matters (*e.g.,* civil rights violations, review of agency orders) and where the government is a party. In most situations satisfying the requirements of federal jurisdiction (all diversity cases and most federal question cases), the federal and state courts have concurrent jurisdiction (rather than exclusive federal jurisdiction). That is, either court has judicial power to hear the case. However, some federal statutes require that certain actions be tried only in federal court.[10] Unless the case is

6. *See Owen Equipment & Erection Co. v. Kroger,* 437 U.S. 365, 98 S.Ct. 2396, 57 L.Ed.2d 274 (1978).

7. *See Franchise Tax Bd. v. Construction Laborers Vacation Trust,* 463 U.S. 1, 77 L.Ed.2d 420 (1983); *Skelly Oil Co. v. Phillips Petroleum Co.,* 339 U.S. 667, 70 S.Ct. 876, 94 L.Ed. 1194 (1950).

8. *See Louisville & Nashville R. Co. v. Mottley,* 211 U.S. 149, 29 S.Ct. 42, 53 L.Ed. 126 (1908); *T.B. Harms Co. v. Eliscu,* 339 F.2d 823 (2d Cir.1964), *cert. denied* 381 U.S. 915, 85 S.Ct. 1534, 14 L.Ed.2d 435 (1965).

9. *See Merrell Dow Pharmaceuticals Inc. v. Thompson,* 478 U.S. 804, 106 S.Ct. 3229, 92 L.Ed.2d 650 (1986).

10. *See, e.g.,* 28 U.S.C.A. §§ 1333 (admiralty), 1334 (bankruptcy), 1338 (patent and copyright).

one of exclusive federal jurisdiction, the plaintiff may file either in state court or in federal court.[11]

The existence of proper federal question jurisdiction over a claim in plaintiff's complaint often permits the court to hear all other claims plaintiff has against the defendant(s), even where the other claims standing alone would not qualify for federal jurisdiction. The test is whether the non-federal claims and the federal claim(s) arise out of a "common nucleus of operative fact." [12] If they do, the court can hear all claims. However, pendent claim jurisdiction is a doctrine of discretion. Thus, if the lone federal claim is dismissed prior to trial, the court may dismiss the claims arising under state law (without prejudice so that plaintiff may refile in state court) or may, less commonly, retain the state law claims for trial.

A variant of pendent claim jurisdiction is pendent party jurisdiction, which has proven doctrinally complex and has never been greeted warmly by the Supreme Court. In pendent party jurisdiction, a party in a case properly before the court asserts a claim against a new party outside the litigation but without the ability to independently satisfy diversity or federal question jurisdiction as to that party or claim. Like pendent claim jurisdiction pendent party jurisdiction is constitutional because Article III of the Constitution confers federal judicial authority over entire "cases and controversies." However, in *Finley v. United States,*[13] the court rejected an attempted assertion of pendent party jurisdiction in a case arising under the Federal Tort Claims Act,[14] stating that it would not read jurisdictional statutes broadly to permit pendent party jurisdiction since this would result in the addition of an entirely new party to the litigation (as opposed to merely permitting additional claims against a party that was already involved in the joy of federal court litigation).

In other words, if Congress wanted the courts to assert pendent party jurisdiction, it must state so clearly so that even a strict interpretation of the jurisdictional statute would support such an exercise of jurisdiction. In late 1990, Congress did just that. In the course of passing a much larger bill (the Civil Justice Reform Act of 1990), Congress codified the doctrine of pendent claim jurisdiction and provided that in federal question cases pendent jurisdiction "shall include claims that involve the joinder or intervention of additional parties." [15] However, this newly enacted broad pendent party jurisdiction is not available in

11. *See, e.g., Yellow Freight System v. Donnelly,* 494 U.S. 820, 110 S.Ct. 1566, 108 L.Ed.2d 834 (1990) (claims under Title VII of the 1964 Civil Rights Act, 42 U.S.C.A. § 2000e *et seq.,* may be brought in either state or federal court).

12. *See United Mine Workers of America v. Gibbs,* 383 U.S. 715, 86 S.Ct. 1130, 16 L.Ed.2d 218 (1966).

13. 488 U.S. 815, 109 S.Ct. 52, 102 L.Ed.2d 31 (1988).

14. 28 U.S.C.A. § 1346(b).

15. *See* 28 U.S.C.A. § 1367 (1990). In the new statute, Congress used the term "supplemental jurisdiction" rather than "pendent jurisdiction." We read the terms as synonymous in context and prefer the term pendent jurisdiction as this has been long used in the case law and commentary.

actions founded solely on diversity jurisdiction or by litigants seeking joinder or intervention if "exercising supplemental jurisdiction over such claims would be inconsistent with the jurisdictional requirements of section 1332" [16] (*e.g.*, where the pendent party is non-diverse or the claim against it is for $50,000 or less). In addition, the statute specifically gives the courts discretion to refuse pendent party jurisdiction in several instances.[17] Federal courts also have broad discretion to "abstain" from hearing a claim or case for other reasons discussed in 4.5.6 and 4.5.7.

§ 3.1.2 Personal Jurisdiction

In addition to a court's having jurisdiction over the subject matter of a lawsuit, the court must also have jurisdiction over the defendant. Personal jurisdiction requires that there exist some relationship between the judicial forum and the defendant. This relationship typically includes some nexus or contact the defendant voluntarily has within the territorial jurisdiction of the court. A defendant will only be subject to the jurisdiction of a court if there exists some connection between the defendant and the forum. Notions of due process, fair play, and substantial justice require minimum contacts.[18] Personal jurisdiction will usually be based on one or more of the following facts:

1. The defendant resides within the jurisdiction.
2. The defendant is incorporated, has a place of business, does business within the forum, or is licensed by the forum.
3. The defendant has expressly consented to jurisdiction, *e.g.*, in a contract provision.
4. The defendant has impliedly consented to jurisdiction, *e.g.*, the defendant owns property in the state.
5. A statute imposes jurisdiction over the defendant, *e.g.*, a nonresident motorist who drives through a state may become subject to the jurisdiction of that state.
6. The defendant voluntarily appears in the state and is personally served.

Section 4.5.2 explains some of these factors in more detail.

"Long-arm" statutes enacted by each state may provide a court with jurisdiction over non-resident defendants who have a single or infrequent contact with a state. These statutes typically confer jurisdiction over a defendant who commits a tort, executes a contract, owns property,

16. *See* 28 U.S.C.A. § 1367(b).

17. *See* 28 U.S.C.A. § 1367(c)(1)-(4) (court may decline to exercise jurisdiction where a state law claim substantially predominates or is novel or complex, where federal claims have been dismissed, or in other "compelling circumstances").

18. But less minimal than they used to be, *see World-Wide Volkswagen Corp. v. Woodson,* 444 U.S. 286, 100 S.Ct. 559, 62 L.Ed.2d 490 (1980); *Kulko v. Superior Court,* 436 U.S. 84, 98 S.Ct. 1690, 56 L.Ed.2d 132 (1978), *rehearing denied* 438 U.S. 908, 98 S.Ct. 3127, 57 L.Ed.2d 1150 (1978) (use of long-arm jurisdiction significantly curtailed).

or benefits from a state. Federal courts sitting in diversity jurisdiction cases apply the service rules of the forum state in addition to the service rules set forth in Rule 4. Both state and federal courts may have both proper jurisdiction over a defendant and the means to obtain service on the defendant.

In 1993, Fed. R. Civ. P. 4 was substantially amended to provide for "last resort" national personal jurisdiction in cases of federal substantive law by service upon defendants who have sufficient contact with the United States even if they are not sufficiently linked enough to any single state to be subject to that state's general jurisdiction. In addition, new Rule 4 specifically authorizes quasi-in-rem jurisdiction under limited circumstances (which you might have thought was dead after *Shaffer v. Heitner*, 433 U.S. 186, 97 S.Ct. 2569, 53 L.Ed.2d 683 (1977).

The 1993 changes also established a strengthened "waiver" of service procedure that can be used to lower service costs or ease service on nonresident defendants. The defendant has some incentive to comply: by waiving service, it gets 60 days to answer (rather than the usual 20 days established by Rule 12); defendants who wrongly refuse waiver are subject to paying for the plaintiff's costs of effecting service. In addition, revised Rule 4 spells out the preferred means of effecting service on foreign defendants, principally the Hague Convention, an international treaty regarding service of process.

Jurisdiction may also be obtained through in rem or quasi-in-rem jurisdiction. In rem jurisdiction provides a court with jurisdiction over property within its territorial jurisdiction. For example, a court has jurisdiction to determine the ownership of real property or personal property located within its boundaries. Quasi-in-rem jurisdiction provides a court with jurisdiction over a matter not related to the property but involving the owner of the property within its jurisdiction. For example, a resident of a state may claim quasi-in-rem jurisdiction over a personal matter with a non-resident who owns property in the state. In rem jurisdiction is constitutionally sound and fair. Quasi-in-rem jurisdiction often involves a constitutional question of whether there is a sufficient connection between the defendant and the judicial forum for jurisdictional purposes.[19]

§ 3.1.3 Venue

Venue. Jurisdiction refers to the power of a judicial system to hear a case. Venue refers to the place of trial within that judicial system. For example, any federal district court may have jurisdiction to hear a case, but venue may be proper in only certain specific districts. Venue is largely a matter of convenience. States usually have venue statutes or rules which define proper venue as the place where the defendant resides, where the cause of action arose, where the defendant is doing business, where the defendant has an office, or where the plaintiff

19. Shaffer v. Heitner, 433 U.S. 186, 97 S.Ct. 2569, 53 L.Ed.2d 683 (1977).

resides. In federal cases, including federal question and diversity cases, venue is proper where all the defendants reside or where the cause of action arose. If the defendant is a corporation, venue is proper whenever the corporation is subject to personal jurisdiction.[20]

These factors may be identical to the factors which determine proper subject-matter and personal jurisdiction, or they may differ. Jurisdiction and venue must be separately analyzed, and the appropriate factors applied separately. If a court does not have jurisdiction the case must be dismissed. If a court does not have venue that court may be able to transfer the case instead of dismissing it.[21] A state court of general jurisdiction will usually be able to transfer a state case to the proper state judicial district. Likewise, a federal judge will be able to transfer a federal case to the federal district which has proper venue. The exercise of venue is a matter of discretion. A court may exercise the doctrine of *forum non conveniens* and decide not to hear a case because it would be fairer to the parties, more convenient for the witnesses, and more efficient if the case were heard by another court. However, the general rule is that the plaintiff's choice of forum will not be lightly disturbed unless compelling facts exist in favor of another forum.[22] Federal courts may transfer a case to a more convenient forum rather than dismiss it.[23]

Recent changes in the general federal venue statute clarified that, for venue purposes, a claim may arise in more than one jurisdiction, essentially clarifying existing case law.[24] The 1990 Civil Justice Reform Act also created a provision for occasional "venue by necessity," which provides that venue is proper in any "judicial district in which any defendant may be found if there is no district in which the action may otherwise be brought."[25]

§ 3.2 PLEADINGS IN GENERAL

Modern pleading practice provides a simplified approach to the initiation of litigation.[1] The modern procedures, commonly referred to as "notice pleading," are intended to provide just that: notice to the opposing party of the pleader's claims or defenses. The elements of a cause of action do not need to be plead, nor do evidentiary facts necessary to prove a claim or defense. A complaint should advise the defendant of the major facts alleged, the nature of the legal claim or claims asserted, and the relief requested. An answer advises the plain-

20. 28 U.S.C.A. § 1391.

21. Fed.R.Civ.P. 12(b)(3); 28 U.S.C.A. § 1406.

22. *Gulf Oil Co. v. Gilbert,* 330 U.S. 501, 508, 67 S.Ct. 839, 91 L.Ed. 1055 (1947).

23. 28 U.S.C.A. § 1404.

24. *See Leroy v. Great Western United Corp.,* 443 U.S. 173, 99 S.Ct. 2710, 61 L.Ed.2d 464 (1979), *on remand* 602 F.2d 1246 (5th Cir.1979) (suggesting that claim may arise in more than one district for venue purposes but not finding multiple venues by claim in instant case).

25. 28 U.S.C.A. § 1391(a) (1991).

§ 3.2

1. For an excellent yet brief background of the history of pleading and the intra-bar battles that led to the pleading rules of the Federal Rules of Civil Procedure, *see* Fleming James, et al., Civil Procedure §§ 1.3–1.8, 3.1–3.6 (4th ed. 1992).

tiff of the defendant's position with respect to the claims and may include affirmative defenses. If the defendant wants to pursue a counterclaim, it must be plead as any other claim. Discovery is intended to permit a party to obtain detailed information about the claims and defenses and the facts supporting the parties' positions.

In the federal courts, the general rules of pleading content and format are for the most part set out in rules 7 through 14. Rule 7 outlines the pleadings allowed and the proper format for motions. Rule 8 establishes the general rules of pleading. Rule 9 addresses pleading special matters. Rule 10 establishes the technical form of pleadings. Rule 11 addresses the ethical obligations of counsel in signing pleadings. Rule 12, in addition to governing attack on the pleadings by motion (a subject discussed in section 4.1), establishes the 20–day time period for responding to a complaint. Rule 13 governs counterclaims and cross-claims. Rule 14 addresses third-party practice.

Although it is important to be aware of all of the civil rules, because any of them may affect a particular pleading or motion, knowledge of these eight rules and perhaps a few others will normally enable a lawyer to place a claim in suit, answer a complaint, bring in additional parties, and generally act like a lawyer, at least in form if not substance. In addition to the above rules, Rule 4 concerning the form and content of the summons and service of process will prove helpful, at least to plaintiff's counsel. Knowing Rule 6 concerning computation of time often proves a handy way to avoid malpractice. Rules 19 to 25 govern the substantive aspects of adding, changing, or deleting parties to a lawsuit. Effective use of Rules 13 and 14 requires knowledge of these rules as well.

State courts usually provide similar rules governing these aspects of litigation. Many state rules today mirror the federal rules. However, many state rules are also somewhat stricter and more archaic than the federal rules, which have moved away from pleading formalism. This book will generally discuss pretrial procedure in the context of the federal rules, occasionally noting significant areas in which state procedure diverges from federal. However, each practitioner must know the particular pleading standards, including the local civil rules, of a jurisdiction.

Although Federal Rule 7(b) discusses motions, a motion is not technically a pleading within the meaning of the rules. Rule 7(a) recognizes only six pleadings—the complaint, the answer (including any counterclaims or cross-claims), a reply to a counterclaim, a reply to a cross-claim, a third-party complaint, and an answer to a third-party complaint. Nothing else counts as a pleading, no matter how common or important it might be. This distinction between pleadings and motions is not, however, of great moment. Rule 7(b) provides that the format and signature requirement of pleadings applies to motions as well.

In general, the Rules on their face tell the attorney all that is required for basic pleading. Prior to the adoption of the federal rules in 1938, pleading was often highly stylized, governed by common law, rigid codes, or local custom. Common law forms of pleading typically required a party to state with specificity the details of a claim and to conform to very technical, formalistic rules. The failure of a party, however inadvertent or minor, to comply with these rules often resulted in an adverse decision. Courts and critics became increasingly intolerant of the injustice this formal system created. The federal rules significantly simplified the requirements of pleading. Although courts initially were reluctant to give full effect to the simplified aspects of the Federal Rules, the 1957 Supreme Court case of *Conley v. Gibson* [2] established that the courts were to read the rules as written rather than require greater specificity or information or legal efficacy in a pleading than required by the federal rules.

In *Conley,* the Court held that a plaintiff's complaint should not be dismissed for failure to state a claim unless it was beyond doubt from the face of the complaint that the plaintiff could prove no set of facts entitling it to relief. This liberal standard has meant that Rule 12(b)(6) motions to dismiss for failure to state a claim are usually granted only when the plaintiff has pursued a cause of action not recognized in existing law.

Although *Conley* dealt with the complaint, its approach to interpreting the federal rules has affected judicial views of all pleadings and motions, which are now liberally construed. The basic approach of the federal rules and courts is to permit pleading that fulfills the basic requirements of notice and framing. Fact development is left for disclosure and discovery. Legal development is left for motion, hearing, or trial. Although there remain tricky technical areas and traps for the unwary, particularly regarding third-party practice and joinder, the lawyer who reads the rules literally and acts accordingly will seldom lose a case on a technicality or technical knock out.

When in doubt, reading the rule should resolve the doubt. Proper pleading begins there. Although some states have more restrictive pleading practices, these, too, are increasingly found in the state civil rules and not hidden in obscure statutes or cases. Where questions arise that are not resolved by the language of the rules, reference to the annotated rules of the jurisdiction or a treatise will usually resolve the problem. In true cases of first impression, Rule 8(f), which provides that pleadings shall be construed to do substantial justice, provides guidance and statutory authorization for the triumph of substance over form.

§ 3.3 THE COMPLAINT

§ 3.3.1 Functions of the Complaint

Initiating Litigation. First and foremost, the complaint starts the litigation. In federal court, the action commences when the complaint is

2. 355 U.S. 41, 78 S.Ct. 99, 2 L.Ed.2d 80 (1957).

filed with the clerk of court. In some states, service of the complaint upon the defendant begins the action. The starting gun qualities of the complaint are important for two reasons. First, the date on which the action was begun determines whether the plaintiff has met the applicable statute of limitations. Second, the commencement date of the case determines other important deadlines in the lawsuit such as the time in which to answer or otherwise plead or when the matter will be set for pretrial conference before the judge.

Providing Notice of Claims. The complaint also places the defendant on notice of the plaintiff's claim. Normally, this comes as no surprise to the defendant, who has probably already received phone calls or a demand letter from the plaintiff or counsel. Often, the parties have engaged in settlement discussions before futility prompts litigation. The notice function has historically caused the most controversy concerning the sufficiency of the complaint. Predictably, defendants and lawyers trained under the old code pleading system argued that the complaint must specify in detail the facts giving rise to a cause of action and the legal elements and justification of the lawsuit. Just as predictably, plaintiffs and advocates of notice pleading argued that a general description of the subject matter of the controversy and the rationale of liability should suffice. The latter group has carried the day. Even so, a complaint will not survive a motion to dismiss or a motion for a more definite statement if the defendant can rightly ask "Where's the beef?" or "What is plaintiff talking about?" or "Do I know this character?"

Providing Notice of Issues. The complaint also frames the issues of the litigation, setting forth the subject matter (*e.g.*, facts, transactions, witnesses) of the dispute and the legal claim arising from it. If the complaint alleges five claims for relief, five legal battles will be fought. If plaintiff alleges only the perceived strongest claim, this defines the legal battleground. Similarly, counterclaims, cross-claims, and third-party complaints will establish other issues in the case. In framing the issues, the complaint (as well as other pleadings) need not be internally consistent regarding the relief sought. Rule 8(e) specifically authorizes pleading in the alternative. This permits the plaintiff to plead one legal claim based upon a particular construction of the facts while pleading an alternative legal theory of relief based upon different facts. For example, the plaintiff may allege negligence in one paragraph and allege in another that the injury was intentional.

Providing Notice of Relief Sought. The complaint, as part of its definition of issues, states the relief sought by the plaintiff. Each complaint must contain a demand for judgment.[1] The complaint thus serves the essential function of putting the plaintiff on the road to rectifying an unhappy situation. Whether the plaintiff's complaint seeks a declaratory judgment, an injunction, an accounting, compensatory damages, punitive damages, reopening of a previous case, or other

§ 3.3

1. Fed.R.Civ.P. 8(a).

available relief, the complaint sets parameters for the future conduct of the litigation.

Defining Scope of Disclosure and Discovery. In defining issues, the complaint also defines the permissible scope of discovery. Rule 26 requires automatic disclosure of material relevant to matters pleaded with particularity and also makes relevant for discovery purposes any matter reasonably calculated to lead to the discovery of admissible evidence (*see* section 5.3). The issues raised in the complaint and responses to the complaint will therefore establish the scope of automatic disclosure and discovery in the action.

Disclosure and discovery are also affected by who is named as a defendant in the complaint. Rule 33 interrogatories (Chapter 7), Rule 34 requests for production of documents (Chapter 8), and Rule 36 requests for admissions (Chapter 9) can be addressed only to parties in the litigation. Depositions may be taken of parties and non-parties, although non-parties must be subpoenaed in order to compel their attendance (Chapter 6). Naming a person as a party may therefore be a wise tactical move because it may require disclosure and permit discovery that would otherwise not be required or readily obtainable. Asserting a frivolous or meritless claim for this reason is not proper, however.

Seeking Discoverable Information. The complaint itself may function as a discovery device. Counsel may draft the complaint to attempt to "flush out" the defendant's legal and factual position in the litigation through particularized or selective pleading. When plaintiff's counsel goes beyond the notice pleading required under the rules, this often indicates a complex case (requiring a detailed complaint to adequately inform the defendant and the court) or an effort to pin down the opposition by forcing the defendant to admit or deny a number of specific averments. By doing this, counsel appropriately makes the complaint a type of early request for admissions.

Surviving a Motion to Dismiss. The information contained in a complaint will be considered by the court if the defendant brings a motion to dismiss under Rule 12 for failure to state a claim upon which relief may be granted. It is advisable for a plaintiff who anticipates that a defendant will bring such a motion to draft the complaint with sufficient detail to establish a claim without any doubt. If the substantive law governing the claim is clear, it may also be effective to use the phrasing of the relevant case or statute in stating the claim. For example, if a statute applies to claims for punitive damages and permits the recovery of punitive damages for conduct which is "willful and malicious," it may be desirable to use that language in the complaint.

§ 3.3.2 Timing of the Summons and Complaint

A civil action usually comes into being when the complaint is filed with the clerk of court. The plaintiff's attorney prepares a summons to be signed by the clerk and served with the complaint. State practice varies. An adequate summons is contained in Official Form 1 of the Federal Rules of Civil Procedure:

[Caption]

To the above-named Defendant:

You are summoned and required to serve upon ______, plaintiff's attorney, whose address is ______, an answer to the complaint which is served upon you, within 20 days after service of this summons upon you, exclusive of the day of service. If you fail to do so, judgment by default will be taken against you for the relief demanded in the complaint.

____

Clerk of Court

Amendments to Federal Rule 4 which took effect in 1993 also provide for a "waiver of service" procedure (Rule 4(d)) and two new official forms for requesting or waiving service (Forms 1A and 1B, respectively). The penalty for refusing to waive service when one is properly subject to the court's jurisdiction is payment of plaintiff's service costs. The 1993 Rule 4 changes also address service in foreign countries and provide for nationwide service of process and personal jurisdiction in very limited circumstances (so limited we will say no more).

An action must be commenced before the applicable statute of limitations has run. Determining this date may involve complex questions of equitable tolling or may be relatively straightforward. For example, if an adult plaintiff-to-be is hit by another automobile driver on August 13, 1980 at the Minnesota Twins game,[2] and the statute of limitations is two years, plaintiff had best place the matter into suit by August 13, 1982. The time may be extended if the plaintiff was under some disability whereby the running of the limitations period was tolled, but before relying on tolling the lawyer must be certain that it applies.

In federal court, there exists an additional technical timing consideration. As previously mentioned, the action begins when the complaint is filed with the clerk. Thereafter, plaintiff must serve the complaint within 120 days of filing or the court may dismiss the action on its own motion.[3] Because such dismissal is without prejudice, plaintiff can always file a second complaint and get a second 120–day period in which to attempt to effect service. However, if the plaintiff files the complaint less than 120 days prior to the running of the statute of limitations, the service deadline in effect becomes a statute of limitations deadline. In most states, where the lawsuit begins with service and where filing may not even be required until the plaintiff seeks to place the matter on the trial calendar, the service deadline is always the statute deadline.

2. This is an unlikely occurrence since there were so few Twins patrons at that time to crash into one another. Paid attendance at that game was 11,615. *But see* 1987 and 1991 World Series (where there were more than enough patrons to do so).

3. Fed.R.Civ.P. 4(j).

A less rigid timing question concerns when to resort to litigation. Some statutory causes of action require that the plaintiff first make a demand for compensation upon the defendant-to-be before commencing litigation. For example, before a party may sue a city or county in many states the party must first serve a notice of claim upon the governmental entity. These notice of claim provisions frequently require the notice of claim to be served on the governmental entity within a short period of time after an injury. Even where this is not required, a demand letter or at least telephone negotiation usually is good practice. However, in negotiating with the opposition, an attorney should not forget (for plaintiffs) deadlines such as the statute of limitations, and (for defendants) time limits for moving to change venue or petitioning for removal. The best rule of thumb in this area is to confer with the client and adopt a negotiating position and an acceptable bottom line before approaching the opposition and requesting satisfaction. Depending upon their reaction alternative approaches include continued talking, getting more strident, making a written demand, or drafting, filing, and serving the complaint. Many defendants won't settle without being sued, but a demand may be useful to convince the client that litigation is necessary to obtain relief. Occasionally, where the plaintiff has a very strong case or the defendant faces a runaway verdict (as in case of a severe personal injury), or faces punitive or exemplary damages (as in an antitrust claim), or a rash of suits after a first lawsuit draws attention (as in securities fraud cases), the defendant may wish to settle silently and quickly without putting the plaintiff to the trouble of suit. Usually, this only happens in fairy tales or to the big gunners of the plaintiff's bar, a group from which you are presumably excluded, at least for now, by virtue of having purchased this law-school text.

In discussing timing in this section, we have assumed that counsel has already decided that a valid claim exists. This should be determined after consultation with the client, brainstorming, legal research, and fact investigation. Obviously, counsel should take the time and effort necessary to make this threshold analysis before worrying about strategic and tactical concerns.

§ 3.3.3 Judicial Forum

The forum, at least initially, can be whatever the plaintiff wants. To name the court in the caption and file the complaint there effects a choice of forum. Of course, if the lawsuit has no business being in that jurisdiction, it will probably not stay there. Some clerk's offices may even refuse to accept a complaint for filing if it contains no reference on its face to the jurisdiction as being either the location of the subject matter of the litigation or at least one of the parties. Thus, both practical considerations and the ethical constraints of Rule 11, and the Code of Professional Responsibility, and the Model Rules of Professional Conduct should prompt counsel to consider where the litigation should really begin.

The determination of which forum is proper involves the consideration of four factors:

1. Does the forum have subject-matter jurisdiction?
2. Does the court have personal jurisdiction over the defendant?
3. Is venue proper?
4. Can service of process be obtained on the defendant?

Service of Process. Service of process provides the defendant with notice of the litigation. Proper service of process involves two issues. The first is constitutional: has the defendant been afforded sufficient notice and an opportunity to be heard? This constitutional standard requires the defendant to receive the best possible and practical notice available. Usually this means that the defendant be personally served or somehow receive actual notice of the litigation. This standard also requires the defendant to be afforded sufficient time and opportunity to respond to the complaint. Usually this means a written response within a reasonable number of days. The second issue involving service of process is regulatory: has the defendant been served in accordance with the regulations of the judicial forum? All courts have adopted service of process rules, augmented by statutory enactments, which delineate proper service of process. The most common methods of providing actual notice are:

(1) personal service, in which a defendant is personally served with a copy of the complaint,

(2) substitute service, in which a copy is left at the domicile of the defendant with a person of suitable age and discretion,

(3) service by personal delivery of a copy to an officer or managing agent of a corporation,

(4) service on a public corporation by personal delivery of a copy to the proper government official, and

(5) the posting of the complaint on the defendant's property and service by mail on the defendant.

In cases involving non-resident defendants, service will usually be proper if it is delivered by certified or registered mail, typically if a long-arm statute provides the court with jurisdiction. In other cases where the defendant cannot be located, then service by publication may be appropriate.

Usually any adult, other than a party, is authorized to serve the summons and complaint. In federal and state courts a sheriff or private process server, or law firm non-attorney, will serve the process. In federal court, a federal marshal may serve process if the court so orders.

Selecting the Forum. After determining the available forums, plaintiff must choose the preferred forum, a decision involving several considerations, including:

1. Procedural and evidentiary differences of the forums;

2. The judges of the courts, their known and probable attitudes, as well as their reputations for competence and fairness;

3. The jury panels and their geographic and philosophical makeup.

4. The time of year and latitude of the courthouse.

5. The governing appellate court, its precedents, approaches, and activism in reviewing trial courts.

6. The likely quality of opposing counsel in different forums. Lawyers in federal court actions are frequently more experienced and more effective trial attorneys than state court practitioners.

7. The trial calendar and likely time required to bring the matter to trial in the different forums.

8. The relative convenience of different forums for the client, key favorable witnesses, but not just for plaintiff's counsel. Unfortunately, too many cases are brought in wrong or inappropriate forums because the plaintiff's lawyer was too lazy to travel to the right jurisdiction or too cheap to refer the case to another lawyer and lose a potential fee.

9. Whether the attorney is afraid of taking the bus.

10. The inconvenience to the defendant and opposing counsel. Even if counsel can't find a forum perfectly suited to the plaintiff and counsel, in picking an alternative site one should avoid a place that gives the opposition the convenience advantage. Of course, if the least convenient forum has the best law and jury for the plaintiff's case, go there anyway.

Other factors may also be considered. The important thing is to make a reasoned decision, and not simply to file the action the same way as the previous one.

§ 3.3.4 Parties to the Action

At least initially, the plaintiff may choose the parties to the lawsuit as well as its location. The first task is to determine who to put on the plaintiff's team. Sometimes the contemplated action will be cleaner and neater if pursued alone. On other occasions, the plaintiff will find safety, credibility, and legal and financial resources in numbers. In these cases the attorney may wish to approach other potential plaintiffs and ascertain whether they want to join the litigation. The Code of Professional Responsibility or the Model Rules of Professional Conduct place some limits on counsel's efforts to promote litigation. Counsel considering approaching other potential plaintiffs should consult the applicable sections in their jurisdictions. Normally, such contact is acceptable so long as counsel believes the claim of the potential plaintiffs has merit.

Where a case presents a large number of equally meritorious and sympathetic plaintiffs and joinder is impractical, counsel should consider commencing a class action. Section 3.11, discusses class actions in some detail. Where the client is an insurance company that has paid an insured for loss caused by the acts of another, counsel should consider subrogation. In subrogation, the insured permits the insurance company to sue the party causing the damage under the name of the insured, a surely more sympathetic figure in the eyes of the jury. Usually, the insured has something to gain as well by seeking recovery of deductibles and coinsurance not covered by the insurance policy. By joining forces, both parties, insured and insurer, can seek recovery more economically.

Choosing defendants also requires creativity and judgment. First, all potentially liable parties should be identified, as should the theories of liability, the supporting facts, and the resources of the potential defendant for satisfying a judgment. In picking the defendants, the plaintiff will want to consider the merits of its case against all. Naming too many defendants with tenuous liability can dilute the plaintiff's strongest case against the really culpable defendant. Conversely, focusing on one defendant can unduly limit the plaintiff's chances of full recovery.

The civil procedure rules of the federal courts and most state courts are liberal in joining parties. Usually parties with claims stemming from the same transaction and occurrence and which involve common questions of law and fact will be proper parties. Fed.R.Civ.P. 17 governs real parties in interest including parties who sue in a representative capacity, *e.g.*, executors and guardians. Rule 19 covers the joinder of persons needed for the just adjudication of an action. If complete relief cannot be afforded to the present parties in a case or if the rights of a non-party will be adversely affected then those non-party persons may need to be added to the lawsuit. The common law notions of indispensable and necessary parties have been merged in this rule. Rule 20 details the considerations involved in the permissive joinder of parties. The preference of most jurisdictions is to encourage and permit all persons who have an interest to join or be joined in a lawsuit. If the inclusion of too many parties creates problems or confusion then severance or separate trials may be appropriate or parties may later be dropped. See section 12.1.

Counsel ordinarily does best by naming as defendants those against whom the plaintiff has a non-frivolous case. Generally, more defendants will more often begin attacking each other and aiding the plaintiff's case both for negotiations and for trial, although occasionally a united front of many defendants will make the jury wonder whether so many others can be wrong and the plaintiff right. Naming all reasonably justified defendants also lessens the possibility that the named defendants can point an accusing finger at someone not in the litigation, thereby convincing the jury that although someone wronged the plaintiff, that someone is not in the courtroom and subject to liability.

Naming an entity as a defendant also subjects it to the discovery tools available against a party, *e.g.*, interrogatories, requests for production, non-subpoena depositions, requests for admissions. The identity of the parties also affects evidentiary matters. For example, the out-of-court statements of a non-party are hearsay and not admissible at trial for the truth of any matter asserted unless one of the exceptions to the hearsay rule should apply. Out-of-court statements of a party are defined by the Federal Rules of Evidence as non-hearsay and may be admitted into evidence absent some other basis for objection.[4]

As the reader has now discerned, we advocate erring on the side of over-inclusion rather than under-inclusion of defendants. However, counsel must also consider the cost of prosecuting an action against multiple defendants and weigh this accordingly. In addition, counsel may successfully name the target defendant and let that defendant bring third-party complaints against other potential defendants. This forces the target defendant to shoulder the lion's share of the cost and effort in pursuing discovery against the third-party defendants. If this discovery indicates that the plaintiff has a meritorious case against these parties, the plaintiff can then seek leave to amend its complaint to assert claims directly against these defendants. The plaintiff will come out empty-handed if the jury assesses liability against only the third-party defendants because these parties pay up only if the defendant is found liable to the plaintiff.

A final word on party selection—it is important to get it right on the caption and in the pleadings. Misnaming or misidentifying the opposing parties normally is not fatal and can be cured by amendment. However, egregious misnaming or misservice may allow the true targets to escape the complaint until the statute of limitations has run. Where the government or its agents are the defendants, misnaming may permit them to have the action dismissed or prevent jurisdiction from attaching.

§ 3.3.5 Issues in the Complaint

As previously noted, the complaint frames the issues. The question then is how many to frame in drafting the complaint. Attorneys differ markedly in this area. Some belong to the kitchen sink school and favor pleading every conceivable claim available against the defendants. Others prefer the rifle to the shotgun and plead only the strongest claim or claims, reasoning that additional claims, even those with some merit, will only confuse the jury or dilute the impact of the strongest claims.

Which approach is right? That depends on which author is asked at which time of the day according to his last brush with drafting a complaint. Sometimes the case suggests one real and strong theory of relief. In these cases, the rifle approach seems best. In many cases, however, a determination of the relative strength of the claims must await discovery, perhaps even trial. In these cases, there is nothing pejorative about the shotgun approach. Of course, if one of the pellets later appears to be a wild shot, plaintiff's counsel should be prepared to

4. Fed.R.Evid. 801.

seek voluntary dismissal of the claim before the issue is sent to the trier of fact. This approach serves both ethics and credibility.

The inclusion of an additional claim for relief may also be an attempt by plaintiff's counsel to create new law. A routine case may become an unusual one with the inclusion of a claim which has not yet been explicitly recognized by the court appearing in the caption (or by higher courts it is required to follow). This tactic has both advantages and disadvantages. If the present state of the law does not provide a plaintiff with a clear claim for relief, then the inclusion of a new cause of action will be necessary. This may also prompt the opposing attorney to view the case from a more serious perspective, increasing the chances of a favorable settlement. If the plaintiff does have a recognizable cause of action, then the inclusion of a novel claim may complicate an otherwise straightforward case. This may also result in a shadow being cast over the otherwise credible claims.

In reality every existing cause of action was first brought by a plaintiff who, in retrospect, was courageous. Earlier and less ambitious plaintiffs and their attorneys may then appear to be fools, or at least cowards. It is not easy to predict the impact the inclusion or exclusion of a novel claim may have on a case. It is appropriate in some cases for a plaintiff's lawyer to endure raucous laughter from the defendant's lawyer upon reading the complaint. The novel claim may also increase the cost of litigation, a factor which all parties must consider.

So long as counsel holds a good faith belief in multiple claims for relief, it is permissible to plead them and use them for negotiation and settlement value. So long as the plaintiff's complaint does not read like a Monty Python transcript, defendants facing several theories of liability are forced to face the possibility that one of them may work. This should encourage negotiated settlement, especially if the various claims will require extra (and expensive) discovery.

In pleading the claim or claims for relief, the plaintiff must walk the fine line between pleading facts sufficient to state a claim for relief but avoiding pleading evidence or conclusions of law. If the distinction sounds like a matter of degree, that's probably because it is. Pleading often lies in the eyes of the beholder. Counsel should apply common sense and decorum in drafting the averments. The complaint should say enough to establish the claims to the desired level of specificity but refrain from labeling a particular incident as negligence, breach of contract or the like.[5] Instead, after the facts are set forth, a broad averment is sufficient at the end of the complaint that states that defendant has been negligent or breached its contract. This puts the defendant on notice of the nature of the legal claim and the facts from which it arises but avoids pleading only conclusions of law.

5. For a more detailed discussion of the analytical bases for fact/law distinction, *see* Fleming James & Geoffrey Hazard, Civil Procedure §§ 3.6–3.7 (3d ed. 1985).

§ 3.3.6 Content of the Complaint

Although Rule 8 and most of its state court counterparts require only a short and plain statement of the facts entitling the plaintiff to relief and a demand for relief, the well-pleaded complaint should meet a number of formal and substantive requirements. Rule 10 establishes the basic format for federal court complaints. These are the main parts of a complaint:

1. Caption;
2. Body;
3. Request for Relief; and
4. Signature.

Caption. The complaint should be captioned with the name of the court, including the applicable division within the district, the names (and addresses in some jurisdictions) of the parties, and the civil action number of the case, and the designation of the pleading (*e.g.*, complaint, answer). In the complaint, the case caption must state the names of all parties. In subsequent pleadings, the name of the first plaintiff and defendant followed by *et al.* may be used.

The specific arrangement of the various parts of a caption on the page is normally a matter of local custom. It is generally a good idea to conform to the local custom since it reinforces the judge's hoped for understanding of your competence.

Body of Complaint. The body of the complaint contains the allegations of fact and description of the plaintiff's claims. The averments of the complaint should be set forth in separate paragraphs, with each paragraph limited insofar as possible to a single set of circumstances. Each paragraph should be numbered and may be referred to by number subsequently in the complaint. Arabic or roman numbers may be used, depending on the preference of the attorney and local custom. Roman numbers, however, appear archaic, and can be cumbersome in lengthy complaints. Later in the complaint, counsel may restate by reference the averments of any preceding paragraph. In addition, the statements in another pleading may be adopted by reference in the instant pleading. This normally does little for the complaint, which is by definition the first pleading of the case except in unusual circumstances. In pleading the existence of a key document, the plaintiff may have it attached to the complaint as an exhibit. This is probably a good practice for crucial documents, but is unnecessary for many less-important documents.

The paragraphs of averment may be very brief or may be somewhat longer so long as Rule 10's spirit is observed. Although long averment paragraphs may attempt to lure the defendant into admitting too much and trapping itself, this style of pleading is generally disfavored and violates the thrust of the federal rules. Besides, the defendant can probably get leave to amend if it appears that the admission of an allegation resulted through inadvertence. It is nobler to be right than cute. Averment paragraphs should be long only where the complexity of the claim makes short averments too fragmented to present the claim in a cogent way.

The federal rules and similar state counterparts do not require a complaint to plead legally required elements stating a cause of action. Such matters of proof are left for trial. Plaintiff need only state facts setting forth a claim entitling relief. The purpose of the claim is to give the defendant notice of the nature of the claim.

In practice, the well-drafted complaint will usually include the following:

1. A description of the parties, both the plaintiffs and defendants;

2. A recitation of the events giving rise to the dispute;

3. An allegation of any demand made to the defendant and the failure to satisfy the demand, as well as any other conditions precedent to making the claim;

4. A reference to the legal nature or source of the cause of action;

5. An allegation of injury to the plaintiff proximately or directly resulting from the defendant's acts;

6. A statement of the damages;

7. In federal court, a statement of the basis for jurisdiction as required by Rule 8(a)(1). In state court, jurisdiction should be apparent from the pleading of a recognized cause of action;

8. Averments of specialized matter such as specific pleading where required (*e.g.,* actions for fraud and libel), allegations of special damages (those not normally thought to flow proximately from the injury alleged), or requests for equitable relief.

In pleading, counsel should have no trouble coming up with an adequate complaint form. It may look something like this:

STATE OF MITCHELL
COUNTY OF SUMMIT
IN DISTRICT COURT

Northstar Oil Company,	
Plaintiff	
	COMPLAINT
v.	
	Civil Action No. ________
Southstar Oil Corporation,	
	Jury Trial Demanded
Defendant	

For its Complaint, Plaintiff Northstar Oil Company ("Northstar") states:

1. Northstar is a corporation organized under the laws of Mitchell with its principal place of business in Summit, Mitchell.

2. Defendant Southstar Oil Corporation ("Southstar") is a corporation organized under the laws of Grand, with its principal place of business in Lexington, Grand.

3. On January 1, 1993, Southstar offered to sell Plaintiff fuel oil at ten dollars ($10.00) per barrel.

4. On January 2, 1993, Northstar accepted Southstar's offer and ordered 30,000 barrels of fuel oil at the $10.00 per barrel price.

5. Southstar failed to deliver fuel and in a letter dated January 10, 1993, informed Northstar that it would not be performing the contract.

6. As a result of Southstar's failure to deliver, Northstar was forced to purchase 30,000 barrels of fuel oil at $15.00 per barrel.

7. As a result of Southstar's breach of its agreement with Northstar, Plaintiff Northstar has suffered damages of one hundred fifty thousand dollars ($150,000.00).

WHEREFORE, Plaintiff Northstar requests Judgment as follows:

1. Judgment in favor of Plaintiff Northstar and against Defendant Southstar in the amount of one hundred fifty thousand dollars ($150,000.00) plus interest and costs to the extent recoverable by law.

2. Such other relief as the interests of justice may require.

Dated: January 26, 1994.

____

Cara Commercial
Laissez & Faire
123 Commodity Place
Commercetown, New York 00000
(212) 000–0000

Counsel for Plaintiff
Northstar Oil Company

Plaintiff could plead more specific averments such as an OPEC oil embargo announced in January 1993, or anything else that might lend strength to the claim. This is, however, not necessary. Plaintiff may also, in most jurisdictions, plead a much less specific complaint. A complaint reduced to its bare minimum might look like this:

> 1. During January 1993 Defendant breached a contract with Plaintiff to sell 30,000 barrels of oil at $10 a barrel, causing Plaintiff damages of $150,000.

This rather concise complaint will survive a motion to dismiss because it complies with the rules of notice pleading, such as they are. Rule 84 provides that the forms contained in the Appendix of Forms to the Federal Rules of Civil Procedure are sufficiently detailed pleadings under the rules. A review of these forms reveals the brevity acceptable and encouraged under the rules. However, because a complaint may serve several functions (as discussed in Section 3.3) a longer and more detailed complaint is usually desirable.

Despite the basic simplicity of what is required to state a claim under modern pleading rules, many turn out looking like this:

> 1. On or about January 10, 1993, Defendant wrongfully and with malice aforethought breached its contract with Plaintiff for the sale of 30,000 barrels of fuel oil at a cost of $10.00 per barrel, said cost having been fraudulently misrepresented to Plaintiff by Defendant and having caused Plaintiff to suffer severe damages as a result of being coerced and forced to buy higher priced fuel oil due to a sudden surge in price between the time the contract was made and Defendant's breach thereof.

Although convoluted and less informative, the second example would probably survive a motion to dismiss in most jurisdictions. However, the attorney who drafted it might not survive the ridicule of colleagues who read such a pleading. Additionally, it is probably easier to deny its allegations than those of the more carefully drafted claim.

Suggested averments for complaints appear in many form books. Many of these forms are appropriate and well-drafted, but many may be inappropriate or even horrendously drafted. The danger in relying on form books is the temptation to plagiarize the forms. This temptation is, unfortunately, especially great when the lawyer does not understand the differences between alternative language or does not know the reason for or effect of particular phrases. The most effective use of form pleadings is to adapt those suggestions that are reasonable and to reject suggestions that appear to be unnecessary or inappropriate under the facts of a particular case or the law of a particular jurisdiction. The same analysis applies to the use of previously drafted complaints as guides. Too often the pleadings relied on are either deficient themselves or are tailor-made, but for the other, different case. Word processing has made the ability to carry forward generations of ill-conceived pleadings and forms not only possible, but widely available.[6] Certain types of cases will easily lend themselves to form pleadings. Many family law pleadings and credit default cases may be composed using a prearranged form. Caution must still be exercised to make certain that each pleading, from whatever source, is suited to the specific needs of the particular case. Examples of complaints appear in the problems at the end of this chapter and in the case files in Appendix B.

Some terms of pleadings have taken on lives of their own, having acquired specialized meanings. Some of these terms serve useful purposes, others deserve to go the way of the Dodo bird. The following include some of the more common terms:

> 1. "*On or about* ... ". This phrase prefaces a date or time, and attempts to avoid establishing a certain date when the pleader is

6. One court has criticized the reuse of interrogatories from an earlier case, observing that they had "all been produced by some word-processing machine's memory of prior litigation," and relieving the recipient from having to respond. *Blank v. Ronson Corp.*, 97 F.R.D. 744, 745 (S.D.N.Y.1983). Similar opprobrium awaits attorneys recklessly using prepared pleadings.

not certain of it. Under modern pleading rules, an allegation of a date or time is considered material, and by pleading the date or time the pleader makes a judicial admission of that date. Qualifying the date by "on or about" results in the pleading not constituting an admission. If the pleader is certain of the date, there is no need to rely upon this unnecessary cautionary phrase.

2. "*Upon information and belief* ...". This phrase is intended to convey the notion that the plaintiff is unsure of some facts and is pleading based upon hearsay information, rumor, or intuition. This phrase is necessary in an affidavit, which otherwise must be made on personal knowledge. Since modern pleading rules do not require pleadings to be made on personal knowledge, there usually is no need for this phrase in a pleading.

3. "*At all times material and relevant to this case* ...". This phrase is used to describe the timing of a continuing condition or event. It is often unnecessary, because specific dates can be provided if necessary. Moreover, it is an open invitation to a denial of the fact. Because the phrase has no precise or clearly understood meaning, no attorney could admit that a fact was true "at all times material and relevant to this case."

4. "*(hereinafter sometimes referred to as '_______').*" As in "Plaintiff National Committee for the Demise of Clean Mudhens (hereinafter sometimes referred to as "Mudhens") ...". Simply ("Mudhens") is sufficient and much less cumbersome. ("NCFDCM") is a much less acceptable alternative. If there is another entity in the action with similar initials, the complaint will look like alphabet soup and will be unintelligible. It is much easier to refer to all the parties by a shortened name which is either an English word contained in the full name, or by a descriptive word related to their role in the action ("Distributor"), ("Dealer"), or ("Owner").

Some claims must be plead with specificity. Counsel should also consult Rule 9 to ensure that any matters that must be pleaded specially have been so averred. Rule 9 actually reads more like a list of things that no longer must be pleaded specially since the adoption of the federal rules. However, state court versions of Rule 9 may not be so liberal and should be consulted with care. Rule 9 provides that fraud, mistake, and conditions of mind must be pleaded with specificity. New Rule 26(a) on disclosure, enacted in 1993, provides that a lawyer's obligation to provide disclosure is triggered only where facts in a complaint are "alleged with particularity" (see § 5.3.5). Courts interpreting the new disclosure requirement will undoubtedly look to Rule 9(b) law to determine what constitutes sufficient detail and particularity. The 1993 changes also offer an opportunity for strategic attorney behavior. Assume the plaintiff wants to get right to discovery without awaiting defendant's disclosure or making disclosures of its own. So long as it will not engender a dismissal of the case, plaintiff may wish to plead vaguely in order to avoid triggering a round of disclosure and its attendant problems and delay. Federal Rule 9 also states that allegations of time and place are material. This means that once pleaded, the pleader is stuck with the times and places averred as though they were admissions.[7] This rule can have consequences for later evidentiary matters as well as the statute of limitations. In cases where rigid adherence to the rule would work injustice, the averment may be cured by amendment. But, as the saying goes, better to get it right the first time.

Rule 11 requires that counsel plead facts that are believed in good faith to be true. Where complete knowledge is lacking, the plaintiff may make averments based upon any reasonable source.

§ 3.3.7 Forms of Relief

Pleading complaints resembles life generally. To get results, one usually has to ask for it (or beg or grovel). After the facts have been set forth and the basic legal claims referenced, the plaintiff must make a claim for relief. The well-drafted complaint in the body or in the *ad damnum* (Wherefore) clause will generally ask for:

1. *A compensatory award of X dollars.* Many jurisdictions require that the complaint merely set forth a general compensatory request such as "in excess of $10,000" in order to avoid the public relations request for "$20 billion dollars and Defendant's DeLorean automobile." It is advisable to aver generally so as not to get boxed into a specific amount that later is abandoned by the plaintiff but used by the defendant to suggest inconsistency. Even if not required, "in excess of *X*" demands are useful and safe. Specific numbers should be saved for negotiating sessions, discovery responses (but only to the extent needed to be candid), and proof at trial.

   Attorneys should take care to plead special damages properly where required. General damages are those that normally flow from the defendant's conduct. Special damages are all other damages. Special damages, or "specials," must be specifically pleaded and proved in order to be recovered. Most damages are general, but certain damages, such as medical bills, lost wages, and substitute help wages, are considered special damages because they are not inevitable, but flow from the particular situation of the plaintiff.[8]

2. *An award of punitive damages,* where warranted by the applicable law under the set of facts pleaded by plaintiff. Punitive damages may be sought "in an amount sufficient to deter Defendant from similar conduct in the future." This form is related to the purpose of punitive damages and does not tie the pleader to a specific number.

7. *Kincheloe v. Farmer,* 214 F.2d 604 (7th Cir.1954), *cert. denied* 348 U.S. 920, 75 S.Ct. 306, 99 L.Ed. 721 (1955); 5 Charles A. Wright & Arthur R. Miller, Federal Practice and Procedure § 1308 (2d ed. 1990).

8. For a listing of types of special damages associated with common causes of action, *see* Fleming James & Geoffrey Hazard, Civil Procedure § 3.18 (2d ed. 1977).

3. *Declaratory, injunctive, or other equitable relief* (*e.g.*, an accounting, replevin) where appropriate under the circumstances and desired by the plaintiff.

4. *Plaintiff's costs and disbursements* incurred in prosecuting the action. Recoverable costs and disbursements will vary from jurisdiction to jurisdiction. The two terms encompass a fixed and limited docket fee or statutory costs, filing fees, out-of-pocket expenses for service of process and obtaining subpoenas, witness fees, and other expenses.

5. *Attorneys' fees* incurred in prosecuting the action if available under the circumstances of the case. Attorneys' fees will be recoverable only in limited circumstances. Generally, attorneys' fees can only be recovered if an agreement between the parties or a specific statute authorizes recovery of fees.

6. *A catchall clause* asking for "such other relief as the interests of justice may require." This phrase adds little or nothing to the pleading. If subsequently discovered facts justify other remedies the pleadings may be amended to conform to those facts. Amendment and supplementation of pleadings are discussed in section 3.12. The presence or absence of this phrase is not likely to affect the court's decision on whether to permit amendment. It has been a part of pleadings for generations and is still prevalent today even if it does serve little purpose.

In addition to requesting equitable relief in the complaint, the plaintiff may require interim equitable relief such as a preliminary injunction or a temporary restraining order. This should be sought in a separate motion and supporting papers filed and served on the heels of the complaint. Motions for provisional relief are discussed in Section 12.5.

§ 3.4 SIGNING OF PLEADINGS

Every pleading must be signed by the attorney of record or the party if an attorney has not appeared for the party. Typically the address and telephone number of the signer will either be required by rule or included as part of practice. Some states require lawyers to include their attorney registration numbers on all pleadings as well.

Pleadings need not be verified unless required by statute or some other reason exists for verification. Verification of a pleading essentially converts the pleading into an affidavit. Verifying a complaint permits it to serve as an affidavit to counter a motion for summary judgment and may obviate preparing a second affidavit.

The signature of an attorney or unrepresented party serves several purposes.[1] Signing constitutes a certification that the attorney has read the pleading, that there exists a good faith basis for the allegations

§ 3.4

1. *See* Fed.R.Civ.P. 11.

made, and that the pleading is not interposed for the delay or other improper purposes. The willful violation of the rule or the inclusion of other inappropriate information not only permits the opposing party to seek to have the pleading stricken as sham or frivolous, but also subjects the attorney to disciplinary action.

§ 3.5 ETHICS OF PLEADINGS

In the '90s and beyond, an essential element of proper pleading will be conformance to the ethics of pleading, which are now reasonably well codified. Counsel should be aware of several ethical rules that specifically address pleadings. Federal Rule 11 provides that the signature of an attorney on a pleading constitutes certification that counsel has read the pleading and determined that there is good ground to support it, and that the pleading is not interposed for delay. A signature in violation of this oath can result in the court striking the pleading and imposing disciplinary sanctions against the signing attorney. Similar sanctions are available if the pleading contains scandalous or indecent matter.

Rule 11 had historically been little used or invoked, but that changed dramatically after the 1983 Amendment of Rule 11 expanded and strengthened the rule which was again amended in 1993 to tone down the courts' newfound zeal. Although common law also provides for certain sanctions against the litigant who prosecutes an action in bad faith, most judicial attention has focused on Rule 11 and 28 U.S.C.A. § 1927.[1] Section 1927 provides that whenever an attorney multiplies proceedings in a case unreasonably and vexatiously, counsel may be personally required to pay the opposition's costs incurred due to the misconduct.

To benefit from this rule, the saintly party usually has to be a prevailing party as well. However, there is no logical need for this restriction. A party may ultimately lose on the merits of a case but nevertheless have been victimized by a pleading through having prepared defenses to frivolous claims upon which the victor did not ultimately succeed. Similarly, motion mania by the victor may not have influenced the result but may have cost the opposition a good deal of money. Even a big loser on the merits may still have been needlessly damaged by scandalous or indecent matter.

Unreasonable and unfounded discovery requests or responses to discovery requests are a frequent source of delay, multiplication, vexatiousness and frivolity. These discovery practices have built-in sanctions under Rule 37. These sanctions are discussed in section 10.5. However, some of the worst discovery abuses, such as intransigent stonewalling, often do not require a motion or pleading by the guilty party, thus limiting the use of the pleading rules of ethics in this regard. But Rule

§ 3.5

1. *See, e.g., Van Berkel v. Fox Farm & Road Machinery,* 581 F.Supp. 1248 (D.Minn.1984).

37, if properly and aggressively employed by the courts, does not require additional help.

Disciplinary Rule 1–101 of the ABA Code of Professional Responsibility, which has been adopted nearly completely by most states, forbids a lawyer from violating a DR, engaging in dishonest conduct, or engaging in conduct "prejudicial to the administration of justice." Although this DR is not specifically directed toward pleadings and motions, it clearly forbids unethical pleading practice. DR 7–102 is more directly focused on advocacy ethics and forbids counsel from filing suit or asserting a position or any other action merely for delay, harassment, or malicious injury. The DR specifically forbids advancing a claim or defense that is unwarranted under existing law. Thus, under these Code sections, which have the force of law in most states, knowingly false motion documents or motions made for an improper purpose, are illegal as well as unethical.

At this juncture, we need to remind the reader of the unique system of legal regulation existing in most states. The actual legal requirements of the profession, from admission, to maintaining good standing, to defining what is ethical, rests with the state supreme courts which promulgate the ethical rules for the self-regulating bar.

In practice, the rules adopted by many state high courts are heavily influenced by the recommendations of state bar associations and whatever select committees recommend rule adoptions and changes. These local forces are in turn heavily influenced by the ABA model, which ordinarily provides the base from which the state groups begin work. Most of the ABA-passed recommendations (the product of years of committee work modified and ratified by the ABA House of Delegates) will be enacted by the states and their codes will closely resemble the ABA model. At least, that's what happened with the Code of Professional Responsibility, passed by the ABA in 1969 and largely the law of the American legal profession by the mid–1970s.

In 1983, the ABA passed the Model Rules of Professional Conduct, which are somewhat more innovative, comprehensive, and therefore more controversial than the Code, which sought to memorialize the general understanding of the profession. The Model Rules have attempted more clearly to deal with problems of modern legal practice—*e.g.,* large firms, branch offices, conflicting client loyalties, and in-house counsel—and have also attempted to more closely grapple with the tension between the attorney's duties to the client (*e.g.,* confidentiality) and to the system (*e.g.,* preventing fraud, perjury, and injury to others). As a result, the Model Rules, even after being toned down by the inevitable compromise of the ABA's legislative process, are more controversial than the Code and have not been as quickly rubber-stamped by state supreme courts. In addition, increasingly sophisticated state bar regulators have modified the Rules more substantially than they did the Code. Therefore, in considering any discussion of the Model Rules in this or other sections, remember that the Rules may not yet be the law in your state and may not become the law at all. However, the Model Rules regarding litigation practice are not substantial changes from the Code.

Model Rule 3.1 requires that counsel bring only meritorious claims and defenses, that the documents have a legal basis or at least a good faith argument for extending the law (read this "not as far out as the things you used to put on law school exams"). Model Rule 3.2 requires that counsel make reasonable efforts to expedite litigation so long as this is consistent with the client's interests. Model Rule 3.3 requires candor toward the court and contains language that is stronger about the duty to reveal perjury or facts necessary to prevent fraud by the client than the Code's admonition. Lawyers are also required to disclose all facts, even the adverse ones, in an ex parte proceeding. Finally, Model Rule 3.4 requires fairness to the opposition, and forbids discovery intransigence, evidence destruction, innuendo, witness tampering, and frivolous discovery motions.

Perhaps the greatest incentive to be ethical is a practical one. If counsel wants to have credibility with the court, opposing counsel, and within the local legal community, all things which any sane lawyer will want and need in the long run, counsel will observe the rules of ethics. Judges can sense hokey pleadings and motions and, while they may not assess sanctions as often as they should, they will remember the near-sham papers and this undoubtedly colors the court's thinking on close call motions, evidentiary rulings, jury instructions, and other procedural matters such as scheduling.

Every litigator will someday need to be given a break by the court or opposing counsel. Some have that need repeatedly. Thus, in pleading and other areas of litigation, the cardinal rule is the golden rule. Most important, counsel must retain credibility with the tribunal, something usually will be irretrievably lost if the lawyer brings specious motions and claims. Someday, counsel might have a creative legal theory that is justified by the facts. Why preclude a chance to win that case by becoming known as a lawyer whose motions and pleadings are as crude and finely drawn as a howitzer blast. Remember the little child who cried wolf? Above all, counsel must take seriously the attorney's function as an officer of the court. Counsel's task is to provide the best representation feasible within the rules and the client's ability and willingness to pay; counsel's job is not to try to make a sure loser a winner by fabricating claims, defenses, law, facts, or anything else.

§ 3.6 DRAFTING TECHNIQUES

§ 3.6.1 Goals of Complaint

In drafting a complaint, counsel has a good deal of flexibility, operating within a framework of relatively few rules. As long as the averment paragraphs tell the recipient and the court something about the case and are not too long, too laden with superfluous or scandalous matter, and not too full of blatant legal conclusions, the complaint will probably pass judicial muster.

However, counsel should not aim merely to avoid a motion to dismiss or to strike. The complaint should not only fulfill its basic functions under the rules but also accomplish something for the plaintiff. Typical goals of the complaint are to:

(1) Alert the defendant that the plaintiff will no longer be a pacifist;

(2) Impress opposing counsel with the competence of plaintiff's counsel;

(3) Identify the issues in dispute between the parties;

(4) Establish the basis of claims for relief, both to the court and to the opposition;

(5) Establish a scope of disclosure and discovery and targets of discovery consistent with the plaintiff's needs; and

(6) Conform to form requirements and customs of local practitioners.

§ 3.6.2 Drafting Techniques

Although these goals and the method of achieving them will vary from case to case, the following drafting techniques are ordinarily best suited to getting the most impact from the complaint.

1. *Be Precise but Brief.* Don't say "over the past ten years," say "On October 1, 197X, January 15, 197X, etc." Follow the command of Rule 10 and use the shortest feasible averment paragraphs consistent with your goals. This forces the defendant to meet specificity with specificity, revealing more clearly to you the legal and factual position. Even where the facts at issue are involved or complex, stick to the short paragraph insofar as feasible. When setting forth the plaintiff's version of reality, attempt a level of detail sufficient to show entitlement to relief and a potentially strong case but avoid attempting to prove the case in the complaint. "If it doesn't help you, it hurts you" is a useful maxim to remember in pleading and brief writing.

The precision with which a complaint is drafted also affects the process of disclosure. Under Federal Rule 26(a), automatic disclosure requirements are made as to matters related to disputed facts pleaded with particularity. Greater detail in drafting the complaint is needed to trigger these disclosure obligations.

2. *Use Objective Words.* Loaded descriptions of the events at hand may be useful in closing arguments but only undermine credibility in the complaint. In addition, argumentative terms may turn factual averments into conclusions of law or scandalous matter, providing the defendant with grounds for a motion to dismiss or to strike. The need to report in objective terminology does not require

that the plaintiff plead a weak case. Rather, the plaintiff should set forth the facts, perhaps even selectively, and let them speak for themselves. In pleading fraud or grounds for punitive damages, the plaintiff in most jurisdictions must use words with negative connotative value, providing counsel an outlet for venom. After all, the court requires it. But where the court does not, plead with restraint in language.

3. *Attach Documents as Exhibits.* A useful tool in letting favorable facts speak for themselves is reference to a document such as a contract or an incriminating letter by the opponent. The document should be attached as an exhibit to the complaint as allowed by Fed.R.Civ.P. 10(c). The documents, especially those authored by the opposition, add credibility to the complaint. However, avoid the tendency to turn the complaint into a replica of the phone book unless all those documents are truly central to the case. Mere relevance is not enough. Less crucial documents can be left out of the complaint and proved up at trial.

4. *Structure the Complaint.* Complaints which include a single cause of action or simple claims can be easily and logically structured. The provisions listed in section 3.3.6 provide an outline appropriate for those complaints. Complaints that include multiple claims or causes of action based upon different or additional facts present some difficulty in composing a readily understood complaint. In those situations the most efficient way to compose the complaint is for the plaintiff first to set forth preliminary matter (party identification, jurisdiction) and then plead the basic facts underlying the relations of the parties and the events of the lawsuit. These factual averments should be prefaced with a heading such as "First Claim for Relief (Breach of Contract)" or "Count I (Negligence)." At the conclusion of these preliminary factual averments, the plaintiff may then plead the averments entitling legal relief such as "Defendant failed to deliver the corn" and "As a result of Defendant's non-delivery, plaintiff suffered damages in excess of $10,000."

The second count based on a different legal claim or a related but different set of facts can then follow. The plaintiff should denominate the next legal claim, *e.g.*, "Second Claim for Relief (Fraud)." The plaintiff can begin this claim by restating the averments set forth in paragraphs *X* to *Y* of the first claim and should then state any additional facts relevant to the second claim, *e.g.*, "Defendant knew it had no corn but told plaintiff it did," "Plaintiff relied on Defendant's statement and rented a corn masher at a cost of *X* dollars". Then, the plaintiff must set forth the legal contentions related to the second claim, *e.g.*, "As a result of relying on Defendant's statement, Plaintiff was damaged in the amount of *X* dollars", "Defendant's conduct in making a knowing misstatement upon which it knew Plaintiff would rely was malicious." In this example, the plaintiff would then claim entitlement to punitive damages using the language of the applicable statute or case law in the jurisdiction. At the end, the demand for relief should set forth the relief sought in connection with each claim. The claim can also be labeled a count or cause of action. However, the rules require only a claim entitling relief, and we prefer this language although we, like most everyone else, frequently lapse into less apt but familiar terminology. An outline of a multiple count complaint may look like this:

STATE OF MITCHELL
COUNTY OF SUMMIT
IN DISTRICT COURT

Northstar Oil Company,

Plaintiff,

v.

Southstar Oil Corporation,

Defendant,

COMPLAINT

Civil Action No. ________

Jury Trial Demanded

For its complaint, Plaintiff Northstar Oil Company ("Northstar") states:

FIRST CLAIM FOR RELIEF
(Breach of Contract)

1.
2.
3.

[Allegations in separately numbered paragraphs similar to those found in the Complaint on page 99.]

SECOND CLAIM FOR RELIEF
(Fraud)

4.
5.
6.
7.
8.

[Allegations that Southstar never intended to provide the promised oil at the agreed price and that Northstar relied to its detriment on Southstar's fraudulent statements incurring damages.]

THIRD CLAIM FOR RELIEF
(Punitive Damages Under a State Statute)

9.
10.
11.

[Allegations that Southstar's conduct was sufficiently knowing and blameworthy to merit a punitive award sufficient to punish it and deter future misbehavior.]

PRAYER FOR RELIEF

WHEREFORE, Plaintiff Northstar requests the following:

1. Damages on the Contract plus interests and costs.

2. Damages for Fraud.

3. Punitive damages under statute or common law.

4. Other relief as may be required.

Dated: January 26, 1994.

____

Cara Commercial
Laissez & Faire
123 Commodity Place
Commercetown, New York 00000
(212) 000–0000

Counsel for Plaintiff
Northstar Oil Company

Using this same modified format in a claim involving an exploding widget used while remodeling the house, a plaintiff homeowner might allege negligence for the first claim for relief, breach of warranty as a second claim, and strict liability as a third claim.

5. *Balance Factual and Legal Contentions.* The general rule of pleading is that the complaint (and all other pleadings as well) should set forth facts and identify the legal issues and not plead conclusions of law. A reasonable description of an event that provides the opposing party with sufficient factual and legal information will usually be sufficient. Pleading either a factual or legal extreme may not be acceptable. A complaint devoid of an explanation of the specific legal claim or that only includes a conclusion of law will fail to meet pleading requirements. The academic distinction between contentions and conclusions is of interest mainly to academics. In the real world unless a complaint reads like a hybrid of Tropic of Cancer and Blackstone's Commentaries, no right-minded defendant will attack it for pleading legal conclusions. If a complaint reads like a campaign brochure, the judge may prevent it from being read to the jury, but complaints, unlike criminal indictments, are seldom read to the jury or introduced in evidence.

6. *Be Restrained in Requesting Relief.* Demands for billions of dollars or for an order requiring the defendant to read this book do little to enhance a plaintiff's case. Grossly inflated claims have little utility, and may be counter-productive. Ask for what the plaintiff is entitled. Depending on the jurisdiction, *ad damnum* clauses such as "in excess of $10,000" may be most appropriate. At the time suit commences, the full extent of damages may not be known. Often, crucial information about damages is in a defendant's possession, requiring discovery before a more precise amount can be claimed. In addition, this technique, without blatantly overstating damages, alerts the defendant to its substantial exposure on the case, a tactic likely to aid settlement. However, the plaintiff must bear in mind that the defendant is equally aware of most facts at issue and has its own mental calculation of possible damages. Plaintiff is unlikely to scare the opponent into settlement by pleading big numbers.

7. *Attempt to Answer the Complaint.* After a proposed complaint has been drafted it may be useful to attempt to answer it from the perspective of the opposing counsel. This technique will usually reveal some deficiencies which may be alleviated with proper editing. A proposed paragraph that would have been automatically denied from the first draft may be crafted to require an admission. It doesn't always result in tangible results, but it may be of value. Because statements in the pleadings are admissions, it is useful to make sure that there are no inadvertent mistakes.

§ 3.6.3 Alternative Complaint Forms

The structure of a complaint will be influenced by the nature of the claims and the complexity of the facts and issues. Some complaints, particularly federal court complaints and major state court complaints, will be structured in a way that presents the information in an alternative format to notice pleading. Federal court complaints often contain headings which describe groups of paragraph allegations relating to jurisdiction, the parties, the facts, causes of action, and remedies. This format provides a readily understandable way to present the case. An outline of a federal class action complaint may resemble this:

Introduction

The initial paragraph concisely explains the nature of the case.

Jurisdiction

This paragraph or two cites the source of jurisdiction for the federal court.

Parties

These paragraphs describe information about the parties.

Class Action

Several paragraphs detail those factors of Rule 23 which provide the bases for the class action.

Facts

These allegations describe the events giving rise to the action.

Causes of Action

These sections delineate the claims, similar to the format of a multiple count complaint.

Remedies

The concluding paragraphs summarize the relief sought.

Several of these headings may be merged or eliminated. Other headings may apply and be used. The introductory paragraph provides a short description of the case to help the judge, law clerk, and opposing lawyer understand the case. This paragraph may be unnecessary. Whatever format is used and whatever headings are included should serve one or more goals of the complaint.

§ 3.6.4 Federal Court Civil Cover Sheet

Some information about a federal court case will need to be provided on a form called a "Civil Cover Sheet" which must be obtained from the federal court clerk. A sample appears on this page. The complaint must still contain information necessary for a well-plead complaint and to obtain specific relief. For example, checking yes in the Jury Demand box does not satisfy the requirement of the plaintiff to properly demand a jury trial. A separate demand still needs to be made.

JS 44
(Rev. 07/89)

CIVIL COVER SHEET

The JS-44 civil cover sheet and the information contained herein neither replace nor supplement the filing and service of pleadings or other papers as required by law, except as provided by local rules of court. This form, approved by the Judicial Conference of the United States in September 1974, is required for the use of the Clerk of Court for the purpose of initiating the civil docket sheet. (SEE INSTRUCTIONS ON THE REVERSE OF THE FORM.)

I (a) PLAINTIFFS	**DEFENDANTS**
(b) COUNTY OF RESIDENCE OF FIRST LISTED PLAINTIFF ____________ (EXCEPT IN U.S. PLAINTIFF CASES)	COUNTY OF RESIDENCE OF FIRST LISTED DEFENDANT ____________ (IN U.S. PLAINTIFF CASES ONLY) NOTE: IN LAND CONDEMNATION CASES, USE THE LOCATION OF THE TRACT OF LAND INVOLVED
(c) ATTORNEYS (FIRM NAME, ADDRESS, AND TELEPHONE NUMBER)	ATTORNEYS (IF KNOWN)

II. BASIS OF JURISDICTION (PLACE AN × IN ONE BOX ONLY)

☐ 1 **U.S. Government Plaintiff**
☐ 3 **Federal Question** (U.S. Government Not a Party)
☐ 2 **U.S. Government Defendant**
☐ 4 **Diversity** (Indicate Citizenship of Parties in Item III)

III. CITIZENSHIP OF PRINCIPAL PARTIES (PLACE AN × IN ONE BOX FOR PLAINTIFF AND ONE BOX FOR DEFENDANT)

(For Diversity Cases Only)

	PTF	DEF		PTF	DEF
Citizen of This State	☐ 1	☐ 1	**Incorporated or Principal Place of Business in This State**	☐ 4	☐ 4
Citizen of Another State	☐ 2	☐ 2	**Incorporated and Principal Place of Business in Another State**	☐ 5	☐ 5
Citizen or Subject of a Foreign Country	☐ 3	☐ 3	**Foreign Nation**	☐ 6	☐ 6

IV. CAUSE OF ACTION (CITE THE U.S. CIVIL STATUTE UNDER WHICH YOU ARE FILING AND WRITE A BRIEF STATEMENT OF CAUSE. DO NOT CITE JURISDICTIONAL STATUTES UNLESS DIVERSITY)

V. NATURE OF SUIT (PLACE AN × IN ONE BOX ONLY)

CONTRACT

☐ 110 Insurance
☐ 120 Marine
☐ 130 Miller Act
☐ 140 Negotiable Instrument
☐ 150 Recovery of Overpayment & Enforcement of Judgment
☐ 151 Medicare Act
☐ 152 Recovery of Defaulted Student Loans (Excl. Veterans)
☐ 153 Recovery of Overpayment of Veteran's Benefits
☐ 160 Stockholders' Suits
☐ 190 Other Contract
☐ 195 Contract Product Liability

REAL PROPERTY

☐ 210 Land Condemnation
☐ 220 Foreclosure
☐ 230 Rent Lease & Ejectment
☐ 240 Torts to Land
☐ 245 Tort Product Liability
☐ 290 All Other Real Property

TORTS

PERSONAL INJURY

☐ 310 Airplane
☐ 315 Airplane Product Liability
☐ 320 Assault, Libel & Slander
☐ 330 Federal Employers' Liability
☐ 340 Marine
☐ 345 Marine Product Liability
☐ 350 Motor Vehicle
☐ 355 Motor Vehicle Product Liability
☐ 360 Other Personal Injury

PERSONAL INJURY

☐ 362 Personal Injury—Med Malpractice
☐ 365 Personal Injury—Product Liability
☐ 368 Asbestos Personal Injury Product Liability

PERSONAL PROPERTY

☐ 370 Other Fraud
☐ 371 Truth in Lending
☐ 380 Other Personal Property Damage
☐ 385 Property Damage Product Liability

CIVIL RIGHTS

☐ 441 Voting
☐ 442 Employment
☐ 443 Housing/Accommodations
☐ 444 Welfare
☐ 440 Other Civil Rights

PRISONER PETITIONS

☐ 510 Motions to Vacate Sentence
Habeas Corpus
☐ 530 General
☐ 535 Death Penalty
☐ 540 Mandamus & Other
☐ 550 Other

FORFEITURE/PENALTY

☐ 610 Agriculture
☐ 620 Other Food & Drug
☐ 625 Drug Related Seizure of Property 21 USC 881
☐ 630 Liquor Laws
☐ 640 R.R. & Truck
☐ 650 Airline Regs
☐ 660 Occupational Safety/Health
☐ 690 Other

LABOR

☐ 710 Fair Labor Standards Act
☐ 720 Labor/Mgmt. Relations
☐ 730 Labor/Mgmt. Reporting & Disclosure Act
☐ 740 Railway Labor Act
☐ 790 Other Labor Litigation
☐ 791 Empl. Ret. Inc. Security Act

BANKRUPTCY

☐ 422 Appeal 28 USC 158
☐ 423 Withdrawal 28 USC 157

PROPERTY RIGHTS

☐ 820 Copyrights
☐ 830 Patent
☐ 840 Trademark

SOCIAL SECURITY

☐ 861 HIA (1395ff)
☐ 862 Black Lung (923)
☐ 863 DIWC/DIWW (405(g))
☐ 864 SSID Title XVI
☐ 865 RSI (405(g))

FEDERAL TAX SUITS

☐ 870 Taxes (U.S. Plaintiff or Defendant)
☐ 871 IRS—Third Party 26 USC 7609

OTHER STATUTES

☐ 400 State Reapportionment
☐ 410 Antitrust
☐ 430 Banks and Banking
☐ 450 Commerce/ICC Rates/etc.
☐ 460 Deportation
☐ 470 Racketeer Influenced and Corrupt Organizations
☐ 810 Selective Service
☐ 850 Securities/Commodities/Exchange
☐ 875 Customer Challenge 12 USC 3410
☐ 891 Agricultural Acts
☐ 892 Economic Stabilization Act
☐ 893 Environmental Matters
☐ 894 Energy Allocation Act
☐ 895 Freedom of Information Act
☐ 900 Appeal of Fee Determination Under Equal Access to Justice
☐ 950 Constitutionality of State Statutes
☐ 890 Other Statutory Actions

VI. ORIGIN (PLACE AN × IN ONE BOX ONLY)

☐ 1 Original Proceeding
☐ 2 Removed from State Court
☐ 3 Remanded from Appellate Court
☐ 4 Reinstated or Reopened
☐ 5 Transferred from another district (specify)
☐ 6 Multidistrict Litigation
☐ 7 Appeal to District Judge from Magistrate Judgment

VII. REQUESTED IN COMPLAINT:

CHECK IF THIS IS A **CLASS ACTION** ☐ UNDER F.R.C.P. 23

DEMAND $

Check YES only if demanded in complaint:
JURY DEMAND: ☐ YES ☐ NO

VIII. RELATED CASE(S) (See instructions): IF ANY

JUDGE ____________ DOCKET NUMBER ____________

DATE SIGNATURE OF ATTORNEY OF RECORD

UNITED STATES DISTRICT COURT

INSTRUCTIONS FOR ATTORNEYS COMPLETING CIVIL COVER SHEET FORM JS-44

Authority For Civil Cover Sheet

The JS-44 civil cover sheet and the information contained herein neither replaces nor supplements the filings and service of pleading or other papers as required by law, except as provided by local rules of court. This form, approved by the Judicial Conference of the United States in September 1974, is required for the use of the Clerk of Court for the purpose of initiating the civil docket sheet. Consequently a civil cover sheet is submitted to the Clerk of Court for each civil complaint filed. The attorney filing a case should complete the form as follows:

I. (a) Plaintiffs - Defendants. Enter names (last, first, middle initial) of plaintiff and defendant. If the plaintiff or defendant is a government agency, use only the full name or standard abbreviations. If the plaintiff or defendant is an official within a government agency, identify first the agency and then the official, giving both name and title.

(b) County of Residence. For each civil case filed, except U.S. plaintiff cases, enter the name of the county where the first listed plaintiff resides at the time of filing. In U.S. plaintiff cases, enter the name of the county in which the first listed defendant resides at the time of filing. (NOTE: In land condemnation cases, the county of residence of the "defendant" is the location of the tract of land involved).

(c) Attorneys. Enter firm name, address, telephone number, and attorney or record. If there are several attorneys, list them on an attachment, noting in this section "(see attachment)".

II. Jurisdiction. The basis of jurisdiction is set forth under Rule 8 (a), F.R.C.P., which requires that jurisdictions be shown in pleadings. Place an "X" in one of the boxes. If there is more than one basis of jurisdiction, precedence is given in the order shown below.

United States plaintiff. (1) Jurisdiction is based on 28 U.S.C. 1345 and 1348. Suits by agencies and officers of the United States are included here.

United States defendant. (2) When the plaintiff is suing the United States, its officers or agencies, place an X in this box.

Federal question. (3) This refers to suits under 28 U.S.C. 1331, where jurisdiction arises under the Constitution of the United States, an amendment to the Constitution, an act of Congress or a treaty of the United States. In cases where the U.S. is a party, the U.S. plaintiff or defendant code takes precedence, and box 1 or 2 should be marked.

Diversity of citizenship. (4) This refers to suits under 28 U.S.C. 1332, where parties are citizens of different states. When Box 4 is checked, the citizenship of the different parties must be checked. (See Section III below; federal question actions take precedence over diversity cases.)

III. Residence (citizenship) of Principal Parties. This section of the JS-44 is to be completed if diversity of citizenship was indicated above. Mark this section for each principal party.

IV. Cause of Action. Report the civil statute directly related to the cause of action and give a brief description of the cause.

V. Nature of Suit. Place an "X" in the appropriate box. If the nature of suit cannot be determined, be sure the cause of action, in Section IV above, is sufficient to enable the deputy clerk or the statistical clerks in the Administrative Office to determine the nature of suit. If the cause fits more than one nature of suit, select the most definitive.

VI. Origin. Place an "X" in one of the seven boxes.

Original Proceedings. (1) Cases which originate in the United States district courts.

Removed from State Court. (2) Proceedings initiated in state courts may be removed to the district courts under Title 28 U.S.C., Section 1441. When the petition for removal is granted, check this box.

Remanded from Appellate Court. (3) Check this box for cases remanded to the district court for further action. Use the date of remand as the filing date.

Reinstated or Reopened. (4) Check this box for cases reinstated or reopened in the district court. Use the reopening date as the filing date.

Transferred from Another District. (5) For cases transferred under Title 28 U.S.C. Section 1404(a). Do not use this for within district transfers or multidistrict litigation transfers.

Multidistrict Litigation. (6) Check this box when a multidistrict case is transferred into the district under authority of Title 28 U.S.C. Section 1407. When this box is checked, do not check (5) above.

Appeal to District Judge from Magistrate Judgment. (7) Check this box for an appeal from a magistrate's decision.

VII. Requested in Complaint. Class Action. Place an "X" in this box if you are filing a class action under Rule 23, F.R.Cv.P.

Demand. In this space enter the dollar amount (in thousands of dollars) being demanded or indicate other demand such as a preliminary injunction.

Jury Demand. Check the appropriate box to indicate whether or not a jury is being demanded.

VIII. Related Cases. This section of the JS-44 is used to reference relating pending cases if any. If there are related pending cases, insert the docket numbers and the corresponding judge names for such cases.

Date and Attorney Signature. Date and sign the civil cover sheet.

(rev. 07/89) GPO : 1989 - 237-312

§ 3.7 DEFENDANT'S PLEADINGS

§ 3.7.1 The Answer

The defendant must respond to each of the plaintiff's numbered averment paragraphs. The typical responses are:

1. Denial;
2. Admission;
3. Partial denial and partial admission; and

4. Denial for reason (*e.g.* insufficient information) of inability to admit or deny.

The defendant may include these responses through a separate paragraph for each of the responses or may list all of its admissions in one paragraph, while listing denials in the next, and those as to which the defendant is without knowledge or information sufficient to form a belief in the next.

Fed.R.Civ.P. 8 generally requires that the defendant do one of these four things in response to each numbered paragraph of the complaint. If a particular paragraph contains material that the defendant must admit and material the defendant will deny, the answer should respond accordingly, stating which averments of paragraph *X* are admitted and which are denied. Since under Rule 8(d) all averments to which defendant does not specifically respond are deemed admitted, defendants will usually add a catchall paragraph denying each and every averment of the complaint except as otherwise admitted. This is a sound practice.

Defendants are permitted under Rule 8 and most state rules to deny generally everything averred in the complaint. This is, however, a poor practice and defeats the purpose of pleading as a device for framing the issues and actual points of controversy for the parties. It should only be used if in fact there exist good faith reasons justifying a general denial. If time is critical and there is insufficient time to answer, an extension of time should be obtained, in order to obtain information to permit a more specific answer. In addition, a general denial does not put in issue topics such as capacity or conditions precedent, which under Rule 9 must be specifically challenged. However, an answer may use a general denial coupled with the pleading of affirmative defenses. The case files in Appendix B contain examples of various forms of answers.

§ 3.7.2 Affirmative Defenses

Certain matter must be set forth as an affirmative defense before the defendant will be permitted to raise these defenses to the plaintiff's claims. Nineteen specific affirmative defenses such as accord and satisfaction, contributory negligence, estoppel, fraud, duress, statute of frauds, and statute of limitations are set out in Fed.R.Civ.P. 8(c). In addition, defendant must plead "any other matter constituting an avoidance or affirmative defense."

The purpose of an affirmative defense is to provide notice to the plaintiff about the defenses and prevent surprise at trial. A defendant should plead as an affirmative defense any substantive defense based on statute or case law. In essence, an affirmative defense occurs when the defendant does not deny the truth of the plaintiff's averments but goes on to contend that, even if the plaintiff's averments are true, other facts prevent the plaintiff from obtaining relief from defendant. Whenever this is the substance of one of the defense positions, it should be pleaded as an affirmative defense.[1]

If an affirmative defense is not pleaded in the answer, the defendant is generally precluded from raising this defense at trial but may seek to amend the answer to correct the deficiency. Jurisdictions vary on how stringently they enforce the rule on waiver of affirmative defenses. As a basic practice, defense counsel should not count on grace from the court but plead all potentially available affirmative defenses. This sometimes results in a kitchen sink answer setting forth practically every defense listed in Rule 8(c). This response borders on an ethical violation. With just a bit of care and thought, counsel can limit the affirmative defenses to those realistically capable of applying to the case after more facts are known.

In lieu of an answer or as part of the answer, the defendant may make any of the motions set forth in Rule 12 and discussed in Chapter 4. Other motions provided for in the rules may also occasionally be apt at this juncture but this is relatively rare. Like the complaint, the answer may allege alternative theories and claims, even if they are inconsistent. As discussed in Section 11.1, Rule 12 defenses alleging lack of personal jurisdiction, improper venue, insufficiency of process, and insufficiency of service of process are waived by the defendant if not made by motion within the 20 days allowed for responding to the complaint. These defenses are also waived if not raised as affirmative defenses in the answer.[2]

The affirmative defense, unlike the claims of the complaint, need only be pleaded generally (*e.g.*, "Plaintiff is estopped from claiming damages from Defendant"). However, better practice is to set forth, in addition to the affirmances and denials of the complaint's allegations, additional facts relevant to telling the defendant's side of the story. A generally phrased statement of a defense does not impose automatic disclosure obligations on the parties, while a defense pleaded with particularity will trigger these additional disclosure. A defendant may plead affirmative defenses on account of the facts set forth earlier in the answer. On occasion, the affirmative defense may be very strong, unlike the boilerplate affirmative defenses so frequently pleaded in order to preserve the defense. When the affirmative defense is good, the defendant may wish to plead it with the detail found in a good complaint.

Example of answers and affirmative defenses appear in the case files in Appendix B. A sample of an answer to the original Northstar Complaint on pages 99–100, with multiple affirmative defenses, is:

§ 3.7

1. *See* Fleming James & Geoffrey Hazard, Civil Procedure § 4.5 (3d ed. 1985).

2. Fed.R.Civ.P. 12(h)(1).

STATE OF MITCHELL
COUNTY OF SUMMIT
IN DISTRICT COURT

Northstar Oil Company,

Plaintiff

ANSWER

v.

Civil Action No. _______

Southstar Oil Corporation,
Defendant.

Defendant Southstar Oil Corporation ("Southstar"), for its answer, states as follows:

1. Southstar admits that it is incorporated in Grand and but denies that its principal place of business is Lexington, Grand.

2. Southstar denies the allegations of paragraphs 3 through 7 of Plaintiff's complaint.

3. Southstar is at this time without information and belief sufficient to form a response to Paragraph One of Plaintiff's Complaint.

Dated: February 22, 1994.

____

Darryl Defense
Stone & Wall
123 Main Street
Commercetown, New York 00000
(212) 000–0000

Counsel for Defendant
Southstar Corporation

§ 3.8 COUNTERCLAIMS, CROSS-CLAIMS, AND THIRD-PARTY COMPLAINTS

§ 3.8.1 Generally

The Rules of Civil Procedure provide three tools by which a defendant in an action may assert claims against persons already parties to the action or against third persons who are not parties—the counterclaim, the cross-claim, and the third-party claim.

Counterclaims, cross-claims, and third-party claims may all be included in the defendant's initial pleadings as a matter of right, without the need for motion for leave of court. In later stages of litigation, however, leave of court is necessary to assert these claims. These devices also generate many motions attacking their propriety. For example, including third-party claims may result in motions for separate trials of the main action and the third-party claims, for continuance of trial, for additional discovery, or for leave for the third-party defendant to serve a "fourth"-party claim.

§ 3.8.2 Counterclaims

Counterclaims occur when a party defending a claim asserts its own claim against the original claimant. Under modern practice, both legal and equitable counterclaims can be asserted. The amount of the counterclaim can exceed the amount of the initial claim. It must be a mature claim but its legal theory or factual base need not be identical to the claimant's claim. Counterclaims may only be asserted against an "opposing party." Example of a counterclaim appears in some of the case files in Appendix B.

Counterclaims may be either compulsory or permissive, a distinction determined by the relationship between the initial claim and the counterclaim. Failure to assert a compulsory counterclaim results in its being barred in later litigation. Fed.R.Civ.P. 13(a) makes a counterclaim compulsory if it arises from the same transaction or occurrence that forms the basis of the opponent's claim. In a strict sense, the claim is not "compulsory," for the court will not compel a party to assert it. If the counterclaim is not asserted, however, the party will not be allowed to assert it at a future time.[1] Bar by operation of Fed.R.Civ.P. 13(a) exists only as to those claims that were in existence and capable of being plead at the time the answer or other responsible pleading was served. Similarly, a party need not assert as a counterclaim a claim that is already the subject of another civil action or one that requires joinder of third persons over whom the court cannot exercise jurisdiction if necessary.[2]

Fed.R.Civ.P. 13(b) governs permissive counterclaims. It establishes the outer limits of what claims may properly be asserted. A party may assert as a permissive counterclaim any claim against an opposing party without regard to whether it arises from the same transaction or occurrence or has any other factual or legal connection to the claimant's claim. Because these counterclaims are permissive, there is no bar if they are not asserted in the initial suit.

Permissive counterclaims raise two special types of motions. First, there must be an independent basis for subject-matter jurisdiction over permissive counterclaims,[3] and motions to dismiss on this basis frequently occur. Second, because of the extremely liberal rules of joinder, a court may desire to separate the trials of the claim and the permissive counterclaim. Fed.R.Civ.P. 42(b) and similar state court rules specifically authorize separate trials, and the assertion of a wholly unrelated permissive counterclaim presents one of the stronger cases for ordering separate trials.

One important, and occasionally overlooked, form of counterclaim is a claim on which the statute of limitations has run. Although such a claim cannot be asserted for affirmative relief, if it operates as a setoff or acts in the nature of recoupment, the defendant can probably assert it

§ 3.8

1. *See* 6 Charles A. Wright & Arthur R. Miller, Federal Practice and Procedure § 1404 (2d ed. 1990).

2. *See Dragor Shipping Corp. v. Union Tank Car Co.*, 378 F.2d 241 (9th Cir.1967).

3. *See, e.g., McCaffrey v. Rex Motor Transportation, Inc.*, 672 F.2d 246 (1st Cir. 1982).

notwithstanding the statute of limitations.[4] In addition, some courts hold that the filing of the claim in the main action tolls the statute of limitations as to counterclaims, at least as to compulsory counterclaims.[5]

Procedural rules typically permit a party to assert counterclaims not initially raised by the new pleading. Specifically, Fed.R.Civ.P. 13(e) permits a party to obtain leave to assert an after-acquired claim. Fed. R.Civ.P. 13(f) permits a party to assert as an omitted counterclaim one that should have been plead earlier. Leave of court must be obtained for either amendment to allow an omitted counterclaim or supplementation to allege an after-acquired counterclaim. It pays to be on time. In many cases leave of court can be obtained upon stipulation of the parties. If a stipulation cannot be obtained, the potential counterclaimant should move for leave as quickly as possible. No fixed deadline exists for bringing a motion for leave, however, and counterclaims may be permitted by amendment to conform to the evidence, or even after trial,[6] but not after retirement from practice.

§ 3.8.3 Cross-Claims

Cross-claims may be broadly defined as any claims a party may have against any other non-opposing party to the action which arise out of the same occurrence or transaction as the main action or counterclaims in that action. Like counterclaims, if a cross-claim is proper when served it does not become defective if the main action is dismissed as to the party against whom the cross-claim is asserted, or if that party becomes an opposing party through realignment of the pleadings.[7] Cross-claims do not require independent grounds for federal jurisdiction since they, like compulsory counterclaims, are considered within the court's ancillary jurisdiction. However, dismissal of the main action may destroy subject-matter jurisdiction and require dismissal of the cross-claim standing alone.[8]

Cross-claims may be asserted as a matter of right in the cross-claimant's initial pleadings. Claims wholly unrelated to the main action may not be asserted as cross-claims. If the cross-claim lacks an affirmative claim for relief and actually constitutes a defense, it is subject to dismissal. All cross-claims are permissive in that the rules do not require a cross-claim to be asserted in order to avoid being lost or barred. However, failure to assert a cross-claim could result in collateral estoppel against the party failing to assert the cross-claim.

4. *See, e.g., City of Grand Rapids v. McCurdy,* 136 F.2d 615 (6th Cir.1943).

5. *See generally* 6 Charles A. Wright & Arthur R. Miller, Federal Practice and Procedure § 1419 (2d ed. 1990).

6. *See, e.g., Dale Benz, Inc. v. American Casualty Co.,* 303 F.2d 80 (9th Cir.1962), *rehearing denied* 305 F.2d 641 (9th Cir. 1962).

7. *See, e.g., Shapiro v. Gulf, Mobil & Ohio Railroad Co.,* 256 F.2d 193 (7th Cir. 1958).

8. *See, e.g., Federman v. Empire Fire & Marine Insurance Co.,* 597 F.2d 798 (2d Cir.1979).

Procedural rules may or may not establish timing requirements for cross-claims. Fed.R.Civ.P. 13 offers no guidance as to when cross-claims may be asserted. They clearly may be included in an otherwise timely pleading without leave of court. Thereafter, although there is no clear requirement in the rules, a party seeking to assert a cross-claim should obtain leave of court, which ordinarily will be liberally granted. If the proposed cross-claim is improperly asserted or fails to state a claim, the opposing party should lodge an immediate objection or make a motion to dismiss to avoid constructive waiver.

§ 3.8.4 Third-Party Claims

Third-party practice is a prolific source of motions. Although third-party claims may be asserted as of right in an initial pleading, or within a limited number of days thereafter, motions concerning third-party claims are frequently necessary. Often, the defendant is not aware of the possible derivative liability of another until after this specific period. In addition to questions of timeliness, third-party claims can also raise questions of court jurisdiction and the third-party defendant's susceptibility to service of process. To obtain service in federal court, the third-party defendant must be within the forum state or within 100 miles from the place of trial.[9]

A party defending a claim may bring into the action a non-party who may be liable to the defendant if the defendant is found liable on the main claim. This procedure is also known as impleader. The purpose of permitting impleader is to promote judicial efficiency by reducing the number of actions necessary to resolve a dispute. Impleader is also available to a plaintiff defending a counterclaim. Similarly, a third-party defendant may implead "fourth"-party defendants.[10]

The nature of the third-party claim differs somewhat from the complaint or counterclaim. These latter claims aver that the opposing party is at fault and owes something to the claimant. In contrast, the third-party claim does not say that the defendant is blameless and the third-party defendant is at fault. Rather, the third-party claim states that if the defendant is found liable, the third-party defendant should indemnify the original defendant because of the third-party defendant's legal wrongs. If the original defendant contends that it is not responsible but that fault of a non-party caused the plaintiff's harm, the defendant should attempt to persuade the plaintiff to name the non-party as a defendant or to have it involuntarily joined as a defendant in the action.

As a practical matter, the defendant will seldom care so much. If the sole original defendant is not found liable, that party suffers no harm. If the defendant is found liable, indemnity may be available from the third-party defendant. See, civil procedure rules aren't so dumb

9. Fed.R.Civ.P. 4(f).

10. *See, e.g., Pabellon v. Grace Line*, 191 F.2d 169 (2d Cir.1951), *cert. denied* 342 U.S. 893, 72 S.Ct. 201, 96 L.Ed. 669 (1951).

after all. If the case is tried, the jury will be asked to assess the liability of all parties before it and may not know whether the defendants are original, added, or third-party. The jury's apportionment of fault controls the amount and proportion of indemnification between defendants.

If a motion for leave to serve a third-party complaint is made and in order, it should ordinarily be granted if "timely." Although there is no statement of the timeliness requirement in the rule, courts may not grant a motion made so late in the proceedings that trial would be delayed, or undue prejudice to the parties would result. The court can also deny leave if the third party claim is obviously non-meritorious. Timeliness is an especially important factor in the eyes of many courts because the third-party defendant, not having been a party to the litigation, is likely to need a substantial period of time to prepare the case for trial. Some state and federal courts have adopted local rules that establish fixed time limits by which any motion to implead a third-party must be brought.

Because of the liberal rules permitting impleader, the rules also contain specific provisions for making an action manageable. Fed. R.Civ.P. 14(a) permits any party to move to strike a third-party claim or for its severance or separate trial. Each of these motions may be made regardless of whether the third-party claim was asserted as of right or later with leave of court. By granting leave to permit a third-party claim, the court does not limit its power to later strike it or sever it. As a practical matter, however, the court is more likely to sever the claim than strike it altogether having granted leave.

Even without the specific language of Rule 14(a), the federal court or a state court operating under the federal format would be authorized by Fed.R.Civ.P. 42(b) to order a separate trial and by Fed.R.Civ.P. 21 to order severance. The court has broad discretion in determining whether severance or separate trials are appropriate. Ultimately, the court must balance the efficiencies of single trial against the complexities that a single trial would engender. That balancing process must be done on a case-by-case basis. Prejudice to one or more of the parties is often a determinative factor. If severance would work no hardship on any party and would simplify the proceedings, it should be granted.[11]

§ 3.8.5 Tactical Summary

In formulating any of the offensive-defensive pleadings, the defendant mirrors plaintiff in the drafting of the pleading. The defendant should identify the target of the claim, state the facts giving rise to the claim, plead jurisdiction (unless pleading a compulsory counterclaim or cross-claim, in which case the court has ancillary jurisdiction over the matter), aver compliance with any conditions precedent or other requirements of statute or case law, state the applicable legal basis of the claim, plead injury and damages or right to indemnity, and plead requested

11. *See Sporia v. Pennsylvania Greyhound Lines,* 143 F.2d 105 (3d Cir.1944).

relief, or any other special averments. In pleading these, counsel should employ the same format of short, numbered paragraphs with precise, brief, and objective language as found in a well-drafted complaint.

Counsel must also give some thought to whether even to assert a claim. Skilled lawyers may recommend dispensing with even meritorious counter-, cross-, and third-party claims in the interest of brevity, simplicity, cost-saving, or any other reason. Realistically, this will occur only when the offensive-defensive claim is small and potentially confusing and, often, expensive to prosecute as well. As a general rule, all claims and parties related to a dispute should be brought before one court for resolution. That's normally simpler, cheaper, and more likely to result in justice. However, strategy may argue for keeping some parties out of the action so that they do not present a united front adverse to the client or introduce tangential issues distracting from what is the main event.

The assertion of a valid counterclaim may result in a favorable tactical reaction from an opponent. The "defendant" no longer is merely defending the case, but is now an attacker. This conversion from defense to offense may significantly affect the plaintiff's attitude toward resolution of the case, particularly regarding settlement. The defendant is not first seeking a stand-off but is also seeking affirmative relief. It is therefore advantageous for a defendant to assert any valid counterclaims in an answer.

§ 3.9 REPLIES

A party who is served with a counterclaim will have to answer it as if it were a complaint. An answer to a counterclaim is called a reply and Fed.R.Civ.P. 8 requires that it be denominated as such. Cross-claims and third-party claims usually must also be answered. However, affirmative defenses and factual averments need not and should not be answered with another pleading. The court may order on its own motion or permit a reply to affirmative defenses and other averments.[1] Counsel will seldom bother for leave to respond since the rules automatically deem any matters raised in an answer denied without any further pleading.[2]

The reply to a counterclaim normally looks like a streamlined answer. The first paragraph may include the averment paragraphs admitted, the second may list the averment paragraphs denied, and the third may list those averment paragraphs where respondent is without knowledge or information sufficient to form a belief as to the truth or falsity of the statements.

§ 3.9

1. *See* 5 Charles A. Wright & Arthur R. Miller, Federal Practice and Procedure § 1185 (2d ed. 1990).

2. *See* Fed.R.Civ.P. 12.

Plaintiff may then want to set forth additional facts and plead affirmative defenses to the counterclaim such as setoff, accord and satisfaction, estoppel, or fraud. If the counterclaim triggers a counter-counter claim, the plaintiff should plead the facts showing entitlement to relief and the relief requested, just as in a complaint. This rarely occurs when the plaintiff faces a compulsory counterclaim but may arise when facing a permissive counterclaim. At this juncture, the plaintiff should also raise any available Rule 12 motions or defenses attacking the counterclaim.

All this is only to alert the reader to what can be done, not to suggest that it be done in every case. As a general rule, replies to counterclaims should be short and sweet. An example of a reply is contained in the case files in Appendix B.

Although Fed.R.Civ.P. 8(d) and similar state rules provide that the failure to deny averments in a responsive pleading is an admission, this rule also states that averments in pleadings that do not require a response are automatically avoided. Counsel need get excited only about counterclaims denominated as such and third-party complaints. Answers to cross-claims and third-party claims, since they more often raise facts and legal issues outside the complaint, frequently require a response more closely resembling a defendant's answer in detail and length. The general format and rules of the answer, including the strategic considerations involving all motions, will normally apply, and examples appear in the case files in Appendix B.

§ 3.10 INTERVENTION AND INTERPLEADER

Claims of third parties may also be resolved through the use of two procedural devices: intervention and interpleader. Intervention permits someone who is not a party to an action to protect his or her interests by joining the litigation. Intervention may be a matter of right or may be permissive. Fed.R.Civ.P. 24 and similar state rules govern the procedures relating to intervention and establish when intervention is a matter of right and when it is permissive. Intervenors must proceed by way of motion in either case, although the court has little discretion to deny intervention as of right. Following intervention, the intervenor is a party to the action for all purposes.

Interpleader is a procedure whereby a person holding property subject to multiple conflicting claims may require all claimants to have their claims resolved in one action. Intervention relieves the party holding the property—frequently called the stakeholder—from having to risk multiple lawsuits or inconsistent results or judgments. A common example of such a stakeholder is an insurer faced with multiple claims from different beneficiaries. The stakeholder may either commence an interpleader action as a plaintiff, naming all claimed beneficiaries as defendants or, if one claimant sues the insurer, it can require all the other claimants to interplead by its answer. Fed.R.Civ.P. 23 and similar state court provisions govern interpleader actions. The federal rule once required the stakeholder to abandon any interest, claim, or defense in the property as a condition precedent to permitting interpleader. Now a party may invoke interpleader even if it contests the claims of all the claimants. Interpleader is also governed by federal statute. Since the statute allows nationwide service of process and liberal venue, it is widely used.[1]

§ 3.11 CLASS ACTIONS AND SPECIAL PLEADING SITUATIONS

Class action litigation requires special pleading and motions by the named plaintiffs and by the defendants. Motions concerning class actions and the process of class action certification and case management are more fully discussed in Section 12.4. Although class actions are not subject to special pleading rules with respect to specificity and content, class action complaints and responses are generally more involved and detailed. Usually the parties will pattern their pleadings after the specific class-action prerequisites contained in Rule 23.

If a class action complaint is a shareholders derivative action against or on behalf of a corporation, Fed.R.Civ.P. 23.1 requires the complaint to be verified, *i.e.,* subscribed and sworn to, by the plaintiff or by the attorney. Rule 23.1 imposes additional procedural requirements on derivative suit plaintiffs. Plaintiffs must allege that the action is not collusive and that demand for correction by the corporation has been made on the directors, and must explain the directors' failure to take action. Other than in derivative actions, pleadings seldom need be verified. Bankruptcy petitions, removal petitions, and bills of costs must be verified. There are other situations in which the pleadings must be verified, but they are not frequently encountered.[1]

Although not so denominated in the rules of procedure, certain civil actions have historically been disfavored by the courts. Greater specificity has been required in such complaints. Libel and slander, malicious prosecution, and abuse of process actions are common examples.[2] During the 1970s and 1980s, a number of courts, particularly in the Third Circuit, also imposed heightened pleading requirements for civil rights claims. This misreading of Rules 8 and 9 should presumably come to a halt in light of a 1993 Supreme Court decision rejecting this approach.[3]

§ 3.12 AMENDMENT OF PLEADINGS

§ 3.12.1 Introduction

On his beginning day, the young attorney was called to the office of one of the senior partners, who cautioned him that "there are virtually

§ 3.10

1. 28 U.S.C.A. § 1397.

§ 3.11

1. *See* 5 Charles A. Wright & Arthur R. Miller, Federal Practice and Procedure § 1335 (2d ed. 1990). Condemnation proceedings also have special pleading rules in federal court and many state courts. See Fed.R.Civ.P. 71A.

2. *Id.* at §§ 1245–46.

3. *Leatherman v. Tarrant County Narcotics Intelligence & Coord. Unit,* ___ U.S. ___, 113 S.Ct. 1160, 122 L.Ed.2d 517 (1993), *on remand* 993 F.2d 1177 (5th Cir.1993).

no mistakes made by a lawyer that can't be remedied, if you're honest enough to admit the mistake and take affirmative steps to remedy it." Whatever the merit of the remainder of the senior partner's advice, she was largely right about rectifying miscues. Undoubtedly, a lawyer's initial failing doesn't help matters, but unlike botched open heart surgery, the failings of the legal professional are at least theoretically remediable. This is especially true for pleading defects. Like the general pleading rules, the rules of amendment are concerned with substance and justice rather than form, and are liberally construed.[1] Pleadings can even be conformed to the evidence presented at trial.[2]

In federal court, amendment of a pleading is permitted as a matter of right if made prior to service of a responsive pleading such as an answer or motion for summary judgment.[3] State rules often establish an absolute time limit as well, *e.g.*, 20 days, regardless of the opponent's tardiness in serving a responsive pleading. Thereafter, amendment is permitted only by leave of court. Ordinarily, amendment is liberally granted where justice so requires, so long as permitting amendment does not irreparably prejudice another party or require a substantial, last-minute delay in the trial. Supplemental pleadings may also be appropriate in order to allege transactions, occurrences or events that have taken place since the date of the original pleading. Usually a party must bring a motion to serve a supplemental pleading.[4] The difference between a motion to amend the pleadings and a motion to supplement relates to the timing of the underlying events giving rise to the motion: if those events occurred before the action was commenced, then the complaint should be amended, if they occurred after the action was commenced, the complaint should be supplemented. The following sections discuss in detail the process of making a motion for leave to amend or supplement a pleading.

§ 3.12.2 The Standards for Permitting Amendment

Rule 15(a) governs amendment of federal pleadings. It permits amendment as of right if the amended pleading is filed and served before the opponent has served a responsive pleading. Responsive pleadings are those permitted by Rule 7(a): the answer and reply if permitted. Rule 12(b) motions to dismiss and summary judgment motions are not responsive pleadings. A party may amend of right after the opposition has made a Rule 12(b) or Rule 56 motion.[5] If the pleading to be amended does not require a response, the amended pleading must be filed within 20 days of the date that the original pleading was served. The amended pleading not requiring a response can be served within a

§ 3.12

1. *Foman v. Davis,* 371 U.S. 178, 83 S.Ct. 227, 9 L.Ed.2d 222 (1962), *on remand* 316 F.2d 254 (1st Cir.1963); *Conley v. Gibson,* 355 U.S. 41, 78 S.Ct. 99, 2 L.Ed.2d 80 (1957).

2. Fed.R.Civ.P. 15(b).

3. Fed.R.Civ.P. 15(a).

4. *See* Fed.R.Civ.P. 12(d).

5. *La Batt v. Twomey,* 513 F.2d 641 (7th Cir.1975).

reasonable time thereafter, but must be filed with the court within the 20–day period to obtain amendment of right.

If the party seeking to amend misses these deadlines, it must either obtain written consent of the adverse party to amend the pleading or file a motion for leave of court to amend. Rule 15(a) states that "leave shall be freely given when justice so requires." This language has been liberally interpreted by the Supreme Court.[6] Ordinarily, leave will always be granted if amendment is sought in the early or middle stages of the litigation. In general, courts have expressed a preference for granting leave to amend and, if necessary, providing additional time and discovery to avoid prejudice to the respondent rather than denying the amendment. In complicated cases, the court weighs factors such as the movant's delay, good or bad faith, motive, and harm if the amendment is denied against the harm to respondent if the amendment is permitted weighed on a scale preset according to the remoteness and necessity of the subject matter of the amendment.[7] Of course, the parties can always stipulate to amendment, a wise course in most situations in light of the liberality of Rule 15(a).

Any number of pleadings can be amended for any number of reasons. A frequent use is to correct deficiencies such as failure properly to allege standing, jurisdiction, the proper and necessary elements of a removal petition, to correct misnaming of parties, or to rectify a defect that would result in Rule 12(b)(6) dismissal. Amendment can obviously be used to add claims and defenses, and can also be used to change the legal theory of a claim or defense, the amount of damages, or the remedy sought.

Amendment is also frequently used to add, drop, or substitute parties,[8] or the capacity in which persons participate in the action.[9] Some courts have held that amendments seeking to add or drop parties are subject to Rule 21, which governs parties to an action, rather than the general amendment rule, Rule 15.[10] Other courts have found Rule 15 applicable to changes of parties regardless of, or in addition to, Rule 21.[11] The distinction is largely one of semantics. The primary distinction is that Rule 21 does not provide for addition or deletion of parties by right or by written consent of the adverse party as does Rule 15(a).

One cardinal rule is that amendments which would destroy federal jurisdiction (*e.g.* adding a non-diverse party or dropping the only federal

6. *Foman v. Davis,* 371 U.S. 178, 83 S.Ct. 227, 9 L.Ed.2d 222 (1962), *on remand* 316 F.2d 254 (1st Cir.1963).

7. *Foman v. Davis,* 371 U.S. 178, 83 S.Ct. 227, 9 L.Ed.2d 222 (1962), *on remand* 316 F.2d 254 (1st Cir.1963); *Zenith Radio Corp. v. Hazeltine Research, Inc.,* 401 U.S. 321, 91 S.Ct. 795, 28 L.Ed.2d 77 (1971), *rehearing denied* 401 U.S. 1015, 91 S.Ct. 1247, 28 L.Ed.2d 552 (1971).

8. *See, e.g., Ames v. Vavreck,* 356 F.Supp. 931 (D.Minn.1973) (substitution). Certain substitutions are governed by Rule 25.

9. *See, e.g., Armani v. Crucible Steel Co. of America,* 7 F.R.D. 344 (N.D.N.Y.1947).

10. *Jones v. Electrodyne Co.,* 224 F.Supp. 599 (W.D.Mo.1963).

11. *See, e.g., Ahmad v. Independent Order of Foresters,* 81 F.R.D. 722 (E.D.Pa. 1979).

question claim) are not permitted and will ordinarily be denied.[12] Although denial of leave is unusual, it is not rare. Typical reasons for denying leave to amend are:

1. Attempted addition of new claims late in the case; [13]

2. Prejudicing respondent by attempting to create much more complex, expensive litigation; [14]

3. Creating confusion through newly interjected issues; [15]

4. Continuance to avoid prejudice to respondent would cause undue delay; [16] and

5. Amendment would be futile because the amended pleading is subject to summary disposition.[17]

Rule 15(b) permits the pleadings to be amended to conform to the evidence presented at trial where issues not raised in the pleadings are tried by the express or implied consent of the parties. This can be done even after judgment has been entered. If one party begins to introduce matter not raised in the pleadings, the other party should promptly object. At this juncture, the party introducing the new matter may orally move for amendment of the pleadings. This motion for leave to amend is subject to the same standards and considerations outlined above but is less likely to be liberally granted.

Rule 15(c) governs whether amendments to a pleading relate back to the date of the original pleading sought to be amended. It simply states that a claim or defense made in an amended pleading relates back to the date of the original pleading if the amended claim or defense "arose out of the conduct, transaction, or occurrence set forth or attempted to be set forth in the original pleading." If the amendment changes the party against whom a claim or defense was originally made, it is subject to more stringent standards for relation back. Where the amendment changes parties, the amendment must relate to the facts of the original pleading and the new party must have both (1) had notice of the original action with the applicable statute of limitations, and (2) known or should have known that the action would have been against it but for the mistake of identity. The notice of the action need not be formal and need not be the result of any pleadings or papers in the original action received by the new party.[18] Some courts had allowed a reasonable time

12. *But see Webb v. Clarion Resources, Inc.,* 95 F.R.D. 491 (N.D.Tex.1982) (permitting addition of parties, requiring remand to state court, but assessing attorney's fees against movant).

13. *See, e.g., Zinser v. Continental Grain Co.,* 660 F.2d 754 (10th Cir.1981), *cert. denied* 455 U.S. 941, 102 S.Ct. 1434, 71 L.Ed.2d 652 (1982).

14. *See, e.g., Wealden Corp. v. Schwey,* 482 F.2d 550 (5th Cir.1973).

15. *See, e.g., Izaak Walton League of America v. St. Clair,* 497 F.2d 849 (8th Cir.1974), *cert. denied* 419 U.S. 1009, 95 S.Ct. 329, 42 L.Ed.2d 284 (1974).

16. *See, e.g., Triangle Industries, Inc. v. Kennecott Copper Corp.,* 402 F.Supp. 210 (S.D.N.Y.1975).

17. *McGovern v. American Airlines, Inc.,* 511 F.2d 653 (5th Cir.1975).

18. *Craig v. United States,* 413 F.2d 854 (9th Cir.1969), *cert. denied* 396 U.S. 987, 90 S.Ct. 483, 24 L.Ed.2d 451 (1969); *Simmons v. Fenton,* 480 F.2d 133 (7th Cir.1973).

for service after a complaint was filed within the limitations period but received after the statute had run.[19] The Supreme Court disapproved these cases and held that an amended pleading correcting a misnamed defendant did not relate back if served after expiration of the statute of limitations even though served with the 120–day time limit of Rule 4.[20] Amendments to Rule 15(c) in 1991 overturned the Court's decision and permit relation back where the proper defendant has received notice within the time provided for service of process.

§ 3.12.3 Procedure

Amendment of right can be obtained merely by filing and serving the amended pleading within the time limits of Rule 15(a). Where leave of court is required, so too is a motion for leave unless the adverse party consents in writing. Like other motions, the motion for leave should be made in writing, should state its grounds, the applicable rules or statutes, and should be accompanied by a notice of motion and a memorandum of law. Affidavits may be useful to prove facts creating a stronger argument for permitting amendment. Although notice of a motion for leave to amend must be given to all other parties to the action, it is not necessary to give notice to non-parties who might be interested in the motion. If leave is granted and they are served, non-parties may present any arguments they may have in their responsive pleadings or in a motion under Rule 12. Most courts hold a hearing or oral argument on the motion for leave to amend, although this is not required. Many courts require the hearing to be scheduled before the motion is made and noticed in the motion. The actual motion for leave can be made at any time prior to judgment, but should be made as soon as the need for amendment is realized, preferably in the first half of the litigation time line.

In attempting to obtain leave to amend, the movant will wish to make the amendment seem reasonable, essentially a fine tuning of the original pleading and one that works no hardship to the opposing parties. If the amendment is demonstrably something new, the movant will want to show why it is necessary in the instant case and why it was not pleaded originally, even if the reason was oversight by counsel. The party opposing the motion for leave will want to characterize the amendment as new matter that prejudices it, belongs in another case, and should have been raised sooner by the movant.

If leave to amend is granted, the movant must file and serve the new, improved pleading within a reasonable time, preferably as soon as possible. The other party has 10 days to respond to the pleading, unless

19. *Kirk v. Cronvich,* 629 F.2d 404 (5th Cir.1980).

20. *See Schiavone v. Fortune,* 477 U.S. 21, 106 S.Ct. 2379, 91 L.Ed.2d 18 (1986) (and because this was a defamation action, the limitations period was a short 1 year; in addition, the defective original pleading was served upon an agent for the proper defendant, who obviously knew the exact identity of plaintiff's target defendant).

otherwise specified by the court or stipulated to by the parties. An amended pleading filed and served supercedes the original pleading, unless the amended pleading specifically refers to and incorporates the earlier pleading.[21] Defects in the second pleading are not cured by a properly pled analogous portion of the first document.[22] However, incorporation by reference is cumbersome, confusing, and risks greater error and traps for the unwary. The better practice is to seek leave to file an amended pleading which is complete in itself. It is important to remember that, although the former pleading ceases to exist as a pleading in the case, statements in that document continue to be admissible as judicial admissions.[23]

An order granting or denying a motion for leave to amend is not a final, appealable order unless it meets the standards for interlocutory appeal set forth in the collateral order doctrine, an unlikely occurrence. A denial of a motion to amend to seek injunctive relief is not an order denying an injunction (and hence appealable under 28 U.S.C.A. section 1292(a)). On appeal, the trial court's decision denying the motion will be viewed according to the abuse of discretion standard.

§ 3.13 SUPPLEMENTATION OF PLEADINGS

§ 3.13.1 Introduction

Rule 15(d) permits supplementation of pleadings. Because amendment and supplementation are closely linked conceptually and discussed in the same federal rule, they are often intermingled or confused, usually to no great detriment, because the liberal standards of Rule 15 and federal policy of resolving disputes between the parties in one action apply to both.

Rule 15(d) permits a party, upon reasonable notice and such terms as are just and proper, to serve a supplemental pleading "setting forth transactions or occurrences or events which have happened since the date of the pleading sought to be supplemented." A supplemental pleading addresses things that occurred after the litigation commenced. An amended pleading addresses things that existed but were not pleaded at the time of the original pleading. Amendment of right is permitted under some circumstances. Supplemental pleading always requires leave of court, which always requires a motion. Examples of a supplemental pleading are new claims of damage incurred since the action commenced,[1] changing the nature of the relief sought (*e.g.,* from recis-

21. *International Controls Corp. v. Vesco,* 556 F.2d 665, 669 (2d Cir.1977), *cert. denied* 434 U.S. 1014, 98 S.Ct. 730, 54 L.Ed.2d 758 (1978).

22. *Bullen v. De Bretteville,* 239 F.2d 824, 833 (9th Cir.1956), *cert. denied* 353 U.S. 947, 77 S.Ct. 825, 1 L.Ed.2d 856 (1957).

23. *Stacy v. Aetna Casualty & Surety Co.,* 484 F.2d 289 (5th Cir.1973).

§ **3.13**

1. *Smith, Kline & French Laboratories v. A.H. Robins Co.,* 61 F.R.D. 24 (E.D.Pa. 1973).

sion to damages),[2] pleading additional defenses,[3] otherwise adding to an answer, and pleading events occurring subsequent to the action, where those events are of significant enough moment to require pleading rather than mere proof at trial.[4] New parties necessitated by new events can also be added by supplemental pleading.[5] Now you know why there is confusion over defining amended and supplemental pleadings. A sane person might easily find the change in relief requested or the amount of damages claimed to be amended original pleadings rather than supplemental pleadings.

Perhaps the purest example of a supplemental pleading is a new claim for relief in the complaint or a new counterclaim made due to an event occurring after commencement of the litigation. Rule 13(e) specifically provides that a claim which matures or was acquired after service of the original answer or response may "be presented as a counterclaim by supplemental pleading." If a counterclaim is asserted under Rule 13(e), it is not subject to the rule regarding compulsory counterclaims since this applies only to claims arising out of the same transaction or occurrence that existed prior to the litigation and was the subject of the case at the time suit commenced.[6] If the court applies the relation back doctrine to the supplemental pleading, it will be done according to the same considerations involving relation back of amended pleadings. The same is true of supplemental pleadings and changing parties. Some courts have read Rule 15(d) as permitting only supplemental pleadings between the existing parties to the case while others have permitted supplemental pleadings that add or change parties.

As with amended pleadings, the court has fairly broad discretion in deciding the motion, perhaps more with supplemental pleadings since these can usually be the subject of subsequent litigation with no injustice to the movant. Nevertheless, the federal pleading policy favors resolution of disputes in one action and thus encourages the court to permit the new claim.

§ 3.13.2 Procedure

The procedure for seeking leave to make a supplemental pleading mirrors that for the motion for leave to amend. As noted above, there is no supplementation of right, only by leave of court. The motion for leave to supplement should be in writing, should state grounds and applicable rules, and be accompanied by notice of motion, a memo of law, and probably affidavits or other exhibits establishing that something has

2. *City of Texarkana v. Arkansas, Louisiana Gas Co.,* 306 U.S. 188, 59 S.Ct. 448, 83 L.Ed. 598 (1939).

3. *Slavenburg Corp. v. Boston Insurance Co.,* 30 F.R.D. 123 (S.D.N.Y.1962).

4. *Kimmel v. Yankee Lines, Inc.,* 125 F.Supp. 702 (W.D.Pa.1954), *affirmed* 224 F.2d 644 (3d Cir.1955) (supplemental answer pleaded res judicata based on state court judgment entered after federal action commenced).

5. *Griffin v. County School Board,* 377 U.S. 218, 84 S.Ct. 1226, 12 L.Ed.2d 256 (1964), *motion granted* 377 U.S. 950, 84 S.Ct. 1627, 12 L.Ed.2d 496 (1964).

6. *Stahl v. Ohio River Co.,* 424 F.2d 52 (3d Cir.1970).

happened since the last pleading to require supplementation. The general rules regarding hearings are equivalent to those concerning motions to amend.

If the supplemental pleading is permitted, the other side must respond according to the terms of the order granting leave to supplement. Since the supplemental pleading involves something newer than the amended pleading, courts will generally allow 20 days to respond. As noted above, supplemental pleadings can involve changes that do not require a response. Rule 15(d) states that the time to respond shall be stated in the court's order granting leave if the court "deems it advisable that the adverse party plead to the supplemental pleading." On review, the appellate court will apply the abuse of discretion standard.[7]

Although the rule says nothing specific about timing, the motion for leave should be made as soon as practicable after the new event and should also be made well prior to any possible statute of limitations and relation back problems. The motion can be made at any time, even after judgment.[8]

PRACTICE PROBLEMS

MAJOR ISSUES IN POTENTIAL LITIGATION BETWEEN HOT DOG ENTERPRISES AND TRI–CHEM

The major issues include:

- Whether the vinylidene chloride component of Bond–Mor undergoes dehydrochlorination (chemical decomposition) when mixed with cement systems.
- Whether dehydrochlorination continuously releases chloride ions and causes corrosion of common steel placed in cement systems as reinforcement or as ties or connectors in cement systems.
- Whether the corrosion of reinforcing steel creates significant expansion forces causing cracking and structural failure of cement systems.
- Whether the use of Bond–Mor as an additive to brick and mortar results in numerous building failures.
- Whether Tri–Chem issued a "warning" to Bond–Mor building owners leading them to believe that if Bond–Mor had been used with protected metal it would not cause or accelerate corrosion.
- Whether Tri–Chem's internal research disclosed that free inorganic chloride ions were released from Bond–Mor's Latex base.

7. *McHenry v. Ford Motor Co.*, 269 F.2d 18 (6th Cir.1959).

8. *Otis Elevator Co. v. 570 Building Corp.*, 35 F.Supp. 348 (E.D.N.Y.1940).

- Whether Tri–Chem knew that Bond–Mor dehydrochlorinated in the presence of the cement used in mortar, releasing chloride ion, which causes corrosion of the steel in contact with Bond–Mor mortar.

POTENTIAL DEFENSES BY TRI–CHEM

The major defenses include:

- Whether damages to Bond–Mor distressed buildings result from inadequate compensation for thermal stress or differential movement.
- Whether the combination of water, air, and iron causes rust, whether or not Bond–Mor is present in a mortar or concrete.
- Whether cracking is a result of freeze-thaw activity.
- Whether cracking is caused by the use of extremely porous mortar which allows excessive moisture to seep into the masonry.
- Whether fissures in masonry are caused by the creep of the structure and differential settlement.
- Whether mortar in filled horizontal expansion joints and shims not removed during construction cause brick panels to stack one on top of the other.
- Whether causes other than or in addition to dehydrochlorinated Bond–Mor damage buildings *e.g.*, the use of rigid restraint panels, design errors, thermal movements, or a lack of functioning vertical and horizontal expansion joints.

POTENTIAL CAUSES OF ACTION

Fraud: Tri–Chem had knowledge or reason to know the corrosion effects of Bond–Mor or Latex used in contact with metal. Tri–Chem fraudulently concealed this knowledge from the architectural, construction, and engineering trades and from customers as part of its scheme to defraud plaintiff and others, and to delay or avoid damage altogether for Bond–Mor induced corrosion and other product defects. Tri–Chem stated to architects, contractors, engineers, and customers:

> Tri–Chem had extensively tested Bond–Mor for at least 10 years prior to 1990.
>
> Tri–Chem had successfully used Bond–Mor in masonry construction in Westland, California, the location of Tri–Chem's headquarters.
>
> Extensive testing and field applications verified that Bond–Mor:

Was suitable for use in brick construction containing embedded steel.

Was less permeable to oxygen and moisture penetration that conventional mortar.

Was suitable for use in a wet environment.

Created a bond between brick and mortar which resulted in a wall at least four times the strength of conventional masonry walls.

Did not require normal protective measures to prevent corrosion.

Strict Liability in Tort: When Tri–Chem represented and sold Bond–Mor for use in the construction of plaintiff's buildings, Bond–Mor was in defective condition when it left Tri–Chem's possession and control because Tri–Chem knew or should have known that Bond–Mor caused the corrosion of metal embedments usually found in brick and masonry construction using Bond–Mor, and that such corrosion caused, among other things, the brick and masonry to crack and fall from the buildings. In addition, Tri–Chem knew or should have known that after a period of time mortar with Bond–Mor would lose the ability to bond bricks so that the brick and masonry of the plaintiff's buildings will crack and fall from the building. Bond–Mor was, therefore, defective and Tri–Chem failed to warn of the defective characteristics described above. Bond–Mor was unreasonably dangerous to the users or consumers of such product.

Breach of Warranty and Negligent Misrepresentation: Tri–Chem represented and warranted, expressly and impliedly, that Bond–Mor was an advanced and proper chemical additive for mortar in masonry construction, was of merchantable quality, and that it was fit for use in masonry construction such as that of the plaintiff's buildings. Tri–Chem knew or reasonably should have known that such representations and warranties were false and misleading or made the same without knowledge as to the truth or falsity, and intended and knew or should have known that plaintiff would rely upon these representations and warranties:

Intentional Misrepresentation: Tri–Chem made numerous false representations. These false representations were material, false, and misleading. Tri–Chem fully intended to defraud plaintiff. Plaintiff believed and relied upon these representations. These representations caused damage.

Negligence. Tri–Chem had a duty to use ordinary and reasonable care to develop, manufacture and sell Bond–Mor. Tri–Chem failed to use ordinary reasonable care and was negligent in the following particulars:

Failing to develop Bond–Mor properly.

Failing to test Bond–Mor properly.

Failing to manufacture Bond–Mor free from defect.

Failing to warn adequately of Bond–Mor's defects and dangers.

Breach of Continuing Duty to Warn: Tri–Chem had knowledge of the defect and damages caused by Bond–Mor and such knowledge created a continuing duty to inform ultimate consumers such as the plaintiff.

Punitive damages: In most jurisdictions a showing of fraud or intentional misrepresentation will permit a claimant to recover punitive damages where it can show, by clear and convincing evidence, that defendant acted with willful indifference to the rights of others.

Counsel fees: Deceptive trade practices/consumer protection acts may permit the recovery of attorney's fees as well.

STATUTE OF LIMITATIONS

Tri–Chem's fraudulent concealment of the defective nature of Bond–Mor tolled any applicable statutes of limitations. Plaintiff could not and did not discover the defective condition of Bond–Mor until 1988.

Chapter Questions

Preparing a Complaint

1. Outline a complaint for your client assigned by your instructor. Consider:

(a) What functions (§ 3.3.1) and goals (§ 3.6.1) the complaint will serve.

(b) What the forum will be.

(c) Which parties will be included in the complaint.

(d) What issues will be included in the complaint.

(e) How the complaint will be structured.

(f) What allegations will be generally alleged and what disputed facts will be stated with particularity.

(g) What relief will be sought.

(h) What will be excluded from the complaint.

Complaint Drafting Exercises

Draft each complaint and include a caption, body, relief clause, and signature. Draft appropriate allegations generally and draft some disputed fact allegations with particularity.

2. You represent Hot Dog Enterprises in a lawsuit against Tri–Chem (Chapter 1).

3. You represent Pat LaBelle in *LaBelle v. Mitchell Arts Council* (Case G).

4. You represent Martha Giacone in *Giacone v. City of Mitchell* (Case D).

5. You represent Juanita Vasquez in *Vasquez v. Hot Dog Enterprises* (Case F).

6. You represent Mack and Meg Luger in *Luger v. Shade* (Case H).

7. You represent Hot Dog Enterprises in a lawsuit against Tri–Chem (Chapter 1).

8. You represent Pat LaBelle in *LaBelle v. Mitchell Arts Council* (Case G).

9. You represent Martha Giacone in *Giacone v. City of Mitchell* (Case D).

10. You represent the Mitchell Computer Club in *Mitchell Computer Club v. Rainbow Computer* (Case E).

11. You represent Juanita Vasquez in *Vasquez v. Hot Dog Enterprises* (Case F).

Redrafting Complaint Exercises

12. Assume in *Northern Motor Homes v. Danforth* (Case I) an associate attorney for the law firm representing Northern Motor Homes drafted the following proposed complaint. Redraft it.

DISTRICT COURT

County of West

State of Summit
Northern Motor Homes,
a Summit Corporation,

vs.

John Danforth &
Joan Danforth

COMPLAINT

Plaintiff for its Complaint and cause of action against the Defendants, John and Joan Danforth, assert the following claims and allegations:

I.

Northern Motor Homes is a Summit corporation organized under the laws of Summit and doing business in the State of Summit at all times material to this litigation.

II.

Based upon information and belief, John and Joan Danforth are residents of the City of Mitchell, residing at 1479 Laurel.

III.

On or about March 25, 19XX, John Danforth and Joan Danforth (hereinafter the Danforths) signed, agreed to, and executed a contract with Plaintiff Northern Motor Homes (hereinafter Northern).

IV.

This contract called for the Danforths to pay a cash price of $8,000 and installments of $299.12 a month for 60 (sixty) months commencing the month after the contract date on June 25, 19XX and continuing until the last payment was paid.

V.

The Danforths breached this contract by failing to abide by its terms.

VI.

Clause 4 of the Contract stated: "If Buyer defaults in any payment . . . Seller shall have the right, at its election, to declare the unpaid portion of the Total of Payments of this contract to be immediately payable and due."

VII.

As a result of the Danforth's default, the Danforths owe Northern (the Seller) the balance of the payments totalling $9,510.33.

VIII.

Northern has fulfilled all its obligations under the contract.

IX.

Defendants Danforths voluntarily and knowingly entered into the retail installment contract with the Plaintiffs.

WHEREFORE, Plaintiff Northern Motor Homes prays that this court will enter a judgment in its behalf and against the Defendants for $9,510.33, plus costs and disbursements, plus reasonable attorney's fees authorized under clause 5 of the contract, plus interest, plus any other relief this Court deems proper and appropriate.

____

____

Doten and Krause
1000 First State Bank
Mitchell, Summit
789–1234

Preparing a Responsive Pleading

13. Outline a responsive pleading for your client assigned by your instructor. Consider:

(a) What functions and goals it will serve.

(b) What parties will be included.

(c) What issues will be included.

(d) How the pleading will be structured.

(e) What relief will be sought.

(f) What will be excluded from the pleading.

14. You represent Tri–Chem in *Hot Dog Enterprises v. Tri–Chem* (Chapter 1).

15. You represent the City of Mitchell in *Giacone v. City of Mitchell* (Case D).

16. You represent Mitchell Arts Council in *LaBelle v. Mitchell Arts Council* (Case G).

17. You represent the Rainbow Computer Company in *Mitchell Computer Club v. Rainbow Computer* (Case E).

18. You represent HDE in *Vasquez v. Hot Dog Enterprises* (Case F).

Answer Drafting Exercise

Draft each pleading and include a caption, body, relief clause, and signature. Draft an answer to the complaint you or a classmate drafted or that appears in the case. Include all appropriate affirmative defenses, counterclaims, cross claims, and third-party claims.

19. You represent Tri–Chem in *Hot Dog Enterprises v. Tri–Chem* (Chapter 1).

20. Assume the complaint that appears in Problem 12 has been served. You represent the Danforths in *Northern Motor Home v. Danforth* (Case J). Draft an answer.

21. You represent the City of Mitchell in *Giacone v. City of Mitchell* (Case D).

22. You represent the Mitchell Arts Council in *LaBelle v. Mitchell Arts Council* (Case G).

23. You represent Hot Dog Enterprises in *Vasquez v. Hot Dog Enterprises* (Case F).

24. You represent the Rainbow Computer Company in *Mitchell Computer Club v. Rainbow Computer* (Case E).

25. Assume the Lugers sue Shade, Develco, and Gotbucks. You represent Sam Shade in *Luger v. Shade* (Case H).

26. Assume the Lugers sue Shade, Develco, and Gotbucks. You represent Develco in *Luger v. Shade* (Case H).

27. Assume the Lugers sue Shade, Develco, and Gotbucks. You represent Gotbucks in *Luger v. Shade* (Case H).

Pleading Problems

28. You represent Mike LaBelle in *Miyamoto v. Snow Cat* (Case C). After you conduct your preliminary investigation before commencing a lawsuit you interview Mike again. He confirms the information that you learned that Mariko told others and him that she loved to ride the snowmobile as fast as it could go and that he and Mariko did not have a happy marriage and that he planned to leave after the December holidays and file for a divorce. Does this information affect your judgment about filing a complaint on behalf of Lee Miyamoto against Snow Cat? Why or why not? What factors influence your judgment?

29. You have been retained by the Mitchell Computer Club in *Mitchell Computer Club v. Rainbow Computer* (Case E). After you interview each of the club members you determine that several of them were not defrauded by Rainbow and that several others do not want to sue Rainbow. How does this information affect your judgment about what complaint to file and serve? What would you do?

30. You represent Mitchell Arts Council in *LaBelle v. Mitchell Arts Council* (Case G). Fran Barnoff advises you that there was a contract of employment for 30 weeks with Pat LaBelle and that the Board of Trustees ordered Fran to intentionally breach that contract. How does this information affect your judgment about how you should respond to the Complaint of Pat LaBelle? What would you do?

*

CHAPTER 4

MOTIONS ATTACKING THE PLEADINGS AND JURISDICTION

Yossarian was moved very deeply by the absolute simplicity of Catch–22 and let out a respectful whistle.

"That's some catch, that Catch–22. It's the best there is," he observed.

Joseph Heller

Catch–22

§ 4.1 MOTIONS ATTACKING THE PLEADINGS

§ 4.1.1 Generally

The considerations applicable to drafting pleadings are discussed in Chapter Three. This section examines the tools available to attack pleadings prepared by adversaries.

Notice pleading and the modern policy of liberal construction of pleadings have reduced the value of attacking pleadings. Attack on the form of a pleading often only buys time, wins a race to the courthouse, or embarrasses opposing counsel, but does not alter the outcome on the merits. Amendment of the pleadings in the interests of justice is also now liberally allowed. Unless a proposed amendment is made willfully late and without any reasonable basis, the court will probably grant it.

§ 4.1.2 Attacks on Service of Process

A successful motion to dismiss for insufficiency of process (Rule 12(b)(4)) or insufficiency of service of process (Rule 12(b)(5)) will not prevent the action from going forward in either a second form or in the same action after the service defect has been cured. Dismissal on these bases is almost always without prejudice and is not a judgment on the merits.

A meritorious motion attacking process or service is, however, a legitimate delaying tactic. But to use it so, counsel should have a meritorious reason for seeking delay, such as to commence a new action as plaintiff in the same or another forum or gather critical information during the pendency for the motion attacking service. Such motions can also be of some value in highlighting the opposition's failure to strictly follow the rules. But, this goal is a two-edged sword, since the movant may easily be perceived as a hypertechnical nerd.

The parties may be racing to the courthouse and the opponent may win but with defective service or process. A successful motion attacking this can result in dismissal which, though without prejudice, destroys the first in time priority of the opponent's action. Thus, the motion can affect forum, case posture, and other practical issues. In some cases, a successful dismissal because of defective service/process can result in a reinstituted action commenced after the statute of limitations has run. Usually, however, the respondent can easily avoid this by asking the court merely to quash the service and obtaining leave of court to perfect defective service without dismissal of the action.[1]

The two types of attacks on service of process should be distinguished. First, pursuant to Rule 12(b)(4), the defendant may make a motion to dismiss the complaint for insufficiency of process. This motion attacks the adequacy of the content of the summons,[2] the requirements of which are set forth in Fed.R.Civ.P. 4(b) and in most state rules or statutes. For example, the motion may attack the failure of the summons to state that an answer is required within 20 days and that default will be entered if no answer is served. Second, the defendant may move to dismiss pursuant to Rule 12(b)(5) for insufficiency of service of process. This motion attacks not the contents of the summons, but the manner of delivery.[3] If for example, the plaintiff intended to commence the action by personal service of the complaint, but the process server opted for "sewer service" and made an affidavit of personal delivery, the motion would properly be made pursuant to Rule 12(b)(5). The Rule 12(b)(5) motion is much more common.

§ 4.1.3 The Applicable Law

Federal Rule 4 governs service of process in federal court actions. The rule sets forth the procedure for obtaining a summons from the clerk of court upon filing the action, the form of the summons, and the persons who can serve the summons. Rule 4(d) describes the proper means of effecting personal service upon individuals, infants and incom-

§ 4.1

1. *Picking v. Pennsylvania Railroad Co.,* 151 F.2d 240 (3d Cir.1945), *rehearing denied* 152 F.2d 753 (1945).

2. *Merz v. Hemmerle,* 90 F.R.D. 566, 567 n. 1 (E.D.N.Y.1981).

3. *Yox v. Durgan,* 298 F.Supp. 1365 (E.D.Tenn.1969).

petents, corporations, and governments and government officials. Rule 4(d)(7) further provides that service may be made on individuals, infants and incompetents, and corporations, in any manner set forth by federal statute or the law of the forum state. This enables federal court plaintiffs to utilize the long-arm statutes of the forum state. The Advisory Committee on the Federal Civil Rules has suggested a number of changes in Rule 4; including a provision to encourage parties to waive service and a provision authorizing nationwide service in some cases as well as nationwide personal jurisdiction for federal claims against certain defendants.

§ 4.1.4 Procedure

As previously noted, the proper means of attacking process or service is through either Rule 12(b)(4) or (5). If this attack is not raised in the party's first motion in lieu of an answer or in the answer itself as an affirmative defense, the right to attack on these bases is deemed waived.[4] If the defendant first raises the issue in its answer, it should follow with a specific Rule 12 motion as shortly thereafter as feasible. Although raising the process or service deficiency in the answer technically preserves it, no court will dismiss a case on either basis after proceedings are well underway. Once the motion is made, plaintiff bears the burden of proving proper service of process by a preponderance of the evidence.[5] An affidavit of service is prima facie evidence of service, but the parties may contest this affidavit by separate affidavit or other evidence.[6] Courts have shown an increasing tendency in recent years to place substance over form concerning service and will accept service not expressly authorized by the applicable rules if the defendant actually received the summons and complaint.[7]

Courts usually hold hearings on motions attacking service. The court may in its discretion permit some limited discovery concerning questions of receipt and notice. Dismissal without prejudice is usually the most the movant can expect. Dismissal under 12(b)(4) or (5) is never an adjudication on the merits, but would constitute a final appealable order. Denial of such a motion does not create a final order.

§ 4.2 ATTACK ON THE FORM AND SPECIFICITY OF THE PLEADINGS

All that a claimant need present is a short and plain statement of the facts establishing jurisdiction, the facts showing entitlement to relief, and a demand for judgment.[1] Of these, only the statement of facts

4. Fed.R.Civ.P. 12(g) & 12(h)(1); *Phillips v. Baker,* 121 F.2d 752 (9th Cir.1941), *cert. denied* 314 U.S. 688, 62 S.Ct. 301, 86 L.Ed. 551 (1941).

5. *Klishewich v. Mediterranean Agencies, Inc.,* 42 F.R.D. 624 (E.D.N.Y.1966).

6. *Hicklin v. Edwards,* 226 F.2d 410 (8th Cir.1955).

7. *See, e.g., Stonewall Insurance Co. v. Horak,* 325 N.W.2d 134 (Minn.1982).

§ 4.2

1. Fed.R.Civ.P. 8(a).

showing entitlement to relief is crucial.[2] Thus, counsel will ordinarily have little use for the motions in this chapter.

Nevertheless, when sufficiently deficient pleadings appear, the following motions are the usual modes of attack:

1. Motion for a more definite statement (Rule 12(e)), where the pleading is so vague or ambiguous that defendant cannot reasonably be expected to draft a response;

2. Motion to strike (Rule 12(f)), where the pleading contains prejudicial or scandalous matter, is redundant, or asserts a clearly legally insufficient defense;

3. Motion to dismiss a complaint or strike a claim under Rules 12(b)(6) & 12(f) for failure to properly plead special matters (where the pleading fails to comport with Rules 8 and 9); and

4. Motion for numbering of paragraphs and separation of claims under Rules 10(b) & 12(e).

Motions for a more definite statement are not available to attack pleadings that do not require a response.[3] Occasionally, a complaint is both confusing and unnumbered. Rule 10(b) requires separate claims and defenses be in separately numbered paragraphs. A separate motion under Rule 10(b) or to strike under Rule 12(e) can seek conformity with the rule, although the rule itself does not make any direct reference to a motion to enforce it.[4]

Only where the pleading contains matter that could defame or otherwise injure if widely disseminated is a motion to strike wise. The motion for more definite statement is sometimes used to force a more specific pleading more vulnerable to a motion to dismiss for failure to state a claim. However, this is generally considered an unethical or improper use of the motion.[5]

Despite our general disenchantment with formal attacks, they are occasionally necessary or useful. Motions for a more definite statement may be useful where the complaint fails to identify a statute or ordinance allegedly violated, consists of mere legal conclusions, or fails properly to match claims with parties in multi-party and claim cases. Motions to strike may be granted not only for the presence of scandalous matter, but to remove unnecessary evidentiary detail that prejudices the defending party. Large, potentially prejudicial, specific allegations of damages (the oft-reported billion-dollar lawsuit) might also be stricken.

The procedure for bringing a motion to strike, for a more definite statement, or to challenge a legal defense mirrors that of other pretrial

2. *Conley v. Gibson,* 355 U.S. 41, 78 S.Ct. 99, 2 L.Ed.2d 80 (1957).

3. *Citizens Trust Co. v. New England Dredge & Dock Co.,* 260 F.Supp. 800 (D.Conn.1966).

4. *Michigan Gas & Electric Co. v. American Electric Power Co.,* 41 F.R.D. 462 (S.D.N.Y.1966) (Rule 10(b)); *Elwonger v. Career Academy, Inc.,* 54 F.R.D. 85 (E.D.Wis.1971) (Rule 12(e)).

5. *See Lodge 743, International Association of Machinists, AFL–CIO v. United Aircraft Corp.,* 30 F.R.D. 142 (D.Conn.1962).

motions. Where the pleading attacked requires a response, the motion should be made prior to response or within 20 days if no response is required.[6] Once made, the motion tolls the time for response during its pendency. The right to make a Rule 12(e) motion is waived if not made prior to the required responsive pleading or within the 20–day period. If the motion is granted, the movant has ten days to correct the defective pleading (*e.g.*, make it more definite or less scandalous). If the claimant fails to do so, the court may make further orders as are just, including dismissal of the pleading. If the motion is denied, the movant must respond promptly to the original pleading.[7]

Neither the grant nor the denial of a motion attacking pleading form and specificity will be a final, appealable order. Appeal will await disposition of the case. The standard of review will be basically plenary, since pleading form is usually a purely legal matter except insofar as the trial court decided facts (*e.g.*, defendant's inability to respond) peculiar to the case rather than as a matter of law.

§ 4.3 FAILURE TO PLEAD SPECIAL MATTERS

§ 4.3.1 Introduction

Like attacks on form, attacks on pleadings because they fail to properly plead special matters are ordinarily not cost-effective. Occasionally, the attack on specificity is useful. For example, if litigants are racing to the courthouse in the same or differing jurisdictions, being the first in time or the plaintiff may be useful. In these cases, a dismissal without prejudice may not keep the opponent out of court, but will set the litigation back chronologically. Similarly, the motion to dismiss a vague or ambiguous complaint or claim is a legitimate delaying tactic which can give the client time to forge its litigation position, close the deal, make the public offering, or arrange a settlement. However, where the movant facing an excessively general pleading alleging fraud or mental state is tempted to learn more or pin the opponent down through the motion to dismiss for failure to plead special matters, counsel should lie down until the feeling goes away. Discovery exists for these purposes. The motion, even if technically proper, is usually not wise.

§ 4.3.2 Available Attacks on Pleading Specificity

Federal Rule 9 specifically addresses specificity and provides that certain matters must be pleaded with varying degrees of detail. Actually, Rule 9, which should also be read in conjunction with Rule 8's general pleading standards, embodies in a nutshell the federal rules. It reads more as a list of things that no longer need to be specifically pleaded than it does a roster of what requires detail. For example, Rule 9 states that capacity to sue or be sued, conditions precedent, official acts or documents, and the existence of a foreign or domestic judgment need

6. *See* Fed.R.Civ.P. 12(a) & 12(f).
7. *See* Fed.R.Civ.P. 12(a) & 12(e).

only be pleaded, not that they be pleaded in detail. For example, Rule 9(c) provides that it shall be sufficient pleading specificity to "aver generally that all conditions precedent have been performed or have occurred."

Rule 9(b) does provide that claims of fraud or mistake "shall be stated with particularity." However, malice, intent, knowledge, and other mental states need only be averred generally. Rule 9(c) states that averments of time and place are material and must be "considered like all other averments of material matter." Translated into English, this does not mean that time and place be specifically stated.[1] Allegations of time and place are binding admissions on the pleader.[2] This can become important if a statute of limitations defense is made. However, a claimant can seek leave to amend time and place allegations and may, under appropriate circumstances, escape the painted-in corner.[3] "On or about" averments are permissible so long as they give the respondent some idea of the relevant time.

Special damages, which are usually liquidated or capable of expression as a sum certain, must be "specifically stated." General damages are often defined as injury proximately resulting from defendant's conduct which the law presumes to exist from the statement of the claim.[4] Special damages are necessary consequences of the wrong that have flowed from the particular circumstances of the case.[5]

Rule 9(h) refers to admiralty and maritime claims, permitting but not requiring the claim to be identified as one in admiralty. No greater degree of specificity is required for such claims. If the claim is designated as one in admiralty, the special provisions of Rules 14(c) (broader third-party practice), 38(e) (restricted right to jury trial), and 82 (more liberal venue rules) apply. A failure to plead the case as one in admiralty or maritime law can be readily cured by timely amendment.[6] An admiralty action claim must otherwise establish valid federal subject-matter jurisdiction. Where admiralty and conventional claims are inextricably wrapped, hybrid procedures may result.

Perhaps the only seriously adjudicated specificity requirement of Rule 9 is its admonition that fraud be pleaded with particularity. Specificity disputes ensue both to protect reputations,[7] and to prevent a frivolous or undeveloped fraud claim from being used to make arguably relevant a discovery fishing expedition.[8]

§ 4.3

1. *Keunzell v. United States,* 20 F.R.D. 96 (N.D.Cal.1957).

2. *Kincheloe v. Farmer,* 214 F.2d 604 (7th Cir.1954), *cert. denied* 348 U.S. 920, 75 S.Ct. 306, 99 L.Ed. 721 (1955).

3. *Hellebrand v. Hoctor,* 222 F.Supp. 81 (E.D.Mo.1963), *affirmed* 331 F.2d 453 (8th Cir.1964).

4. *Radio Electronic Television Corp. v. Bartniew Distributing Corp.,* 32 F.Supp. 431 (S.D.N.Y.1940).

5. *Burlington Transportation Co. v. Josephson,* 153 F.2d 372 (8th Cir.1946).

6. *Doucet v. Wheless Drilling Co.,* 467 F.2d 336 (5th Cir.1972).

7. *See In re Commonwealth Oil/Tesoro Petroleum Corp. Securities Litigation,* 467 F.Supp. 227, 250 (W.D.Tex.1979).

8. *Goldman v. Singer Co.,* 89 F.R.D. 436, 438 (S.D.N.Y.1981); *Benoay v. Decker,* 517 F.Supp. 490 (E.D.Mich.1981) *judgment affirmed* 735 F.2d 1363 (6th Cir.1984).

Although Rule 9's specificity requirements are not draconian, those imposed by statute or common law often are. For example, when suing the United States, an exception to sovereign immunity must be specifically pleaded.[9] In some jurisdictions, specific pleading is required in civil rights actions in order to weed out frivolous claims.[10] In historically disfavored actions such as libel, slander, and malicious prosecution, particularized pleading is often required.[11] Fed.R.Civ.P. 23.1 requires specific pleading of pre-litigation attempts to gain relief from the corporation in shareholders' suits.[12] Claims that fraudulent conduct has tolled the statute of limitations must be pleaded with particularity.[13] But, as noted above, these are the exceptions, and not the general rule.

All else being equal, defendants have the greater specificity burden. Rule 8(c) sets forth 19—count 'em 19—specific affirmative defenses that must be set forth in defendant's answer or first responsive pleading or they will be considered waived. These affirmative defenses are (1) accord and satisfaction; (2) arbitration and award; (3) assumption of risk; (4) contributory negligence; (5) discharge in bankruptcy; (6) duress; (7) estoppel; (8) failure of consideration; (9) fraud; (10) illegality; (11) injury by fellow servant; (12) laches; (13) license; (14) payment; (15) release; (16) res judicata; (17) statute of frauds; (18) statute of limitations; and (19) waiver. In addition, Rule 8(c) requires that any other matter constituting an avoidance or affirmative defense be pleaded in the answer. Failure to plead an affirmative defense when answering generally will be held to be a waiver of the right to present the affirmative defense at trial, unless the defense is tried by consent.[14]

§ 4.3.3 Strategy, Tactics, Procedure

The proper vehicles for attacking a failure to plead special matters are (1) a motion to dismiss the claim due to the failure to state a claim (Rule 12(b)(6)); (2) a motion for a more definite statement (Rule 12(e)); or (3) a motion to strike the claim involved (Rule 12(f)).

Most states follow the federal theory of pleadings, and state rules of civil procedure are increasingly being revised to resemble the federal rules. However, state practice on pleading specificity is still one area of difference that the practitioner must know. Worse yet, the state practice may be one embodied in case law or an obscure statute rather than the state civil rules. As a general rule, states will be more likely to require specific pleading of some matters, usually state of mind, official

9. *Jewell v. United States,* 27 F.Supp. 836 (W.D.Ky.1939).

10. *Rotolo v. Borough of Charleroi,* 532 F.2d 920, 922 (3d Cir.1976).

11. *See, e.g., Arvey Corp. v. Peterson,* 178 F.Supp. 132 (E.D.Pa.1959) (time and place to be pleaded with particularity in libel action).

12. *Lawson v. Baltimore Paint & Chemical Corp.,* 298 F.Supp. 373 (D.Md.1969).

13. *Rutledge v. Boston Woven Hose & Rubber Co.,* 576 F.2d 248, 250 (9th Cir. 1978).

14. *Blonder-Tongue Laboratories, Inc. v. University of Illinois Foundation,* 402 U.S. 313, 91 S.Ct. 1434, 28 L.Ed.2d 788 (1971), *on remand* 334 F.Supp. 47 (N.D.Ill. 1971), *judgment affirmed* 465 F.2d 380 (7th Cir.1972), *cert. denied* 409 U.S. 1061, 93 S.Ct. 559, 34 L.Ed.2d 513 (1972).

acts, judgments, or conditions precedent. States may also require detailed pleading of certain conditions such as malice, wilfulness, or specific intent, even though not generally requiring specificity for "state of mind" generally. In addition, where states require pleading with particularity, the level of detail required is often greater than that which would satisfy a federal court. In federal cases, the degree of particularity or need to plead an affirmative defense is procedural under the *Erie* doctrine, but the burden of proof on the affirmative defense is determined by state law in diversity cases.

If a party wishes to attack a pleading for failure to properly plead a special matter, the motion should be made before a responsive pleading is due. If no response is required, the motion should be made as soon as feasible. If the opponent has failed to plead an affirmative defense, the best response is no motion at all. Claimant should press forward toward trial. If the affirmative defense is later pleaded or argued, counsel should move to have it dismissed on grounds of waiver.

Affidavits are seldom useful in motions attacking pleadings. The grant or denial of any of the above motions concerning failure to plead special matters is not a final order and will seldom fit an exception pursuant to 28 U.S.C. section 1291(b) or the collateral order doctrine permitting immediate appeal of interlocutory orders. Appellate review of these orders almost always must await resolution of the case on the merits. Only where a particularly egregious trial court decision has or may have systemic importance (*e.g., Conley v. Gibson*) will the appellate court (federal or state) get very excited about reviewing these types of motions.

§ 4.4 ATTACK ON SUBSTANCE OR LEGAL ADEQUACY OF THE PLEADINGS

§ 4.4.1 Dismissal for Failure to State a Claim

Although obtaining dismissal of the complaint on its face is not easy, it is available. Rule 12(b)(6) specifically authorizes it as the modern replacement for the code pleading demurrer. A successful 12(b)(6) motion directed at plaintiff's essential case is an adjudication on the merits although a Rule 12(b)(6) dismissal granted because of technical deficiencies in the complaint will not legally foreclose a second lawsuit by the plaintiff.[1]

Although this motion is more substantive than those previously discussed in this chapter, it is similarly susceptible to overuse. The successful 12(b)(6) motion must be clear and convincing to be granted. The complaint will not be dismissed merely because the plaintiff's theory of causation is attenuated or because it seems unlikely that the facts alleged can be proven. Such matters will be taken as true for purposes

§ 4.4

1. *Ballou v. General Electric Co.,* 393 F.2d 398 (1st Cir.1968), *on remand* 310 F.Supp. 476 (D.Mass.1970), *judgment affirmed* 433 F.2d 109 (1st Cir.1970), *cert. denied* 401 U.S. 1009, 91 S.Ct. 1253, 28 L.Ed.2d 545 (1971).

of deciding the motion.[2] Counsel facing the weak case will often be better off conducting sufficient discovery and seeking summary judgment and a merits adjudication rather than filing the Rule 12 motion that is unlikely to be granted.

As previously noted, all claims made by the plaintiff will be taken as true for purposes of deciding the motion. According to the pleading standard set forth in the federal rules as interpreted by case law, the complaint will be dismissed only where it appears that, beyond doubt, plaintiff has stated no set of facts that would entitle it to relief. Thus, the motion accepts everything said by the claimant and then, based on this version of reality, determines whether those facts would entitle plaintiff to any legal relief. If the answer is no, the complaint should be dismissed.

The 12(b)(6) motion works best where the weakness in the claim is legal and doctrinal rather than factual. For example, the motion may be very effective to attack a pleading on grounds of:

1. Statute of limitations has run (where a factual equitable tolling issue is not present);

2. Seeking recovery from a defendant cloaked in immunity;

3. Plaintiff lacks standing;

4. The dispute is moot;

5. Dispute is not an actual case or controversy or is unripe;

6. There exists no private right of action for the violation claimed;

7. The plaintiff's legal theory of recovery is one repeatedly rejected by courts of the applicable substantive jurisdiction (*e.g.*, wrongful life claims).

Although the 12(b)(6) motion may not be as generally useful as the summary judgment motion, it remains a useful tool for terminating frivolous litigation at the earliest possible stage and reducing the costs of discovery, more involved motions, and full litigation.

In actions claiming libel, slander, malicious prosecution, abuse of process, or other disfavored actions, the courts are noticeably more receptive to the motion to dismiss or for judgment on the pleadings. Where affidavits or matters outside the record are considered, the motion to dismiss is converted to one for summary judgment and the court should give notice of the conversion to all parties. Additionally, the court should permit additional submissions on the issue since a grant of summary judgment would be an adjudication on the merits.[3]

2. *Gardner v. Toilet Goods Association*, 387 U.S. 167, 87 S.Ct. 1526, 18 L.Ed.2d 704 (1967).

3. Fed.R.Civ.P. 12(b); *Beacon Enterprises, Inc. v. Menzies*, 715 F.2d 757 (2d Cir. 1983).

§ 4.4.2 *Judgment on the Pleadings*

Rule 12(c) authorizes judgment on the pleadings upon a motion made after the close of the pleadings. The motion may be brought at any time after the pleadings are closed, but sufficiently before trial that trial is not delayed. The pleadings, as set forth in Rule 7(a), are the complaint, other pleadings making claims (counterclaims, cross-claims, and third-party complaints), and the permitted responsive pleadings. When the claims have been made or the time for making them has passed, the pleadings are closed and a motion for judgment on the pleadings is appropriate.

Like a Rule 12(b)(6) motion, a Rule 12(c) motion is converted to one for summary judgment if matters outside the pleadings are presented and not excluded. Notice of the conversion and opportunity to be heard must be given to all other parties. Unlike a motion to dismiss, a grant of judgment on the pleadings is a decision on the merits, with the graver consequences entailed by that distinction. As with the motion to dismiss, the court deciding on the pleadings accepts as true the allegations of the non-movant, including contravention of what the movant has alleged.[4] Parties may bring Rule 12(b) defenses which they neglected to raise in an answer or Rule 12(b) motion through the Rule 12(c) motion, except that venue, lack of personal jurisdiction, process, and service of process are waived and are not permitted under the guise of a motion for judgment on the pleadings.[5]

§ 4.4.3 *Procedure*

The motion to dismiss for failure to state a claim, like all Rule 12 motions, should ideally be filed in lieu of the answer. However, the Rule 12(b)(6) motion, like Rule 12 motions to dismiss for lack of subject-matter jurisdiction and to dismiss for failure to join an indispensable party, are not waived if made after an answer has been filed. When the 12(b)(6) motion is made in lieu of the answer, it tolls the time within which an answer is required should the motion be denied.

The Rule 12(b)(6) and Rule 12(c) motions, like almost all motions, should be in writing. This general rule is nearly ironclad regarding these motions, since they by nature ask the court to decide fine points of law and are made (or should be made) well in advance of hearing or trial and outside the heat of battle. The motion should be properly scheduled where so required by local rule or custom and should be accompanied by a notice of motion and a memorandum of law. Affidavits are not proper unless used to prove a collateral point (*e.g.*, that movant is not in default even if the motion is filed late because plaintiff's service was defective, etc.) or unless the movant intends to convert either motion into a summary judgment motion as set forth in the last sentence of Rule

4. *Hospital Building Co. v. Trustees of Rex Hospital,* 425 U.S. 738, 96 S.Ct. 1848, 48 L.Ed.2d 338 (1976), *appeal after remand* 691 F.2d 678 (4th Cir.1982), *cert. denied* 464 U.S. 890, 104 S.Ct. 231, 78 L.Ed.2d 224 (1983).

5. Fed.R.Civ.P. 12(h).

12(b). If the movant plans on introducing affidavits or any other exhibits, the Rule 12 motion will be treated as a Rule 56 motion and the better procedure is to label it a summary judgment motion from the start.

The grant of a Rule 12(b)(6) motion is a final, appealable order. The denial of the motion is interlocutory and not appealable absent some exception to the general policy permitting appeals only of final orders. Only rarely will denial of this Rule 12 motion meet the criteria for being considered appealable as a collateral order.

§ 4.5 MOTIONS ATTACKING JURISDICTION

§ 4.5.1 Motions to Dismiss for Lack of Subject-Matter Jurisdiction

A judgment rendered in a court lacking jurisdiction is void:[1] further prosecution of a jurisdictionless action wastes everybody's time. In addition, the subject-matter jurisdiction dismissal motion provides a bonus for defense counsel because it is a permissible delaying tactic. Motions to dismiss for lack of subject-matter jurisdiction are most often encountered in federal court motion practice. A federal court is a court of limited jurisdiction, and can act only when a party correctly invokes its jurisdiction. There is no federal court of "general" jurisdiction. Under long-standing principles of federal-state relations, judicial power not within the specific jurisdiction of the federal courts is reserved to the state courts. By contrast, state courts are courts of general jurisdiction. Rarely will a motion attacking subject-matter jurisdiction succeed in a state court. When the case is brought in the wrong state court, the judge will frequently order transfer rather than dismissal.

Because a judgment obtained in a court lacking subject-matter jurisdiction is void, a defense of lack of subject-matter jurisdiction may be raised at any time. The court can even dismiss a case for lack of subject-matter jurisdiction after certiorari has been granted. Rule 12(h)(3) specifically provides that "[w]henever it appears by suggestion of the parties or otherwise that the court lacks jurisdiction of the subject matter, the court shall dismiss the action."

Fed.R.Civ.P. 12(b)(1) governs this motion. The motion should be made before an answer or other responsive pleading is filed or as soon thereafter as counsel is aware of the probable jurisdictional defect. In all other respects, the moving party should observe the procedural requirements applicable to all Rule 12 motions generally. As with the other enumerated grounds for dismissal contained in Rule 12(b), the subject-matter jurisdiction dismissal may be joined to other Rule 12 rationales for dismissal, and should be filed within the 20–day response time set by Rule 12(a). Lack of subject-matter jurisdiction is also grounds for vacating a judgment under Fed.R.Civ.P. 60(b)(4), and cannot

§ 4.5

1. *Stewart v. United States,* 199 F.2d 517 (7th Cir.1952).

be cured by stipulation of the parties.[2] The Rule 60(b)(1) motion also avoids the strict application of the 20–day response deadline, and can be made at any juncture.

Furthermore, the plaintiff contesting the motion cannot rest upon pleadings alleging subject-matter jurisdiction but must affirmatively prove the existence of jurisdiction by a preponderance of the evidence.[3] Thus, although the defendant is the moving party, the burden of proof is on the plaintiff. Where a permissive counterclaim is pleaded by a defendant, the plaintiff may move for dismissal of the counterclaim for lack of subject-matter jurisdiction. If the defense counterclaim is compulsory (arising out of the same transaction or occurrence that is the subject-matter of plaintiff's complaint) and the court had subject-matter jurisdiction over the complaint, the court will have ancillary subject-matter jurisdiction over the compulsory counterclaim. The motion to dismiss for lack of subject-matter jurisdiction is also favored in that it will ordinarily be the first motion considered by the court, and if it is granted, no other motion will be considered.[4]

The parties cannot confer valid subject-matter jurisdiction by stipulation. Courts usually hold hearings to determine jurisdictional facts. A court may weigh the probative value of competing affidavits in deciding a subject-matter jurisdiction dismissal motion.

Because subject-matter jurisdiction often turns on issues of fact, the court should permit each side sufficient discovery to prove its version of jurisdictional reality and to inform the court so that a correct ruling can be made.

If the defendant overlooks a jurisdictional problem or facts emerging at a later date suggesting the absence of jurisdiction, a Rule 12(b)(1) motion should be made immediately. If the party discovering probable lack of jurisdiction stands silent hoping to win on the merits but holding the motion in reserve, counsel has acted unethically.

The grant of a Rule 12(b)(1) motion is without prejudice, and is not an adjudication on the merits of the claims. Dismissal for lack of subject-matter jurisdiction is not a judgment on the merits, and has no res judicata effect. Such dismissal is a final order, immediately appealable. On appeal, the reviewing court will grant deference to the trial court's fact findings, applying the "clearly erroneous" standard of review. Appellate review of the trial court's legal conclusions is plenary and without deference to the lower court.

2. *Neirbo Co. v. Bethlehem Shipbuilding Corp.,* 308 U.S. 165, 60 S.Ct. 153, 84 L.Ed. 167 (1939).

3. *McNutt v. General Motors Acceptance Corp.,* 298 U.S. 178, 56 S.Ct. 780, 80 L.Ed. 1135 (1936); *Mortensen v. First Federal Savings & Loan Association,* 549 F.2d 884, 891 (3d Cir.1977), *on remand* 79 F.R.D. 603 (D.N.J.1978).

4. *Bell v. Hood,* 327 U.S. 678, 66 S.Ct. 773, 90 L.Ed. 939 (1946). *But see Troup v. McCart,* 238 F.2d 289 (5th Cir.1956) (ruling on subject-matter dismissal motion can be deferred where decision on motion is intertwined with merits of case).

§ 4.5.2 *Motions Attacking Personal Jurisdiction*

In litigation, as in sports, the home team usually has an advantage. Thus, the defendant sued in a distant or inconvenient forum will almost certainly seek dismissal grounded on lack of personal jurisdiction. If the defendant loses the motion due to barely sufficient contacts with the forum state, step two is a motion to dismiss for improper venue or to transfer venue. Unlike the motion to dismiss for lack of subject-matter jurisdiction, the personal jurisdiction dismissal motion must be made prior to a responsive pleading or it is deemed waived. A party may also waive its right to contest personal jurisdiction through an appearance, admission in a pleading or discovery response, as well as by stipulation.

A motion to dismiss for lack of personal jurisdiction, where properly made, contends that the defendant does not have sufficient contact with the forum to make the exercise of personal jurisdiction proper by the instant court. In essence, a Rule 12(b)(2) motion becomes, once the technical requirements of federal or state process have been met, a constitutional question that asks: Does the defendant have sufficient contact with the forum state that the exercise of personal jurisdiction over it by the court will not offend traditional notions of due process, fair play, and substantial justice?[5] The overarching question may sound lofty and has given the Supreme Court occasion for dispute and shifting doctrine in recent years. In practice, however, the questions to ask are more mundane:

Does defendant do business in the state?

Has it otherwise consented to jurisdiction?

Has defendant or its agents visited the state?

How often?

For what purpose?

How recently?

Has defendant shipped anything into the state?

Has it caused any harm in the state?

Was the harm foreseeable?

Has it advertised in the state?

How much?

How directly?

Each case turns on its own facts, but general rules have emerged for particular causes of action, defendants, and state "long-arm" statutes.

Where a motion attacking personal jurisdiction is made, plaintiff bears the burden to prove jurisdiction by a preponderance of the evidence and may not rest upon the mere allegations of its pleadings unless

5. *See Rush v. Savchuk*, 444 U.S. 320, 100 S.Ct. 571, 62 L.Ed.2d 516 (1980), *on remand* 290 N.W.2d 633 (Minn.1980); *World–Wide Volkswagen Corp. v. Woodson*, 444 U.S. 286, 100 S.Ct. 559, 62 L.Ed.2d 490 (1980).

they are uncontroverted by the movant.[6] Plaintiff and defendant will both be permitted reasonable discovery directed toward only the jurisdictional issue pending the court's ruling.[7]

The motion to dismiss for lack of personal jurisdiction should comport with general motion format, should be timely made (within the time permitted to respond to the complaint) and should precede any responsive pleading on the merits or any appearance in the action by the defendant or counsel. The Rule 12(b)(2) motion should be joined with any other Rule 12 motions which defendant wishes to make although, as previously noted, the court should decide subject matter and personal jurisdiction issues before addressing other bases for dismissal.

The grant of a Rule 12(b)(2) motion is a final, appealable order but is not a judgment on the merits and has no res judicata effect. The denial of the motion is not a final order and may only be reviewed after disposition on the merits in the absence of a proper trial court certification for interlocutory review pursuant to 28 U.S.C. section 1292(b) or application of the collateral order doctrine. On appeal, the trial court's fact findings will be reviewed under the "clearly erroneous" test while legal analysis is reviewed de novo.

Where the plaintiff is faced with a likely dismissal on a Rule 12(b)(2) motion (or any Rule 12 motion for that matter), counsel should note the applicable statute of limitations. If the statute has run in the interim between filing of the complaint and decision on the dismissal motion, plaintiff should request that the action be transferred to a forum which will have jurisdiction over the action and the defendant. Courts are authorized by statute to do this in venue matters and have also transferred rather than dismissed actions where the issue is personal jurisdiction. However, without subject-matter jurisdiction, the court has no power to transfer the action and courts are reluctant to so exercise their jurisdiction in a manner not clearly constitutional.

§ 4.5.3 Motions Seeking Non-Exercise of Jurisdiction

Some claims are within the permissible scope of federal jurisdiction, but nevertheless are subject to dismissal in the court's discretion. This motion to dismiss or abstain is based upon the federal courts' prudential authority to refuse to exercise available jurisdiction.

The motion seeking non-exercise of jurisdiction is seldom, if ever, appropriate in state court. Because state courts have general judicial power while federal courts possess limited judicial power, the considerations of federalism and federal-state comity will rarely prompt the state court not to exercise jurisdiction. The only significant instances of a state court "abstention" occur when the state court case involves the

6. *Welsh v. Gibbs,* 631 F.2d 436, 438–439 (6th Cir.1980), *cert. denied* 450 U.S. 981, 101 S.Ct. 1517, 67 L.Ed.2d 816 (1981); *O'Hare International Bank v. Hampton,* 437 F.2d 1173, 1176 (7th Cir.1971).

7. *Fraley v. Chesapeake & Ohio Railway Co.,* 397 F.2d 1 (3d Cir.1968), *on remand* 294 F.Supp. 1193 (W.D.Pa.1969).

same subject matter as a state or federal administrative proceeding or where the parties have agreed to arbitrate the dispute.

The possibility of non-exercise of available jurisdiction is a consequence of history, the American system of constitutional government, the limited jurisdiction of the federal courts, and the tradition of federalism. The most common grounds for seeking non-exercise of jurisdiction are:

1. The presence of pendent state claims subject to dismissal;

2. The availability of federal judicial abstention pursuant to the *Younger, Pullman, Burford,* or *Colorado River* doctrines;

3. The improper presence of an ancillary claim;

4. Failure to exhaust state remedies; and

5. The presence of other means of dispute resolution which must precede federal adjudication.

§ 4.5.4 Motions Seeking to Dismiss Pendent State Claims

Federal courts have jurisdiction to decide the entire case or controversy before then. Where a properly pleaded federal claim invokes federal jurisdiction, the court may hear and decide state law claims also arising out of the dispute between the parties whenever the state and federal claims "derive from a common nucleus of operative fact," and where the claims are sufficiently related that a plaintiff "would ordinarily be expected to try them all in one judicial proceeding." [8]

Once pendent jurisdiction is properly invoked, the court may even decide the state claims first in order to promote the policy of avoiding decisions on federal issues, particularly constitutional questions, whenever possible.[9] However, when a state or the functional equivalent of the state is a defendant, the constitutional power to exercise pendent jurisdiction conflicts with the Eleventh Amendment, and may only be exercised when the state defendants have acted so far outside their authority as to shed the cloak of sovereign immunity.[10]

Although pendent jurisdiction is permitted, its exercise is not required. The court may dismiss the state claims if "considerations of judicial economy, convenience and fairness to [the] litigants" weigh in favor of their dismissal, and may also dismiss pendent claims to avoid unnecessary decisions of state law.[11] Where the federal claims are dismissed prior to trial, the case for dismissing pendent state claims grows stronger. The court has discretion, however, either to dismiss or

8. *United Mine Workers of America v. Gibbs,* 383 U.S. 715, 86 S.Ct. 1130, 16 L.Ed.2d 218 (1966). *Gibbs* is now essentially codified by 28 U.S.C.A. § 1367 (1990).

9. *Ashwander v. Tennessee Valley Authority,* 297 U.S. 288, 346–348, 56 S.Ct. 466, 482, 483, 80 L.Ed. 688 (1936) (Brandeis, J., concurring), *rehearing denied* 297 U.S. 728, 56 S.Ct. 588, 80 L.Ed. 1011 (1936).

10. *Pennhurst State School & Hospital v. Halderman,* 463 U.S. 1251, 104 S.Ct. 45, 77 L.Ed.2d 1458 (1983).

11. *United Mine Workers of America v. Gibbs,* 383 U.S. 715, 726–727, 86 S.Ct. 1130, 1139, 16 L.Ed.2d 218 (1966).

decide the remaining state claims, depending upon the stage of the litigation and whether the state claims are closely tied to a question of federal policy.[12]

Pendent jurisdiction applies only where the state and federal claims involve the same parties. In other words, there must be a federal law basis for the presence of each party in the case in the absence of all but extraordinary circumstances.

§ 4.5.5 Motions to Dismiss Ancillary Claims

Pendent jurisdiction refers only to the court's review of both state and federal claims arising from the same facts. Where federal jurisdiction rests on diversity and a court with proper jurisdiction over the main action decides claims or joins parties outside this main action, it does so on the basis of ancillary jurisdiction. Ancillary jurisdiction is a doctrine which allows a federal court to exercise jurisdiction over all matters related to the central matter properly before the court even though it does not have separate subject-matter jurisdiction over the related matters. Concerns of fairness to litigants, judicial economy and avoiding multiple litigation also buttress the concept of ancillary jurisdiction.

Ancillary jurisdiction cannot be exercised in some situations where its use would clearly contradict the normally strict judicial views of federal subject-matter jurisdiction. The major procedural examples of this limit on ancillary jurisdiction are:

1. Joinder of parties under Rule 20;
2. Permissive intervention under Rule 24(b);
3. Permissive counterclaims under Rule 13(b); and
4. Joinder of claims under Rule 18 unless the state and federal claims are so closely related that they are merely different grounds supporting the same causes of action.

Of these limits on ancillary jurisdiction, the most important and inflexible concern the identity of the parties. For example, joinder of a non-diverse party cannot be accomplished by use of ancillary jurisdiction no matter how closely linked that party is to the main action.[13] However, a recent federal statute (28 U.S.C.A. § 1367(a) (1990)) permits courts to take "supplemental jurisdiction" of sufficiently related claims, even where they require joinder of new parties, so long as this does not destroy diversity jurisdiction. A non-diverse party cannot be permitted to intervene under Rule 24(b), but may intervene as of right under Rule 24(a).

Ancillary jurisdiction has been held applicable to:

1. Compulsory counterclaims under Rule 13(a);

12. *Rosado v. Wyman,* 397 U.S. 397, 402–405, 90 S.Ct. 1207, 1212, 1213, 1214, 25 L.Ed.2d 442 (1970), *on remand* 322 F.Supp. 1173 (E.D.N.Y.1970), *judgment affirmed* 402 U.S. 991, 91 S.Ct. 2169, 29 L.Ed.2d 157 (1971).

13. *Aldinger v. Howard,* 427 U.S. 1, 96 S.Ct. 2413, 49 L.Ed.2d 276 (1976).

2. Joinder of parties to respond to a compulsory counterclaim under Rule 13(h);

3. Cross-claims under Rule 13(g);

4. Third-party claims under Rule 14;

5. Joinder of interwoven claims under Rule 18;

6. Interpleader under Rule 22; and

7. Intervention as of right under Rule 24(a).

§ 4.5.6 the Abstention Doctrines

Federal courts are courts of limited jurisdiction and state courts have always been viewed as the front line of the nation's judiciary. This tradition has spawned several abstention doctrines encouraging, and occasionally mandating, federal courts to refrain from adjudicating cases that are thought to be more properly within state court jurisdiction. Each abstention doctrine is slightly different, some more commanding than others.

Younger Abstention. This doctrine is named after the case clearly articulating its requirements, *Younger v. Harris.*[14] Where an action seeks an injunction of state criminal prosecution begun prior to the federal action the court should abstain unless a federal injunction is necessary to prevent immediate, irreparable injury, or where there is some evidence of bad faith or harassment in the state proceedings, or where the state statute upon which prosecution is based is "patently invalid" under federal law.[15] The rationale for *Younger* abstention is that the state court criminal defendant (who is usually the plaintiff challenging the state law and his or her prosecution) can raise any federal arguments against conviction in the state proceeding.

The *Younger* doctrine has been held applicable to state civil proceedings antecedent to a criminal prosecution seeking closure of obscene movie theaters and to civil actions to collect state taxes. It is probably safe to state that *Younger* abstention applies whenever the federal suit seeks to restrain state court civil proceedings commenced by the state.

Pullman Abstention. This federal abstention doctrine was established in *Railroad Commission of Texas v. Pullman Co.*[16] The doctrine applies to federal actions challenging state action as contrary to the United States Constitution. If the case involved also presents unsettled state law questions which may be dispositive of the controversy, the federal court may refrain from hearing the case pending the parties' resort to the state courts.

Pullman abstention is less draconian than *Younger* abstention. Under *Pullman* abstention, the federal court usually retains jurisdiction

14. 401 U.S. 37, 91 S.Ct. 746, 27 L.Ed.2d 669 (1971).

15. *Younger v. Harris,* 401 U.S. 37, 91 S.Ct. 746, 27 L.Ed.2d 669 (1971).

16. 312 U.S. 496, 61 S.Ct. 643, 85 L.Ed. 971 (1941).

and refrains from action for a "reasonable" time, rather than dismissing the case as in *Younger*. Federal courts also have greater discretion to determine the applicability of *Pullman* abstention, whereas the criteria for *Younger* abstention are comparatively obvious and inflexible. Under the *Pullman* doctrine, only where the state law question is both difficult and unclear is the federal court more or less obligated to abstain. Where the applicable state laws are clearly unconstitutional, *Pullman* abstention is inappropriate.[17]

Burford Abstention. This abstention doctrine is set forth in *Burford v. Sun Oil Co.*,[18] and states that federal courts should abstain from the exercise of jurisdiction where exercising jurisdiction would create needless conflict with the state's administration of its own regulatory scheme, thereby affecting issues of substantial local importance that transcend the federal court case. *Burford* abstention is particularly appropriate where the state law questions are difficult or where the state courts or state administrative agencies have special expertise in interpreting the state law or controversy involved. In *Burford* abstention, as in *Younger* abstention, the federal action will normally be dismissed, not merely stayed.

Federal courts have long been loathe to adjudicate controversies which essentially involve state property disputes, even where some federal basis for jurisdiction has been asserted.[19] This policy stems from the doctrine of comity, the notion that controversies over real property are peculiarly local regardless of the legal issues involved, and the practical belief that state courts have particular expertise in adjudicating certain types of real property disputes (*e.g.*, boundary disputes, non-navigable water rights, adverse possession, and easements). Consequently, federal courts have dismissed cases involving real property disputes where the action does not present a federal question issue which outweighs the real property character of the action. It is not entirely clear whether this historical practice of the federal courts is a separate category for declining to exercise jurisdiction, such as the domestic relations exception, or whether "real property abstention" is simply a form of *Burford* abstention.

Colorado River Abstention. Although the federal courts have been reluctant to label it abstention, they have long recognized another abstention category. We will call it *Colorado River* abstention because it was most comprehensively discussed by the United States Supreme Court in *Colorado River Water Conservation District v. United States.*[20] Under this doctrine, an action is dismissed or placed in suspense because

17. *Harman v. Forssenius,* 380 U.S. 528, 85 S.Ct. 1177, 14 L.Ed.2d 50 (1965).

18. 319 U.S. 315, 63 S.Ct. 1098, 87 L.Ed. 1424 (1943), *rehearing denied* 320 U.S. 214, 63 S.Ct. 1442, 87 L.Ed. 1851 (1943).

19. Note, John D. Echeverria, Land Use Regulation, The Federal Courts, and the Abstention Doctrine, 89 Yale L.J. 1134 (1980).

20. 424 U.S. 800, 96 S.Ct. 1236, 47 L.Ed.2d 483 (1976), *rehearing denied* 426 U.S. 912, 96 S.Ct. 2239, 48 L.Ed.2d 839 (1976).

of the existence of concurrent state court proceedings involving the same parties and controversy.

A number of Supreme Court cases have applied *Colorado River* abstention, even decades prior to the *Colorado River* decision.[21] Although the doctrine is limited and largely within the court's discretion, the usual course of action in exercising this type of abstention—dismissal—is as powerful as that of *Younger* or *Pullman* abstention. This form of abstention is particularly appropriate where the federal action is a declaratory judgment action.[22]

A variant of *Colorado River* abstention occurs when two parallel federal court proceedings exist. In these cases, the same considerations will be applied by the courts, but there is a lower standard for dismissal since a federal court will retain jurisdiction in any event.[23]

Classroom Abstention. After reading all this, you must question your priorities in life.

§ 4.5.7 Miscellaneous "Abstention" or Quasi-Abstention Provisions

Although they are not generally denominated as "abstention" cases, there exist a number of other small categories of cases in which a federal court will decline to exercise jurisdiction.

Most common among this category are causes of action which require the federal court plaintiff to exhaust specified administrative or legislative remedies or to satisfy conditions precedent to invoking federal subject matter jurisdiction. Exhaustion of state judicial remedies is, however, not normally required.[24] Examples of these situations include applications for habeas corpus relief from state court confinement,[25] actions to overturn the administrative denial of social security benefits,[26] and actions to overturn various administrative agency rulings.[27] The existence of an arbitration agreement in a contract pertaining to the subject matter of the lawsuit provides another basis for seeking quasi-abstention.[28]

21. *Brillhart v. Excess Insurance Co. of America,* 316 U.S. 491, 62 S.Ct. 1173, 86 L.Ed. 1620 (1942), *rehearing denied* 317 U.S. 704, 63 S.Ct. 23, 87 L.Ed. 562 (1942); *Pacific Live Stock Co. v. Lewis,* 241 U.S. 440, 36 S.Ct. 637, 60 L.Ed 1084 (1916).

22. *Brillhart v. Excess Insurance Co. of America,* 316 U.S. 491, 62 S.Ct. 1173, 86 L.Ed. 1620 (1942), *rehearing denied* 317 U.S. 704, 63 S.Ct. 23, 87 L.Ed. 562 (1942). *See also Will v. Calvert Fire Insurance Co.,* 437 U.S. 655, 663–665, 98 S.Ct. 2552, 2557, 2558, 57 L.Ed.2d 504 (1978), *on remand* 586 F.2d 12 (7th Cir.1978). *But see* 437 U.S. at 668, 98 S.Ct. at 2560 (Brennan, J., dissenting).

23. *Kerotest Manufacturing Co. v. C-O-Two Fire Equipment Co.,* 342 U.S. 180, 72 S.Ct. 219, 96 L.Ed. 200 (1952).

24. *City Bank Farmers' Trust Co. v. Schnader,* 291 U.S. 24, 54 S.Ct. 259, 78 L.Ed. 628 (1934).

25. 28 U.S.C.A. § 2254.

26. 42 U.S.C.A. § 405.

27. *See, e.g.,* 28 U.S.C.A. § 1341 (state tax collection challenges) & 1342 (utility rate orders).

28. *See* Federal Arbitration Act, 9 U.S.C.A. § 2.

A judge-made exception to the duty to exercise federal subject-matter jurisdiction is domestic relations abstention. Even though the diversity statute [29] provides for jurisdiction without regard to the subject matter of the action, federal courts have long refused to hear diversity cases involving divorce, child support, and related domestic relations matters.[30] A similar exception, also judge-made, causes federal courts to decline to probate a will or administer a decedent's estate.[31]

Considerations of federalism also militate against federal court interference in state court actions, which doctrine has been codified into law. The Anti–Injunction Act, 28 U.S.C.A. section 2283 (1982), provides:

> A court of the United States may not grant an injunction to stay proceedings in a State court except as expressly authorized by Act of Congress, or where necessary in aid of its jurisdiction, or to protect or effectuate its judgments.

The language of the Act is strictly construed, and the Act may not be avoided through clever redefinition or sophistry.[32] For example, the Act cannot be avoided by directing the injunction at a party rather than the state court,[33] or by seeking a declaratory judgment with the effect of an injunction.[34]

§ 4.5.8 Removal and Remand

Defendants who are sued in state court should consider whether the controversy may be removed to federal court and whether they are likely to benefit from the federal forum. Conversely, plaintiffs who have chosen the state court will want to seek the remand of cases improperly removed to federal court.

The federal judicial code provides a comprehensive set of standards and procedures for removal and remand.[35] Perhaps the most difficult aspect of removal is deciding whether to remove. This decision is largely subjective, and must be decided after considering many factors which cannot be readily balanced. Among those factors are:

1. Relative quality of state and federal judges;

29. 28 U.S.C.A. § 1332.

30. *Linscott v. Linscott,* 98 F.Supp. 802 (S.D.Iowa 1951). Breach of a contract or state court divorce decree providing for specific alimony or child support payments will give rise to a breach of contract claim within the court's diversity jurisdiction if all other requirements for diversity jurisdiction are met. *See Harrison v. Harrison,* 214 F.2d 571 (4th Cir.1954), *cert. denied* 348 U.S. 896, 75 S.Ct. 217, 99 L.Ed. 704 (1954).

31. *In re Broderick's Will,* 88 U.S. (21 Wall.) 503, 22 L.Ed. 599 (1874).

32. *See Atlantic Coast Line Railroad Co. v. Brotherhood of Locomotive Engineers,* 398 U.S. 281, 90 S.Ct. 1739, 26 L.Ed.2d 234 (1970).

33. *See Atlantic Coast Line Railroad Co. v. Brotherhood of Locomotive Engineers,* 398 U.S. 281, 90 S.Ct. 1739, 26 L.Ed.2d 234 (1970); *Oklahoma Packing Co. v. Oklahoma Gas & Electric Co.,* 309 U.S. 4, 60 S.Ct. 215, 84 L.Ed. 447 (1940), *rehearing denied* 309 U.S. 693, 60 S.Ct. 465, 84 L.Ed. 1034 (1940).

34. *Cunningham v. A.J. Aberman, Inc.,* 252 F.Supp. 602 (W.D.Pa.1965), *affirmed* 358 F.2d 747 (3d Cir.1966).

35. *See* 28 U.S.C.A. §§ 1441–1451.

2. Judicial experience with substantive law of this case (may favor either state or federal);

3. Differences in state and federal procedure;

4. Comparative conditions of each court's docket;

5. Differences in methods of assigning matters to individual judges;

6. Relative differences in state and federal jury panels.

To be removable, a case commenced in state court must usually be one which could have been commenced in federal court. The statute specifies that certain actions otherwise qualifying may not be removed. Thus, an action brought pursuant to the Federal Employers Liability Act (FELA), the Jones Act, state workers' compensation laws, or against a common carrier for shipment loss under 49 U.S.C.A. section 11707 which has an amount in controversy of $10,000 or less cannot be removed to federal court.[36] Some statutes in addition to the general removal statute provide for removal of certain actions by federal government agencies who are sued.[37] The Foreign Sovereign Immunities Act adds a section to the removal statute (28 U.S.C.A. section 1441(d)) to permit a foreign state sued in state court to remove and obtain a bench trial in order to avoid possible prejudice of an American jury.

To be removable on the basis of federal question jurisdiction, federal law must be an *essential* ingredient of the plaintiff's claim. An action is not removable if a defense to the action invokes federal law or requires an interpretation of federal law.[38] A cross-claim or counterclaim invoking federal law similarly will not provide the basis for removal.[39] The removal statute (28 U.S.C.A. § 1441(c) also permits a case to be removed even if it contains a "separate *and* independent" claim arising under federal law (i.e., not based on diversity) that would, if sued upon alone, confer valid federal jurisdiction. Thus, a case with one federal claim in a 26–count complaint may be removed to federal court. However, the trial court has discretion to remand to state court those claims in the case for which state law predominates.

Where there is complete diversity between plaintiff and defendants, the defendants may remove the action if all the defendants are not citizens of the forum state and join in the removal petition within the required time.[40] Complete diversity must usually exist both at the time

36. 28 U.S.C.A. § 1445.

37. *See, e.g.,* 12 U.S.C.A. § 1819(4) (FDIC may remove state actions to which it is a party).

38. *See Gully v. First National Bank in Meridian,* 299 U.S. 109, 57 S.Ct. 96, 81 L.Ed. 70 (1936); *La Chemise Lacoste v. Alligator Co.,* 506 F.2d 339 (3d Cir.1974), *cert. denied* 421 U.S. 937, 95 S.Ct. 1666, 44 L.Ed.2d 94 (1975), *rehearing denied* 421 U.S. 1006, 95 S.Ct. 2408, 44 L.Ed.2d 674 (1975).

39. *American Oil Co. v. Egan,* 357 F.Supp. 610 (D.Minn.1973).

40. *Gableman v. Peoria, D. & E. Railroad Co.,* 179 U.S. 335, 21 S.Ct. 171, 45 L.Ed. 220 (1900); *Superior Fish Co. v. Royal Globe Insurance Co.,* 521 F.Supp. 437 (E.D.Pa.1981).

the action is commenced and at the time the removal petition is filed.[41] A corporation is a citizen both of its state of incorporation and its principal place of business. An unincorporated association or partnership is a citizen of each state where its members or partners reside.[42]

An action may be removed even if the state proceeding is procedurally defective or the state court lacks personal jurisdiction over a defendant. After removal, these procedural defects may be cured or the action may be dismissed based upon the procedural defects or lack of personal jurisdiction.[43]

The removal statute sets forth specific procedural requirements for removing an action to federal court. This statute will normally be strictly construed.[44] The defendant seeking removal must file a petition for removal with the local federal district court within 30 days after receipt (by service or otherwise) of the summons and complaint. The removal petition must be filed prior to entry of judgment in the state court action. The petition must be verified, and contain a short and plain statement of the facts which make the action removable. The statute requires that copies of all process, pleadings, and orders served on the removing party in the state court action accompany the petition.[45] All defendants must join in the petition for removal, and all defendants must be entitled to demand removal for themselves if they were sued separately.[46] The petition for removal should be addressed to the judges of the applicable federal district court.

A removal petition must be filed within 30 days or it is of no effect. Because removal is a matter of the court's subject-matter jurisdiction, the 30–day limit cannot be extended. If the petition is not timely filed, the federal court is without jurisdiction to hear the matter, and it must remand the case to state court. Regardless of when a diversity action becomes subject to federal jurisdiction (*e.g.* through deletion of a nondiverse party), there can be no removal after one year has passed from commencement of the action.

After the removal petition is filed, the removing party must "promptly" give notice of the filing to the clerk of the state court and to the other parties to the action. The state court proceeding comes to a complete halt and the file is transferred to the federal court. The case

41. *Kellam v. Keith,* 144 U.S. 568, 12 S.Ct. 922, 36 L.Ed. 544 (1892).

42. *Great Southern Fire Proof Hotel Co. v. Jones,* 177 U.S. 449, 20 S.Ct. 690, 44 L.Ed. 842 (1900).

43. *See* 28 U.S.C.A. § 1448; *Savarese v. Edrick Transfer & Storage, Inc.,* 513 F.2d 140 (9th Cir.1975).

44. *See Shamrock Oil & Gas Corp. v. Sheets,* 313 U.S. 100, 61 S.Ct. 868, 85 L.Ed. 1214 (1941).

45. 28 U.S.C.A. § 1446(a).

46. *Transport Indemnity Co. v. Financial Trust Co.,* 339 F.Supp. 405 (C.D.Cal. 1972). 28 U.S.C.A. § 1441(c) permits an entire state court case to be removed if it has within it a separate and independent claim which would be removable if used on alone. This provision has been given a restrictive interpretation by the United States Supreme Court, however, and is rarely used. *See American Fire & Casualty Co. v. Finn.,* 341 U.S. 6, 71 S.Ct. 534, 95 L.Ed. 702 (1951). *See generally* 14 Charles A. Wright, et al., Federal Practice and Procedure § 3724, at 629–30 (2d ed.1985).

remains in the federal court unless and until it is remanded, and all further papers must be filed in the federal court.

If the state court action as originally commenced was not removable, but is later amended so as to become removable, receipt of the amended pleading initiates the running of a 30–day period for filing a removal petition. To avoid default, a removing defendant is still required to answer the complaint within 20 days of receipt of the summons and complaint, or five days after filing the removal petition, whichever is longer.[47]

Removal petitions no longer need be accompanied by a surety bond as security to indemnify the plaintiff for costs and disbursements incurred if the case is not removable or was improperly removed. However, an improperly removed action may, on remand, subject the removing party to an order requiring payment of actual expenses, including attorneys' fees, to the party obtaining remand.

The federal court is authorized to remand the case to state court, upon the motion of a party or *sua sponte,* if at any time before final judgment "it appears that the case was removed improvidently and without jurisdiction." In doing so, the court may order the removing party to pay costs and disbursements. The clerk for the federal court must mail a certified copy of the remand order to the state court clerk (presumably accompanied by the record), whereupon the action may continue to proceed in state court.

Motions for remand to state court are frequently brought on the following grounds:

1. Petition not filed within 30 day period;
2. Absence of a federal cause of action in the plaintiff's claim;
3. Demand made by resident defendant on diversity grounds;
4. Lack of complete diversity;
5. Failure to have all defendants to join in petition; and
6. Absence of subject matter jurisdiction in state court action.

Orders for remand are not reviewable "on appeal or otherwise" unless the case was remanded pursuant to the statute providing for removal of a state court prosecution in conflict with civil rights laws guaranteeing racial equality.[48] However, in rare and extraordinary cases, where remand is clearly in error, mandamus review of remand orders has been permitted.[49] Ordinarily, however, the party claiming wrongful remand must complete the state court proceedings through appeal and seek a writ of certiorari to the United States Supreme Court, an unlikely and certainly burdensome means of obtaining federal appellate review of an erroneous remand.

47. Fed.R.Civ.P. 81(c).

48. 28 U.S.C.A. § 1447(d).

49. *See Thermtron Products, Inc. v. Hermansdorfer,* 423 U.S. 336, 96 S.Ct. 584, 46 L.Ed.2d 542 (1976) (remand of otherwise valid removal on sole basis of crowded federal docket reversed).

§ 4.6 PRIOR PENDING ACTIONS AND STAYS

A recurring problem for the courts is the action commenced by a party in one court after that party has been sued in another action or court. This situation presents unique problems, and the attorney facing such a situation has a number of potential remedies available. Among the potential solutions are the following:

1. Dismissal of one of the actions, presumably the one later filed;

2. Issuance of an order enjoining the party commencing the second action from prosecuting it;

3. Transfer of one action to the court in which the other action is pending, and consolidation; and

4. Staying the later-filed action pending outcome of the first action.

Courts prefer to require that one action, rather than two, decide a single dispute, and will usually take one of these paths to resolve the problem of separate cases dealing with the same parties or issues.

A stay is a temporary cessation of the instant case pending the occurrence of some future event, usually the completion of some other proceeding. A court may also stay one aspect or procedure in the case (*e.g.*, prejudgment attachment or garnishment) until the case is adjudicated. Federal Rule 62 specifically addresses stays of enforcement of judgment pending appeal and is beyond the scope of this book. For purposes of this section's discussion, a stay is not a temporary restraining order or a preliminary injunction, modes of equitable relief addressed in § 12.5. In many cases, however, a court order staying an action is similar in effect to a TRO or preliminary injunction. Many courts will also reinforce their stay orders with injunctive relief. Other than pursuant to Rule 62, stays of execution are found on the late, late show, when the governor calls with a pardon just before the switch is thrown. State and federal statutes may also specifically provide for stays of judicial proceedings in certain contexts.

Although the party moving for a stay of proceedings need not ordinarily prove irreparable harm, it does need to show that the ongoing court action is unnecessary, at least at the time of the motion. Realistically, when discussing stays, we speak of stays of civil court actions. A frequent ground for a stay motion is the presence of a prior or ongoing pending action concerning the same controversy or facts or issues in the action in which the stay is sought. The prior action need not be judicial. Court cases can in some circumstances be stayed because of ongoing administrative proceedings or arbitrations. The Federal Arbitration Act provides that written agreements to arbitrate disputes are enforceable in either state or federal court, where the underlying activity is in interstate commerce.

A grant or denial of a stay motion is not a final order subject to appeal under 28 U.S.C.A. § 1291. Neither are decisions on stays appealable as grants or denials of injunctions under 28 U.S.C.A. § 1292(a). However, the stay order may become appealable pursuant to 28 U.S.C.A. § 1291(a) where coupled with a decision on a motion for injunctive relief. Depending on the stakes and the legal questions involved in the stay motion, the decision on the stay may be certified for immediate appeal by the court pursuant to 28 U.S.C.A. § 1292(b). Stay decisions are somewhat more likely to meet the requirements of the collateral order doctrine than are decisions on the average motion. On appeal, the standard of review is whether the trial court abused its discretion in granting or denying the stay.

§ 4.7 MOTIONS TO TRANSFER VENUE

Venue refers to the place where an action should be tried, and therefore, where an action should be filed. The United States Supreme Court has observed that venue is "primarily a matter of convenience of litigants and witnesses." [1] Statutes define venue, *i.e.,* which districts are proper for the commencement of actions. Statutes and common law give additional direction to the courts. The federal rules offer little guidance on matters of venue: Rule 12(b)(3) permits improper venue to be raised by motion, Rule 12(h) requires the defense to be raised in the first pleading or motion, and Rule 41(b) provides that a dismissal for improper venue is normally made without prejudice. Rule 81 clarifies that the rules neither extend or contract the scope of statutory venue provisions.

The distinction between venue and jurisdiction is clear and important—venue can be agreed to or waived by the litigants, but the parties cannot confer subject-matter jurisdiction, which encompasses judicial authority, on a court.[2]

If venue is improperly laid initially, the court can dismiss the action or, in certain instances, may transfer the action to a proper venue. The court must decide venue at the threshold. If venue is proper under the applicable statutes, the court cannot dismiss the action, but may transfer it in appropriate cases.

Proper venue depends on the nature of the action. Local actions may be brought only where the property involved in the action is located. Local actions involve those generally thought of as *in rem* actions, and other actions which are closely related to an individual court. All other actions are transitory actions. The distinction between local actions and transitory actions is not a clear one, and the courts have compounded the question by confusingly viewing it alternatively as one of venue or of

§ 4.7

1. *Denver & Rio Grande Western R.R. Co. v. Brotherhood of Railroad Trainmen,* 387 U.S. 556, 560, 87 S.Ct. 1746, 1748, 18 L.Ed.2d 954 (1967).

2. *Leroy v. Great Western United Corp.,* 443 U.S. 173, 180, 99 S.Ct. 2710, 61 L.Ed.2d 464 (1979), *on remand* 602 F.2d 1246 (5th Cir.1979).

jurisdiction. There is no general federal law that determines the venue of local actions. The question of proper venue in local actions is thus a matter of common law.

Venue in transitory actions is determined completely by statute.[3] Three general venue statutes govern venue of all transitory actions in the federal courts for which no special venue statute applies.[4] In addition, hundreds of special venue statutes apply to individual types of actions. If a special statute applies to an action, it will control over the general venue statutes.[5]

In federal court diversity actions, venue is proper in any district in which all defendants reside, are subject to personal jurisdiction, or in which "a substantial part of the events or omissions giving rise to the claim occurred" or where significant disputed property is located. In cases in which jurisdiction is based, in part, upon federal question jurisdiction, venue is also proper in any district in which all defendants reside, or in which something substantially related to the claim occurred. If defendants reside in different districts within one state, venue is proper in any district in the state. In addition, if there is no district that satisfies the claim or defendant residence criteria for venue, venue in a case founded on federal question jurisdiction may be proper in "a judicial district" in which any defendant may be found.[6]

In multiple-party litigation, a district where the claim arose is frequently the only proper venue. Determining "where the claim arose" is a difficult and confusing task. The question is a matter of federal law.[7] The courts have struggled to create a test to determine where a claim arose, and have not been particularly successful. Courts have created at least three different tests, and have applied those tests inconsistently.[8] The United States Supreme Court cast considerable doubt over what may be a proper test in 1979, and also intimated that a claim may arise in more than one district for venue purposes;[9] a view confirmed by Congress when it amended the venue statute as part of the Civil Justice Reform Act of 1990. 28 U.S.C.A. § 1391 now provides that venue is proper when a "substantial part" of the claim arose in the district.

3. *See, e.g., Blank v. Bitker,* 135 F.2d 962 (7th Cir.1943).

4. 28 U.S.C.A. §§ 1391–1393.

5. *Fourco Glass Co. v. Transmirra Products Corp.,* 353 U.S. 222, 77 S.Ct. 787, 1 L.Ed.2d 786 (1957); *see also* American Law Institute, Study of Division of Jurisdiction Between State and Federal Courts, Official Draft, Appendix F 498–501 (1969).

6. *See* 28 U.S.C.A. § 1391(a) and (b).

7. *Leroy v. Great Western United Corp.,* 443 U.S. 173, 183 n. 15, 99 S.Ct. 2710, 2716 n.15, 61 L.Ed.2d 464 (1979), *on remand* 602 F.2d 1246 (5th Cir.1979).

8. *See, e.g., Sherman v. Moore,* 86 F.R.D. 471 (S.D.N.Y.1980) ("place of injury" test); *Hodson v. A.H. Robins Co.,* 528 F.Supp. 809, 813 (E.D.Va.1981), *affirmed* 715 F.2d 142 (4th Cir.1983) ("weight of contacts" test); *Lamont v. Haig,* 590 F.2d 1124 (D.C.Cir.1978) ("substantial part of events or omissions" test).

9. *See Leroy v. Great Western United Corp.,* 443 U.S. 173, 184–185, 99 S.Ct. 2710, 2717, 61 L.Ed.2d 464 (1979), *on remand* 602 F.2d 1246 (5th Cir.1979).

Because dismissal may be an unduly harsh measure for remedying an inconvenient forum, 28 U.S.C.A. § 1404(a) permits a court to transfer an action to another district. That statute provides:

> For the convenience of parties and witnesses, in the interest of justice, a district court may transfer any civil action to another district or division where it might have been brought.

This provision is applicable to any civil action, including cases removed from the state courts.[10] Because of the limited jurisdiction of the state courts, the power to transfer actions to a different jurisdiction may not be present in state court proceedings. Some state courts may, however, be authorized to direct the plaintiff to commence an action in a new forum, and have the plaintiff do so by threatening dismissal under the state venue provision.

Venue may also be challenged under the federal common-law doctrine of *forum non conveniens,* a doctrine that permits the dismissal of an otherwise proper action solely for the reason that the action was brought in a district which is inconvenient for trial. The doctrine only applies to actions in which subject-matter and personal jurisdiction are proper and in which venue lies. If a defect in jurisdiction or venue exists, the court will dismiss or transfer the case on that basis, and not under *forum non conveniens.*

Dismissal under *forum non conveniens* is not proper unless an alternative forum exists which could exercise jurisdiction over all the parties and which could enter all requested relief.[11] Because dismissal is invariably a drastic remedy, *forum non conveniens* dismissal will be ordered only in extreme circumstances. The movant must make a strong showing that the alternative forum is significantly more convenient. The adoption of a statute permitting transfer of an action brought in an inconvenient forum, 28 U.S.C.A. § 1404(a), has significantly reduced the use of dismissal under *forum non conveniens.* The doctrine has continued importance, however, and may be the only remedy for the action brought in an inconvenient forum where the alternative forum is a state court or a foreign country's courts.

In addition to the venue provisions governing all federal court actions, a special statute, 28 U.S.C.A. § 1407 permits change of venue in "multidistrict" cases. It provides for the temporary transfer of federal cases from one district to another for the purpose of conducting consolidated and coordinated pretrial proceedings. Although transfer under this statute is normally made only for pretrial proceedings, experience under the statute indicates that an action, once transferred, is unlikely to return to its original venue for trial.[12] Once transfer is ordered under the statute, the transferor court relinquishes all jurisdiction and power

10. *See Reyno v. Piper Aircraft Co.,* 630 F.2d 149, 157 (3d Cir.1980), *reversed on other grounds* 454 U.S. 235, 102 S.Ct. 252, 70 L.Ed.2d 419 (1981) *rehearing denied* 455 U.S. 928, 102 S.Ct. 1296, 71 L.Ed.2d 474 (1982).

11. *See, e.g., Gulf Oil Corp. v. Gilbert,* 330 U.S. 501, 67 S.Ct. 839, 91 L.Ed. 1055 (1947).

12. *See* Lauter, Mastering MDL, 6 Nat. L.J. 1, 24–25, 32 (Nov. 21, 1983).

over the proceedings. Any motions which are then pending are transferred, with the rest of the file, for all further handling by the transferee court.[13]

The statute permits transfer either upon the motion of a party or on initiation of the Judicial Panel on Multidistrict Litigation. The Judicial Panel has promulgated its own rules of procedure which supplement the Federal Rules of Civil Procedure.[14]

Transfer under 28 U.S.C.A. section 1407, generally the first step in consolidating numerous actions, amounts to a change of venue for pretrial purposes. This statute, for example, supersedes the general venue statute and special venue statutes.[15] The Judicial Panel has held that the transfer for pretrial purposes supersedes traditional considerations of "venue," including the traditional requirement that there be personal jurisdiction over a defendant by the transferee court:

> [D]efendants' argument regarding the unavailability of a single district with jurisdiction over all parties is misdirected. Transfer of civil action pursuant to 28 U.S.C. § 1407 is for pretrial purposes only and the fact that all parties are not amenable to suit in a particular district does not prevent transfer to that district for pretrial proceedings where the prerequisites of Section 1407 are otherwise satisfied.... Succinctly, venue is not a criterion in deciding the propriety of transfer under § 1407.[16]

So there.

There are three statutory criteria for transfer under the statute, and all three criteria must be met before transfer is proper:

1. The actions must share common issues of fact;
2. Transfer must be for the convenience of parties and witnesses; and
3. Transfer must advance the just and efficient conduct of the actions.

The mere existence of common issues of fact does not mandate transfer, as the other criteria must be met as well.[17] Additionally, if a party stipulates as to the common issues, then no common issues will exist, and transfer will not be appropriate.[18] The presence of common issues of law has no effect on transfer: it is neither a necessary nor sufficient

13. *In re Upjohn Co. Antibiotic "Cleocin" Products Liability Litigation,* 508 F.Supp. 1020 (E.D.Mich.1981). For a comprehensive treatise on transfer under this statute, see David F. Herr, Multidistrict Litigation (1985, Supp. 1989).

14. *See* Rules of Procedure of the Judicial Panel on Multidistrict Litigation, *reprinted in* 28 U.S.C.A. § 1407, at 186.

15. *Matter of New York City Municipal Securities Litigation,* 572 F.2d 49, 51 (2d Cir.1978).

16. *In re Aviation Products Liability Litigation,* 347 F.Supp. 1401, 1404 (J.P.M.D.L. 1972).

17. *See In re Photocopy Paper,* 305 F.Supp. 60, 61 (J.P.M.D.L.1969).

18. *See In re Swine Flu Immunization Products Liability Litigation,* 464 F.Supp.

condition for transfer.[19]

The Panel's only function is to determine if transfer is appropriate under the statute. In practice, the Judicial Panel applies standards more detailed than those of the statute to determine the transfer issue. In addition to the attitudes of the parties towards transfer, the Panel has set forth a number of other factors it will consider in determining whether transfer and consolidation for pretrial proceedings is appropriate. These factors include, but are not limited to:

1. Convenience of counsel;
2. Convenience of witnesses;
3. Minimizing of duplicative discovery;
4. Possibility of conflicting rulings;
5. Pendency of at least one action in the proposed transferee district;
6. Progress of discovery at the time of proposed transfer;
7. Docket conditions;
8. Familiarity of transferee judge with issues raised;
9. Availability of judicial resources;
10. Number of actions pending in district; and
11. Size of litigation.[20]

In practice, any factor which might have an impact on the Panel's determination of the appropriateness of transfer under the statute may be considered.

The most common motion involving multidistrict litigation is a motion for transfer. That motion must be filed with the Panel, and served upon all parties or their attorneys in all pending actions. Additionally, the clerk of court in each district where an action is pending must be provided a copy of the motion. Upon the filing of a motion for transfer, all parties must designate a single attorney as counsel of record before the Panel within ten days. Response to the motion for transfer is due within 15 days. The Panel Rules contain additional provisions that must be carefully followed.

In addition to motions for initial transfer, a party may seek to add a later-filed action to the multidistrict cases or may learn of another previously pending case that should be part of the multidistrict group. Such cases are known as "tag-along" actions, and a case may be given "tag-along" status by filing a motion for it. Whenever a case comes to

949 (J.P.M.D.L.1979).

19. *Compare In re Air Crash Disaster at Huntington, W.Va. on Nov. 14, 1970,* 342 F.Supp. 1400 (J.P.M.D.L.1972) *with In re Eastern Airlines, Inc. Flight Attendant Weight Program Litigation,* 391 F.Supp. 763 (J.P.M.D.L.1975).

20. *See, e.g., In re Bristol Bay, Alaska, Salmon Fishery Antitrust Litigation,* 424 F.Supp. 504 (J.P.M.D.L.1976) (witness convenience and discovery duplication); *In re Eastern Airlines, Inc. Flight Attendant Weight Program Litigation,* 391 F.Supp. 763 (J.P.M.D.L.1975) (docket conditions).

the attention of the Clerk of the Panel (this usually occurs by motion of a party), the clerk is authorized to enter a conditional transfer order transferring the action to a court where previously transferred cases are pending. The conditional order is served on all parties, but transfer does not occur for 15 days in order to give the parties an opportunity to object to transfer.[21] The Panel Rules provide for motions for extension of the various time limits, and reasonable requests are frequently granted by the clerk of the Panel. The Panel Rules contain detailed requirements for all other motions.

Section 1407 clearly contemplates that multidistrict actions will be handled in the transferee court for pretrial proceedings, and then remanded to the courts in which they were initially filed for trial. In practice, remand seldom occurs. One common reason for not remanding is the settlement or resolution of the case on motion in the transferee court. The transferee court can consider a motion for change of venue under one of the general or special venue statutes, and can essentially "transfer" the cases to itself for trial. Remand is ordered by the Panel, not the transferee court, and any party may move for remand at any time, a motion likely to be denied by the Panel if sought before the transferee court certifies the actions ready for remand and trial.

§ 4.8 JOINDER OF PARTIES

§ 4.8.1 Joinder Generally

There is a wide variety of motions which may be used to effect the joinder of additional parties to an action or which may be necessitated by another party's joinder of parties. Joinder initially may be accomplished in a pleading (see § 3.3.4), but may result in motions if that joinder is improper or if circumstances change.

Parties are commonly added by amending a pleading to name additional parties as adverse parties. This process is governed by Rule 15. Similarly, parties may be added to an action by third-party pleadings, which are discussed in § 3.8.4. These motions are used where a party voluntarily seeks to add parties. Occasionally, however, a party may seek to compel some other party to add a party to the action.

Fed.R.Civ.P. 19, which establishes the criteria for joinder, technically does not authorize the court to order parties joined in the action, although the courts routinely exercise this power by indicating that the action will be dismissed if certain parties are not joined. In fact, because dismissal is viewed as exceptionally harsh, courts are quite likely to explore compelling the joinder rather than dismissing the action. If the court can prevail upon the party to join a party, even on pain of a threatened dismissal, there will not be any appealable, or even ultimately reviewable, decision. This procedure appeals to the pragmatic side of trial judges.

21. Panel Rules 9 & 10, *reprinted in* 120 F.R.D. 251 (1988).

A party may also seek to compel joinder of a proper party who is not initially named. Thus, if an action is commenced by a party not a real party in interest as defined in Rule 17, a defendant may compel the joinder of the proper party plaintiff. The court's interest in compelling joinder in these circumstances is to insure that the defendant will be given res judicata protection if it prevails in the action.

§ 4.8.2 Class Actions

Class actions present a prolific source of motions. The bulk of these motions result from the inherently complex nature of class suits, and not intrinsically from their status as class actions under Fed.R.Civ.P. 23. The most frequent motions in class actions are motions for certification or decertification of classes, and motions to approve settlement. The law of class actions is extensive and is complex. The discussion here is limited to the more common motions, and does not constitute a primer on handling class actions.

Before a case can proceed as a class action it must be certified as an appropriate class action, and the class must be defined. Certification calls for a two-step analysis. First, the court must determine if the four requirements of Fed.R.Civ.P. 23(a) are met. These requirements, known informally as the numerosity, commonality, typicality, and representivity requirements, must each be met. These four requirements amount to threshold requirements: only if they are met does the court reach the question of whether the action may be maintained as a class action. Fed.R.Civ.P. 23(b) establishes the kinds of actions which may be maintained as class suits. The different types of class actions are frequently referred to by the subdivision of Rule 23 under which they are maintained.

Class actions are permitted in order to achieve judicial efficiency in handling claims, particularly claims that are too small individually to be the subject of an action. The class action device is also intended to prevent a multitude of similar civil actions. In any motion relating to class action certification, the parties should direct the argument to these intended benefits.

A motion for class certification is required by Fed.R.Civ.P. 23(c)(1). That rule requires that the motion be brought "as soon as practicable after commencement of an action." Courts expect the motion to be brought at the earliest time consistent with there being no prejudice to any of the parties. The motion for certification is usually brought by the attorneys for the class representatives, but any party may move to have the certification question decided. Many courts have rules which supplement Fed.R.Civ.P. 23, and require a motion for certification to be brought within a fixed period, frequently 90 days, after the action is commenced. The court may also enter a certification order on its own motion.

A motion for certification should ask for certification under a particular subdivision of Rule 23(b), and should be supported by affidavits or other evidence establishing that the four requirements of Rule 23(a) and the requirements of a subdivision of Rule 23(b) have been met. Orders granting or denying certification are not appealable.

If certification is denied, certification may nonetheless be sought at a later date. A certification order can be made expressly conditional upon the happening of future events. For example, the court can conditionally certify a class pending refinement of the definition of the class or the change of representative parties.[1] An even more important change in the certification order will be the entry of an order decertifying the class. If decertification is ordered, the action will be allowed to proceed, with only the class representatives. Decertification may occur where the facts or law have changed following the initial certification order.[2] Modification of the certification order may also be sought by the class representatives. One such motion would be for determination that the conditions for certification under a conditional order have been met, and that certification should be made final. For example, the class representatives may seek to expand the scope of the class.[3]

Rule 23(d) gives the trial court authority to enter a wide variety of orders to control and manage class actions. The rule allows court orders to:

(1) determine the course of the proceedings;

(2) require notice be given in such manner as the court may direct to some or all of the members of any step in the action;

(3) impose conditions on the representative parties or on intervenors;

(4) require that the pleadings be amended to eliminate any matter; and

(5) deal with similar procedural matters.

Motions for orders under the rule may be brought by any party to the action, and may be brought at any time during the pendency of an action. Many of the managerial powers contained in Rule 23(d) are also found in the *Manual for Complex Litigation.*

Class actions are the only civil actions which cannot be settled by the parties without court approval. Fed.R.Civ.P. 23(e) directs that class actions "shall not be dismissed or compromised without the approval of the court." The rule also requires notice of any proposed settlement be given to all members of the class in a manner determined by the court. The rule applies to all actions commenced as class actions, regardless of whether a class has been certified. One of the purposes of this rule is to prevent the class representatives from obtaining settlement on favorable

§ 4.8

1. *Page v. Curtiss-Wright Corp.,* 332 F.Supp. 1060 (D.N.J.1971).

2. *See, e.g., Vuyanich v. Republic National Bank of Dallas,* 723 F.2d 1195 (5th Cir.1984), *rehearing denied* 736 F.2d 160 (5th Cir.1984), *cert. denied* 469 U.S. 1073, 105 S.Ct. 567, 83 L.Ed.2d 507 (1984).

3. *See Coleman v. Block,* 100 F.R.D. 705 (D.N.D.1983) (state-wide class expanded to national class on motion).

terms as to their own claims in return for unjustified abandonment or compromise of the claims on the non-representative class members.

Notice of the proposed settlement as required by the rule serves two important purposes. First, it gives the affected parties an opportunity to object to the settlement, or "opt-out" of the class. This will allow the parties to protect their own rights, and will also provide the court a useful gauge of the fairness of the settlement. Courts are very interested in learning how the class members react to the notice of proposed settlement, and have frequently based their decisions to approve a settlement on the low rate of objections.[4] Second, notice of compromise is necessary to insure that class members do not continue to rely erroneously on the presumption that an action is proceeding on their behalf. This may be significant since the statute of limitations would be tolled on class claims during the pendency of an action, but the tolling would cease when class status is denied or the action abandoned.[5]

§ 4.8.3 Intervention

Intervention is the process by which a non-party may become a party to an action. Motions to intervene are governed by Fed.R.Civ.P. 24, which creates a two-tier classification of motions to intervene: intervention as of right and permissive intervention. As the name makes clear, if the rule authorizes intervention of right the court is virtually required to grant the motion. The court has considerably more discretion in considering motions for permissive intervention. In addition to the standard for granting the motion, however, the distinction in the rule may have important ramifications on related questions of jurisdiction and appealability.

A party may intervene of right in two circumstances under Fed. R.Civ.P. 24(a): (1) if a federal statute grants an unconditional right to intervene, or (2) if the party claims an interest in the subject matter of the litigation and is so situated that the disposition of the action will adversely affect that interest and that interest is not adequately represented by the existing parties.

There are relatively few statutes granting parties an absolute right to intervene. For example, the Attorney General of the United States has an unconditional right to intervene in any action challenging the constitutionality of any Act of Congress if the federal government (or any agency) is not already a party.[6] Intervention of right occurs more frequently in the federal courts under the second section of Fed.R.Civ.P. 24(a). The party seeking to intervene under this section of the rule must establish three things:

4. *See, e.g., Archer v. Cuisinarts, Inc. (In re Cuisinart Food Processor Antitrust Litigation),* 38 Fed.R.Serv.2d 446 (D.Conn. 1983).

5. *See, e.g., American Pipe & Construction Co. v. Utah,* 414 U.S. 538, 94 S.Ct. 756, 38 L.Ed.2d 713 (1974), *rehearing denied* 415 U.S. 952, 94 S.Ct. 1477, 39 L.Ed.2d 568 (1974).

6. 28 U.S.C.A. § 2403. For additional examples, see generally 7A Charles A. Wright & Arthur R. Miller, Federal Practice and Procedure § 1906 (2d ed. 1986).

1. The party claims an interest relating to the property or transaction which is the subject matter of the action;

2. The party is so situated that the disposition of the action may as a practical matter prejudice his or her ability to protect that interest; and

3. The interest is not adequately protected by the present parties to the action.

Actually, although the courts address this as a three-part test, the would-be intervener does not have the burden of showing the third factor. If the first and second factors are established, the burden will be on the party opposing intervention to show adequate representation.

There is no clear standard for determining whether the potential intervenor's "interest" is sufficient under the rule. The United States Supreme Court has refined the question somewhat by stating that the interest must be "a significantly protectable interest."[7] With that guidance from the Supreme Court, the trial courts have taken a wide range of positions regarding intervention of right.[8] Interests which justify intervention of right include property interests, and any interest which would be barred by *res judicata* or collateral estoppel if judgment were rendered. *Res judicata* is not, however, the test to determine if the party's interest will be adversely affected. Less onerous dangers and harms are sufficient to meet the second part of the three-part test.[9] The standards applied to determine if the would-be intervener's interest is adequately represented are an amalgam of practical and legal considerations. If the interests are not represented at all, or are truly adverse (such as would support a cross-claim or counterclaim), representation is clearly not adequate. The danger of collusion is also considered by the court.[10] The court also reviews the energy or diligence of the existing representative.

Courts have wide latitude to determine if permissive intervention is appropriate. Under Fed.R.Civ.P. 24(b) all that is necessary for permissive intervention is a statute giving a conditional right to intervene (any federal statute which mentions intervention but does not grant an absolute right to intervene so as to allow intervention of right fits in this category) or the existence of a single common issue of law or fact. There is no requirement that the common issues predominate as in Fed. R.Civ.P. 23(b)(3), or even that there be common issues as in Fed.R.Civ.P. 23(a)(2). In order to obtain leave for permissive intervention, however, the would-be intervener must convince the court to exercise discretion to permit it. The most important thing considered by the court will be the

7. *See, e.g., Smuck v. Hobson,* 408 F.2d 175, 181 (D.C.Cir.1969).

8. *Donaldson v. United States,* 400 U.S. 517, 531, 91 S.Ct. 534, 542, 27 L.Ed.2d 580 (1971).

9. Try Shepardizing *Donaldson* if you don't believe us. *Or see* 7A Charles A. Wright & Arthur R. Miller, Federal Practice and Procedure § 1908 (2d ed. 1986). Don't, however, try to find that signal in the Bluebook.

10. The various situations are discussed in greater detail in 7A Charles A. Wright & Arthur R. Miller, Federal Practice and Procedure § 1908 (2d ed. 1986).

effect intervention will have on the parties to the action and the prompt resolution of the dispute.[11]

Courts favor the resolution of as many disputes as possible in a single suit. The intervention provisions of Rule 24 reflect the overall philosophy of the rules favoring joinder and consolidation. A party seeking leave to intervene should show to the court that the interests of the courts and all parties will be served by allowing intervention. The court will be performing a balancing of interests on a motion to intervene, and it is necessary to establish that failure to permit intervention will cause hardship to the movant.

A motion to intervene must be served on all parties to the action. The motion should not be granted *ex parte*. The motion must be accompanied by a proposed pleading, and that pleading must state a claim or defense.[12]

The most important procedural requirement for motions to intervene is the requirement of Fed.R.Civ.P. 24(a) & (b) that the motion be "timely." What is "timely" is a matter for the sound discretion of the trial court.[13] The court is likely to apply a test for timeliness which considers the would-be intervener's conduct in not seeking intervention earlier (a la laches) and the prejudice which will occur to the existing parties.

Fed.R.Civ.P. 25 creates the standards for substitution of parties. Although often formally a matter for motion practice, most motions for substitution are either approved upon stipulation of the parties or are summarily granted by the court. Substitution of parties may occur because of death, incompetency, or transfer of interest in the litigation. A change in public officials holding office involved in the litigation may also prompt substitution. In addition, substitution may be appropriate where an action is commenced by a person who is not the real party in interest under Rule 17(a). Similarly, substantive law may permit or require substitution in cases not governed directly by the rules. For example, courts will routinely permit trustees in bankruptcy or receivers to be substituted in actions because of their powers under the substantive law.

Fed.R.Civ.P. 25 expressly provides for substitution in several circumstances:

Death. Fed.R.Civ.P. 25(a) permits substitution in the event of death if the death does not result in the extinguishment of the cause of action. The issue of whether a cause of action survives is a question of substantive law, and is frequently covered by so-called "survival" statutes.[14] Federal causes of action are governed by federal common law. Fed.

11. *See, e.g., Degge v. City of Boulder, Colo.,* 336 F.2d 220 (10th Cir.1964).

12. *Hirshorn v. Mine Safety Appliances Co.,* 186 F.2d 1023 (3d Cir.1951).

13. *See FMC Corp. v. Keizer Equip Co.,* 433 F.2d 654 (6th Cir.1970).

14. *See generally* Note, Survival of Actions Brought Under Federal Statutes, 63 Colum.L.Rev. 290 (1963).

R.Civ.P. 25(a) applies only to natural persons, and not to "death" of a corporation by dissolution.[15]

Rule 25(a) requires that substitution be sought within 90 days after service of a written "suggestion" of death on the record. If no motion for substitution is made within 90 days after the suggestion of death is made upon the record, the court may dismiss the action, but may also excuse the failure to bring the motion within 90 days.[16] Any party to the action may move to have the substitution take place.

Incompetency. Substitution of an incompetent party's representative for the incompetent is authorized by Fed.R.Civ.P. 25(b). Substitution for incompetency follows the same procedures as for substitution upon death of a party, and will also look to the substantive law for the effect incompetency will have on whether an action can continue to be prosecuted by or against the incompetent.

Transfer of Interest in Action. Substitution may also be appropriate where a party transfers its interest in the litigation or the subject matter of the litigation. Fed.R.Civ.P. 25(c) permits substitution to take place in the event of transfer of an interest, but does not require substitution. The rule specifically permits the action prosecuted by or against the original party to proceed and a judgment in the action will have full res judicata effect even as to the unnamed transferee.[17] There is no time limit for seeking substitution under Rule 25(c). The motion may be made by any party to the action, or by the transferee.

Rule 25(c) covers a wide variety of transfers which may justify substitution. Assignment of the cause of action may permit substitution, as may a contractual undertaking to be liable for the obligation sued upon. Sale of property which is the subject of litigation may also make substitution appropriate even if the interest in the litigation was not specifically assigned or assumed.

Other Circumstances Permitting Substitution. Courts have permitted substitution to take place in other situations not specifically addressed by Rule 25. For example, courts routinely permit the substitution of a party by name for a party named as a "John Doe" or "Jane Roe" in the initial pleading. Although this may be done by amendment under Rule 15, the procedure allows for the substitution to take place. Similarly, Rule 17 allows substitution to take place if an action is not commenced by the real party in interest. Rule 17 directs that dismissal not be ordered until the parties have an opportunity to effect ratification, joinder or substitution.

15. *Lawrence Warehouse Co. v. Defense Supplies Corp.,* 168 F.2d 199, 206 (9th Cir. 1948), *vacated on other grounds* 336 U.S. 631, 69 S.Ct. 762, 93 L.Ed. 931 (1949), *rehearing denied* 337 U.S. 921, 69 S.Ct. 1151, 93 L.Ed. 1730 (1949).

16. *See, e.g., Ten v. Svenska Orient Linen,* 87 F.R.D. 551 (S.D.N.Y.1980) (dismissal refused because of hardships on litigants even though delay was inexcusable).

17. *International Rediscount Corp. v. Hartford Accident & Indemnity Co.,* 425 F.Supp. 669 (D.Del.1977).

The motion and notice of hearing must be served upon all the parties to the action in accordance with Fed.R.Civ.P. 5, and upon any non-parties affected by the motion as required under Fed.R.Civ.P. 4. Any party or the affected third person may object to the substitution.

PRACTICE PROBLEMS

1. You represent Tri–Chem. Hot Dog Enterprises has sued Tri–Chem. The complaint includes claims based on violation of Federal and State Deceptive Trade Practices Act, negligence, and products liability. The complaint seeks recovery for the following damages:

> (1) Costs to replace the existing bricks and remodel the exterior, (2) damages for lost business income because customers failed to frequent the restaurant due to the defective exterior, and (3) punitive damages.

Your legal research reveals the applicable state substantive law has not recognized the recovery of lost business income or punitive damages based on the causes of action alleged.

(a) Plan a motion to dismiss these claims for relief.

(b) Draft such a motion and any supporting documents.

(c) You represent HDE. Plan a response to the motion to dismiss.

(d) How will the motion to dismiss be decided?

2. You represent HDE in *Vasquez v. Hot Dog Enterprises* (Case F). Juanita Vasquez has included a cause of action based upon an employment covenant of good faith and fair dealing. Your legal research indicates that the state supreme court in the applicable jurisdiction has not recognized such a cause of action.

(a) Plan a motion to dismiss this cause of action.

(b) Draft such a motion and supporting documents.

(c) You represent Juanita Vasquez. Plan a response to the motion.

(d) How will the motion be decided?

3. You represent a plaintiff injured by bricks falling from the HDE restaurants in Kansas. You plan to serve and file a lawsuit against HDE on behalf of your client.

(a) What courts have subject matter jurisdiction and why?

(b) What jurisdictions have personal jurisdiction over HDE and why?

(c) What factors influence your decisions to sue HDE in a particular jurisdiction?

(d) Assume you plan to sue in Kansas state court. Plan how you would serve process on HDE.

(e) Assume you plan to sue in federal district court in Kansas. Plan how you would serve process on HDE.

(f) Assume you plan to sue HDE in Delaware, in either state or federal court. Plan how you would serve process on HDE.

(g) Assume you plan to sue HDE in Minnesota, in either state or federal court. Plan how you would serve process on HDE.

4. You represent HDE in its potential lawsuit against Tri–Chem.

(a) What courts have subject matter jurisdiction over the action.

(b) What courts have personal jurisdiction over Tri–Chem.

(c) Select a federal court in which to sue Tri–Chem. Plan how you would serve process on Tri–Chem.

(d) Select a state jurisdiction in which to sue Tri–Chem. Plan how you would serve process on Tri–Chem.

5. You represent the Defendant Whirling Dervish Lathes in *Rheinwald v. Whirling Dervish Lathes* (Case I). The plaintiff has sued WDL in Forestland state court based on tort claims for damages in excess of $50,000.

(a) Plan a petition for removal to federal court.

(b) Draft a petition for removal to federal court, including supporting papers.

(c) Do you really want to remove this action? Why or why not?

6. You represent Tri–Chem. HDE has properly sued Tri–Chem in state court in Minnesota based on violations of federal statutes.

(a) Plan a petition for removal of the federal court.

(b) Draft a petition for removal to federal court.

(c) What factors influence your decision whether to remove this case from state to federal court?

7. You represent Shop Format in *Rheinwald v. Whirling Dervish Lathes* (Case I).

(a) Plan a motion to dismiss for lack of personal jurisdiction for any of the potential defendants. Use a local state long-arm statute and Constitution as your guide.

(b) Draft such a motion.

(c) Include all necessary affidavits, exhibits, or other supporting papers in your draft motion.

(d) How will the motion be decided?

8. You represent HDE and the plaintiff injured from falling bricks at HDE's restaurant brings a lawsuit in federal district court in Delaware.

(a) Plan a motion to transfer venue.

(b) Draft such a motion and supporting papers.

(c) How will the motion be decided?

9. You represent HDE, and the plaintiff in Problem 8 instead brings a lawsuit in state court in Delaware.

(a) Plan a motion to dismiss based on forum non conveniens.

(b) Draft such a motion.

(c) How would a motion be decided?

10. You represent Tri–Chem. HDE brings a lawsuit in federal district court in Minnesota for damages to its Kansas restaurant.

(a) Plan a motion to transfer.

(b) Draft such a motion.

(c) How will the motion be decided?

11. You represent Tri–Chem. HDE has brought a lawsuit in state court in Minnesota for damages to its Kansas restaurant.

(a) Plan a motion to dismiss based on forum non conveniens.

(b) Draft such a motion.

(c) How will the motion be decided?

12. You represent HDE. You decide to sue Tri–Chem in federal court based on the violation of a federal statute which provides a private cause of action for fraudulent and deceptive practices occurring in interstate commerce and through the United States mail. You also want to bring claims for relief based upon negligence and products liability.

(a) Plan a federal court complaint including federal and state claims.

(b) Draft such a complaint.

(c) Where is venue appropriate in federal court.

(d) Select a state jurisdiction to sue the defendant. Where is venue appropriate within this jurisdiction?

(e) You represent Tri–Chem. Plan a motion to dismiss the state claims from the federal court complaint. How will the motion be decided?

13. You represent Juanita Vasquez in *Vasquez v. Hot Dog Enterprises*. Your legal research indicates that Ms. Vasquez has causes of action based upon violations of federal civil rights and employment statutes, state employment statutes, and breach of contract.

(a) What factors influence your decision whether to bring this lawsuit in federal court or state court?

(b) Plan a federal court complaint including the state claims.

(c) Where is venue appropriate in federal court.

(d) Select a state jurisdiction to sue the defendant. Where is venue appropriate within this jurisdiction?

(e) You represent HDE. Plan a motion to dismiss the state claims from the federal court action. How will the motion be decided?

14. You represent Tri–Chem. Hot Dog Enterprises properly sues Tri–Chem in federal district court for claims based on federal and state statutory violations, negligence, and products liability.

(a) Tri–Chem has a breach of contract claim against HDE for failure to pay $15,000 for Bond–Mor supplies. Can Tri–Chem assert this claim against HDE in this federal lawsuit? Explain.

(b) Tri–Chem has proper third party claims against the contractor who constructed the HDE restaurant buildings in Kansas which are the subject matter of the federal court litigation. Can Tri–Chem bring this third party complaint against the general contractor in the federal lawsuit? Explain.

(c) Assume HDE sues both Tri–Chem and the architect in the same federal district court lawsuit. The architect has a claim against Tri–Chem for $12,000 in consulting fees for work done for Tri–Chem on the buildings in Kansas. Can the architect assert this claim against Tri–Chem in this federal court lawsuit? Explain.

15. You represent HDE. A sole proprietor who supplied and delivered hot dog buns to HDE at its restaurants in Kansas sues HDE for personal injuries and property damage to her delivery truck caused by falling bricks. Can this sole proprietor properly assert this claim in the federal court action. Explain.

(a) HDE has a claim against the sole proprietor based on the fact that the sole proprietor, when backing up the delivery truck, slammed into the restaurant building, causing damages of $58,000. Can HDE assert this claim against the sole proprietor in the federal court action. Explain.

(b) HDE has a proper third party action against Tri–Chem for defective construction causing the bricks to fall at its Kansas restaurants. Can HDE assert this claim against Tri–Chem in the federal court action? Explain.

(c) Assume the sole proprietor sues HDE and the general contractor. The general contractor has a claim against HDE for failure to pay $54,000 as part of the construction contract amount due. Can the general contractor assert its claim against HDE in a federal lawsuit? Explain.

16. *Buckley v. New York Post Corp.*, 373 F.2d 175 (2d Cir.1967). Buckley, a resident of Connecticut, brought this action in the Superior Court of Fairfield County in that state, against New York Post Corporation, a Delaware corporation having its principal place of business in New York City, to recover damages for libel. He claimed that two editorials appearing in April 1965 had been published maliciously and with reckless disregard of the truth. The *Post,* having removed the action to the United States District Court, sought dismissal on the ground that it was not subject to service of process in Connecticut.

Buckley asserted that two sections of Connecticut's "long-arm" statute . . ., G.S. §§ 33–411(c)(3) and (4), gave the court jurisdiction. The sections subject a foreign corporation to suit in the state "on any cause of action arising" as follows:

> (3) out of the production, manufacture or distribution of goods by such corporation with the reasonable expectation that such goods are to be used or consumed in this state and are so used or consumed . . .; or
>
> (4) out of tortious conduct in this state, whether arising out of repeated activity or single acts. . . .

Answers to interrogatories disclosed that for a two-year period ending May 1, 1965, an average of 1,707 copies of the daily and 2,100 copies of the weekend edition of the *Post* were distributed to persons in Connecticut . . .; that the Post received news dispatches relating to Connecticut from the Associated Press in New York City and from five Connecticut contributors; that it carried advertisements for not more than 15 Connecticut resorts once or twice weekly during the spring and summer, for four Connecticut restaurants once a week, and for three New York stores which indicated a Connecticut branch in some of their advertising. The figures as to papers distributed to persons and corporations in Connecticut did not include copies sold in New York City with the expectation they would be taken into Connecticut by residents returning home from work; the number of these was stated to be "indeterminable."

(a) As counsel for the defendant *New York Post,* how would you proceed?

(b) As counsel for the *Post,* draft a motion to dismiss for lack of personal jurisdiction. What other supporting documents should accompany the motion.

(c) As counsel for the *Post,* outline your memorandum in support of your motion.

(d) As Buckley's counsel, outline your memorandum in opposition.

(e) As judge, decide the motion.

17. *Troutman v. Modlin,* 353 F.2d 382 (8th Cir.1965). On October 26, 1964, James Gooch set out from Arkadelphia, Arkansas, to attend a Democratic Party dinner and rally in Little Rock, Arkansas. Traveling with him, as passengers in his car, were three friends; among them, Jim Modlin. On Interstate Highway 30, near Little Rock, the automobile operated by Mr. Gooch collided with the rear of an automobile operated by James Wilder, as both vehicles were proceeding in an easterly direction in the left-hand (north) traffic lane. Highway 30, at this point, has two lanes for eastbound traffic and, on the other side of a median, two lanes for westbound traffic.

After the collision, the two vehicles stopped in the traffic lane in which the accident had occurred. The occupants of both vehicles alighted, but remained in the vicinity of the cars. Shortly thereafter, a vehicle operated by Clarence Troutman, also traveling in an easterly direction in the left-hand lane, approached the scene of the accident. Jim Modlin, apparently seeking a position of safety, ran from the highway onto the median. Clarence Troutman, instead of turning his vehicle into the right-hand eastbound lane to avoid the accident, swerved to the left and onto the median. His vehicle struck Mr. Modlin, who later died of the injuries he sustained.

Mrs. Modlin, as administratrix of her husband's estate, brought suit against Troutman in the Circuit Court of Clark County, Arkansas, praying for a judgment for Modlin's estate in the amount of $2,000, and for herself, as widow, and for each of their four minor children in the amount of $100,000. Because of the existence of diversity of citizenship between plaintiff and defendant, the action was removed to the United States District Court for the Western District of Arkansas, and tried to a jury.

(a) As counsel for Troutman plan a third-party complaint against Gooch, seeking contribution as provided by Ark.Stat.Ann. §§ 34–1001–34–1009 (1947).

(b) Draft such a complaint.

(c) As Troutman's counsel, plan the removal petition. Can Modlin's estate seek remand after service of the third-party complaint?

(d) Draft such a petition and necessary supporting papers.

(e) As Gooch's counsel, either plan an answer to the third-party complaint or a motion to dismiss it. Upon what grounds would you move?

(f) Draft such an answer or motion.

18. Ronny Rodman and Vin Missich are shopping in Haddod's (located in Mitchell) when they are stopped, frisked, roughed up and detained by a store security guard, Lillian Garcia. When policeman Arnold Schwartz arrives, he detains the boys for another tongue lashing, saying they were lucky to get away with it this time. All the while, there has been no evidence of shoplifting by the boys, who later bring an action for damages for false imprisonment, slander, and assault and battery. Plaintiffs, minors, charged that the security employee of defendant had searched them and falsely accused them of shoplifting.

(a) As counsel for Plaintiffs plan a complaint against Haddod's, the employee, the policeman and the city.

(b) Draft such a complaint.

(c) As the attorney for the city, plan a Rule 12(b)(6) motion and outline the supporting memorandum.

(d) Draft such a motion.

(e) As plaintiffs' counsel, outline the memorandum in opposition.

(f) If plaintiffs brought the suit in state court but alleged a deprivation of federal rights, would the city want to remove the action to federal court? Why?

(g) Draft the removal petition and any necessary supporting papers.

(h) Assume Mitchell Tribune, a local newspaper, reported the incident in a story that stated the boys were guilty of shoplifting. Plaintiffs wish to assert a defamation claim. Plan an amended complaint and move for leave to file it.

(i) Draft such an amended complaint and motion.

(j) The Tribune wishes to remove the amended complaint to federal court. Plan a petition to remove and any necessary supporting papers.

(k) Draft such a petition.

(*l*) As plaintiffs' counsel, plan a motion to remand the action to state court and outline the supporting memorandum. Do you really want to remand? Why?

(m) Draft such a motion.

19. You are counsel to the Mitchell *Enquirer,* a local newspaper, which is served with the following complaint.

Lester Cheese)
v.) Civil Action No.
Mitchell Enquirer)

Plaintiff Lester Cheese is a decent, God-fearing, home-loving, friendly human being.

II.

Defendant Mitchell *Enquirer* is an instrument of the devil, a scandal-sheet concocted to further the nefarious intentions of leftist humanists and sympathizers throughout the U.S. and Canada.

III.

Throughout its sordid history, the *Enquirer* has defamed and derogated Lester Cheese, in the most wanton and willful way, displaying its true pink colors and entitling plaintiff to punitive damages in an amount of $1 million as well as an apology from the spineless worm who owns the *Enquirer.*

Wherefore, plaintiff demands a judgment of $1,000,000.

(a) How do you respond to this complaint? (Remember, civil commitment isn't as easy as it used to be.)

(b) Draft a motion attacking both the specificity of the complaint and moving to strike or dismiss for any other reasons you can think of. If Cheese had made a breach of contract claim, could you attack the specificity?

20. Originally, Martha Giacone in *Giacone v. City of Mitchell* (Case C) sued the water company only for breach of contract. Now, she has retained you as her attorney.

(a) Plan an amended complaint and a motion to amend the complaint to assert any additional cause of action available to your client.

(b) Draft such an amended complaint and motion.

(c) Can you plead anything that will allow recovery of attorney's fees? What?

(d) Outline a memorandum in opposition to the amended complaint.

21. You represent Phoenix Airlines headquartered in Mitchell. Walter Clark is an airplane broker once engaged by Phoenix to sell a large used airplane from the Phoenix fleet. After six months, Clark had not succeeded and Phoenix sells the plane through another broker. Clark, who thought he had an exclusive contract, is furious and sues for breach in federal court in Mitchell. Discovery ensues. Clark, a resident of Switzerland, refuses to disclose certain business data, claiming the secrecy protections of the Swiss Penal Code. The federal court rejects his claim and orders him to disclose the data. Fed up with American justice, Clark takes a new tack. He obtains a writ of attachment initiated in an action in Honduras and uses the Honduras writ as the basis for obtaining a similar writ in Costa Rica. When the next Phoenix flight hits Costa Rica, Clark hits it with his writ and ten armed guards, three of whom are pilots, fly the craft to Cuba. Fortunately for Phoenix, Castro wants no part of an operator like Clark and arranges for the plane's return and Clark's quick trip to Switzerland.

(a) As counsel for Phoenix, plan a counterclaim against Clark in the still pending federal action in Mitchell.

(b) Draft such a counterclaim.

(c) Plan a motion for leave to serve the supplemental counterclaim and outline the memorandum in support.

(d) Draft such a motion.

(e) Clark, no quitter, now sues Phoenix in Switzerland. Plan a motion to dismiss or stay the Swiss suit on the basis of the U.S. action.

(f) Draft such a motion.

22. *J.M. Blythe Motor Lines Corp. v. Blalock,* 310 F.2d 77 (5th Cir.1962). The appellee, Jean Blanchette Blalock, invoking federal jurisdiction on the ground of diversity of citizenship, brought an action against J.M. Blythe Motor Lines Corporation and Richard B. Kingery claiming damages for personal injuries resulting from a highway collision between an automobile in which she was a passenger and a truck of the defendant corporation negligently operated by its employee Kingery. The complaint fixed the place of the collision on Pelham Parkway in the City and State of New York, and fixed the time of the collision as December 4, 1956. The complaint was filed on November 29, 1960.

The Corporation and Kingery answered, denying negligence and asserting that the collision was caused by the negligence of the driver of the car in which she was a passenger. The answer also asserted:

"That as and for a further additional and affirmative defense, the Defendants state the above cause is regulated by the Statute of Limitations as set out in Section 49 of the New York Practices Act which statute limits actions to three (3) years for personal injuries arising out of negligence and that it affirmatively appears from the pleadings herein that the within accident occurred more than three (3) years last past since the filing of the instant suit."

(a) As defense counsel, plan a motion for judgment on the pleadings and outline the arguments for the supporting memorandum.

(b) Draft such a motion.

(c) As plaintiff's counsel, how do you get out of this pickle? Plan the appropriate motion, necessary supporting papers, and memorandum outline to do it. Remember, actions that would support suspension or disbarment are not responsive to the question.

(d) Draft such a motion and papers.

(e) As judge, decide the motions.

23. Assume that this is the complaint filed by plaintiffs in *Mitchell Computer Club v. Rainbow Computer* (Case E).

Mitchell Computer Club)
v.) Civil File No.
Rainbow Computer Company)

The Rainbow Computer Company lied to the Mitchell Computer Club in not providing new software programs to the Club.

II.

Rainbow is clearly trying to defraud the Club, entitling the Club members to cancel their deal with Rainbow and get their money spent to date back plus costs.

Wherefore, Plaintiff seeks a judgment in excess of $50,000.

(a) Plan a motion on behalf of defendant Rainbow Computer Company to dismiss the complaint for failure to plead fraud with particularity. Will you win or lose on this issue?

(b) Draft such a motion.

(c) What else is wrong with the above complaint? List the possible (and at least arguably) legitimate motions you can make attacking the complaint.

(d) Draft one of the motions, a form order accompanying the motion and outline the arguments for a memorandum of law in support of the motion.

24. In *Luger v. Shade* (Case H), Gotbucks commences an action in Gothamtown seeking a declaratory judgment that he is

the true and correct owner of the condo in question. The defendants are Develco, Shade, and the Lugers.

(a) As counsel for the Lugers, what do you want to do in response? List all potential (but not too flaky) responses before reaching a decision.

(b) As Lugers' counsel, draft a motion to dismiss the Gothamtown action for a lack of personal jurisdiction and outline the memorandum in support.

(c) As counsel for Shade and Develco, do you like or loathe Gotbucks' Gothamtown action? What can you do in response? What should you do in response?

(d) As Lugers' counsel, plan a counterclaim against Gotbucks. What potential counterclaims do you legitimately have? Does it depend on what facts Gotbucks knew and when? If so, can you properly plead a counterclaim against Gotbucks at this time? Which one?

25. In *Giacone v. City of Mitchell* (Case D), there is now another twist. After the suit is filed, the water department agrees to come out and reconnect the water during the pendency of the litigation if Giacone agrees not to seek interim equitable relief. The main water valve is located on the exterior cinder block basement wall. While attempting to turn on the valve the service person negligently breaks the water pipe resulting in structural damage to the wall and causing water to flood Giacone's basement. The damage to her personal property in the basement amounted to $2,000 and the damage to her house amounted to $3,000.

(a) As counsel for Giacone, plan a supplemental complaint.

(b) Draft such a complaint.

(c) As counsel for Plaintiff Giacone, draft a motion for leave to file the supplemental complaint and outline the supporting arguments.

(d) Assume the service person was temporarily hired by the water department from Benito's Temporaries. As counsel for the City, plan a third-party complaint against Benito's.

(e) Draft such a complaint.

(f) As counsel for the city, draft a motion for leave to file the third-party complaint and outline the arguments in support.

26. In *Luger v. Shade* (Case H), you represent Gotbucks.

(a) Draft a cross-claim against the co-defendants.

(b) Assume that the eve of trial is near. Draft a motion to amend Gotbucks' answer to assert the cross-claim. Outline the supporting memorandum.

(c) Before you run to court, what should you consider doing? Draft something that does it.

(d) As counsel for Develco, draft a motion to dismiss the Gotbucks cross-claim. Outline the supporting memorandum.

27. Structural Products Institute (SPI) is a national trade association for masonry and other construction companies. In the 1980's, SPI sought to revive a declining industry by promoting research to develop the compound allowing for the construction of prefabricated brick panels in walls without reinforcement. Subsequently, Tri–Chem developed Bond–Mor.

Tri–Chem participated in the affairs of SPI in an attempt to promote its product through this national trade association. Tri–Chem entered into a contract with SPI to establish intensive field development projects regarding the use of Bond–Mor. In cooperation with architects, engineers, and contractors, Tri–Chem paid SPI $50,000 to defer SPI's expenses.

Tri–Chem further participated in the affairs of SPI, and SPI promoted Tri–Chem products through articles and technical notes published in construction industry trade journals. Employees of SPI suggested to architects, engineers, and contractors that Bond–Mor be used in their construction projects.

Hot Dog Enterprises sues Tri–Chem for violation of federal and state laws, negligence, and product liability. You represent Structural Products Institute. SPI has an interest in intervening in the lawsuit to represent its interests and the interests of other members in the trade association.

(a) Plan a motion in the action. Is it of right or permissive?

(b) Outline the memorandum in support.

(c) Draft a motion.

(d) Draft a proposed order.

(e) Will the motion be granted?

28. Assume in *Luger v. Shade* (Case H) that Gary Gotbucks has not been named as a defendant. He contacts you and seeks to intervene.

(a) Plan a motion to intervene.

(b) Draft the motion and proposed order. What is the basis for and theory of Gotbucks' intervention?

(c) Outline a memorandum in support.

(d) As his lawyer, will you advise him to go through with the action? What other means of protecting his interest might there be?

29. Assume the court permits Gotbucks to intervene in *Luger v. Shade* (Case J).

(a) Plan his responsive pleading. What claims does he have to assert? Assume Luger seeks specific performance of the townhouse sale.

(b) Draft an appropriate responsive pleading.

*

PART THREE
DISCOVERY PRACTICE

*

CHAPTER 5
THE SCOPE

Ask and you shall receive. Seek and you shall find.

Matthew 7:7

§ 5.1 PURPOSES OF DISCOVERY

Discovery rules and procedures serve many functions in the litigation process, including:

- Supplementation of pleadings.
- Early and thorough disclosure of information by all sides.
- Some equalizing of the investigative resources of both sides without allowing one side to take undue advantage of the other.
- Limited exploration into the adversary's camp to discover its perceptions of the facts and case.
- Documentation of testimony and preservation of documents.
- Isolation of issues and determination of material and undisputed facts.
- Promotion of negotiated settlements.
- Fostering of trial verdicts based upon accurate presentations and informal arguments, not on surmise and surprise.
- Providing an economical method of resolving disputes.

All of these functions are essential to the maintenance of our current litigation system. It is fair to ask which came first—the purposes or the system. The answer, of course, is both, because neither could exist without the other. Discovery is an integral part of the litigation process and the acceptance of that view will make this chapter and this book more understandable and useful. For many lawyers discovery merely gets in the way of going to trial, and that attitude accounts for much of the misuse of discovery devices. Discovery for other lawyers seems to be the best way to avoid or delay going to trial, and that attitude, too, accounts for its share of the abuse of discovery procedures. But for most lawyers, discovery constitutes an effective, efficient, and economical means of representing a client involved in litigation, a perspective which in itself fosters such a system.

Discovery allows an attorney to know as much about a case, with limitations, as the opposing attorney knows. The facts, opinions, conclusions, theories, and even trial preparation materials in some cases are there for the asking. Discovery permits a lawyer to review and probe the good, the bad, and the indifferent from the safety of the office before settlement, and long before trial. Just as trial lawyers develop their own systems of trial notebooks, which they use to present and argue a case at trial, so also discovery provides attorneys with a system to develop a case to present and argue during negotiations. A thorough use of discovery leaves few reasons for two reasonable attorneys seeking to satisfy their clients' best interests to decide to go to trial instead of negotiating a settlement.

Amendments to the Federal Rules of Civil Procedure, effective on December 1, 1993, have dramatically changed the nature and purpose of discovery. Parties in districts which follow the new rules must now disclose information in addition to engaging in discovery. We call this new process "disclovery."

The primary purpose of the revised discovery rules is to require parties to disclose information to other parties without any discovery request. This disclosure is to provide opposing parties with information, witnesses, facts, and expert opinions which relate to specifically alleged facts. These new rules will promote and accelerate the early exchange of supportive and adverse information between parties, will eliminate the need for some discovery requests, and will accelerate settlements because parties will be able to evaluate cases more quickly. Or so it is hoped.

The present formalized discovery system promotes the use of informal discovery exchanges by lawyers. The very existence of the rules encourages lawyers to use more efficient and economical means to exchange information. Bilateral trading of documents, cooperative bartering of information, mutual alteration of procedures, and informal enforcement of the rules, all have come about because the discovery rule procedures are somewhat more costly, more formal, and less efficient.

Newton discovered long ago, in another context, that every advantage has a disadvantage. So also with discovery. It can be expensive. It may cause delay. It may force the other side to prepare a case better. It may prompt the other side to react with additional discovery, and it can be abused. A danger lurks in simply relying on the rules and failing to apply the theories and rationales supporting the particular rule. An understanding and application of the reasons for the rule is the best way of determining how the rule should be interpreted and applied. The rules should not be applied automatically or mechanically; they require the understanding of a legal philosopher and the application of a legal artist. A practitioner has to be both.

§ 5.2 SCOPE OF DISCOVERY

Rule 26 defines the boundaries of what is and what is not discoverable. Subsections of Rule 26 define the limits and impose restrictions on the scope of discovery relating to:

1.	Required Initial Disclosures	26(a)(1)
2.	Expert Testimony Disclosures	26(a)(2)
3.	Pretrial Disclosures	26(a)(3)
4.	Form of Disclosures	26(a)(4)
5.	Methods to Discover Additional Information	26(a)(5)
6.	Relevancy	26(b)(1)
7.	Discovery Limitations	26(b)(2)
8.	Privilege	26(b)(3)
9.	Trial Preparation Materials	26(b)(3)
10.	Attorney Mental Impressions	26(b)(3)
11.	Witness Statements	26(b)(3)
12.	Expert Opinions	26(b)(4)
13.	Privilege/Trial Preparation Claims	26(b)(5)
14.	Protective Orders	26(c)
15.	Sequence and Timing of Discovery	26(d)
16.	Supplementation of Responses	26(e)
17.	Discovery Conference and Planning	26(f)
18.	Signing of Discovery Requests and Responses	26(g)
19.	The LSAT score of the opposing lawyer	

This chapter explores these provisions of Rule 26, some other provisions which involve procedural matters, and some discovery strategies relating to the scope of disclosure and discovery.

§ 5.2.1 Timing and Sequence of Discovery

Federal Rule 26(d) explicitly states that formal discovery—depositions, interrogatories, document production requests, requests for admissions—may not commence until the parties have met and conferred to discuss discovery and other issues. Section 5.3.8 explains the timing of this conference. This rule further provides that discovery may be accelerated by agreement of the parties or a court order if circumstances support early discovery. Rule 26(d) also states that methods of discovery may be used in any sequence and the use of one method by a party does not delay the use of another method by another party.

§ 5.3 METHODS OF DISCOVERY

The federal rules of civil procedure and similar state rules initially require parties to affirmatively disclose information to each other without the need for any discovery request. The scope and type of information to be disclosed is explained in § 5.3.1. Federal and all state jurisdictions permit five major discovery devices:

1. Depositions upon oral examinations or written questions;
2. Written interrogatories;
3. Production of documents or things or permission to enter upon land or other property, for inspection and other purposes;
4. Physical and mental examinations;
5. Requests for admissions.

Although these devices will be explained in detail in separate chapters, a summary description of each will provide a better understanding of the applications of Rule 26.

Depositions. A deposition is a sworn statement made by a witness before a notary or other officer authorized to administer oaths. The deponent may be a party or any person who has information. The deposition is usually conducted orally, the attorney who requested the deposition typically examining and cross-examining the deponent, with the opposing attorney in attendance. The questions and answers are usually transcribed and later prepared in transcript form. A deposition may be conducted using written questions submitted by the requesting attorney and read to the deponent by the officer.

Written Interrogatories. Interrogatories are written questions submitted to a party to be answered in writing under oath. This discovery device is particularly suitable for information involving specific factual data or witness and document information.

Production of Documents. A party may require another party to provide documents and tangible things for inspection and copying or to permit entry onto land or access to other property for inspection, testing, or sampling. A party may be able to obtain the same access to documents, things, and land from a non-party through a subpoena duces tecum under Rule 45.

Physical and Mental Examinations. A party may be able to obtain a physical or mental examination of another party if the condition of that person is in controversy and if there exists good cause for an examination. These types of examinations usually occur in personal injury litigation.

Requests for Admissions. Responses to requests for admissions determine the truth of certain matters and the genuineness of documents. This device not only discovers information, but also narrows the disputed issues for trial.

The provisions of Rule 26 relating to the scope of discovery apply, with some exceptions, with equal force to all five of these devices. The extent of what is and what is not discoverable is virtually the same, regardless of the device used to obtain the information. Each device has some inherent limitations that affect the practical scope of discovery, but what cannot be obtained through one discovery device can usually be obtained through another.

§ 5.3.1 Disclosure Information

Federal Rule 26 now requires three types of information to be affirmatively disclosed by a party without the need for a discovery request from an opposing party:

1. Rule 26(a)(1) requires initial disclosures of specific information regarding witnesses, documents, damages, and insurance agreements. The remainder of this section explains these disclosures.

2. Rule 26(a)(2) imposes on parties the duty to disclose information regarding expert testimony and expert reports sufficiently in advance of the trial to provide opposing parties a reasonable opportunity to prepare for trial based upon this expert testimony. Section 5.8.3 explains this duty to disclose and its timing in detail.

3. Rule 26(a)(3) imposes on parties an additional duty to disclose evidence that may be offered at trial. Section 5.11.2 explains these pretrial disclosures and their timing in detail.

All these disclosures required by Rule 26(a) must be in writing, signed, served, and properly filed with the court. Rule 26(a)(4) imposes these requirements to assure disclosures are made in accordance with the rules.

§ 5.3.2 Initial Disclosure

New Rule 26(a) requires early disclosure of four types of basic information that customarily have been obtained through formal discovery requests. This rule eliminates the need for certain discovery requests and forces parties to exchange the required information.

Rule 26(a)(1) requires the following specific disclosures "relevant to disputed facts alleged with particularity in the pleadings":

> (A) The identity (name, address, and telephone) of each person likely to have discoverable relevant information and the identification of the subject of the information.
>
> (B) A copy of or description of documents, data compilations, and tangible things that are relevant.

§ 5.3.3 Disclosure of Individuals

Rule 26 (a)(1)(A) requires the disclosure of the names of all witnesses and all persons who have knowledge of relevant information, including individuals who may not testify at trial. All persons with such information should be disclosed, whether or not their testimony will be supportive of the position of the disclosing party. As officers of the court, counsel are expected to disclose the identity of those persons who may be used by them as witnesses or who, if their potential testimony were known, might reasonably be expected to be deposed or called as a witness by any of the other parties. The purpose of requiring the disclosure of the subjects known by a person is to assist the other parties in determining whether a deposition is necessary.

§ 5.3.4 Disclosure of Documents

Rule 26(a)(1)(B) requires the disclosure of all documents, computer data, and things in the possession, custody, or control of a party. This rule replaces the need for a party to submit routine document production requests to the other party. The description of the documents, data, and things should be sufficient to allow opposing parties to make an informed decision concerning which documents might need to be examined, and to frame their document requests in a manner likely to avoid disputes resulting from the wording of the request. All potentially relevant documents, including supportive and non-supportive documents must be disclosed.

This rule does not require the production of documents, but only requires a disclosure of their identity and description. A party may prefer to provide copies of the documents rather than describe them, and the rule permits a party to do so. The rule allows a disclosing party to choose between disclosing the existence of the documents and providing a copy. If a disclosing party choose only to identify their existence and not to provide copies, the other party may by a Rule 34 request require the disclosing party to produce the documents in accord with Rule 34.

Disclosing parties are very likely to want to provide copies of supporting documents or other documents that may accelerate the settlement process. Similarly, a disclosing party may decide to disclose only the identity of documents, which may contain adverse information, without providing copies.

A party receiving a Rule 26(a)(1) disclosure will and should routinely serve a Rule 34 request for production of all documents not provided. The requesting party may include in the Rule 34 request the description of the documents provided by the disclosing party. This practice will eliminate squabbles over Rule 34 definitions and description requests.

The rule protects the disclosing party by preserving defenses to the disclosed documents. A party disclosing the existence of documents under Rule 26(a)(1)(B) does not waive its right to object to the production of those documents pursuant to a Rule 34 request on the basis of privilege, work product, relevancy, or any other applicable objection. This preservation will reduce the chances that a disclosing party will balk at disclosing the existence of documents which it claims are privileged or otherwise protected.

§ 5.3.5 Disputed Facts Alleged With Particularity

Rule 26(a)(1)(A) and (B) limit disclosures to information that is "relevant to disputed facts alleged with particularity in the pleadings." This phrase is likely to become infamous. Some of the words in this phrase are brand new to the world of litigation, and some of the terms have a current meaning and usage. Federal Rule of Procedure 9 uses the phrase "with particularity" referring to allegations of fraud and related claims.

There appear to be three primary factors which will determine whether this phrase will prompt meaningful disclosures or will result in satellite litigation regarding Rule 26 disclosures:

1. *How a party pleads its case.* It appears that if a party includes allegations "with particularity," disclosures must be made about these allegations. It appears that if a party uses broad, vague, and conclusory allegations, disclosures need not be made about these allegations. A party who does not want to disclose information will be inclined to use such notice pleading allegations.

A party who prefers to disclose supporting information of documents may allege these facts "with particularity." This type of allegation would trigger disclosure requirements. A potential discovery problem in stating allegations with particularity may arise if a party fails to disclose properly in accord with new Rule 26(a). Sanctions may be imposed upon a party who fails to comply with the required disclosure provisions. An attorney may choose to avoid the potential imposition of sanctions by using notice pleading and informally disclosing the information or documents to the other parties.

Other words in the new phrase may also create new problems. For example, the word "facts." Is not always easy to distinguish between a fact and an opinion. While the rules of evidence attempt to do so, the rules of civil procedure do not. For another example, the word "disputed" may also create its own disputes. In some cases, it will be ambiguous whether a fact is disputed at the time the pleading is drafted. This uncertainty may continue to exist even after the attorneys attempt to discuss what issues are in dispute.

2. *The meeting of the parties.* Rule 26(f) requires that the parties meet to discuss the nature and basis of the claims and defenses, to make or arrange for Rule 26(a)(1) disclosures, to discuss the possibility of a prompt settlement or other resolution of the case, and to develop a proposed discovery plan. The meeting may be in person, or by telephone, or by other electronic transmission. It is during this meeting that the application of this phrase to the pleadings should be discussed by the parties, or more accurately, by the attorneys for the parties. It may be that this discussion will resolve problems regarding the application of this phrase. It is likely, that in some cases the attorneys will be unable to agree on what is required to be disclosed. Whether these meetings will result in agreements, or whether these get togethers will result in conflagrations will be up, in part, to the attorneys.

3. *Common sense.* Attorneys need to and should use common sense in interpreting this phrase. It may be that a lack of common sense has caused many of the current discovery problems. The develop-

ment of the appropriate level of common sense begins long before law school.

§ 5.3.6 *Damages*

Rule 26(a)(1)(c) also requires a party to initially disclose information about damages: "A disclosing party who seeks recovery for damages must disclose: the computation of the damages and all documents or other evidentiary material on which the computation is based, including materials relating to the nature and extent of the injury suffered but excluding documents or other evidentiary materials which are privileged or otherwise protected from disclosure." This rule imposes an initial burden on a plaintiff, or on a counter-claimant, who seeks damages to disclose the specific damages, how the damages were computed, and documents and materials which support the computation.

This rule operates as the equivalent of a Rule 33 Interrogatory and a Rule 34 request for production of documents regarding damages. The rule restricts the disclosure of documents to documents that are discoverable and that are not privileged or protected by work product or other reasons and to those that are reasonable available to a party. Subdivision (c) also requires the disclosing party to make available "for inspection or copying as under Rule 34 the documents or material to be produced." A disclosing party may choose to provide a copy of the documents and materials or to permit the other parties to inspect and copy the original computation documents and materials.

§ 5.3.7 *Insurance Agreements*

Rule 26(a)(1)(D) requires a disclosing party to provide "any insurance agreement" which "may be liable to satisfy part or all of a judgment" or which may "indemnify or reimburse for payments made to satisfy the judgment." Section 5.6 explains this rule.

§ 5.3.8 *Timing of Initial Disclosures*

Rule 26(a)(1) requires that the initial disclosures, unless otherwise stipulated or ordered by the court, shall be made within 10 days after the parties meet in accord with Rule 26(f). This meeting usually occurs early in a case.

The time of the meeting will generally be left to the parties as long as the meeting is held at least 14 days before a scheduling conference is held or before a scheduling order is due under Federal Rule 16(b). In cases in which no scheduling conference is held, the meeting must ordinarily be held within 75 days after the defendant has first appeared in the case, requiring initial disclosures to be made 85 days after the appearance of a defendant. It will often be useful, particularly if the complaint includes broad claims for the parties to have their Rule 26(f) meeting early in the case, perhaps before the defendant has answered the complaint or had time to conduct a full investigation.

§ 5.3.9 Scope of Preliminary Investigation

Rule 26(a)(1) explains what information should and can be disclosed. The rule provides: "A party shall make its initial disclosures based upon the information then reasonably available to it and is not excused from making its disclosure because it is not fully completed its investigation of the case or because it challenges the sufficiency of another party's disclosures or because another party has not made its disclosures." This provision of the rule requires a party to complete its investigation of the case before it makes disclosures and eliminates two potential excuses for not disclosing information: that the party has not made this disclosure or that it has not made sufficient disclosures. What is "reasonably available" to a party will need to be interpreted by courts as judges determine how to apply the principles, the spirit, and the letter of new Rule 26.

A party must make a reasonable inquiry into the facts of the case. What is a reasonable investigation and what is information reasonably available to a party will depend upon a number of factors. The investigation will vary based upon the following factors: (1) the complexity of the issues, (2) the location, number, and availability of witnesses and documents, (3) any prior working relationships between the attorney and the client, and (4) how long the party has to conduct an investigation. A party is not excused from the duty of disclosure merely because an investigation remains incomplete. A party must make initial disclosure based on the pleadings and information reasonably available at the time. Supplemental information obtained as the investigation continues should be supplemented in accord with Rule 26(e).

§ 5.3.10 Modifications

The new disclosure provisions of Federal Rule 26 can be varied by stipulation between the parties, by court order relating to a specific case, by standing judicial order relating to certain types of cases, or by local rule. A court may require parties to disclose additional information without a discovery request, may modify the information to be disclosed, or may exempt all or particular types of cases from disclosure requirements. A significant number of the federal district courts have exempted some or all cases from the disclosure rules.

It is especially important for attorneys to realize that they can mutually agree to modify any or all of the disclosure requirements in a particular case. This situation requires the agreement of all the parties and their attorneys, which requirement may reduce its availability in many cases. Nonetheless, if the disclosure rules are or appear to be inappropriate for a particular case, the attorneys can create their own set of rules to apply.

§ 5.4 RELEVANCY: WHAT IS DISCOVERABLE

Rule 26(b)(1) explains what is discoverable:

> *In General.* Parties may obtain discovery regarding any matter, not privileged, which is relevant to the subject matter involved in the pending action, whether it relates to the claim or defense of the party seeking discovery or to the claim or defense of any other party, including the existence, description, nature, custody, condition and location of any books, documents, or other tangible things and the identity and location of persons having knowledge of any discoverable matter. It is not ground for objection that the information sought will be inadmissible at the trial if the information sought appears reasonably calculated to lead to the discovery of admissible evidence.

This rule and interpretive case law provide vast leeway to discover nearly everything there is to know about a case. Granting or denying discovery is a matter within the broad discretion of the trial court.[1] The party who opposes discovery carries a "heavy burden" of showing why discovery should be disallowed.[2] We all know that discovery may constitute a "fishing expedition." [3] What we need to know is what kind and how many fish we can catch, so we need to explain the four specific standards which define the scope of discoverable information.

1. *Non-privileged Matter Relevant to the Subject Matter Involved in the Pending Action.* Courts have construed this clause liberally,[4] declaring that this rule envisions generally unrestricted access to sources of information.[5] The term *subject matter* relates to any matter in a case; it does not limit itself to the merits of a case, nor does it distinguish between substantive concerns and procedural matters.[6] Questions about liability and damages, jurisdiction and venue, have been held to be clearly discoverable.[7]

Court descriptions have further broadened the boundaries of relevancy. The term *relevant* encompasses any matter "that bears on or that reasonably could lead to other matter that could bear on any issue that is or may be in the case." [8] Requests for discovery should be considered relevant if there is any possibility that information sought may be relevant to the subject matter of the action.[9]

§ 5.4

1. *See, e.g., Pettway v. American Cast Iron Pipe Co.,* 576 F.2d 1157 (5th Cir.1978), *cert. denied* 439 U.S. 1115, 99 S.Ct. 1020, 59 L.Ed.2d 74 (1979), *appeal after remand* 721 F.2d 315 (11th Cir.1983), *cert. denied* 467 U.S. 1243, 104 S.Ct. 3515, 82 L.Ed.2d 824 (1984).

2. *See Blankenship v. Hearst Corp.,* 519 F.2d 418, 429 (9th Cir.1975).

3. *Hickman v. Taylor,* 329 U.S. 495, 507, 67 S.Ct. 385, 91 L.Ed. 451 (1947).

4. *Mitsui & Co. (U.S.A.) Inc. v. Puerto Rico Water Resources Authority,* 79 F.R.D. 72, 80 (D.Puerto Rico 1978).

5. *Heathman v. United States District Court for Central District Cal.,* 503 F.2d 1032, 1035 (9th Cir.1974).

6. 4 Moore's Federal Practice ¶ 26.56[1], at 26–117 (2d ed. 1989) (hereinafter cited as Moore's Federal Practice).

7. *See Sinclair Refining Co. v. Jenkins Petroleum Process Co.,* 289 U.S. 689, 691–696, 53 S.Ct. 736, 77 L.Ed. 1449 (1933).

8. *Oppenheimer Fund, Inc. v. Sanders,* 437 U.S. 340, 351, 98 S.Ct. 2380, 2389, 57 L.Ed.2d 253 (1978).

9. *Detweiler Brothers, Inc. v. John Graham & Co.,* 412 F.Supp. 416, 422 (E.D.Wash.1976), *citing* 8 C. Wright & A. Miller, Federal Practice and Procedure § 2008, at 47 (1970 & Supp. 1991).

Opinions, contentions, and conclusions have also been declared discoverable under related rules. Rule 33(b) specifically provides that an interrogatory will not be objectionable merely because a question involves an opinion or contention; Rule 36 permits requests for admissions that involve opinions of fact. The "matter" discoverable under Rule 26 includes opinion and conclusion questions. Any discovery device may be used to obtain such information.[10]

The discovery standard of relevancy is not limited by the evidentiary standard of relevancy.[11] It is much broader in scope and encompasses any information that relates to the subject matter of a case regardless of its admissibility at trial.[12] This includes information exclusively within the knowledge or possession of the other side and information already known to the discovering party,[13] as well as information equally available to the interrogator as a matter of public record.[14] This latter type of request for known information is consistent with the discovery theory that knowing what others know and what they know that others know is useful and appropriate information. This type of information has been held to be discoverable not because it necessarily produces new information but because it permits a party to verify facts for use as admission requests, an equally valid discovery purpose.[15]

It is difficult to define relevancy systematically because the variety of legal and factual settings provide an infinite number of questions relating to it. Numerous examples that help define the line between the relevant and the irrelevant appear in other publications.[16]

Limits are placed on the use of discovery. The Supreme Court recently reminded the trial courts to "not neglect their power to restrict discovery where" appropriate.[17] The rules do not permit a party "to roam in shadow zones of relevancy and to explore matter which does not presently appear germane on the theory that it might conceivably become so." [18] Questions regarding the plaintiff's motives in instituting a lawsuit and in fee arrangements will usually be held irrelevant, but not in all cases.[19] Questions concerning discussions between the plaintiff and the plaintiff's attorney prior to the filing of the complaint, the manner in which plaintiffs were solicited, fee arrangements, and other information concerning the institution of the action have been denied,

10. 4 Moore's Federal Practice ¶ 26.-56[3], at 26–168 (2d ed. 1984).

11. Fed.R.Civ.P. 26(b), Notes of Advisory Comm.—1946 Amendments, reprinted in 28 U.S.C.A. § 153.

12. *Freeman v. Seligson,* 405 F.2d 1326, 1335 (D.C.Cir.1968).

13. *See* 8 C. Wright & A. Miller, Federal Practice and Procedure § 2014, at 110–111 (1970 and Supp. 1991).

14. *Petruska v. Johns–Manville,* 83 F.R.D. 32, 35 (E.D.Pa.1979).

15. *Wilmington Country Club v. Horwath & Horwath,* 46 F.R.D. 65, 66 (E.D.Pa. 1969).

16. *See* 4 Moore's Federal Practice ¶ 26.56[1], at 26–128 (2d ed. 1984).

17. *Herbert v. Lando,* 441 U.S. 153, 177, 99 S.Ct. 1635, 1649, 60 L.Ed.2d 115 (1979).

18. *In re Surety Association of America,* 388 F.2d 412, 414 (2d Cir.1967), *quoting Broadway & Ninety–Sixth Street Realty Co. v. Loew's, Inc.,* 21 F.R.D. 347, 352 (S.D.N.Y. 1958).

19. *See* 4 Moore's Federal Practice ¶ 26.52[2], at 26–157 to –160 (2d ed. 1984).

because it was "difficult to see how an inquiry into the circumstances surrounding the instigation of the action could affect the substance of the claim." [20]

Courts balance the competing interests of parties in deciding whether to order disclosure of certain information. The interests of one party may outweigh the discovery interests of another party, especially when the use of the discoverable information serves only a limited purpose. One court has held that a discovery request for information for use as possible impeachment material at trial does not outweigh another party's interest in preserving the privacy of certain information.[21]

But no single definition delineates the exact boundaries of discovery. We seem to be left with analogies as the final determinant:

> The exactitude of discovery, the lawyer's tool for factfinding, properly lies somewhere between the acuity of the surgeon's scalpel and the carpenter's hammer. Ideally, the lawyer probes for facts with the precision and delicacy of a cardiologist incising the aorta to receive a by-pass vehicle. Realistically, the lawyer's factfinding search shares a closer propinquity with the carpenter's trade and pounds much more bluntly.[22]

2. *Matters Relating to the Claim or Defense of Any Party.* The range of subject matter extends to claims and defenses asserted by any party, including the party seeking discovery. Controverted issues involving jurisdictional matters are an appropriate area for discovery.[23] Damage claims as well as liability issues are discoverable.[24] The subject matter of "potential" issues that may be available to a party may also be discoverable.[25] Matters supporting additional claims or defenses may be uncovered through discovery, and a party may seek information to ferret out these possible claims or defenses.

Information involving "similar" transactions may also be discoverable.[26] The practices or policies of a party similar to the acts or conduct involved in the pending claims or defenses may be discoverable if they show some habit or pattern. The time span of the discoverable subject matter of a case may be extended to include events after the litigation began. A case involving continuing claims or defenses will make such post-complaint matter relevant. Discovery may also be available regarding matters involved in motions to reopen or vacate a judgment under

20. *Foremost Promotions, Inc. v. Pabst Brewing Co.,* 15 F.R.D. 128, 130 (N.D.Ill. 1953).

21. *Williams v. Thomas Jefferson University,* 343 F.Supp. 1131, 1132 (E.D.Pa. 1972).

22. *Roesberg v. Johns–Manville Corp.,* 28 Fed.R.Serv.2d 1170, 1183 (E.D.Pa.1972).

23. *Data Disc, Inc. v. Systems Technology Associates, Inc.,* 557 F.2d 1280, 1285 (9th Cir.1977).

24. *General Instrument Corp. v. General Diode Corp.,* 41 F.R.D. 1, 3 (D.Mass.1966).

25. Manual of Federal Practice § 5.24, at 300 (Rudolf W. Fischer, et al., eds., 2d ed. 1979).

26. *See Laufman v. Oakley Building & Loan Co.,* 72 F.R.D. 116, 120 (S.D.Ohio 1976).

Rule 60 [27] and to enforce a judgment by examining a judgment debtor to determine assets.[28]

One proposal to amend the discovery rules suggested limiting the scope of discovery to any matter "relevant to the issues raised" by any party rather than to the "subject matter" of the case.[29] Another suggestion proposed that the phrase "relevant to the subject matter" be replaced with the standard "relevant to the issues raised by the claims and defenses of any party." [30] The rejection of these proposals by the Supreme Court maintains the current broad scope of discovery. The Supreme Court has reaffirmed the broad scope of discovery extending beyond the issues raised by pleadings, because discovery helps define and clarify issues and because discovery assists in shaping the merits.[31]

Specific claims and issues will, however, affect the discoverability of some information. Inquiries into the financial status of a party will usually be disallowed unless there is a specific claim of punitive damages against that party for reckless or wanton conduct.[32] Information about the claims of non-parties may become relevant to a case if the habits, prior conduct, or past practices of a party are in issue.[33]

A recent addition to Rule 26 provides another means to establish the scope of discovery. Rule 26(f) permits discovery conferences and allows a judge to restrict the extent of discovery by identifying the issues, establishing a discovery plan, and setting limits on discovery. This relatively new format provides another means for an attorney to attempt to limit discovery by seeking such a conference and persuading a judge or magistrate to establish reasonable bounds.

3. *The Existence, Description, Nature, Custody, Condition, and Location of Documents and Tangible Things, and the Identity and Location of Persons Having Knowledge of Any Discoverable Matter.* This clause clarifies that tangible things are discoverable and that individuals as sources of information are also discoverable. These individuals need not necessarily have firsthand information. It is sufficient if they have knowledge of any discoverable information, which includes hearsay sources.[34] This provision does not refer to inquiries into the "contents" of documents because the first factor, which allows discovery of subject matter, includes the contents of documents.

27. *H.K. Porter Co. v. Goodyear Tire & Rubber Co.,* 536 F.2d 1115, 1122 (6th Cir. 1976).

28. *Caisson Corp. v. County West Building Corp.,* 62 F.R.D. 331 (E.D.Pa.1974).

29. Advisory Committee on Civil Rules, Preliminary Draft of Proposed Amendments to the Federal Rules of Civil Procedure (March 1978), reprinted in 77 F.R.D. 613, 626–627 (1978).

30. *See* American Bar Association, Section of Litigation, Report of the Special Committee for the Study of Discovery Abuse (1977).

31. *Oppenheimer Fund, Inc. v. Sanders,* 437 U.S. 340, 351, 98 S.Ct. 2380, 2389, 57 L.Ed.2d 253 (1978).

32. *Renshaw v. Ravert,* 82 F.R.D. 361, 363 (E.D.Pa.1979).

33. *Johnson v. W.H. Stewart Co.,* 75 F.R.D. 541, 543 (W.D.Okl.1976).

34. Fed.R.Civ.P. 26(b), Notes of Advisory Comm.—1946 Amendments, reprinted in 28 U.S.C.A. § 154.

4. *Information Reasonably Calculated to Lead to the Discovery of Admissible Evidence.* This standard further broadens the scope of discovery by stating that both inadmissible and admissible evidence is discoverable and that information likely to lead to admissible evidence is also discoverable. This includes any type of trial evidence, including impeachment information and any sources or leads about potential trial evidence.[35] Indeed, one of the benefits resulting from a broad scope of discovery is this opportunity to explore, discover, and establish new information that supports another theory or that bolsters a previously unsupported allegation.

These four standards, when applied together, create a very broad scope of discoverable information. The "reasonably calculated" standard, when joined with the "subject matter" standard, provides a requesting attorney with rule-sanctioned reasons to justify and support requests for information relating to almost anything about a case. There are limits, of course. Rule 26 subsections narrow this broad scope; legitimate objections to certain information also narrow the scope. These limitations reflect the balanced discovery philosophy that if a party wants to go discovery fishing, that party ought to catch no more than a reasonable and sufficient limit. The Supreme Court has emphasized the need for reasonable discovery restraints by declaring that the discovery provisions must be applied " 'to secure the just, speedy, and inexpensive determination of every action.' "[36]

These rules, cases, and definitions frame the theory of the scope of discovery. Practice, experience, and economics frame the practicalities of the extent of discovery. These practicalities in turn frame three specific approaches to what is discoverable.

First, you can ask for everything you want to discover, whether you professionally believe it to be discoverable or not. The experience of many attorneys confirms that what one attorney thinks to be discoverable, another lawyer believes never to be discoverable. The broad standards of Rule 26 account for the wide divergence of opinion regarding the discoverability of various types of information. Sometimes there will be a collective opinion regarding some information, confirmable in a published judicial decision. More often the professional opinions of practitioners and the myriad of unreported and unknown lower-court opinions determine what is or is not discoverable in a specific case. These differences in approach to practice become magnified when local customs, specialized traditions, and the adversary process add other factors. Your doubts about the discoverability of something may not match your adversaries' doubts. Ask and you may receive.

Second, you can ask only for those things you have the time and finances to pursue. Your time and your client's finances will determine the practical extent of discovery in a case. The theoretical scope of

35. *See* 8 Charles A. Wright & Alan R. Miller, Federal Practice and Procedure § 2015, at 113–121 (1970, Supp. 1994).

36. *Herbert v. Lando,* 441 U.S. 153, 177, 99 S.Ct. 1635, 1649, 60 L.Ed.2d 115 (1979), *quoting* Fed.R.Civ.P. 1.

discovery will be limited by the actualities of economics and strategy. Local restrictions on the number of interrogatories, the termination of discovery at a set time before trial, and the scope of pretrial conference orders may affect what is requested.

Third, you can ask for information you intend to obtain through court order if your request is refused by the opposing attorney. Many judges, when confronted with the issue of whether to allow something to be discovered, permit such discovery—for several reasons. One, the rules clearly favor liberal disclosures, and judges like to follow the rules. Two, reported opinions allowing discovery outnumber cases prohibiting discovery, and judges like to go with the numbers. Three, an attorney who takes the time and effort to prepare a motion, memorandum, and proposed order, all for some bit of information, must be convinced that the information ought to be disclosed. Judges will respect that conviction and may not want to second-guess that judgment. Four, courts recognize that the value of the information sought usually outweighs the burden discovery places on the responding party, and courts like to weigh things. Five, there is less likelihood of being reversed on appeal if discovery is permitted and judges do not like to think themselves wrong. Seek and you may find.

§ 5.5 PRIVILEGE

§ 5.5.1 Analysis

Rule 26(b)(1) explicitly declares privileged matter to be non-discoverable. Privilege in discovery contexts is the same as that defined by the rules of evidence.[1] No general privilege secures a person from providing information, but the law of evidence has established specific privileges that permit a person to withhold information in certain reasonably well-defined circumstances. What is and what is not privileged for discovery purposes is defined by constitutional provisions, statutory law, common law, the rules of evidence, and cases interpreting them.

This section outlines privileged information encountered in discovery in both federal and state proceedings. Detailed analysis of federal case law, state decisional and statutory laws, and uniform rules on privileges appear in considerable detail elsewhere,[2] so our purpose is to summarize the status of federal and state law privileges in order to inform you regarding proper discovery requests and responses.

The existence of a privilege is one of the few claims that will legitimately stonewall discovery inquiries. Attorneys therefore need to become familiar with the limits of privilege to determine just what

§ 5.5

1. *Mitchell v. Roma,* 265 F.2d 633, 636 (3d Cir.1959).

2. Jack B. Weinstein & Margaret A. Berger, Weinstein's Evidence (1980); 4 Moore's Federal Practice ¶ 26.60–.66 (2d ed. 1989); 8 John H. Wigmore, Evidence in Trials at Common Law §§ 2190–2396 (McNaughton rev. 1961) (hereinafter cited as Wigmore, Evidence); 8 Charles A. Wright & Arthur R. Miller, Federal Practice and Procedure §§ 2016–2034 (1970 & Supp. 1994).

information can properly be sought and when objections and refusals to respond can properly be interposed. But familiarity can be difficult to achieve because the law of privileges seems to be constantly developing. There is no common agreement defining the present status of privileges, and this lack of consensus compounds the confusion surrounding many privileges.

The rule of privilege provides protection to communications occurring in privileged relationships. The following elements usually need to be present to create a privilege, though they neither apply in all situations nor to all privileges:

> 1. The communication must originate in confidence with an understanding that the information will not be disclosed;
>
> 2. The element of confidentiality must be essential to a full and satisfactory maintenance of a relationship between individuals or must serve a vital governmental or public need;
>
> 3. This relationship or need must be one which in the opinion of the community ought to be fostered;
>
> 4. The injury that would occur by disclosure must outweigh any benefit gained by the disposition of litigation based upon the information.[3]

The following questions and responses explore some of these factors. Not all privileges or situations will involve these questions; some circumstances will involve other criteria. These questions do, however, provide a framework for an initial analysis of the existence and applicability of a privilege.

1. *Was the Information Intended to Be a Confidential Communication?* The basic rationale for privileges is the need to retain the confidential character of the information. This confidentiality must usually be present to support the existence of a privilege, although, for example, it need not be present to create a marital testimony privilege between spouses.

2. *Was the Privilege Properly Asserted?* A party must usually refuse to reveal the information voluntarily. The disclosure of such data, even with an objection, may well constitute a waiver of the privilege. A party may not assert a privilege during discovery and plan to waive that privilege at trial.

3. *Who is the Holder of the Privilege?* The privilege is a personal right and usually belongs to the person who communicates the information.[4] Some privileges will belong to someone else. The holder can assert the privilege, and often the individual or organization who received the information can assert it on behalf of that person. For example, the client is the holder of the attorney-client privilege, and

3. 8 Wigmore, Evidence § 2285 (McNaughton rev. 1961).

4. *See Hudson Tire Mart, Inc. v. Aetna Cas. & Sur. Co.*, 518 F.2d 671 (2d Cir.1975).

either the client, or the attorney on behalf of the client, may assert the privilege.

4. *Is the Information Discoverable From Another Source?* Information which is communicated in a confidential manner may be obtainable from another source. Data communicated to a government agency, for example, will be protected but may be obtainable or provided to another source, such as an independent investigator. An attorney may not be compelled to disclose facts a client has communicated, but the client may be deposed regarding such facts.

5. *Are the Data Discoverable Through Another Discovery Device?* Information obtainable through a discovery device that does not breach a confidence will be preferred to a method that delves into privileged matter.

6. *Does Another Privilege Protect the Data?* Information not sheltered by one privilege may be protected under another privilege. For example, the attorney-client privilege may not protect certain communications, while the privilege against self-incrimination may.

7. *Has the Party Claiming the Privilege Maintained the Confidential Nature of the Information?* The privileged data will lose their protected status if the party claiming the privilege voluntarily discloses such information to a non-privileged source.

8. *Has the Privilege Been Waived in Whole or in Part Through Some Disclosure?* The person who holds the privilege is the one who may waive it. Inadvertent disclosure may or may not result in a waiver. Partial disclosure of the subject matter of a topic will usually constitute a waiver of the entire subject matter. Some situations will permit selective declaration of a privilege. For example, the privilege against self-incrimination may be selectively asserted.[5]

9. *Which Party has the Burden to Establish the Existence of the Privilege?* The party claiming the privilege has the burden to show its existence and application through facts and persuasion.

10. *Is the Motion Seeking Disclosure or Protection Properly Before the Court?* The party seeking disclosure will bring a Rule 37 motion. A party seeking protection will seek a Rule 26 motion. Courts, by local rule, standing order, or expectations, may require the attorneys to attempt to resolve the dispute before seeking judicial relief.

11. *Has the Requesting Party Proved a Need for the Information?* The information must otherwise be discoverable under the provisions of Rule 26(b), and it may be necessary for the party seeking the information to explain why the information is needed.

12. *What are the Interests of the Party Seeking Discovery?* Usually the requesting party needs the information for the litigation. The party's interest is that of having access to information to be able to assess the case accurately and to prepare the issues for trial properly.

5. *See In re Master Key Litigation,* 507 F.2d 292, 294 (9th Cir.1974).

13. *What are the Interests of the Party Claiming the Privilege?* These interests parallel the interests in keeping certain communications confidential: to preserve the integrity of relationships or to further governmental interests. The exact interest will depend upon the particular privilege.

14. *What are the Interests of the Public?* Discovery and testimonial exclusionary rules and privileges contravene the fundamental principle that "the public has a right to every man's evidence." [6] A countervailing public interest may be promoted by protecting certain communications. These conflicting public interests must be weighed.

15. *Which Interests Prevail?* The existence and applicability of privileges will be strictly construed. Courts will create or apply them only in situations where the rationale for non-disclosure transcends the "normally predominant principle of utilizing all rational means for ascertaining truth." [7] The courts will weigh all the competing interests and decide what is protected and what must be disclosed.

16. *Have the Parties Provided Enough Information Through Affidavits and Memos Regarding the Privilege?* Parties can assist judges in weighing these competing interests by providing the court with the facts of the situation and by explaining their positions.

17. *Is an In Camera Inspection of the Privileged Matter Necessary?* A judge may need to review the communicated information to determine whether indeed it falls within a privileged classification. Federal Rule of Evidence 104(a) suggests this procedure may be improper in some cases, but judges will be inclined to review the allegedly privileged matter and then excise the privileged matter from the non-privileged matter.

18. *Is the Privilege Absolute or Qualified?* The application of almost any privilege to a specific situation will render that privilege qualified and not absolute. The court determines the extent of the qualifications in its assessment of the competing interests of the parties and public.

19. *Will a Protective Order Permitting Limited Disclosure Protect the Privileged Information?* Rule 26(c) provides the court with discretion to shape an order limiting the disclosure of privileged information. This opportunity is used, for example, with some frequency regarding trade secrets.

20. *What Privilege Law Applies? Federal Common Law? Federal Statutory Law? State Law? Which State Law?* Evidence Rule 501 provides the answers and case law interprets this rule.

21. *Why Was This Case Assigned to Me in the First Place?*

6. *United States v. Bryan,* 339 U.S. 323, 331, 70 S.Ct. 724, 730, 94 L.Ed. 884 (1950), *rehearing denied* 339 U.S. 991, 70 S.Ct. 1018, 94 L.Ed. 1391 (1950), *quoting* 8 Wigmore, Evidence § 2192 (McNaughton rev. 1961).

7. *Elkins v. United States,* 364 U.S. 206, 234, 80 S.Ct. 1437, 1454, 4 L.Ed.2d 1669 (1960).

The courts and parties review these and other questions in determining the existence and applicability of a privilege. The following subsections explain the sources of privileges in the federal system. Federal Evidence Rule 501 lists the various sources of privilege for federal cases:

1. The United States Constitution;
2. Acts of Congress;
3. Rules prescribed by the Supreme Court;
4. Common law interpreted in light of reason and experience.

§ 5.5.2 Privilege Under the United States Constitution

Privileges based upon constitutional rights include protection against self-incrimination, the right of privacy, and governmental secrecy.[8]

Non-party witnesses may refuse to disclose information if that information may incriminate them. A non-party deponent or a person responding to a subpoena duces tecum may decide not to disclose certain incriminating materials. The asserted privilege in many of these situations may well be absolute and, if so, a Rule 37 motion brought by the requesting party will be denied.

The Fifth Amendment privilege is a personal privilege; it allows a person to refuse to provide testimony or information against himself or herself. The privilege does not protect information or documents in the possession of a third party,[9] however, even including the client's attorney. Nor can the privilege be claimed by a corporation.

A party may or may not be able effectively to assert a self-incrimination privilege in a civil suit. Though a party can never be forced to waive a privilege, courts have held that a party cannot both seek affirmative relief and assert a privilege to block inquiries about those affirmative claims.[10] These holdings reflect the trial rule that a witness cannot testify on direct examination and then claim a privilege on cross-examination about matters made relevant by the direct. The trial rule is based on the rationale that a party cannot assert a privilege as a shield if the party is using the information to wield a sword.

Nevertheless, the assertion of a privilege by a plaintiff will not automatically justify dismissal of an action. While some courts have imposed such a sanction against a party who sought affirmative relief,[11]

8. *Campbell v. Gerrans,* 592 F.2d 1054, 1056 (9th Cir.1979).

9. *Couch v. United States,* 409 U.S. 322, 328, 331, 93 S.Ct. 611, 615–617, 34 L.Ed.2d 548 (1973).

10. *See Kastigar v. United States,* 406 U.S. 441, 92 S.Ct. 1653, 32 L.Ed.2d 212 (1972), *rehearing denied* 408 U.S. 931, 92 S.Ct. 2478, 33 L.Ed.2d 345 (1972).

11. *See Kisting v. Westchester Fire Insurance Co.,* 290 F.Supp. 141 (W.D.Wis. 1968), *affirmed* 416 F.2d 967 (7th Cir.1969).

others have balanced the interests of the competing parties and imposed less restrictive alternatives.[12]

The right to privacy forms a more obscure source of privilege rights. In practice, the right to privacy may be raised as an objection to a discovery question seeking information about a party's personal or financial matters. In theory, the right stems from a variety of constitutional provisions including the First, Fifth, and Fourteenth Amendments.

Those courts that have considered privileges based upon privacy balance those privacy rights with the opposition's legitimate need to obtain the information.[13] The typical balancing tests employ several factors:

1. The scope of the invasion of privacy. The broader the breach of confidentiality, the less likely the discovery will be permitted; the narrower the breach of privacy the more likely the request will be granted.

2. The needs of the opposition for the information. The more necessary the information is, the more likely it will be obtainable; the less vital it is, the less likely it will be available.

3. The status of the person or corporation claiming the privilege. If the claimant is a party, it is more likely that discovery will be allowed; if not a party, it is less likely to be allowed.

4. The availability of the information from another source. If a source is exclusive, it is more likely that the source will be required to disclose the information; if there are other sources, it is less likely that the requested source will be forced to disclose the information.

5. The specific kind of privacy invaded. The more "sacred" the right, the less likely it will be revealed; the less vital the privilege, the more likely it will be revealed. A "sacred" right might include freedom of the press and rights of reporters not to divulge sources of information. A less vital interest might be confidential financial records.

Discovery that has sought access to government information has been opposed by the governmental claims of constitutional privileges. Typical claims include military secrets, executive privilege, and state secrets. The Supreme Court has recognized that these claims are not absolute.[14] Such information is discoverable under limited circumstances and can be protected through the provisions of a protective

12. *Campbell v. Gerrans,* 592 F.2d 1054 (9th Cir.1979).

13. *Lora v. Board of Education of the City of New York,* 74 F.R.D. 565, 576–577 (E.D.N.Y.1977).

14. *United States v. Nixon,* 418 U.S. 683, 712, 94 S.Ct. 3090, 3109, 41 L.Ed.2d 1039 (1974).

order.[15]

§ 5.5.3 *Privilege Under Acts of Congress and State Legislatures*

Congress and state legislatures have adopted and will continue to adopt statutes creating privileges in certain specific situations. Many of these statutes do not directly create an evidentiary privilege, but rather prohibit governmental agencies or employees from disclosing reported information to individuals or the general public. Specific categories include: accident reports, trade secrets, confidential information, statistics, "insider" information, immunity, information about national defense and security, and the privacy and identity of the reporter of the information. These privileges are usually qualified and not absolute; some but not all such information may be discoverable.[16]

§ 5.5.4 *Privilege Under Supreme Court Rules*

The United States Supreme Court and state supreme courts have promulgated rules that restrict the disclosure of information. Various sections of the Federal Rules of Civil Procedure restrict the disclosure of discovery information in a way parallel to the characteristics of a privilege. Rule 26(b)(3) limits the scope of discovery involving trial preparation materials and work product. Rule 26(b)(4) governs discoverable information concerning experts. Rule 26(c) provides a court with discretion to protect a party from any discovery causing annoyance, embarrassment, oppression, or undue burden or expense. Rule 35, which provides for physical and mental examinations of parties, operates as a waiver of the common law physician-patient privilege. State civil procedure rules have similar provisions.

These rules cannot be properly identified as privileges, but they have been described as providing "qualified immunity from discovery."[17] By whatever name, they continue to restrict certain types of information from disclosure.

§ 5.5.5 *Common Law Privileges*

Federal Rule of Evidence 501 establishes privileges based on "the common law as interpreted by the courts of the United States in the light of reason and experience." In 1972 the Supreme Court submitted to Congress a number of specific privileges contained in its proposed Rule 501 to create a detailed set of privilege rules and standards. Congress decided not to enact these specific privileges because the legislators, lawyers, commentators, and evidence experts could not agree

15. *Dellums v. Powell,* 561 F.2d 242 (D.C.Cir.1977), *cert. denied* 434 U.S. 880, 98 S.Ct. 234, 54 L.Ed.2d 160 (1977).

16. *See Association for Women in Science v. Califano,* 566 F.2d 339, 346 (D.C.Cir. 1977).

17. *Kirkland v. Morton Salt Co.,* 46 F.R.D. 28, 30 (N.D.Ga.1968).

about which privileges should be created, codified, modified, or eliminated. Congress instead adopted Rule 501 "to provide the courts with flexibility to develop rules of privileges on a case-by-case basis." [18] The proposals contained in Rules 502 through 513, even though rejected by Congress, have significant effect on this development. These proposed rules act as "standards" that federal courts may employ as "comprehensive guide[s] to the federal law of privileges." [19]

Federal courts are also free to reject the suggestions contained in the proposed rules. The Supreme Court did so in *Trammel v. United States* by redefining the scope of the husband-wife privilege.[20]

The following subsections summarize the extent of the attorney-client privilege specifically and outline the status of other specific privileges derived from these proposed rules and from common law, state statutes, and state decisional law.

§ 5.5.6 Attorney-Client Privilege

The attorney-client privilege is the oldest of the privileges involving confidential communications. The privilege encourages "full and frank communication between attorneys and their clients and promote[s] broader public interests in the observance of law and administration of justice." It recognizes that "sound legal advice or advocacy ... depends upon the lawyer being fully informed by the client." [21] The privilege exists between a client and the client's attorney. A client has a privilege to refuse to disclose and to prevent any other person from disclosing confidential communications with a lawyer or a representative of the lawyer. The character of this privilege raises several questions regarding the applicability and extension:

1. *Is the Information That Is Communicated Privileged?* No. A client can be questioned about what he or she knows, even though that knowledge has been communicated to the lawyer, unless, of course, there exists another claim of privilege, such as self-incrimination. The mere fact that a client communicates certain information to an attorney does not enshroud that information with the privilege. "The privilege only protects disclosure of communications; it does not protect disclosure of the underlying facts by those who communicated with the attorney." [22] "For example, the client may not be asked a question: 'What did you tell your attorney about the amount claimed as a business expense?', but may be asked the question, 'Did you spend the amount claimed as a business expense for meals or for travel?' " [23]

18. *Trammel v. United States,* 445 U.S. 40, 47, 100 S.Ct. 906, 63 L.Ed.2d 186 (1980).

19. Weinstein's Evidence ¶ 501[03] at 501–28.

20. 445 U.S. 40, 100 S.Ct. 906, 63 L.Ed.2d 186 (1980).

21. *Upjohn Co. v. United States,* 449 U.S. 383, 101 S.Ct. 677, 66 L.Ed.2d 584 (1981).

22. *Upjohn Co. v. United States,* 449 U.S. 383, 395, 101 S.Ct. 677, 685, 66 L.Ed.2d 584 (1981).

23. Note, The Attorney and His Client's Privileges, 74 Yale L.J. 525, 546–47 (1964).

2. *Does the Privilege Extend to the Identity of a Client?* Not normally.[24] But the identity of a client is usually privileged if disclosure would implicate the client.

3. *Does the Privilege Cover Fee Arrangements Between an Attorney and a Client?* Not usually.[25] But the privilege will protect such fee information to avoid incriminating the client.

4. *Are Written Communications Privileged?* Yes, to the extent that any of the contents are privileged.[26] The mere transfer of any materials or documents or tangible things from a client to a lawyer does not render these items confidential. A Rule 34 request for production will compel the production of factual documents whether they are in the attorney's possession or the client's possession.

5. *Are Communications by the Lawyer Privileged?* Yes, if the requirements of the rule are fulfilled.[27] The privilege normally extends both to the client's communication and to the attorney's response and advice.[28] The mere communicating of legal advice does not preclude that legal theorizing from being discovered. Rules 33 and 36 permit discovery concerning matters which relate the law to the facts involved.

6. *Are Acts of the Client That Are Observed by His or Her Attorney Privileged?* Usually. Information communicated in any form will be privileged as long as the other facets of the privilege rule are met. The act of rolling up a sleeve to show a lawyer a hidden scar is part and parcel of the privileged communication.[29]

7. *Does the Privilege Extend to Communications Inadvertently Overheard by Eavesdroppers?* Perhaps. The client may be able to invoke the privilege to prevent testimony by a third person who overhears a communication intended to be confidential.[30]

8. *Who May Claim the Privilege?* The privilege belongs to and is for the benefit of the client, not the attorney. The client determines when the privilege is to be asserted or waived. The attorney typically raises it on behalf of the client.[31]

9. *What is the Status of the Privilege With Regard to Corporate Clients?* This question has not been authoritatively answered. A corporate client functions differently from an individual client, and this fact affects communications and confidentiality. Corporations have many individuals of different status with relevant information about a case; much of this information involves both business and legal concerns; and

24. *United States v. Hodge & Zweig,* 548 F.2d 1347, 1353 (9th Cir.1977).

25. *See United States v. Ponder,* 475 F.2d 37, 39 (5th Cir.1973).

26. *Colton v. United States,* 306 F.2d 633, 639 (2d Cir.1962), *cert. denied* 371 U.S. 951, 83 S.Ct. 505, 9 L.Ed.2d 499 (1963).

27. *Mead Data Central, Inc. v. United States Department of the Air Force,* 566 F.2d 242, 254 & n. 25 (D.C.Cir.1977).

28. *Upjohn Co. v. United States,* 449 U.S. 383, 101 S.Ct. 677, 66 L.Ed.2d 584 (1981).

29. McCormick's Evidence § 89 (1972).

30. McCormick's Evidence § 75 (1972).

31. *United States v. Baskes,* 442 F.Supp. 322, 327 (N.D.Ill.1977).

many of the corporate agents, as well as the employees, may be eyewitnesses to an event. Courts have faced these problems and have developed a number of alternative approaches to apply the attorney-client privilege to corporate clients:

1. *The Unlimited Approach.* All confidential communications between a corporate officer, employee, or director with an attorney create a privilege.[32]

2. *The Subject-matter Test.* Communications are privileged if: (a) an employee makes the communication at the direction of a supervisor, and (b) the subject matter is related to the employee's job duties.[33]

3. *The Modified Subject-matter Test.* Five requirements must be met to establish the attorney-client corporate privilege under this approach:

(a) The communication is made for the purpose of securing legal advice;

(b) The employee making the communication does so with the direction of the employee's corporate superior;

(c) The superior makes the request so that the corporation could secure legal advice;

(d) The subject matter of the communication is within the scope of the employee's corporate duties; and

(e) The communication is not disseminated beyond those persons who, because of the corporate structure, need to know its contents.[34]

4. *The Upjohn Approach.* The Supreme Court has reviewed the corporate client privilege and declined to establish a firm rule concerning its scope.[35] The decision rejected lower-court decisions that attempted to restrict the scope of the privilege, but it did not delineate specific factors. However, the Court's assessment of the privilege question resembled the modified subject matter approach and squarely rejected the control group. In *Upjohn*, the communications protected by the Court were matters within the employee's corporate duties and were elicited through confidential interviews with lawyers. The concurring opinion of former Chief Justice Burger suggested the following detailed criteria as creating a privilege:

> The attorney must be one authorized by the management to inquire into the subject and must be seeking information to assist counsel

32. *United States v. United Shoe Machinery Corp.*, 89 F.Supp. 357, 358 (D.Mass. 1950).

33. *Harper & Row Publishers, Inc. v. Decker*, 423 F.2d 487, 492 (7th Cir.1970), *cert. granted* 397 U.S. 1073, 90 S.Ct. 1523, 25 L.Ed.2d 820 (1970).

34. *Diversified Industries, Inc. v. Meredith*, 572 F.2d 596, 609 (8th Cir.1977).

35. *Upjohn Co. v. United States*, 449 U.S. 383, 101 S.Ct. 677, 66 L.Ed.2d 584 (1981).

in performing any of the following functions: (a) evaluating whether the employee's conduct has bound or would bind the corporation; (b) assessing the legal consequences, if any, of that conduct; or (c) formulating appropriate legal responses to actions that have been or may be taken by others with regard to that conduct.[36]

10. *In What Situations Does the Privilege Not Exist?* No privilege arises in situations in which a client seeks legal advice to commit a crime or fraud, an attorney commits malpractice, or a client fails to pay an attorney for professional services.[37]

11. *When Does the Attorney–Client Privilege Terminate?* The privilege lasts forever; it survives even after the attorney-client relationship ends. The privilege also extends beyond the client's death. The client or a personal representative may waive all or part of the privileged communications. Certain conduct by a client will also operate as a waiver; for example, a client who reviews documents to refresh recollection waives the privilege as to those documents.[38]

§ 5.5.7 Other Specific Privileges

The following privileges apply in the various situations that give rise to confidential communications. Not all these privileges are recognized by all jurisdictions. The privileges designated 1 through 9 below represent the more commonly accepted privileges in federal and state courts. The remaining privileges represent situations that act as a bar to disclosure in some state jurisdictions:

1. Marital spousal privileges are of two types: a privilege not to testify against a spouse regarding any information, and a privilege not to disclose confidential communications between spouses. The former privilege as defined by the Supreme Court for federal cases is available only to the witness spouse and the other spouse can neither compel nor foreclose testimony.[39] The interspousal privilege affords protections to confidential marital communications and neither spouse can disclose such information without the consent of the other.[40]

2. Communications with clergy will be deemed privileged to protect the confidence of the disclosures.[41]

36. *Upjohn Co. v. United States,* 449 U.S. 383, 403, 101 S.Ct. 677, 66 L.Ed.2d 584 (1981) (Burger, C.J., concurring), *citing with approval Diversified Industries, Inc. v. Meredith,* 572 F.2d 596 (8th Cir.1978), *and Harper & Row Publishers, Inc. v. Decker,* 423 F.2d 487 (7th Cir.1970).

37. *See Matter of Doe,* 551 F.2d 899, 900–901 (2d Cir.1977).

38. *Bailey v. Meister Brau, Inc.,* 57 F.R.D. 11, 13 (N.D.Ill.1972).

39. *Trammel v. United States,* 445 U.S. 40, 53, 100 S.Ct. 906, 63 L.Ed.2d 186 (1980).

40. *Trammel v. United States,* 445 U.S. 40, 51, 100 S.Ct. 906, 63 L.Ed.2d 186 (1980).

41. *Wolfle v. United States,* 291 U.S. 7, 14, 54 S.Ct. 279, 280, 78 L.Ed. 617 (1934).

3. Trade secrets and other confidential business communications will be protected by privileged status.[42]

4. Political vote privileges protect a voter from disclosing his or her vote.[43]

5. The required-report privilege protects the confidentiality of reports and returns required by law to be filed with the government.[44]

6. Governmental privileges exist for (a) military, diplomatic, and state secrets, (b) governmental opinions and recommendations, (c) investigatory law enforcement files, (d) and freedom-of-information exemptions.[45]

7. The identity of an informer privileged.[46]

8. A general physician-patient privilege has been created by case law and statute. Many exceptions to this privilege narrow the privilege severely.[47]

9. A limited psychotherapist-patient privilege covers confidential personal revelations of a patient.[48]

10. An optometrist-patient privilege operates similarly to the physician-patient privileges.[49]

11. The hospital-and-medical-review-committee privilege is applicable to staff discussions evaluating the adequacy of provisions for hospital care.[50]

12. A grand-jury privilege provides protection and secrecy to grand-jury testimony.[51]

13. The teacher-pupil privilege restricts disclosures of communications between teachers and their students.[52]

14. The social service and juvenile workers and children privilege protects communications between probation and welfare workers and juveniles.[53]

15. A counselor-pupil privilege applies to communications between licensed counselors and school students.[54]

42. Advisory Committee's Note to Proposed Evidence Rule 508, 56 F.R.D. 248 (1973).

43. 8 Wigmore, Evidence § 2214, at 163–164 (McNaughton rev. 1961).

44. *Association for Women in Science v. Califano,* 566 F.2d 339, 344 (D.C.Cir.1977).

45. *See* McCormick's Evidence § 107 (1972).

46. *Carl Zeiss Stiftung v. V.E.B. Carl Zeiss, Jena,* 40 F.R.D. 318, 331 (D.D.C. 1966), *affirmed,* 384 F.2d 979 (D.C.Cir. 1967), *cert. denied* 389 U.S. 952, 88 S.Ct. 334, 19 L.Ed.2d 361 (1967).

47. *See United States v. Meagher,* 531 F.2d 752, 753 (5th Cir.1976), *cert. denied* 429 U.S. 853, 97 S.Ct. 146, 50 L.Ed.2d 128 (1976).

48. Standard 504 contained in proposed Fed.R.Evid. 504.

49. West's Rev.Code Wash.Ann. 18.53.-200.

50. *Bredice v. Doctors Hospitals, Inc.,* 50 F.R.D. 249 (D.D.C.1970).

51. West's Rev.Code Wash.Ann. 10.27.-090.

52. Nev.Rev.Stat. 49.291.

53. N.M.R.Evid. 509.

54. Nev.Rev.Stat. 49.290.

16. An accountant-client privilege applies to communications between a professional accountant and a client.[55]

17. A scholar's privilege has been recognized in federal court decisions to promote the free flow of confidential information and sources necessary to scholarly research.[56]

18. Tax returns enjoy a qualified privilege, protecting against disclosure, unless such information is vital and unavailable from any other source.[57]

19. Business privileges protect confidential business contracts, customer lists, and other business matters.[58]

20. A judicial privilege protects persons engaged in judicial decisionmaking processes (including governmental officials and judges and juries) from disclosing the mental processes employed in formulating judgments.[59]

21. Qualified privileges exist for news sources, usually based on "shield" laws or First Amendment protections.[60] Editorial processes and mental impressions have been held discoverable in libel cases.[61]

§ 5.5.8 Objections to Claims of Privilege

The mechanics of how a party objects to a discovery request or the basis of a claim of privilege depends upon the applicable procedural law. Federal Rule 26(b)(5) requires that an objecting party identify and describe the privileged information and materials being withheld without revealing the underlying protected information. The scope and extent of the description of the privileged information upon what is sought to be protected. In most cases, a description which reveals the existence of the privileged document or information, the identity of the person who created the document or who knows the information, the time when the document was created or who the information became known, and the purpose for its existence would be an adequate description. It is possible that the disclosure of the existence of the privileged information or materials may be a waiver of the privilege. This should only occur in rare circumstances because, otherwise, parties would be inclined to claim generally that the disclosure of the existence of the privileged information and materials violates the privilege, effectively emasculating this rule.

55. *Couch v. United States,* 409 U.S. 322, 93 S.Ct. 611, 34 L.Ed.2d 548 (1973).

56. *United States v. I.B.M. Corp.,* 83 F.R.D. 92 (S.D.N.Y.1979).

57. *Federal Savings & Loan Insurance Corp. v. Krueger,* 55 F.R.D. 512 (N.D.Ill. 1972).

58. *See Maritime Cinema Service Corp. v. Movies En* Route, Inc., 60 F.R.D. 587 (S.D.N.Y.1973).

59. These persons may have to disclose factual matters. *Standard Packaging Corp. v. Curwood Inc.,* 365 F.Supp. 134, 136 (N.D.Ill.1973).

60. *See, e.g.,* 12 Okl.St.Ann. § 2506; *Branzburg v. Hayes,* 408 U.S. 665, 92 S.Ct. 2646, 33 L.Ed.2d 626 (1972).

61. *Herbert v. Lando,* 441 U.S. 153, 99 S.Ct. 1635, 60 L.Ed.2d 115 (1979).

State rules may permit a party to effectively object to a request for information on the basis of privilege with a general objection, without having to identify specifically the privileged information or materials. The federal rule requiring specific objections allows the discovering party to determine whether the claim or privilege is valid. State rules which allow general objections make it difficult for a discovering party to determine whether or not the claim or privilege is legitimate. In all jurisdictions, a party may bring a motion seeking an order disclosing the information claimed to be privileged and testing the legitimacy of the objection.

§ 5.6 INSURANCE AGREEMENTS

Insurance information must be disclosed. Federal Rule 26(a)(1)(D) requires a party to affirmatively disclose any insurance agreements covering the events or transaction of the case, including liability insurance policies. A party may provide a copy of the insurance policy or make a policy available for inspection or copying. State rules typically allow opposing parties to seek discovery information by submitting a discovery request, such as an interrogatory or a document production request.

Yes, Santa Claus is discoverable. What are the reasons for this? (1) Because insurance is an asset created specifically to satisfy the claim; (2) because the insurance company ordinarily controls the litigation; (3) because information about coverage is available only from the defendant or his insurer; and (4) because disclosure does not involve a significant invasion of privacy.[1]

These rationales do not extend to other potential assets of a party. Other assets that may be available to satisfy a judgment become a proper subject for discovery only after a trial in a supplementary proceeding to enforce the judgment.[2] Insurance coverage differs from other assets because it is the insurance carrier and not the insured who coordinates and controls the defense of claims, and because all attorneys in the action will be able to make a realistic appraisal of a case based upon the facts and not upon speculation. The amount of coverage will affect the timing of settlement and the avoidance of unnecessary litigation. A moderate coverage policy will encourage a settlement not exceeding its limits. A large coverage policy may delay a reasonable settlement. Money has a way of strengthening the merits of some cases.

Interrogatory questions may uncover more information about the existence of insurance. A Rule 34 request for production will reveal the policy itself if it has not already been disclosed.

§ 5.6

1. Fed.R.Civ.P. 26(b)(2), Notes of Advisory Comm.—1970 Amendments, reprinted in 28 U.S.C.A. § 155.

2. Kent Sinclair, Federal Civil Practice 539 (1980).

§ 5.7 TRIAL PREPARATION MATERIALS

§ 5.7.1 Introduction

Courts over the past decades have considered discovery requests seeking the disclosure of every imaginable type of information. Cases considering these requests include the seminal decision of *Hickman v. Taylor,*[1] which spawned the "work-product" doctrine. Subsequent judicial decisions developed the scope of work product by applying other doctrines such as "qualified privilege," "good cause," "relevancy," and "litigation materials."[2] Subsequent amendments to the discovery rules codified some of these decisions and created the "trial preparation materials" rule.

There continues to exist a fair amount of confusion regarding what is and what is not discoverable from efforts made and materials prepared in anticipation of litigation or for trial. This confusion stems in part from the use and misuse of various terms, including *work product.* This term means different things to different lawyers, judges, and justices.[3] The Supreme Court has contributed both to the continuing vitality of the work-product doctrine and to the confusion surrounding its definition. The Court in a review of the work-product rule stated that the doctrine "has been *substantially* incorporated in Federal Rule of Civil Procedure 26(b)(3)" and then only 47 words later stated that "Rule 26(b)(3) *codifies* the work-product doctrine."[4] It is indeed fair to ask: Which is it?

This section will avoid such confusion by employing the terminology defined in Rule 26(b)(3) and by avoiding other terms manufactured by well-meaning jurists and commentators. This rule does not contain the phrases *good cause* or *work product.* We begin with a true/false analysis of this matrix and continue with an elaboration of Rule 26 provisions.

True or False?

1. Trial Preparation materials are documents and tangible things prepared in anticipation of litigation or for trial.

True. Anyone who can think knows that.

2. Trial preparation materials are discoverable only upon a showing of substantial need and undue hardship under Rule 26.

§ 5.7

1. 329 U.S. 495, 67 S.Ct. 385, 91 L.Ed. 451 (1947).

2. The Supreme Court has declared the trial preparation work-product doctrine a qualified privilege. *United States v. Nobles,* 422 U.S. 225, 237–238, 95 S.Ct. 2160, 2169, 2170, 45 L.Ed.2d 141 (1975). Circuit and district court judges frequently fail to define precisely or accurately the doctrine they employ to allow or restrict discovery. *See* Fed.R.Civ.P. 26(b)(3), Notes of Advisory Comm.—1970 Amendments.

3. The term *work product* was coined in the argument of the Hickman v. Taylor case before the Third Circuit. The Court of Appeals thought the phrase accurately described what the court held to be excluded from discovery. *Hickman v. Taylor,* 153 F.2d 212, 223 (3d Cir.1945), *cert. denied* 328 U.S. 876, 66 L.Ed.2d 1337, 90 L.Ed. 1645 (1946).

4. *Upjohn Co. v. United States,* 449 U.S. 383, 398–399, 101 S.Ct. 677, 66 L.Ed.2d 584 (1981) (emphasis added).

True. Anyone who can read knows that.

3. Documents and tangible things not trial preparation materials are discoverable through a Rule 34 request.

Maybe. Maybe not. Some documents and tangible things may not be discoverable because they are irrelevant or privileged. Other documents and tangible things will be discoverable merely for the asking.

4. Documents containing the written impressions, conclusions, opinions and legal theories of an attorney are never discoverable through discovery.

True. Period.

5. A party or witness cannot obtain a copy of a statement made by that party or witness.

False.

6. Witness statements and investigative file materials are not discoverable.

Some are. Some are not. It depends.

Rule 26(b)(3)

> [A] party may obtain discovery of documents and tangible things otherwise discoverable . . .

This provision limits the scope of the rule to the disclosure of written documents or tangible things. Other forms of discovery requests are not covered. Some materials will not be discoverable because they may be irrelevant as defined by Rule 26(b)(1) or because they contain privileged matter. A Rule 34 request will produce all other documents or tangible objects unless they are trial preparation materials.

> . . . prepared in anticipation of litigation or for trial for that party or by or for that party's representative (including his attorney, consultant, surety, indemnitor, insurer, or agent) . . .

This clause is the rule's definition of trial preparation materials. The definition seems circular: trial preparation materials are materials prepared for trial or in anticipation of litigation. The definition includes materials comprising a case file, including investigation matters, witness statements, file memos, letter correspondence, legal memoranda, lawyer and staff notes, client communications, trial notebooks, and other documents and tangible things. The rule itself does not detail criteria that determine which of these materials will be classified as trial preparation materials in a particular case. Case law has developed factors that, when applied, determine the nature of the materials. These factors can be categorized into three questions:

WHO assembled the materials?

WHEN were the materials gathered?

WHY were the materials collected and for whom?

These three factors are not independent of each other. A court may consider all three factors in determining whether some requests seek trial preparation materials or may decide that one of the factors controls the fate of the materials.

The WHO. The key figure is the lawyer. The presence or involvement of an attorney in the investigation process is a significant factor in classifying the materials. The presence of a lawyer is not a requirement; documents created and gathered by non-lawyers may be trial preparation materials;[5] the involvement of an attorney does not automatically convert materials into trial preparation matters.[6] However, the inclusion of a lawyer may cause materials to be considered to have been prepared in anticipation of litigation.[7]

The WHEN. The time when materials were prepared will affect their classification. Materials gathered during litigation usually become trial preparation materials. Documents and tangible things prepared after a cause of action has arisen but before litigation has been initiated may or may not be trial preparation matters.[8] Materials assembled before the maturation of a legal claim may be trial preparation materials depending upon how imminent the claim was and upon the timing of subsequent litigation.[9]

The WHY. The Federal Advisory Committee Notes add some gloss to the definition of trial preparation materials by excluding three categories of materials according to their assembled purpose: (1) materials assembled "pursuant to public requirements," (2) materials assembled in the "ordinary course of business," and, naturally, (3) materials assembled "for nonlitigation purposes."[10] The first category excludes as trial preparation materials documents that are prepared under a duty pursuant to statute or regulation.[11] The second category eliminates materials because the inherent nature of a business or activity makes such preparation useful or necessary regardless of the existence of litigation or because such materials are customarily collected other than for litigation.[12] The third category by definition excludes materials if the reason they were collected was for a non-litigation purpose.

Need the non-litigation purpose be the primary reason why the materials were gathered? A significant reason? A secondary reason? The answer to these questions has not yet been definitively provided by case law. The "primary purpose" reason appears to be more consistent

5. *See Bredice v. Doctors Hospital, Inc.,* 50 F.R.D. 249, 251 (D.D.C.1970).

6. *See* 4 Moore's Federal Practice ¶ 26.-64[3] (2d ed. 1989).

7. *See Thomas Organ Co. v. Jadranska Slobodna Plovidba,* 54 F.R.D. 367 (N.D.Ill. 1972).

8. *Spaulding v. Denton,* 68 F.R.D. 342, 346 (D.Del.1975).

9. *See McDougall v. Dunn,* 468 F.2d 468 (4th Cir.1972).

10. Fed.R.Civ.P. 26(b)(3), Notes of Advisory Comm.—1970 Amendments, reprinted in 28 U.S.C.A. § 156.

11. *Galambus v. Consolidated Freightways Corp.,* 64 F.R.D. 468, 472 (N.D.Ind. 1974).

12. *Thomas Organ Co. v. Jadranska Slobodna Plovidba,* 54 F.R.D. 367, 371 (N.D.Ill.1972).

with other provisions of Rule 26 than the other reasons. One indicium of a non-litigation purpose is the tone of the materials: are they impartial and without an adversarial tone? The more partisan the materials are, the more likely they will be declared trial preparation materials.

> [All trial preparation materials will be discoverable only] upon a showing that the party seeking discovery has substantial need of the materials in the preparation of his case and that he is unable without undue hardship to obtain the substantial equivalent of the materials by other means....

A party has the burden to demonstrate both "substantial need" and "undue hardship" to obtain access to trial preparation materials. A requesting party must first show substantial need by demonstrating that the materials are very important to the preparation of the case,[13] and then showing that the substantial equivalent cannot be obtained without undue hardship. This latter factor has been met in a number of situations. Courts have ordered trial preparation documents to be disclosed when witnesses became unavailable,[14] memories of witnesses faded over time,[15] reports were made contemporaneously with or shortly after an event,[16] witnesses became hostile and antagonistic,[17] or the opposing party possessed surveillance films made of a party.[18]

Courts have ruled that parties fail to demonstrate substantial need and undue hardship if witness statements could be obtained from other sources, such as personal interviews and depositions.[19] The cases that have reviewed requests for trial preparation materials have involved the disclosure of witness statements and correspondence between parties' employees or agents,[20] but not other materials from investigative files. This is because practitioners seek to obtain witness statements and party correspondence rather than other file materials, perceiving that they stand little chance of obtaining other categories of trial preparation materials.

§ 5.7.2 Objections to Trial Preparations Materials

The federal rules require that a party provide specific information when withholding materials based on a claim of trial preparation materials. Federal Rule 26(b)(5) requires an objecting party to identify the nature of the protected materials. The purpose of this rule is to allow the party seeking the information to determine whether the documents

13. *Rackers v. Siegfried,* 54 F.R.D. 24, 26 (W.D.Mo.1971).

14. *See Hilton v. Contiship Corp.,* 16 F.R.D. 453 (S.D.N.Y.1954).

15. *Teribery v. Norfolk & Western Railway,* 68 F.R.D. 46, 48 (W.D.Pa.1975).

16. *See Gillman v. United States,* 53 F.R.D. 316, 319 (S.D.N.Y.1971).

17. *Mitchell v. Bass,* 252 F.2d 513, 518 (8th Cir.1958); *see also Xerox Corp. v. I.B.M. Corp.,* 64 F.R.D. 367 (S.D.N.Y.1974).

18. *Snead v. American Export–Isbrandtsen Lines, Inc.,* 59 F.R.D. 148, 151 (E.D.Pa.1973).

19. *United States v. Chatham City Corp.,* 72 F.R.D. 640 (S.D.Ga.1976).

20. *See* 4 Moore's Federal Practice ¶ 26.64[4] (2d ed. 1989).

appear to be trial preparation materials. The federal rule does not allow general trial preparation objections to be made. Many state court rules do not require a description of the materials withheld and permit general objections to be asserted.

The extent of the description required by the federal rules depends upon the information sought to be protected. In most cases, a description which reveals the existence of the trial preparation document, the identity of the person who created the document, the time when the document was created, and the purpose for its creation would be an adequate description. In some cases, this description would reveal underlying protected information and a narrower description would suffice.

§ 5.7.3 Witness Statements

Rule 26(b)(3) explicitly makes two types of statements discoverable merely for the asking and without having to show substantial need and undue hardship: (1) a party can obtain the party's own statement from another party; (2) a witness can obtain a copy of the witness's statement from any party. This provision of the rule also defines a statement as either "a written statement signed or otherwise adopted or approved by the person making it," or as "a stenographic, mechanical, electrical, or other recording, or a transcription thereof, which is a substantially verbatim recital of an oral statement by the person making it and contemporaneously recorded." These definitions include the following types of statements among others:

1. A statement written and signed by the party or witness;
2. A statement typed by someone else and signed by the party or witness;
3. A statement prepared by a third person and initialed by a party or witness;
4. A statement written by someone else and corrected by a party or witness;
5. A tape-recorded conversation of a party or witness interview;
6. A telephone-recorded interview of a party or witness;
7. A statement of a party or witness in the presence of a court reporter which is later transcribed;
8. Diagrams or drawings made by a party or witness.[21]

Who writes or prepares the statement is irrelevant; the party or witness need only sign, adopt, or approve it. Whether the party or witness is aware of being recorded is irrelevant for purposes of this rule. Whether the statement is made in anticipation of trial or not is also irrelevant.

21. *Parker v. Carroll,* 20 Fed.R.Serv.2d 698, 700–701 (D.D.C.1974).

Investigation decisions determine whether a party or witness statement falls within one or the other categories of this rule. If a recorded statement is made during an interview, that statement or a later transcript becomes discoverable. If a recorded statement is not made, a written statement can be prepared after the interview and later signed, adopted, or approved by the witness, making it discoverable. It is an important tactic to decide whether a statement should be preserved and whether it should be preserved in a form that becomes discoverable. This decision will depend upon a myriad of factors in a case, including the type of witness (friendly, neutral, or adverse), the timing of the statement, the purpose for the statement, and other discovery options.

A party who seeks to obtain the party's own witness statement from an opponent is entitled as a matter of right under the rules to a copy. All other statements can be obtained from an opponent (unless voluntarily disclosed) only after a showing of need and hardship. Likewise, a litigant can obtain a copy of any witness statement from a witness by persuading the witness to request a copy from an opposing party and then to give a copy of the statement to the litigant.

Certain information obtained from witnesses may not be discoverable. Oral statements made to an attorney by a witness contained in the lawyer's notes and memoranda are not discoverable. The Supreme Court has declared this information protected as part of "the attorney's mental processes in evaluating the communications." [22]

§ 5.7.4 Attorney Mental Processes

Some materials are exempt from disclosure. Rule 26(b)(3) provides in part that "the court shall protect against disclosure of the mental impressions, conclusions, opinions, or legal theories of an attorney or other representative of a party concerning the litigation."

This portion of the rule explicitly defines and protects specific categories of trial preparation materials. These categories reflect the holding of the Supreme Court in *Hickman v. Taylor,* which declared secure the mental impressions and beliefs of an attorney.[23] This doctrine protects the effectiveness of the lawyer's work by preserving such materials from discovery. No showing of substantial need or undue hardship will justify its disclosure.

The "mental impressions" of an attorney need to be distinguished from trial preparation materials and privileged matter. Material that includes factual information, as distinguished from opinion, is trial preparation material discoverable upon a showing of substantial need and undue hardship, whereas the attorney's opinion remains exempt from discovery. Matters discussed between an attorney and a client may

22. *Upjohn Co. v. United States,* 449 U.S. 383, 401, 101 S.Ct. 677, 66 L.Ed.2d 584 (1981).

23. 329 U.S. 495, 509–512, 67 S.Ct. 385, 392–394, 91 L.Ed. 451 (1947).

be privileged under the attorney-client privilege, whereas mental impressions of an attorney remain protected through Rule 26(b)(3).

Applying the protections of Rule 26 raises three questions:

1. *Is This Protection Absolute?* No one knows. The Supreme Court has faced this exact question and declined to answer it. The Court, in *Upjohn Co. v. United States,* did hold that an attorney's mental impressions "cannot be disclosed simply on a showing of substantial need and inability to obtain the equivalent without undue hardship." [24] The Court left open the question whether attorneys' mental impressions may be discoverable in rare situations.

There are limits placed upon an attorney's ability to create exempt materials. One court held that an attorney cannot protect a verbatim witness statement from disclosure by including its text in an evaluative memorandum prepared for litigation.[25] Another court held that an attorney's involvement in creating information does not automatically convert such data into exempt information. One party sought to discover the calculations of damages in a case, and the responding party refused to disclose the calculations, claiming that the information contained attorneys' work efforts. The court rejected this position, stating that even though lawyers developed the information, the damage calculations must be disclosed because that information would be presented at trial.[26] This analysis is consistent with other cases, which declare factual information to be discoverable even if gathered through attorney's efforts.

2. *Does This Protection Extend to Non-written, Intangible Matters?* While Rule 26(b)(3) explicitly exempts written mental impressions, opinions, conclusions, and legal theories from discovery, Rules 33 and 36 expressly permit the discovery of interrogatory information and admissions relating to the application of law to fact. A Rule 34 request seeking documents may be properly objected to as requesting materials that are exempt from discovery. An attorney may be obligated to disclose some opinions and legal theories in response to interrogatories under Rule 33(b), but will be entitled to maintain the confidentiality of those memos and documents containing this information which are prepared for internal use.[27]

Case law has extended the protection afforded a lawyer's mental impressions, opinions, conclusions, and legal theories to oral deposition requests. Courts have established certain guidelines detailing the scope of deposition questioning of a deponent. Those guidelines prohibited questions about any matter that revealed "counsel's mental impression" concerning the case, including specific areas and general lines of inquiry discussed by opposing counsel with the deponent, and any facts to which

24. 449 U.S. 383, 401, 101 S.Ct. 677, 66 L.Ed.2d 584 (1981).

25. *Mervin v. FTC,* 591 F.2d 821, 825 (D.C.Cir.1978).

26. *Wheeling–Pittsburgh Steel Corp. v. Underwriters Laboratories, Inc.,* 81 F.R.D. 8, 12 (N.D.Ill.1978).

27. *See Natta v. Hogan,* 392 F.2d 686, 693 (10th Cir.1968).

opposing counsel appeared to have attached particular significance during conversations with the deponent.[28]

The Supreme Court in *Upjohn* appears to make no distinction between the forms of the attorney's mental impressions as affecting their discoverability. The materials sought to be discovered in *Upjohn* were notes and memoranda made of oral witness interviews.[29] The Court protected these materials because they revealed attorney's mental processes. The rationale underlying this protection would apply to discovery requests seeking to reveal the attorney's memory of the oral interviews, including interrogatories and depositions.

3. *Can This Protection Be Waived?* Some situations will require the disclosure of protected information. One situation involves the subject matter of a lawsuit. If the mental processes of an attorney are an issue in a case, such as in a legal malpractice case, they will be discoverable. Another situation involves waiver by the statements or conduct of the client or of the attorney acting for the client.

Case law has restricted the extent of waivers by holding that the subject-matter waiver doctrine does not always apply to these protections. This doctrine declares that partial or inadvertent disclosure of some information constitutes a waiver of all information relating to the subject matter.[30] The subject-matter doctrine does apply to the attorney-client privilege and to trial preparation materials that do not contain an attorney's mental impressions, opinions, conclusions, or legal theories.[31] Courts have not applied the subject-matter waiver to mental impression materials because they have found that inadvertent or partial disclosure can be controlled and that the public policy supporting protection continues to operate even if the protection has been reduced.[32] This means that protected information could be disclosed selectively or inadvertently without constituting a waiver of the protection afforded the preserved materials.

§ 5.7.5 Practice Considerations

The party claiming that materials are trial preparation materials has the burden to show just that. The party who claims substantial need and undue hardship has that burden to carry. Judges who have some doubts about the status of documents and tangible things have the discretion to review such materials in camera before making a decision.[33]

28. *Ford v. Philips Electronics Instruments Co.*, 82 F.R.D. 359, 360–361 (E.D.Pa. 1979).

29. *Upjohn Co. v. United States*, 449 U.S. 383, 101 S.Ct. 677, 66 L.Ed.2d 584 (1981).

30. *See, e.g., Duplan Corp. v. Deering Milliken, Inc.*, 540 F.2d 1215, 1223 (4th Cir.1976).

31. *United States v. Nobles*, 422 U.S. 225, 238–239, 95 S.Ct. 2160, 2170, 45 L.Ed.2d 141 (1975), *on remand* 522 F.2d 1274 (9th Cir.1975).

32. *United States v. Nobles*, 422 U.S. 225, 238–241, 95 S.Ct. 2160, 2170, 45 L.Ed.2d 141 (1975), *on remand* 522 F.2d 1274 (9th Cir.1975); *Duplan Corp. v. Deering Milliken, Inc.*, 540 F.2d 1215, 1223 (4th Cir.1976).

33. *See Hamilton v. Canal Barge Co.*, 395 F.Supp. 975, 978 (E.D.La.1974).

In sum, the most accurate and reliable measure of the applicability of the trial preparation doctrine continues to be a reasonable and complete reading of Rule 26. This approach triggers the consideration of the following and other questions relating to trial preparation information:

Do the materials sought constitute the mental impressions, opinions, conclusions, or legal theories of an attorney or representative of the party? If so, they are protected from discovery.

Do the documents requested constitute materials prepared in anticipation of litigation or for trial? If so, they are trial preparation materials protected from discovery absent further demands by the other party.

Does the other party claim a substantial need for such materials, which can only be otherwise obtained through undue hardship? If so, such material will be discoverable excluding attorney mental processes.

Does the other party or a witness seek his or her own statement? If so, it will be discoverable.

§ 5.8 EXPERTS

§ 5.8.1 Introduction and Categories of Experts

Discovery concerning experts frequently includes discovery of their identity, their opinions, and facts known to them. Additionally, discovery may include background information on the bases for any opinions and other factors relating to what the experts know.

In state courts, the nature and extent of discoverable expert information varies widely depending upon the applicable rules of the jurisdiction. In federal court, Rule 26 governs the discoverability of expert information. Section 5.8.2 provides an analysis useful in determining the discoverability of expert information in state court jurisdictions. Section 5.8.3 explains what is discoverable from experts in federal court cases.

§ 5.8.2 Types of Experts

The specific rules of civil procedure applicable in a state court case determines what is discoverable from an expert and how it is discoverable. The rules range from very liberal rules which permit a wide range of discovery to more restrictive rules that narrow available discovery. A method of analyzing what is and what is not discoverable includes a determination of the type of expert involved. There are five major types of experts:

Trial experts. A trial expert is an individual who will testify at trial or who is identified by a party as an expert who is likely to testify at trial. The general rule is that a party can discovery everything about this type of expert including the expert's identity, experience, opinions, and basis of opinion. Most states allow this expert to be deposed to obtain this information; some states restrict discovery to interrogatory questions and answers.

Retained or Specially Employed Experts. This type of expert is an individual who is retained or specially employed by a party in anticipation of litigation or to assist in the preparation for trial. Information about this type of expert is generally very limited, if anything is permitted to be discovered. Many states only permit the discovery of the identity of this type of expert and nothing more. The reason supporting such restrictive disclosure is that this expert assists the attorney in a case and does not have any factual information or any opinions that will be evidence in the case. If this expert were to testify, the expert would be a trial expert and more information would be discoverable.

Employee Experts. Experts who are employees of a party are generally treated as any other employee of a party for discovery purposes. Typically, broad discovery is available from any party agent or employee, including an employee who is an expert or who has expert information. An employee expert may be a full-time or part-time employee. An expert who is an independent contractor would more likely be categorized as a retained or specially employed expert.

An "Actor" Expert. Witnesses who acquire their information as participants or viewers involved in the occurrence or transaction giving rise to the lawsuit are "actor" experts. Often they are parties to the case, and their expertise or conduct is an issue in the case (*e.g.*, a defendant physician in a medical malpractice case). An actor expert may be called upon to serve three possible roles during discovery: that of an adverse party or agent, that of an eyewitness, or that of an expert. The general rule is that their identities and facts known to them will be discoverable and that their opinions may or may not be discoverable depending upon the specific role they play in the case.

Informally Consulted Expert. An "informally consulted" expert is an expert who has been approached by a party for some information or an initial opinion but who will not testify at trial, has not been retained or specially employed, is not an employee of the party, and is not an actor in the case. It is common for a party or attorney initially to discuss a case and informally consult with an expert to determine the expert's opinion. The general rule is that nothing is discoverable from or about an informally consulted expert.

After an expert has been categorized as one or more of these types, the attorneys should review the applicable state rules of civil procedure and determine what is discoverable and how the information is to be discovered from such an expert.

§ 5.8.3 Expert Discovery in Federal Cases

Federal Rule 26 includes two sections regarding expert information and testimony: Rule 26(a)(2) provides for the disclosure of expert testimony. Rule 26(b)(4) provides for the discovery of information from experts. The term "expert" regarding disclosure and discovery is the same term used with respect to scientific, technical, and other specialized matter under the Federal Rules of Evidence.

Rule 26(a)(2) requires a party to reveal two specific types of required disclosures:

1. Rule (a)(2)(A) requires that a party "disclose to other parties any person who may be used at trial to present evidence under Rule 702, 703, or 705 of the Federal Rules of Evidence." This subdivision requires the disclosure of the identity of any potential trial expert. The definition of who a trial expert is to be is resolved by a reference to the rules of evidence governing expert testimony.

2. Rule 26(a)(2)(B) requires that a disclosure "be accompanied by a written report prepared and signed by the witness" with respect to "a witness who is retained or specially employed to provide expert testimony in the case or whose duty is as an employee of the party regularly involved in giving expert testimony." This subdivision requires a report to be prepared by those trial experts who are retained or specially employed or who are employees of the party, and this report must be disclosed. This rule requires that: "The report shall contain a complete statement of all opinions to be expressed and the basis and reasons therefore; the data or other information considered by the witness informing the opinions; any exhibits to be used in a summary of or support for the opinion; the qualifications of the witness, including a list of all publications authored by the witness within the proceeding 10 years; the compensation to be paid for the study and testimony; and a listing of any other cases in which the witness has testified as an expert at trial or by deposition within the proceeding four years."

Now that is full disclosure. The purpose of this disclosure is to provide the other parties with the complete testimony to be presented by the experts and all documentary evidence. The requirement that all exhibits or charts be disclosed eliminates, or substantially reduces, the argument that materials furnished to experts to be used in forming their opinions are protected from disclosure or discovery because of privilege or other reason. The written report, complete with all documents and exhibits, must be signed by the witness and should be written in a way that reflects the testimony that will be given by the witness.

Rule 26(e)(1) requires the disclosure of any material changes made in the opinions of an expert from whom a report is required, including changes in the written report or testimony given at a deposition.

A disclosing party has a substantial incentive to comply with this disclosure rule because revised Rule 37(c)(1) contains the sanction that the party will not ordinarily be permitted to use any expert testimony on direct examination not disclosed in accord with Rule 26. The timing of the disclosure of expert information under Rule 26(a)(1)(B) will typically be determined by a scheduling order pursuant to Federal Rule 16(b).

Rule 26(b)(4) governs the discoverability of additional expert testimony:

1. Rule 26(b)(4)(A) states that: "A party may depose any person who has been identified as an expert and whose opinions may be presented at trial." This new rule specifically permits the deposition of all trial experts, which reflects current practice. This subdivision specifies that a deposition shall not be conducted of an expert who is required to provide a written report in accord with 26(a)(2)(B). This will make certain that the deposition will occur after the expert has prepared testimony and supporting documents.

2. Rule 26(b)(4)(B) allows a party through interrogatories or by deposition to discover facts known or opinions held by an expert who has been retained or specially employed by another party and who is not expected to testify at trial upon a showing of exceptional circumstances. This rule infrequently applies to cases because of the special requirements and unusual circumstances.

3. Rule (b)(4)(C) repeats the provisions of the current rule regarding the compensation of experts. Parties may agree to bear their own cost and not seek compensation because they may be seeking discovery information from each other's experts.

The parties by written stipulation can modify these disclosure requirements in any way. A court by order or local rule may similarly waive or impose additional obligations.

§ 5.9 SUPPLEMENTATION

Rule 26(e) imposes a continuing duty to supplement disclosures and discovery responses. The duty to supplement extends to all forms of discovery requests, including interrogatories, depositions, requests for production, and requests for admissions. The courts within their sound discretion will interpret Rule 26(e) and apply the disclosure duty to appropriate situations.

Rule 26(e) requires a party to supplement disclosure and discovery responses that are "incomplete or incorrect" in "some material respect" and if the additional corrective information has not been otherwise made known to the other parties during the discovery process or has been provided to them in writing. There is no obligation to provide complete or correct information if the other parties learn about the supplemental information.

The rule imposes a duty to supplement all disclosures "in appropriate intervals." Supplementation need not be made as each new item of information is learned by a party, but should be made at appropriate intervals during the discovery period, and with special promptness as a trial date approaches. A scheduling order may specify the time or times when supplementation should be made. Rule 26(e) also explicitly extends the duty to supplement disclosures to expert information contained in a report or through a deposition and requires that these additions or changes be made by the time the party's disclosures under Rule 26(a)(3) are due.

Subdivision 26(e)(2) establishes a "duty seasonably to amend a prior response to an interrogatory, request for production, or requests for admission." This duty does not extend to deposition testimony, with the exception of deposition testimony by experts pursuant to 26(a)(2)(B). Changes in deposition testimony may be made by correcting a deposition transcript. A witness who testifies differently at trial from a deposition transcript may be impeached.

The term "seasonably" will depend upon the facts and circumstances of each case. A party who delays for several months the disclosure of supplemental information may be barred from doing so because it is not timely. The more the supplemental responses affect a party's trial preparation and presentation, resulting in undue prejudice, the more likely a court will determine a supplementation is not done seasonably.

A party can use additional discovery requests for obtaining supplemental information and make certain that responses are complete and correct. A party may serve additional discovery requests including interrogatories and requests for production. Or an attorney may stipulate with opposing counsel attorney to supplement and update all or selected previous discovery requests. Or a party may seek a court order during a pretrial conference or hearing requiring additional supplemental disclosures.

§ 5.10 PROTECTIVE ORDERS

§ 5.10.1 Introduction

The discovery rules include a provision protecting attorneys from each other. Rule 26(c) permits a party, or anyone involved in a discovery request, to bring a motion seeking a court order and protection from some aspects of discovery.

A sample motion will resemble the following form:

[Caption]

Plaintiff moves this court for an order pursuant to Rule 26(c) [describe relief sought]. A copy of a proposed order is attached to this motion.

There exists good cause to support this motion in that [explain reasons for order, such as assertion of privilege or explanation of undue burden or expense or annoyance, embarrassment, or oppression].

This motion is based upon the notice, pleadings, records, and files in this action; the supporting affidavits of [party, or witness, or attorney]; the attached memorandum of law [if necessary or appropriate]; and oral and documentary evidence to be presented at the hearing on the motion [if anticipated].

____

[Signature]

Before a party may bring a Rule 26(c) motion in federal court the movant must confer—either in person or by telephone—with the other parties in a good faith effort to resolve the discovery dispute. The movant must explain these efforts in a written certification which accompanies the protective order motion. The purpose of this provision is to encourage the parties to resolve their differences without the need for court intervention and to rely upon the court for a protective order only if the parties are unable to mutually resolve their problems.

The movant has the burden to show "good cause" why justice requires protection from "annoyance, embarrassment, oppression, or undue burden or expense."[1] The rule balances one party's need for information with another party's right to certain protections. Indeed, the issue involved with most motions for protective orders "is not whether the court is going to allow parties to embark upon a fishing expedition, but whether the court may make the voyage more pleasant for those who are required to become passengers by the Rules of Civil Procedure."[2]

Information obtained by a party through the discovery process may be used in any way that the law permits, subject to the provisions on protective orders. "The implication is clear that without a protective order, materials obtained in discovery may be used by a party for any purpose...."[3] The movant's burden to show the necessity for a protective order includes a particular and specific demonstration of facts as distinguished from general and conclusory statements. This demonstration must be made through the submission of affidavits or the introduction of evidence or information supporting the grounds of the motion.[4]

The person seeking the protective order may have to take some steps to preserve the right to obtain the order. A deponent cannot fail to attend a properly noticed deposition and later seek a protective order against such discovery.[5] A party cannot seek protection from interrogatories or requests for productions or admissions without first filing timely and appropriate objections to such requests.[6] Local rules may also affect the right of a party to seek a protective order. The failure to comply with a rule that requires counsel to confer with the opposing party in good faith to resolve issues before filing motions raises the risk of the protective order's being denied on a procedural basis.[7]

§ 5.10

1. *See Reliance Insurance Co. v. Barron's,* 428 F.Supp. 200 (S.D.N.Y.1977) (burden); *Lincoln American Corp. v. Bryden,* 375 F.Supp. 109 (D.Kan.1973) (annoyance, expense, and embarrassment).

2. *Twin City Federal Savings & Loan Association v. American Title Insurance Co.,* 31 F.R.D. 526 (W.D.Mo.1962).

3. *In re Halkin,* 598 F.2d 176, 188 (D.C.Cir.1979).

4. *See Lewis v. Capital Mortgage Investments,* 78 F.R.D. 295 (D.Md.1977).

5. *Hudson Tire Mart, Inc. v. Aetna Casualty & Surety Co.,* 518 F.2d 671 (2d Cir. 1975).

6. 4 Moore's Federal Practice ¶ 26.68, at 26–492 (2d ed. 1989).

7. *Quaker Chair Corp. v. Litton Business Systems, Inc.,* 71 F.R.D. 527 (S.D.N.Y. 1976).

Attorneys will often stipulate to provisions protecting discovery information. These provisions may be incorporated into a stipulation signed by the attorneys or may be incorporated into a proposed order jointly submitted to a court for routine approval. Reasonable attorneys will be able to accommodate each other's needs through stipulations without becoming involved in contested motions for protective orders. The reasons supporting a protective order will usually correspond to the nature and scope of the protective orders sought. Rule 26(c) lists a number of available protective orders. The following subsections discuss them.

§ 5.10.2 That Discovery Not Be Had

Courts have granted protective orders prohibiting discovery of parties and witnesses because of ill health; [8] if a discovery request is submitted to a party at the eleventh hour, in an untimely fashion; [9] and if discovery questions do not pursue legitimate needs, but instead constitute an attempt to take advantage of trial preparation efforts.[10] Courts will preclude discovery from one person until other individuals who appear to have more knowledge of the facts have been examined.[11]

§ 5.10.3 That Discovery Be Had Only on Specified Terms and Conditions

Courts have explicit power to control the time and place of conducting discovery if the parties themselves are unable to reach agreement.[12] Courts have considered the financial positions of the deponent and the parties in designating a place for the deposition [13] and have declared that the lengthy examination of a sick or elderly deponent may not be permitted.[14] Courts have also scheduled the sequence of discovery in appropriate circumstances, by requiring the taking of a deposition before the disclosure of documents and by requiring responses to interrogatories before the taking of depositions.[15] Simultaneous submission of interrogatories and requests for production have been coordinated by court order in cases involving multiple defendants.[16] Likewise, simulta-

8. *Celanese Corp. v. Duplan Corp.*, 502 F.2d 188 (4th Cir.1974), *cert. denied* 420 U.S. 929, 95 S.Ct. 1128, 43 L.Ed.2d 400 (1975).

9. *Global Maritime Leasing Panama, Inc. v. M/S North Breeze Nav. Co., Ltd.*, 451 F.Supp. 965 (D.R.I.1978).

10. *Schweinert v. Insurance Co. of North America*, 1 F.R.D. 247 (S.D.N.Y. 1940).

11. *See Salter v. Upjohn Co.*, 593 F.2d 649 (5th Cir.1979).

12. *Detweiler Brothers, Inc. v. John Graham & Co.*, 412 F.Supp. 416 (E.D.Wash. 1976).

13. *Leist v. Union Oil Co. of California*, 82 F.R.D. 203 (D.Wis.1979).

14. *De Wagenknecht v. Stinnes*, 243 F.2d 413 (D.C.Cir.1957), *cert. denied* 355 U.S. 830, 78 S.Ct. 44, 2 L.Ed.2d 43 (1957).

15. *Smith v. China Merchants Steam Navigation Co., Limited*, 59 F.R.D. 178 (E.D.Pa.1972).

16. *Rochester Gypsum Co-operative, Inc. v. National Gypsum Co.*, 23 Fed.R.Serv.2d 355 (E.D.Pa.1976).

neous disclosure of discovery information will be ordered, in certain cases, if the information would influence either side's response.[17]

Litigants may seek protective orders preventing the disclosure of discovery information to the public and to the press. Court rulings have not been uniform in dealing with these issues, but the courts do recognize the privacy interests of litigants and the public interest in limiting the use of the fruits of discovery to the litigation process and not permitting the use of discovery to obtain information for other purposes.[18] The right to confidentiality is balanced against the First Amendment rights of the press and the public to know what transpires in open court and open court files. The claimed right of free access to discovery materials has been rejected, however, and protective orders may be issued to protect the valid interests of litigants to keep discovery confidential. Nonetheless in the absence of a protective order, discovery materials may be freely disseminated.[19]

§ 5.10.4 That Discovery Be Had Only by a Particular Method

One court has restricted discovery to interrogatories and denied a party the opportunity to take a deposition, because the interrogatory answers supplied sufficient information in light of the apparent lack of a meritorious claim by the discovering party.[20] Another court ordered a party to proceed by way of an oral deposition rather than by written interrogatories because the court questioned the purpose and motive of the discovering party and because the deposition would be sufficient to produce the information.[21] Courts are inclined to substitute one mode of discovery for another to protect someone's health, by substituting a written deposition for an oral deposition.[22] Courts base their choice of a discovery device in part upon the interest to be served by the information sought.

§ 5.10.5 That Certain Matters Not Be Inquired Into

Courts have limited the inquiry of discovery requests to specific, limited topics. Discovery inquiries into privileged matter or burdensome or oppressive requests will be restricted by protective orders.[23] Discov-

17. *Davis v. General Motors Corp.,* 64 F.R.D. 420 (N.D.Ill.1974).

18. *See Seattle Times Co. v. Rhinehart,* 467 U.S. 20, 104 S.Ct. 2199, 81 L.Ed.2d 17 (1984), *cert. denied* 467 U.S. 1230, 104 S.Ct. 2690, 81 L.Ed.2d 884 (1984); *Tavoulareas v. Washington Post Co.,* 724 F.2d 1010 (D.C.Cir.1984), *on rehearing* 737 F.2d 1170 (1984).

19. *See In re Halkin,* 598 F.2d 176, 188 (D.C.Cir.1979).

20. *Shirley v. Chestnut,* 603 F.2d 805, 807 (10th Cir.1979).

21. *Fishman v. A.H. Riise Gift Shop, Inc.,* 68 F.R.D. 704, 705 (D.V.I.1975).

22. *See* James L. Underwood, A Guide to Federal Discovery Rules 86 (1980).

23. *See* Fed.R.Civ.P. 26(c), Advisory Comm. Notes—1970 Amendments.

ery issues have been limited to those issues raised in a motion for summary judgment.[24]

§ 5.10.6 That Discovery Be Conducted With No One Present Except Persons Designated by the Court

In wrestling with the question of who may be present during a deposition and who may have access to certain discovery information, courts have generally declared that discovery proceedings must take place in public and become part of the public record, unless some compelling reason exists for denying public access to the proceedings.[25] Courts have also claimed for themselves the authority to limit who attends depositions, even excluding parties to a lawsuit.[26] One court recognized that such exclusion should be rarely granted, but itself excluded a party from a deposition to protect the other party from embarrassment or ridicule.[27] Another court precluded deponents from attending the depositions of other deponents because of the subtle and sensitive issues of the case.[28]

Restricting attendance at depositions helps control the dissemination of discovery information when deemed necessary. For example, the disclosure of discovery information has been restricted exclusively to a party's trial counsel for use in preparation of the trial because of the confidential nature of the information.[29] Other courts have ordered information to be disclosed selectively to other participants in the trial process, such as experts.[30]

An example of a written assurance signed by a participant in the litigation process follows:

[Caption]

I, [insert name, business position, and address], being duly sworn, state that:

1. I reside at [address].

2. I have read and fully understood the Protective Order dated ______, 19__.

3. I am engaged as a [insert description of position] on behalf of ______ in the preparation or conduct of the action entitled [title of action].

4. I am fully familiar with and agree to comply with and be bound by the provisions of the order.

24. *See Scroggins v. Air Cargo, Inc.*, 534 F.2d 1124, 1133 (5th Cir.1976), *rehearing denied* 540 F.2d 1085 (1976).

25. *American Telephone & Telegraph Co. v. Grady,* 594 F.2d 594, 596 (7th Cir. 1978), *cert. denied* 440 U.S. 971, 99 S.Ct. 1533, 59 L.Ed.2d 787 (1979).

26. *Beacon v. R.M. Jones Apartment Rentals,* 79 F.R.D. 141, 142 (N.D.Ohio 1978).

27. *Galella v. Onassis,* 487 F.2d 986, 997 (2d Cir.1973).

28. *See Beacon v. R.M. Jones Apartment Rentals,* 79 F.R.D. 141 (N.D.Ohio 1978) (whether the defendants engaged in unlawful discriminatory housing practices).

29. *Scovill Manufacturing Co. v. Sunbeam Corp.,* 61 F.R.D. 598, 602 (D.Del. 1973).

30. *See Gentron Corp. v. H.C. Johnson Agencies, Inc.,* 79 F.R.D. 415, 418 (E.D.Wis. 1978).

5. I will not divulge to persons other than those specifically authorized by the order, and will not copy or use, except solely for the purpose of this action, any information obtained pursuant to the order except as expressly permitted by the court.

6. For the purposes of enforcing compliance with this order, I irrevocably submit to the jurisdiction of the United States District Court for the [district] and appoint the clerk of the court as agent for the service of process, pleadings, and other papers in connection with all claims arising out of this written assurance.

____

[Signature of Affiant]

[Notary Subscription]

Non-parties have challenged protective orders that denied them access to certain information. Government investigators, who sometimes need information the access to which has been restricted by a court order, have challenged protective orders denying them information disclosed through discovery. In reviewing these orders, courts balance the government's need for the information with the civil litigant's need for privacy.[31] Parties also have sought to prevent discovery disclosure to non-party individuals on the grounds that such disclosure may foment additional litigation. One court rejected this view and declared that collaboration among lawyers and other persons to distribute discoverable information is appropriate, may reduce time and money expended in similar proceedings, and promotes "effective, speedy, and efficient representation."[32] Where disclosure has occurred only in reliance on a protective order, however, the courts are disinclined to allow later dissemination of the material.

§ 5.10.7 That a Deposition Be Sealed and Opened Only by Order of the Court

Courts may issue protective orders which require that the discovered information be sealed and filed with the court. This procedure prevents unnecessary disclosure of discovered information. Some courts have adopted local rules that achieve the same result in all cases, or limit the right of persons other than counsel of record to obtain access to the deposition.

§ 5.10.8 That a Trade Secret or Other Confidential Information Not Be Disclosed or Be Disclosed Only in a Designated Way

Courts may also restrict access to trade secret information until such disclosure is necessary to adjudicate the case. The primary factor courts consider in determining the appropriateness of this type of protective order is the degree to which the disclosure of such confidential

31. *See Martindell v. International Telephone & Telegraph Corp.*, 594 F.2d 291 (2d Cir.1979).

32. *Patterson v. Ford Motor Co.*, 85 F.R.D. 152, 154 (W.D.Tex.1980).

information will place a party in a significant competitive disadvantage with another party or with competitors.[33] This main factor can be subdivided into four criteria: "(1) the extent to which information is known outside the business; (2) the extent to which information is known to those inside the business; (3) measures taken to guard the secrecy of the information; and (4) the value of the information to the business and its competitors." [34]

§ 5.10.9 That Parties Simultaneously File Discovery Responses

This provision is most often involved in patent cases, to prevent one side from being influenced by, and altering its own responses because of, information gained through discovery from the other side. It is available in other situations, however, and may be a useful discovery tool.

§ 5.10.10 That the Court Make Any Order Which Justice Requires

This catch-all section will occasionally be used by courts to justify protective orders in situations other than the specific situations enumerated in Rule 26(c). The clause reflects the broad discretion a court has to shape discovery and has been used to justify a court's direct supervision of discovery or the appointment of a master to do so.

§ 5.10.11 Summary

Any party may seek a protective order providing for one or more of the above-enumerated provisions. A non-party in an appropriate case may obtain permission to intervene for the limited purpose of supporting, opposing, or modifying a protective order.[35]

Judges consider various factors when exercising their discretion to grant or deny protective order motions, depending on the facts and circumstances of the particular case. Some general criteria include: (1) the harm caused by the disclosure of information must be substantial and serious; (2) the protective order must be drawn precisely; and (3) there must be no alternative way of protecting the interest of the party seeking the protective order.

Courts also have discretion to modify a protective order.[36] The party or persons seeking modification must either show that the original order was granted improvidently or show some extraordinary circumstance or compelling need requiring disclosure. Parties and witnesses

33. *Parsons v. General Motors Corp.*, 29 Fed.R.Serv.2d 175, 177 (N.D.Ga.1980).

34. *Reliance Insurance Co. v. Barron's*, 428 F.Supp. 200, 203 (S.D.N.Y.1977).

35. *See, e.g., Martindell v. International Telephone & Telegraph Corp.*, 594 F.2d 291, 294–295 (2d Cir.1979).

36. *American Telephone & Telegraph Co. v. Grady*, 594 F.2d 594, 596 (7th Cir. 1978), *cert. denied* 440 U.S. 971, 99 S.Ct. 1533, 59 L.Ed.2d 787 (1979).

should be entitled to rely upon the enforceability of an original protective order. Courts also have the inherent power to review information in camera or to permit opposing counsel to participate in such in camera proceedings.

Protective orders will reflect the circumstances of a particular case. An order may need to include provisions for abstracts and indexes of classified information,[37] or may require a party or witness to return all documents and copies of discovery information at the close of litigation.[38] Because some provisions of a protective order will be difficult to enforce, courts have considered this fact in determining whether a protective order should be issued at all.

The reasons why someone may obtain a protective order are limited only by the creativity of the attorney seeking protection. The extent of the burden the movant must shoulder will vary depending on the type of relief sought. The more protective the relief, the more persuasive the good-cause showing must be. The reasons that support the court's decision to grant or deny motions are similarly limitless. Judges balance the conflicting interests of the various parties and attempt to fashion a remedy that reflects those interests. Rule 26(c) motions for protective orders will often be a response to a motion under Rule 37 brought by the opposition seeking an order compelling discovery. Rule 37(a) allows the court to enter a protective order upon the denial of a motion to compel discovery even if the objecting party does not move for such a protective order.

§ 5.11 OVERALL DISCOVERY STRATEGY

§ 5.11.1 Discovery by Agreement

A substantial amount of discovery is exchanged by agreement of attorneys. Rule 29 encourages such agreement by making any stipulation, other than one changing certain time limits, enforceable as if it were adopted by rule. Such a stipulation may be equivalent to a court order. Federal Rule 29 provides:

> Unless otherwise directed by the court, the parties may by written stipulation (1) provide that depositions may be taken before any person, any time or place, upon any notice, and in any matter may be taken and may used by other depositions, and (2) modify other procedures governing or limitations placed upon discovery, except the stipulation extending the time provided in Rule 33, 34, and 36 for responses to discovery may, if they would interfere with any time set for completion of discovery, hearing of a motion, or for a trial, be made only with the approval of the court.

37. *See Duplan Corp. v. Moulinage et Retorderie de Chavanoz,* 509 F.2d 730, 736–737 (4th Cir.1974), *cert. denied* 420 U.S. 997, 95 S.Ct. 1438, 43 L.Ed.2d 680 (1975), *appeal after remand* 540 F.2d 1215 (4th Cir.1976).

38. *Haykel v. G.F.L. Furniture Leasing Co.,* 76 F.R.D. 386, 391 (N.D.Ga.1976).

This rule allows attorneys to agree to conduct discovery to meet the specific needs of their client in a case. Specific provisions of discovery rules may also provide attorneys with explicit authority to vary discovery procedures. Attorneys may disclose information, exchange documents, and schedule depositions without formally complying with the rules of civil procedure. These agreements may need to be memorialized in a written stipulation or may be enforceable by an oral agreement between the attorneys, depending upon the applicable rule. As a practical matter, while some rules including Rule 29, require a written stipulation, the attorneys may vary the rules based on their oral agreement because no attorney objects to the lack of the written stipulation. In federal cases, it is a better practice to use a written stipulation when required because the judge may expect such stipulation to be filed and to ensure the agreement will be enforceable. In state cases allowing informal compliance with the rules, a written agreement may be unnecessary.

A written stipulation is a document containing the agreement and signed by all the parties or by all the attorneys representing parties in a case. A confirming letter signed and sent by one attorney to another is not a formal written stipulation, although it may be a basis to prove that the receiving attorney agreed to a change and waived any objection to the non-compliance with the rule. Stipulations between attorneys are frequently used to allow more interrogatories than those provided by the rules, permit medical examinations, exchange expert reports, and regulate depositions.

Judges generally favor the use of stipulations because they allow the parties to fashion an efficient and economical discovery plan and because they reduce the need for court intervention. The primary limitation placed or the use of stipulations is the inability of attorneys to extend time limits for certain discovery responses. The reason for this restriction is to prevent litigants from unnecessarily prolonging the trial of a case and to reserve to the court the power to control scheduled proceedings. A judge may impose a sanction against parties or for an agreement not authorized by the rules. However, unless there has been an inordinate delay causing prejudice to a party, judges appear to prefer applying the so-what doctrine and ignore the rule violations. In cases where a judge has issued a scheduling order or imposed discovery cutoff dates, these orders control and prevent attorneys unilaterally changing the dates except with permission of the court. While judges may wink at the attorneys non-compliance with the rule, they enforce what steadfast eyes their own orders.

A sample stipulation and order follows:

[Caption]

[Plaintiff] and [defendant] stipulate that the time to respond to the [describe discovery request] shall be extended from [scheduled date or new date or number of days].

[Responding party] needs more time to respond because [explain reasons].

A court may issue an order upon the filing of this stipulation without any notice or hearing. The order shall take effect upon the filing and receipt of the order upon the [responding attorney] through the mail.

____

[Signatures]

Upon the stipulation of the parties,

IT IS ORDERED that [party] shall have until [new date] in which to respond to the [describe discovery request] served and filed by [party].

Dated: This ______ day of ______, 19__.

____

Judge

The uses of stipulations are endless, and an attorney who approaches discovery with a cooperative attitude may frequently obtain discovery which would not be obtainable by motion. The first effective step in any discovery plan may be asking the opposing lawyer mutually to agree on specific discovery steps. The worst that can happen is that your ideas will be rejected. It will not have been the first time, nor will it be anywhere near the last.

§ 5.11.2 Planning a Discovery Program

Rule 26(d) provides that discovery methods may be used in any sequence. This provision eliminated the priority system for determining the timing of discovery, which had the party who first noticed or demanded discovery proceeding with discovery before the opposition could proceed. The current provision envisions discovery proceeding concurrently, eliminates any fixed priority regarding discovery, and provides courts with the clear power to establish priority if need be.

Procedural rules vary regarding the sequence and timing of discovery. Federal rules establish specific procedures for the regulation of discovery. Some state cases proceed without any set schedule, with discovery exchanges occurring randomly. Other cases include an informal, unwritten schedule resulting in timely discovery exchanges.

Federal Rule 26(f) requires parties to confer and develop a discovery plan. This plan is to contain a mutual agreement by the parties or their separate, different views concerning:

- What disclosures will be made, and any change in the timing and scope of these disclosures.
- What discovery requests will be served, when responses will be due, and when discovery should be completed.
- What changes will be made in any of the applicable discovery rules.
- What additional pleadings may be served.

- What motions may be brought and when.
- Any other issues that affect litigation.
- Why the attorneys went to law school and decided to become litigators.

All attorneys of record and all unrepresented parties must be present or represented at the meeting and attempt in good faith to agree on a discovery plan. Defendants must participate even if they have not yet filed an answer or brought a Rule 12 motion. The rule requires the parties to meet as soon as practical after the case has been filed and served, and, typically, the parties should meet within 60 to 90 days after the complaint have been served.

A sample report including a discovery plan may look like this:

Form 35.

REPORT OF PARTIES' PLANNING MEETING

[Caption and Names of Parties]

1. Pursuant to Fed.R.Civ.P. 26(f), a meeting was held on __(date)__ at 17 __(place)__ and was attended by:

__(name)__ for plaintiff(s)

__(name)__ for defendant(s) __(party name)__

__(name)__ for defendant(s) __(party name)__

2. Pre–Discovery Disclosures. The parties [have exchanged] [will exchange by __(date)__] the information required by [Fed.R.Civ.P. 26(a)(1)] [local rule ______].

3. Discovery Plan. The parties jointly propose to the court the following discovery plan: [Use separate paragraphs or subparagraphs as necessary if parties disagree.]

Discovery will be needed on the following subjects: __(brief description of subjects on which discovery will be needed)__

All discovery commenced in time to be completed by __(date)__. [Discovery on __(issue for early discovery)__ to be completed by __(date)__.]

Maximum of ______ interrogatories by each party to any other party. [Responses due ______ days after service.]

Maximum of ______ requests for admission by each party to any other party. [Responses due ______ days after service.]

Maximum of ______ depositions by plaintiff(s) and ______ by defendant(s).

Each deposition [other than of ______] limited to maximum of ______ hours unless extended by agreement of parties.

Reports from retained experts under Rule 26(a)(2) due:

from plaintiff(s) by __(date)__

from defendant(s) by __(date)__

Supplementations under Rule 26(e) due __(time(s) or interval(s))__.

4. Other Items. [Use separate paragraphs or subparagraphs as necessary if parties disagree.]

The parties [request] [do not request] a conference with the court before entry of the scheduling order.

The parties request a pretrial conference in (month and year).

Plaintiff(s) should be allowed until (date) to join additional parties and until (date) to amend the pleadings.

Defendant(s) should be allowed until (date) to join additional parties and until (date) to amend the pleadings.

All potentially dispositive motions should be filed by (date).

Settlement [is likely] [is unlikely] [cannot be evaluated prior to (date)] [may be enhanced by use of the following alternative dispute resolution procedure: [______]].

Final lists of witnesses and exhibits under Rule 26(a)(3) should be due

from plaintiff(s) by (date)

from defendant(s) by (date)

Parties should have ______ days after service of final lists of witnesses and exhibits to list objections under Rule 26(a)(3).

The case should be ready for trial by (date) [and at this time is expected to take approximately (length of time)].

[Other matters.]

Date: ______

(Added Apr. 22, 1993, eff. Dec. 1, 1993.)

Parties may be unable to agree on a discovery plan for a number of reasons. If the reasons are legitimate, the written report should indicate the differences. If the reasons appear to a party to be illegitimate, that party may seek sanctions against the offending party in accord with Rule 37(g). In some cases, disagreements may exist because the conference between the attorneys occurs too early and an extension or delay of the issuance of the final report may result in a subsequent agreement.

After the parties submit a discovery plan and report to the court, a judge will typically issue a scheduling order establishing deadlines for discovery, motions, and pretrial disclosures. Judges typically establish these schedules based upon administrative and judicial guidelines for the disposition of cases. Judge have to report the status of their case docket to an administrator in their jurisdiction, and the scheduling deadlines for cases reflect the time deadlines imposed on judges by administrative rules and guidelines.

The initial discovery and litigation plan of a case will be affected by subsequent pretrial disclosures. As a case approaches trial, the parties will need to exchange additional information about trial evidence and procedures. The details of these pretrial orders depends upon the applicable procedural rules and pretrial orders issued by a judge in a case. Federal Rule 26(a)(3) and similar state rules require specific pretrial disclosures which require parties to provide each other with the following evidentiary information: (1) the name, address, telephone number of each witness the party may call at trial (2) the designation of those witnesses whose testimony is expected to be presented by means of a deposition, (3) an appropriate identification of each document or other exhibit including summaries of evidence that may be offered at trial. These disclosures must be made at least 30 days before trial, unless otherwise directed by the court which may commonly occur through a scheduling or pretrial order. The timing of the disclosures represents an effort to provide sufficient time for final trial preparation for cases that do not settle and to allow lawyers to bring motions a reasonable time before trial challenging the introduction of some of this evidence. See § 15.3.

§ 5.11.3 Factual Stipulations

The process of discovery may be supplanted or supplemented by stipulations between attorneys regarding the facts. The decision whether to suggest, accept, reject, or modify a fact stipulation proposal depends upon the accuracy and completeness of the stipulation, the amount of time and expenses saved, and the impact such a proposal has upon strategic considerations. Such stipulations may be drafted as formal, written agreements, or read into a deposition transcript, or included as part of a pretrial agreement, or reserved for the trial record. The attorneys are free to reach any reasonable agreement regarding the effect the stipulation has on evidentiary, trial, and other litigation elements.[39] The components of such agreements may include some of the following alternative statements, in addition to factual recitals:

1. The witness, if asked the proper questions, would testify that . . .;

2. The facts may be received as evidence at the trial without the laying of any additional foundation;

3. The documents are authentic, genuine, and admissible as evidence;

4. The contents of the stipulation constitute evidence for trial and may be introduced as evidence at the request of either party;

5. Neither party may object to the introduction or receipt of the facts as evidence;

6. The parties waive all objections to the introduction and receipt of the contents of the stipulation as evidence;

7. The contents of this stipulation may be received in evidence on behalf of any party as permitted by the Federal Rules of Evidence, to the same extent as if the witness so testified at a deposition or preliminary hearing or motion hearing or trial;

8. The facts recited in this stipulation remain subject to evidentiary objections interposed by either party.

39. *See Seay v. International Association of Machinists,* 360 F.Supp. 123 (C.D.Cal.1973).

§ 5.12 PRE-COMPLAINT DISCOVERY: RULE 27

§ 5.12.1 Introduction

There are two situations in which it would be helpful, if not essential, to engage in some discovery prior to the formal initiation of litigation. One circumstance involves insufficient information with which to frame a pleading. Another involves the preservation of evidence that may not be available later. The rules do not provide any mechanism to obtain discovery in the former situation, but do provide a pre-litigation device to preserve testimony through Rule 27.

If you do not have sufficient data to frame a complaint, you have to do the best you can in drafting a complaint and then proceed with discovery to obtain the required information; you can then follow discovery with the drafting of an amended complaint. Notice pleading allows for skeleton complaints, and you will ordinarily be able to obtain sufficient discovery before being dismissed. Rule 27 is not available to obtain facts with which to base a complaint where there exists no prospective loss of testimony. Courts have continually denied petitions under Rule 27 on the grounds that the rule cannot be used for the purpose of ascertaining facts to be used in drafting a complaint.[1]

In the second situation, Rule 27 allows for taking a pre-complaint deposition for the purpose of perpetuating testimony and preserving evidence. Situations arise that delay the formal start of a lawsuit, causing potential trial evidence to become irrevocably lost. A Rule 27 proceeding is an ancillary or auxiliary procedure to prevent a delay of justice by preserving testimony that would otherwise be lost before the matter to which it relates can become ripe for a judicial determination.[2]

§ 5.12.2 Procedures

In the arsenal of discovery devices available to the practitioner, Rule 27 has limited use. The rule's procedures will be most useful to preserve some specific bit of information or evidence likely to be lost unless it is preserved. Three specific procedural conditions must be met before its provisions become operational:

1. The matter must be "cognizable in any court in the United States . . ." At the time of the filing of the petition, the expected action must fall within the jurisdiction of the federal courts. A Rule 27 proceeding must be supported by the jurisdictional grounds of the underlying anticipated lawsuit.

2. The petition must be filed "in the district of the residence of any expected adverse party." This provision determines the proper venue for filing the petition.

§ 5.12

1. *In re Gurnsey,* 223 F.Supp. 359 (D.D.C.1963).

2. *De Wagenknecht v. Stinnes,* 250 F.2d 414 (D.C.Cir.1957).

3. The petition must contain a caption setting forth the name of the petitioner and other matters. An accepted form is: "In the Matter of the Petition of Yoda to perpetuate the testimony of the Force."

§ 5.12.3 Contents of the Petition

The petition itself includes the several specific elements outlined in Rule 27 and a request for the specific relief sought. Necessary elements include:

1. Petitioner must expect to be a party to a specific action. Petitioner may be a plaintiff or a potential defendant.

2. Petitioner must presently be unable to bring the action or to cause it to be brought.

3. Petitioner must have an interest in the subject matter of the expected action.

4. Petitioner must state the facts that petitioner desires to establish by the proposed testimony. This statement of facts may be a brief, generalized description that allows the judge to determine whether the facts justify being perpetuated. The scope of such information resembles the scope of discovery under Rule 26 in that the information sought need not be admissible in trial, but only reasonably likely to lead to admissible evidence.

5. Petitioner must enumerate the reasons why petitioner desires to perpetuate the information. This factor requires a demonstration of the likelihood that the evidence sought will be lost or suffer a significant decline in quality because of the unavoidable reasons for delay that prevent the action from presently being brought.

6. Petitioner must supply the names or description of persons expected as adverse parties, and their addresses.

7. Petitioner must list the names and addresses of persons to be examined and describe the substance of the testimony expected to be elicited from each. A general description of the hoped-for information will usually suffice to meet the standard and provide the court with enough information to determine the legitimacy of the petition. This summary, when coupled with the other affidavit facts, provides adequate information to the court.

8. Petitioner must request relief. The petitioner must ask for an order authorizing the petitioner to proceed with the perpetuation of the testimony. The request will commonly be for a deposition, but may also be for written answers to interrogatories, responses to requests for production, or examinations under Rule 35.

§ 5.12.4 Other Provisions

Rule 27(a)(2) sets forth the provisions regarding notice and service of the petition. Rule 27(b) also allows proceedings to perpetuate testimony during a pending appeal of an action. This provision recognizes that the lengthy interval between the conclusion of a trial and an appellate judgment may diminish the quantity and quality of evidence. Witnesses may die, physical evidence may deteriorate, memories may fade.

PRACTICE PROBLEMS

Disclosure

1. Prepare a concise outline listing the categories of information and documents that must be affirmatively disclosed by a party in federal court:

   A. Regarding allegations of disputed facts stated with particularity.

   B. Regarding expert information.

   C. Regarding pretrial disclosures.

   D. Regarding other issues or subject matter of a case.

2. Prepare a concise outline listing the categories of the information and types of subject matter a party may seek from another party through discovery requests and methods in federal court.

3. Prepare a time chart listing the timing and deadlines of required disclosures and the use of discovery methods in federal court cases.

4. Review the complaint and the answer and counterclaim appearing Northern Motor Homes vs. Danforth (Appendix B, Case J). Assume the federal rules of civil procedure apply to these cases. Determine what affirmative disclosures the pleading party must make under Federal Rule.

Relevance

5. During the litigation of Hot Dog Enterprises vs. Tri–Chem, the plaintiff HDE submits interrogatories to defendant Tri–Chem seeking the following information relating to its claims based on fraud and products liability and actual and punitive damages:

   (a) Information regarding all complaints which buildings owners, contractors, and architects have communicated to the defendant about Bond–Mor since its development.

   (b) The names of all building owners which defendant knows own buildings constructed with Bond–Mor.

   (c) The names of all contractors Tri–Chem has solicited to use Bond–Mor.

(d) Financial information showing the net worth of Tri–Chem.

(1) What reasons would you advance on behalf of the defendant Tri–Chem that this information is irrelevant?

(2) What reasons would you advance on behalf of the plaintiff HDE that this information is relevant?

(3) If you were the judge, how would you decide and why?

(4) What other ways might these requests be drafted to make the request more clearly relevant?

6. Tri–Chem deposes Casey Pozdak, HDE Chairperson, and asks questions seeking the following information:

(a) Whether Pozdak has ever been arrested or convicted of any criminal or traffic offense.

(b) Information regarding other law suits HDE has been involved in over the past 10 years.

(c) All information regarding the construction of the HDE restaurant buildings in Kansas.

(d) The names of all HDE employees who have worked in the restaurant in Kansas.

(1) What reasons would you advance on behalf of the plaintiff HDE that this information is irrelevant?

(2) What reasons would you advance on behalf of the defendant Tri–Chem that the information is relevant?

(3) If you were the judge, how would you decide and why?

(4) What other ways might these requests be drafted to make them more clearly relevant?

7. In *Vasquez vs. Hot Dog Enterprises* (Case F), the attorney for HDE deposes Juanita Vasquez and asks her questions seeking the following information:

(a) The names, addresses, and telephone numbers of all men whom she has dated socially since she was 18.

(b) Whether she has had sexual relations or otherwise been intimate with any former or current employees of HDE.

(c) Information regarding any counseling or treatment she has received from any psychiatrist, psychologist, or other counselor.

(d) Facts to support her claim that she has suffered emotional distress.

(1) What reasons would you advance on behalf of the plaintiff Vasquez that this information is irrelevant?

(2) What reasons would you advance on behalf of the defendant HDE that this information is relevant?

(3) If you were the judge, how would you decide and why?

(4) What other ways might these requests be phrased to make the request more clearly relevant?

8. In *Giacone vs. City of Mitchell* (Case D), Martha Giacone individually meets with her attorney in her attorney's office and discusses the following:

(a) Facts regarding her utility services and bills.

(b) Facts regarding her communications with employees of the Department of Water with the City of Mitchell.

Defendant City of Mitchell submits interrogatories asking the following questions:

Explain everything you told your lawyer regarding your utility bills and utility services.

Describe all communications you had with any employee of the City of Mitchell Department of Water regarding your utility bill and services.

(a) Is this information discoverable? Why or why not?

(b) How can these requests be drafted to make them more relevant?

9. During the client interview between Martha Giacone and her attorney, her lawyer renders legal advice about her situation and alternative remedies.

(a) Is this information discoverable? Why or why not?

(b) What type of legal information may be discoverable?

(c) What discovery devices are available to obtain appropriate types of legal information?

10. Martha Giacone, prior to first visiting her attorney, prepares a written statement detailing the facts of her utility dispute and gives this statement to her attorney who places it in the law office file.

(a) Is this memo discoverable? Why or why not?

(b) If, during the course of the attorney-client interview, the lawyer obtains additional facts from the client and wrote that information down in the memo, would the memo or that portion of the memo be discoverable? Why or why not?

11. Before Hot Dog Enterprises sues Tri–Chem, the following occurs:

(a) The attorney for HDE dictates a memorandum to the file summarizing the client interview with Pat LaBelle.

(b) The attorney for HDE has a conference with a law partner regarding the facts, legal theories, and strategies of a potential law suit and subsequently prepares a memo summarizing the discussion.

(c) The attorney has the same discussion with a paralegal with the law firm.

(d) The attorney has the same discussion with an expert witness retained by HDE and the law firm to help investigate a potential law suit.

(e) During the course of legal research, the attorney makes handwritten notes of citations, case notes, and summaries of the law.

(1) Is any of this information discoverable by Tri–Chem? Why or why not? Through interrogatories, requests for production, or depositions?

12. After HDE retains an attorney, but before a law suit is brought against Tri–Chem, the attorney personally begins an investigation by interviewing some eyewitnesses, visiting the restaurant buildings, and summarizing the information in a file memo.

(a) Is that memo or any portion of it discoverable? Why or why not?

(b) Is the information somehow discoverable from the attorney?

(c) Is the information some how discoverable from the eyewitnesses interviewed by the attorney? How?

(d) The attorney hires an independent private investigator who conducts the investigation and prepares a memo for the attorney. Is that memo or any portion of it discoverable from the attorney?

(e) If the private investigator retains a copy of the memo and places it in a file in the investigator's office, is a copy of the memo discoverable from the investigator? Why and how, or why not?

13. At its restaurant in Kansas, some of the bricks which fell hit a customer. Government regulations require HDE to investigate the accident and prepare a report, which is then filed in the company's records and with the government. Is that report discoverable by the customer from HDE in a subsequent law suit brought by the customer against HDE? Explain your answer.

14. HDE has a policy of keeping personnel, evaluation, and termination records which are prepared and maintained by supervisors and kept in the personnel office. HDE fires an employee who subsequently sues HDE claiming job discrimination. Are

the records maintained by HDE regarding that employee discoverable by that employee in this litigation? Explain your answer.

15. The Vice President for Production of Hot Dog Enterprise receives a telephone call from a vendor complaining that the vendor did not receive payment for hot dog ingredients delivered to HDE. The Vice President asks the manager to prepare and file a written report detailing whether the supplies were received and whether or not they were paid. Several months later the vendor sues HDE for breach of contract. Is the report discoverable by the vendor in this litigation with HDE? Explain your answer.

16. While cutting grass one sunny Saturday afternoon, Casey Pozdak witnessed an accident in which a neighbor, Mark, is injured by a lawn mower operated by another neighbor, Helen. Mark retains a lawyer who contacts both Casey and Helen and interviews them.

(a) The attorney for Mark prepares a statement in Casey's own handwriting, which Casey signs, and he has Helen write out her story in her own handwriting and date it, but does not have her sign it. Subsequently, Mark sues Helen for negligence. Can Casey or Helen obtain a copy of their own statements? Why and how, or why not?

(b) Suppose that the attorney does not obtain a written statement from Helen. The attorney returns to his office and dictates a memorandum from his notes. Is the memorandum discoverable by Helen? Why or why not?

(c) Suppose that the attorney does not obtain a written statement from Helen. Instead, the attorney contemporaneously records the conversation with Helen on tape without her knowledge or permission. Is the tape or transcript of the tape or the tape information discoverable by Helen?

17. A worker at the manufacturing plant of Hot Dog Enterprises is injured on the job. A co-worker observes the accident and, at the request of a HDE manager, writes down her eyewitness account, signs the statement, and gives it to the manager, who forwards it to the worker's compensation department of the company. The injured worker brings an action against HDE for the injury. Can the co-worker's statement be obtained by the plaintiff through discovery? Why and how, or why not?

18. During the annual July 4th softball tournament at the national headquarters at the Hot Dog Enterprises, an employee starts a fight with Pat LaBelle after Pat slides into the employee at second base. An HDE attorney suggests that Pat write a report of the incident and place it in the employee's personnel file. Pat does so. Subsequently, HDE fires the employee. The employee sues HDE for breach of employment contract. Is Pat

LaBelle's statement discoverable by the employee during discovery? Explain.

19. In *Hot Dog Enterprise vs. Tri–Chem*, the defendant submits interrogatories to the plaintiff seeking the following information:

(a) All individuals interviewed by or contacted by the plaintiff regarding this litigation.

(b) The identities of all witnesses who provided information or statements to the plaintiff.

(c) All persons who have knowledge relating to the subject matter of this case.

(d) The names of all witnesses that plaintiff will call to testify at the trial.

(1) You are the judge. Which, if any, of this information is discoverable and why?

20. Tri–Chem has monthly management meetings involving the company president, general counsel, six division managers, and a secretary. They discuss company matters at these meetings, and a written memorandum of each meeting is prepared by the secretary and distributed to the eight attendants. In October, Hot Dog Enterprises sent a letter to the president of Tri–Chem alleging that damages to HDE's restaurant buildings in Kansas were caused by the failure of Bond–Mor and detailed the factual basis and legal consequences of HDE's claims. The president of Tri–Chem jotted notes on the letter, indicating her reaction to the contents, and distributed copies to the general counsel and the six division managers. The president then placed two matters on the agenda for the November meeting: (1) Tri–Chem's general advertising campaign regarding Bond–Mor, and (2) the October letter from HDE.

Both matters were discussed during the November meeting, and the subsequent meeting memorandum contained paragraphs summarizing the discussions. During December, the general counsel of Tri–Chem requests a memo from the advertising manager of Tri–Chem regarding his response to the claims in the HDE letter. The product manager from Tri–Chem received a copy of the letter from Tri–Chem to HDE and wrote in the margins:

> "This is the same old problem we've always had. We need to get these bricks and mortar back for testing, or at least to hide the real damaging evidence."

The advertising manager then asked each of his three supervisory advertising personnel to submit to him individual memos with their reactions to the HDE letter, which he had distributed to them. The advertising manager received all three memos in

December and wrote one reply memo in January to the Tri–Chem general counsel. In February, HDE sued Tri–Chem, claiming violation of Federal and State Deceptive Trade Practices statutes, negligence, and product liability. The general counsel of Tri–Chem then personally interviewed each of the three supervisory advertising personnel and recorded the summaries of the interviews in separate memos placed in her files. Tri–Chem retained the law firm of Burn & Albright to defend it in litigation. Burn personally met with the president of Tri–Chem and with each of the six division managers and prepared notes at such interviews, which he placed in his office file.

(1) What positions would you advance on behalf of the plaintiff HDE to obtain all of these memos?

(2) What positions would you advance on behalf of defendant Tri–Chem protecting these documents from disclosure?

(3) As the judge, which of the documents would you rule discoverable:

(a) The October letter from HDE contained handwritten notes by the president of Tri–Chem.

(b) The paragraph summarizing the November meeting discussions.

(c) The letter from Tri–Chem to HDE with the production manager's notes.

(d) The three December memos from the advertising personnel to the advertising manager.

(e) The January memo from the advertising manager to the general counsel.

(f) The February interview memos prepared by the general counsel.

(g) The Burn notes.

21. Hot Dog Enterprises has sued Tri–Chem alleging that the use of Bond–Mor to construct its restaurant buildings in Kansas violated the Deceptive Trade Practices Act and constituted negligence and products liability. Tri–Chem retains you to defend it in this litigation. You conduct a thorough search of all company documents. Your research uncovers all of the documents appearing in Case A in Appendix B.

(1) Plaintiff HDE submits a properly drafted request for production of documents seeking the disclosure of "all documents containing information relevant to the subject matter of this litigation" and "documents relating to the research, development, marketing, advertising, production, and distribution of Bond–Mor." Which of the above documents or portions of them, would you disclose to HDE? What posi-

tions would you advance in refusing to disclose any of these documents, or portions of them?

(2) During your investigation you interview a number of Tri–Chem managers. They advise you that there existed many other documents including memorandums regarding Bond–Mor which were destroyed. Some of these documents were destroyed in the ordinary course of document destruction by Tri–Chem because it is impossible to retain all documents. Some of these documents were destroyed because there was some concern that litigation may ensue and it would be better for Tri–Chem that such documents did not exist. What would you do in response to this information? Would you ask the managers to prepare a list or a summary of documents that were destroyed? Why or why not?

(3) Assume the same facts as in paragraph (2) above. One of the managers tells you that she believes while the hard copy of the documents have been destroyed the data may exist on computer disks and tapes. What would you do in response to this information? Would you ask that a search be conducted for this data on the computer to obtain a hard copy? Would you disclose the existence of this information if the other side properly requests such information? Would you advise Tri–Chem to destroy such computer disks and tapes? Would you affirmatively advise Tri–Chem not to destroy the computer disks and tapes? Would you advise Tri–Chem of the consequences of destroying the computer tapes and disks and leave the decision of destroying such information to your client?

22. A plaintiff is injured as a result of the bricks falling from HDE's restaurant buildings in Kansas when the plaintiff visited the restaurant. The treating physician of the plaintiff composes a written opinion about the physical condition of the plaintiff at the request of the plaintiff's attorney who intends to call the doctor as an expert at the trial. The physician also met with the attorney for the plaintiff and gave an oral opinion regarding the plaintiff's condition. HDE is the defendant. What information must plaintiff affirmatively disclose under Federal Rule 26(a)? What information may HDE discover from the plaintiff regarding information known by, and testimony of the expert physician: Why and how, or why not?

23. A chemist at Tri–Chem is a full-time employee in the Product Development Division and was reassigned to spend one year with a retained outside law firm that represents Tri–Chem in its litigation against HDE regarding Bond–Mor. The chemist during this time conducts non-destructive tests, provides written test reports to Tri–Chem and the law firm, and meets with the

attorneys for the firm and renders oral opinions and written memorandums. What is discoverable by HDE? What must be disclosed by Tri–Chem under Federal Rule 26(a)? Why and how, or why not?

24. Tri–Chem hires an engineer who is a full-time university professor to provide it with an expert opinion regarding one of its products known as roofoam.

(a) Prior to any problems with roofoam or the potential litigation, the professor provides Tri–Chem with an oral opinion and a written report regarding test conclusions about roofoam.

(b) Tri–Chem is sued in a product liability case by plaintiff who claims roofoam to be defective. Tri–Chem again retains the full-time university professor to provide it with an opinion regarding whether roofoam was defective. The expert provides both an oral report and a written report to Tri–Chem.

(1) Which of this information, if any, must be disclosed by Tri–Chem under Federal Rule 26(a) in the product liability case?

(2) Which of this information, if any, is discoverable by the plaintiff in the product liability case?

25. Dr. Ellis has a national reputation as an expert in the treatment of lower-back problems and has been conducting a two-year research treatment program for individuals with lower-back pain. Herb visits him in March, complaining of chronic lower-back pain, and after tests Dr. Ellis accepts him as a patient in the research treatment program, recommends surgery for reduction of his enlarged disc, and performs the surgery in April. Herb continues to experience the same chronic back pain after surgery. Dr. Ellis recommends a physical therapy program for him, but Herb has too much pain and cannot continue with the program. In June, Herb contacts another back specialist, who places Herb on a hanging-traction program. During July, Herb's back pain subsides and Herb can engage in normal physical activities. In August, Dr. Ellis completes the two-year research project, which has involved 50 patients, and prepares a final report, which he publicly releases. In September, Herb sues Dr. Ellis for medical malpractice. Which of the following will be discoverable by the lawyer for Herb and why and how?

(a) Results from the March test that Dr. Ellis conducted on Herb.

(b) The surgery X-rays and records.

(c) Dr. Ellis' opinion on why Herb continued to suffer lower-back pain from April through July.

(d) The files and records of the 50 patients involved in the research project.

26. Tri–Chem is sued for the negligent installation of roofoam and hires two experts, Maxi and Kyle. Maxi submits a written report to Tri–Chem which supports the position of the company's engineers. Kyle submits a report which concludes that the Tri–Chem's engineers were negligent in installing roofoam.

(a) The company retained Maxi as an expert. What, if anything, must be disclosed by Tri–Chem? What, if anything, may the plaintiffs obtain from Tri–Chem regarding the opinions of Maxi? Explain.

(b) Tri–Chem retains Kyle as an expert but does not use him or his report for anything further in this litigation. What, if anything, must be disclosed by Tri–Chem? What, if anything, may the plaintiff discover regarding the opinion of Kyle? Explain.

(c) Assume the company pays Kyle for the initial report and then dismisses Kyle. What, if anything, must be disclosed by Tri–Chem? What, if any, may the plaintiff obtain from Tri–Chem regarding the opinion of Kyle? Explain.

27. The answers to interrogatories of Hot Dog Enterprises provide a plaintiff injured by its falling bricks with the names of all eyewitnesses to the incident. Subsequent to such answers, HDE learns of another key eyewitness. Must HDE disclose this information? Why and how, or why not?

28. Tri–Chem submits to HDE on May 1st all documents it has relating to telephone conversations between Tri–Chem employees and HDE. Subsequent investigation by Tri–Chem uncovers another relevant telephone message, with notes of a conversation between employees of the parties. Must Tri–Chem disclose this information to HDE? Why and how, or why not?

29. Hot Dog Enterprises is involved in litigation with one of its franchisees regarding a lease. The attorney for HDE deposes the plaintiff, who testifies that she had said nothing to HDE about a lease in a meeting on August 10th. After the deposition, the plaintiff advises her attorney that she recalls asking two questions in the meeting about the lease on August 10th. Must the plaintiff disclose this information to HDE? Why and how, or why not?

30. Hot Dog Enterprises sues Tri–Chem for millions of dollars in damages to its corporate headquarters building constructed with Bond–Mor. HDE asserts claims based on Deceptive Trade Practices, negligence, and products liability.

(a) Your law firm represents Tri–Chem. You are assigned the task of preparing a protective order for the disclosure of any information Tri–Chem must make to HDE through interrogatories, requests for production, or depositions. Outline a list of the issues and topics to be included in this protective order.

(b) Your law firm represents HDE. You anticipate that either Tri–Chem will refuse to disclose information unless a stipulated protective order exists between Tri–Chem and HDE or that a judge would require reasonable restrictions in a protective order regarding information sought from Tri–Chem by HDE. Outline a list of issues and topics to be included in a protective order.

31. In *Luger v. Shade* (Case H), on March 1, the attorney for the Plaintiffs served a notice of deposition on Defendants Shade and Develco. This notice scheduled the deposition of Sam Shade for March 30. On March 8 the attorney for Defendant Shade served notices of depositions on the Plaintiff Lugers and the Defendant Develco. These notices scheduled the depositions of the Lugers for March 22 and 23. On March 10 the attorney for the Lugers wrote a letter to the attorney for Sam Shade and explained that the Lugers would not appear on March 22 and 23 or at any time for their depositions until after Sam Shade had been deposed on March 30.

(a) As the attorney for Shade, what are your options? What would you do?

(b) As either attorney, how would you attempt to resolve this problem without court intervention?

The attorney for Sam Shade seeks a protective order permitting Shade to be deposed after the Lugers.

(c) As the attorney for Shade, what arguments would you advance on Shade's behalf to have the depositions of the Lugers taken first?

(d) As the attorney for the plaintiffs, what argument would you advance on the Lugers' behalf that the deposition of Shade should be taken first?

(e) As the judge, how would you decide and why?

32. In *Luger v. Shade* (Case H), Plaintiffs have sued Defendant Develco and submitted a request for production of documents seeking the financial records of Develco. In response, Develco seeks a protective order.

(a) As either attorney, how would you attempt to resolve this problem without court intervention?

(b) As the attorney for Develco, what arguments would you advance on its behalf?

(c) As the attorney for the Lugers, what arguments would you advance on their behalf?

(d) As the judge, how would you decide and why?

33. In *Luger v. Shade* (Case H), the plaintiffs submit interrogatories upon Defendant Shade asking Shade about (A) his personal wealth and finances, (B) his personal insurance coverage, and (C) his use of illegal drugs. In response, Shade seeks a protective order from having to answer these questions.

(a) As either attorney, how would you attempt to resolve this problem without court intervention?

(b) As the attorney for Shade, what arguments would you advance on his behalf?

(c) As the attorney for the Lugers, what arguments would you advance on their behalf?

(d) As the judge, what would you decide and why?

34. Veronica Mikita, Casey Pozdak's daughter, is a senior law student at Summit College of Law, a private law school. Summit has a student Honor Code which states, in part, that:

> A student who has knowledge that another student has cheated in an exam must report this offense to the Code Committee. The failure to so report shall constitute a violation of the Code and subject the student to appropriate disciplinary action by the Code Committee.

Mikita has a classmate, Randall Lee, who told her that he had cheated in a take home exam with two other classmates by working together to prepare answers. The Dean of Summit learned of Veronica's knowledge of this cheating episode and arranged to meet with her to discuss the matter.

Prior to that meeting Veronica met with Professor Phebe O'Connell who discussed the problem with Veronica. When Veronica met with the Dean she refused to answer any questions claiming she did not have to provide any information to the Dean.

When the Dean met with Professor O'Connell the Professor explained that Mikita had not sought legal advice from O'Connell, but that O'Connell considered the conversation confidential because of a professor/student privilege. The Dean unilaterally expels Mikita claiming that he has the discretion to do so, notwithstanding the procedural provisions of the Honor Code, because her silence indicated that she had violated the Code.

Mikita sues the law school in a civil suit seeking reinstatement as a student. The defendant law school notices the deposition of Professor O'Connell.

You represent the Professor. Mikita advises you that she considers her conversations with Professor O'Connell confidential and privileged. Summit has no statute or case law creating a professor/student privilege. What options do you have? What would you do?

35. Bernie worked for Hot Dog Enterprises at its corporate headquarters and was caught stealing $2,400 of computer equipment and software. HDE contacted the police and county attorney and described the theft. Then the HDE lawyer initiated a civil lawsuit based on conversion against Bernie seeking a money judgment for the stolen property which was not recovered. Bernie retains you to represent him in both the potential criminal action as well as the civil action. You contact the county attorney who tells you that she may or may not prosecute because the police have not been able to locate the person who bought the stolen goods. Bernie tells you that he did steal the property and that HDE failed to pay Bernie $1,200 in salary for his last two weeks of work. HDE notices Bernie's deposition in the civil suit. What options do you have? What do you do?

36. You supervise the litigation section of your law firm. There has recently been some confusion among the lawyers regarding the application of Rule 26(b)(3) and the creation of trial preparation materials. You decide to draft a concise memo detailing the considerations that will assist the attorneys in determining what documents become trial preparation materials, both before and after litigation. Prepare such a memo.

37. Because of your reputation, you have been asked to address a litigation committee of the federal bar association. You select as your topic Rule 26(b)(3) and what information is exempt from discovery as attorney mental impressions, conclusions, opinions, or legal theories. Prepare a concise memo summarizing considerations that will assist litigators in determining what information falls within the protected attorney mental processes and what falls outside the purview of the rule and is subject to disclosure.

38. You are a lawyer with Tri–Chem. The general counsel for Tri–Chem has become concerned with the current developments relating to the attorney-client privilege as applied to corporations. She has asked you to prepare a concise list of considerations that will assist all corporation lawyers in determining whether their conversations with corporate officers, managers, and employees fall within the range of communications protected by the privilege. Prepare such a memo.

39. You represent Tri–Chem in defense of a class-action lawsuit brought by three named plaintiffs and more than 100 unnamed class members. The plaintiffs have brought the class action under a state consumer fraud act that permits such actions and allege that Roofoam Insulation failed to reduce, in hundreds of buildings owned by the class members, utility expenses as advertised by Tri–Chem. The state rules of civil

procedure relating to class actions are identical to Federal Rule 23. The plaintiffs have submitted interrogatories to your client seeking information about customers. You plan to obtain information from the plaintiffs about the alleged claims. Prepare a concise memo explaining:

(a) What information the plaintiffs can obtain regarding customers.

(b) What discovery can and should be initiated by you at this stage of the litigation.

40. Prepare a concise memo planning a discovery program. Your memo should:

1. Explain what information you want to obtain.
2. Identify what information might need to be disclosed affirmatively by a party.
3. Describe the discovery devices you plan to use to obtain that information.
4. Explain the sequence of those discovery devices.
5. Describe what information might be better obtained through informal investigation.

(a) Prepare such a discovery plan for the plaintiff HDE in its litigation over Bond–Mor against Tri–Chem.

(b) Prepare such a discovery plan for Tri–Chem in its litigation with HDE.

(c) Plan such a discovery plan for the defendant in *Northern Motor Homes v. Danforth* (Case J).

(d) Plan such a discovery plan for the plaintiff in *Burris v. Warner* (Case K).

(e) Plan such a discovery plan for the plaintiffs in *Luger v. Shade* (Case H).

(f) You represent HDE in its litigation against Tri–Chem. Meet and confer with opposing counsel and develop a discovery plan in accord with Federal Rule 26(f).

(g) You represent Tri–Chem in its litigation with HDE. Meet and confer with opposing counsel and develop a discovery plan in accord with Federal Rule 26(f).

41. *Martin v. Reynolds Metals Corp.*, 297 F.2d 49 (9th Cir.1961).

Reynolds Metals Corp. owns property near Troutdale, Oregon, west of the Sandy River, on which it operates an aluminum reduction plant. Paul Martin also owns property nearby, east of the river, on which he raises cattle. Martin claims that, since 1955, fluorides emanating from the Reynolds' plant have been discharged on their lands and into the water, killing 174 cattle that ate vegetation and drank water contaminated by the fluorides. Reynolds expects to be sued by Martin and cannot itself bring or cause the action to be brought. Reynolds also alleges that it has not, in fact, damaged Martin, and it believes that certain information and data will demonstrate that Martin's cattle have not been damaged, which include:

- The fluorine content of samples of forage, feed, air, water, soil, vegetation and mineral supplements taken periodically from areas where livestock are being pastured.
- Physical examinations of such cattle, including photographs.
- The fluorine content of bone and tissue samples taken from cattle which have died or which have been slaughtered.

On two occasions, Reynolds asked permission to examine Martin's lands and cattle, and on one occasion asked him to advise it if any cattle died, so that Reynolds might examine them. Martin denied these requests because he is accumulating this information. Reynolds desires to take Paul Martin's deposition "for the purpose of eliciting from him information concerning present plans for the disposition of the cattle owned by him which are presently being pastured upon the lands as well as information from him concerning cattle which he may have removed from said lands to be pastured in other areas." Martin believes he has been damaged but does not know whether he will sue.

(a) As counsel for Reynolds, plan a Rule 27 Petition and proceeding.

(b) Draft such a Rule 27 Petition and all necessary supporting documents.

(c) As counsel for Martin, oppose the petition and request.

(d) As the judge, decide.

CHAPTER 6
DEPOSITIONS

Where Weaver's Needle casts its long shadow at four in the afternoon, there you will find a vein of rose quartz laced with gold wire—and you will be rich beyond your wildest dreams.

—The Legend of the Lost Dutchman Gold Mine and Superstition Mountain

§ 6.1 AN OVERVIEW OF THE DEPOSITION PROCESS

§ 6.1.1 Advantages of Depositions

You can search for information by deposing a witness or another party. You may never be able to depose the Lost Dutchman or become all that rich, but depositions do serve several purposes and offer advantages in discovery efforts. Depositions help you to:

1. Explore and obtain information from the other side through prepared and spontaneous, flexible follow-up questions;
2. Determine what a deponent knows and does not know;
3. Pin down a deponent to a particular story;
4. Assess the witness's demeanor to determine what type of trial witness that person would be;
5. Confront an adversary deponent with damaging information or probe the deponent about weaknesses in the case prior to trial;
6. Preserve testimony to be used later as admissions, impeachment evidence, or for other evidentiary or cross-examination purposes at trial.

§ 6.1.2 Disadvantages of Depositions

Depositions have some disadvantages, though they are usually outweighed by their advantages:

Haydock,Fund.Pretrial Lit.3E--10

1. Depositions can be expensive.

2. Depositions may force the other side to prepare or may trigger counter-depositions, but it is poor practice indeed to prepare a case relying on the hope that the other attorney is a stumblebum.

3. Depositions also educate witnesses. Being deposed helps one learn the testifying process as well as what to say and what not to say in testimony.

4. A discovery deposition also preserves the testimony of the opposing party or adverse witness, the transcript of which can be used at trial should that deponent be unavailable then.

On balance, depositions are the best discovery devices available. They allow you into the other side's camp to gather information, view, understand, and evaluate the opposition, its witnesses, and its case. They should be used (or attempted) in every case, except in those cases in which you can look yourself in the mirror and say, "Even F. Bennett Day Nizer would not depose in this case." So much for the disadvantages.

§ 6.1.3 Scope of Depositions

Rules of civil procedure, customary procedures, and local practice provide the basic procedural framework for the taking and using of depositions. These ground rules vary to some extent from attorney to attorney, from law firm to law firm, and from area to area. This chapter explains the spectrum of depositions rules, customs, and practice and describes strategies and tactics for the taking and using of depositions.

Federal rules 26, 29, 30, and 32 encourage and provide attorneys and judges with the authority to customize deposition practice. Rule 26(g) requires attorneys to discuss discovery plans including the scope of depositions. Rule 29 continues to provide attorneys with the ability to vary the rules to allow depositions to be taken efficiently and economically. Changes to Rule 26 and 30 allow judges by order and by local rule to restrict or expand the new rules applicable to depositions. One of the primary goals of these rule changes is to provide attorneys and judges with the flexibility to control the scope, number, time, and procedures regarding depositions. Similar state rules also provide this flexibility.

§ 6.1.4 Timing of Depositions

When a deposition may be taken depends upon the applicable rules of civil procedure. Federal Rule 26 permit depositions to be scheduled only after the parties have met and conferred about a discovery plan, which conference may occur 60 to 90 days after the filing of the law suit. Federal Rules 30(a) and 29 permit counsel to schedule depositions at any time they mutually agree by written stipulation and to seek leave of court to take an early deposition if they cannot agree. See Federal Rules 30(a) and 29. State rules typically allow depositions to be taken without leave of court by plaintiff 30 days after service of the summons and complaint and permit defendant to schedule a deposition any time after receiving a summons and complaint.

Federal Rule 30(a)(2) designates three specific situations when leave of court is required to schedule a deposition:

1. When more than 10 depositions would be taken. Section 6.1.5 discusses the 10–deposition limit.

2. When the person to be examined has already been deposed. This rule prohibits a person from being deposed more than once. This requirement does not apply to incomplete depositions that are temporary recessed or adjourned for the convenience of the deponent or counsel to gather additional materials. Uncompleted depositions may be completed by the telephone, if the parties agree, particularly if significant travel costs are incurred or if there are only a few remaining questions.

3. Before the attorneys have met and conferred in accord with Rule 26(b), unless a deponent is about to leave the United States. If the person to be examined will be unavailable for examination in the United States because the person is expected to leave this country, a deposition may be scheduled based on a notice and a written certification containing supporting facts.

Some state court jurisdictions also limit the number of depositions that may be taken. The limited number may be anywhere from three to ten. The attorneys usually have the power to vary this number, and, in all jurisdictions, the attorneys may seek leave of court to expand or restrict this number.

Strategy considerations will prompt depositions to be scheduled at the earliest practical time during litigation. Early examination preserves more accurate testimony, permits more time to investigate the facts obtained and to research the issues uncovered, and commits the deponent to testimony early on in the litigation. Further, early deposition may prompt a ready settlement on advantageous terms. Attorneys, especially defense attorneys, may schedule a plaintiff's deposition as soon as possible to evaluate the extent of the claim properly. A successful deposition by the defendant in many of these cases forces an early and economical settlement.

In some situations, however, a deposition should be scheduled later in the litigation. A delayed deposition permits the attorney to be better informed on the areas of inquiry. Investigation may be necessary to prepare properly for the deposition; other discovery devices may produce helpful information. The timing of a deposition may also depend upon other depositions yet to be taken. A deponent at a later deposition may have the advantage of either having attended an earlier deposition or having read the transcript of an earlier deposition, which may influence his or her version of what happened or otherwise affect the testimony. To avoid this problem, depositions of adverse parties or witnesses may be scheduled back to back, on the same or subsequent days. A deposition may need to be taken just before or even during a trial if a witness belatedly becomes available. This latter situation should arise only infrequently.

§ 6.1.5 *Number of Depositions*

Federal Rule 30(a)(2)(A) establishes a limit on the number of depositions parties may take unless they agree otherwise or obtain leave of court. No more than ten depositions may be taken by one side in a case. The purpose of the rule is to obviously limit the number of depositions unless the parties agree or the court orders otherwise. The rule is intended to require the attorneys to agree on a cost effective discovery plan for cases involving a significant number of depositions.

The rule states that a deposition may not be scheduled if: "A proposed deposition will result in more than 10 depositions being taken under this rule or Rule 31 by the plaintiffs, or defendants, or by third party defendants." This provision restricts each side of the case to ten depositions, irrespective of the number of parties on a side. In multi-party cases, the attorneys will need to confer and agree on whose depositions need to be taken. If parties in any case believe that more than 10 depositions are needed and are unable to agree on additional depositions, court intervention may be sought under Rule 30(a)(2).

Rule 30(a)(2) states that leave of court "shall be granted to the extent consistent with the principles stated in Rule 26(b)(2)," which is the general rule regarding the scope and relevancy of discovery. This provision should encourage courts to grant reasonable requests for more depositions, or fewer depositions. Parties who believe the number of depositions to be taken in a case, even if less than ten, is excessive have support under Rule 26(c) to seek restrictions on whose deposition may be taken.

§ 6.1.6 *Location of Depositions*

Rule 30(b)(1) provides that the attorney taking the deposition has the right to specify where it will be held. Plaintiffs and their agents can be required to attend depositions in the district where the action is pending. Depositions of a corporation's officers or employees are ordinarily taken at its principal place of business. Special circumstances, such as hardship or financial burden to a party, may also affect the location of a deposition. Depositions are frequently held in the examining attorney's office; often in the court reporter's office; occasionally in a courthouse; sometimes in the opposing attorney's office; and at times in the deponent's office. The exact location of the deposition largely depends upon your convenience and what effect you want the location to have on the deponent. Although holding the deposition in your office may be convenient, holding it in a records office may make it more convenient for you to inspect and copy documents obtained through the deposition. Again, holding the deposition in the office of the deponent's attorney may make the deponent comfortable amidst familiar surroundings, whereas holding it in a courthouse may be imposing and threatening to a deponent. Attorneys occasionally wrangle over location. A court reporter's office may offer neutral ground, or a protective order regarding location may be obtained.

§ 6.1.7 Time Allocated to Depositions

How long a deposition is scheduled for and how long it lasts usually depends upon how much reasonable time is needed to complete a deposition. The notice of deposition typically states the beginning time of the deposition and that it will continue until completed. Many depositions take a few hours, some take several hours, and still others take one hour. And, then, there are those that take more than one day. Some courts limit the time for a deposition. These jurisdictions have recognized that modern depositions have increasingly expanded in length with examining attorneys asking many tangentially relevant questions and opposing lawyers slowing down the deposition by objections and unnecessary breaks. All jurisdictions permit a party to seek a court order establishing a time limit for a deposition or extending a time limit imposed by rule or local order. An examining attorney can request more time, if needed, as long as the questions and areas are relevant. An examining attorney can also seek an order controlling unnecessary interference and inappropriate objections by a defending attorney, thus making the deposition shorter. Another idea to control the time limit of depositions is to prevent lawyers from being paid by the hour for depositions. Right. Federal and state rules encourage parties to use the deposition time wisely with the threat that sanctions, including reasonable costs and attorneys fees, may be imposed upon any person responsible for impeding or delaying a deposition.

§ 6.1.8 Non-Party Depositions

Deposition notices do not compel the attendance of non-party witnesses at depositions. Service of a Rule 45 subpoena is required to get their attention. The clerk of the district court where the deposition is to be taken issues the subpoena. Rule 45(d)(1) specifies that "[p]roof of service of a notice to take a deposition ... constitutes sufficient authorization for the issuance of the subpoena by the clerk of district court for the district in which the deposition is to be taken. . . ." It's that simple.

It is almost that simple to schedule the deposition of a non-party witness to be taken in another district. Some of these deponents will be residents of the district in which the deposition is to be located; others will be non-residents. Rule 45(d)(2) explains the difference:

> A resident of the district in which the deposition is to be taken may be required to attend an examination only in the county wherein he resides or is employed or transacts his business in person, or at such other convenient place as is fixed by an order of court. A nonresident of the district may be required to attend only in the county wherein he is served with a subpoena, or within 40 miles from the

place of service, or at such other convenient place as is fixed by an order of court.

District courts have broad discretion in designating the location of non-party examinations. Non-party witnesses usually are not required to travel distances just for the convenience of the parties. Corporations are usually deposed at their principal place of business or where the corporate examinee resides. A non-party witness designated as a deponent for a corporation, association, or governmental agency may be able to limit the deposition location to the places authorized by Rule 45(d)(2).

The party seeking the deposition has the burden to show the capacity of the prospective deponent: that is, whether the deponent is a party or non-party. This burden is easily and obviously met in most situations. But not in all. Occasionally a question will arise as to whether a prospective deponent, usually a corporation's employee, is a non-party witness or an agent of a party. The nature of the relationship between the deponent and the party at the time of the incident and at the time of the deposition determines the answer. A former employee of a corporation must be subpoenaed to a deposition.

A party who has a relationship with a deponent may have some responsibility for making sure the deponent attends the deposition. A party may be responsible for producing a deponent who is a relative or a former agent, for example, or a former corporate employee whom the party now controls through a wholly-owned subsidiary.

Depositions of non-party witnesses in a lawsuit pending in a state court, other than the state of the deponent's residence, may be arranged pursuant to the subpoena rules of the deponent's jurisdiction. This subpoena process usually mimics the federal procedures and ordinarily provides the examining attorney with an order as a routine matter.

A party who seeks to review or obtain documents from a non-party may or may not need to schedule a deposition to do so depending upon the applicable rules of procedure. In federal cases, Rule 45 allow a party to serve a subpoena duces tecum on a non-party ordering the party to produce and permit inspection of documents without having to appear at a deposition. This procedure saves the non-party the time and expense from having to bring the documents to a deposition.

In many state court jurisdictions, a party must schedule a deposition in order to obtain documents in the possession of a third party. A notice of deposition must accompany the subpoena duces tecum served on the third party. In these state jurisdictions, an attorney who seeks documents from a non-party but who does not need to take that person's deposition may have a number of options. The attorney may first request the non-party to voluntarily disclose the documents without the need for a subpoena and notice of deposition. The attorney may also stipulate with the opposing lawyer to vary the deposition rules and not provide a notice of a deposition with the subpoena duces tecum, although this practice may be prohibited by rule. Or an attorney may schedule the deposition, have the non-party appear and produce the documents, and then immediately conclude the deposition. Whatever alternative an attorney attempts must not only comply with the applicable rules but must also not violate any protections provided a non-party who, usually, is not involved directly in the litigation.

§ 6.2 PRELIMINARY DEPOSITION CONSIDERATIONS

The taking of depositions requires the consideration of several matters that affect the deposition. These considerations include proper notice, who can attend a deposition, who can be brought to a deposition, and how to ensure that the deponent brings the necessary documents to the deposition.

§ 6.2.1 Noticing the Deposition

Rule 30(b) requires the party taking a deposition to provide reasonable written notice to all parties to the action, specifying the time, place, and person to be deposed. The minimum time permissible to notice a deposition should be a reasonable amount of time dependent upon the circumstances and may be governed by specific time requirements established by rule. Federal Rule 32 states that a party who receives less than 11 days notice of a deposition may seek a court order rescheduling the deposition. This rule, while not mandating a minimum 11 day notice, encourages lawyers to schedule depositions after this notice period. In state cases, applicable rules or court decisions may require "reasonable" notice or may set a specific period of time, such as five days.

Federal Rule 30(b)(2) also permits parties to designate in the notice of deposition the method by which the deposition shall be recorded. A deposition may be recorded by stenographic means (with a reporter who uses a stenograph machine) or by sound (audio recording) or by sound and video (a video recording). The federal rule allows the party noticing the deposition to choose the method of recording without the need to obtain agreement of other counsel or approval of the court. In many state court jurisdictions a party noticing a deposition must obtain consent of the other attorneys or permission of the court to take a deposition other than by the stenographic method. These jurisdictions do not permit a deposing attorney to unilaterally choose to have a deposition recorded by audio or video means, but do permit such recording if the other attorney agrees or a court issues an order.

Changes in the scheduled time may be, and routinely are, made by agreement between counsel. Rule 29 permits the lawyers to set their own scheduled date and the time is usually negotiable between the attorneys. A mutually convenient time can be arranged in a variety of ways: a telephone call to the opposing attorney confirming the arrangements with a written notice, a letter to the opposing attorney suggesting a number of alternative times and dates, a cover letter with the formal notice suggesting that the opposing attorney contact you if the time is inconvenient, or a stipulation.

[Caption]

[Plaintiff] and [Defendant] hereby stipulate and agree that the deposition of [name of deponent] shall be taken by [plaintiff/defendant] on oral examination at [place], [address], on ______, 19__, at [time] __ m. Notice of the time and place of this deposition as required by Rule 30 is waived. [Add any other stipulations.]

____

[Signature]

Examples of written notice sufficient to compel the attendance of an individual party or corporate deponent to the deposition include:

[Caption]

To: Each party and attorney for each party.

PLEASE TAKE NOTICE that the deposition of [name of deponent] will be taken by oral examination pursuant to the ______ Rules of Civil Procedure before [name of court reporter] or other person authorized by law to administer oaths at [location], at [city and state] on [date] at [time] __ m. The method of recording this deposition will be [stenographic/audio recording/videotape/other (specify)].

The deposition will continue from day to day until completed. You may appear and examine the witness.

____

[Signature]

[Caption]

To: Each party and attorney for each party.

PLEASE TAKE NOTICE that the deposition of [name of corporate party] through the testimony of [name of witness], its [title of deponent], will be taken by oral examination pursuant to the ______ Rules of Civil Procedure before [name of court reporter] or other person authorized by law to administer oaths at [location], at [city and state] on [date] at [time] __ m. The method of recording this deposition will be [stenographic/audio recording/videotape/other (specify)].

The deposition will continue from day to day until completed. You may appear and examine the witness.

____

[Signature]

Depositions may be scheduled at any time during regular business hours, and during other hours for good reasons. Recesses will be necessary for rest and recuperation for everyone present at the deposition. Adjournments may become necessary if the deponent needs time to search for some information or make some other inquiries or if the subject matter of the deposition is still developing. You should feel free to discuss deposition format and the timing of recesses, lunch, and other breaks with the other attorney.

Rule 30(g) explains what may happen to the attorney who notices the deposition but fails to appear or fails to obtain the attendance of the court reporter or deponent. Such an attorney may be ordered to pay to the other party the amount of the reasonable expenses incurred, including reasonable attorney's fees. Reasonable expenses include travel expenses, per diem, and fees for both the deponent and the other attorney(s). If a witness promised to attend the deposition but fails to appear, the examining attorney will be liable for reasonable expenses, unless the witness would not have attended because of illness even if subpoenaed. So set your clock to make sure that you show up, check with the reporter to make certain he or she shows up, and double-check with the deponent.

An attorney is not required to attend a deposition of a non-party, nor even of a party not his or her client. Rule 30(c) does permit an attorney not attending to submit written questions to be answered by the deponent. But the decision not to attend may have later, unanticipated ramifications. Failure to attend a properly noticed deposition may operate as a waiver of any objection the attorney has to the admissibility of the deposition testimony.

§ 6.2.2 Persons Present at the Deposition

The people present during the deposition are:

1. *The Deponent.* All persons who have information relevant to the subject matter or are likely to provide admissible evidence may be deposed. This includes parties, witnesses, and other persons. The problems encountered with identifying corporate deponents is resolved by Rule 30(b)(6), which permits a party to name as the deponent a public or private corporation or a partnership or association or governmental agency and describe with reasonable particularity the matters on which examination is requested, and require the organization so named to designate one or more officers, directors, or managing agents, or other persons who consent to testify on its behalf.

Rule 30(b)(1) solves the further problem of an unknown deponent, by allowing a party to identify the deponent with a "general description sufficient to identify him or the particular class or group to which he belongs." An example of such a notice is:

[Caption]

To: Each party and attorney for each party.

PLEASE TAKE NOTICE that the deposition of [name of corporate party] will be taken by oral examination pursuant to the Federal Rules of Civil Procedure before [name of court reporter] or other person authorized by law to administer oaths at [location], at [city and state] on [date] at [time].

[Name] Corporation is directed, pursuant to Rule 30(b)(6) of the Rules of Civil Procedure, to designate one or more officers, directors, managing agents, or other persons who consent to testify on its behalf on each of the subject matters set forth below:

1. [Describe with reasonable particularity the matters of the examination.]

The deposition will continue from day to day until completed. You may appear and examine the witness.

____

[Signature]

These rules provide the examining party with the best of all possible discovery worlds. If the examining attorney knows who should be deposed, that person can be designated. If the examining attorney only knows the area to be discovered, the opposing party must designate the person who knows that information. If in the course of the examination, the deposing attorney discovers additional officers, agents, or employees who know something, they can be deposed later. Who could ask for anything more?

2. *The attorney(s)* representing the deponent and the attorneys representing the parties. A deponent who is either a witness or a party has a right to have an attorney present; and all parties to an action have a right to have their respective attorneys present, even though those attorneys may not represent the deponent.

3. *The notary public* who administers the oath and the *officer* who records the testimony. Usually, this will be one and the same—the court reporter. This person can have someone assist him or her during the deposition, for instance, to operate a tape recorder or a video camera.

4. *The parties* (individual parties and designated representatives of corporate parties) to an action have a right to sit in during all depositions. Rule 30(b)(1) requires that a deposition notice be provided each party, implying that all parties have a right to be there. The prevailing view is that parties have an absolute right to be present during a deposition.[1] They have a right to be present during all stages of a trial, and the logical extension of this right would include deposition proceedings. They often do not attend because there is no reason to. A court has discretion to limit a party's attendance, but this limiting order is issued only rarely, as in the case of a party who may ridicule or harass a party deponent.[2]

Sometimes strategic reasons dictate having parties there. For example, their presence may assist in obtaining complete and accurate testimony from the deponent (the deponent may be the only other eyewitness), or their presence may help them prepare for their own deposition. Conversely, there are reasons not to have a party present. For instance, a party may react to some of the testimony and disrupt the deposition, or a party may expect an attorney to be aggressive rather than conciliatory, thereby affecting the attorney's performance. Sometimes there are even reasons to object to a party's being present. The attorney representing the deponent may object to the influence the

§ 6.2

1. *See* Annot., 70 A.L.R.2d 685, 752–753 (1960).

2. *See, e.g., Gallella v. Onassis,* 487 F.2d 986, 997 (2d Cir.1973).

party's presence has on the deponent (the party may be the deponent's employer) or may object to the party's being present during confidential testimony. The only way to bar another party's attendance, however, is to obtain a protective order under Rule 26(c)(5).

A corporation, association, or governmental agency may be able to have two individuals present during a deposition. One person would be designated to represent the organization as a party representative. Another person would be designated as the representative deponent pursuant to Rule 30(b)(6).

5. *Witnesses.* Whether a witness or potential deponent in a case may attend another deposition depends upon the rules of procedure and court decisions. Federal Rule 30(c) provides that witnesses and potential deponents may attend the deposition unless they are excluded by agreement of all the parties or by a court order. This rule prohibits a witness or potential deponent from being automatically excluded from a deposition merely at the request of a party.

A witness or potential deponent may be excluded if all the parties agree or if a party obtains a court order pursuant to Federal Rule 26(c)(5). A potential deponent may be appropriately excluded from a deposition to avoid any unfair advantage a future deponent may gain by attending an earlier deposition of another deponent. An excluded witness may also be prohibited from reading or otherwise being informed about the testimony provided in earlier depositions.

The attendance of potential deponents and witnesses in depositions taken in state court cases depend upon the applicable state rules and state court decisions. Most states do not restrict the attendance of the witness or potential deponent unless other parties agree or a party obtains an appropriate court order, which is similar to federal rules and practice.

6. *Third Persons.* May third persons (interested persons, or just plain members of the public) attend a deposition? Is a deposition a public hearing? Can tickets be sold? Rule 26(c)(5) permits protective orders allowing a deposition to proceed "with no one present except persons designated by the court." This implies that anybody may attend unless restricted by a protective order. Further, Rule 29 allows attorneys to establish their own rules for the conduct of the deposition, thus implying that the attorneys may mutually exclude whomever they want from a deposition. But the attorney's power to exclude may be limited: the court reporter at the deposition is a court officer and may be the one deciding who may or may not attend. The rules are silent on this matter, with no indication one way or the other. Some commentators believe that the court reporter has no such right.[3]

Some courts have declared depositions to be private proceedings closed to the public. A 1912 decision held that preliminary proceedings

3. *See, e.g.,* 2 J. Hetland & O. Adamson, Minnesota Practice 12 (1970); *Queen City Brewing Co. v. Duncan,* 42 F.R.D. 32, 33 (D.Md.1966).

to a trial, including depositions, are private.[4] In 1913, a federal statute was enacted, rejecting this view and specifically declaring depositions in antitrust matters to be open to the public.[5] This special statute does not apply to any other type of deposition. One court has declared that this limited statute is clear evidence of congressional intent to preserve the private nature of depositions.[6] This same court reasoned that deposition inquiries may probe into all sorts of information, much of which will be inadmissible at trial.

The deposition's purpose is markedly different from trial and subject to different protections. The trial judge determines what is admissible and so protects parties from the indiscriminate disclosure of irrelevant private information. But no one determines the relevancy of discovery information. This would support the conclusion that such information should be deemed private until disclosed at trial, but that the public does not have a right to be present unless a court rules otherwise. Courts have restricted the attendance of individuals present at depositions because of privacy considerations, because the examining party seeks to obtain the independent recollection of a deponent without influence by other depositions, and because such a person would be properly excluded from hearing such testimony at trial. This last reasoning fails to take into account the availability of the deposition transcript to such a witness.

Usually, third persons will not attend a deposition, and ordinarily attorneys do not invite them. However, somebody—an interested observer, a member of the press, or a member of the general public—may want to attend. More often, an attorney wants a third person present for tactical reasons (to influence the deponent), while an opposing attorney objects to that person's being present, also for tactical reasons (to avoid their becoming familiar with the testimony). Rule 26 allows attorneys mutually to restrict the attendance of third persons to a deposition, but if they are unable to agree on who should be present, they will either have to compromise the dispute or seek a protective order or a Rule 37 sanction. Courts that issue such orders must balance the First Amendment rights of the third person (usually the press) with the privacy rights of the litigant. Courts have restricted attendance of a third person (a newsperson) at a deposition and sealed the subsequent transcript.[7] Courts, including the Supreme Court, also have denied third persons access to information in criminal cases, protecting the defendant's right to a fair trial through prior restraint.[8]

Before a deposition, you will need to consider several tactical questions relating to the persons present at the deposition: Whose presence

4. *United States v. United Shoe Machinery Co.,* 198 Fed. 870, 876 (D.Mass.1912).

5. Publicity in Taking Evidence Act, 15 U.S.C.A. § 30 (depositions for use in suits in equity open to the public).

6. *See United States v. I.B.M. Corp.,* 82 F.R.D. 183, 185 (S.D.N.Y.1979).

7. *Times Newspapers, Limited (of Great Britain) v. McDonnell Douglas Corp.,* 387 F.Supp. 189, 197 (C.D.Cal.1974).

8. *Nebraska Press Association v. Stuart,* 427 U.S. 539, 96 S.Ct. 2791, 49 L.Ed.2d 683 (1976).

would favorably affect the deposition in your client's behalf? Should you advise the opposing attorney of your intentions? Should you assume that anyone may attend, unless the opposing attorney has obtained a protective order or has asked you to agree mutually to exclude all but essential individuals? Should you ask the opposing attorney whom he or she plans to invite to the deposition? Should your deposition notice indicate whom you will bring? Should you advise the deposing attorney that you are bringing someone else besides the deponent to the deposition?

§ 6.2.3 Ensuring Production of Documents and Materials

You may want a deponent to bring some documents or tangible things to the deposition. Rule 30(b)(5) allows you to compel the disclosure of such documents from a party at a deposition, by attaching to the deposition notice a Rule 34 request for production of documents or tangible things. Rule 45(b) permits you to compel disclosure from a non-party deponent by serving a subpoena duces tecum commanding the person to bring the designated documents and tangible things to the deposition. Rules 34 and 45 operate in a similar fashion, not only to allow inspection, but also to permit the copying of documents. Rule 45 also allows a court to modify or quash an unreasonable or oppressive subpoena, or to condition the disclosure of such materials on the advancement, by the examining party and to the deponent, of the reasonable costs of production. Rule 45 expressly permits use of a subpoena to obtain documents from a non-party without the fanfare of a deposition.

Using one or the other of the document disclosure methods may prove very revealing and prevent frustration at the deposition. You will have the opportunity to review documents with the deponent and to receive an explanation of their contents from the deponent. You will also be able to avoid the response from some deponents, "Golly, by now the smoking paper is back on my office desk engulfed in flame."

§ 6.3 RECORDING THE DEPOSITION

Rules 28(a) and 28(c) require that an officer authorized to administer oaths be present for the taking of a deposition and that this officer cannot be a relative, employee, or attorney of any of the parties or attorneys or otherwise be financially interested in the action. This disinterested court officer is usually a reporter, typically from an independent court reporting firm. Rule 30(c) allows someone other than the officer who put the witness under oath to record the testimony, as long as this other person is under the direction of the officer and the officer is personally present. The party who notices the deposition will pay for the officer's time and the costs of reporting.

The party who notices the deposition, as explained in § 6.2.1, chooses the method of recording. A party who did not notice the deposition may also have a choice regarding how the deposition is recorded. Federal Rule 30(b)(3) permits any party to designate another method to record the deponent's testimony in addition to the method specified by the person taking the deposition. The additional record of transcript is made at that party's expense, unless the court orders otherwise. These provisions allow other parties at their own expense to record a deposition any way they prefer. A party planning to do so must provide notice to the deponent and all of the parties. For example, the party noticing the deposition may schedule a deposition to be recorded by stenographic means, and, another party may arrange for an additional video recording after giving notice to all the other parties. Many state court jurisdictions permit only the party noticing the deposition to designate the method of recording and do not permit other parties to arrange for other methods of recording unless all parties are agreeable or a court issues the appropriate order.

§ 6.3.1 The Deposition Transcript

There is no general requirement that a recorded deposition be transcribed, although, typically, a transcript will be made of the recorded deposition. Any party may arrange for and pay for a transcript, although it is most common for the party taking the deposition to want and obtain a transcript. Federal Rule 26(a)(3)(B) and Federal Rule 32(c) require a party to arrange for and pay for a transcript if that party relies upon the testimony of a deponent as evidence at trial or in support of a motion. Any party in a case, if no other party requests a transcript, may order a transcript and be responsible for paying for it. Parties not requesting a transcript may order a copy of the recorded transcript (which usually costs less than the original transcription), or may use another party's transcript if agreed to by that party and if not violative of an applicable rule or practice.

§ 6.3.2 Telephone and Remote Electronic Depositions

Rule 30(b)(7) specifically authorizes telephone and remote electronic depositions by written stipulation or court order. The rule also defines the location of a telephone deposition to be the district within which the deponent answers the questions, that is, where the deponent is when responding.

The purpose of the rule is to publicize and encourage the use of telephone and other electronic methods of taking depositions. Telephone depositions can be an ideal way to obtain information efficiently and economically. What about effectively? The decided disadvantage is the lack of visual means to determine the deponent's credibility. Other remote electronic means, such as satellite transmission, provide an audio and video presentation. Video, telephone, and new technological advances will promote the use of these deposition methods. Jules Verne was right.

Telephone depositions take place as conference calls and follow procedures similar to ordinary face-to-face depositions. The officer swearing in the deponent may be on the telephone with the examining attorney or in the room with the deponent. Placement depends in part upon how the deposition is recorded, by stenographic recording or through electronic recording.

§ 6.3.3 *Electronic Recording of Depositions*

Federal Rule 30 explicitly recognizes the use of audio and video tape depositions. There was a time, in the pioneer days of electronic depositions, that courts were reluctant to allow such methods of recording. Now, the federal rules, and similar state rules, readily permit electronic recording of depositions. Tape recorders and videotape recorders are two electronic devices used to record depositions.

Safeguards that help ensure the accuracy and trustworthiness of recordings include the following suggestions:

1. High quality recording equipment should be tested before being used.

2. A back-up system should be used in case the primary recording method fails.

3. The person who operates and monitors the equipment should be an expert.

4. In videotape depositions, the appearance and demeanor of the participants should not be distorted by selective camera or sound recording techniques.

5. In audio recordings the speakers should identify themselves whenever necessary for clarity of the record.

6. Another party may record the deposition by another method, creating another source of what occurred.

7. An attorney may record a deposition with a tape recorder as long as the recording is unobtrusive and does not interfere with the deposition.

8. The original electronic recording should be labeled, placed in a sealed container, and immediately delivered to counsel or the court for storage and safe keeping.

In state court cases where the rules do not explicitly authorize the use of electronic recording methods, an agreement of the parties or a court order may allow such method. The agreement or order may contain specific safeguards to ensure the accuracy and completeness of the recording.

§ 6.3.4 *Videotaped Depositions*

Videotaped depositions provide an excellent technique for preserving the testimony of a witness who will not be available for trial. Videotaped recordings have some distinct advantages over conventional stenographic recordings. They show facial expressions, physical posture, demeanor, reactions, exhibits, all in living black and white or color. A videotaped deposition preserves not only what is said, but how it is said, as well as the setting, atmosphere, and conduct of the proceedings. You need only attend a deposition and later read the bare transcript, comparing it to what really happened during the deposition, to realize the night-and-day difference. The videotaped deposition can significantly strengthen the negotiation posture of a case and significantly affect trial results. Showing a videotape to a jury will have substantially more impact than the mere reading (unless you are a Tracy or a Hepburn) of a transcript. Both stenographic and electronic recordings can capture the testimony of a deposition, but only a videotape can recreate the tears, tension, and tactics.

Deponents need to be prepared as if they were going to appear on television, which in effect they will be. They need to select wearing apparel that not only will improve their appearance at the deposition, but will also be appropriate for color videotape. The presence of a camera will make some deponents more nervous, while others may become preoccupied with the camera rather than focused on the attorney's questions. These and other factors need to be reviewed with the deponent before appearing in front of the cameras.

Careful consideration must also be given to the placement of people and equipment. A professional technical crew is necessary to place and operate the camera(s) and the recorder, and to monitor the recording. The equipment is not difficult to operate, but there is a difference between a novice and a professional. The better the technicians, the better the videotaped deposition. The camera or cameras will capture all of the events, including the questioning, the responses, the objections, and any discussion.

There exists a Uniform Audio–Visual Deposition Act, which regulates the procedures to be employed in a videotaped deposition.[10] The act provides that any deposition may be recorded by audio-visual means without a simultaneous stenographic record and without approval of the opposing party or a court. Another party is entitled to make a stenographic or audio record (and bear the expense) and is also entitled to a copy of the videotape recording (at no expense). The act further dictates that the audio-visual record is an official record, along with any transcript later prepared by an official court reporter; that such a deposition may be used for any purpose and under any circumstances in which a stenographic deposition may be used; and that the notice of subpoena for videotaped deposition must state that the deposition will be recorded by audio-visual means.

The procedures to be observed during the deposition include:

1. The deposition must begin with statements explaining the identity of the operator, case, deponent, the date, time, and place, parties, and any stipulations.

10. Uniform Audio–Visual Deposition Act, reprinted in 12 Uniform Laws Annotated 11 (Supp.1981).

2. Counsel must identify themselves on camera.

3. The oath must be administered on camera.

4. The ending of one tape and the beginning of another tape must be announced on the audio recording portion.

5. The deposition must end with statements that the deposition has concluded and with any stipulations regarding custody of the tapes or exhibits.

6. The deposition must be indexed by a time generator or another method established by court rules. A video counter will provide an external means of indexing the deposition and may be enhanced with a timer indicating the length of segments. A time-date generator provides an internal indexing means, by placing the elapsed tape time in minutes and seconds, and the date, if necessary, in one corner of each frame of the videotape.

7. Objections and instructions not to answer, and other comments by the deponent's counsel, will proceed as in a stenographic recorded deposition.

8. The video recording may be edited or altered only by court order or approval.

9. The original recording, any later edited copies, and all exhibits must be immediately filed with the court.

10. Reasonable expenses incurred with a videotaped deposition may be taxed as costs.

The act finally provides that the supreme court can establish additional standards for audio-visual deposition recordings.

Since there is usually no going off the record in a video deposition, everything will be recorded, and the videotape may require editing for appropriate use during trial. Equipment currently on the market makes editing relatively easy. The time-date generator provides an index for any objectionable section; sections can be located by highspeed playback machines, which compress the recording into a much shorter period of time while maintaining an understandable audio.

Videotapes may be edited in a number of ways. The operator can black out the objectionable part, suppressing both the audio and video portions, and proceed to the next segment at either normal speed or fast-forward. This method may cause the operator to under- or over-shoot the next segment, creating some delay and perhaps confusion. The operator can black out the audio portion only, and allow the video image to remain. This procedure will be distracting to the jurors and will not be appropriate for long edits. The operator could also opt to make a second videocassette, omitting all objectionable matter. This process can be expensive and must be planned in advance of the trial, but is the most effective way.

Continuing technical advances will ease the fears judges and lawyers have of mechanical things and make videotaped depositions more reliable and effective than traditional stenographic recordings. Costs are still a barrier to widespread video use and will continue to be a major factor until videotape equipment becomes as commonplace in law firms as yellow-page advertisements.

§ 6.3.5 Reducing the Cost

The costs of depositions include the charge for the court reporter during the deposition and for the transcription of the testimony after the deposition. Court reporters charge an hourly or daily rate for the deposition and a per-page rate for the transcript. The bulk of the recording costs will ordinarily be involved in the transcription expenses, unless you have a deponent who spells words during the deposition. Deposition costs may be advanced by the attorney as long as the client remains ultimately liable for such costs.

The preceding sections have, in bits and pieces, suggested ways of reducing deposition costs (excluding attorney's fees). A deposition need not be transcribed. An attorney anticipating this can take notes during a deposition to record and remember vital information. Ordering a transcript can be delayed until a later stage of the case, and then only if necessary. An attorney can use the deposition filed with the court instead of ordering an individual copy. The attorneys together could order the deposition transcribed and split the costs; they could agree that a deposition of a certain deponent should be taken and split all costs for the deposition. Such a deponent may be important to both sides, may refuse to speak to either side, or may be unavailable for the trial and yet have information both parties need. The attorneys could stipulate to modify the deposition proceedings and to employ a notary public to conduct a tape-recorded deposition. The rules now allow and encourage telephone depositions where appropriate. Judges are inclined to issue orders altering the traditional deposition to reduce costs.

Some attorneys are willing to bargain away some discovery rights to gain the agreement of opposing counsel to take an inexpensive deposition. For example, an examining attorney may agree to waive the right to submit any interrogatories on the topics covered by the deposition. This type of agreement, in the appropriate case, will allow for sufficient discovery while saving the expenses involved seeking a Rule 26 order.

The extent of cost reduction depends upon the creativity and willingness of the attorneys involved to reduce expenses. Both parties may gain through cooperative approaches—cost reductions may justify taking a deposition in a case involving a client with insufficient funds or little at stake.

Federal statute 28 U.S.C.A. § 1915 provides indigent civil litigants with an opportunity to proceed *in forma pauperis*. Subdivision (a) provides, "Any court of the United States may authorize the commencement, prosecution, or defense of any suit, action or proceeding ... without prepayment of fees and costs or security ...." This provision affords the district court broad discretion in determining the applicability of the statute to a case.[11] Such fees or costs advanced by the court will be taxed as costs and reimbursed to the court, should the *in forma pauperis* party prevail. The statute does not explicitly permit depositions to be funded. It is up to the court in each action to exercise its discretion and decide whether or not to advance costs for depositions and pretrial discovery.[12] Courts have authorized the payment of costs of taking, transcribing, and making copies of depositions.[13] Some courts impose a burden on the indigent party to provide the court with information enabling it to determine the reasonableness and necessity for pretrial discovery costs.[14] The specific criteria vary from court to court. A motion, affidavit of indigency, a proposed order, and perhaps an attorney affidavit, ordinarily are sufficient for a motion hearing on your request.

Courts have discretion to order that costs be shared or borne by the opposing party. Some districts have local rules which allocate costs. A party may have to pay for the travel costs of the opposing deponent, and a reasonable attorney's fee for the opposing lawyer, if a deposition occurs beyond a certain distance from the courthouse. The party taking the deposition ordinarily pays the associated expenses of transcription and filing. A district court has discretion to require one party to bear the deposition costs of another party, particularly if the examining party has raised important public issues or has no financial resources.[15]

Some deposition costs will be reimbursable to a prevailing party (or to the court if the party proceeded *in forma pauperis*). Court reporter fees "for all or any part of the stenographic transcript necessarily obtained for use in the case" may be taxed as costs.[16] The stenographic transcript includes depositions and related costs. The trial court has the discretion to tax as costs those deposition expenses reasonably necessary to the case.[17]

Rule 54(d) outlines recoverable costs and provides that they may be taxed by the clerk on one day's notice and may be reviewed by the court upon a motion served within five days after such notice. The prevailing party typically completes a form provided by the clerk, who then decides who pays what, subject to court review.

§ 6.3.6 The Record

The reporting officer at the deposition has the responsibility under the rules to record all testimony and all objections occurring during the deposition. Ordinarily a reporter will record everything said by anyone

11. *Jones v. Morris,* 590 F.2d 684, 687 (7th Cir.1979), *cert. denied* 440 U.S. 965, 99 S.Ct. 1513, 59 L.Ed.2d 780 (1979).

12. *See Ebenhart v. Power,* 309 F.Supp. 660, 661 (S.D.N.Y.1969).

13. *See Douglas v. Green,* 327 F.2d 661, 662 (6th Cir.1964) (appellant must show a need for such copies).

14. *See United States v. Banks,* 369 F.Supp. 951, 955 (M.D.Pa.1974).

15. *See Haymes v. Smith,* 73 F.R.D. 572, 575 (W.D.N.Y.1976).

16. 28 U.S.C.A. § 1920(2).

17. *Bailey v. Meister Brau, Inc.,* 535 F.2d 982, 996 (7th Cir.1976).

present. Federal Rule 30(b)(4) specifies how an officer is to conduct and begin a deposition. This rule requires the officer begin with a statement on the record that includes: "(a) the officer's name and business address; (b) the date, time and place of the deposition; (c) the name of the deponent; (d) the administration of the oath or affirmation to the deponent; and (e) identification of all persons present." This rule further states that if a deposition is recorded other than stenographically, by video or audio means, "the officer shall repeat items (a) through (c) at the beginning" of each recorded tape or other recording method. The revised rule further provides: "at the end of the deposition, the officer shall state on the record that the deposition is complete and set forth any stipulations made by counsel concerning the custody of the transcript or recording and the exhibits, concerning other pertinent matters." This rule speaks for itself.

The attorneys should make certain that the record is accurate and complete by:

1. Speaking clearly;

2. Having the deponent speak clearly;

3. Proceeding at a pace appropriate for the reporter;

4. Spelling difficult names and words (or providing a written list of them);

5. Allowing a deponent to finish an answer without interruption (unless the interruption is intentional);

6. Reducing all conduct, gestures, and inaudible responses to verbal descriptions, noting for the record what the witness or attorney did;

7. Avoiding superfluous comments, ("O.K., now, let me ask you this," "I see," "Strike that"), repeating answers, and unnecessary arguments ("I object and let me read three pages from Wigmore that will explain why . . .");

8. Not asking multiple questions;

9. Refraining from asking negative pregnant questions such as, "Then you didn't apply the brakes until after the impact, did you?" (a yes or no answer establishes nothing definite);

10. Not throwing Federal 2d reporters at each other.

Everything that goes on during a deposition should be recorded. There are occasions when going off the record will be necessary or be requested by an attorney. If the attorneys agree to go off the record, the court reporter will abide by their request. If one attorney requests going off the record but the other attorney refuses, the court reporter should continue to record. The reporter is an officer of the court for purposes of the deposition and does not have an obligation to obey either attorney. The fact that one attorney has noticed the deposition and hired the reporter does not give that attorney an employer's right to order the reporter to do things.

Going back on the record will occur when either attorney or both attorneys suggest it; a reporter will record the suggestion. Occasionally statements are made, agreements are reached, or things are done off the record that must be included on the record. Whenever these situations occur, one attorney need only verbalize or summarize on the record what happened off the record and obtain the recorded "agreed" from the other attorney.

§ 6.3.7 *Court Reporters and Depositions*

Court reporters are an integral part of a deposition. They provide another perspective on depositions and attorney involvement. Some of their more telling observations, obtained from interviews, follow:

1. The abilities of court reporters vary as much as the abilities of attorneys, and the accuracy and completeness of the resulting record and deposition transcript depend in part on the abilities of the reporter.

2. The advent of recording equipment has proven beyond a doubt that court reporters make mistakes. Some of the errors are within their control; some are not. The deposition process itself builds in mistakes and guarantees that human errors will occur. Consider all the possibilities of error in this sequence of events:

(a) The deponent says something aloud, sometimes imperfectly;

(b) The reporter transcribes the statement accurately, while simultaneously listening to more talk;

(c) The reporter reads and interprets those notes;

(d) The reporter dictates the contents into a tape recorder;

(e) The typist listens carefully to the dictated recording;

(f) The typist types everything accurately and completely.

Moreover, all reporters have particular difficulties with words that sound like other words, with lengthy numbers, with troublesome language, with peculiar information, and with technical data. Mistakes are inevitable even with the use of computer disk recording equipment.

3. Some reporters will use tape recorders, along with their steno machine, as a reference source, if they have difficulty with their transcription. Also, court reporters usually have no objection if an attorney brings a tape recorder (but another attorney may object).

4. Life should be made as easy as possible for reporters by doing simple things, like providing them with a copy of the deposition notice containing the necessary information, allowing them the choice of where to sit, spelling difficult names or words during the deposition, furnishing them with a glossary of technical terms, providing them with a copy of anything that is read into the record, allowing them a break at least every 90 minutes, and asking them at the end of the deposition if they need anything for preparation of the record.

5. Reporters may or may not transcribe everything they hear "on the record" and may or may not "edit" the final transcript. Approaches vary. Some reporters record everything they hear, including "private" conversations between a deponent and counsel, if they are still on the record and if they are within earshot of the reporter. Others do not record such conversations, nor do they record offhand statements that in their opinion have no bearing on the deposition. Should they transcribe these things, they may edit them when they read and dictate their notes.

6. Some reporters may voluntarily "clean up" the transcript. They may eliminate false starts by an attorney, occasions when an attorney misspeaks, or unnecessary examining habits such as "O.K., I see, let me ask you this." Some will eliminate lengthier comments by lawyers, such as repeating an answer or a partial, unfinished question. Most will edit statements and comments made by a deponent only rarely. They may alter the sequence of an answer that a deponent completes while the attorney is still asking the question. This occurs with "yes or no" answers or short responses. That is, the deponent may respond before the attorney has finished asking the question. The reporter then places the response after the question, and not in the middle of it.

7. Court reporters do tend to listen to the attorney who has hired them. Many obey that attorney outright. The reporter may side with the hiring attorney during deposition incidents, including conflicts between the attorneys about going off the record, or breaks, or what the deponent just said or did. Reporters realize that if they do not do things the way the hiring attorney expects, they will not be employed again, and that some other loyal and obedient court reporter will be hired. There are limits, however, since court reporters also realize their obligations not to compromise the accuracy or completeness of a deposition nor the integrity of the system.

8. Some reporters do not do anything unless they are told to. They do not swear in a deponent unless asked; they do not mark a document unless asked; they do not go back on the record after going off the record unless they are told. Other reporters may suggest something be done, if in their opinion one of the attorneys has made a procedural mistake.

9. All reporters charge about the same: an hourly or daily rate plus an amount for the original transcription and one copy. An average deposition produces about 40 pages of transcript per hour.

10. Most reporters believe that the attorneys involved have the primary obligation and burden to arrange and preserve a "recordable situation" during a deposition. But there is another perspective: reporters are officers of the court and also have an obligation and burden to ensure that a deposition results in an accurate and complete recording. This requires the reporter to be impartial, a sometimes difficult position for someone who is being paid by only one (usually) of the parties. Reporters have varying understandings of their roles and

loyalties during a deposition, understandings that lead to their varying approaches on the above and related elements of a deposition.

§ 6.4 PREPARING FOR THE DEPOSITION

From your first law-school exam you know that you had to prepare thoroughly for the questions and the answers in order to do well. So also with a deposition.

Preparation of a case requires familiarity with your file and all other sources of factual information and legal claims and defenses relating to the case. Preparation also requires a grasp of the applicable legal doctrines and overall discovery strategies. Further, it demands knowledge of both the subject matter of the deposition and what the deponent knows about that topic. This includes experts and lay witnesses. If the deponent is an eyewitness to an auto accident, you should be familiar with the location, site, topography, area and other matters relating to the accident. If a deponent is an expert engineer, then you should be versed in whatever specialized engineering area the deposition will cover.

An assessment of the deponent is extremely beneficial to proper preparation of the case. Your best source of information may be your own client or a friendly witness who knows the deponent. You should seek whatever information will assist you: gauge the deponent's ability to communicate, degree of common sense, amount of education, extent of sophistication, stability of emotional reactions, physical appearance, and any particular strengths or weaknesses relevant to the deposition. If you do not have access to anyone with such information, you will then be limited to making these and other determinations during the early stages of the deposition.

Preparation further requires a determination of the purpose or purposes of the deposition. There may be more than one purpose. There may be a primary purpose with secondary considerations. The purpose may even change during a deposition. Because depositions serve countless specific purposes in a case, their length varies. You may schedule a one-week deposition for one deponent, and only a 30-minute deposition for another, to elicit some bit of information or to pin down a deponent on some matter. But an initial decision must be reached regarding why you are taking a deposition and what goals you hope to achieve.

With assessments of the factual, legal, and personality aspects of the deposition, you can now decide upon the approach to take toward the deponent and your overall strategy. Different purposes necessitate different approaches and different strategies. If you want to obtain reams of information, then a friendly, sympathetic approach may best yield that result. If you wish to pin down a deponent, a stern and controlled strategy may attain that goal. If you want to confront a deponent, an aggressive, distant approach may best achieve that purpose. If you want to preserve testimony for trial, a cooperative formal approach appropriate for trial may obtain such testimony. A generally formal and rigid line of questioning that produces limited responses to leading questions may produce a deposition that a court will restrict as to use.[1] A cooperative, informal approach that permits a deponent to tell a story spontaneously, coupled with a controlled and aggressive approach concerning selected topics, may produce a deposition for all seasons.

No amount of preparation will fully prepare you for everything, but the more preparation you do, the better you will be able to respond appropriately during a deposition, the more foresight you will have to anticipate problems, and the better you will be able to take advantage of later opportunities. On the other hand, over-preparation may have its drawbacks. You may establish your line of questioning and form your theories of the case and then proceed during the deposition to obtain specific answers and confirm specific theories. But the responses during a deposition may make your questions or theories inappropriate. You need to be flexible enough to adapt various lines of questions and explore new theories. The valuable part of the deposition is the opportunity you have both to prepare what you want to do and to remain open to unplanned things and to asking spontaneous questions. The answers obtained during a deposition may form a new approach to the case or create new issues, claims, and demands you could not anticipate, because the examination itself uncovers the requisite information. Rather than fit the deposition answers to your case, you may want to fit a theory, approach, claim, or demand to the deposition information.

§ 6.4.1 Outline Organization

The Boy Scouts and Girl Scouts are correct: Be prepared. If there is one absolute rule that should be followed it is: Prepare a complete and detailed outline for the deposition. The degree of detail depends upon several factors, one of which is your level of experience. The more experience you have, the less exhaustive the outline need be. Maybe.

A few attorneys are able to conduct an effective deposition without extensive written notes, relying upon an organization they have created in their minds. Some lawyers rationalize their lack of written preparation by thinking they can do this. Not many can. Most of us have too many things going on in our minds (or not enough mind for things to go on in) and need a written outline. It is difficult, if not impossible, for most of us to perform several skills at one time. You too may have found it difficult, for example, to stay awake, to think, and to respond in your law-school classes. Similarly, during a deposition, it may be difficult to talk, listen, observe the deponent, think, decide on a tactical maneuver, and formulate the next question, all in one brief moment. It is much more difficult to do all that when you experience the peer pressure and tensions that may accompany the deposition.

§ 6.4

1. *Stonsifer v. Courtney's Furniture Co., Inc.,* 474 F.2d 113, 115 n. 2 (10th Cir.1973).

A thorough, planned and well-organized outline of what you want and need to cover during the deposition allows you the time to concentrate on your essential listening and observing skills. It also impresses the opposing attorney with your professional preparedness, prevents important topical areas from being omitted, allows you the flexibility to follow tangents spontaneously, prevents unintentional repetitious questioning, eliminates your having to guess what else you should cover during a deposition, reduces deposition time, and so saves your client money. Form books containing discovery lists for specific cases are sources for ideas about what to ask. After preparing a draft of an outline, you can review it and eliminate superfluous or unimportant areas.

The outline should be organized in some logical, chronological, or associational (organized by issues, claims, defenses, situations) sequence. Though as a strategic maneuver you may decide to skip around, and not to ask questions in a logical order during the deposition, your preparation of the outline should be orderly to avoid omitting topics. It is generally advisable not to write out all your questions, but only those important ones that need to be carefully phrased to elicit a certain response. Questions seeking vital admissions, leading questions that may confuse or trap the deponent, important foundation questions, and questions that will be asked at trial may need to be written out. Preparing too many questions may reduce your flexibility during the deposition, make you sound like a Double Jeopardy contestant, and take too long.

The rules of evidence should not unduly influence you in your preparation of the outline or in seeking information during the deposition. The evidentiary rules govern admissibility for trial purposes, not for discovery purposes. Unless the deposition is solely to preserve testimony for trial, you need not become preoccupied with what is or is not a proper question or an admissible answer. Sometimes it is best to forget the rules of evidence completely (easier for some of us than for others) and probe for triple and quadruple hearsay, for the worst evidence, for unauthentic documents, and for gossip and baseless opinions. All this may still not uncover the smoking paper, but it is certain to make things more fun.

The structure of your outline should also suit your personal and professional preferences. Its organization should be easy to read and easy to follow. Space should be allowed for you to make notes, record dandy responses by the deponent, or just to doodle, even if you are not a Yankee.

§ 6.4.2 Deposition to Preserve Testimony

Depositions are usually conducted in order to gather information from the deponent. But some depositions are taken for a more specific purpose: to preserve testimony. The strategies involved in taking this latter type of deposition differ dramatically from the strategies relating to discovery depositions. The decision to take a preservation deposition depends upon the availability of the deponent for trial. The testimony of a deponent who will not or may not be able to testify at trial may be considered by the factfinder in five specific situations noted by Rule 32(a)(3):

1. The deponent dies before trial;
2. The witness is more than 100 miles from the trial site;
3. The deponent is imprisoned, ill, or infirm;
4. The witness cannot be subpoenaed for the trial;
5. Exceptional circumstances exist.

The examining attorney may anticipate one of these situations and decide to take a deposition to preserve testimony for trial.

Preservation depositions are taken of witnesses who have information supportive of the examining attorney's case; the deponents would testify at trial for the examining attorney. The deposition question-and-answer format parallels the direct examination format. The deposing attorney attempts to duplicate what would be the direct examination of this witness during trial. Witnesses can consist of deponents who are friendly or neutral and those who are unfriendly. In preserving the testimony of a friendly or neutral witness, consider:

1. Questions that elicit the reasons the deponent will be unavailable;

2. Using trial techniques to make the direct examination effective, such as simple, understandable questions structured to create and maintain interest;

3. Responsive answers detailing the necessary information, including sufficient foundation explanations;

4. Questions and answers designed to be read or summarized at trial;

5. Avoiding objectionable questions, such as leading questions, except to develop testimony.

Preservation depositions of unfriendly witnesses involve some different considerations since they usually seek admissions from an opposing party or expert or lay witnesses. The question-and-answer format parallels adverse direct examination with its use of leading questions to gain specific information and to control the witness. In all preservation depositions the examining attorney must be concerned that all questions and answers will be admissible at the trial.

These approaches differ markedly from discovery depositions, which are more free-wheeling and less concerned with trial matters. But depositions may not all be neatly divided into preservation or discovery classes. Because a deposition often serves several purposes, some of its parts may seek to elicit supportive admissions, while others attempt to discover information or reduce credibility and establish impeachment material. The examining attorney must be flexible enough to adapt the applicable strategies to the respective parts of a deposition.

The attorney representing the deponent must also be aware of the strategies involved in preserving testimony. That attorney must determine whether the deponent will be available at trial. If the witness will be unavailable, the attorney may want to schedule a deposition to preserve testimony, in addition to any discovery deposition noticed by the opposition. If this is not done, the only transcript available for trial will be the deposition transcript conducted as a cross-examination. It may not contain all the information necessary for trial and will certainly not be in a direct-examination format. So the deponent's attorney may have an interest in questioning the deponent to preserve information. If concise, this questioning could occur during the attorney's opportunity to "rehabilitate" the deponent.

§ 6.5 TAKING THE DEPOSITION

Taking the deposition involves a number of procedures and considerations, which are discussed in detail in the subsections that follow.

§ 6.5.1 Preliminary Procedural Matters

Rule 30(c) provides that the deposition officer shall put the witness under oath or affirmation (if the witness has valid objection to taking an oath) and shall personally, or by someone acting under his or her direction, record the testimony of the deponent. The more common oath and the occasional affirmation are usually routine matters. If the examination proceeds and the witness has not been sworn, the witness must either ratify the prior testimony or answer each question again. The officer must record certain information, including the caption of the case, the persons present, and the appearances of the attorneys. Most reporters obtain that information from the deposition notice and from one or more of the attorneys.

§ 6.5.2 The Demeanor of the Attorneys

Attorneys have an obligation to conduct themselves during a deposition as if they were at trial. Judges have so held, as passages from two opinions make clear:

> [T]he stenographic record of the examination before trial of Mr. Nimis clearly shows conduct on the part of counsel which would not have been indulged in were the testimony taken before a judge or in open court; nor would it have been indulged in, and certainly if indulged in, would not have been permitted, if it occurred in the trial of the action. There seems to be no reason why, therefore, counsel should conduct themselves upon an examination before trial

any differently than in the trial of the case.[1]

> The federal rules envision that discovery will be conducted by skilled gentlemen [*sic*] of the bar, without wrangling and without the intervention of the court. The vision is an unreal dream. Regrettably, hostility and bitterness are more the rule than the exception in unsupervised discovery proceedings. Perhaps this is inevitable, for litigation at all stages and under the best of circumstances is fertile ground for conflict. The opposing self-interests of the parties, as each vies for advantage, often spawns not only bitterness but abuse of the discovery process.[2]

It is improper for an attorney to interfere with a fair examination of a deponent and to engage in any conduct that the attorney knows would not be allowed in the presence of a judicial officer. Commentators have explained the appropriate demeanor of an attorney at a deposition. The Federal Advisory Committee which drafts official comments to the rules states: "In general, counsel should not engage in any conduct during a deposition that would not be allowed in the presence of the judicial officer."

Questionable attorney conduct can usually be controlled by peer pressure, by noting such conduct on the record, by asking the offending attorney to stop, and if all else fails, by seeking a protective order or Rule 37 sanctions. Rule 30(d) describes the situation and procedures available to seek relief from improper conduct by an attorney (or a deponent):

> At any time during the taking of the deposition, on motion of a party or of the deponent and upon a showing that the examination is being conducted in bad faith or in such manner as unreasonably to annoy, embarrass, or oppress the deponent or party, the court in which the action is pending or the court in the district where the deposition is being taken may order the officer conducting the examination to cease forthwith from taking the deposition, or may limit the scope and manner of the taking of the deposition as provided in Rule 26(c). If the order made terminates the examination, it shall be suspended for the time necessary to make a motion for an order. The provisions of Rule 37(a)(4) apply to the award of expenses incurred in relation to the motion.

The demeanor of the attorneys during a deposition must be balanced by a number of considerations: appropriate trial decorum, aggressive and spirited advocacy, the purpose of the deposition conduct, the need for maintaining a cooperative approach, peer pressure, and the best interests of the client. Whatever the attorney does, should be done with a reason.

§ 6.5

1. *Detective Comics, Inc. v. Fawcett Publications, Inc.,* 4 F.R.D. 237, 239 (S.D.N.Y. 1944).

2. *Harlem River Consumer Co-operative, Inc. v. Associated Grocers of Harlem, Inc.,* 54 F.R.D. 551, 553 (S.D.N.Y.1972).

§ 6.5.3 *Stipulations*

"Usual stipulations, counsel?"

"Huh? Oh, sure, yes, indeed, certainly, by all means."

What stipulations? One of the attorneys may suggest, usually at the beginning or at the conclusion of the deposition, that the "standard" or "usual" stipulations apply to the deposition proceedings. The other attorney may mumble agreement without a consensus reached on what the stipulations are. The court reporter may specify in the transcript some version of the standard stipulations. Conversely, the other attorney may insist that some stipulations be specified and that others are unnecessary or undesirable. (Beginning stipulations that detail procedures governed by the rules are no longer necessary. A stipulation may state that the deposition is taken pursuant to the "Rules of Civil Procedure," but that statement serves no purpose, because the rules do indeed apply.) There are some legitimate reasons for a beginning procedural stipulation. For instance, in a deposition in a case involving many parties, a stipulation that an objection by one attorney will be deemed to have been made by all opposing attorneys can save time and prevent confusion. Stipulations can be agreed upon at any time during a deposition. Typical concluding stipulations will be reviewed in § 6.8.1.

§ 6.5.4 *Introductory Statements and Questions*

Some customary introductory requests and explanations include the following:

1. An agreement from the opposing attorney that everything has proceeded properly and correctly up until that moment, to prevent him or her from later raising objections to the formalities, is usual. However, because Rule 32(d) provides that objections to the reporter's qualifications and to the taking of the deposition will be waived unless made prior to the beginning of the deposition or when the disqualification becomes known, such a request may invite an objection that would have been waived.

2. A statement, identifying who is present at the deposition, should be made. The court reporter will usually note the appearances of counsel and the deponent at the beginning of the deposition transcript. Some attorneys prefer describing in the record who is there, so that the court reporter and the deponent know who is who. Most attorneys leave that matter to the court reporter, who obtains the necessary information from the notice of the deposition and case caption.

3. An explanation of whom the attorney represents may be helpful. This may not be necessary for a party deposition, but will be for a witness or multiparty deposition. An attorney who does not represent a witness, but represents the adverse party, cannot counsel that witness during the deposition and may not have standing to object to all questions. Some attorneys, however, will insist on objecting, and it is

not clear what they can or cannot do. A request for an explanation will lay the ground rules for the remainder of that deposition.

4. Explanations and questions directed to the deponent will vary, depending upon the deposition approach and the relationship the deposing attorney wants to establish with the deponent. Traditional opening explanations, which help put the witness at ease and which serve as aids in preventing later inconsistent testimony, might go something like this:

Examining attorney: Mr. Witness, I am Jeffrey Haddock, and I represent the Cookie Monster in this lawsuit. Do you understand what a deposition is? (*Or,* Has your attorney explained to you what a deposition is?) (*If no, explain in detail. If yes, continue on:*)

I am going to ask you a series of questions about the incident involved here, and the reporter will take down your answers. If at any time you don't understand any question, please tell me and I will repeat or rephrase the question. If you answer a question, I will assume that you understood it. Is this understood and acceptable to you? (*The witness will invariably say yes.*)

This deposition will be transcribed by the reporter, and everything that is said here today will be recorded. At the trial, all the testimony you give will be available in booklet form, and if I ask you the same questions then that I will ask you today, and if your answers then differ from the answers given today, you may expect to be asked to account for the difference in your answers. Do you understand this? (*The witness again will usually answer yes, and some attorneys will continue with the following explanation:*)

Your testimony today is under oath, as if you were in a court of law. You have sworn to tell the truth, and if you fail to do so, adverse consequences may result. Do you understand this?

These explanations, which can be varied or modified, may establish some rapport with the witness. They will also effectively prevent witnesses from claiming at trial that they did not understand the questions asked, or understand that they would be asked the questions again, or that they were under oath. This portion of the deposition can be read at the trial for impeachment purposes. Other attorneys will not be this specific with the explanations or may omit the last explanation, because they do not want to suggest that the witness be cautious about answering questions.

Your opening explanations, statements, or questions will affect the atmosphere you want to create at the deposition. If you want to establish a friendly, informal relationship, your initial remarks should have a friendly, informal character to them. If you want to create a stern, formal atmosphere, your remarks should be stern and formal. Deponents will react to your opening. You can attempt to make them feel at ease or attempt to make them feel uneasy. You may not wish to employ any of the traditional openings and may prefer to begin immediately with the factual questioning. Whatever you decide, it must be planned.

§ 6.5.5 Handling Exhibits

Exhibits are best handled with the hands. A variety of exhibits may be available during the deposition. You may have had the deponent bring some materials and objects pursuant to Rule 34 or Rule 45. The deponent may voluntarily bring some documents or may use some materials to refresh his or her recollection. You may wish to question the deponent about things in your possession. Some attorneys read the exact nature of the document production request under Rule 34 or 45 into the record and then ask whether the documents brought to the deposition are responsive to such request, because there is no formal written response. The question and the answer make clear whether the disclosing side has fully or partially responded to the request. Attorneys also read into the record a description of the documents available at the deposition or have the deponent read part of the document being reviewed into the record. This makes clear what provision is being referred to, but it can be unnecessary and time-consuming. In these situations, the beginning and end of the provision can be noted on the record, or the deponent can mark the provision being reviewed.

Part of this identification process includes the marking of the deposition exhibits. The rules require that exhibits be marked for one reason: so that the record is clear regarding the identity of the exhibit and references made to it by the deponent and attorneys. The record would be confusing if an exhibit were not described in some fashion, to distinguish it from other exhibits. The record would also be lengthier than necessary if exhibits were referred to by some description including title, date, signatures, contents, or whatever. The process is simple. The reporter marks an exhibit upon request of either attorney. Such a request may be made before the deposition starts, particularly if there are numerous exhibits, to save time later. Some attorneys merely hand the exhibit to the reporter and ask the reporter to mark it. Others describe the thing to be marked at least once on the record. For example:

Attorney: Reporter, please mark as Plaintiff's Exhibit 1 this three-page will, dated October 1, 1978, signed by Howard Hughes and witnessed by Saint Peter and Bugs Bunny.

Reporter, please mark as Defendant's Exhibit A this pale pink eraser, approximately two inches long and one inch wide, bearing the initials *R.N.*

All documents and objects should be marked before they are used, and all subsequent references to the exhibit should include the exhibit identification. For example:

Attorney: I hand you this letter, marked Plaintiff's Exhibit 2, and ask you whether that is your *X* on the bottom of page 3.

You may prefer showing the exhibits to the opposing attorney before you hand them to the deponent, particularly if the attorney is not familiar with the exhibit. It is professional courtesy to do so, and an experienced opposing attorney will insist on reviewing the exhibit before or with his or her client. Witnesses often discuss exhibits without identifying them, and you may need to clarify the record by designating the exhibit number or letter of the document or object they discuss. Further, you may want the exhibits marked by the witness with initials or a specific mark, to designate significant portions of the exhibit the witness acknowledges or describes.

Part of the process of introducing exhibits in a deposition parallels the process of their introduction at trial, but there are some differences. There is no need to "offer" an exhibit at a deposition, because it automatically becomes part of the record, and any objections to the receipt of such an exhibit will be determined by the judge at trial. Likewise, while there is usually no need to lay a foundation before questioning the deponent about the exhibit, there may be reasons for doing so. The answers to foundation questions may produce sufficient information, helping you to compose later a Rule 36 admission request relating to the genuineness and authenticity of the document, or to frame a stipulation. The foundation questions may need to be asked at trial, and the answers to such questions at the deposition make trial preparation more effective and efficient. Lastly, a deposition transcript with exhibit foundation answers makes possible the introduction of such exhibits at trial, if the deponent is unavailable to testify.

Rule 30(b)(1) describes what happens to the exhibits after the deposition. The intent of the rule is to permit an attorney to offer copies for marking and annexation to the deposition. These copies are the "substitute," and the originals used during the deposition would not be attached to the transcript, but would be returned to the party who provided them. These original documents must be retained and made available to the other party should the need arise. The deposition and the exhibits will be filed with the court in due course. Some clerk's offices will not accept the filing of non-paper exhibits like blueprints or x-rays, so other filing arrangements for the originals must be made by the attorneys involved.

§ 6.5.6 Discovery of Materials

Rule 34 is the appropriate discovery device to obtain copies of documents and things, but a deposition provides you with the opportunity to uncover the identity and location of materials and to request that you be allowed to inspect and copy such materials. Your request will not necessarily be complied with, but more often than not, professional courtesy and the spirit of cooperation will prompt the other attorney to agree to your request.

You can ask questions concerning how thorough the search for the documents produced pursuant to Rule 34 was. A detailed inquiry into the mechanics of the search may indicate that some potential sources of documents were overlooked, and you can insist that such documents falling within the Rule 34 request be produced. Your questioning may also uncover documents the deponent used to refresh his or her recollection in preparing for the deposition. You have a right to review these documents. Courts require their disclosure, relying upon Rule 30(c) and Federal Rule of Evidence 612, which permit depositions to proceed in the same fashion that direct and cross-examination proceeds at trial.[3] Courts have required documents to be disclosed that were protected by the attorney-client privilege, because the use of documents to refresh recollection operated as an effective waiver of such privilege.[4]

You may insist that all documents discovered during a deposition be produced before the deposition terminates, during a break, or at a later date when the deposition has been continued. You may also uncover the existence and identity of documents not requested and not used to refresh recollection. You should seek an agreement from the other counsel during the deposition to allow you to review and copy these documents.

Any such agreement concerning the disclosure of documents and things should be reflected in the deposition record. If you are the attorney seeking the information, be certain the record reflects what the other attorney has agreed to provide and the date or deadline by which such things will be disclosed. For example:

Examining Counsel: The record will reflect that Mr. Smith has agreed to allow me to inspect and copy all correspondence exchanged between the plaintiff and defendant in September 1992, and that the records will be made available in defendant's office at 10:00 A.M., May 1, 1993. Would you further agree to provide me with a copy of the contract, dated November 1, 1992, signed by both parties?

Other Attorney: Yes.

Examining Counsel: Would you please mail me a copy within ten days?

Other Attorney: Yes.

These recitations should detail the contents of the agreement and the date. If the other attorney fails to provide such access or copies, the requesting attorney can still submit a Rule 34 request buttressed by the previous agreement.

If you are the attorney who has been asked for something, you may cooperate with the other attorney unless you have good reason not to. Do not give things away until you first have had the chance to review the items yourself. You do not want to disclose something without having reviewed its contents and appraised its discoverability.

3. *Prucha v. M & N Modern Hydraulic Press Co.,* 76 F.R.D. 207, 209 (W.D.Wis. 1977).

4. *Wheeling–Pittsburgh Steel Corp. v. Underwriters Labs., Inc.,* 81 F.R.D. 8, 10–11 (N.D.Ill.1978).

An agreement on the deposition record to disclose documents raises the question of its enforceability. Does this commitment compel such disclosure without a formal Rule 34 request? May the attorney renege on the agreement and insist upon a Rule 34 request? The answer depends upon the circumstances. The attorney who changes positions must have a good-faith, substantial reason for doing so, compelling enough to convince the other attorney not to initiate a Rule 37 motion, and sufficient to avoid the imposition of motion expenses and attorney's fees by a judge. The opposing lawyer must decide whether to serve a Rule 34 request before enforcing the deposition through Rule 37. Rule 34 does not appear to be the exclusive way to obtain access to documents. Stipulations can be enforced.

§ 6.5.7 Confidential Information

The deponent's attorney may refuse to disclose documents or reveal information, by claiming that the materials are confidential or privileged. These grounds may become the basis for an instruction not to answer a question. You must anticipate these situations and be prepared to counter such positions. Rule 26(c)(7) permits parties to obtain a court order preserving the confidentiality of information. This order can be obtained by a motion or a stipulated agreement between counsel. These agreements can be made upon the record at a deposition, later confirmed in writing and approved with a court order.

The significant terms of these agreements include the scope of the confidential materials (what is confidential and what is not) and who has access to the information. Usually the attorneys, a party or a representative of a party, and an expert will have access to the confidential information. Details, such as which attorneys and how many, which party representatives, and how many experts, will be negotiated by the attorneys. Problems relating to confidential matters can be anticipated and resolved prior to the deposition, so that the information or documents can be readily disclosed during the deposition itself.

§ 6.5.8 Reacting to Objections

Your opponent has a right to make proper (and limited) objections during a deposition, though no one is authorized to rule on the objections at that time. Ordinarily, your reaction to an objection is to proceed and insist on an answer to the question. Rule 30(c) provides that "[e]vidence objected to shall be taken subject to the objection" and shall be "noted by the officer" upon the record and "the examination shall proceed." Section 6.7.4 describes the proper making of appropriate objections. As the examining attorney, your primary concern with objections is to prevent them from interfering with your taking the deposition.

The opposing attorney may or may not specify the grounds for the objection. Federal rules and practice require specific objections. If you are uncertain why the attorney has objected, you may want to ask for specific or explanatory grounds for the objection. Sometimes you will ask a question that you know is poor, and if there is an objection, you will know why. You can then decide either to rephrase the question or withdraw it. At other times you will ask what you think is a perfectly proper question, and still receive an objection. If you are uncertain, you may want to ask the attorney the grounds, or you may want to proceed and insist upon an answer. Your reaction will largely depend upon the specific type of objection raised:

1. If an objection to the form of the question is raised, then you should decide whether to rephrase the question. It may be improper, unclear, or not understandable. Rule 32(d)(3)(B) validates such objections. You may decide it is proper, and insist on an answer as originally stated.

2. If an objection cites lack of foundation, you will probably want to establish the foundation through additional questions. If the deposition is to preserve testimony, then most likely you will want to lay the proper foundation. But even if you have no intent to preserve testimony and do not care whether there is a sufficient foundation, you will nonetheless care about conducting a probing, intensive deposition, and so, again, you will ask questions to establish foundation. Rarely will there be situations in which you do not want to inquire about how a witness knows something.

3. If it is an objection based on relevancy or competency, you may be able to cure the objection by rephrasing the question or by asking a series of clearly relevant questions. If so, do it. If not, insist on an answer. Rule 32(d)(3)(A) authorizes such objections.

4. If the objection is based on any other grounds, ignore it and obtain your requested answer from the deponent. If the deponent is unsure of what to do, insist on an answer to the question. You have a right to the answer regardless of the nature of the objection.

5. If the attorney objects and properly instructs the deponent not to answer, you will find it impossible to extract an answer. Section 6.7.5 explains the proper use of instructions not to answer. You may ask the witness to make the refusal clear, if he or she does refuse to answer. But the rules prohibit the use of bamboo shoots inserted in the fingernails. If there is an objection to your question, do not ask the other attorney if he or she is instructing the witness not to answer. There is no sense in putting ideas in his or her head, even though there may be room.

6. If the opposing attorney persists in an instruction, your recourse is to seek a court order under Rule 37, compelling an answer. To obtain such an order you must present to the judge the actual wording of the objectionable question, preferably in an excerpt from the transcript containing the objectionable question. It is possible to submit an affidavit describing what happened, but it is much better practice to have the reporter mark the passage and prepare the excerpt from the deposition for the judge to read.

At the time the instruction not to answer is interposed, you should make certain that the transcript clearly and accurately details what happened. The transcript should reflect the following:

1. The question;
2. The objection;
3. The instruction not to answer;
4. The deponent's refusal to answer;
5. The reason supporting the refusal.

The sanctions available under Rule 37 need to be sought only occasionally, because the importance of the question diminishes as the time, effort, and expense in obtaining the answer mounts. Rarely is there an adjournment of the deposition to seek an immediate court ruling. Usually the deposition will continue and the order will be sought later. The deposing attorney may be able to avoid the problem, either by asking the same question later in a different form or by agreeing with the other attorney to obtain a partial answer to the question.

Reacting to objections should not include arguing with the other attorney about the correctness or appropriateness of the objection. There is no need to try to persuade the attorney because the question must be answered regardless. There may be a reason, however, to discuss with an attorney an instruction not to answer—if you do change the attorney's mind, it will save you a trip to the courthouse. Otherwise, arguing over objections wastes time, often tips the witness to the reason you asked the question in the first place, and allows the witness more time to conjure up a response.

If an attorney insists on interposing frequent objections to your questions, there are several ways you can handle the situation. You may suggest that the record reflect a continuing objection to all or certain of your questions, to avoid the other attorney's continually interrupting with objections. You may tactfully remind the other attorney that nearly all objections are preserved for trial and that there is no need for most objections. You may advise the other attorney that such unnecessary objections unduly interfere with the deposition and that such conduct is improper under the rules. Or you can, in egregious situations, seek a protective order or a Rule 37 sanction. If all else fails, you could ask the attorney for his or her home address.

§ 6.5.9 Controlling Interference

The primary concern of the deposing attorney is to maintain control over the deposition procedures. The preceding sections have described situations and suggested approaches allowing the attorney to prevent interference and maintain control. But interference may stem from the opposing attorney, the deponent, or strategy considerations.

Rules of civil procedure and court decisions prohibit an attorney from interfering with the deposition. Section 6.7.6 describes what an attorney representing a deponent may properly do during a deposition. These restrictions will not deter some attorneys from attempting to interfere. You may counter interfering tactics with the following approaches:

1. Insist the rules be followed. Applicable rules usually prohibits the efforts of the other attorney to interfere with the deposition, and you should advise the attorney of the existence of these rules.

2. Insist that court decisions regulating deposition practice be followed. There may be reported judicial decisions in a jurisdiction, or from a jurisdiction that has the same or similar rules, that regulate what an attorney may do and that admonish counsel from unnecessarily interfering with the deposition. Advise the attorney of these cases or read such prohibitions from a relevant case to the attorney on the record.

3. Record everything that occurs. Especially record all nonverbal conduct by the opposing attorney, whether it involves passing a note to the witness, whispering in the deponent's ear, signaling the witness, conferring with the client, or other conduct affecting the testimony.

4. Establish reasonable ground rules. Explain instructions at the beginning or during a deposition explaining conduct that is permissible or that will not be tolerated.

5. Insist that the deponent respond to your question and only to your question and advise the opposing attorney not to testify. Insist on complete answers and interrupt rambling responses.

6. Admonish an attorney from unnecessarily conferring with the deponent. Some jurisdiction and courts may prohibit an attorney from counseling a client during a deposition, or even during a recess. If these restrictions apply, advise the attorney and deponent of their inability to consult with each other.

7. Advise the opposing attorney that you will telephone a judge to seek a ruling regarding the improper behavior. If the interfering conduct continues, telephone the judge assigned to a case, or the chief judge, or contact the clerk or administrator's office and ask for an available judge to resolve the dispute. If a judge is available, explain the problem to the judge over a speaker phone in the presence of the other attorney and ask the court for a ruling.

9. In unusual cases in which the opposing attorney is uncontrollable, suggest or reschedule the deposition to be held in a courthouse or before a referee, magistrate, or judge who can control the situation.

10. Advise the opposing attorney that if the conduct continues the deposition will be adjourned and a protective order will be sought. If the inappropriate conduct continues, continue the deposition and notice a motion seeking a protective order.

You may decide to interrupt the deposition for reasons of strategy. Occasionally your preparation may not be complete, and you may need a break to obtain some more information or to rethink your approach to the deposition. Or the deponent may not be prepared to respond fully to a question, and you may want an adjournment to allow the witness to obtain some data or to review some materials. The deposition may uncover some documents, and you may want a recess to study them before continuing with the deposition. The other attorney may suggest a recess or lunch break during a deposition. Before acceding to such a request, you should be certain to complete a full segment of the deposition, in order to prevent a conference between the deponent and the attorney during the break that could lead to alterations or supplementations in the testimony later.

§ 6.5.10 Concluding Questions and Considerations

The examining attorney may wish to end the examination with several broad questions on the record to make clear that the witness has both understood everything and told all. Questions such as "Have you understood all the questions you answered?" or "Did you reveal all the facts you were asked about?" usually produce affirmative or "to the best of my recollection" responses and nothing further. They may bolster the impeachment value of the testimony. Other concluding questions have different purposes. "Do you wish to change any of your answers?" may produce a quick no or a statement from the deponent's attorney that the deponent has a right to read the transcript and to make any appropriate changes at that time. "Do you wish to say anything else?" is a stab-in-the-dark question, hoping that the witness will somehow say something damaging. This question may also prompt an objection that the question is too broad. Neither question will usually have any useful purpose.

Some examining attorneys advise deponents that they have an obligation to provide supplementary answers to the deposition questions if they recall any additional information after the deposition or if they need to update some answers. This supplementation commitment may or may not be mandatory under Rule 26(e). The opposing attorney may interrupt such an explanation and suggest that he or she will advise his or her client accordingly.

Rule 30(c) allows examination of the deponent by his or her counsel or attorneys representing other parties. This examination will occur after you have completed your questioning. You have an interest in making certain the other attorney receives that opportunity. If the opportunity has not been provided to an attorney, the deposition could be considered incomplete by a court and useless as evidentiary or even impeachment material. So it is good practice to ask on the record whether the other attorney has any questions of the deponent before ending a deposition.

Examining attorneys usually allow the other attorney to ask a reasonable number of questions for rehabilitation purposes. Questions that become excessive in number allow you to take the position that your deposition of the deponent has formally ended because the examination has become a deposition to preserve testimony. You can then advise the other attorney that you will no longer pay the reporter. You could decide to be difficult (particularly if you have something else scheduled at that time) and leave. You probably should cooperate, however, and stay to listen to the answers and ask more questions after the examination. You can negotiate with the other attorney to assume the extra costs associated with the lengthened deposition.

§ 6.6 DEPOSITION QUESTIONING STRATEGIES

Some deposition questioning techniques are almost mandatory in application and will be used in every deposition. Techniques should not require any thinking; they should simply be implemented. Inexperienced or unsuccessful attorneys use a number of techniques that flag their inexperience or contribute to their losing percentages. They make interesting grist for analysis when formulated as precepts:

- *Don't Pay Close Attention to the Deponent's Responses. It is hard enough to ask the questions, and if you must also listen closely to the answers, well, it might be too much for you. For example:*

  Deponent: All right, so I am not the real deponent. I didn't think you would ever find out. My name is. . . .

  Counsel: Excuse me, let's take a short recess. I have to call and reserve a racquetball court for this afternoon.

- *Don't Observe the Witness.* Witnesses may react in the most telling ways to certain questions. Their body posture and facial expressions may indicate their nervousness, or tension, or what seems to be an inconsistent answer. This all means nothing. For example:

  Counsel: You were driving 105 miles per hour through the grade-school parking lot at the time you hit the milk carton, correct?

  Deponent: Not really. *(Thud.)*

  Counsel: Your client looks awfully uncomfortable. Must be the flu. How about a recess?

- *React Visibly to Damaging Information.* Experienced attorneys will impassively and neutrally respond to the most damaging information without indicating what surprises, bothers, disturbs, or pleases them. It may be better for your psyche (although not your law practice) to release your primal instincts as your case disintegrates before your eyes. For instance:

  Deponent: I remember the exact words your client spoke immediately after the accident. She said, "It was all my fault. I was 100 percent negligent, you were zero percent negligent." In fact, I wrote it down in this document in front of 38 impartial eyewitnesses, all of whom signed in the presence of three notaries.

Counsel: I got good grades in law school, I never complained about the bar exam, why should my career be tarnished?

- *Ask Complex, Unclear Questions, Chock Full of Legalese.* Successful attorneys prefer using simple, clear questions, so that the deponent understands and that the questions will be appropriate for evidentiary or impeachment use later at trial. It may sound better to your blue-book ear if you ask discombobulated questions. For example:

  Counsel: Allow me to recapitulate your previous testimony, which you have provided us with this day in immediate response to my direct question relating to the doctrine of incorporeal hereditaments, did you or did you not commit this act perpetrated on my client, the plaintiff in this civil action, file number....

- *Do Not Be Curious.* If you are trying to find out what information the other side has or what the deponent knows, don't probe, don't ask follow-up questions, don't be inquisitive, and don't ask questions merely because you don't know or understand something. Keep your puzzlement to yourself. You have enough things to remember already and there is little use in becoming confused with the facts. But, above all, don't be curious or ask questions you suspect may reveal damaging information. What you don't know won't hurt you. For example:

  Deponent: I told your client that it was probably going to be what we call a fornistan, but he insisted, and the next day....

  Counsel: Oh, a fornistan, sure. How long have you been a deponent?

- *Assume Everything Is in Your Best Interests.* Depositions can be significantly reduced in time, scope, and expense if you make assumptions about what happened, instead of asking question after question to discover what actually did happen. This guessing game also reduces the amount of actual information and evidence available for trial, making your trial notebook lighter and making it easier on the law clerk who carries your briefcase to court. For example:

  Counsel: State your name.

  Deponent: Number 6746.

  Counsel: Were you driving your car on the date this accident occurred?

  Deponent: Yes.

  Counsel: Thank you. No further questions. I'm bright enough to know what happened.

- *Insist on Generalizations and Conclusions, Not Factual Responses.* Experienced and successful attorneys insist on factual responses to factual questions. They know that most people tend to use generalized, conclusory words to describe things. They know that words have more than one meaning. They know that to prove a case at trial they need facts and admissible evidence, not generalizations and assumptions. They know they have to ask continually the key questions in depositions: "How do you know?" "What facts do you have to support that statement?" They know they may have to repeat or rephrase a question over and over again, until the witness answers with a factual description or retracts a prior response. They know there are many reasons a witness will reach a conclusion without having any data to support that position. They know that follow-up factual questioning often reduces a conclusion to a guess. But that process takes knowledge, patience, and persistence. It is much simpler to take what a witness says at face value and go on. After all, witnesses would not say anything unless they saw everything, remembered everything, and were able to recall at a later date everything that had happened, communicating it clearly in unequivocal words. Attorneys can all do that. But then, attorneys are supposed to be perfect. For example:

Counsel: Did Mr. Danforth sign the contract?

Deponent: Yes, of course.

Counsel: How do you know?

Deponent: Well, I saw his name on the bottom line. I assume he signed.

Counsel: You did not see him sign, did you?

Deponent: No.

Counsel: Then, you don't know if he signed the contract, do you?

Deponent: No.

Counsel: Did Mr. Danforth read the contract?

Deponent: Oh, yes.

Counsel: How do you know?

Deponent: He sat in the room with me for a while with the contract.

Counsel: Did he just glance over parts of the contract?

Deponent: I don't know.

Counsel: Did you observe his eyes as he looked at the contract?

Deponent: No.

Counsel: Did he say anything to indicate he read the contract?

Deponent: No. But he didn't say he didn't read it.

Counsel: You don't know whether he read it or not, do you?

Deponent: No. I thought so. I assumed he read it. I guess . . . all right, I confess. I read it. It took me about two minutes. The content was boring. So was your client.

It works every time.

There are a number of other strategic and tactical options that must be considered before and during the deposition and that affect its direction and success. The precise strategies to be employed will depend on the purposes of the deposition. The following subsections detail these tactical alternatives. Keep in mind that not all the strategies need to be considered in every deposition: each has its place and moment.

§ 6.6.1 *Specific Techniques: How to Probe*

- *Insist on Responsive Answers.* Attorneys should ordinarily insist that witnesses fully and accurately respond to the questions. But witnesses may respond in different fashions.

  They may respond "I don't know," and they may not know. The best you can do is follow up and ask why they don't know, particularly if they should know something.

  They may summarily respond "I don't know," but further questioning may be necessary to make certain they have no information. Follow-up questions may include: "Did you know something in the past?" "You don't know, or you don't presently remember?" "Is it your testimony today that you do not have any personal knowledge to answer that question?"

  They may respond "I don't know for sure," but you are more interested in their estimate or even their guess about something. You can lead the deponent with "bracketing" questions to elicit some response:

  Deponent: I don't know for sure.

  Counsel: Wait until I ask a question. How far from the intersection was Mr. Haydock's motorcycle when you first saw the motorcycle?

  Deponent: I don't know for sure.

  Counsel: Was the distance less than 400 feet?

  Deponent: Yes.

  Counsel: Was the distance more than 200 feet?

  Deponent: Yes.

  Counsel: Was it more or less than 300 feet?

  Deponent: I'm not sure. I really don't know.

  Counsel: You are sure, though, that it was less than 400 feet and more than 200 feet, is that correct?

  Deponent: Yes.

They may respond "I think so" or "probably" or "I'm not certain, but I believe so." You have to decide whether to follow up with further questions seeking a more definite answer, or a yes or no, or "I don't know." If the less-than-certain response is favorable, further inquiries may erode that favorable effect or may solidify that answer. If the response is unfavorable, further inquiries may erode or solidify that response. Your assessment of the situation and potential responses should be your guide.

They may respond "I don't recall" or "I don't remember." You have to decide whether you want to attempt refreshing their recollection or to leave the response as is. You may want to ask if there is anything that may refresh their recollection. It is usually important during a deposition to discover not only what the deponent knows but also what he or she does not know. If the deponent does not recall something, you can follow that response with "Then it is possible that. . . ."

They may respond with a selective memory, remembering only favorable information. It is the task of the examiner to refresh the deponent's recollection of other, perhaps damaging, information.

They may respond with an emerging pattern of ambiguous or evasive or incomplete answers. You then have to decide whether to ask questions that continue to elicit such responses. The deposition transcript will then show a witness who knew little, was evasive, and who will be worthless as a witness for the opposition.

- *Decide Upon a Structured Approach.* Some attorneys employ a standard questioning approach to obtain complete information about an event. One such technique includes: (1) asking general, open-ended questions to which the deponent provides narrative answers; (2) following up with specific, closed-ended questions that clarify and probe such answers; (3) concluding with questions that verify another version of the event to pinpoint similarities and differences between the accounts (without being obvious). This or other structured approaches assist the examining attorney in exhausting a particular area before moving on to another.
- *Encourage the Deponent to Talk and Ramble.* This, of course, depends on what the deponent says. The response may be self-serving and should be discouraged. It may be relevant or irrelevant. Loquacious witnesses sooner or later tend to disclose some damaging information or to say something inconsistent.
- *Go From General to Specific.* Often depositions seek information about both general and specific practices performed by the deponent. You must decide whether you want to have the deponent first explain the general, normal practices, then follow with questions delving into specific practices relevant to the litigation, or

vice versa. The former approach may lock a witness into a particular version or force the witness later to explain inconsistencies between the normal practice and the practice questioned in the litigation.

- *Proceed in a Logical Order or Shift the Subject Matter of the Questions Frequently and Suddenly.* A logical, orderly tactic should produce more and reliable information from the deponent. A haphazard, helter-skelter approach may cause difficulty for the deponent and result in confusing and inconsistent responses. Either tactic or a modified strategy requires organization and planning.
- *Explain What You Want.* You can explain or instruct the deponent to answer in certain ways. You may tell the deponent exactly what it is you want. For example: "Tell me everything that you said and everything that he said." "Please explain, step by step, what happened, describing everything you saw." Or, "Answer the next questions either yes, no, or 'I cannot answer yes or no.'" These directions keep you and the deponent on the same track and establish a clearer record.
- *Repeat Questions.* You may repeat questions. Repeat questions. Not with the exact words each time. Sometimes answers to questions change if asked at different times during the deposition. This tactic also makes it difficult for a less-than-honest deponent, who may have some difficulty remembering what was said previously. You may also have to repeat a lengthy line of questions relating to a series of separate events. This can become tedious and boring, but it may be your task to persevere.
- *Short-Circuit Questions.* Depositions often involve inquiries into related documents or incidents and, rather than repeat an entire detailed line of questions for each document or incident, you may ask: "Would your answers pertaining to Exhibit 1 generally pertain to Exhibit 2 as well?" This shortened inquiry may be objected to as overly broad and may cause you to miss some detail.
- *Lead the Witness.* You may want to lead the witness with factual or leading questions because you want to obtain some responses that support your particular theories of the case. They can help you create a certain impression or perspective of a deponent, particularly regarding the deponent's memory. For example, if you want to establish that a deponent has a poor grasp of the circumstances of an auto accident, you should ask leading questions such as: "This accident happened very quickly. This was a frightening experience for you. You became tense anticipating the crash. You were moving at the time of the collision." If you want to establish that a deponent had a good grasp of what happened, you should ask leading questions such as: "You have a vivid memory of this event. You were especially alert because of the potential danger. You had a clear view of the scene. You

were concentrating very intensely at the time of the collision." The more factual the leading questions are, the more likely an adverse deponent will have to agree with your question. For example, "You were wearing your sunglasses, you moved down before the impact." The more conclusory your leading question, the greater leeway the deponent has to disagree.

- *Take Notes.* You may want to take notes during a deposition, to record a response or to frame later questions on a topic. Notetaking may affect the deponent. Your writing causes you to lose eye contact with the deponent, who may naturally speak more slowly as you write or stop until you are done. Deponents may wonder why you are taking notes of some responses and not others, causing the deponents to expand or, more likely, limit their responses. Suspicious of your notetaking, and concluding that some of their responses are more important than others, they become more cautious and guarded.
- *Pace the Deposition.* Be aware of the time, rhythm, and pace of the deposition. A pace, or varying paces, that achieves your goals should be maintained. Fast-paced questioning tends to keep your mind alert and quick, while forcing responsive answers and providing less time for the deponent to think about less-than-honest responses. But a quick pace may also discourage lengthy narratives by the deponent, interrupt responses, and make it difficult for you to keep track of what was asked and to remember what was said. Slower-paced questioning may eliminate these deficiencies by sacrificing the advantages. Whatever pace occurs, fast, slow, or moderate, you must be aware of it and what effect it has on the deposition.

§ 6.6.2 *Specific Techniques: What to Ask*

- *Ask Anything and Everything.* Should you ask "why" questions, leading questions, potentially harmful questions, or questions inadmissible for trial? Most depositions seek factual information, so you ordinarily want to probe, explore, and press deponents for information until their memory is exhausted. All kinds of information should be elicited—the good, the bad, the neutral, and especially the harmful information, because discovery is the place and means for you to uncover the weaknesses as well as strengths in your case. Many depositions seek to know the reasons something happened or people have done something. They require "why" and opinion questions. Depositions with narrower purposes and scope do not call for such detailed and thorough questioning.
- *Ask Who, What, When, Where, Why and How Questions.* These questions will usually produce detailed information, clarifying and supplementing a deponent's narrative response.

- *Employ Closing Questions.* As the deposition progresses from topic to topic, you should consider whether you have taken enough precautions to prevent the deponent from legitimately modifying or adding to his or her testimony later. One such device is the use of wrap-up questions, such as "Have you told us absolutely everything that you remember happening at that time?" Or, "Did she say anything else to you on the telephone that you have not testified to?" Or, "Do you have any other information relating to the incident that you have not disclosed?"
- *Probe the Source of the Information.* A deponent often provides information without clarifying whether that information is based upon personal observation or knowledge, hearsay, inference, or assumption. You are well advised to determine its exact source.

  Questions about other sources of information also make the witness more accountable for his or her story. If the deponent thinks you have no corroborating or contrary source of information, he or she may be inclined to exaggerate. If the deponent realizes that you have access to another source, he or she usually attempts to formulate a story consistent with that source. Accountability reduces the chances of exaggeration and increases the likelihood of accuracy.
- *Detail Conversations.* Deponents usually provide a summary of a conversation when asked what was said. The examining attorney must then decide whether to seek clarifications through detailed questions and thus to determine whether the answer is (1) an impression of what was said, (2) a paraphrase of who said what, (3) a close approximation of what was said, (4) an exact quotation, or (5) some other recollection. Probing questions not only detail a deponent's story but also reflect on the deponent's credibility.
- *Compare Stories.* Your client or witness usually has a different version of what occurred from that of an adverse deponent. You must obtain sufficient information during the deposition to compare the conflicting versions. You may want the deponent to know that your questions are based upon information you have gained from another source, or you may want the deponent not to realize you are verifying another version. A deponent who senses that your questions are based upon contrary information may become more cautious in answering. The timing of such questions will also affect your use of this technique. In order not to influence the deponent's story, first ask narrative and neutral questions to obtain information. Or if you do hope to influence the response, ask suggestive, leading questions.
- *Ask About Feelings, Emotions, Opinions, Thoughts, and Attitudes.* Too often, examining attorneys limit their questions to what happened and what was said or observed. Other levels of questions may produce helpful information. "What were you thinking? What was your attitude? What judgment did you make

about that person? What is your opinion? How were you feeling at that moment? What did that sound like? Did you notice any smell?" Questions dealing with thoughts, attitudes, judgments, opinions, feelings, emotions, impressions, and sense perceptions often explain the reason for some event and may lead to more information about it. Responses to these questions add another dimension to the typical, fact-oriented deposition.

- *Inquire About Witnesses and Documents.* Whether a witness answers a question completely or incompletely, you should consider asking whether anyone else might have more information or whether there are any documents and things which might reveal more information. Questions about witnesses, documents, material things, and persons with information should be routine and asked periodically during a deposition. The related technique of "working a document" during a deposition involves asking various sorts of questions designed to authenticate the document, to inquire into its creation or meaning, or to place the document in a favorable perspective.
- *Have the Deponent Draw a Diagram.* Drawing a diagram may make it easier for the deponent to testify accurately and for you to understand the testimony. It also commits the deponent to a specific diagram. Many cases involve visual aids and demonstrative evidence at the trial, and depositions of witnesses in these cases should include some visual diagram for the witness's testimony. Diagrams composed by a witness during a deposition cannot be changed for the trial, except that a deponent will ordinarily not be expected to draw a diagram to scale. Specially prepared trial diagrams are drafted by an attorney with an artist and are usually drawn to scale.
- *Review Pleadings and Materials.* The deponent may be able to add to, explain, be surprised by, or become confused by legal materials. A party deponent may not be sufficiently familiar with his or her pleadings, answers to interrogatories, and other statements to deal with them directly. Deponents have a difficult time if not properly prepared to respond fully and persuasively to such broad questions as "Your complaint alleges that 'Plaintiff suffered actual damages amounting to $60,000.' What facts do you have to support that claim for damages?" Or, "Your answer denies a complaint allegation that 'defendant acted negligently.' Upon what facts do you base your denial?"
- *Place the Deponent at a Specific Time.* Questions causing the deponent to place himself or herself back in time at a particular event often help the deponent to recall more of the incident. These are called retrospective questions. You may wish to place the deponent at a time before he or she spoke to his or her attorney about the incident or about the deposition, in order to

get at the witness's recollection before it may have been influenced by conversations with the attorney.

§ 6.6.3 Specific Techniques: How to React

- *Use a Gauge.* You usually have some means of determining whether the deponent has told everything and whether it is reasonable to believe the deponent's response. Time is one such gauge. The deponent may testify that a conversation occurred during a ten-minute interval. This period of time can assist you in determining whether the witness has explained the complete event and conversation. You merely approximate the time it would take to do or say what the deponent testified to and match that with the time. You usually have to allow some additional time for events or conversation that the deponent testifies he or she does not remember. This total will help you determine whether the deponent has told you everything or whether you need to probe further. The deponent who tells you the conversation lasted ten minutes, and then only describes three minutes' worth, needs to be questioned further.
- *Suggest a Mistake.* Many depositions involve something that occurred as a result of someone's mistake, and deponents may refuse to admit their involvement in that mistake. The foil to such a position is simple: you ask the deponent whether it is inevitable that, on occasion, a mistake is made. After all, no one or no practice is perfect.
- *Seek an Admission.* Depositions produce information that can be phrased in the form of an admission. A deponent may be influenced by the examiner's specific or leading question, and agree with the question. But an examining attorney often proceeds to question a deponent, seeking to obtain an admission the deponent refuses to make. Though it is equally important to establish this contrary position, too often this questioning becomes repetitive and argumentative as the examining attorney attempts to force the deponent to agree with the admission. The examiner may fare better by probing into the basis for the deponent's reply rather than attempting to persuade by argument.
- *Pursue an Admission.* What should you do when the deponent makes an admission and you want to get the specifics? You must make a judgment: if you pursue the questioning, will the deponent attempt to retract or soften the admission, or will such detailed questioning firm up the admission? Proceeding and probing the grounds of the admission is probably best: it is better to uncover information in a deposition than not to explore the area.
- *Summarize Previous Testimony.* The deponent may say something favorable, though not in the most favorable language. You can summarize what was said in more favorable words and ask

the deponent if your statement is correct. Or a deponent may say one thing at one time, add another thing later, and, still later, make another modification. You can summarize everything said and ask the deponent if your summary is accurate. You cannot testify, but summarizing may be the next best thing.

- *React to the Deponent's Disposition.* Witnesses display various dispositions in a deposition. They are friendly, confused, neutral, indifferent, partial, withdrawn, outgoing, aggressive, hostile, or some combination of these. You have to decide whether the deponent's disposition helps or hurts your approach and how to react to it. Should you respond in kind? Or to the contrary? Should you alert the deponent to his or her visible disposition? Should you attempt to control or change the disposition? Should you have it reflected in the record?
- *Appear Disbelieving.* Your disbelief may cause some deponents to second-guess their response. Questions such as "Are you sure?" affect an uncertain deponent. Some deponents become anxious and wonder whether they are indeed certain or sure. Your disbelief of their responses may cause them to change a "yes" to a "probably" or a "no" to a "possibly." Other deponents may become confused and believe that they made some mistake; still other witnesses may become paranoid and believe that you have proof supporting your disbelief, with which you can confront them.
- *Undermine the Deponent's Credibility.* You must occasionally decide whether to attempt to impeach the deponent during a deposition. If you have some impeaching materials or indications that a deponent is wrong or is testifying to bizarre happenings, you have to decide whether to do anything in response. You can choose to ignore it and go on, or to doubt the information and intimate to the deponent that you have contrary information without disclosing it, or to challenge the testimony directly by disclosing impeaching material and not saving it for trial. This last tactic may backfire, giving the deponent an opportunity to prepare to counter such evidence at the trial; but with open discovery, the other side may discover such impeaching material in any event, without your voluntarily disclosing it. You should avoid arguing with the deponent, unless the tactic appears to succeed and the opposing attorney just sits there, ever so meek and humble.
- *Ask About the Deponent's Memory.* You can ask factual questions to determine the extent of the deponent's memory. You can also ask directly: "Would you consider your memory a good or poor memory concerning that event?" This may produce a self-serving response, no good to you, but also may lock the deponent into a position which you can use for contrast later, particularly if a cautious witness with a selective or poor memory claims to have a good memory. The opinion question can extend to other areas,

such as "Did you have an excellent view?" "Were you able to hear everything that was said?"

- *Be Persistent.* During a deposition you may become bored with the tedious questioning, resigned to the damaging information, or put off by the opposing lawyer. These situations can affect your effectiveness as an examiner, and may require additional effort, patience, persistence, and time from you.
- *Make Assessments.* In most depositions one seeks to obtain information from a deponent and to assess that deponent as a witness. After each such deposition you should put yourself in the place of the opposing lawyer and ask "Will that deponent be an effective witness at trial?" One of your main purposes during a deposition is to have the opposing attorney leave the deposition answering that question in the negative.

What to do regarding these tactics during a deposition often requires a split-second judgment on your part. Experience will help you refine that judgment ability, but anticipating situations, rehearsing how you will react in certain circumstances, and preparing for the deposition will also assist in refining that decision-making process.

§ 6.6.4 Specific Techniques: Deposing the Expert

Despite specialization, each expert witness provides some common areas for examination. Rule 26 sets forth the various categories of experts and the discovery devices to be used to obtain information. Rule 33 interrogatories may reveal certain information regarding the background, opinions, and reasoning of an expert. Depositions can produce additional information. Each expert should be examined regarding the specific areas of his or her expertise, but a general list of topics can also be explored with most experts, including the following:

- Their qualifications;
- Their opinions;
- The bases of their opinions;
- The sources of information relied upon in forming their opinions and bases;
- Their fees and whether they expect to testify for their party in the future;
- The number of times they have testified for plaintiffs and defendants in previous cases;
- Insufficient information, tests, or sources of information they have relied upon;
- The degree of probability of their opinions;
- Possible causes or explanations contrary to their opinion;

- Their familiarity with any treatises useful to the examining attorney's case.

Inquiry into these areas serves several of the purposes of deposing an expert: to explore the details of the expert's opinion, to prepare for cross-examination of that expert at trial, and to provide information necessary to counter or impeach the expert's testimony through the opinion of the deposing attorney's own expert at trial. These topics are not complete, but they should be considered, and their review may lead to additional areas of inquiry.

Deposition inquiries of an expert may be subject to some limitations, including: (1) The information sought must pertain to matters within the expert's knowledge and expertise; (2) hypothetical and opinion questions must be based on the facts in the case; (3) questions cannot be so broad as to require the expert to do research to provide an answer.

§ 6.7 REPRESENTING THE DEPONENT

The attorney representing the deponent serves a vital and important function in the deposition process. Some attorneys view the role as a passive one. They prefer to stay in the background. But lawyering functions require you to be as active and involved in the deposition as the examining attorney. You do not have many questions to ask, but there are many ways to participate actively in the proceedings.

The following subsections focus on the functions of deponent representation and also discuss the ancillary functions involved in attending depositions of non-client deponents.

§ 6.7.1 Selecting the Deponent

The notice of deposition usually designates the person to be deposed. Sometimes the other attorney may wish to depose someone you know does not have the information sought. You must decide whether to tell the other attorney, and perhaps suggest someone else to be deposed (and save everyone concerned wasted time and effort) or to appear at the deposition and snicker. Rule 30(b)(6) permits the deposing attorney merely to designate the subject matter of a deposition to be taken of a corporation, governmental agency, or other organizational party. The rule permits you to select the deponent or deponents and to designate or limit the matters on which they will testify. Whom do you and your client select? Obviously, you pick the person or persons who have information relating to the subject matter of the deposition. But what if there is more than one such know-everything witness? Then you should select:

> Someone astute enough to understand the questions he is asked and to perceive what motivates opposing counsel to ask them;
>
> Someone articulate enough to phrase answers that will read well when transcribed;

Someone resourceful enough to phrase what he says so as to make the best of the strengths of your case and to de-emphasize its weaknesses to the extent legitimately possible; and

Someone of character, a witness who will speak the truth and whose phraseology and tone of voice will manifest his candor and accuracy.[1]

Should you find such a witness, you should consider using that person for all your depositions regardless of the subject matter. If the deponent is that good, what he or she doesn't know won't matter.

§ 6.7.2 General Deponent Preparation

Your preparation of the deponent should include a complete and thorough preparation of the general elements of any deposition and of the specific elements of a particular case.

Preparing a deponent takes time and involves expense. You can reduce some of that effort by providing the deponent with written deposition instructions before meeting with him or her. A short set of general instructions appears on the following page, and a set of detailed deponent instructions appears in Appendix A.

The value of detailed written instructions is considerably enhanced by a preparation conference with your deponent. There you can emphasize or modify major points, provide additional instructions, and answer any remaining questions. You may even have your client observe a videotape of a simulated deposition designed to educate a prospective deponent.[2]

INSTRUCTIONS ON WHAT NOT TO DO
DURING A DEPOSITION

OR

IF YOU DO ANY OF THESE THINGS I WILL
IMMEDIATELY
WITHDRAW FROM THE CASE

1. Do not pretend that you do not know me.
2. Do not call me "doctor," "hey, you," or use my middle name in front of the other attorney.
3. Do not dress for the deposition like a zombie, look like a turkey, or wear two-tone leisure or pants suits.
4. Don't faint during the deposition. If you feel a faint coming on, lean away from me so you don't fall on me.

§ **6.7**

1. Walter Barthold, Attorney's Guide to Effective Discovery Techniques 111 (1975).

2. *See* Roger S. Haydock & John Sonsteng, National Institute for Trial Advocacy, Demonstration Videotape, Deponent Preparation (1980).

5. Do not respond "huh" when the other attorney asks you your name.
6. Do not eat during the deposition.
7. If the other attorney asks whether you are a party in the action, do not ask what time it starts.
8. If the other attorney asks about your major expenses, do not point to me.
9. If I ask you any questions during the deposition, do not laugh.
10. If I close my eyes during the deposition or slip out of my chair, don't poke me. It's all part of a strategic ploy on my part to make the other attorney think I'm a dolt.
11. Don't yelp when I tap your foot. If I tap once, it means you misunderstood the question. If I hit it twice, it means you made a mistake. If I stomp on it three times, it means you just lost the case.

§ 6.7.3 Specific Deponent Preparation

Your witness must understand the intricacies of depositions and all facets of your case. While the previous section dealt with general preparation, this section offers guidelines on specific preparation relating to the actual subject matter of the deposition.

- *Explain What the Case Is All About to the Witness.* You may have previously discussed the case with a client, but an updated explanation will aid understanding. You want to make certain the witness understands not only what is happening but why it is happening. Use ordinary, everyday English, not law-school legalese, to outline the issues and theory, to detail what you have to prove, to explain the burden the other side has, and to indicate where that witness fits in the case. A witness will answer questions more knowledgeably, perceive the motives of the other attorney more easily, understand the impact of the answers more clearly, and be more at ease and confident during the deposition.
- *Review the Facts and File.* The deponent may have provided you with information earlier, but nonetheless you must review this information. It will help refresh the witness's recollection and may generate additional information. You should inform deponents about facts they may not know. You may have notes to refresh their recollection, documents and objects they should see, or other information in your file they should know about.

  You should go over everything in the file that will be relevant to the deposition. Pleadings, discovery responses, statements, letters, materials, affidavits, you name it, the deponent should see it if it has any bearing on the subject matter of the deposition. Remember that documents a deponent reviews to refresh recollection may be discoverable, and this possibility may limit your disclosure.

- *Explain Conflicting Stories.* You accept it as a fact of legal life that your witness's story will differ from the other side's and perhaps even differ from your other witnesses' stories, but the witness may not expect or understand this. You should explain that this is normal and that they should tell the truth using their best recollection, and not attempt to harmonize their story with someone else's version.
- *Be the Devil's Advocate.* Tell your witness what you know about the examining attorney. It is essential that you explain the type and scope of questions the deposing attorney will probably ask. You may want to use practice questions and have yourself or another attorney from your law firm simulate the deposition by asking questions. You may want to use a tape recorder so the witness can listen to the responses and learn some strengths and weaknesses. You may want, in important cases, to use video equipment to provide witnesses with the opportunity to see themselves.

The preparation of a deponent who is a witness and not a client varies from the suggestions presented in these two sections. The attorney can still approach the witness and explain many of the previous instructions and all facets of the case if the witness does not have a lawyer. However, the attorney does not represent that witness and therefore cannot render legal advice or pursue matters that conflict with the client's best interests, nor instruct the witness about what to do during the deposition. Your preparatory explanation and instructions will then differ accordingly, to take into account the different relationship between you and the non-client deponent.

§ 6.7.4 Raising Objections During the Deposition

You have a right to object to any questions posed to any deponent, including client and non-client deponents. If you make an objection, you should also state the ground for the objection. Whether your objection is correct or not, the examining attorney still has a right to insist on an answer, unless you instruct the client not to answer. Usually little purpose is served by a detailed explanation of the objection or an argument over the merits of the objection, unless you have legitimate strategic or procedural reasons for so doing.

Rule 32(d) describes the situations requiring objections during depositions. Subsection (1) provides that all errors and irregularities in the deposition notice are waived unless a written objection is promptly served upon the party giving the notice. The requirement places the burden on the opposing party to raise any problem with the notice. This rule prevents a party who fails to appear at a deposition from relying on a technical defect. Not all errors or irregularities may give rise to this written objection requirement. Some may not be obvious in a notice. Even the listing of an incorrect date or location is not necessarily an error or irregularity, if the other party or deponent had otherwise been advised of a different time or place.

Subsection (2) provides that any objection based upon the disqualification of an officer who takes the deposition is waived, unless it is made before the taking of the deposition begins or as soon thereafter as the disqualification becomes known or could have been discovered with reasonable diligence. Disqualification situations are rare.

Subsection (d)(3)(B) details the objections that must be made concerning other errors. Any irregularities occurring at the deposition, regarding the taking of the examination, the oath or affirmation, the conduct of the parties, or "errors of any kind which might be obviated, removed, or cured if promptly presented," are waived unless seasonable objection is made at the deposition. For example, an opposing lawyer who is aware that a deponent has not been sworn will be unable to raise this objection later, because an objection made during the deposition would have provided timely notice and an opportunity to the party taking the deposition to cure the error.

The same subsection also applies this "seasonable objection" standard to the form of the questions and answers during the examination. Improper questions by an examining attorney that can be corrected at the deposition must be objected to in order to preserve the objection for trial. Examples of such form objections to inappropriate questions and responses include vague, confusing, ambiguous, misleading, complex, compound, argumentative, incomplete hypothetical questions; misquoting the deponent; non-responsive answers. Most depositions allow leading questions because the deponent is an adverse party, an agent, or a hostile witness, and a leading objection in those depositions will be improper. The decision whether to object under the requirements of this rule is determined by whether the error produced by the objectionable question or answer can be obviated during the deposition by an objection to the form of the question.

Rule 32(d)(3)(A) delineates another situation requiring an objection to be made during a deposition: objections to the competency, relevancy, or materiality of testimony are not waived by a failure to make them before or during a deposition, unless the ground of the objection is one that might have been obviated or removed if presented at that time. The Federal Rules of Evidence have eliminated immateriality as an objection, and competency objections are not common. But relevancy objections are available and common. The official comments to this subsection offer no example of such situations nor any explanation for this subsection.

What situations require making a relevancy objection to avoid waiving such objection? Clearly, information discoverable during a deposition includes much evidence that will not be relevant for trial purposes. The scope of relevancy under Federal Rule of Civil Procedure 26 for deposition purposes far exceeds the scope of relevancy under Federal Rule of Evidence 401 for trial purposes. Since deposition questions seeking information that will be irrelevant for trial purposes are common and proper, the concern of the deponent's attorney is to object to those irrelevant questions which, if objected to, could somehow be cured by the examining attorney.

The failure to object to certain questions during depositions will result in the waiver of underlying rights. A client is also bound by an attorney's failure to raise a timely objection. For example, Rule 26(b) makes privileged matter non-discoverable. A procedural lapse by a deponent's attorney in neglecting to object to inquiries into privileged matter during a deposition will operate as a waiver of the substantive protections. A later objection at trial to such inquiries will be overruled because of the waiver that occurred during the earlier deposition. Objections to privileged or other matters sought from a deponent will be necessary to preserve those objections and will also be preliminary to an instruction from the deponent's attorney not to answer the question.

Some attorneys, because of the uncertainty of the need to object to certain questions, prefer entering into a stipulation at the start of the deposition, stating, "It is stipulated that all objections to questions and answers shall be reserved by each party, except objections to the form of the question." Other attorneys perceive no need for this agreement and prefer having the rules control.

Objections will sometimes actually work: an attorney will not pursue an answer after an objection to a question. An objection says, in effect, that the objecting attorney believes the question is improper or seeks non-discoverable information, and that belief has some effect on the thinking of the other attorney. This is particularly true in depositions involving both experienced and inexperienced attorneys. The experienced attorney may attempt through peer pressure and objections to limit the scope of the examination, and the inexperienced attorney may be convinced enough not to insist on answers. This is also true in situations in which the examining attorney has doubts about the legitimacy of the question or the hoped-for response. The objecting attorney may be right and the examining attorney may agree.

The proper way to make an objection is to state the objections specifically and concisely and in a non-argumentative and non-suggestive manner. While you may have a right or need to make an objection, the objection should not be made in an effort to interfere with a deposition or frustrate the purpose of the deposition. The Federal Advisory Committee, in an effort to reduce the frequency and use of objections during depositions, explains: "Depositions frequently have been unduly prolonged, if not unfairly frustrated, by lengthy objections and colloquy, often suggesting how the deponent should respond. While objections may be made during a deposition, they ordinarily should be limited to those that under Rule 32(d)(3) might be waived if not made at that time." Federal and state court decisions have also recognized that the interposing of frequent and unnecessary objections constitutes abusive and improper deposition practice.

Tactical ramifications will also affect your judgment about whether you should object or not. For example, the examining attorney may inquire into the deponent's opinions on other matters without asking for foundation or establishing the witness's competency. Your objection to lack of foundation may prompt the examiner to consider the defect in the inquiry and to rectify it by asking foundation questions and obtaining more detailed responses and consequently more information. If you need or want that information detailed in the deposition, you should object. If you do not want the other attorney probing further, you should not object. You must decide during depositions not only whether you have a proper objection but also whether tactically it is wise to object. Many depositions are relatively objection-free, and you should not feel unfulfilled as an attorney if a deposition passes without your having to object to anything more substantial than the shape of the table.

§ 6.7.5 Instructing the Deponent Not to Answer

An instruction not to answer occurs when the attorney representing the deponent advises the deponent not to answer a question which is objectionable. The instruction not to answer may accompany the making of the objection or may follow an objection if the deposing attorney insists on an answer. In most jurisdictions, instructions not to answer may only be utilized in a few, limited situations. Federal Rule 30(d) provides: "A party may instruct the deponent not to answer only when necessary to preserve a privilege, to enforce a limitation on evidence directed by the court or to present a [protective order] motion."

With regard to the assertion of a privilege, an objection and instruction not to answer may be made to preserve a privilege. The reason why a claim of privilege is a legitimate reason to instruct not to answer is that a subsequent answer may constitute a waiver of the privilege. The objecting party may also have to describe the specifics of the privileged information, and cannot merely assert a general objection. The examining attorney can ask questions designed to seek specific information about the legitimacy of the privilege such as the identity, existence, nature, and type of information withheld.

With regard to the limitation of evidence directed by a court, an objecting party may instruct the deponent not to answer to comply with the court order. An examining attorney may not inquire into an area which has been determined by a judge to be inappropriate. A judge may have issued such a ruling as part of a scheduling order or a protective order restricting discovery.

With regard to instructions not to answer to enable a party to seek a protective order motion, Federal Rule 30(d)(3) permits a party to bring a motion to restrict a deposition on the grounds that it "is being conducted on bad faith or such a matter as unreasonably to annoy, embarrass, or oppress the deponent or party." To comply with this rule, an objecting attorney must object on the ground of bad faith, annoyance, embarrassment, or oppression before instructing not to answer. Questions that seek information beyond the scope of discoverable information pursuant to the applicable rules of discovery may be considered bad faith and harassing questions, and appropriate for an instruction not to answer. Questions that are objected to on the grounds of irrelevancy or hearsay are not usually considered to be bad faith or harassing. In some cases there will be a bright line and in other cases there will be a fine line, regarding what are bad faith and harassing inquiries.

Judges and commentators have concluded that instructions not to answer a question can be more disruptive and more abusive than the making of unnecessary objections. Many judges are inclined to severely restrict the use of instructions not to answer. Courts that support the limited use of instructions not to answer reason that the harm caused by having to seek a court order to determine the legitimacy of an instruction not to answer and the consequent delays in the deposition far exceed the mere inconvenience to a witness of having to answer a question. Some federal judges and state court judges limit instructions not to answer to questions seeking privileged information. These rulings are more restrictive of the federal rule and further reduce the defending attorney's use of instructions not to answer.

If you have no legitimate reason supporting your instruction not to answer, you have abused your role as an advocate and subject yourself and your client to sanctions. You may and should instruct not to answer only if the rules and law permit such an instruction. A judge may impose monetary sanctions on you personally and may impose more severe sanctions on a party for the improper use of an instruction not to answer.

With regard to non-client deponents, an attorney who does not represent the deponent cannot advise that deponent not to answer a deposition question. The attorney may suggest to the witness that the question may not be answered, or that a privilege may exist, but the witness must decide how to respond. Neither an examining attorney or another attorney may suggest or advise a non-client deponent to answer a question or to suggest that a privilege may be waived if a conflict of interest exists. D.R.7–104 prohibits an attorney from rendering advice to a person who may have a conflict of interests with the attorney's client. A non-party deponent may have an interest different than the interest to be protected on behalf of a client during a deposition, rendering an attorney representing such a client unable to provide any suggestions or advice to a non-party deponent.

§ 6.7.6 Protecting the Deponent

The law varies among jurisdictions and among judges as to what is permissible conduct by an attorney in properly protecting a deponent.

What is a legitimate or inappropriate reason will depend upon the circumstances, the applicable rules, and judicial decisions. The following situations reflect a range of acceptable conduct to unacceptable behavior.

If you did not hear a question, you can properly ask a court reporter to read the question back.

If you did not understand the question, you may not be able to ask that the question be read back. It is critical for the deponent to understand the question, and not necessarily you, although if you do not understand the question it may not be possible to determine whether an objection should be made.

If the deponent becomes fatigued, you can assist upon a recess. Even if the other attorney objects, the deposition cannot continue if you or the deponent leave the deposition room for a brief rest to overcome the fatigue.

If the deponent forgets something or answers inappropriately, you may not properly request a recess in order to talk to your deponent client. The examining attorney has a right to obtain information from the deponent and not from you or your reminding the deponent of the story. The tactic of taking a recess to prepare a client for an answer or to correct an answer is usually inappropriate and constitutes an abuse of deposition procedures.

If a deponent has answered a question and begins to ramble, you can interrupt and object to any further answer on the ground that the deponent has answered the question. If the witness is being non-responsive and unnecessarily volunteering information, you may properly object, and, in effect, remind your client not to ramble.

If a deponent has difficulty remembering a fact, you may not interrupt and volunteer the information. The examining attorney has a right to determine what the deponent knows, not what you know. It may be appropriate to correct an obvious misstatement of a deponent if the information is inconsequential or if everyone else is confused by the answer. Your interest in doing so is to provide accurate information and not to unnecessarily interfere with the deposition.

If a deponent has difficulty providing an answer which is contained in a document, it is inappropriate for you to show the deponent that document and provide the answer. The examining attorney has a right to assess the memory of the witness without reference to a document.

If a deponent is shown a document by the examining attorney during the deposition and is immediately asked questions about the document, if may be appropriate for you to remind the deponent that he or she may review the entire document or specific provisions before answering any questions. It is also appropriate for you during the deposition to review the document for purposes of making a proper objection. It is inappropriate for you to confer with your client or take a break in an effort to influence the testimony about the document.

If it appears to you that your client deponent needs to consult with you, or if the deponent specifically asks to consult with you during a deposition, you may or may not be able to do so. Some courts and some jurisdictions prohibit an attorney from consulting with their client deponent during a deposition and during any recesses of the deposition. The rationale for this restriction is that the attorney has an opportunity to prepare the deponent before the deposition and consultations during a deposition will unfairly influence the testimony of the deponent. Another rationale is that an attorney does not have a right during trial to consult with a client during cross-examination and may not have a right to consult during a break in the trial. Most courts and jurisdictions permit attorneys to reasonably consult with a client during a deposition and during a break in the deposition. The rationale permitting consultation is that there is no one present during a deposition to monitor the proceedings and there are no rules of evidence restricting questions and responses. These protections, which are available at trial but not during a deposition, justify a client and an attorney consulting with each other.

It is improper during a deposition for you to whisper in your client's ear, signal the client with some gesture or facial expression, interpose an improper objection, testify or attempt to testify, or otherwise interfere with the deposition.

The appropriateness or impropriety of lawyer conduct can be assessed by relating the behavior to the purposes of a deposition. A deposition provides an opportunity to obtain factual information and determine what a deponent knows. Conduct that interferes with this purpose is improper. Conduct that attempts to protect the deponent while not interfering with the goal of the deposition will be appropriate. Lawyers who attempt to protect clients using improper tactics may be controlled by the examining attorney, as explained in § 6.5.9. Or they may be admonished and sanctioned by a court.

Federal Rule 30(d)(2) specifically authorizes a court to impose sanctions on any person who frustrates "the fair examination of the deponent." A court which finds that if any impediment, delay, or other conduct of an attorney has frustrated the fair examination of a deponent may impose upon the attorney or party, or both, appropriate sanctions, including reasonable costs and attorney's fees.

§ 6.7.7 Questioning the Deponent

Rule 30(c) allows you to "cross-examine" the deponent. That term is actually a misnomer because usually the deponent is your client or a friendly witness, and you have no need or urge to cross-examine. You may want to ask the deponent some questions at the end of a deposition, and you should proceed as if you were conducting a direct examination. If you did conduct a cross-examination and used leading questions, the other attorney would be able properly to object to these questions, and to move later to strike responses to your questions, which, when granted by a court, renders such deposition testimony inadmissible.

In what situations should you question your client deponent? Usually, the best question is no question—the sooner the deposition is over without the deponent mispeaking, the better. Ordinarily, your preparation of the deponent does not include any preparation of questions. If you ask questions, you run the risk of the deponent not understanding why you are asking a question or responding to it in a different fashion from what you expected. Further, the more questions you ask, the more information you provide the other side; the more questions you ask, the more time the other attorney has to think about what else to ask; and the more questions you ask, the more chance the other attorney has to ask still more questions.

Still, on some occasions you will need to ask questions. You must conduct a thorough direct examination to preserve the testimony of a deponent who either will not or may not be available at the trial. You must consider the possibility that your deponent will not be available for trial. Death, illness, being outside the jurisdiction of the court, or unforeseen circumstances may prevent the deponent from testifying. The only available testimony will appear in the deposition transcript, which will probably not contain all the information you need for trial and which will certainly not be in a format that will strengthen your case. Or, in other circumstances, if during the deposition the deponent did not have an opportunity to complete and answer or to explain a response, you may want to ask some questions, using that opportunity to clarify or supplement the record before the deposition ends.

Again, if the deponent made a misstatement or forgot to provide some known information, you may want to ask some questions to correct or complete the record. Or you may want to put on the record some testimony that you perceive bolsters your position for negotiations. You can then point to definite evidence in the transcript to support your position, rather than relying upon your paraphrasing of what your witness would say. You must remain alert for any areas that you may want to inquire into after the examining attorney has completed his or her questioning. Detailed rehabilitative questions may be necessary in light of these considerations.

Trouble may arise when the attorney representing the deponent begins to ask a lot of questions at the end of an informational deposition. The attorney who noticed the deposition is paying for the reporter's time, and if that attorney thinks the opposing lawyer is ranging far afield in such examination, the lawyer should be advised that the deposition will come to an end unless there is some agreement on sharing expenses. If you prolong the cross-questioning, you ordinarily become obligated to pay your fair share of the deposition costs.[3]

Rule 30(c) permits an attorney who cannot or chooses not to participate in the oral examination nevertheless to ask questions of the deponent. The attorney may serve written questions in a sealed envel-

3. *See Wheeler v. West India Steamship Co.*, 11 F.R.D. 396, 397–398 (S.D.N.Y.1951); *Baron v. Leo Feist, Inc.*, 7 F.R.D. 71, 72 (S.D.N.Y.1946).

ope on the party taking the deposition, and that party shall give the envelope to the reporter, who will ask the deponent the questions and record the answers. Obviously this is not the best way to proceed. However, if the deposition occurs in a distant location, if the deponent is not a party or a significant witness, or if you are only interested in objective information, it is an available device.

§ 6.8 CONCLUDING THE DEPOSITION

After all the questioning has been completed, there are a number of concluding matters relating to the deposition and the transcript to consider: stipulations, reviewing the deposition, signing of the deposition, changes in the record by the deponent, and filing of the deposition.

§ 6.8.1 Stipulations

Attorneys at the conclusion of a deposition, or at the beginning, suggest that certain stipulations be made on the record concerning: (A) reviewing the deposition by the deponent, (B) reviewing the deposition by other attorneys, (C) signing the deposition, (D) changes in the deposition by the deponent, (E) filing of the deposition, (F) all of these. If you chose either A, B, C, D, E, or F, at least you are not wrong. These represent common stipulations in some jurisdictions. Some attorneys lump them all together under the public of "usual stipulations" and seek to have them waived. Some examining attorneys expect and ask the attorney representing the deponent to explain to the deponent, on the record, the effect of these various stipulations ("Counsel please instruct your client . . ."). Whatever you do, you should have a reason for doing it. If you do not understand what the usual stipulations are, you should not agree to them. If you do not want to or need to instruct your client regarding stipulations, you should not do so. What should you do? Read on.

§ 6.7.2 Review of the Deposition by the Deponent

A deponent has a right to review the deposition after it is completed. The deponent may read a transcript of the deposition or review the recording. Some jurisdictions require that the deponent before completion of the deposition, request on the record to review the deposition. Some jurisdictions require a deponent to review the deposition unless the deponent waives the right or opportunity to do so. Federal Rule 30 states that a deponent before completion of the deposition may request that the deponent review the transcript or a recording within 30 days after receiving a copy of the deposition or after being notified by the officer that the transcript or recording is available. Jurisdiction typically place a time limit on when the deponent may review a deposition.

The deponent should request to review the deposition: (A) always, (B) all the time, or (C) every time. If you chose A, B, or C, you have a natural instinct to be a litigator. The deposition contains the deponent's testimony. It is critical that the testimony be complete and accurate. It may well be that the stenographic notes contain some errors or that some glitch caused the recording system to malfunction. The reporter or recording may have had difficulties with the recording of some names, amounts, dates, or other specific data. The transcript may include incorrect statements, or misspellings, that can become the basis for an alleged admission or impeaching statement. The deponent may not have spoken clearly resulting in the recording of an inaccurate or incomplete answer. Or it may be that the deponent made a mistake in an answer and needs to change that answer. These are reasons why a deponent, and the deponent's attorney, should on the record of the deposition request that it be reviewed and not waive the opportunity to do so. After receiving the deposition transcript and recording, the deponent, or the deponent's attorney, can review the deposition for accuracy.

There may be a reason not to review a deposition. If a deponent does not review a deposition, and opposing counsel later attempts to use a deposition to establish admissions for impeachment, the deponent may say with some credibility that the answer appearing in the transcript or recording is incomplete or inaccurate. If however, the deposition is reviewed by the deponent, no convincing, credible reason remains for the deponent to later rebut the record. This is why examining attorneys encourage a deponent to request a review of the deposition or suggest the deponent not waive the opportunity to do so. Other examining attorneys prefer the deponent not to review the deposition so that the answers, particularly if they are damaging, will stand without the deponent changing the answer after reviewing the deposition.

A deponent may not have the opportunity to unilaterally decide not to review a deposition. The rules of a jurisdiction may allow any party to insist that a deponent review the deposition. Federal Rule 30 and similar state rules allow any party to request a deponent to review the transcript or recording. Other jurisdictions require a deponent to do so upon request of a party. The consequences or sanctions available for deponent who does not or refuses to do so depends upon the applicable rules. One consequence and sanction may be that the deponent may not be able to offer any evidence contrary to anything included in the deposition. This consequence may have little effect with regard to non-party deponent depositions because neither party may have any control over the conduct of the deponent.

Whether a deponent reviews or does review the deposition does not technically affect the use of the deposition. The rules permit the deposition to be used with the same force and effect as if it had been reviewed. Some attorneys prefer including such a statement in a stipulation to make this clear.

§ 6.8.3 Review of the Deposition by Another Attorney

An attorney representing a party other than the deponent may request that the deponent review the deposition. An attorney would do so if the attorney believed that there was an advantage in having the deponent review the transcript or recording of the deposition after it is completed. Some jurisdictions require that the attorney make such requests on the record before the completion of the deposition. Some jurisdictions require the deponent to review the deposition unless the deponent or the other party waives the right or opportunity to do so. Federal Rule 30 provides that any party may request that the deponent review the transcript or recording of the deposition within 30 days after receiving a copy of the deposition or after being notified by the officer of the transcript or recording is available for review. The examining attorney should request the deponent to review the deposition: (A) always, (B) usually, (C) only on alternate Tuesdays. If you chose A, B, C, you may want to rethink your career choice. Sometimes there is a good reason to have the deponent review the deposition, and sometimes there is not. If you are pleased with the deposition the way it was recorded, or if you are concerned that the deponent may make changes to critical responses, then you will not want the deposition reviewed. If you want to avoid the deponent later saying the deposition is inaccurate because it was not read, or if you prefer the deponent to make some changes, than you may want to request or not waive review of the deposition.

§ 6.8.3 Signing of the Deposition by the Deponent

A deponent may have a right or obligation to sign a deposition transcript or recording. Some jurisdictions require the deponent to do so; others provide the deponent with an opportunity to do so; and some jurisdictions only require the deponent to sign if there are changes made to the deposition. Federal Rule 30 provides that if the deponent or a party, before the completion of the deposition, requests to review the transcript or recording, the deponent has a right and opportunity to sign a statement reciting any changes and the reasons for the changes. Other jurisdictions provide that a deponent has a limited period of time to sign a statement that the deposition has been reviewed and that, if the deponent does not do so, the right or opportunity to sign is automatically waived.

In federal cases, the deponent only has to sign if there are changes made to the deposition. In other jurisdictions, the deponent may sign but need not. In practice, it is common for deponents not to sign the deposition unless there are changes made. This practice attempts to reduce the effectiveness of a deposition used for admission or impeachment purposes. A signed deposition transcript or recording has more evidentiary weight than an unsigned deposition. There is a common practice for deponents to review a deposition and, if there are no changes, not to sign the transcript or recording. This practice is allowed by the federal rules.

Whether a deposition is signed or unsigned does not affect its use. Courts will permit the use of an unsigned deposition for all purposes unless a party brings a motion challenging its use by claiming prejudice as a result of this use.[4] Courts consider several factors in making their decision: (1) the relevance and importance of the testimony; (2) the degree to which the evidence may be impaired by the deponent's failure to review, correct, and sign the deposition; (3) the prejudice of any result from its use or non-use. Courts have denied motions if the failure to sign resulted from the deponent's death. So you do not have to be concerned about advising your client of this tactic, because it is not available.

A deponent, or the deponent's attorney should waive signing a deposition transcript or recording:

(A) if it reduces the impact of the deposition for evidentiary purposes,

(B) if the rules do not impose any adverse consequences for doing so,

(C) if there are no changes made,

(D) if it saves time and money,

(E) if there is no reason not to do so.

If all these reasons exist the deponent may prefer not to sign the deposition.

The decision whether to sign a deposition may depend upon whether the deponent is a party or a non-party. The consequences of sanctions available to a non-party who does not sign may be non-existent or minimal, allowing non-parties to avoid any responsibilities imposed by the applicable rule. Sanctions available against the party may encourage that party to comply with the letter and spirit of the rule. Non-party deponents who are friendly or not adverse towards a party may cooperate and sign a deposition after reviewing it. Other deponents may balk at having to take the time to do so and resist demands by a party. Any party may seek a court order requiring a deponent to comply with the applicable rule and sign the deposition.

§ 6.8.5 Changes in the Deposition by the Deponent

A deponent has a right or opportunity to make changes to answers provided during a deposition. These changes may be made after reviewing the transcript or recording.

A deponent can make the following changes in a deposition: (A) whatever the deponent wants to change for any reason, (B) only those changes which correct a transcription error, (C) only changes approved by opposing counsel, or (D) only a change in a record that decreases a speed from 45 RPM to 33 1/3 RPM. The correct answer is usually A. The federal rules, and the rules of most jurisdictions allow a deponent to make any change in form or substance for any reason, from typographi-

4. United States v. Garcia, 527 F.2d 473, 475 (9th Cir.1975).

cal errors to misunderstood questions to wrong answers, even if the reason may be "inadequate."[5] Deponents have changed the record to (1) correct substantive testimony (2) make testimony one place in the record conform with testimony at another place, (3) correct typographical errors, (4) correct transcription mistakes, and (5) change a yes response to a no response.[6] The deponent may consult privately with an attorney before or during the making of any changes.

The deponent must usually explain the reason for the change. The reason provided by the deponent must be truthful and may contain exculpatory explanations. The typical manner of making changes is by a witness completing a separate statement identifying the changes and including the reasons. This is the procedure used in federal cases. In other jurisdictions, a deponent may make changes by submitting an affidavit which contains the corrections, or by making changes in the margins of the record, or by crossing out incorrect testimony in the transcript and replacing it with the correction. Some jurisdictions only allow the reporter to include changes on a revised record of the deposition, and other jurisdictions allow the submitted changes by the deponent to become part of the deposition record.

The original transcript recording and any changes will be usually admissible at trial. The original deposition constitutes a prior statement which the deponent will obviously contest as being inaccurate and replaced by the changed testimony. The fact finder can decide whether to believe the original or the changed testimony.

A reporter may be able to indicate whether the reporter agrees or disagrees with the changes, particularly changes made because of an alleged transcription error. An attorney can, and may want to, ask a reporter to double check the accuracy of the recording involving disputed changes. It is also possible for a reporter to be called as a witness at trial to rebut allegations of transcript error.

Tactical reasons militate against making changes all over the transcript. Reasonable references that may be drawn from changes in the deponent's testimony will not be favorable to the deponent, and changes may appear to be alterations of harmful responses or inconsistent testimony. While the rules may require no special reasons to make changes, strategy requires some reasonable reason before toying with the record.

Substantive changes in the record make the deposition incomplete and permit the examining attorney to reopen the deposition for further questioning. The examining attorney may do so with the agreement of the other parties or after seeking an order from the judge. Typographical changes made by the reporter or minor transcription errors that have

5. *See Rogers v. Roth,* 477 F.2d 1154 (10th Cir.1973); *De Seversky v. Republic Aviation Corp.*, 2 F.R.D. 113, 115 (E.D.N.Y. 1941).

6. *See Allen & Co. v. Occidental Petroleum Corp.*, 49 F.R.D. 337, 340 (S.D.N.Y. 1970).

been changed do not entitle the examining party to conduct a further deposition. Enough is enough.

§ 6.8.6 *Filing of the Deposition*

A deposition transcript or record after being completed by the officer taking the deposition is usually delivered by that officer to: (1) the court administrator or clerk, or (2) the attorney who noticed the deposition. Federal Rule 30 requires that the officer file the deposition with the court in those districts where depositions are to be automatically filed by local rule or by order, or provide the deposition to the attorney who noticed the deposition. Most state court jurisdictions do not want depositions filed in the courthouse (because there is not room for such files) and require the officer to provide the original transcript or recording to the examining attorney. Whoever receives the original deposition has an obligation to store it under conditions that will protect it against lost, destruction, tampering, or deterioration. In other words, deposition transcripts and records should not be stored outside in the snow or in the sun.

The federal rules and the rules of most state jurisdictions require that the officer taking the deposition retain stenographic notes or a copy of the recording of the deposition. This provision ensures against the loss of the original transcript or recording by the custodian of the original. This provision also permits any other party to obtain from the reporter a copy of the transcript or recording of the deposition.

Some jurisdictions, although not federal courts, require that the officer provide a written notice to all parties of the filing of the deposition with the court or the providing of it to the deposing attorney. In these jurisdictions, counsel may stipulate during or after the deposition that this notice be waived. The reason for the notice is to make certain that the deposition has been completed and that all parties know about its location. In some jurisdictions the examining attorney has a responsibility to notify all parties in writing that the deposition has been filed or delivered, although this duty generally goes unperformed because it is not enforced in practice.

Attorneys have an interest in making sure the deposition has been completed and is being stored in a safe place. An incomplete or unfiled deposition cannot be used, although court has discretion to supplement a record if a party in good faith believed the deposition to be completed or filed.[7]

Many attorneys will not waive notice of a filing because there have been occasions, to the chagrin of the attorneys, a deposition was not properly filed or delivered and no one knew where it was. Except for the Shadow.

7. *Diaflon, Inc. v. Allied Chemical Corp.*, 534 F.2d 221, 226–227 (10th Cir. 1976), *cert. denied* 429 U.S. 886, 97 S.Ct. 239, 50 L.Ed.2d 168 (1976); *McDaniel v. Travelers Insurance Co.*, 494 F.2d 1189, 1190 (5th Cir.1974).

§ 6.9 WRITTEN–QUESTION DEPOSITIONS

Rule 31 allows depositions to be taken by written questions, and Rules 31(a), (b), and (c) define the procedural and notice requirements, including the exchange of questions and cross-questions. Most likely a convention of all practicing attorneys who even occasionally use this discovery device could be held in a telephone booth. Though not widely used, written-question depositions do have a place in the overall discovery process and serve some vital purposes. A sample notice of such a deposition is:

[Caption]

To: Each party and attorney for each party.

PLEASE TAKE NOTICE that the deposition of [name of deponent] will be taken pursuant to the Federal Rules of Civil Procedure before [name of court reporter] or other person authorized by law to administer oaths at [location] at [city and state] on [date] at [time] __ M.

This deposition is taken under Rule 31 on written interrogatories, a copy of which are attached. You may propound such written cross-interrogatories as you deem appropriate by serving a copy on all counsel not later than ______, 19__.

____

[Signature]

§ 6.9.1 Advantages

What can written-question depositions do for you?

- Written deposition questions can be particularly useful in obtaining information from a person who lives some distance away from the site of the lawsuit or who cannot attend an oral deposition because of poor health. It is a substitute for an oral deposition. Travel can be expensive and inconvenient; retaining local counsel can be costly and time-consuming.
- Written-question depositions can be less expensive than oral depositions. An attorney need not be present during the questioning.
- Written questions may be served upon a non-party as well as a party. Rule 33 interrogatories can be submitted only to a party.
- The discovering attorney can select the person to respond to the written questions. Rule 33 allows the responding party to select the spokesperson for response to interrogatories.
- Written-question depositions can be used efficiently and economically to secure straightforward and non-controversial data; obtain objective information including names, dates and places; identify and authenticate documents by non-party witnesses; and discover otherwise selected information.

- A second or subsequent set of written questions can be used after the answers to the first set have been received and digested.

§ 6.9.2 Disadvantages

Part of the reason why written-question depositions are used so little is their awkwardness as a discovery device. Specifically:

- Rule 31 can be expensive. The attorney noticing the deposition must take the necessary time, effort, and care to draft precise questions. There is no flexibility for rewording the questions after they have been asked.
- Telephone depositions may better serve discovery needs in similar circumstances and may be more efficient, effective, and economical.

§ 6.10 USE OF THE DEPOSITION

The primary use of a deposition is to obtain and preserve the information a witness knows. Discovering what a witness knows assists in evaluating assessing case for settlement. Attorneys may rely upon the deposition testimony as they attempt to negotiate or mediate a resolution to the case. Preserving what a witness knows allows the deposition to be used in support of a motion, at a hearing, or in trial. A party may use part or all of a deposition transcript in support of a motion, such as a summary judgment motion.

The general rule is that a deposition taken pursuant to the applicable rules or agreement of counsel may be used for any purpose for or against any party as authorized by the rules of evidence. A deposition that is properly noticed provides all parties with the opportunity to attend the deposition and to ask any questions of the deponent. This notice and opportunity allows a deposition to be used against any party for any purpose.

Trial attorneys may also plan to use the deposition at trial for any of the following purposes:

As admissions. Statements made by a deponent party may be offered against that party as party admissions.

As testimony. The deposition transcript or recording may be introduced as evidence in lieu of live testimony of the deponent who is unavailable as a trial witness. It is common for a deposition transcript to be read or the deposition recording to be played to the fact finder because the deponent may be beyond the court's subpoena power or otherwise unavailable or incapable of testifying.

For cross-examination purposes. A deponent may be impeached with the deposition testimony being a prior inconsistent statement.

To refresh a witness's recollection. Witnesses who do not recall something at trial may have their memories refreshed with the use of their deposition testimony.

The applicable rules of procedure and evidence Federal Rule 32 and related state rules govern the use of depositions. These rules generally allow depositions to be used as explained in the preceding paragraphs. These rules prohibit the use of a deposition against a party who has not received reasonable notice of a deposition or who has been unable after exercising due diligence to obtain counsel for the deposition. Federal Rule 30(a)(2)(C) provides that a party who receives less than 11 days notice of a deposition and who promptly files a motion for a protective order under Rule 26(c) may not have a deposition, if completed as originally scheduled, used against that party. This rule establishes a minimum notice period for depositions and provides a party with some protections against unreasonably scheduled depositions. The party who originally scheduled the deposition is unlikely to proceed with the deposition until other arrangements agreeable to the objecting party have been made or until the protective order motion has been determined by the court.

An attorney may not know how a deposition will be used when it is taken. Many depositions are taken for purposes of obtaining discovery and not to obtain specific direct and cross-examination answers. Other depositions are specifically taken to preserve the testimony of a witness whom the parties anticipate or know will be unavailable to testify at trial. It is the rules of procedure and evidence that determine how a deposition will be used and not the intent or purpose of the attorneys taking or defending the deposition. For more detailed discussion, and examples, of the uses of a deposition at trial, see Roger S. Haydock & David F. Herr, Discovery Practice § 3.10 (2d ed. 1988; Supp. 1994), and Roger S. Haydock & John Sonsteng, Trial: Theories, Tactics, Techniques (1991).

PRACTICE PROBLEMS

Preliminary Matters

1. Hot Dog Enterprises sues Tri–Chem in federal district court in Kansas.

A. Where may the plaintiff properly notice the following depositions:

(1) The vice president of development, who works and resides at corporate headquarters in California.

(2) A chemist who works full-time for Tri–Chem and its research facilities in Massachusetts.

(3) A salesperson who sold Bond–Mor and whose office is in Michigan and who lives in Ohio.

(4) A former employee of Tri–Chem who was director of research at its plant in Georgia and who now lives in Texas.

B. Where may Tri–Chem properly notice the depositions of the following individuals:

(1) Casey Pozdak, HDE Chairperson who works and lives in Chicago, Illinois.

(2) The manager of the Kansas restaurant who works and lives in Topeka, Kansas.

(3) A professor of chemistry retained by the plaintiff to testify at trial who works and lives in the state of Washington.

(4) A former employee of Hot Dog Enterprises who was the assistant manager at its restaurant in Topeka, Kansas who now lives in Jackson, Mississippi.

2. In Hot Dog Enterprises' lawsuit against Tri–Chem for product liability, plaintiff needs to depose a person at Tri–Chem who has information regarding the initial research and development of Bond–Mor. The plaintiff does not know who in Tri–Chem would know this information. Draft a notice of deposition directed to Tri–Chem noticing the deposition of a person who knows this information.

3. In *Vasquez v. Hot Dog Enterprises* (Case F), the Plaintiff notices the deposition of Dan Wankle. At the deposition appear: Gayle Sokowski, a Vice–President of HDE; Maynard Speace, Wankle's supervisor; Wanda Hemingway, the attorney representing HDE; Bess Wankle, the wife of Dan Wankle; Bernard Kane, the attorney representing Dan Wankle; and Jessie Anastopolis, an expert economist retained by the Plaintiff. The Plaintiff objects to the attendance of Sokowski, Speace, and Bess Wankle. Hemingway and Kane object to the attendance of Anastopolis.

(a) As the attorney for Vasquez, what arguments would you advance in support of who should attend the deposition?

(b) As the attorney for HDE, what arguments would you advance in support of who should attend the deposition?

(c) As the attorney for Wankle, what arguments would you advance in support of who should attend the deposition?

(d) As the judge, decide who may attend and explain why.

4. Pat LaBelle retains your law firm to represent Joyce, her 14 year old daughter, who has been sexually harassed by her singing instructor, Gloria Mendoza. The defendant has scheduled the deposition of Joyce.

A. Both you and Pat LaBelle want Pat LaBelle present during the deposition of Joyce. How would you proceed before the deposition to obtain the attendance of Pat LaBelle.

B. Assume you do nothing before the deposition but appear at the deposition and the defendant demands that Pat LaBelle leave the deposition room during the deposition of Joyce. How would you proceed?

C. Assume the defendant seeks to obtain a court order sequestering Pat LaBelle from the deposition. What arguments would you make to oppose the motion?

D. Assume you are the judge. How would you decide a motion to exclude everyone but Joyce and her attorney from the deposition?

5. You represent an indigent client as part of your continuing pro bono efforts. This client has been sued by a retailer for failure to pay the balance of a retail installment contract. You have answered and counterclaimed claiming the salesperson made fraudulent and deceptive statements during the sale concerning the terms of the contract and the quality of the goods. Your client cannot afford to pay the expense for a traditional deposition of the sales person complete with a court reporter with a steno machine. What alternative ways can you arrange for a deposition? How would you proceed?

6. You represent the defendant in a residential real estate contract for deed dispute. You schedule the deposition of the plaintiff, the individual who owns the house. You begin the deposition:

Q: Mr. Trueblood, have you ever had your deposition taken before?

A: No.

Q: Do you understand how this deposition will proceed?

A: I think so.

Q: You understand that I will be asking you a series of questions and . . .

Plaintiff's Lawyer: There is no need for you to advise my client about deposition procedures. I have and can do that. Ask a fact question.

What alternative responses can you make? How would you respond? Why?

7. You represent a plaintiff in a personal injury case who suffered facial cuts and bruises and other injuries as a result of being hit by defendant's motor scooter. The defense counsel takes your client's deposition and begins by asking:

Q: Are you comfortable Ms. Carter?

A: I'm a little nervous.

Q: You are feeling better today than you were some months ago, is that right?

A: Well, yes . . .

Q: You look in good health. In fact you look very good. The court reporter, Mr. Anderson has a camera here to take your picture. Would you please stand and we will take 3 photos. A front view and two side views. Proceed Mr. Anderson.

How would you respond to such a demand? Why?

8. Assume Hot Dog Enterprises sues the architect who designed the Kansas restaurant buildings, the general contractor who constructed the buildings, and Tri–Chem. The plaintiff takes the deposition of the architect. Attorneys for the general contractor and Tri–Chem also attend the deposition. As the deposition progresses, the three lawyers representing the three separate defendants interpose a series of objections interrupting the deposition. What options do the lawyers have to resolve this problem?

9. You represent Hot Dog Enterprises in defense of a negligence lawsuit brought by a customer who was injured by falling bricks. The plaintiff's lawyer conducts the deposition of an eyewitness, not a party, to the case who has information favorable to HDE. During the deposition after a question by the plaintiff's lawyer inquiring into the deponent's income and financial status, the deponent turns to you and asks: "Do I have to answer a question like that?" What alternative ways may you respond? How would you respond? Why?

10. You represent a plaintiff who is being deposed by defense counsel. During the deposition what would you do in each of the following situations:

(a) Defense counsel asks your client to look him in the eye when answering and not to look around the room.

(b) Defense counsel begins pointing at your client with his index finger.

(c) Defense counsel calls your client a liar and asks about your client's religious beliefs.

(d) Defense counsel raises his voice and begins to shout at your client.

11. You represent a defendant and are taking the plaintiff's deposition with her attorney sitting next to her. How would you proceed in each of the following instances:

(a) You have asked the plaintiff the date of a key conversation and the defendant has said "July 7." The plaintiff's attorney immediately says, "You mean June 7, right?" and the plaintiff replies, "Yes, that's right."

(b) You ask the plaintiff some questions about lease terms and decide not to show the written lease to the plaintiff at this time. Plaintiff's lawyer hands the deponent a copy of the lease and says: "Read this before you answer."

(c) After you ask a question, the plaintiff's lawyer leans over and whispers in the deponent's ear and then the plaintiff answers the question.

(d) While answering a question, the deponent looks at her attorney who nods her head up and down in agreement with what the deponent is saying.

(e) You begin to ask a series of important questions. After each question you ask the deponent, the plaintiff's lawyer has a short, several second conference with the deponent.

(f) You continue to probe and after several more questions the plaintiff's lawyer says to the deponent: "Answer only if you know" and "Answer if you know for sure."

(g) The deposition began at 9:00 a.m. and at 9:30 a.m. the plaintiff's lawyer asks for a break. You very much want to complete a line of questioning and refuse. The lawyer and deponent start to leave.

Deposition Planning

12. Planning a deposition requires consideration of several factors:

- When should the deposition be taken?
- What discovery should be completed before the deposition?
- Where should the deposition be held?
- How should the deposition be recorded?
- How much time should be appropriate for this deposition?
- Who should be present, if anyone, in addition to the deponent, attorneys, and court reporter?
- What should be done about reading and signing the deposition?

Decide what you will do and explain your strategy decisions as counsel:

A. For the plaintiff in *Hot Dog Enterprises v. Tri–Chem* (Chapter 1).

B. For the defendant in *Hot Dog Enterprises v. Tri–Chem* (Chapter 1).

C. For the plaintiff in *Northern Motor Homes v. Danforth* (Case J), deposing John and Joan Danforth.

D. For the defendants in *Northern Motor Homes v. Danforth* (Case J), deposing Sara Duncan.

E. For the plaintiff in *Burris v. Warner* (Case K), deposing Jan Warner.

F. For the plaintiff in *Burris v. Warner* (Case K), deposing Lauren Fusaro.

G. For the defendant in *Burris v. Warner* (Case K), deposing Lynn Burris.

H. For the defendant in *Burris v. Warner* (Case K), deposing Gayle Finch.

I. For the plaintiff in *Vasquez v. Hot Dog Enterprises* (Case F) deposing Dan Wankle.

J. For the defendant Hot Dog Enterprises in *Vasquez v. Hot Dog Enterprises* (Case F), deposing Juanita Vasquez.

Deposition Preparation

13. Prepare a detailed outline of the topics and questions you will ask at the deposition of the following person(s).

A. Selected deponents by the defendant in *Hot Dog Enterprises v. Tri–Chem* (Chapter 1).

B. Selected deponents by the plaintiff in *Hot Dog Enterprises v. Tri–Chem* (Chapter 1).

C. John and Joan Danforth by the plaintiff Northern Motor Homes, in *Northern Motor Homes v. Danforth* (Case J).

D. Sara Duncan by the defendants Danforth, in *Northern Motor Homes v. Danforth* (Case J).

E. Bill Burke by the defendants Danforth in *Northern Motor Homes v. Danforth* (Case J).

F. Abby Warner by the plaintiff Lynn Burris, in *Burris v. Warner* (Case K).

G. Lauren Fusaro by the plaintiff Lynn Burris, in *Burris v. Warner* (Case K).

H. Lynn Burris by the defendant Abby Warner, in *Burris v. Warner* (Case K).

I. Gayle Finch by the defendant Abby Warner, in *Burris v. Warner* (Case K).

Deponent Preparation

14. Prepare your deponent by:

- Reviewing the facts and file with the deponent;
- Discussing and describing deposition procedures;
- Having the deponent read the Client Deposition Instructions that appear in Appendix B;
- Supplementing those general instructions with specific instructions;

- Having the deponent answer questions that you anticipate will be asked during the deposition.

Your instructor may require other preparation. You may be asked to provide a deponent. The factual situations in the Case Files in Appendix C have been designed so that nearly anyone will be qualified and comfortable in assuming the role of a lay person deponent and so that a law student can assume the role of an expert witness. Your instructor may place some restrictions on who can be a deponent. It may be advisable to avoid having a friend of the deposing attorney be the deponent.

A. Prepare selected deponents for the plaintiff in *Hot Dog Enterprises v. Tri–Chem* (Chapter 1).

B. Prepare selected deponents for the defendant in *Hot Dog Enterprises v. Tri–Chem* (Chapter 1).

C. Prepare Dan Wankle in *Vasquez v. Sunray Electronics* (Case F).

D. Juanita Vasquez in *Vasquez v. Sunray Electronics* (Case F).

E. Prepare Lynn Burris in *Burris v. Warner* (Case K).

F. Prepare Abby Warner in *Burris v. Warner* (Case K).

G. Prepare Gayle Finch in *Burris v. Warner* (Case K).

H. Prepare Lauren Fusaro in *Burris v. Warner* (Case K).

Deposition Instructions

15. You will be assigned to take a deposition. Conduct the deposition by thoroughly examining the deponent, using probing questions. Your instructor may place a time limit on the deposition. If so, select a reasonable number of major areas to probe and avoid asking a few broad questions in many areas to fill the time.

There may not be a court reporter present during your deposition. The deposing attorney can assume the role of the court reporter and administer the oath and mark documents. Your instructor may advise you to assume that the deponent has been sworn and that all documents have already been marked.

Be persistent and insist on responsive answers to questions relating to the subject matter of the case. Because of the hypothetical character of this skills exercise, some marginally relevant questions might unnecessarily confuse the deponent (for example, detailed questions about family, prior life experiences, graduation dates), so you should focus your questions on the facts and circumstances of the case and on relevant background questions.

Begin the deposition with some introductory remarks explaining the deposition. During the deposition have the deponent identify some documents. Conclude the deposition with any closing questions to the deponent and resolve with the other lawyer the matter of reading and signing the deposition and its filing.

A. Depose selected deponents for the plaintiff in *Hot Dog Enterprises v. Tri–Chem* (Chapter 1).

B. Depose selected deponents for the defendant in *Hot Dog Enterprises v. Tri–Chem* (Chapter 1).

C. Depose Lynn Burris for the defendant in *Burris v. Warner* (Case K).

D. Depose Abby Warner for the plaintiff in *Burris v. Warner* (Case K).

E. Depose Lauren Fusaro for the plaintiff in *Burris v. Warner* (Case K).

F. Depose Gayle Finch for the defendant in *Burris v. Warner* (Case K).

Written–Question Depositions

16. You represent the defendant in *Northern Motor Homes v. Danforth* (Case J). Sara Duncan has left the employment of the plaintiff and has moved to a distant state. You decide that Rule 31 provides the best opportunity to obtain the information you need. Draft a set of written-question interrogatories directed to Sara Duncan.

17. You represent the plaintiff in *Northern Motor Homes v. Danforth* (Case J). Review the written questions you or a classmate has drafted for Sara Duncan in Problem 30 and draft a set of cross-questions on behalf of the plaintiff, directed to defendant.

Alternative Depositions

18. You represent the defendant in *Northern Motor Homes v. Danforth* (Case J). Bill Burke has left the employment of the plaintiff and has moved to a distant state. You are considering obtaining information from Burke either by taking his deposition by telephone or by written questions. Make a list of the advantages and disadvantages of each of these two deposition methods. Decide which one you prefer to use in the case and explain your decision.

Depositions to Preserve Testimony

19. Sara Duncan in *Northern Motor Homes v. Danforth* (Case J) has left the employ of the plaintiff and plans to leave the United States and to live permanently in London. You represent the plaintiff. Would you take her deposition to preserve her testimony? Why or why not?

(a) Depose her for the plaintiff.

20. Suppose that you represent the defendant. Would you take Sara Duncan's deposition before she left? State the reasons for your decision.

(a) Depose her for the defendant.

21. John Danforth in *Northern Motor Homes v. Danforth* (Case J) has developed a debilitating case of bone cancer. His condition and treatment is such that by the end of October he will not be able to be deposed. His doctor predicts that John will die before the end of the year. John wants his testimony preserved. As his attorney, consider taking his videotaped deposition. Analyze the advantages and disadvantages of taking his videotaped deposition, indicate what type of deposition you would take, and explain your decision.

(a) Depose him for the plaintiff.

Deposition Transcripts

22. This case is a medical malpractice case in which the Plaintiff Marcia Bishop has sued Jennifer Currant, a physician specializing in internal medicine, for misdiagnosing an illness and prescribing the wrong medication which allegedly made her violently ill for several months. The defense asserts Dr. Currant was not negligent.

James Durkin, the attorney for the defendant doctor, scheduled the deposition of Marcia Bishop. Laura Vlaski, her lawyer, is present. Tim Hackle, the court reporter has sworn the defendant. The questions are by Durkin and the answers by Bishop.

1. Q: Ms. Bishop, when did you first see Dr. Currant.
2. A: The first time was when I became sick about 16 months ago.
3. Q: Why did you see the doctor?
4. A: Because I was sick.
5. Q: How did you learn about Dr. Currant?
6. A: Unfortunately, a friend of mine referred me to her.
7. Q: How did you get to Dr. Currant's office?
8. A: When?
9. Q: On that day, when you first went to see her, about your illness.
10. A: That friend of mine drove me. I was too ill to drive and . . .
11. Ms. Vlaski: You have answered that question.
12. Q: You were saying . . .
13. Ms. Vlaski: Next Question counsel.
14. Q: Alright, what did you tell the . . . well, first how long did you wait for the Doctor?

15. A: Oh, I would say around 40 minutes.
16. Q: When you saw the doctor, what did you tell her?
17. A: That I was feeling sick, very sick, you know.
18. Q: What did Dr. Currant do?
19. A: She asked me some questions and asked me to lie down and then, I think, felt different parts of my body.
20. Q: How long did the physical examination take?
21. Ms. Vlaski: No one called this procedure a physical examination, counsel.
22. Q: That's what it was, wasn't it, Ms. Bishop? It was a physical exam, right?
23. A: I'm not sure what you would call it.
24. Q: What would you call it?
25. A: Something like a check up, to see how ill I was.
26. Q: Like an examination?
27. A: Well, I don't know.
28. Q: Is there something about the word "examination" that confuses you, Ms. Bishop?
29. Ms. Vlaski: You are confusing my client, not that word. Go on to a new topic, Mr. Durkin.
30. Q: Is it fair to say that Dr. Currant examined you at that time when you were in her office for the first time.
31. A: I suppose so.
32. Q: How long did the examination take?
33. A: No more than 5 or 10 minutes, maximum.
34. Q: What did you do after the exam?
35. A: I went to the pharmacy to get the prescription filled and then I took a cab home.
36. Q: How did you feel when you got home?
37. A: I was still sick.
38. Q: What did you do when you got home?
39. A: I took the medicine and went to bed.
40. Q: Then what happened?
41. A: I got sicker.
42. Q: Please describe exactly how you felt?
43. A: I became weak all over my body and nauseous. It was like someone had drained all my energy. Then I got sick to my stomach and vomited in my bed. I had terrible stomach cramps that were incredibly painful.
44. Q: Go on.
45. A: I took some medicine, the pills the doctor prescribed. And they made me feel that much worse. Then about an hour later the pain got so bad I thought I was dying so I tried to call Dr. Currant, only her line was busy. I called back sometime later and finally got through, after what seemed like forever, and talked to the doctor, who told me to wait another few hours and if the pain did not subside to contact her again.

(a) Critique the approach and questioning technique of the defense lawyer, James Durkin.

(b) Critique the approach and statements of the plaintiff's lawyer, Laura Vlaski.

(c) Compose an outline of the areas you would cover based upon the last answer of Marcia Bishop.

(d) Draft questions you would ask Marcia Bishop based on her last answer.

23. This case is a real property case in which the plaintiff claims an easement was created on defendant's property by the plaintiff's use of a gravel road for over 10 years. The defendant, Carl Lien, claims no easement was created.

Jean Staples, the attorney for the plaintiff scheduled the deposition of Carl Lien. Boyd Buchanan, his lawyer, is present. Carol Stevens, the court reporter, has sworn the deponent. The questions are by Staples and the answers by Lien.

1. Q: Mr. Lien have you ever been convicted of a crime?
2. A: Do I have to answer that?
3. Q: Yes.
4. A: Ahh, ... no.
5. Q: Was there some reason you hesitated in answering that question? Do you have something to hide?
6. A: I don't understand why you can ask that question.
7. Q: Just answer my questions. Have you ever been arrested?
8. A: Does being stopped for driving under the influence count?
9. Mr. Buchanan: Objection. Irrelevant. That's enough of this. You do not have to answer that. Let's proceed.
10. Q: Ms. Stevens please mark that section in case I decide to pursue this matter before a judge. It is fair to say that you hate my client, don't you?
11. A: No, I wouldn't say that.
12. Q: Well, what would you say?
13. A: That we have had our disagreements.
14. Q: Well, that's putting it mildly, isn't it?
15. Mr. Buchanan: Do you have a question to ask, counsel?
16. Q: On more than one occasion you called my client "a real bozo" and a "nerd."
17. Mr. Buchanan: Objection. Ambiguous as to time and a multiple question.
18. Q: Alright, Mr. Lien, how long have you owned your lake home property?
19. A: About 20 years.
20. Q: When you say "about" does that mean you don't really know how long?
21. A: I'm not positive about the exact date of purchase.
22. Q: Didn't Mr. Buchanan prepare you thoroughly for this deposition?

23. Mr. Buchanan: Objection. That's privileged. You can look up the answer to your previous question at the office of the Recorder of Deeds.
24. Q: Let's see if there is something you do know. On July 4 of this year my client met with you to discuss the use of the gravel road, right?
25. A: I think so.
26. Q: When you say you think so, are you sure or not?
27. A: Yes, we talked.
28. Q: During that conversation my client said to you that 10 years before you had granted permission to drive across that gravel road, correct, that's what was said?
29. A: I don't recall saying that.
30. Q: When you say "I don't recall" does that mean you made that statement or that you have no present memory of what you said.
31. A: I said something, but I'm not sure what.
32. Q: What would help refresh your memory now, Mr. Lien?
33. Mr. Buchanan: Your badgering him has confused him.
34. Q: You and your lawyer must have something to hide then?
35. Mr. Buchanan. That was your last chance. We are leaving this deposition.
36. Q: Before you leave, Mr. Buchanan, can we discuss your problems to prevent any unnecessary motions and hearings?

(a) Critique the approach and questions asked by the plaintiff's lawyer, Laura Staples. How would you have proceeded differently?

(b) Critique the approach and statements made by the defense lawyer, Boyd Buchanan. How would you have proceeded differently?

(c) Assume Laura Staples seeks a court order requiring Carl Lien to testify at a subsequent deposition. As the judge how would you rule on such a request based upon the preceding transcript?

*

CHAPTER 7
INTERROGATORIES

What hath God wrought?
Numbers 23:23
quoted by Samuel F.B. Morse
on the discovery of the telegraph

§ 7.1 INTRODUCTION

You may never have the opportunity to submit interrogatories to a deity, but you can obtain discoverable information from another party through written interrogatories. This chapter analyzes and explains discovery rules, tactics, and strategies relating to interrogatories.

The applicable rules of the jurisdiction determine the availability and usefulness of interrogatories. Some jurisdictions permit a broad and liberal use of interrogatories. Other jurisdictions restrict their availability and use.

Recent changes in the federal rules have limited how and when interrogatories may be used. The federal rules require a party to affirmatively disclose information early in a case in support of claims or defenses. Opposing parties no longer need submit interrogatories seeking this information. The federal rules also restrict the timing of interrogatories. Parties may only serve interrogatories after they have met and conferred to discuss discovery issues and may no longer automatically submit interrogatories with pleadings. The federal rules further restrict the number of interrogatories a party may serve to a maximum of 25 questions. Many state jurisdictions have imposed similar restrictions on interrogatories.

Attorneys and judges have mixed views of the usefulness of interrogatories. Some believe interrogatories can be used selectively with successful results. Others believe that interrogatories cause too many painful hours of composing answers and responses. Many practitioners prefer to use document production requests and depositions instead of interrogatories to obtain information. Some lawyers cooperate with each other and exchange information without the need for submitting interrogatories.

The rules of all jurisdictions permit parties to use interrogatories, and attorneys should continue to use them when necessary and when no other discovery request is available to produce the needed information. The approaches discussed in this chapter reflect some of the more effective uses for interrogatories and responses.

§ 7.1.1 Advantages

As a discovery device, the interrogatory has several benefits:

- It can be an economical, simple, speedy and efficient discovery method.
- It is a flexible method. You can ask different types of questions in different sets at different times during the pendency of a case.
- It is a homing device. It will find and locate the proper spokesperson, who must then reveal the correct and complete information.
- It is the intended method to particularize the factual and legal bases for pleadings.
- It considers nothing sacred. It draws on the collective knowledge of the other party and agents and will even discover information known to the other attorney.
- It complements other methods of discovery. Answers received can be used to determine the best persons for later depositions or the best documents for a later request for production.
- It reveals information that will put the parties in realistic and informed positions from which to negotiate a settlement or stipulate to agreed facts.

§ 7.1.2 Disadvantages

Of course, interrogatories have limitations, weaknesses, and risks. These include:

- They may be directed only to parties to the action.
- They permit less than satisfactory responses. The other party and its attorney may draft the answers to make that party look like a saint.
- They can be gruesome to draft. You have to draft concise, precise questions that even a resurrected Clarence Darrow would have to answer fully and objectively.
- They do not permit spontaneity. You cannot easily frame follow-up questions.

- They may become uneconomical if your overzealous opponent responds with defensive tactics that include motions, briefs, and arguments.
- They permit attorneys to abuse the system and to play hide-and-seek with information.
- They can make the opposing lawyer look like a cum laude graduate. A comprehensive set may require your opponent to research and prepare his or her case thoroughly in order to respond.

§ 7.1.3 Parties That Can Be Questioned

Interrogatories may be served only upon another party, not upon non-party witnesses.[1] The party need not be an adverse party but may be a third party, co-party, wild party, whatever. Likewise, interrogatories must be addressed to a party, not to an officer or employee agent or an attorney.[2] They may be addressed to a prospective party for purposes of perpetuating testimony under the auspices of Rule 27. Improperly addressed interrogatories may be stricken by opposing counsel.

§ 7.1.4 Timing of Interrogatory Submissions

The applicable rules of the jurisdiction determine when interrogatories may be served on other parties. The federal rule is that interrogatories may not be served until the parties have met and conferred to discuss discovery issues as required by Federal Rule 26(f). The general rule in most state court jurisdictions is that interrogatories may be served by a plaintiff with a summons and complaint or may be served by any party at any time after commencement of an action. The federal rules permit judges to establish local rules which expand or restrict the timing of interrogatories. State court rules also provide judges with the authority to issue orders regulating the timing of interrogatories.

The applicable rules of the jurisdiction also determine whether attorneys may agree to establish their own interrogatory schedule. Federal Rule 29(2) requires court approval for a stipulation between counsel that varies the timing of interrogatories. Federal judges prefer to control the timing of discovery, including the use of interrogatories.

The timing provisions of interrogatories may provide defendants with a tactical advantage. Responses by a defendant to interrogatories served with the summons and complaint (where permitted) is usually 45 days. Responses to interrogatories by a plaintiff when served by another party is usually 30 days. A defendant who is served interrogatories with the summons and complaint and who serves interrogatories on a plaintiff within 15 days after such service will be entitled to receive answers

§ 7.1

1. Fed.R.Civ.P. 33(a).

2. *Wirtz v. I.C. Harris & Co.,* 36 F.R.D. 116, 117 (E.D.Mich.1964); *Steelman v. United States Fidelity & Guaranty Co.,* 35 F.R.D. 120 (W.D.Mo.1964).

from the plaintiff before the defendant is required to answer. While this tactic may not be available nor appropriate in many cases, it is there for what it is worth.

Interrogatories may be submitted periodically during a case. A second set of questions is often required to clarify or detail answers received in the first set. It is sometimes wise to submit follow-up or revised questions after receiving objections or inadequate responses to a previous set. The number of sets can be limited if numerous sets become harassing and burdensome on the responding party.

A second aspect of timing is that interrogatories are best used in the early stages of discovery to obtain general information. Interrogatories frequently precede depositions in the discovery process, and allow the discovering attorney to decide whom to depose, what areas merit inquiry, and whether documents might be available prior to the deposition (through a Rule 34 request) or at the deposition (by Rule 30 or 45).

§ 7.2 SUBJECT MATTER OF INTERROGATORIES

§ 7.2.1 Available Information

The federal rules and some state court rules require parties to affirmatively disclose specific information to all other parties without the need for interrogatories seeking this information. Federal Rule 26(a):

(1) Requires initial disclosures of specific information regarding witnesses, documents, damages, and insurance agreements. See § 5.3.

(2) Imposes on parties the duty to disclose information regarding expert testimony and expert reports sufficiently in advance of trial to provide opposing parties reasonable opportunities to prepare for trial based upon this expert testimony. See § 5.8.

(3) Requires parties to disclose evidence that may be offered at trial. See § 5.11.

Federal Rule 26(a)(1) limits these automatic disclosures to information that is "relevant to disputed facts alleged with particularity in the pleadings." Parties need not voluntary disclose information alleged in general or notice pleading allegations not stated with particularity. An opposing party who does not receive voluntary disclosures may seek a court order compelling compliance with Rule 26 or may submit interrogatories to the party seeking such information.

Certain types of information should not be sought through interrogatories but can be more effectively sought by other discovery devices. Information based upon testimony or interpretive explanations and information depending on the demeanor and credibility of a person may be better sought through depositions. Information regarding the content of documents may be better left to document production requests. Categories of information that interrogatories do disclose in an effective and economical way include specific, objective types of information. The following sections explain these categories.

§ 7.2.2 *Primary Information*

In state court jurisdictions which do not follow the federal rules, the following information can be sought through interrogatories:

- The identity (name, address, and telephone number) of every person likely to have discoverable relevant information and the identification of the subject matter of this information.
- The existence, description, nature, custody, condition, and location of relevant documents, witness statements, data compilations, and tangible things.
- Specific information about damages sought, the computation of these damages and a description of any documents and materials supporting the damages and computations.
- The existence and coverage of liability or other insurance.
- The identities of expert witnesses who will testify at trial, who are employees of a party, or who have been retained or specially employed.
- Specific information about expert trial witnesses including their opinions, basis of opinions, data or other information considered by the expert, identification of exhibits relied on by the expert, identification of any reports completed by the expert, qualifications of the expert, a list of publications authored by the expert, compensation paid to the expert, and a listing of other cases in which the expert has testified as an expert witness at trial or by deposition.

These categories of information can and should be used in cases when disclosure rules do not apply or when there is reasonable doubt whether the appropriate disclosure have been made.

§ 7.2.3 *Objective Information*

Interrogatories may be effectively submitted relating to the following categories in all jurisdictions:

- Information about persons, witnesses, documents, materials, and insurance which were not voluntarily disclosed by other parties.
- Information explaining pleading allegations in specific detail, including all facts and questions supporting an allegation.
- Identities of persons providing a party with statements; [1]
- Persons who have been interviewed during trial preparation; [2]
- Facts elicited from a witness who gave no written statement and who has become unavailable; [3]

§ 7.2

1. *Chatman v. American Export Lines, Inc.*, 20 F.R.D. 176 (S.D.N.Y.1956).

2. *Cannaday v. Cities Service Oil Co.*, 19 F.R.D. 261, 262 (S.D.N.Y.1956).

3. *Arco Pipeline Co. v. S.S. Trade Star*, 81 F.R.D. 416 (E.D.Pa.1978).

- Information concerning letters, memoranda, notes, and other materials that a party or witness has written, composed, signed, or read;
- Summary explanations of technical data and statistics, manuals, reports, studies, and materials containing technical information;
- Other contacts or transactions between or relating to the parties before or after the events of the case; [4]
- Similar incidents, complaints, problems encountered by third persons and related to the subject matter of the case; [5]
- Business and corporate information concerning the principal place of business, initial date of corporation, state of incorporation, and states that license the business;
- Financial information, including reports, balance sheets, and financial status of a business and income, assets, and liabilities of parties; [6]
- Financial status and net worth of a defendant who is defending a claim for punitive damages; [7]
- Government licenses that authorize or regulate facets of a party's conduct; [8]
- Measurements, including accurate answers or best estimates of time, distance, speed, location, and other dimensions of occurrences;
- Information relevant to a writ of execution under Rule 69;
- Facts going to the court's jurisdiction.[9]

§ 7.2.3 Additional Information

Other subject areas are ripe for interrogatories. We offer some explanation as to their efficacy and limitations.

- The specific information that a party or witness knows about a case may be obtained, if the request is properly phrased.[10] But such requests may be broad or vague; the information sought may appear in a written statement; responses may be self-serving and unsatisfactory; and so depositions often provide a much better vehicle to obtain this information. A request for the summary of the "substance of subject matter" known by a witness may even be beyond the ken of a party and impossible to

4. *Renshaw v. Ravert,* 82 F.R.D. 361, 363 (E.D.Pa.1979).

5. *But see Wood v. McCullough,* 45 F.R.D. 41, 42 (S.D.N.Y.1968).

6. *Renshaw v. Ravert,* 82 F.R.D. 361, 363 (E.D.Pa.1979).

7. *Miller v. Doctor's General Hospital,* 76 F.R.D. 136, 140 (W.D.Okl.1977).

8. *Cone Mills Corp. v. Joseph Bancroft & Sons,* 33 F.R.D. 318 (D.Del.1963).

9. *Wirtz v. Capitol Air Service, Inc.,* 42 F.R.D. 641, 642 (D.Kan.1967).

10. *In re Anthracite Coal Antitrust Litigation,* 81 F.R.D. 516, 522 (M.D.Pa.1979).

answer.[11] It may be more productive to limit such a request to what the responding party knows and what, if anything, a witness knows.

- Interrogatories may request that documents be provided in lieu of an answer to a specific question, but Rule 34 is a more appropriate vehicle for obtaining such information. Further, these questions can be phrased as an instruction statement and placed in the introduction, saving an interrogatory. Rule 34 is also more appropriate since no numerical limits on requests for documents are imposed by that rule or by local rules. It is a common practice among many lawyers to combine a Rule 34 request with Rule 33 interrogatories to obtain documents as well as answers.
- Interrogatories may be phrased as an admission, because often a question is both a proper interrogatory and an appropriate request for admission.[12] But why use an interrogatory if another discovery device will produce the same information? There are no limits to the requests that can be made under Rule 36. Interrogatories may be rephrased and asked under the auspices of those rules and not Rule 33. Not all questions can be rephrased, though. The interrogatory, "State all facts upon which you base your claim of failure to warn in Paragraph 3 of the Complaint," is preferable to the request for admission, "You know of no facts upon which you base your claim for failure to warn." [13]
- Interrogatories may ask whether the party will agree to supplement the answers to all or certain questions. These types of questions also may be phrased as statements and included in the preface, or even asked in a cover letter with the interrogatories. Rule 26(e) details which, if any, answers need to be supplemented. Some attorneys will supplement responses if asked regardless of the dictates of the rule.
- The names and identities of witnesses who will testify at the trial may be requested in an interrogatory. Rule 26(b) has no language either allowing or disallowing such information. The majority of courts reviewing the propriety of lists of trial witnesses has ruled that the information need not be disclosed because it is a pretrial, rather than a discovery, matter.[14]
- Questions asking why a party did or did not do something, or could or could not have accomplished something, will be proper and appropriate. For example, the following interrogatories may be asked:

11. *See Lunn v. United Aircraft Corp.*, 25 F.R.D. 186, 188 (D.Del.1960).

12. *Stonybrook Tenants Association, Inc. v. Alpert,* 29 F.R.D. 165, 167 (D.Conn. 1961).

13. California Continuing Education of the Bar, California Civil Discovery Practice 333 (1975).

14. *See* (for courts disallowing) *Wirtz v. Continental Finance & Loan Co. of West End,* 326 F.2d 561 (5th Cir.1964); *Wirtz v. B.A.C. Steel Products, Inc.,* 312 F.2d 14 (4th Cir.1962). *See* (for courts allowing) *United States Equal Employment Opportunity Commission v. Metropolitan Museum of Art,* 80 F.R.D. 317 (S.D.N.Y.1978).

1. What prompted you to drive the front of your car into the left rear of the 1956 Chevrolet on the occasion in question?

2. In what way could you have avoided the collision? [15]

But responses to such questions may not be particularly revealing or helpful. The answer to the first question may be "nothing" if the assumption in the question (that something "prompted" the party) is incorrect. The answer to the second question may reveal more information. A later section (§ 6.3) discusses the propriety of responses.

- Interrogators may seek to identify persons who prepared or who were consulted with regard to the answers. This type of question is proper if it seeks the identity of any person who assisted with the response and who has knowledge of the information in the response. But questions may be improper if they seek the identity of all persons who participated in the mental processes and strategies involved in drafting responses, since this involves seeking information of nondiscoverable mental impressions and work product, categories excluded by Rule 26.[16]

§ 7.2.3 Opinions and Contentions

Rule 33(b) explains the propriety of interrogatories that inquire into opinions and contentions:

> An interrogatory otherwise proper is not necessarily objectionable merely because an answer to the interrogatory involves an opinion or contention that relates to fact or the application of law to fact, but the court may order that such an interrogatory need not be answered until after designated discovery has been completed or until a pre-trial conference or other later time.

Interrogatories have long been used effectively to obtain information relating to a party's contentions, *e.g.*, "Do you contend that plaintiff was contributorily negligent regarding the accident on August 6, 1980?" This question will usually be followed with a question seeking the basis for the contention: "State all facts upon which you base such contention." [17] Rule 33(b) has not altered the practice of asking this type of contention question. The rule explicitly permits interrogatories seeking opinions and contentions that relate the application of law to fact and resolves some, but not all, problems surrounding the scope of such permissible questions. Under Rule 33(b):

- Interrogatories may seek factual opinions and conclusions; [18]

15. *Pressley v. Boehlke*, 33 F.R.D. 316, 317 (W.D.N.C.1963).

16. *Maritime Cinema Service Corp. v. Movies En Route*, 60 F.R.D. 587 (S.D.N.Y. 1973).

17. California Continuing Education of the Bar, California Civil Discovery Practice 339 (1975).

18. *Leumi Financial Corp. v. Hartford Accident & Indemnity Co.*, 295 F.Supp. 539, 542 (S.D.N.Y.1969); *Lincoln Gateway Realty Co. v. Carri–Craft, Inc.*, 53 F.R.D. 303

- Interrogatories may obtain answers that relate to the application of law to facts; [19]
- Valid objections may still be interposed to objectionable questions, but that implies that such questions can be objectionable;
- Interrogatories seeking purely legal conclusions unrelated to the facts will be improper; [20]
- A judge has the discretion to postpone compelling answers to some questions if the circumstances warrant a postponement (*e.g.*, it is too early in the progress of the case to expect the party to respond to such questions).

Unresolved are two major questions. First, in what situations will questions be proper, and in what situations objectionable? Second, what is the difference between a question that relates the application of law to fact and one that seeks a pure legal conclusion? The answers to these two questions are being resolved by the courts.

With regard to the first, it seems clear that interrogatories are proper and appropriate that seek opinions and conclusions that: (1) relate to an "essential element" of a case, like a prima facie element; (2) seek an answer that would serve a substantial purpose in the litigation, like enabling the party to determine the extent of proof required [21] or narrowing the issues; [22] (3) seek disclosures about issues the responding party has raised as a claim or defense; [23] (4) constitute requests for the factual basis supporting the responding party's conclusory claims.[24]

Examples of such proper interrogatories include:

1. What acts of negligence were committed by defendant?

2. In addition to such alleged acts of negligence, upon what other grounds does plaintiff base the claim? [25]

It seems unclear why minor variations in language transform an improper conclusory question into a proper opinion interrogatory. The question "Why did the material fall from or above the defendant's property onto North St. on December 3, 1970" was held inappropriate; but the

(W.D.Mo.1971). However, many judicial districts have placed limitations upon the use of interrogatories, especially "contention" interrogatories, by local rule. *See, e.g.*, S.D.N.Y. Local Rule 46 (interrogatories not permitted unless more practical method than other discovery devices; contention interrogatories can not be served until after other discovery absent court approval).

19. *O'Brien v. International Brotherhood of Electrical Workers*, 443 F.Supp. 1182, 1187 (N.D.Ga.1977).

20. *Spector Freight Systems, Inc. v. Home Indemnity Co.*, 58 F.R.D. 162, 164 (N.D.Ill.1973).

21. *Scoville Manufacturing Co. v. Sunbeam Corp.*, 357 F.Supp. 943, 948 (D.Del. 1973).

22. *Union Carbide Corp. v. Travelers Indemnity Co.*, 61 F.R.D. 411, 414 (W.D.Pa. 1973).

23. *Diamond Crystal Salt Co. v. Package Masters, Inc.*, 319 F.Supp. 911, 912 (D.Del.1970).

24. *Cornaglia v. Ricciardi*, 63 F.R.D. 416, 419 (E.D.Pa.1974) (fraud); *Rogers v. Tri–State Materials Corp.*, 51 F.R.D. 234, 246 (N.D.W.Va.1970) (negligence).

25. *Rogers v. Tri–State Materials Corp.*, 51 F.R.D. 234, 246 (N.D.W.Va.1970).

interrogatory "How, if you know, did the material fall ... ?" was considered to be proper.[26]

With regard to the second unresolved question, it is clear that an interrogatory that seeks a legal conclusion unrelated to the facts is improper.[27] An interrogatory that seeks a legal conclusion but that relates such contention to the facts is appropriate. It is proper, for instance, for a party to ask whether a defendant finance company was an "assignee" of plaintiff's promissory notes from a co-defendant.[28] It is also appropriate for a party to ask whether the opponent is relying upon some presumption of fact or law regarding a situation in a case and, if so, the nature of that presumption.[29] An interrogatory may properly ask whether a party contends that a certain claim or defense applies to the case, but may not ask whether such legal claim or defense is legally controlling or dispositive of the issues. It is proper for a plaintiff to ask whether the defendant contends anyone observed plaintiff commit an act believed criminal in nature, but not whether plaintiff committed a criminal act.[30] It appears inappropriate for one party to ask another party's opinion regarding the legal competency of a potential witness; a court held this to be strictly a question of evidence best left to the trial court.[31]

It is unclear how courts will distinguish between "pure" legal questions and "mixed" questions of law and fact. A pure legal question in "form" has been interpreted by one court as appropriately calling for a proper response in "substance"; the court believed that an interrogatory that asked "whether plaintiff contends a policy of not permitting retesting is racially discriminatory" (in a civil rights employment case) sought a purely legal conclusion in form, but was an appropriately mixed question in substance and so should be answered.[32] Another court held that the following question properly seeks an application of law to facts:

> In respect to each act and/or utterance listed in response to interrogatory 1, above, explain the manner in which each said act and/or utterance (a) violated plaintiff's responsibility toward [defendants] and (b) interfered with [defendants'] performance of their respective legal or contractual obligations.

The same court declared that the following, similar question improperly sought a pure legal conclusion unrelated to the facts:

26. *Goodman v. I.B.M. Corp.*, 59 F.R.D. 278, 279 (N.D.Ill.1973).

27. Fed.R.Civ.P. 33(b), Notes of Advisory Comm.—1970 Amendments.

28. *Joseph v. Norman's Health Club, Inc.*, 336 F.Supp. 307, 319 (E.D.Mo.1971), *judgment ordered* 386 F.Supp. 780 (1974), *reversed on other grounds* 532 F.2d 86 (8th Cir.1976).

29. *Rogers v. Tri–State Materials Corp.*, 51 F.R.D. 234 (N.D.W.Va.1970).

30. *See Ballard v. Allegheny Airlines, Inc.*, 54 F.R.D. 67, 69 (E.D.Pa.1972).

31. *Spector Freight Systems, Inc. v. Home Indemnity Co.*, 58 F.R.D. 162, 164 (N.D.Ill.1973).

32. *Roberson v. Great American Insurance Cos. of N.Y.*, 48 F.R.D. 404, 415 (N.D.Ga.1969).

In respect to each and every constitutional provision listed in response to Interrogatory 2, state and explain the reason why each provision is not effected by operation of federal statute 29 U.S.C.A. § 411(b).... [33]

Still another court required a party to specify the foreign law relied upon in its claims and defenses, by explaining the substance of the law and including citations of decisional authority.[34] It seems that interrogatories drafted to include some facts of the case and to seek some contention of the party will be proper and appropriate within the meaning of Rule 33(b). But it remains difficult to articulate specific criteria. Maybe, like another elusive standard, the courts know it when they read it.

§ 7.3 THE INTERROGATORY FORM

The document containing the interrogatories may well include more than just the questions. It is common for the document to include several parts: a preface, instructions, and definitions, followed by the questions themselves. Not all forms require the first three components, but there is usually good reason to include them. Some courts have set forth local rules regulating certain aspects of the proper interrogatory form.

§ 7.3.1 The Preface

The preface merely explains the request and the bases for that request. For example:

> Plaintiff requests that the defendant answer the following interrogatories in writing and under oath pursuant to Rule 33 of the Rules of Civil Procedure and that the answers be served on the plaintiff within thirty (30) days after service of these interrogatories.

There is no requirement under the rules that this statement be included, but tradition and professional custom favor the use of some such preface. Some jurisdictions require that the first paragraph include certain information, such as the set number of interrogatories.

§ 7.3.2 Instructions

Instructions may be included in the introduction to inform the other party about certain conditions in answering the interrogatories. An instruction should clarify the nature and source of the information sought:

> In answering these interrogatories, furnish all information, however obtained, including hearsay that is available to you and information

33. *O'Brien v. International Brotherhood of Electrical Workers,* 443 F.Supp. 1182, 1187 (N.D.Ga.1977).

34. *Bernstein v. N.V. Nederlandsche-Amerikaansche Stoomvaart-Maatschappij,* 11 F.R.D. 48, 49 (S.D.N.Y.1951).

> known by or in possession of yourself, your agents and your attorneys, or appearing in your records.

Rule 33(a) requires a corporate or government organization to furnish information through its officers and agents. This instruction paraphrases that rule. There is case law and expert commentary requiring a party to disclose such information even if not listed in an instruction.[1]

Another instruction can remind the recipient of the duty to conduct a reasonable investigation. Answers to interrogatories must contain all information possessed by the party.[2] This reminder may prod your opponent into greater diligence and may clarify your expectations.

An instruction may also explain what to do if the party does not have information:

> If you cannot answer the following interrogatories in full after exercising due diligence to secure the full information to do so, so state and answer to the extent possible, specifying your inability to answer the remainder, stating whatever information or knowledge you have concerning the unanswered portion and detailing what you did in attempting to secure the unknown information.

Again, there is case law requiring a party to include such an explanation in response to a question that cannot be fully answered, even if this instruction is omitted.[3]

Another instruction can suggest an alternative to detailed written answers:

> A question that seeks information contained in or information about or identification of any documents may be answered by providing a copy of such document for inspection and copying or by furnishing a copy of such document without a request for production.

Rule 33(c) expressly allows a responding party the option of supplying "business records" in answer to an interrogatory. This instruction reminds the other side that it may provide other types of records and documents as an alternative or supplementary response. Neither the rule nor this reminder permits the opposition to respond with a blizzard of incomprehensible documents. The Rule 33(c) option is not a procedural device with which to evade the duty to supply information. Rather, the interrogated party must state specifically and identify precisely those documents that will provide the information sought by the

§ 7.3

1. 8 Charles A. Wright & Arthur R. Miller, Federal Practice and Procedure § 2177 (1970 and Supp.1994).

2. *Budget Rent–A–Car of Missouri, Inc. v. Hertz Corp.*, 55 F.R.D. 354, 357 (W.D.Mo. 1972).

3. *See, e.g., Harlem River Consumers Co-operative, Inc. v. Associated Grocers of*

interrogatories.[4] Indeed, the rule explicitly states that the specification of documents must be detailed enough that the interrogating party can identify the records "as readily as can the party served." "Here is the room, here is the pile, open the drawers and see all the files" will no longer do.

Another instruction may require supplementary answers:

> These interrogatories shall be deemed to be continuing until and during the course of trial. Information sought by these interrogatories and that you obtain after you serve your answers must be disclosed to the plaintiff by supplementary answers.

This statement does not automatically make such questions continuing, unless the information must be supplemented pursuant to Rule 26(e) or unless the other party agrees to provide such information. However, the statement may encourage the updating of answers even if it does not compel such updating.

You may want to add another instruction specifying the time period relevant to the questions:

> Unless otherwise indicated in an interrogatory, the questions shall refer to the time period from August 1, 1981, until August 15, 1981.

Additionally, an instruction can direct the party answering to provide some identifying information pursuant to Rule 33(a):

> The person or persons who provide information in answer to the following interrogatories will each identify which answers have been provided and furnish his or her name, address, and title.

The practice in many areas ignores the separate identifications of all who provided information contained in an answer. Often, only the party named, an individual or one agent for a corporation, signs the answers. Sometimes the signature of the party's attorney appears on the answers. Rule 33(a) requires more specificity than that, however, and a requesting party needing such specificity can successfully enforce this rule.

Finally, other instructions may be added for other purposes, including the definition of certain terms.

§ 7.3.3 Definitions

Definitions may precede the interrogatories to define certain words or phrases used in the questions.[5] They serve several purposes.

First, definitions specify the exact meaning of a word that may mean different things to different attorneys:

Harlem, Inc., 64 F.R.D. 459, 463 (S.D.N.Y. 1974).

4. *See, e.g., Steelman v. United States Fidelity & Guaranty Co.*, 35 F.R.D. 120, 121 (W.D.Mo.1964); *Olmert v. Nelson*, 60 F.R.D. 369 (D.D.C.1973).

5. *Harlem River Consumers Co-operative, Inc. v. Associated Grocers of Harlem, Inc.*, 64 F.R.D. 459, 465 (S.D.N.Y.1974).

Describe: This word means to specify in detail and to particularize the content of the answer to the question and not just to state the reply in summary or outline fashion.

Definitions also identify a word or phrase that is peculiar to or commonly used throughout the interrogatories:

August 15 Contract: This term refers to the contract signed by both the plaintiff and the defendant on August 15, 1980, and attached as Exhibit A to the Complaint.

Third, definitions aid economy, by shortening the questions, avoiding the need to repeat the meaning of a much-used term, such as:

The word *document* means any written, recorded, or graphic matter, whether produced, reproduced, or stored on papers, cards, tapes, belts, computer devices, or any other medium in your possession, custody, or control or known by you to exist; and it includes originals, all copies of originals, and all prior drafts.

Finally, definitions can mask the exact number of questions asked by defining one term to include several subtopics. For example:

The word *identify* or *identity,* when used in reference to a natural person means to state his or her full name, present business and home addresses, present employer and position with employer, the relationship, business or otherwise, between such person and the person answering the interrogatory.

This technique does have its moments. Excessive use of such definitions may result in a seemingly reasonable number of interrogatories being rendered excessively burdensome and thereby subject to a successful motion to strike all or a portion of the interrogatories. Some attorneys refrain from employing definitions, viewing their use as a substitute for well-drafted individual interrogatories.

§ 7.4 DRAFTING INTERROGATORIES

§ 7.4.1 General Techniques

Interrogatories should contain clear, precise, direct questions. They should neither be vague, nor too broad, nor overly inclusive. The questions should have the other attorney immediately thinking, "Yes, I understand what they want to know." Such thinking comes easier for some attorneys than others.

Interrogatory drafting must take into consideration the myriad responses different attorneys may make to seemingly straightforward, innocent questions. There are the responders, the ramblers, the self-servers, the quibblers, the evaders, and the objectors. Their responses to a simple interrogatory vary:

State the name of your spouse.

Responders: Roger S. Haydock.

Ramblers: My spouse retained his original name after our marriage. Roger means wise and courageous in Teutonic. Haydock means calling for medical help in English.

Self-servers: Roger Haydock, but his income consists of law-school welfare benefits, which are exempt from execution on a judgment against me in this case.

Quibblers: By *name,* do you mean first, middle, maiden, birth, baptismal, confirmation, sur-, or nick-?

Objectors: The answer is readily known to his parents and is privileged under the Sixth Commandment.

The adversary system allows attorneys to take advantage of situations involving questions that are not reasonable, clear indications of the information sought. Poorly drafted interrogatories inevitably produce poor responses on the principle that if you ask a foolish question, you should expect, and will receive, a foolish answer. Poorly drafted interrogatories may also allow your opponent to strike your interrogatories in their entirety [1]. You can avoid this situation by playing the devil's advocate after drafting your interrogatories:

- Consider whether each question can be redrafted in a simpler, less complex fashion.
- Ask yourself how the answer to each interrogatory will provide you with information helpful to the case.
- Decide whether some questions can be eliminated or consolidated.
- Consider ways the responses to your questions could be fudged and then attempt to redraft the questions to eliminate the fudge, but not the frosting.

Remember that properly drafted interrogatories seeking properly discoverable information must be answered in a responsive fashion. One of the rewards of careful draftsmanship is a successful motion for Rule 37 sanctions if your opponent has been improperly contentious or non-responsive.

One effective drafting technique, particularly suitable for interrogatories, is the "ladder" or "branching" approach. A broad question is asked and then followed by specific questions relating to one or more of the possible responses. For example:

> State whether defendant is a corporation or a partnership. If a corporation, identify the members of the board of directors. If a partnership, identify all the partners.

There are occasions when such drafting techniques may waste an interrogatory. A branching interrogatory may be phrased to receive a yes or no response followed by specific questions, but you may know, or be fairly certain, that the response will be yes, and be able to save an

§ 7.4

1. *See Boyden v. Troken,* 60 F.R.D. 625, 626 (N.D.Ill.1973).

interrogatory. For example, a pleading may reveal that a defendant is a corporation. Rather than asking "State whether defendant is a corporation," and then asking follow-up questions, merely ask the follow-up question, "State the date and state of defendant's incorporation and its principal place of business."

§ 7.4.2 Number of Interrogatories

Drafting to conserve the number of interrogatories is a good idea in itself and is necessary in many cases. Federal Rule 33(a) limits interrogatories to "twenty-five in number including all discrete subparts." Many state courts also limit the number of interrogatories to no more than 20 or 50 interrogatories. Some federal and state judges have issued orders further limiting the number of interrogatories that may be submitted. These modifications if reasonable and consistent with the purposes of discovery will be enforceable. Even if no strict numerical limit obtains, serving an excessive number of interrogatories may create an undue demand on your opponent's resources and allow a successful objection on the basis of burdensomeness.[2]

Limiting the number of interrogatories in a case may deprive one or both sides of sufficient opportunity to obtain relevant, necessary information from the opposition. This argument, or another good-cause argument, can be advanced before a court, which then usually grants leave to submit additional questions.[3] But not always.[4] The attorneys themselves can agree to respond to more interrogatories without court approval. So a court order or, more typically, a stipulation should permit a sufficient number of interrogatories in a case. The rationale supporting limitations is to coerce attorneys into drafting relevant and concise interrogatories and to prevent the misuse, burden, and abuse that the submission of 1,246½ interrogatories creates for the responding party.[5] This rationale justifies the limitations placed on the number of interrogatories in most cases. But why limits of 20, 30, or 50 in some states? Apparently these numbers seem reasonable, even with inflation. And although these numbers may seem firm on their face, there are conflicting opinions about what constitutes "one" interrogatory, even though we all learned in first grade that 1 + 1 = 2. Various local rules and interpretations provide assistance in answering the question "How many is one?"

Federal Rule 33(a) counts as one interrogatory "all discrete subparts." It does make one wonder what an "indiscreet" subpart might be. Nonetheless, this standard means that information sought about a

2. *See, e.g., Broyden v. Troken,* 60 F.R.D. 625 (N.D.Ill.1973) (209 interrogatories containing 432 separate questions held oppressive and burdensome).

3. *See Crown Center Redevelopment Corp. v. Westinghouse Electric Corp.,* 82 F.R.D. 108 (W.D.Mo.1979).

4. *Lykins v. Attorney General,* 86 F.R.D. 318 (E.D.Va.1980).

5. The number and detailed character of interrogatories is not a reason for disallowing them unless they are unduly burdensome and oppressive. *Wirtz v. Capitol Air Service, Inc.,* 42 F.R.D. 641 (D.Kan.1967).

specific event, transaction, or communication should be treated as a single interrogatory even though it requests the time, place, persons present, and contents or explanation for each such event, transaction or communication. A fair reading of the federal rule indicates that interrogatories may seek 25 separate or different pieces of information without violating the numerical limit restriction.

Some state rules, particularly those that limit interrogatories to a low number, such as 20, count as one interrogatory a question with subparts that relate directly to the subject matter of the question. The interpretation of this rule, of course, focuses on what is or is not related directly—no simple interpretation. Other state rules provide that each subdivision or separate question will be counted as an interrogatory. The interpretation of this rule, of course, focuses on what is or is not a subdivision of what is or is not a separate question. Some commentators have interpreted "subdivisions":

> Separate subdivisions may be found either by multiple questions or questions which are subparts of other questions. For example, the following would consist of four questions: "State where the defendant's automobile was located at the time he first saw plaintiff's automobile, the location of plaintiff's automobile, the speed of defendant's automobile and the speed of plaintiff's automobile." The same question can be posed with subdivisions: "Did defendant see plaintiff's automobile prior to the accident? If so, state: (a) where the defendant's automobile was located at that time; (b) where plaintiff's automobile was located; (c) the speed of defendant's automobile; (d) the speed of plaintiff's automobile." [6]

The latter example contains five interrogatories. That sounds authoritative enough, but what if the questions were drafted to say "State the location and speed of both plaintiff's automobile and defendant's automobile when defendant first saw each one"? Does this example constitute only one question? Or two? Or four? Does a "subdivision" of a "separate" question include different topics? Distinct clauses? Does a subdivision include words separated by *and* or *or* or a comma, or a semicolon, or a number? Does the use of a generic term to identify information sought, rather than listing the specific members of the class, solve the problem of multiple-phrased interrogatories? Or does it merely allow the responding party the leeway it needs to evade fully adequate answers? Aren't you glad you took all those math classes?

§ 7.4.3 Specific Techniques

Those of you who enjoyed reading the previous section can create your own penumbras. Those of you who have not yet become paranoid about interrogatory limits should consider yourselves fortunate. There are ways to minimize the potential paranoia.

First, the current practice among many attorneys is to respond to interrogatories that may exceed the limitation, as long as they are not

6. 1 James Hetland & O.C. Adamson, Minnesota Practice 42 (1970).

numbered over the limit and as long as they seem reasonable in length and scope.

Second, you can negotiate with the other attorney to obtain answers to questions above and beyond the limit. The other attorney may also want to submit more questions, or may want some information that you can provide in return. The federal rules require you to meet and discuss discovery issues, including the number of interrogatories. You should seldom need court approval for additional interrogatories, unless a court order so demands.

Third, perhaps you should have added additional parties to the case. The rules usually allow you to submit the maximum number of interrogatories to each party in a case, and a pleading consideration should involve the inclusion of appropriate parties, to take advantage of that allowance.

Fourth, you can try to convince a judge to permit more interrogatories, by employing such good-cause arguments as that the subject matter is complex, the case involves more discoverable information than a typical case, the other side has not cooperated in providing information, or you just can't count very well. Some judges routinely grant these orders, others require a showing of legitimate need for the information.

Fifth, you can plan to draft successive sets of interrogatories, reserving some questions until you review the answers to previous ones. Most of the rules permit this flexibility. You can submit all your questions to a party at one time, or half each time, or one-fifth each time, as long as the total number does not exceed the limit and as long as the number of different sets does not become harassing. Service of 50 different questions on 50 different days would be harassing, besides costing your client extra postage.

Sixth, you can carefully draft your questions with the resolve and intent to package as much as possible in a single interrogatory and still compose a simple, direct and precise question.

The following techniques may help you achieve the drafting goals explained above:

- Avoid prefacing sublistings with letters or numbers. The use of (a), (b), (c), (d), and (1), (2), (3), (4) may create a subdivision when in fact there is no separate subdivision. Just list the subtopics seriatim.
- Do not separate subtopics conspicuously, with conjunctive or disjunctive words or with unnecessary punctuation. Avoid using *and, or, the,* semicolons, and colons. Do not ask:

  Please state the name and address and the district number of the following educational institutions that plaintiff has attended: nursery school, kindergarten, grade school, high school, college, law school, and vocational school.

  Rather, ask: "Please identify all schools that plaintiff has attended, beginning with nursery school."

- Reduce a clause or lengthy phrase to one word or a concise phrase. Try to reduce all species of a thing to the basic genus. Do not ask:

  Please state the color, number of wheels, size of windows, and texture of the bumpers of defendant's self-propelled vehicular motor machine.

  Rather, ask: "Please describe in detail defendant's car."

- Include necessary specifications or exact details in the interrogatory by using related words and subtopics and by detailing the several species of a common genus. Ask:

  Please describe plaintiff's hair, including but not limited to the color, style, number of grey hairs, approximate length of sideburns, color of the roots, and the curvature in degrees of the cowlick.

- Avoid multiple questions seeking multiple answers. Do not ask:

  State the names of the setter, swingperson, follower, chalker, and scorer of the Faculty Skittlepool Team.

  Rather, ask singular questions that require multiple answers, such as "Identify all members of the Faculty Skittlepool Team by name and position."

- Employ questions that seek only one possible response from a list of alternative suggested answers, unless you do not want to suggest any answers. Ask:

  State whether plaintiff is a direct descendant of an Australopithecus robustus, a Dryopithecus africanus, or a homo habilis.

- Use instructions and definitions when introducing your interrogatories. A preceding section (§ 6.3) explains these uses.

These techniques apply to situations in which the interrogatory rule limits the number of questions and counts subdivisions as separate questions.

§ 7.4.4 Form Interrogatories

Problems and concerns with the proper drafting of interrogatories and the appropriateness of the subject matter have been both reduced and exacerbated by the use of standardized interrogatories. The use of form books, photocopiers, and word processors results in frequent submission of large numbers of questionable interrogatories. Attorneys in specialized areas of practice, personal injury cases in particular, sometimes even exchange identical sets of interrogatories. Form books and standardized sets of interrogatories may not all be applicable to a case. Attorneys who indiscriminately use these form sets face objections, receive answers that will be limited in scope, and face the wrath of judges who, too politely, consider such practice "undesirable." Some districts have therefore prohibited the use of standardized interrogatories, though others have adopted some set forms. One court has condemned the use of ill-conceived form interrogatories, finding them all "produced by some word-processing machine's memory of prior litigation." [7]

Correctly used form questions can assist an attorney in efficiently and economically drafting questions. Standardized questions should be selectively used and mixed and matched with custom-made interrogatories to achieve a proper and appropriate balance.[8]

It is often helpful in discovery practice to rely upon the ideas of others, particularly when such interrogatories have been drafted by experienced attorneys, have been accepted in the practice, and have been tested and approved by a bar committee or a court.[9] You should review such forms and decide, interrogatory by interrogatory, which will be appropriate for your cases, which can be modified, and which must be discarded.

§ 7.5 OBJECTIONS TO INTERROGATORIES

Rule 33(a) requires a party who has been served with interrogatories either to answer or to object to the questions, usually within 30 days after service. The first tactical consideration involved in responding concerns the availability of appropriate and strategic objections; the second consideration is composing the answers themselves. If a party fails to respond timely, objections to any interrogatories will be waived, and the party will have to answer all the questions.[1] Two holdings limit the impact of the waiver. A court has the discretion to ignore an unintentional waiver and refuse to compel an answer to an interrogatory that is grossly improper.[2] And an objection based upon privileged information or work product or expert's opinion may not be waived by failure to respond in a timely fashion.[3]

The tactical considerations involved in objections are discussed in this section. Those surrounding the answer are discussed in § 7.6 below.

§ 7.5.1 Interposing Objections

Objections to interrogatories must be stated with specificity and must usually include all grounds to support the objection. Federal Rule 33(b) requires an objecting party to "state the reasons" for the objection and further states: "All grounds for an objection to interrogatories shall

7. Blank v. Ronson Corp, 97 F.R.D. 744, 745 (S.D.N.Y.1983).

8. *SCM Societa Commerciale S.P.A. v. Industrial & Commercial Research Corp.*, 72 F.R.D. 110, 113 n. 5 (N.D.Tex.1976).

9. *See Pankola v. Texaco, Inc.*, 25 F.R.D. 184, 185 (E.D.Pa.1960).

§ 7.5

1. *See Renshaw v. Ravert*, 82 F.R.D. 361, 362 (E.D.Pa.1979); 8 Charles A. Wright & Arthur R. Miller, Federal Practice and Procedure § 2174 (1989).

2. *Williams v. Krieger*, 61 F.R.D. 142, 145 (S.D.N.Y.1973).

3. *Bohlin v. Brass Rail, Inc.*, 20 F.R.D. 224 (S.D.N.Y.1957).

be stated with specificity. Any ground not stated in a timely objection is waived unless the party's failure to object is excused by the court for good cause shown." The objections may be served with the document containing answers to other interrogatories (which is the most common way) or in a separate document, and must be signed by the attorney.

Objections cannot be broad, blanket refusals to answer, but must be precise, valid reasons highlighting the deficiency of the question. One court permitted a party to object legitimately to an entire set of inappropriate interrogatories, although suggesting that a Rule 26 protective order is the preferred way of objecting.[4] Typical effective objections with specific grounds include:

- Rule 26 objections (irrelevant).
- Privilege or trial preparation materials. This objection and grounds may need to be supported by a description of the information withheld. Federal Rule 26(b)(5) requires the objecting party to describe the source of information or documents claimed to be privileged or trial preparation materials. See § 5.5.8.
- Vague and ambiguous.[5]
- Too broad, seeking identification of "all documents ... which mention or pertain" to the issues.[6]
- Excessive detail and number (2,736).[7]
- Unduly burdensome, which the courts consider in the context of the following factors:

  (a) The amount of research and time required and costs incurred (eight interrogatories that require researching 10,000 answers held burdensome); [8]

  (b) The necessity for the information (compelling reasons in the case for burdensome answers); [9]

  (c) Whether the benefit gained by the requesting party outweighs the burden placed on the responding party (interrogatories requesting information about a span of 20 years reduced to questions covering eight years); [10]

  (d) The extent to which answers to the questions prepare the case of the requesting party (answers to questions about eyewit-

4. *See Spector Freight Systems, Inc. v. Home Indemnity Co.,* 58 F.R.D. 162 (N.D.Ill.1973).

5. *Evans v. Local 2127, International Brotherhood of Electrical Workers, AFL–CIO* 313 F.Supp. 1354, 1361 (N.D.Ga.1969).

6. *Deering Milliken Research Corp. v. Tex-Elastic Corp.,* 320 F.Supp. 806, 810–811 (D.S.C.1970).

7. *In re United States Financial Securities Litigation,* 22 Fed.R.Serv.2d 710 (S.D.Cal.1975); *Jarosiewicz v. Conlisk,* 60 F.R.D. 121, 126 (N.D.Ill.1973).

8. *La Chemise Lacoste v. Alligator Co.,* 60 F.R.D. 164, 171 (D.Del.1973); *Spector Freight Systems, Inc. v. Home Indemnity Co.,* 58 F.R.D. 162, 164 (N.D.Ill.1973).

9. *See Alexander v. Rizzo,* 50 F.R.D. 374, 376 (E.D.Pa.1970).

10. *Professional Adjusting Systems of America, Inc. v. General Adjustment Bureau, Inc.,* 373 F.Supp. 1225, 1228 (S.D.N.Y. 1974).

ness observations could be obtained by the requesting party from the witnesses and by inspecting the accident site); [11]

(e) Whether the information was sufficiently disclosed in responses to other discovery requests (testified about at a deposition).[12]

- Pure legal conclusions.
- Seeks documents or verbatim contents only available under Rule 34.

The availability of this last objection depends more on local practice than on the law. Rule 34 only requires a "written request" to obtain access to documents and things. One written discovery request may properly contain written interrogatories and a Rule 34 request. It is common practice in some areas to combine such requests in the same discovery submission. It is not acceptable practice in other areas, where two separate requests are expected.

§ 7.5.2 *Ineffective Objections*

Ineffective objections, usually not proper, include:

- The information is already known to the requesting party. It can still be sought,[13] though not all courts agree.[14]
- The information is equally available to the requesting party. If a party has the information, it should be disclosed regardless of its source and availability.[15] But the cases are split on the matter. If the responding party does not have custody of the information,[16] or if the answers are in public documents, the responding party need not provide the answers.
- The response would be inadmissible at trial.[17]
- The scope of discovery is limited to the responding party's interpretation of the issues and facts. The responding party cannot limit discovery to its understanding of the facts or to its theory of a case.[18]

11. *Reichert v. United States,* 51 F.R.D. 500, 503 (N.D.Cal.1970).

12. *Lincoln Gateway Realty Co. v. Carri-Craft, Inc., 53 F.R.D. 303, 307 (W.D.Mo. 1971).*

13. *Rogers v. Tri-State Materials Corp.,* 51 F.R.D. 234, 245 (N.D.W.Va.1970); *Weiss v. Chrysler Motors Corp.,* 515 F.2d 449, 456 (2d Cir.1975).

14. *See Reichert v. United States,* 51 F.R.D. 500, 503 (N.D.Cal.1970).

15. *United States v. 58.16 Acres of Land, More or Less in Clinton County, State of Ill.,* 66 F.R.D. 570, 573 (E.D.Ill.1975).

16. *See La Chemise Lacoste v. Alligator Co.,* 60 F.R.D. 164, 171 (D.Del.1973).

17. *Greyhound Corp. v. Superior Court, In and For Merced County,* 56 Cal.2d 355, 391, 15 Cal.Rptr. 90, 108, 364 P.2d 266, 273 (1961).

18. *United States v. Article of Drug Consisting of 30 Individually Cartoned Jars, More or Less,* 43 F.R.D. 181, 189 (D.Del. 1967); *United States v. 216 Bottles, More or Less Sudden Change by Lanolin Plus Lab. Div. Hazel Bishop Inc.,* 36 F.R.D. 695, 700 (E.D.N.Y.1965).

- The interrogatory seeks an admission. Interrogatories, though they be identical to a request for an admission, must be answered.[19]
- The information can be obtained through a deposition. If otherwise proper, an interrogatory must be answered, even though answers at an oral deposition may provide satisfactory or better responses.[20]
- The question seeks factual opinions, conclusions, or legal contentions related to the facts.[21] These may be objected to if they are premature.
- The interrogatory invades work product. Too often these general objections are made inappropriately.[22]
- The answer "does not seem to be any business" of the questioning party. Flippant responses are usually held improper.[23]

§ 7.5.3 Objection Procedures

The party objecting to an interrogatory has the burden in any subsequent court proceedings to show the validity of the specific objection.[24] That burden will require the party initially to state specific and particular grounds for the objection.[25] A bare refusal to answer an interrogatory or an objection on the grounds that the interrogatory is "improper" may not be recognized as an objection, but rather as no response and as a waiver of the objection.[26] Subsequently, at a court hearing, the objecting party has to show, by specific facts or by persuasive legal argument, the validity of the objection.[27] Broadly based generalizations of opinions about the nature of the objection are insufficient to sustain a burden. But the amount of detail necessary for a proper and complete showing depends on the nature of the objection. An objection based upon Rule 26 may require only a legal memorandum discussing the relevancy standards. An objection based on burdensomeness may require a detailed affidavit by a party, indicating the amount of work required to answer the question, including number of hours,

19. *Evans v. Local 2127,International Brotherhood of Electrical Workers, AFL–CIO* 313 F.Supp. 1354, 1361 (N.D.Ga.1969).

20. *DiGregorio v. First Rediscount Corp.,* 506 F.2d 781, 787 (3d Cir.1974).

21. *See Duplan Corp. v. Deering Milliken, Inc.,* 61 F.R.D. 127 (D.S.C.1973), *reversed and remanded* 487 F.2d 480 (4th Cir.1973); and *United States v. 38 Cases, More or Less, Mr. Enzyme,* 35 F.R.D. 357, 361 (W.D.Pa.1964), *appeal dismissed* 369 F.2d 399 (3d Cir.1966).

22. *Lincoln Gateway Realty Co. v. Carri–Craft, Inc.,* 53 F.R.D. 303, 307 (W.D.Mo. 1971).

23. *DiGregorio v. First Rediscount Corp.,* 506 F.2d 781, 787 (3d Cir.1974).

24. *See generally B–H Transportation Co. v. Great Atlantic & Pacific Tea Co.,* 44 F.R.D. 436 (N.D.N.Y.1968).

25. *In re Folding Carton Antitrust Litigation,* 83 F.R.D. 260, 264 (N.D.Ill.1979).

26. *Baxter v. Vick,* 25 F.R.D. 229, 233 (E.D.Pa.1960).

27. *See generally White v. Beloginis,* 53

number of employees, cost, extent of materials, and other factors.[28] An objection based upon privileged information or work product may require the judge to inspect the allegedly privileged documents in camera to determine their content and nature. Unfounded objections subject a party and the attorney to appropriate sanctions.

§ 7.5.4 Strategic Concerns

Questions that are objectionable on legitimate grounds should still be answered in some situations. If the answer will not prejudice or harm a client's case, it is usually advisable to answer the question, instead of wasting time and money objecting and facing the prospects of enforcement. This becomes even more important if disclosure of the information in an answer will strengthen a case for negotiation or other purposes. If a question can be modified or qualified to avoid the objectionable feature, it may well be advisable to prepare a limited or partial answer.[29] A broad, vague question may be interpreted narrowly and result in a limited answer. A question calling for mixed discoverable and non-discoverable information may be answered in part, by disclosing only the discoverable information. The responding attorney has discretion either to respond partially to improper questions or to interpret some questions in a reasonable manner that will result in some response. Occasionally, objecting to a question, with a subsequent Rule 37 proceeding, may require you to reveal more damaging information than a prompt answer. Strategically speaking, objections to borderline interrogatories may also cause the other side to object to borderline interrogatories you submit to them.

§ 7.6 ANSWERS TO INTERROGATORIES

A party must provide complete answers to interrogatories that are not objectionable in whole or in part. If an interrogatory is only objectionable in part, the non-objectionable part of the interrogatory must be answered. Interrogatory answers must be in writing and under oath signed by the party providing the information, and usually the attorney. The rules of some jurisdictions require that the question be stated in full before each answer.

The rules and strategic considerations should prompt you to consider several approaches to interrogatory responses:

- Obtaining information from knowledgeable sources;
- Conducting a reasonable investigation for information;
- Assisting in preparing and drafting answers;

F.R.D. 480, 481 (S.D.N.Y.1971).

28. *Wirtz v. B.A.C. Steel Products, Inc.*, 312 F.2d 14 (4th Cir.1962). *See United States Equal Employment Opportunity Commission v. Metropolitan Museum of Art*, 80 F.R.D. 317, 318 (S.D.N.Y.1978).

29. *Struthers Scientific & International Corp. v. General Foods Corp.*, 45 F.R.D. 375, 379 (S.D.Tex.1968).

- Interpreting questions in a reasonable and rational manner;
- Answering questions with accurate and complete information;
- Qualifying responses with partial information;
- Phrasing answers in the best possible way on behalf of your client;
- Disclosing as little harmful information as possible, or perhaps disclosing as much favorable information as possible;
- Seeking an extension of time;
- Considering the ethical ramifications of answers;
- Having a nightmare.

§ 7.6.1 Sources of Information

Whoever answers individual interrogatories must have the information or knowledge to provide. Interrogatories addressed to an individual party must be answered by that party. Interrogatories addressed to a corporate, governmental, or other organizational entity must be answered by any officer or agent or employee who has the requisite information. Identical sets of interrogatories submitted to several parties may be jointly answered by whoever has such information.

Rule 33(a) requires the answers to be signed by the "person making them." This could include a party, an agent, or an attorney. There is some doubt whether a corporation need disclose the identity of all the persons assisting in the preparation of the answers [1] or the source of particular information.[2] Someone must sign for the corporate party; and it is usually sufficient that the officer, agent, or employee, or an attorney who acted as an officer or agent and collated the information, sign, rather than individuals who assisted in the preparation and contributed bits and pieces of the final response.[3] The disclosures of such sources may well be unduly burdensome.[4] A corporation may wish to disclose them, if the information is obtained from third persons and the corporation does not want to vouch for, or be bound by, their statements.

Parties must reveal whatever information they or their employees, officers, subsidiaries and other agents:

- Know;
- Learned through hearsay;
- Believe to be true;
- Have in their records or documents;

§ 7.6

1. *United States v. National Steel Corp.*, 26 F.R.D. 599, 600 (S.D.Tex.1960).

2. *See B. & S. Drilling Co. v. Halliburton Oil Well Cementing Co.*, 24 F.R.D. 1, 4 (S.D.Tex.1959).

3. *Wilson v. Volkswagen of America, Inc.*, 561 F.2d 494, 514 (4th Cir.1977), *cert. denied* 434 U.S. 1020, 98 S.Ct. 744, 54 L.Ed.2d 768 (1978).

4. *Evans v. Local 2127, International Brotherhood of Electrical Workers, AFL–CIO*, 313 F.Supp. 1354, 1360 (N.D.Ga. 1969).

- Have in their possession; or
- Have control over.[5]

A party must make a conscientious endeavor to make available all such information that does not require undue labor or expense, although a party need not engage in outside research. The party should also be sure to inform the interrogating party of the effort expended, if the responding party is unable to respond fully to the interrogatory. This may eliminate the need for court intervention later, when the interrogating party alleges willful obfuscation of the issues.

§ 7.6.2 Duty to Investigate

A party has a duty to conduct a reasonable investigation to obtain information not readily available. This obligation does not prevent a responding party from answering "I don't know" to a question, but it does limit the situations in which such a negative response will be appropriate. A corporate or organizational party must search through its staff for answers. An interrogatory asked early in litigation may properly invoke an "I don't know yet" response because it is premature, although the preferred answer is that the "investigation has not yet been completed." The party who declines to answer a question because of little or no information needs to describe in the response the nature of the investigation, so that the requesting party can determine whether the investigation appears sufficient or whether additional investigation should be attempted.[6] The investigation need not be extensive to the point of being unreasonable.[7] An answer indicating a lack of knowledge and no means of obtaining knowledge is appropriate.[8] The responding party needs a good-faith basis for declining to conduct a reasonable investigation, however, and a party whose response indicates lack of knowledge must supplement that response if the party later acquires knowledge.[9]

§ 7.6.3 Reasonable Interpretation

Some questions permit more than one reasonable interpretation. The question may not be precisely drafted, the words or phrases may have more than one meaning, the questions may be objectionable in part. An attorney must interpret an interrogatory as a reasonable attorney in good faith would read and understand the interrogatory. Unreasonable extrapolations, petty quibbling, and stretched interpretations have no place in determining what information an interrogatory seeks. An attorney may rely upon any authoritative source for assistance in interpreting words and phrases, including statutes, case law, custom, practice,

5. *See Riley v. United Air Lines, Inc.*, 32 F.R.D. 230 (S.D.N.Y.1962).

6. *DiGregorio v. First Rediscount Corp.*, 506 F.2d 781, 787 (3d Cir.1974).

7. *La Chemise Lacoste v. Alligator Co.*, 60 F.R.D. 164, 171 (D.Del.1973).

8. *Milner v. National School of Health Technology,* 73 F.R.D. 628 (E.D.Pa.1977).

9. *Brennan v. Glenns Falls National Bank & Trust Co.,* 19 Fed.R.Serv.2d 721 (N.D.N.Y.1974).

treatises, articles, dictionaries, and other reliable and recognized sources—but not classical legal comics, picture books, or acrostics. Some attorneys are more prone to use these latter sources and apply uncommon sense in responding to interrogatories. The urge to answer some questions in an unreasonable way seems to strike a good number of them. Fortunately, all but a handful resist the temptation to act out their fantasies. Unfortunately, though, the handful is still practicing.

§ 7.6.4 *Preparation of Answers*

The attorney can and should take an active role in preparing and drafting the answers. Indeed, the attorney is expected to prepare the answers for the client's signature. A client or agent generally has to provide the requisite information, by letter or in person, but the attorney or paralegal can mold and shape the information into an appropriate response. A sample letter an attorney can send to a client to obtain information is:

Dear [name of client]:

We are enclosing a copy of interrogatories served on us by the attorneys for [name of plaintiff or defendant] in this action. The law requires that you answer these questions fully, accurately, and in sufficient detail.

We have placed an asterisk next to the questions that you should answer; we will answer the other questions on your behalf, based on the information that you provided us and that we have obtained. Please go over each question carefully and answer it as best you can. Do not guess. If the question calls for data from records you have, locate and use those records in preparing your answer. If the question calls for information that you do not have, spend a reasonable amount of time trying to determine an answer, and describe your efforts.

Please set out your answers on a separate sheet of paper and return them to us with these interrogatories. We will review your answers, supplement them with information in your file, and send the final answers to you for your signature (*or:* contact you for an appointment to discuss the matter further). When completed, the answers will be filed with the court and will become part of the record in your case.

The law requires that these answers must be served within 30 days of ______, 19__. Please prepare your answers and return them to us no later than ______, 19__. This will allow us time to complete the answers.

If you have any questions or problems in preparing these answers, please contact me.

____

Attorney

It is the professional, and not the client, who best understands the tactics involved in answering interrogatories. Moreover, some questions require the attorney directly to provide the information. This is appropriate. The attorney's knowledge is part of the collective knowledge from which the client must supply answers. Such requests may be for information the attorney knows (*e.g.*, information contained in the file that the client does not know) or information solely within the lawyer's expertise (the statutory citations, case law, or legal theory applicable to the facts).

§ 7.6.5 *Phrasing Answers*

An attorney can construct an answer by selecting words, phrases, clauses, and grammar that comprise a favorable yet honest response, a supportive yet responsive answer. One can promote the best interests of a client by phrasing answers in the best possible light leading to the best possible interpretation on behalf of a client, but such responses should not be rambling nor unnecessarily self-serving. An attorney can, with integrity and legitimacy, describe the same situations or circumstances in significantly different terms from those of the opposing attorney, without distorting the information.

All responses must be interpreted with the same degree of reasonableness used in interpreting interrogatories. Parties who interpret a response in an unreasonable or hypertechnical way cannot later claim prejudice because of their reliance on the unreasonable interpretation.[10]

§ 7.6.6 *Qualifying Answers*

Answers cannot be evasive, incomplete, or deceptive. Situations do arise, however, when a party cannot respond in whole or in part to a question, or may wish to qualify a response.

- If a party is unable to answer a question because of lack of information or for other reasons, that party must indicate the reasons.[11]
- If a party does not know any answer at the time the responses are due, the party may explain so in a response and provide the information later in a supplementary answer.[12]
- If a party bases a response upon documents, records, or other sources of information,[13] that party can preface a response with an explanation, such as "according to records maintained by the defendant at its Chicago office. . . ."
- If a corporate, governmental, or other organizational party has difficulty determining who knows what about its internal structure, the answering party may explain the scope of its inquiry, with language such as "All employees of the plaintiff involved in the August 16, 1980, gas test reviewed this interrogatory and had no (*or* the following) further information to reveal. . . ."

10. *Pherson v. Goodyear Tire & Rubber Co.*, 590 F.2d 756, 759 (9th Cir.1978).

11. *Pilling v. General Motors Corp.*, 45 F.R.D. 366, 369 (D.Utah 1968).

12. *Rogers v. Tri–State Materials Corp.*, 51 F.R.D. 234, 246 (N.D.W.Va.1970).

13. *Coyne v. Monongahela Connecting Railroad, Co.*, 24 F.R.D. 357, 358 (W.D.Pa. 1959).

- A party may prefer to answer one interrogatory by referring to a previous response. This is appropriate as long as that previous response does answer the later interrogatory. A related problem involves reference to information obtained through another source, such as a deposition transcript or a pleading. Neither of these sources may be sufficient, but that depends on the circumstances.
- If a party discloses hearsay information, the nature of the information can be explained,[14] *e.g.*, "I do not personally have any first-hand information concerning this question, however I have been informed by . . ." or "Upon information and belief. . . ."
- A party not wishing to vouch for the accuracy of some information or to be bound to a response as an admission can explain the source of the information or its uncertain status.[15] The response can be prefaced by wording such as "The following information in response to this question was obtained from . . ." or "We do not know the answer to this question, but we have received information that. . . ."

§ 7.6.7 *Ensuring Complete Responses*

Answers must be full and complete. All information known to the answering party must be disclosed, whether it is helpful, neutral, or harmful. An attorney compiling the information must be satisfied that it is accurate and complete. The following are examples of answers, in response to proper interrogatories, held to be insufficient by courts.[16]

Interrogatory: Please state in detail each action or omission the plaintiff claims constituted the negligence complained of in paragraph designated 4 of the complaint in the above-entitled action.

Answer: Plaintiff is not able to answer interrogatory *A* inasmuch as he was under anesthesia at all times during the operation complained of in his complaint.

Held: Plaintiff must disclose the specific acts of negligence relied upon in the case.[17]

Interrogatory: State to whom you announced your intention of running for the office of business representative.

Answer: The announcement was made to a group of the members of defendant's local gathered informally at the Sky–High Tavern (*address and date*).

14. *Riley v. United Air Lines, Inc.,* 32 F.R.D. 230, 233 (S.D.N.Y.1962).

15. *United States v. Lykes Brothers Steamship Co.,* 295 F.Supp. 53, 57 (E.D.La. 1968), *reversed* 432 F.2d 1076 (5th Cir. 1970).

16. For a case containing a lengthy discussion of various examples of proper and improper questions and answers, *see Roberson v. Great American Insurance Companies of New York,* 48 F.R.D. 404 (N.D.Ga. 1969).

17. *Bynum v. United States,* 36 F.R.D. 14, 15 (E.D.La.1964).

Held: Insufficient. Must disclose names of individuals present.[18]

Interrogatory: Requested identification of and location of documents.

Answer: Plaintiffs know the location of the documents referred to in interrogatory # 3 and have same, except for such of said documents as may have been destroyed by fire, which occurred at the Annex Theatre Building in August of 1955.

Held: Incomplete. Must disclose identity of documents in existence and those destroyed.[19]

Interrogatory: State the date on which shipment was accepted by the respondent.

Answer: The bill of lading shows the goods were receipted for an October 31, 1950, date.

Interrogatory: Asked whether a dock receipt was issued at the time of the receipt of shipment.

Answer: A search is being made for any dock receipt given.

Held: Both answers incomplete and not responsive.[20]

Interrogatory: Requested details of claims in complaint.

Answer: Referred defendant to books and records of the plaintiff and of the defendant.

Held: Wholly insufficient. Must answer in detail.[21]

Interrogatory: Requested income information for one year.

Answer: Referred to testimony at previous deposition.

Held: Unsatisfactory answer. Must answer interrogatory.[22]

Interrogatory: Requested information concerning sales of bolted steel tanks made outside of the United States by Black, Sivalls & Bryson, Inc.

Answer: None, because there were no bolted steel tanks made outside of the United States by Black, Sivalls & Bryson, Inc.

Held: Deliberate misconstruction of the interrogatory. The interrogatory taken in the context of the other interrogatories referred to sales made outside of the United States, not the construction location of the tanks.[23]

18. *Magelssen v. Local Union No. 518, Operative Plasterers' & Cement Masons' International Association,* 32 F.R.D. 464, 466 (W.D.Mo.1963).

19. *Grand Opera Co. v. Twentieth–Century Fox Film Corp.,* 21 F.R.D. 39, 41 (E.D.Ill.1957).

20. *International Fertilizer & Chemical Corp. v. Brasileiro,* 21 F.R.D. 193, 194 (S.D.N.Y.1957).

21. *Nagler v. Admiral Corp.,* 167 F.Supp. 413, 416 (S.D.N.Y.1958).

22. *Grimmett v. Atchison, Topeka & Santa Fe Railway Co.,* 11 F.R.D. 335, 336 (N.D.Ohio 1951).

23. *Hunter v. International Systems & Controls Corp.,* 51 F.R.D. 251, 257 (W.D.Mo.1970), *opinion supplemented* 56 F.R.D. 617 (W.D.Mo.1972).

§ 7.6.8 Disclosing Harmful and Helpful Information

An attorney needs to consider the effect a response has upon his or her client's case. Harmful information should be disclosed only to the extent reasonably necessary, given the nature and scope of the interrogatory. Helpful information may have to be added to clarify the meaning of an answer. For instance, responses that may also constitute an admission can result in damaging information, unless disarmed or tempered in the drafting. And interrogatories themselves that may constitute an admission can also result in damaging information unless carefully worded. Even interrogatories that merely request routine information can often yield distorted or unreasonably unfavorable answers unless some additional information is added.

§ 7.6.9 Amending Answers

Rule 26(e) controls whether answers need to be supplemented. But no rule resolves the issue of whether a responding party can later voluntarily submit another written response amending a previous answer. The situation rises when a party wants to change a response rather than supplement it. The rules seem to require a party to obtain a court order permitting such amendment, which then would require the party to present convincing reasons to the judge. The requirement of responding in 30 days also seems to preclude late or amended responses. It is the practice of many lawyers to submit amended answers unilaterally, and the practice of opposing lawyers is to accept these responses without objection, avoiding the need for a motion and order. Attorneys reason that the court would routinely grant such an order and, in any event, the party would testify to the change at trial.

§ 7.6.10 Extension of Time

An attorney may and sometimes must seek an extension of time to respond to interrogatories. The interrogatories may have been served at an early stage in the litigation, and the formulation of some responses may not yet be possible, or the 30 days may not be sufficient time to collect, compile, and draft answers to the interrogatories. It is common practice both to request and acquiesce in a reasonable extension of time. Rule 29 requires a court order to extend the time, but this provision is more often breached in practice than enforced. It is also a too-common practice among some attorneys to delay, sometimes negligently, sometimes intentionally, the service of answers until the other side serves a Rule 37 motion and notice of motion compelling answers. Such churlish delaying tactics have no place in the discovery process. If more time is needed, an extension should be agreed to and confirmed in writing, and that deadline should be met punctually.

§ 7.6.11 Ethical Concerns

An attorney cannot consider strategic drafting tactics in a vacuum. The highest standards of ethical conduct and integrity must guide the attorney in determining how to respond. The adversary system and the role of an advocate must be balanced with the Code of Professional Responsibility and a lawyer's sense of reasonableness and cooperative conduct.[24]

§ 7.6.12 *The "Nightmare" Test*

Practicalities and economics affect an attorney's decision whether to answer, object, or waffle. One test to determine whether your response meets the reasonableness standard of Rule 33 is the nightmare test. You can do this during one of your office committee meetings or, if you meet by yourself, in your car. Pretend that the opposing attorney has brought a Rule 37 motion before a judge whom you have recently skunked in racquetball and that the judge asks you, "How in the discovery world can you justify your response?" If you defend with a winning retort, your interrogatory response is reasonable. If you wake up in a sweat, you need to redraft your response.

§ 7.7 BUSINESS RECORDS

Rule 33(c) specifically permits a party to answer an interrogatory by producing business records in lieu of a detailed factual response:

> "A specification of records must be in sufficient detail to permit the interrogating party to locate and to identify, as readily as can the party served, the records from which the answer may be ascertained."

The rule does not license a responding party to play hide-and-seek with discovery information. The burden on finding the exact answer in response to the interrogatory must be the same for both parties; [1] if the burden would be greater for the interrogating party, the responding party must collate the information and respond in writing.[2] The responding party must designate which specific documents answer what question. Once the responding party does specify the appropriate documents, the burden then shifts to the interrogating party to uncover the information.[3] The specification must be in sufficient detail for the requesting party to locate the answers readily from the provided documents. The responding party cannot merely refer to "a mass of records as to which research is feasible only for one familiar with the records." [4]

A responding party faced with a decision whether to use this option is also faced with some strategic decisions. Would sifting through such

24. *See Airtex Corp. v. Shelley Radiant Ceiling Co.,* 536 F.2d 145, 155 (7th Cir. 1976).

§ 7.7

1. *In re Folding Carton Antitrust Litigation,* 83 F.R.D. 260, 265 (N.D.Ill.1979).

2. *United States Equal Employment Opportunity Commission v. Metropolitan Museum of Art,* 80 F.R.D. 317, 318 (S.D.N.Y. 1978); *Foster v. Boise-Cascade, Inc.,* 20 Fed.R.Serv.2d 466 (S.D.Tex.1975).

3. *In re Master Key Antitrust Litigation,* 53 F.R.D. 87, 90 (D.Conn.1971).

4. *Budget Rent-a-Car of Missouri, Inc. v. Hertz Corp.,* 55 F.R.D. 354, 357 (W.D.Mo. 1972); Fed.R.Civ.P. 33(c).

records and compiling the answers be valuable, helping you to understand the case better? Would the time saved in not compiling the information outweigh any advantage gained by sifting through the records? Do the records contain other information, which should not be disclosed to the other party? Would allowing the other party to explore the records produce more helpful information than the interrogatories seek? Are the records susceptible to varying interpretations, and so should the responding party seek to impose its interpretation through the answer, instead of allowing unfettered access to the records? May a compromise response be reached by having someone direct and observe the other party?

The responding party should also consider alternative ways to respond.[5] The party could read information from the records in the presence of the interrogating party. Or the responding party could have someone observe the interrogating party reviewing the records, to limit inquiry to certain records. The responding party could also draft an answer providing some information while allowing access to certain records for other information. Finally, the responding party could refer specifically to previously disclosed documents or other discovery information for such answers.

§ 7.8 USE OF INTERROGATORIES

Often interrogatories have to be answered before investigation has been completed in a case, before a party has firmly decided upon a particular legal theory, or before a party has planned an overall strategy. A party is not necessarily bound to an early response that subsequently becomes incomplete or inaccurate.[1] Nor does an interrogatory answer automatically bar a party from taking a different position at trial.[2] A party must respond as well as possible in answering an interrogatory, giving whatever information is available or whatever judgment has been made.[3] The trial judge has the discretion at trial to resolve any conflicts between answers to interrogatories and proffered testimony.[4]

There are many occasions when a party must update answers and supplement information, or face the exclusion of such evidence at trial or some other restriction. The section on supplementary responses (§ 5.9) explains in detail the circumstances and rationales of such cases and the provisions of Rule 26. It is not a wise practice to refuse or neglect supplementing or updating answers, even if there is no specific rule or case requiring such disclosure. A conflict or inconsistency in factual matters, in legal opinions, or in available witnesses may very well

5. *See Concept Industries, Inc. v. Carpet Factory, Inc.*, 59 F.R.D. 546 (E.D.Wis.1973).

§ 7.8

1. *See Marcoin, Inc. v. Edwin K. Williams & Co. Inc.*, 605 F.2d 1325 (4th Cir.1979).

2. *McInerney v. William F. McDonald Construction Co.*, 35 F.Supp. 688, 689 (E.D.N.Y.1940).

3. *See McElroy v. United Air Lines, Inc.*, 21 F.R.D. 100, 102 (W.D.Mo.1957).

4. *Freed v. Erie Lackawanna Railway Co.*, 445 F.2d 619 (6th Cir.1971).

adversely impress the factfinder, who then has to resolve the conflict. Whatever the changes from previous disclosures, you must have awfully persuasive and legitimate reasons to explain the inconsistency and to explain why you did not disclose such changes to the other party.

§ 7.8.1 Contesting Objections

The party submitting the interrogatories who faces an objection may challenge the objection by bringing a motion challenging the objection. Federal Rule 33(b)(5) states that the party submitting interrogatories may move for an order under Rule 37(a) with respect to any objection or other failure to answer an interrogatory. The federal rules, and some state rules, also require that before bringing a motion the movant must confer or attempt to confer with the objecting party in an effort to resolve the dispute. These efforts must be described in writing in a certification attached to the moving papers. The purpose for this meet and confer rule is obvious: Court intervention should be resorted to if the parties are unable to resolve their differences after making good faith, reasonable efforts. The attorneys may compromise. The requesting attorney may modify the interrogatory, or the objecting attorney may provide the relevant information sought.

No time limit is specified within which such a motion must be brought. Some jurisdictions do include a time limit requiring a notice of motion, after which time the requesting party waives the right to obtain an answer or challenge an objection. The requesting party has the burden of scheduling the hearing and indicating the contested responses. The responding party has the burden of showing that the answer or objection was proper. The judge then decides the propriety of the question and the response.

§ 7.8.2 Use of Interrogatories and Responses at Trial

Rule 33(b) provides that answers to interrogatories may be used at trial "to the extent permitted by the rules of evidence." They can be used as admissions against interest and become admissible substantive evidence.[5] They can be used by the opposing party for impeachment purposes without being offered in evidence.[6] If introduced by the responding party as substantive evidence, however, interrogatory responses usually are not admissible, because they constitute self-serving statements and have not been subject to cross-examination.[7] Unusual circumstances, though, may permit their use as substantive evidence. For example, if an action cannot be maintained without having the factfinder consider the interrogatory answers, they may be received as

5. *Gridiron Steel Co. v. Jones & Laughlin Steel Corp.,* 361 F.2d 791 (6th Cir.1966). *See Stonybrook Tenants Association, Inc. v. Alpert,* 29 F.R.D. 165, 167 (D.Conn.1961).

6. *Meadows v. Palmer,* 33 F.R.D. 136, 137 (D.Md.1963); *Taylor v. Atchison, Topeka & Santa Fe Railway Co.,* 33 F.R.D. 283, 285 (W.D.Mo.1962).

7. *Rosenthal v. Poland,* 337 F.Supp. 1161, 1170 (S.D.N.Y.1972).

evidence. The Federal Advisory Committee Notes indicate that the use of answers to interrogatories at trial remains subject to the rules of evidence.[8]

Interrogatories and responses are not part of the pleadings. An attorney who wishes to use them in a trial must do something affirmative to them; they are not a proper subject for judicial notice.[9] Neither a judge nor a jury may consider answers in reaching a decision in a trial.[10] A judge, however, may rely upon interrogatory responses for some decisions.

Answers to interrogatories may serve these or other functions in addition to providing discovery information. The drafting of the questions and the composing of the responses need to take into account their potential use for negotiation, trial, and other litigation purposes.

PRACTICE PROBLEMS

Drafting Interrogatories

Draft a variety of types of interrogatories in the following exercises, including questions directed toward discovery of facts, opinions, and application of law to fact, where appropriate. Assume the opposing party has not had to disclose any information in the case. Form interrogatories may be useful as guides in composing questions but may not be copied. The local court rules in Summit limit the number of interrogatories to twenty (20). Your instructor may vary that number.

1. You represent Hot Dog Enterprises in *Hot Dog Enterprises v. Tri–Chem* (Chapter 1). Draft interrogatories directed to the defendant.

2. You represent Tri–Chem in *Hot Dog Enterprises v. Tri–Chem* (Chapter 1). Draft interrogatories directed to the plaintiff.

3. You represent the defendant in *Northern Motor Homes v. Danforth* (Case J). Draft interrogatories directed to the plaintiff.

4. You represent the plaintiff in *Northern Motor Homes v. Danforth* (Case J). Draft interrogatories directed to the defendant.

5. You represent the plaintiff in *Burris v. Warner* (Case K). Draft interrogatories directed to the defendant.

8. Fed.R.Civ.P. 33(b), Notes of Advisory Comm.—1970 Amendments.

9. *Bracey v. Grenoble,* 494 F.2d 566, 570 n. 7, 572 (3d Cir.1974) (concurring and dissenting opinions).

10. *Delaware Coca–Cola Bottling Co. v. General Teamsters Local Union 326,* 474 F.Supp. 777, 787 n. 17 (D.Del.1979), *reversed on other grounds* 624 F.2d 1182 (3d Cir.1980).

6. You represent the defendant in *Burris v. Warner* (Case K). Draft interrogatories directed to the plaintiff.

7. You represent the defendant Snow Cat in *Miyamoto v. Snow Cat* (Case C). Draft interrogatories directed to the Plaintiff.

8. You represent the plaintiff in *Vasquez v. Hot Dog Enterprises* (Case F). Draft interrogatories directed to the defendant.

9. You represent the defendant Hot Dog Enterprises in *Vasquez v. Hot Dog Enterprises* (Case F). Draft interrogatories directed to the plaintiff.

10. You represent the plaintiff in *Giacone v. City of Mitchell* (Case D). Draft interrogatories directed to the defendant.

Reconsidering and Redrafting Interrogatories

11. You represent the defendant Summit Insurance Company in *Pozdak v. Summit Insurance Company* (Case B). Fran Pozdak has sued for breach of contract seeking to recover $250,000 for the fire loss to his building and $1,000,000 for the loss of its contents. You defend claiming Pozdak committed arson which bars recovery under the contract. An associate in your firm prepares a draft of the following interrogatories:

> 1. Identify all persons who know anything relevant to the claims and defenses of this case.
>
> 2. Explain all reasons which support your factual and legal allegations and contentions in paragraph 2 of your Complaint that "Defendant Insurance Company breached its contract with the Plaintiff."
>
> 3. Why did you, several months before the fire, increase your coverage on your building to $250,000 and its contents to $1,000,000?
>
> 4. Have you ever taken any drugs?
>
> 5. If your answer to Interrogatory No. 5 is in the affirmative, explain:
>
> > The circumstances of each event;
> >
> > The identity of all persons present;
> >
> > Whether you ever received treatment for your problem and the time, location, and circumstance of such treatment.
>
> 6. Describe the car you owned on the day of the fire, its mileage before you began your trip to Stacy Lindberg's cabin before July 4, and its mileage after your return from the cabin after July 4.
>
> 7. Explain in specific detail the following information about Jan McCulrone:

(1) When did you hire McCulrone as an employee?

(2) What were the job duties and responsibilities?

(3) How effective or ineffective was McCulrone's work?

(4) When did you fire McCulrone and why?

(5) Explain the law applicable to your contention in paragraph 6 of the Complaint that states "clause 12 of the insurance contract between the Plaintiff and the Defendant is void based on public policy."

(a) Which of these interrogatories would you not submit, and why?

(b) Assume you would submit all, redraft those that need redrafting.

(c) What other interrogatories would you ask, and why?

(d) If you represented Pozdak and received this set of interrogatories, how would you respond to each question? Identify specific objections you would make.

Responding to Interrogatories

12. You represent the plaintiff in *Northern Motor Homes v. Danforth* (Case J). The defendants have submitted the following interrogatories to you and your client. Draft responses to them on behalf of your client:

(a) Describe all oral representations made to defendants by plaintiff regarding the Voyageur Motor Home on May 25.

(b) Describe all facts that support plaintiff's statement, made by Sara Duncan to the defendants on May 25, that the Voyageur Motor Home would get 16 miles per gallon on the highway.

(c) Describe the facts and dates upon which you base your Complaint allegations that defendants have "defaulted" on the retail installment contract.

(d) Describe the defects with the Voyageur Motor Home that caused the problems with the electrical system, engine, transmission, and gas mileage that were allegedly repaired between June 13 and June 22 by Northern Motor Homes.

(e) Why did you not charge the defendants for the repairs completed on July 11?

(f) What law supports plaintiff's refusal to accept defendants' revocation of acceptance of the Voyageur Motor Home? Why does the plaintiff continue to possess the camper in its service lot?

13. You represent the defendants in *Northern Motor Homes v. Danforth* (Case J). The plaintiff has submitted the following interrogatories to you and your clients. Draft responses to them on behalf of your clients.

(a) Describe all facts upon which you base your Answer, denying the statement in paragraph 2 of the Complaint that defendants "have defaulted on the contract."

(b) Describe all "statements" and "representations" plaintiff made to you as alleged in paragraph 3 of the Answer.

(c) Describe the specific amounts and types of actual, consequential, and incidental damages approximating the $15,000 alleged to have been incurred by defendants.

(d) Describe the amount and type of damages for lost vacation and leisure time alleged to have been suffered by defendants.

(e) Explain why you decided not to bring the Voyageur Camper to plaintiff for repairs on Monday, June 26, 19XX?

(f) When and how did defendants revoke acceptance of the Voyageur Motor Home? What law supports defendants' alleged revocation of acceptance?

14. You represent a party in a case to be assigned by your instructor in which another student represents the opposing party. Draft responses to the interrogatories prepared by the student attorney who represents the opposing party.

CHAPTER 8

REQUESTS FOR PRODUCTION AND PHYSICAL EXAMINATIONS

The harpoon was darted; the stricken whale flew forward; with igniting velocity the line ran through the groove—and ran afoul. Ahab stood to clear it; he did clear it, but the flying turn caught him round the neck, and voicelessly as Turkish mutes bowstring their victim he was shot out of the boat.

—Herman Melville
Moby Dick

§ 8.1 INTRODUCTION

You will never have the discovery difficulty Captain Ahab had in inspecting and copying Moby Dick. All you need do is shout "Give Away" [1] and you will have the document or thing from your opponent.

In federal cases, you will not have to shout or ask for anything and you will automatically receive documents and things from the other party. Federal Rule 26(a)(1)(B) requires that a party provide to all other parties documents, data, and things relevant to disputed facts alleged with particularity in the pleadings. This rule requires parties to disclose these materials and replaces the need for the party to submit a Rule 34 document production request for these materials. Federal Rule 26

§ 8.1

1. A whaling term meaning to begin the attack. Not related to a children's game called "Keep Away."

further requires that the parties meet and confer before they may serve each other with document production requests. The purpose of the rule is to have the parties discuss and agree what documents should be exchanged without the need for parties to draft and serve document production requests. In states which do not have a similar disclosure rule, you will need to shout and submit the document production request.

Federal Rule 34 permits any party to obtain from another party the production of documents, property, and tangible things merely by asking, if the materials were not disclosed or exchanged by agreement of the other party. Most state jurisdictions have adopted a rule similar to Rule 34.

Though it is not the exclusive discovery device for making available documents and objects, Rule 34 is the only discovery device that *requires* opponents to produce them. Rule 33(c) allows a responding party to produce business records in lieu of interrogatory answers; Rule 30(f)(1) authorizes documents and things to be produced during a deposition; and Rule 45 permits the discovery of tangible information from non-parties. A party can also request the production of objects and things informally, without relying upon a formal discovery request. But Rule 34 is the only device that has the enforcement capabilities to compel disclosure.

Rule 35 allows physical, mental, or blood examinations of a party. Rule 35 permits such examinations under more restrictive conditions than apply to Rule 34 production. The party to be examined must place his or her physical condition in issue, and an examination is authorized only by court order. These examinations are, however, readily available in the appropriate case, and they can be a useful discovery tool. Physical examinations are discussed in §§ 8.23–8.32.

§ 8.2 SAYING PLEASE

If you can say *please* to the other attorney you can frequently obtain access to documents and things without reliance on Rule 34. Telephone and letter requests frequently result in unilateral or reciprocal exchange of documentary information. It is a common practice for attorneys to forward copies of documents to each other, with each side bearing the rather minimal copying costs. These informal agreements save time and money, but they also have some drawbacks. The disclosing party has the flexibility to define the scope of the request and to decide what relevant documents will be voluntarily turned over. You cannot be certain that all the documents you think you requested were produced. The discovery rules do not provide any specific sanction for the breach of an informal disclosure agreement, although such a breach may constitute an ethical violation.

Formalizing the agreements helps reduce these drawbacks. A letter can be sent after an informal oral agreement, confirming the scope of the request and the expected items. Likewise, a letter sent after production, listing all the things disclosed, can ask whether they comprise all the writings and things requested within certain designated categories. A stipulation can be drafted and executed, listing the terms of the disclosure exchange; the scope of the things requested; and the time, place, and manner of disclosure. The more formal these agreements become, the closer they approximate the time and money involved with a simple Rule 34 request and the less attractive they become as discovery alternatives.

Federal rules encourage parties to exchange materials by agreement. Federal Rule 26(f) requires that the parties meet soon after the complaint has been served to discuss a discovery plan, including the exchange of relevant documents and things. Unless the parties have objections to each other's requests, a significant amount of materials are likely to be voluntarily exchanged by agreement without the need for a Rule 34 request.

Federal Rules 26(c) and 37 also require parties to discuss specific discovery disputes before pursuing a motion to compel discovery. If a party submits a Rule 34 document of production request which is properly objected to by the receiving party, the discovering party may bring a Rule 26(c) motion seeking an order from a court requiring the disclosure of these materials. Before the discovering party can file this motion with the court, the parties must make an effort to discuss the discovery dispute in an effort to resolve the matter without court intervention. A similar effort to discuss a discovery dispute with another party is required by Federal Rule 37 if a party seeks other sanctions for violation of the discovery rules. The intent of all these rules is to require attorneys to discuss problems increasing the likelihood the attorneys can solve their own disputes and to reduce the time spent by judges in reviewing motions and issuing orders.

§ 8.3 THE DOCUMENT DISCLOSURE RULE

Rule 26(a) *ipsa loquitur*:

> "Except to the extent otherwise stipulated or directed by order or local rule, a party shall, without awaiting a discovery request, provide to other parties: ... (B) A copy of, or a description by category and location, of all documents, data compilations, and tangible things in the possession, custody, or control of the party that are relevant to disputed facts alleged with particularity in the pleadings; (C) A computation of any category of damages claimed by the disclosing party, making available for inspection a copy under Rule 34 the documents or other evidentiary material, not privileged or protected from disclosure on which such computation is based, including materials bearing on the nature and extent of injuries suffered; and (D) For inspection and copying as under Rule 34 any insurance agreement under which any person carrying on an insurance business may be liable to satisfy part or all of the judgment which may be answered in the action or to indemnify or reimburse for payments made to satisfy the judgment."

§ 8.4 THE DOCUMENT DISCOVERY RULE

Rule 34 also *ipsa loquitur:*

> "Any party may serve on any other party a request (1) to produce and permit the party making the request, or someone acting on his behalf, to inspect and copy, any designated documents (including writings, drawings, graphs, charts, photographs, phonorecords, and other data compilations from which information can be obtained, translated, if necessary, by the respondent through detection devices into reasonably usable form), or to inspect and copy, test, or sample any tangible things which constitute or contain matters within the scope of Rule 26(b) and which are in the possession, custody or control of the party upon whom the request is served, or (2) to permit entry upon designated land or other property in the possession or control of the party upon whom the request is served for the purpose of inspection and measuring, surveying, photographing, testing, or sampling the property or any designated object or operation thereon, within the scope of Rule 26(b).[1]"

§ 8.5 PARTIES

The rule permits production only from parties. Rule 45 allows obtaining documents and things from non-parties at depositions, hearings, and trials through a subpoena duces tecum. If materials are available from both party and a non-party, it is preferable for a requesting party to use Rule 34 rather than to impose the discovery burden on a non-party through a subpoena.[1] Rule 34 requests can be directed to representative parties in a class action and to absentee class members in certain situations. The request submitted to absent class members must seek documents that are unavailable from the representative parties and must be relevant to a decision of common issues.[2]

§ 8.6 THE SCOPE OF RULE 26 DISCLOSURES

Rule 26 requires a party to disclose initially three types of materials:

1. *Documents, data compilations, and tangible things that are relevant to disputed fact alleged with particularity in the pleadings.* A disclosing party must describe the documents, data compilations or tangible things and may choose to provide a copy to the other side. A party is likely to provide copies of materials that are supportive of positions or that the party wants the other side to have without submitting a Rule 34 request. A party has to disclose all documents that

§ 8.4

1. Fed.R.Civ.P. 34(a).

§ 8.5

1. *See Bada Co. v. Montgomery Ward & Co.,* 32 F.R.D. 208, 209–210 (E.D..Tenn. 1963).

2. *Dellums v. Powell,* 566 F.2d 167 (D.C.Cir.1977), *cert. denied* 438 U.S. 916, 98 S.Ct. 3146, 57 L.Ed.2d 1161 (1978), *rehearing denied* 439 U.S. 886, 99 S.Ct. 234, 58 L.Ed.2d 201 (1978), *on remand* 490 F.Supp. 70 (D.D.C.1980), *judgment affirmed in part and reversed in part* 660 F.2d 802 (D.C.Cir. 1981).

are "reasonably available" but need not necessarily create documents in order to provide some materials to the other parties. This rule only requires the automatic disclosure of materials that may be relevant or available and that relate to allegations of disputed facts alleged with particularity in the pleadings. See § 5.3.5.

2. *All documents or other evidentiary material relating to the computation of damages or to the nature and extent of injuries suffered, and excluding documents and materials which are privileged or otherwise protected from disclosure.* This rule requires a party seeking damages to provide written documentation supporting such damages. The rule protects from disclosure documents that are claimed to be privileged or otherwise protected by a rule of procedure or evidence. See § 5.6.

3. *Insurance Agreements.* A party must disclose the existence of insurance agreements and must provide for the inspection or copying of such agreements by other parties. This rule requires that all liability insurance policies be made available for inspection and copying. Other documents regarding insurance, such as insurance applications, may be discoverable pursuant to a Rule 34 document production request.

Federal Rule 26(a)(2)(B) further requires a party to provide additional disclosures at a later stage of litigation. This rule requires that a party who identifies trial experts must also accompany this disclosure with a written report prepared and signed by the trial expert, or by a witness who is retained or specially employed to provide expert testimony, or by an employee of the party regularly involved in giving expert testimony. The report must contain a complete statement of expert opinions, bases for opinions, data, information, exhibits, qualifications, publications, compensation, and other information. Section 5.8.3 explains these disclosures in detail.

Further, the federal rules require additional disclosures of documents and materials at the pretrial stage of a case. Federal Rule 26(a)(3) requires that a party disclose to all other parties the identification of all exhibits and documents expected to be presented at trial. Ordinarily, the initial disclosure and document production rules would produce these materials before the pretrial stage. See § 5.11.

§ 8.7 THE SCOPE OF RULE 34 REQUESTS

The scope of discovery under Rule 34 is identical with other discovery devices outlined in Rule 26 and explained in § 5.3. "The rule authorizes the broadest sweep of access, inspection, examination, testing, copying, and photographing of documents or objects in possession or control of another party."[1] A showing of good cause is no longer a requirement for requested materials, and the mass of confusing and conflicting case law interpreting "good cause" is now left for legal

§ 8.7

1. 8 Charles A. Wright & Arthur R. Miller, Federal Practice and Procedure § 2206, at 607 (1970 and Supp.1994).

historians. Instead, the Rule 26 standard of relevance establishes the scope of all types of discoverable information. Some courts require a more restrictive standard in some situations: a Rule 34 request that disrupts the opposition's routine, creates a hazard, or may produce only marginally reliable information may require the showing of necessity before a party can obtain access.[2]

The following categories of documents and things are discoverable:

1. *Documents Defined as "Writings, Drawings, Graphs, Charts, Photographs, Phono-records, and Other Data Compilations. . . ."* Anything that contains some written, printed, recorded information or images is discoverable. Such documents can be inspected and copied. A later section (§ 8.19) discusses the effect of the rule on computerized information.

2. *Tangible Things That are Discoverable Under Rule 26.* Any object can be inspected, copied, tested or sampled. Sections 8.17, 8.18, below, discuss testing concerns and procedures.

3. *Land and Other Property.* Such real and personal property may be inspected, measured, surveyed, photographed, tested, and sampled.

Most, if not all, cases involve some sort of documents, and Rule 34 is the routine way of discovering them. A growing number of cases, such as product liability and environmental actions, involve tangible and real property. Increasingly, cases also involve access to property for innovative discovery purposes. Treatment facilities may need to be inspected, relative to their conditions and procedures, in a case seeking better treatment for the residents.[3] An inspection tour of a factory may be necessary to obtain evidence for a product liability or employment-discrimination case.[4] These situations may first require a discovering party to use less intrusive discovery devices, like a deposition, to establish a need for Rule 34 access.[5] Rule 34 may also be an appropriate device to create tangible things for discovery purposes. It may be possible to require a party, for example, to produce a voice exemplar by speaking into a tape recorder.[6]

§ 8.8 POSSESSION, CUSTODY, AND CONTROL

All these documents, things, and property must be in the possession, control, and custody of a party. Possession and custody include both actual and constructive possession and custody, while control means the party has a legal right to obtain the documents.[1] Case law has both clarified and confused the discoverability of various items:

2. *See Belcher v. Bassett Furniture,* 588 F.2d 904, 908–910 (4th Cir.1978).

3. *See Hubbard v. Rubbermaid, Inc.,* 78 F.R.D. 631 (D.Md.1978); *Morales v. Turman,* 59 F.R.D. 157 (E.D.Tex.1972).

4. *Belcher v. Bassett Furniture, Inc.,* 588 F.2d 904 (4th Cir.1978); *National Dairy Products Corp. v. L.D. Shreiber & Co.,* 61 F.R.D. 581 (E.D.Wis.1973).

5. *See* James L. Underwood, A Guide to Federal Discovery Rules 128 (1979).

6. *See Haaf v. Grams,* 355 F.Supp. 542 (D.Minn.1973).

§ 8.8

1. 8 Charles A. Wright & Arthur R. Miller, Federal Practice and Procedure § 2210, at 621–625 (1970 and Supp.1994).

1. Non-party witness statements are considered trial preparation materials, requiring a showing of substantial need and undue hardship before they may be obtained by a party.[2] Because non-party witnesses may obtain their own statement without any special showing, the friendly witness may request a copy at the urging or on behalf of one of the parties.[3]

2. Documents and things in the possession, control, or custody of a party's attorney are discoverable, excluding trial preparation materials and written lawyer mental impressions.[4]

3. Documents of which a party does not have copies, but has a right or opportunity to copy, must be produced.[5]

4. Documents a party possesses, but which belong to a third person who is not a party, may have to be disclosed. A party need not "own" the documents; it is enough if the party possesses them.[6]

5. Documents prepared by or under the direction or supervision of an expert expected to be called at trial, including reports embodying preliminary conclusions,[7] excluding trial preparation materials and lawyers' written mental impressions, are discoverable.

6. Documents and objects that a party possesses, controls, or has custody of are discoverable, even though such records and things may be beyond the territorial jurisdiction of the court.[8]

7. Things and documents in possession of a party's liability insurer are discoverable in an action against its insured, on the basis that the insurer is a real party with an interest.[9]

8. A corporation is required to produce documents held by its subsidiaries.[10]

9. A party has control over income tax returns available from the IRS.[11]

10. Hospital and physician records of a party have been held to be both under the control [12] and not under the control [13] of a patient.

2. Civil Trial Manual 184–185 (ALI–ABA 1974).

3. *Ossenfort v. Associated Milk Producers, Inc.*, 254 N.W.2d 672, 681 (Minn.1977).

4. *In re Ruppert,* 309 F.2d 97, 98 (6th Cir.1962).

5. *Herbst v. Able,* 63 F.R.D. 135, 137 (S.D.N.Y.1972); *Buckley v. Vidal,* 50 F.R.D. 271, 274 (S.D.N.Y.1970).

6. *Societe Internationale Pour Participations Industrielles Et Commerciales, S.A. v. Rogers,* 357 U.S. 197, 200, 204, 78 S.Ct. 1087, 1089, 1091, 2 L.Ed.2d 1255 (1958); *United States v. National Broadcasting Co.,* 65 F.R.D. 415, 419 (C.D.Cal.1974), *appeal dismissed* 421 U.S. 940, 95 S.Ct. 1668, 44 L.Ed.2d 97 (1975).

7. *Quadrini v. Sikorsky Aircraft Div., United Aircraft Corp.,* 74 F.R.D. 594 (D.Conn.1977).

8. *In re Harris,* 27 F.Supp. 480, 481 (S.D.N.Y.1939).

9. *Bingle v. Liggett Drug Co.,* 11 F.R.D. 593, 594 (D.Mass.1951).

10. *Advance Labor Service, Inc. v. Hartford Accident & Indemnity Co.,* 60 F.R.D. 632, 634 (N.D.Ill.1973).

11. *Reeves v. Pennsylvania Railroad Co.,* 80 F.Supp. 107, 109 (D.Del.1948).

12. *Schwartz v. Travelers Insurance Co.,* 17 F.R.D. 330 (S.D.N.Y.1954).

13. *Reeves v. Pennsylvania Railroad Co.,* 80 F.Supp. 107, 109 (D.Del.1948); *Greene v. Sears, Roebuck & Co.,* 40 F.R.D. 14, 16 (N.D.Ohio 1966).

§ 8.9 TIMING OF DISCLOSURES AND REQUESTS

Federal Rule 26 governs the timing of affirmative disclosures. The rule requires document disclosures to be made shortly after the parties have met and conferred pursuant to Federal Rule 26(f). This meeting will typically occur early in the case. Additional disclosures about expert reports occur at later stages of litigation after the party has identified expert trial witnesses. Pretrial disclosure of documents occur at the pretrial stage of litigation.

Federal Rule 34(b) provides that document production requests may not be served before the time specified in Federal Rule 26(d), without leave of court or written stipulation of the other parties. Rule 26(d) states that discovery requests may not be served until the parties have met in accord with Rule 26(f). The parties may vary this time and allow document production requests to be served and responded at any time that does not conflict with the deadline provisions of a court order. This agreement may be common in situations when parties seek documents from each other. Leave of court may be sought in accord with the motion brought under an applicable provision of Rule 26 or Rule 34 or a scheduling order pursuant to Rule 16.

§ 8.10 THE REQUEST PROCEDURE

A party wanting to inspect documents and things or to enter property usually needs merely to serve a request setting forth the what, when, where, and how of the examination. A request may accompany a deposition notice requiring the party deponent to bring certain documents to a deposition. Requests for production may be used in any sequence with other discovery devices to precede or supplement other information. The rule requires that a request: (1) set forth with reasonable particularity a description of the items to be discovered; and (2) specify a reasonable time, place, and manner for making the inspection and copying.

Official Form 24 of the Federal Rules of Civil Procedure contains an illustration of a proper request:

> Plaintiff *A.B.* requests defendant *D.C.* to respond within ______ days to the following requests:
>
> (1) That defendant produce and permit plaintiff to inspect and to copy each of the following documents: [*Here list the documents either individually or by category and describe each of them.*]
>
> [*Here state the time, place, and manner of making the inspection and performance of any related acts.*]
>
> (2) That defendant produce and permit plaintiff to inspect and to copy, test, or sample each of the following objects: [*Here list the objects either individually or by category and describe each of them.*]
>
> [*Here state the time, place, and manner of making the inspection and performance of any related acts.*]

(3) That defendant permit plaintiff to enter [*here describe property to be entered*] and to inspect and to photograph, test, or sample [*here describe the portion of the real property and the objects to be inspected*].

[*Here state the time, place, and manner of making the inspection and performance of any related acts.*]

§ 8.11 REASONABLE PARTICULARITY

How do you know for certain whether the request you have drafted designates the items sought "with reasonable particularity"? You could ask the law-school classmate who stands one rank ahead of you in class standing. Or you could apply common sense. You can never be absolutely certain that your request meets the standard of reasonable particularity, because it is not a standard susceptible to an exact definition; it is, rather, a flexible standard that varies with the circumstances of a case.[1] Descriptions of materials by the subject matter they contain, by particular classification, or by definite time periods, is usually specific enough.[2] Moreover, there is a simple, two-prong test that, if met, reduces recurring nightmares about "reasonable particularity." The request should be sufficient to: (1) allow a person of ordinary intelligence to say "I know what they want;"[3] and (2) permit a judge to determine whether all the requested items have been produced.[4]

Rule 34 allows descriptions of the items sought to be stated with exactitude and precision ("I want the June 27, 2:00 P.M. to 2:45 P.M. tape") or with generally descriptive categorization ("I want all the files that contain the law school's bronzed bluebook exam answers"). However the request is phrased, it must meet the two-prong test described above and must occasionally comply with more stringent requirements imposed by case law. Most courts allow discovery of general categories of items if the description is "easily understood."[5] Some courts expect a party who has knowledge about the documents sought to be specific in designating the items requested.[6] And almost all courts disallow general

§ 8.11

1. *See, e.g., Mallinckrodt Chemical Works v. Goldman, Sachs & Co.*, 58 F.R.D. 348, 353 (S.D.N.Y.1973); *Richland Wholesale Liquors, Inc. v. Joseph E. Seagram & Sons, Inc.*, 40 F.R.D. 480, 481 (D.S.C.1966).

2. *SEC v. American Beryllium & Oil Corp.*, 47 F.R.D. 66 (S.D.N.Y.1968).

3. *See Mallinckrodt Chemical Works v. Goldman, Sachs & Co.*, 58 F.R.D. 348 (S.D.N.Y.1973).

4. 8 Charles A. Wright & Arthur R. Miller, Federal Practice and Procedure § 2211, at 611 (1970 and Supp.1994). The cases do not indicate whether both the attorneys and judges involved must be of "ordinary intelligence."

5. *See Hillside Amusement Co. v. Warner Brothers Pictures, Inc.*, 7 F.R.D. 260, 262 (S.D.N.Y.1944).

6. "Any statements of witnesses" discoverable: *Wilson v. David*, 21 F.R.D. 217, 219 (W.D.Mich.1957). "All photographs" of the accident scene discoverable: *Simper v. Trimble*, 9 F.R.D. 598, 600 (W.D.Mo. 1949). "Disbursement books, canceled checks, check stubs" discoverable: *Michel v. Meier*, 8 F.R.D. 464, 477 (W.D.Pa.1948). "Receipts, settlements, compromises and releases" discoverable: *Walling v. R.L. McGinley Co.*, 4 F.R.D. 149, 150 (E.D.Tenn. 1943). "Documents, records and correspondence" discoverable: *Quemos Theatre* descriptions that are vague, ambiguous, or too broad. Afflicted with this malady are requests seeking, for example, "all diagrams or documents containing drawings," [7] "written communications about financial transactions," [8] "all data relating to certain" facts,[9] or simply "file pertaining to the defendants." [10]

There are better techniques, for example the "33–34 One–Two." You submit a Rule 33 interrogatory asking the other party to describe certain documents, and then after receiving the answer, you submit a Rule 34 request containing the document whose description appears in the interrogatory answer. There is also the "33–34 One." You combine in one document Rule 34 requests with Rule 33 interrogatories. Since Rule 34 merely requires a request to be "in writing," a request, in a set of interrogatories, that a party produce "all documents identified in the preceding answers" is an appropriate Rule 34 request. You can also add a written snicker to your Rule 34 request.

§ 8.12 DRAFTING TECHNIQUES

The drafting suggestions described in the preceding chapter (§ 7.4) on interrogatories apply equally to requests for production. You want to draft with some specificity, to avoid allowing the other side to withhold some documents, while at the same time drafting with enough breadth to make certain that no existing documents escape your attention. Two drafting techniques that may be employed to make requests escape-proof and all-encompassing are: (1) draft requests seeking both specifically designated items and generally described items, and (2) use definitions. For example:

> Furnish all documents concerning any contractual breach by defendant alleged in paragraph 2 of the complaint including but not limited to:
>
> The original and all copies of each letter or written communication between the plaintiff and defendant between May 1, 1991, and August 1, 1991;
>
> All writings submitted by the plaintiff to the Banking Commissioner which contain any reference to the defendant;
>
> All complaints plaintiff received relating to the conduct of defendant from May 1, 1991, to September 1, 1991. Complaints include any writings submitted by any person, corporation, organization, agency or other entity that in any way refer to the alleged conduct of the defendant described in the complaint.

Co. v. Warner Brothers Pictures, Inc., 35 F.Supp. 949, 950 (D.N.J.1940).

7. *Stark v. American Dredging Co.*, 3 F.R.D. 300, 302 (E.D.Pa.1943).

8. *Wharton v. Lybrand, Ross Brothers & Montgomery*, 41 F.R.D. 177, 180 (E.D.N.Y. 1966). *See also Paiewonsky v. Paiewonsky*, 50 F.R.D. 379, 381 (D.V.I.1970).

9. *Dynatron Corp. v. United States Rubber Co.*, 27 F.R.D. 480, 481 (D.Conn.1961).

10. *Balistrieri v. O'Farrell*, 57 F.R.D. 567, 569 (E.D.Wis.1972).

The most important definition is usually the meaning of the word *document,* which can be expanded beyond the definition provided in Rule 34 to include the following, and then attached to a request:

> The term *documents* means all writings of any kind, including the originals and all non-identical copies, whether different from the originals by reason of any notation made on such copies or otherwise, including without limitation, correspondence, memoranda, notes, diaries, statistics, letters, telegrams, minutes, contracts, reports, studies, checks, statements, receipts, returns, summaries, pamphlets, books, interoffice and intra-office communications, notations of any sort of conversations, telephone calls, meetings or other communications, bulletins, printed matter, computer print-outs, teletypes, telefax, invoices, worksheets, all drafts, alterations, modifications, changes, and amendments of any of the foregoing, graphic or oral records or representations of any kind (including, without limitation, photographs, charts, graphs, microfiche, microfilm, videotapes, recordings, motion pictures), and any electronic, mechanical, or electric records or representations of any kind (including, without limitation, tapes, cassettes, discs, recordings, and computer memories).
>
> Whew.

The request for production can include a preface and instructions similar to the introduction to interrogatories (*see* § 7.3) and for the same reasons. A Rule 34 introduction can include one or more of the following or similar statements:

> 1. If your response is that the documents are not in your possession or custody, describe in detail the unsuccessful efforts you made to locate the records.
>
> 2. If your response is that the documents are not in your control, identify who has control and the location of the records.
>
> 3. If a request for production seeks a specific document or an itemized category that is not in your possession, control, or custody, provide any documents you have that contain all or part of the information contained in the requested document or category.
>
> 4. Identify the source of each of the documents you produce.

§ 8.13 TIME, PLACE, MANNER

Rule 34(b) requires that a stated time, place, and manner for inspection and copying be included in the request for production. The date must be scheduled at least 30 days after service of the request because the other party has at least 30 days to respond. The hour usually is during business hours. The place usually is the location of the documents [1] and occasionally the location of some copying equipment. The manner depends on the kind of items requested. The delineation in

§ 8.13

1. *Petruska v. Johns–Manville,* 83 F.R.D. 32 (E.D.Pa.1979).

advance of a specific time, place, and manner can be difficult in some cases, and it is a common practice to use less definite statements in the request. It is sufficient if the requests include an alternative statement such as:

1. The time, place, and manner will be mutually agreed upon by the parties at a later date;

2. The time and place will be determined by the responding party;

3. The production and copying will occur at a specific time and specific place in a specific manner, but the responding party may contact the requesting party to arrange a more convenient time and place;

4. The responding party may make copies of the documents and forward such copies to the requesting party with a bill for the copying expenses.

§ 8.14 RESPONSE

Rule 34 requires the party receiving the request to serve a written response upon the requesting party (and all other parties) within 30 days after service of the request (or within 45 days if the request is served with the summons and complaint). A judge, upon a motion, may shorten or lengthen the time. The responding party may reply in one or more ways to the request.

1. Abracadabra! Produce the requested items according to the suggested time, place, and manner. A party must produce all materials sought that are discoverable in response to a non-objectionable request. Rule 34(b) specifically dictates how a party produces certain documents. It provides that "A party who produces documents for inspection shall produce them as they are kept in the usual course of business or shall organize them and label them to correspond with the categories in the request."

But not always. The requesting party and not the responding party may be required to organize documents if it would take a substantial amount of time to number a large number of documents.[1] A requesting party may also ask for too much. For example, a party may request written compilations of data that the responding party does not have. The responding party can then make available documents containing the data, which the requesting party can then use to make the compilations. This response comports with the duty to respond under Rule 34.[2]

2. Disclose the requested items but at another time, place, and manner agreeable to the requesting attorney.

§ 8.14

1. *United States for Use and Benefit of Schneider, Inc. v. Rust Engineering Co.*, 72 F.R.D. 195 (W.D.Pa.1976).

2. *Webb v. Westinghouse Elec. Corp.*, 81 F.R.D. 431 (E.D.Pa.1978).

3. Serve a written response upon the requesting party, stating that inspection and related activities will be permitted for the designated items or categories at the suggested or at another time, place, and manner.

4. Move for a protective order under Rule 26(c) to safeguard the disclosure of certain items.

5. Ignore the request (although this is not authorized by the rule).

6. Object to the production and state the reasons for the objection. If an objection is made to part of a request, the non-objectionable parts of the request must be satisfied by appropriate production.

The first three responses comprise the typically cooperative response by an attorney. The party producing the documents must do so by organizing and labeling them, to correspond to the discovery requests, or must allow the other party to inspect documents as the documents are kept in the ordinary course of business. This manner of production is clearly mandated by Rule 34. The current rule does not countenance the deliberate or negligent mixture of critical documents with irrelevant documents to obscure the location and importance of the critical ones. The responding party has the obligation to designate specific documents, and should not play games by disclosing edited information or truckloads of immaterial documents.

The fourth response has been discussed in Chapter 5 and may also be the subject of a stipulation between the attorneys.[3] The fifth response is deplorable and is dealt with in detail in Chapter 10 on enforcement of discovery requests. The sixth response has been discussed in the context of objections to interrogatories in Chapter 7, and many of the same considerations apply to objections to requests for production, discussed in the next subsection.

§ 8.15 OBJECTIONS

A responding party may object to part or all of an item or category requested for production and may withhold from discovery the objected-to documents. All objections must be bona fide and provide the responding party with substantial justification for the refusal to disclose. Even if there are valid technical or substantive objections, as a strategic matter you need first to determine whether the harm, if any, in disclosing an item justifies the effort required in opposing discovery, and second, to determine what impact your refusal to disclose may have upon the opposing lawyer's willingness to cooperate with you in your requests for production.

The more common objections[1] to Rule 34 requests state that the documents or items:

3. *See* §§ 4.10 and 4.11.1 for discussion of the use of protective orders and stipulations respectively. *See also Thermorama, Inc. v. Shiller,* 271 Minn. 79, 85, 135 N.W.2d 43, 47 (1965); *Snyker v. Snyker,* 245 Minn. 405, 408, 72 N.W.2d 357, 359 (1955).

§ 8.15

1. An objection that is neither common nor well recognized, but is peculiar to a Rule 34 request by a government agency, is an objection based upon the Fourth Amendment's prohibition against unreasonable

- Are not in the possession, control, or custody of the responding party; [2]
- Are no longer in existence; [3]
- Are not yet prepared; [4]
- Are not discoverable under Rule 34; [5]
- Are irrelevant beyond the scope of Rule 26; [6]
- Are public records and available through requester's own efforts; [7]
- Are trial preparation materials; [8]
- Are mental impressions or opinions of a lawyer; [9]
- Are materials from experts who will not testify at trial; [10]
- Have an 18–minute gap; [11]
- Impose undue burden or expense; [12]
- Are sought through an overbroad request; [13]
- Are sought through a vague and ambiguous request; [14]
- The inspection of property is hazardous or extensively disrupts operations; [15]
- The inspection of land invades the privacy of the property owner; [16]

The party who interposes the objection must show its validity and grounds.[17] This burden may be met by factual affidavits from a party or by legal memoranda from the attorney. In some cases the requesting party may also have a burden. Courts may require a requesting party to

searches and seizures. *See* 8 Charles A. Wright & Arthur R. Miller, Federal Practice and Procedure § 2020, at 585 (1970 and Supp.1994).

2. *See* Fed.R.Civ.P. 34(a)(1).

3. *See William A. Meier Glass Co. v. Anchor Hocking Glass Corp.,* 11 F.R.D. 487, 491 (W.D.Pa.1951).

4. *See Soetaert v. Kansas City Coca Cola Bottling Co.,* 16 F.R.D. 1, 2 (W.D.Mo.1954).

5. *See Haaf v. Grams,* 355 F.Supp. 542 (D.Minn.1973).

6. Fed.R.Civ.P. 26(b)(1).

7. *United Cigar–Whelen Stores Corp. v. Philip Morris, Inc.,* 21 F.R.D. 107 (S.D.N.Y. 1957).

8. Fed.R.Civ.P. 26(b)(3).

9. Fed.R.Civ.P. 26(b)(3).

10. Fed.R.Civ.P. 26(b)(4).

11. Remember Rosemary Woods.

12. Fed.R.Civ.P. 26(c); *Baskerville v. Baskerville,* 246 Minn. 496, 507, 75 N.W.2d 762, 769 (1956).

13. *Biliske v. American Live Stock Insurance Co.,* 73 F.R.D. 124 (W.D.Okl.1977).

14. Documents and things to be produced should be described with reasonable particularity, but the test is a relative one, depending on the degree of knowledge of the requesting party in each particular case. *Roebling v. Anderson,* 257 F.2d 615, 620, 621 (D.C.Cir.1958); *Flickinger v. Aetna Casualty & Surety Co.,* 37 F.R.D. 533, 535 (W.D.Pa.1965).

15. *Belcher v. Bassett Furniture Industries Inc.,* 588 F.2d 904, 908 (4th Cir.1978).

16. *See* Kenneth B. Hughes & Carol E. Anderson, Discovery: A Competition between the Right of Privacy and the Right to Know, 23 U.Fla.L.Rev. 289 (1971).

17. *See* 8 Charles A. Wright & Arthur R. Miller, Federal Practice and Procedure §§ 2206–2207, at 607–614 (1970 and Supp. 1994).

show necessity for the Rule 34 access if such a request creates a hazardous situation or produces minimally reliable information.[18]

Objections to Rule 34 requests, like objections to other discovery requests, must be made in good faith and with care. There exists a temptation, because of the difficulties inherent in complying with a Rule 34 request, to yell "It's impossible." Objections based on undue burdens or overbroad requests are scrutinized by judges and often overruled, because the very nature of discovery renders such requests quite possible. A responding party itself may have created part of the impossibility claimed, because of inadequate record management or poor filing systems or because the materials were maintained in a way that is undecipherable to the requesting party. Courts require responding parties to produce documents in an orderly and understandable way.[19]

The party who receives an objection to part or all of the request may redraft the request to eliminate the objections or may attempt to negotiate with the responding attorney to reach a compromise on disclosure. Courts look very, very kindly on these good-faith efforts to resolve an objection and may mandate by local rule that these efforts be made. A party seeking materials that may place too heavy a burden on the responding party can reduce the burden by offering assistance in collating or collecting documents or by paying the costs of their production.[20] Should these efforts fail, the requesting party may seek a Rule 37 order compelling production or may pout in a corner of a law office.

§ 8.16 CONDUCTING THE EXAMINATION

The extent of your examination depends on the nature of the item. Rule 34(a) provides you with the right to inspect and copy documents; to inspect, copy, test, and sample tangible things; to enter and to inspect, measure, survey, photograph, test, or sample land and property; to observe machinery or manufacturing, production, distribution, and other business processes.

Your inspection and perusal of the requested documents and things should proceed with two primary considerations: (1) Has everything you requested been turned over to you? Or too little? Or too much? (2) Do the records indicate that other relevant documents are still outstanding?

You should maintain some means of listing and identifying the exact documents and things examined. A good record can later quell any questions about what was produced when. You can create such a record with some distinctive mark or initials. Although you need the permission of your adversary if you plan somehow to mark the items, your adversary usually has a similar interest and will cooperate in maintaining an accurate and complete record.

18. *See* James L. Underwood, A Guide to Federal Discovery Rules 131 (1979).

19. *Alliance to End Repression v. Rockford,* 75 F.R.D. 441 (N.D.Ill.1977); *Stapleton v. Kawasaki Heavy Industries Limited,* 69 F.R.D. 489 (N.D.Ga.1975).

20. *See Shang v. Hotel Waldorf–Astoria Corp.,* 77 F.R.D. 468 (S.D.N.Y.1978).

Copying of the items is usually at your own expense. You can arrange to use the adversary's copying equipment and reimburse your opponent or arrange for your own copying facilities. You may wish to photograph or tag some items as physical evidence. The manner of copying or recording is usually one of accommodation and cooperation between the attorneys.

§ 8.17 TESTING

You have a right to test certain items. The decision to test, according to one commentator, turns on a consideration of five questions:

> 1. Is the test I am considering likely to do more harm than good, by destroying or materially altering evidence which, in its present condition, provides vivid proof of the point I am urging?
>
> 2. Is it feasible to consider deferring the testing until the trial, and conducting it as a courtroom experiment?
>
> 3. Will the disadvantages of my proposed testing outweigh whatever I may gain from it?
>
> 4. Am I confident enough of the results of the tests to stake my case on them?
>
> 5. Even if my proposed tests are permissible under the rules of discovery, will the court receive them in evidence at the trial? [1]

Whatever testing you do must be done with the full knowledge of the opponent. Your request for production should spell out in detail what and how you intend to test. It is wise to seek a written stipulation or a court order detailing the testing procedure. This is mandatory if testing destroys or alters material evidence.[2] Testing may then proceed along the lines dictated by the stipulation or order, with an exhaustive or videotaped record made of everything that occurs during the testing.

It is also wise to obtain a test report in the form of a letter, so that you may later claim a privilege or work-product protection for such information. It is not wise, however, to request two reports, one a slanted report to disclose to the opposing side, and the other a "confidential and candid report" for your purposes only. The contents of both reports may be discoverable. The existence of both reports is certainly discoverable and a proper subject for cross-examination at the trial. If a report appears to be incomplete or inadequate, merely request a supplementary report. Their discoverability depends on the status of the expert.[3]

§ 8.17

1. Quoted from Walter Barthold, Attorney's Guide to Effective Discovery Techniques 187–188 (1975) (footnotes omitted).

2. *See City of Kingsport v. SCM Corp.,* 352 F.Supp. 287 (E.D.Tenn.1972).

3. Experts are discussed in § 5.8 of this text. *See also Leininger v. Swadner,* 279 Minn. 251, 156 N.W.2d 254, 259–260 (1968).

§ 8.18 DESTRUCTIVE TESTING

Although most testing under Rule 34 consists of examination and tests that can be repeatedly performed, it is sometimes advantageous or necessary to conduct destructive examinations or tests. Although attorneys have found a need for such testing for years, the recent surge in product liability litigation has dramatically increased the number of requests for destructive testing.

Courts require a specific court order prior to the conducting of destructive tests.[1] Even as a practical matter, however, a party desiring to conduct destructive testing of any evidence should want to obtain an order approving such testing. If an order is not procured, a compelling argument exists at the time of trial to exclude the evidence obtained from the testing on the basis of unfairness, since opposing parties have not had an opportunity to conduct such tests. The destruction itself of the evidence may give rise to an even stronger argument at trial against the party destroying the evidence.[2]

The trial court has discretion in deciding whether to issue an order allowing destructive testing.[3] The court's discretion is normally guided by two factors: the usefulness or need of the discovery to the party requesting it and the prejudice or handicap that will occur to the party or parties opposing destructive testing.[4] The court becomes involved in the destructive testing dispute upon either the motion of the parties seeking testing to compel production of the article to be tested or upon the motion for protective order from the party holding the article to be tested. Most frequently the motion to compel production of the article is met by a motion for a protective order, and both motions are heard at once.

Courts, in attempting to balance the need of the party to obtain information regarding the article with an underlying concern for fairness, generally either deny the right of any party to conduct destructive testing,[5] postpone such testing until shortly before trial, or most frequently, permit the testing under the provisions of a protective order.[6] The terms of such a protective order frequently include:

§ 8.18

1. *Cameron v. District Court, In and For First Judicial Dist.*, 193 Colo. 286, 565 P.2d 925, 931 (1977); *Sarver v. Barrett Ace Hardware, Inc.*, 63 Ill.2d 454, 349 N.E.2d 28, 30 (1976).

2. In a criminal case the introduction of destructive testing results was held to be reversible error. *People v. Dodsworth*, 60 Ill.App.3d 207, 17 Ill.Dec. 450, 376 N.E.2d 449 (1978).

3. "Destructive testing is not a matter of right, but lies in the sound discretion of the trial court." *Cameron v. District Court, In and For First Judicial Dist.*, 193 Colo. 286, 565 P.2d 925, 929 (1977).

4. *See Sarver v. Barrett Ace Hardware, Inc.*, 63 Ill.2d 454, 349 N.E.2d 28, 30 (1976).

5. *Home Insurance Co. v. Cleveland Electrical Illuminating Co.*, 7 Fed.R.Serv.2d 731 (N.D.Ohio 1959); *State ex rel. Crawford v. Moody*, 477 S.W.2d 438 (Mo.App.1972).

6. *Cameron v. District Court, In and For First Judicial Dist.*, 193 Colo. 286, 565 P.2d 925, 931 (1977); *Sarver v. Barrett Ace Hardware, Inc.*, 63 Ill.2d 454, 349 N.E.2d 28, 31 (1976); *Foster–Lipkins Corp. v. Suburban Propane Gas Corp.*, 72 Misc.2d 457, 339 N.Y.S.2d 581 (1973); *Edwardes v. Southampton Hospital Association*, 53 Misc.2d 187, 278 N.Y.S.2d 283 (1967); *Martin v. Reynolds Metals Corp.*, 297 F.2d 49 (9th Cir.1961); *Petruk v. South Ferry Real-*

- A testing plan;
- An opportunity prior to testing for all other parties to examine and photograph the article to be tested;
- A notice to all parties of the testing;
- The right of any party to be present at the testing, with consultants or experts if necessary;
- Careful and thorough recording of test activities and test results;
- The availability of test results to all parties;
- The availability of reports by persons conducting the testing to all parties;
- The right of other parties to take additional samples for similar testing, if material is available.

Although the concern of courts in destructive-testing cases is generally toward preventing a party from being prejudiced in the pending litigation by the destruction of crucial evidence, testing is sometimes also sought that threatens to cause monetary damage to the item being tested. If this situation occurs, the party conducting the testing should be held liable for damages.[7] A practical solution to this problem, perhaps, is for the court to require the parties seeking the tests to post an appropriate bond to protect against any damage that might be done to the article being tested.[8] An attorney should not be misled, however, into thinking that a surety bond will prevent hardship to the party opposing discovery in all respects. If evidence is destroyed by testing in which the party opposing destructive testing is not allowed to participate, the difficulty of proving recovery under the surety bond is no less than the difficulty of proving the underlying action. Thus the surety bond may be an illusory protection to parties opposing destructive testing.[9]

§ 8.19 COMPUTERIZED INFORMATION

Rule 34(a) permits the discovery of any "data compilations from which information can be obtained, translated, if necessary, by the respondent through detection devices into reasonably usable form." In other words, documentary information stored on punched data cards, electronic disks, recording tapes, and computer banks is discoverable. What's more, the responding party must furnish it in a manner understandable to the requesting party and must bear the cost and expense of

ty Co., 2 A.D.2d 533, 157 N.Y.S.2d 249, 255 (1956).

7. *Fisher v. United States Fidelity & Guaranty Co.*, 246 F.2d 344, 350 (7th Cir. 1957).

8. *See Williams v. Continental Oil Co.*, 215 F.2d 4 (10th Cir.1954), *cert. denied* 348 U.S. 928, 75 S.Ct. 341, 99 L.Ed. 728 (1955); *Arkansas State Highway Commission v. Stanley*, 234 Ark. 428, 353 S.W.2d 173, 177 (1962).

9. *See People v. Dodsworth*, 60 Ill. App.3d 207, 17 Ill.Dec. 450, 376 N.E.2d 449 (1978) (reversible error to introduce destructive testing results in criminal case).

compiling the data and translating them into a readable printout or some other machine-readable format.[1]

Courts draw a distinction between producing computer information and designing new computer programs to extract data; they require the former and deny the latter unless the requesting party bears all such programming costs.[2] A party can seek an order protecting it from excessive expenses, and parties can negotiate to share the costs. In some cases a party may prefer to obtain programs or raw data in a format that can be used on that party's computer. In this fashion, by analysis and review, facts may be uncovered that might otherwise remain hidden in a computer printout.

Rule 34 is deliberately broad to accommodate disclosures of all types of information and provides safeguards through Rule 26 and Rule 37 to balance proper disclosures. The courts will need to develop case law guidelines on the manner and means for disclosure of such discoverable information. Complicated questions will arise involving the disclosure of information that can be digested and understood only by another computer and not by people, disclosure of confidential programming systems and non-discoverable material in the computer stores, and disclosure of work-product and trial preparation materials and privileged information contained or generated by computers. These problems will also affect other discovery rules besides Rule 34.[3]

§ 8.20 INDEPENDENT ACTIONS

Rule 34 and Rule 45 are not the exclusive ways to obtain documents and property from a party or a person not a party. Rule 34(c) makes clear that the rules do not preclude an independent action against a non-party person for the production of documents and things and for permission to enter lands. Federal courts have also recognized the availability of such an action.[1] Some state advisory committee notes indicate that an action in the nature of a bill in equity is available.[2]

§ 8.21 PRODUCTION FROM NON-PARTIES

While Rule 34 discovery is available only against parties, unless an independent action is filed, Rule 45 allows for the use of a subpoena duces tecum to compel the production of documents and things from non-party witnesses at depositions, trials, and hearings, but not at other

§ 8.19

1. *Adams v. Dan River Mills, Inc.*, 54 F.R.D. 220 (W.D.Va.1972).

2. *Sanders v. Levy*, 558 F.2d 636 (2d Cir.1976), *reversed on other grounds* 437 U.S. 340, 98 S.Ct. 2380, 57 L.Ed.2d 253 (1978).

3. For more information about discovery and the computer age, *see* 8 Charles A. Wright & Arthur R. Miller, Federal Practice and Procedure § 2218, at 174, 175 (1970 and Supp.1994).

§ 8.20

1. *United States v. 25.02 Acres of Land, More or Less, in Douglas County, State of Colo.*, 495 F.2d 1398 (10th Cir.1974).

2. *See* Minn.R.Civ.P. 34, Notes of Advisory Comm. *See also McGuire v. Caledonia*, 140 Minn. 151, 167 N.W. 425 (1918).

times or places.[1] The scope of discovery under this subpoena is the same as that applicable to Rule 34. This rule protects non-parties from indiscriminate use of discovery procedures, from improper searches and seizures, and from intrusive fishing expeditions.[2] A party should resort to a Rule 45 subpoena only if the documents are unavailable from an adversary or not otherwise available through the requester's own efforts.[3] Although there is no separate "discovery" rule, similar to Rule 34, directed at non-parties and allowing for the inspection and copying of items, the subpoena may command the person to whom it is directed to produce materials, thus allowing for inspection and copying.[4]

There are three methods for obtaining desired documentary materials from non-parties. (1) A Rule 45 subpoena of the documents held or controlled by a nonparty witness, can either seek documents alone or can be used in conjunction with a deposition of the nonparty witness. (2) A motion hearing can be scheduled and a subpoena served upon a person, ordering the non-party to bring designated items. Or (3) a court may issue an order requiring a party to produce documents and things at other times and places.[5] Previously, the failure to schedule a deposition or motion hearing or to obtain a court order rendered a Rule 45 subpoena ineffective.[6] However, amended Rule 45, expressly permits use of subpoenas alone to obtain documents from non-parties (and cut back on some of the fun for lawyers who like nothing better than billing clients for meaningless depositions). Counsel may still wish in some cases to depose the nonparty witness regarding record keeping, missing documents, altered documents, etc. Often, such depositions will work best when they occur after counsel has thoroughly reviewed the documents provided pursuant to a Rule 45 subpoena rather than in conjunction with document production.

The rules specifically detail the scope of such discovery and the protections afforded the non-party who wishes to object to disclosures of such data. Rule 45(d) details the procedures applicable to depositions:

> Proof of service of notice to take a deposition as provided in Rules 30(b) and 31(a) or in a state where the action is pending

§ 8.21

1. *Ghandi v. Police Department of City of Detroit,* 74 F.R.D. 115 (E.D.Mich.1977). A subpoena duces tecum, where there was no notice to take a deposition, nor a hearing, trial, or conference set to be heard by the court, was quashed because of noncompliance with Rule 45.

2. *Premium Service Corp. v. Sperry & Hutchinson Co.,* 511 F.2d 225 (9th Cir. 1975). Plaintiff's request for documents was sweeping and would have placed a tremendous burden on the defendant employees, who would have had to sift and analyze the documents. The court held that the plaintiff's offer to do the sifting itself was unrealistic and constituted an impermissible fishing expedition. *See also* 8 Charles A. Wright & Arthur R. Miller, Federal Practice and Procedure §§ 2208 & 2209, at 2457 (1970, Supp.1994).

3. *In re Penn Central Commercial Paper Litigation,* 61 F.R.D. 453 (D.C.N.Y.1973).

4. *See* 8 Charles A. Wright & Arthur R. Miller, Federal Practice and Procedure § 2452 (1970 and Supp.1994). *See also* James L. Underwood, A Guide to Federal Discovery Rules 136 (1980).

5. *See Eastern States Petroleum Co. v. Asiatic Petroleum Corp.,* 27 F.Supp. 121, 122 (S.D.N.Y.1938).

6. *Ghandi v. Police Department of City of Detroit,* 74 F.R.D. 115 (E.D.Mich.1977).

> constitutes a sufficient authorization for the issuance of subpoenas for the persons named or described therein. The subpoena may command the person to whom it is directed to produce and permit inspection and copying of designated books, papers, documents or tangible things which constitute or contain matters within the scope of the examination permitted by Rule 26(b), but in that event the subpoena will be subject to the provisions of Rule 26(c) and subdivision (b) of this rule.
>
> The person to whom the subpoena is directed may, within 10 days after the service thereof or on or before the time specified in the subpoena for compliance if such time is less than 10 days after service, serve upon the attorney designated in the subpoena written objection to inspection or copying of any or all of the designated materials. If objection is made, the party serving the subpoena shall not be entitled to inspect and copy the materials except pursuant to an order of the court from which the subpoena was issued. The party serving the subpoena may, if objection has been made, move upon notice to the deponent for an order at any time before or during the taking of the deposition.

The rule goes on to describe the location of the deposition, which is indeed geographically limited.[7] The designated documents can be discovered only during the deposition, and the subpoena duces tecum that accompanies a deposition will be quashed if there is no thought by the subpoenaing party to take the deposition of the person served.[8]

Rule 45(b) details further procedures:

> A subpoena may also command the person to whom it is directed to produce the books, papers, documents or tangible things designated therein; but the court, upon motion made promptly, and in any event at or before the time specified in the subpoena for compliance therewith, may (1) quash or modify the subpoena if it is unreasonable or oppressive, or (2) condition denial of the motion upon the advancement by the person in whose behalf the subpoena is issued of the reasonable cost of producing the books, papers, documents or tangible things.

The subpoena describes the documents to be produced. The drafting practices followed or involved with Rule 34 apply as well to subpoenas. You should mix general and specific descriptions of documents with "reasonable particularity," even though this term is nowhere found in Rule 45. Thus, like a Rule 34 request, you can specify documents you want or you can command production of all documentary information relating to a specific matter or issue. You can also combine Rule 45 and

7. "A resident of the district in which the deposition is to be taken may be required to attend an examination only in the county wherein he resides or is employed or transacts his business in person, or at such other convenient place as is fixed by an order of court. A nonresident of the district may be required to attend only in the county wherein he is served with a subpoena, or within 40 miles from the place of service, or at such other convenient place as is fixed by an order of court." Fed.R.Civ.P. 45(d)(2).

8. *McLean v. Prudential Steamship Co.*, 36 F.R.D. 421, 426 (E.D.Va.1965).

Rule 34 in sequence: after reviewing the Rule 45 documents at the deposition, you can submit a Rule 34 request to a party for additional documents.

The grounds for obtaining an order quashing the subpoena duces tecum or limiting its scope mimic the objections available to a Rule 34 request for production. Additional objections may also include the possible ground (1) that the discovering party can obtain such documents and things from a party to the case and should first use a Rule 34 request before employing a Rule 45 request against a non-party,[9] and (2) that a non-party's privacy outweighs a party's need for the information.[10]

The burden to establish that the subpoena should be quashed or modified is on the person seeking the order. The non-party witness served with a subpoena duces tecum clearly has standing to quash or limit it. But in addition to the subpoenaed non-party witness, a party to the action may also have standing to quash or limit it if that party has some personal right or privilege in the subject matter of the subpoena.[11] Rule 45(j) provides that the failure of a party "without adequate excuse" to comply with a subpoena may be deemed contempt of court.

§ 8.22 PRODUCTION FROM THE GOVERNMENT

Parties involved in litigation with the federal government, and frequently with state governments, have the same discovery obstacles they would encounter with non-governmental litigants. The federal Freedom of Information Act (FOIA),[1] however, provides an additional means of obtaining access to governmental records not available in most lawsuits. Statutes similar to the FOIA have been passed in a number of states, giving litigants and potential litigants access to documents in the hands of state governmental agencies.[2]

The Freedom of Information Act was enacted as a means of bringing government activity into the public eye, thus creating an informed electorate and a responsive, open government. Subsequent amendments and the Federal Privacy Act have modified the initial FOIA.

The FOIA allows broad disclosure of documents held by the government, and states that the governmental agencies must release any identifiable agency records in the agency's possession to "any person." No reason need be given for a request under the FOIA. Access to records is provided either by publication in the Federal Register, access at the agency's headquarters, or by making copies available upon re-

9. *Bada Co. v. Montgomery Ward & Co.*, 32 F.R.D. 208, 210 (E.D.Tenn.1963).

10. *Premium Service Corp. v. Sperry & Hutchinson Co.*, 511 F.2d 225 (9th Cir. 1975).

11. *Shepherd v. Castle*, 20 F.R.D. 184, 188 (W.D.Mo.1957).

§ 8.22

1. 5 U.S.C.A. § 552.

2. For a compilation of state acts relating to access to governmental information, *see* Guidebook to the Freedom of Information and Privacy Acts 265–435 (Appendix C) (Robert F. Bouchard & Justin D. Franklin eds. 1980).

quest. Most information is disclosed by an agency's designated information officer, who makes copies available upon request.

The act contains nine specific exemptions to disclosure, and these exemptions are given narrow interpretations by the court in order to effectuate the broad purposes of the FOIA. The exemptions are:

1. Classified defense or national security documents;

2. Agency internal personnel-rule documents;

3. Documents specifically exempted by other statutes;

4. Confidential or privileged trade-secret, commercial or financial information;

5. Interagency or intra-agency memoranda not otherwise discoverable;

6. Personnel and medical files;

7. Law enforcement investigatory records;

8. Documents pertaining to examination and supervision of financial institutions;

9. Geological and geophysical information concerning wells.

The FOIA contemplates a simple procedure for obtaining agency documents and requires the agency to respond within ten days. An appeal is permitted from an adverse decision on disclosure, and the agency must determine the administrative appeal within 20 working days. A party may thereafter commence an action in the court to enjoin the withholding of agency records.[3]

Perhaps the biggest advantage of using FOIA for discovery is that the government may put together a vast *collection* of information for you. For example, the Consumer Products Safety Commission (CPSC) amasses information on injuries involving many types of products, regardless of their manufacturer. Although a product liability action may be commenced against a single manufacturer, the information contained in CPSC files relating to all manufacturers may be very useful. Presumably the information about the particular defendant in your action or intended action will be directly discoverable from that party, while the government records may provide a large collection of cases involving parties from whom discovery would be difficult or expensive. The FOIA is also useful in that it permits "discovery" to take place even prior to the commencement of an action. For a party contemplating litigation with the government, the use of a request for documents under FOIA may be a very useful tool for investigation.

§ 8.23 PHYSICAL EXAMINATIONS

In federal cases, a party before bringing a Rule 35 motion must confer or attempt to confer with the opposing party in an effort to seek

3. 5 U.S.C.A § 552(a)(3).

an agreement regarding the examination. Rules 26(c) and 37 and local rules require a movant to accompany a motion with a written certification explaining these efforts. Many state courts have similar meet and confer rules. Even in the absence of these required rules, it is a wise practice for attorneys to discuss their Rule 35 disputes in an effort to mutually agree to an examination without the need for court intervention.

In practice, most examinations occur as a result of an agreement between attorneys. A sample stipulation is:

[Caption]

[Plaintiff] and [defendant] stipulate and agree, pursuant to Rules 29 and 35 of the Federal Rules of Civil Procedure, as follows:

1. [Plaintiff/Defendant] will [appear/produce] [name of examinee] for [physical, mental, blood] examination at the request of [plaintiff/defendant] on ______, 19__, at [time] __.M.

2. The examination will be conducted at [location].

3. The examination will be conducted by [name of expert].

4. The examination shall include [describe type and scope of examination and tests].

5. The examinee agrees to answer all proper questions submitted.

6. The examinee shall be accompanied during the course of examination by [names of any observers].

7. Good cause exists for this examination.

8. The costs of this examination will be borne by [plaintiff/defendant].

9. The examinee requests a copy of the examination report and [plaintiff/defendant] will supply the report and all other reports of the same condition without any further demand when the report becomes available.

10. A court may issue an order upon the filing of this stipulation without any notice or hearing.

11. The order shall take effect upon filing and receipt of the order upon the attorney for examinee through the mail.

____

[Signatures]

The courts are eager to give effect to stipulations and ratify their use with respect to any physical, mental, or blood examination.[1] The courts recognize that Rule 35 is a device that should be used only if the parties fail to agree on an examination.

Rule 35 applies broadly to any case in which there is controversy about the physical, mental, or blood condition of the person to be examined; it is commonly applied to the examination of an injured

§ 8.23

1. *See Liechty v. Terrill Trucking Co.*, 53 F.R.D. 590 (E.D.Tenn.1971). *See also* discussion in § 4.11.1 of this text.

plaintiff and sought by the defendant or defendants in a personal-injury action. Other types of litigation that may involve Rule 35 examinations include parentage, citizenship, incompetence, and undue influence.[2] These cases typically involve physical, mental, or blood condition questions. And while the condition of a dead body may be ascertained through a Rule 34 procedure for the production of tangibles,[3] conceivably Rule 35 also stands as an additional authority allowing a medical examination of a dead person.

Is a particular party subject to examination? Is the party's physical or mental condition in controversy? Can a significant showing of good cause be made in support of the motion to compel examination? These are all questions that the moving party must answer affirmatively in order to prevail. The Supreme Court has stated that the rule prohibits "sweeping examinations ... automatically ordered merely because the person has been involved in an accident ... and a general charge of negligence is lodged."[4] The Court does not sanction the "routine" ordering of such examinations but instead requires the trial judge to apply the rule "discriminately." Rule 35 practice, however, does not always appear to follow the dictates of this holding. Personal-injury actions involving an auto accident and allegations of negligence routinely prompt a Rule 35 examination. When this occurs, the Rule 35 criteria usually have been strictly met by a claim of serious or permanent physical injury.

The rule creates three standards to be met in obtaining an adverse examination: the physical, mental, or blood condition of an *examinee* must be *in controversy* and *good cause* must be shown for the examination. The trial court has broad discretion in considering and acting upon a Rule 35 request.[5]

§ 8.23.1 The Examinee

The rule applies to all parties, defendants as well as plaintiffs, and extends examinations to include *agents* as well as *persons under control of the party.* An agent of a party is an agent of the party—even a cursory review of your notes on agency will provide that definition. A person under the legal control of the party is a person under legal control of the party—a cursory review of the word "control" will not provide a workable definition here, though. Nonetheless, some situations are clear. The Federal Advisory Committee states that the rule settles "beyond doubt that a parent or guardian suing to recover for injuries to a minor may be ordered to produce the minor for examina-

2. *See* 4A Moore's Federal Practice ¶ 35.03[1] (2d ed. 1994); *Yee Szet Foo v. Dulles,* 18 F.R.D. 237 (S.D.N.Y.1955).

3. *See Zalatuka v. Metropolitan Life Insurance Co.,* 108 F.2d 405 (7th Cir.1939).

4. *Schlagenhauf v. Holder,* 379 U.S. 104, 121, 85 S.Ct. 234, 244, 13 L.Ed.2d 152 (1964).

5. *Coca-Cola Bottling Co. of Puerto Rico v. Negron Torres,* 255 F.2d 149 (1st Cir. 1958); *Bucher v. Krause,* 200 F.2d 576 (7th Cir.1952). *See also* 4A Moore's Federal Practice ¶ 35.04, at 35–21 (2d ed. 1994).

tion." [6] The committee clearly intended the rule to cover a required blood examination of minors in cases involving their paternity.[7] Other situations remain unresolved. Professors Wright and Miller state:

> It is not quite so clear, but it would seem that when a husband has a substantive right to recover for injuries to his wife, the wife is under his legal control for this purpose and he can be ordered to produce her for physical examination.[8]

Control does have its limits. The Federal Advisory Committee Notes state that "an order to 'produce' the third person imposes only an obligation to use good faith efforts to produce the person." [9]

§ 8.23.2 The Controversy

Personal injury cases almost automatically include some condition in controversy. Other cases may also raise the question of whether the plaintiff or defendant voluntarily has placed physical, mental, or blood condition in issue. One party may attempt to place an opponent's condition in controversy. A more pronounced showing of actual "controversy" will be required of a party who initiates the dispute concerning the condition of another. Mere conclusory allegations that a condition is in controversy will not provide the basis for a Rule 35 order.

The party seeking an examination must make a showing beyond a mere allegation that the evidence itself places the condition in dispute. For example, the plaintiff in one personal-injury case clearly placed her physical condition in controversy by asserting physical injuries to her head and body in the complaint. Defendant argued that plaintiff's mental condition was also in controversy, contending that the real question was whether plaintiff's physical condition was affected by her mental condition. This argument was supported by an expert's adverse medical examination report, which found plaintiff to be minimally injured and predicted that plaintiff's residual symptoms would disappear when the litigation settled.[10]

In another illustrative case, the plaintiff in a negligence action, which involved the collision of a bus with a tractor-trailer, sought a Rule 35 examination of the defendant and the bus driver.[11] The plaintiff contended that the bus driver was "not mentally or physically capable" of driving the bus and sought examinations in internal medicine, ophthalmology, neurology, and psychiatry. The plaintiff supported its motion with affidavits alleging that the rear lights of the trailer were visible for one-half mile and that the driver had been involved in a

6. Fed.R.Civ.P. 35(a), Note of Advisory Comm.

7. Fed.R.Civ.P. 35(a), Note of Advisory Comm. The rule conforms to the holding in *Beach v. Beach,* 114 F.2d 479 (D.C.Cir. 1940).

8. 8 Charles A. Wright & Arthur R. Miller, Federal Practice and Procedure § 2233, at 669 (1970, Supp.1994).

9. Fed.R.Civ.P. 35(a), Note of Advisory Comm.

10. *Haynes v. Anderson,* 304 Minn. 185, 232 N.W.2d 196 (1975).

11. *Schlagenhauf v. Holder,* 379 U.S. 104, 85 S.Ct. 234, 13 L.Ed.2d 152 (1964).

previous accident. The United States Supreme Court found sufficient controversy for the ophthalmological examination on the basis of one affidavit, but not for the other three examinations.[12] Two Justices dissented, noting that the record supported a finding that the physical and mental condition of the driver were in controversy and the three examinations would produce highly relevant evidence. The dissenters remarked in a practical and telling observation that such an accident prompts a reasonable person to inquire "What is the matter with that driver? Is he blind or crazy?" [13]

A creative attorney may be able to formulate a persuasive argument that physical, mental, or blood condition is in controversy in a type of lawsuit not ordinarily involving Rule 35 examinations. A defamation action involving alleged defamatory remarks concerning the plaintiff's physical, mental, or blood condition may justify a Rule 35 examination to allow the defendant to establish the defense of truth. The "in controversy" requirement may also be met by a dispute over the right or competence of a party to maintain an action or defense. One court has authorized a mental examination to determine if the plaintiff was capable of understanding the nature and effect of the lawsuit involved.[14] The court issued the order on the authority of both Rule 35 and Rule 17(c), the rule providing for prosecution of actions by representatives of incompetent persons. The court stated that this type of examination would not be permitted as a routine practice and issued the order subject to certain protective provisions.[15] This precedent is not uniform, however. Another court has denied a Rule 35 motion based on similar allegations of controversy.[16]

§ 8.23.3 The Good Cause

Rule 34 may no longer require a showing of good cause for the production of documents, but Rule 35 continues this requirement for compulsory examinations. This good-cause requirement frequently creates difficulty in obtaining a Rule 35 order. The standard for determining the question of good cause goes beyond a mere formality, requiring (1) that the moving party establish that the prospective information meets the relevancy standard of Rule 26 and (2) that the moving party need such information. Courts impose varying burdens upon parties seeking Rule 35 orders, but they routinely grant such motions in personal-injury actions, where physical or mental condition is usually in controversy and "good cause" is self-evident. Courts also grant Rule 35 requests in cases not ordinarily involving questions of mental, physical, or blood conditions, but they impose a higher burden on the party

12. 379 U.S. at 120–121, 85 S.Ct. at 243.

13. 379 U.S. at 123, 85 S.Ct. at 245.

14. *Bodnar v. Bodnar,* 441 F.2d 1103 (5th Cir.1971), *cert. denied* 404 U.S. 913, 92 S.Ct. 232, 30 L.Ed.2d 186 (1971). *See also Buck v. Board of Education,* 17 Fed. R.Serv.2d 165 (E.D.N.Y.1973).

15. *Bodnar v. Bodnar,* 441 F.2d 1103, 1104 (5th Cir.1971), *cert. denied* 404 U.S. 913, 92 S.Ct. 232, 30 L.Ed.2d 186 (1971). *See also Swift v. Swift,* 64 F.R.D. 440 (E.D.N.Y.1974).

16. *See Raymond v. Raymond,* 105 R.I. 380, 252 A.2d 345, 348–349 (1969).

seeking the examination if the proposed examination will be either painful or of dubious probative value. One court declined to order a bone-scan examination because of its questionable value and the potential pain to the party to be examined.[17]

Although higher standards may be imposed in such cases, courts nonetheless order a painful examination or dangerous procedure if appropriate.[18] The determination of good cause involves a balancing approach: weighing the pain, danger, or intrusiveness of the examination against the need for, or usefulness of, the information to be gained. One court suggested that if a party complains about the difficulty and pain involved in an examination, that party could avoid examination by stipulating that no evidence would be introduced at the trial based upon the same or similar type of examination.[19]

Judges wish to avoid the indiscriminate use of Rule 35 examinations and are open to considering rational and deliberative factors before granting an order for one. An attorney who opposes such an examination may be successful in restricting the scope of an otherwise inevitable court order permitting it.

§ 8.24 NUMBER OF EXAMINATIONS

How many examinations must a person undergo under the authority of Rule 35? The rule does not specifically limit the number of examinations, but leaves to the courts the resolution of the question within the framework of the "in controversy" and "good cause" analysis used under Rule 35.[1] Multiple examinations arise in two contexts: (1) a request for a later examination by the same doctor conducting an initial examination, or by a doctor of the same specialty; and (2) a request to have a person examined by a doctor in another specialty.

Rule 35 neither provides for nor prohibits more than one adverse examination. Judges routinely allow the parties to conduct such examinations as will approximately "balance" the parties' positions [2] and are even inclined to balance the number and type of examinations. If a plaintiff has been treated or examined by five doctors, all of whom may testify, the defendant most likely will be able to establish good cause to conduct comparable adverse examinations. If the plaintiff has been examined by a number of specialists, the defendant will probably be able to have the plaintiff examined by doctors in each of these specialties.

Some courts employ a list of factors in applying a balancing approach to the problem of multiple examinations. One court listed four factors to consider before permitting a second examination:

17. *Hernandez v. Gulf Oil Corp.*, 21 Fed.R.Serv.2d 1378, 1379 (E.D.Pa.1976).

18. *See, e.g., Klein v. Yellow Cab Co.*, 7 F.R.D. 169 (N.D.Ohio 1944).

19. *See Klein v. Yellow Cab Co.*, 7 F.R.D. 169 (N.D.Ohio 1944).

§ 8.24

1. *See* 4A Moore's Federal Practice ¶ 35.04 (2d ed. 1994).

2. *See* 4A Moore's Federal Practice ¶ 35.03 (2d ed. 1994).

1. The lapse of time since the initial examination;

2. The amendments to the pleadings or new information raising other contentions;

3. Any lack of cooperation during a first examination; or

4. An incomplete report of the first examination, or an inability of the examiner to testify.[3]

Courts prefer to keep the number of examinations to a minimum.[4] Partial examinations by more than one examiner are usually held equivalent to a complete examination by one examiner and are allowed. One plaintiff sued for personal injuries, claiming whiplash injuries to the spine and extensive aggravation of a pre-existing heart disability. The court required him to submit to two separate examinations, one by an orthopedic specialist and one by a heart specialist.[5] The number and specialties of physicians treating the examinee may also provide guidance to the court to determine what is fair examination by an adversary.

Multiple examinations by the same physician or the same type of specialist require establishing some change of circumstance following the previous examination. The party seeking additional examination must make a strong showing of need for it.[6] One court allowed a second physical examination of a plaintiff when the defendant could not obtain the testimony at trial of the physician conducting the first examination, because he resided outside the jurisdiction of the court and refused to appear voluntarily.[7] One federal court has held that the passage of two years since plaintiff has been required to undergo a physical examination in a state-court action between the same parties was an adequate basis for permitting (and requiring) a second examination.[8] Most courts permit a second examination shortly before trial, or even during trial, if the case has not reached trial for some time following the administration of an initial examination. Experienced trial judges realize that medical experts frequently are reluctant to testify to the present or future condition unless they have examined the patient recently. So second examinations generally are permitted, unless testimony concerning the present physical condition is of little value or the condition at the time of the initial examination has relevance to the issues in the case.

§ 8.25 WHO MAY BE PRESENT DURING THE EXAMINATION?

A contest sometimes arises concerning who will be present during the examination. Obviously, the examinee and the examiner will be present. Frequently the attorney representing the party to be examined

3. *Vopelak v. Williams,* 42 F.R.D. 387 (N.D.Ohio 1967).

4. *See, e.g., Schlagenhauf v. Holder,* 321 F.2d 43 (5th Cir.1963), *vacated on other grounds* 379 U.S. 104, 85 S.Ct. 234, 13 L.Ed.2d 152 (1964).

5. *Marshall v. Peters,* 31 F.R.D. 238 (S.D.Ohio 1962).

6. *Vopelak v. Williams,* 42 F.R.D. 387 (N.D.Ohio 1967).

7. 42 F.R.D. at 389.

8. *Lewis v. Neighbors Construction Co.,* 49 F.R.D. 308 (W.D.Mo.1969).

or that person's physician wants to be present. Occasionally the attorney for the party requesting the examination also wants to attend.

An early case stated that a party obtaining an examination was entitled to have the examination conducted without the examinee's attorney present.[1] This holding no longer reflects the preferred practice. The courts generally make this determination only after considering the circumstances of each case.[2] But a party's request to have an attorney present during the examination is still frequently denied, under the reasoning that denying a party the presence of an attorney expedites the examination.[3] Other courts have adopted the questionable rubric that the doctor in a Rule 35 examination is an "officer of the court" and that examination is not an adversarial process, so there is no need for an attorney.[4] A court also may authorize the presence of an attorney during only a portion of the examination, for example while the doctor takes the case history of the examinee.[5] The party to be examined may obtain protective relief under Rule 26 to prevent the examination from becoming a deposition without benefit of counsel. For example, the order for an examination may specifically limit the scope of the examination, may prohibit the use of any non-medical questions, and may even prohibit the introduction of any evidence relating to statements made by the examinee during the course of the examination.[6]

Courts have generally been more willing to allow the party to be examined to have a physician present during the examination.[7] Although one court has stated that a party has a *right* to have a physician present,[8] most courts consider this question a matter of discretion.[9]

A party seeking the presence of a physician may need to establish that some prejudice or embarrassment would result from the absence of the friendly physician. Some courts may require an affirmative showing that the presence of the physician at an examination conducted by another physician will increase the accuracy of the diagnosis and prognosis, although this reasoning may not be convincing by itself when the courts correctly note that a separate examination can be conducted shortly before or after the court-ordered examination to achieve the same result.[10] Those courts that do deny such requests usually approve

§ 8.25

1. *Dziwanoski v. Ocean Carriers Corp.*, 26 F.R.D. 595 (D.Md.1960).

2. *See* 4A Moore's Federal Practice ¶ 35.04, at 35.24 & n. 11 (2d ed. 1994).

3. *See, e.g., Brandenberg v. El Al Israel Airlines*, 79 F.R.D. 543 (S.D.N.Y.1978); *Warrick v. Brode*, 46 F.R.D. 427 (D.Del. 1969).

4. *See, e.g., Warrick v. Brode*, 46 F.R.D. 427 (D.Del.1969); *The Italia*, 27 F.Supp. 785 (E.D.N.Y.1939).

5. *See* Shepard's Manual of Federal Practice § 5.196 (2d ed. 1979).

6. *See Dziwanoski v. Ocean Carriers Corp.*, 26 F.R.D. 595 (D.Md.1960). *See also Garner v. Ford Motor Co.*, 61 F.R.D. 22 (D.Alaska 1973).

7. *See, e.g., Reese v. Batesville Casket Co.*, 29 Fed.R.Serv.2d 1097 (D.D.C.1980).

8. *Warrick v. Brode*, 46 F.R.D. 427 (D.Del.1969).

9. *Sanden v. Mayo Clinic*, 495 F.2d 221 (8th Cir.1974).

10. *Sanden v. Mayo Clinic*, 495 F.2d 221 (8th Cir.1974).

a consultation between the examining physician and the "friendly" physician.[11]

§ 8.26 PLACE OF EXAMINATION

Where does the examiner examine the examinee?

The location of the examination may be contested.[1] The party may live in one place, the examiner may work in another, and the attorneys may practice in still another district. Previous decisions concerning the location of discovery during litigation may affect the location of the Rule 35 examination. The attorneys by agreement or the court by order can determine the situs of depositions for the case or the allocation of travel expenses between the parties. An additional consideration is the availability of the examining physician to provide testimony at trial. Attorneys who cannot compromise on a location will have to have the matter resolved by a court.

Courts routinely require that a party appear for a medical examination at the place where the action is pending. The courts require a nonresident plaintiff to appear in that district for the Rule 35 examination, on the grounds that the plaintiff selected the forum and should not then be heard to complain about having to appear in that forum for pre-trial proceedings.[2] A plaintiff may show that attending a Rule 35 examination in such a location will be either financially burdensome or medically dangerous, and may convince the court to order the examination held at the plaintiff's residence.[3] In many of these situations, courts require the plaintiff to attend both a deposition and a physical examination on the same or consecutive days in the district where the plaintiff commenced the action, thereby minimizing the burden on all concerned.[4] The increasing use of videotaped deposition testimony will provide more flexibility for determining the location of an adverse examination, particularly when a choice of location pivots on the availability of the examiner to provide testimony during the trial.[5]

§ 8.27 DRAFTING THE DOCUMENTS

The motion to obtain an order for a physical, mental, or blood examination must be in writing. The notice of motion and motion must be served on all parties to the action, and also on the person to be

11. *Swift v. Swift,* 64 F.R.D. 440 (E.D.N.Y.1974).

§ 8.26

1. *See* Commentary, Scope and Manner of Physical Examination before Trial, 3 Fed.R.Serv. § 35a.42, at 713 (1940).

2. *Costanza v. Monty,* 50 F.R.D. 75 (E.D.Wis.1970); *Marshall v. Peters,* 31 F.R.D. 238 (S.D.Ohio 1962); *Pierce v. Brovig,* 16 F.R.D. 569 (S.D.N.Y.1954); *Gale v. National Transportation Co.,* 7 F.R.D. 237 (S.D.N.Y.1946).

3. *Baird v. Quality Foods, Inc.,* 47 F.R.D. 212 (E.D.La.1969); *Stuart v. Burford,* 42 F.R.D. 591 (N.D.Okl.1967); *Warren v. Weber & Heidenthaler, Inc.,* 134 F.Supp. 524 (D.Mass.1955).

4. *Hunter v. Riverside Community Memorial Hospital,* 58 F.R.D. 218 (E.D.Wis. 1972).

5. For a discussion of the use of videotape depositions, *see* § 5.3.3 of this text.

examined (if a non-party). State or local rules may specify that service of the papers must be made at least a fixed period before the hearing.

Rule 35(a) specifically requires the order for examination to state the:

1. Time (and presumably the date),

2. Location of the examination,

3. Manner in which the examination will be conducted,

4. Conditions restricting or relating to the procedures,

5. Scope of the examination,

6. Person or persons who will conduct or be present during the examination, and

7. Physician's golf handicap.

The moving party will undoubtedly desire to provide the court with this detailed information in the form of a proposed order served and filed with the notice of motion and motion. Opposing counsel may prefer to file an alternative proposed order, particularly when the attorney does not contest the examination itself, but only some facets of its procedure. Proposed orders buttress arguments made during the hearing and provide the judge with reasonable written alternatives. Proposed orders can also prevent an examination from being scheduled in the kitchen, by Professor Plum, with a wrench.

An evidentiary hearing rarely is necessary, but the moving party frequently supports the motion for an examination with evidentiary support in the form of affidavits. Local rules may require such an affidavit. The most important reason is that good cause for the examination is not established by arguments, cajoling, citation of authority, or crying. Good cause turns on the facts of the individual case and on the nature of the examination sought. Pleadings alone may be sufficient to show good cause in a personal injury lawsuit, but in a routine case an affidavit of an attorney to support the need for the examination is needed. An affidavit by the examining physician may also be necessary in a case involving an examination that could be intrusive, painful, controversial, or somewhat dangerous. Such an affidavit should explain to the judge (remember, the judge is not likely to be an expert in medicine as well as law) the nature of the procedures to be ordered; the need for them; why less intrusive, painful, or dangerous tests are not satisfactory; and any other information which might assist the judge in making a decision. It may even be advisable to supply an affidavit from a physician who is *not* going to administer the test to establish that the tests are reasonable and required. This independent affidavit may persuade the judge in a close case that the tests sought are appropriate.

The submission of such affidavits requires you to make a tactical decision: do you want to give your opponent indications of your position? Do you want to try to anticipate your opponent's position? You can, of course, submit responsive materials after the hearing and reserve submitting a proposed order or affidavit (except where required by local rule), but these may not have the impact necessary to convince the judge. Your conversation with opposing counsel and the attempt to schedule the examination without resort to a court order probably have already put him or her on notice of your position and provided you with information on the opponent's position. Both sides then know what the arguments will be at the hearing. Why not lay most, if not all, of your cards on the table? That is, assuming you are playing with a full deck.

§ 8.28 SELECTING THE DOCTOR

The most important thing to remember in selecting a doctor to conduct the examination is that, in addition to selecting a medical expert, you are selecting an expert witness. You want to select someone whose examination will be the basis of testimony that the jury would deem credible. Defense attorneys seeking examination of the plaintiff should avoid selecting a physician with a notorious reputation as a biased defense doctor. Testimony from such an expert, indicating a patient's amputated leg will soon grow back, may be music to the defense attorney's ears, but an incredible aria to the jury. The shadow cast by testimony from a suspect expert may fall over the entire case, reducing the credibility of otherwise believable witnesses.

The second most important thing to remember is that the court, not the attorney, selects and appoints the doctor to conduct the examination. Courts usually appoint the doctor sought by the moving party, but they have been quite willing to exercise their power to select a doctor not chosen by counsel. This power will be exercised readily when counsel cannot agree on a doctor to conduct the examination.[1] Some judges honor strenuous objections by opposing counsel to the choice of a physician and appoint another person to conduct the examination.[2] Other judges refuse to excuse a party from an examination by a particular examining physician merely because of an alleged personality conflict between the party and the doctor.[3] This power of the court encourages counsel to select an examining physician whose credentials and professional qualifications are not subject to serious criticism and who is acceptable to the opponent. Employing these criteria is almost certain to gain the court's *imprimatur,* buttresses the witness's status and credibility at trial, and avoids having the jury attribute the doctor's testimony to professional or personal conflict with the opposing party or counsel.

§ 8.28

1. *Liechty v. Terrill Trucking Co.,* 53 F.R.D. 590 (E.D.Tenn.1971); *Stuart v. Burford,* 42 F.R.D. 591 (N.D.Okl.1967); *Pierce v. Brovig,* 16 F.R.D. 569 (S.D.N.Y.1954).

2. *The Italia,* 27 F.Supp. 785 (E.D.N.Y. 1939).

3. *See Wasmund v. Nunamaker,* 277 Minn. 52, 151 N.W.2d 577 (1967).

The kind of doctor you select depends on the matter in controversy, the nature of the examination, and the availability of expert examiners in the field. The typical Rule 35 medical expert comes in all varieties. Do you prefer a family practitioner over a specialist? An internist, a gynecologist, or a surgeon? Ben Casey? Elizabeth Blackwell? This decision also turns on the type of medical expert the opposing party identifies as its treating physician or a potential trial witness or consulting expert. You may have to select examiners to match the qualifications or specialties of the opposing examiners.[4]

§ 8.29 PREPARATION FOR THE EXAMINATION

You must be well-versed in all relevant physical and mental aspects of your case. Your comprehensive understanding of the case ensures that the examining doctor conducts all the tests you need as evidence to support your claims and theories at trial. You need to educate and advise the examiner for the examination.

The expert must be educated on the legal relevance of anything the examination may reveal. The examiner must also be presented with every report, every record, *every anything* which relates to the medical condition of the person to be examined. This helps the expert prepare, and also ensures that his or her eventual report and testimony are not deficient because of incorrect or incomplete underlying data. Since the medical history carries some weight in any examination and diagnosis, the attorney must transmit these records to the doctor, preferably through a conference, however brief, before the examination is to be held. Some practitioners intentionally avoid discussing the detailed facts of the case or the specific claims or theories involved; this avoids the later argument by the opposition that such discussion unduly influenced the doctor's opinion by suggesting desirable examination results in advance of the examination. All practitioners should discuss the examiner's fees.

Fee arrangements with the expert must be made in advance of the examination. A fee dispute might cause the report to be held up, create friction in the relationship of the doctor to the case, or cause unneeded trouble for both doctor and attorney. The expert's fee ordinarily is an hourly rate or a flat fee for the examination and report. These costs must be borne by the party and not by the attorney. The examiner's fee should *not* be contingent on the outcome of the examination or the outcome of the case; the Code of Professional Responsibility prohibits such an arrangement,[1] and the doctor's credibility would likely be

4. Although formal sources exist which might be of assistance in locating a specialist (*see, e.g.*, R. Miller, Lawyers' Source Book § 110 (1971)), these sources do not assist in determining whether particular physicians will be objective, credible, and cooperative witnesses. A more useful source of information is probably your colleagues in the Bar, particularly lawyers who try cases similar to the one for which you need an expert witness.

§ 8.29

1. ABA Code of Professional Responsibility, DR 7–109(c).

impaired at trial. Tradition stamps this practice as the equivalent of bribing a doctor for favorable testimony.

§ 8.30 RESPONDING TO A MOTION FOR EXAMINATION

You may not often want to oppose an examination. When physical, mental, or blood condition are in controversy, the court usually orders a good-faith examination. Furthermore, an adverse examination may be all it takes to settle your case; it certainly gives you a narrower focus for subsequent discussions. Your objections to an examination may then be limited to the scope of the examination, its procedures, or the doctor selected. You may raise these specific objections rather than a general objection to the examination itself.

A separate protective order under Rule 26(c) or a Rule 35 order limits the examination. You may seek protection for your client based upon reasons discussed earlier in this chapter, including an examination involving intrusive, dangerous, untried, bizarre, or painful procedures. You may also seek an order allowing yourself or another expert to be present during the examination. There, your primary task as the opponent is to ensure that the Rule 35 examination proceeds according to the rule. You may be able to gain these advantages by presenting a counter-motion for the appointment of a well-qualified and clearly neutral doctor (if you oppose the physician selected by the moving party), by submitting appropriate affidavits detailing factual information for the court, and by submitting a proposed order embodying your ideas for the Rule 35 examination.

§ 8.31 THE EXAMINATION AND REPORT

The examination itself is a proceeding in which lawyers, if allowed to attend at all, should play bit parts.[1] A physician conducts the examination,[2] the party being examined responds to questions, and the lawyers do not actively participate. Counsel obtaining the examination must avoid the appearance that the examination is essentially a legal rather than a medical examination, and the attorney representing the party being examined must not appear to be overly protective.

The examining physician ordinarily prepares a report of the examination. This formal document should be a detailed statement of the doctor's examination, specific findings, and overall conclusions. A pre-examination conference between the attorney and the examiner may have established other types of information the report should contain. A copy of this report is ordinarily forwarded to the party examined and to any other parties. Rule 35(b) requires such an extra-judicial exchange if requested by the party examined.

§ 8.31

1. *See* discussion in § 6.2.2 regarding who may attend an examination.

2. *In re Mitchell,* 563 F.2d 143 (5th Cir. 1977).

Demand to Produce Medical Reports or Medical Report Authorizations

To: Plaintiff and plaintiff's attorney.

Pursuant to Rule 35 of the Federal Rules of Civil Procedure, defendant requests that you produce within [number] days:

1. Copies of all medical reports previously or subsequently made by any treating or examining medical expert; and

2. Written authority signed by the plaintiff to permit the inspection of all hospital and other medical records concerning the plaintiff's physical, mental, or blood condition.

____

Attorney for Defendant

The request triggers the exchange; the rule itself does not "automatically" require exchange. This demand by the examinee for a copy of the report entitles the party seeking the examination under Rule 35(b) to receive copies of all reports from any examination of the examinee for the same condition, unless the examinee shows inability to obtain the report of the examination of a person not a party. An unsolicited sending of the report does not entitle the party seeking the examination to previous medical records.[3]

The scope of this reciprocity appears limited to similar examinations of the same conditions. If an ophthalmologist's report were completed, the examinee would be required to exchange any ophthalmological reports, but not other types of examinations, like neurological or psychiatric reports.[4] A court may order a doctor to make a written report if no report has previously been made.[5] A physician who fails or refuses to make a report may have his or her testimony excluded if offered at the trial. The rule requires the disclosure only of the examiner's report, including any tests and results, but not hospital records or office records.[6] The examination reports will be, more likely than not, offered as evidence at the trial, and should be prepared with that eventuality in mind.

§ 8.32 WAIVER AND DEPOSITION

The party involved in a case concerning his or her own physical, mental, or blood condition ordinarily has waived any privilege, based on state or federal law, that he or she may have had in the pending action

3. *Hardy v. Riser,* 309 F.Supp. 1234 (N.D.Miss.1970). One court even held that delivery of a report pursuant to court order, rather than request, would not waive the privilege. *Benning v. Phelps,* 249 F.2d 47 (2d Cir.1957).

4. *See* 4A Moore's Federal Practice ¶ 35.06 (2d ed. 1994).

5. *See* Moore's Manual, Federal Practice & Procedure § 15.07(4).

6. *Sher v. De Haven,* 199 F.2d 777 (D.C.Cir.1952), *cert. denied* 345 U.S. 936, 73 S.Ct. 797, 97 L.Ed. 1363 (1953); *Butts v. Sears, Roebuck & Co.,* 9 F.R.D. 58 (D.D.C. 1949).

or any other involving the same controversy.[1] Rule 35(b)(2) specifies that requesting and obtaining a report of an examination or the taking of the deposition of an examiner also acts as the waiver of any privilege. This rule anticipates that the party examined may decide to conduct a deposition of the examiner to obtain information about the examination and an explanation of the report. Subdivision (3) of the same rule makes it clear that Rule 35 does not preclude discovery of a report of an examining physician or the taking of a deposition of the physician in accordance with the provisions of any other discovery rule. The operation of Rule 35 causes a party to lose privileges but also ensures that the same party has sufficient access to discovery devices to obtain information relevant to the privileged examination. At the same time, Rule 26 protects the examined party from unnecessary disclosures of privileged information.

PRACTICE PROBLEMS

Requests for Production

Draft Rule 34 requests for production of whatever documents or things you deem appropriate for the following situations. Form requests may be useful as guides in composing requests but cannot be copied. Assume the opposing party has not had to disclose any of the documents you seek. Draft a reasonable number of requests. Your instructor may specify numerical limits.

1. You represent Hot Dog Enterprises in *Hot Dog Enterprises v. Tri–Chem* (Chapter 1). Draft requests for production directed to the defendants.

2. You represent Tri–Chem in *Hot Dog Enterprises v. Tri–Chem* (Chapter 1). Draft requests for production directed to the plaintiff.

3. You represent the defendants in *Northern Motor Homes v. Danforth* (Case J).

4. You represent the plaintiff in *Northern Motor Homes v. Danforth* (Case J).

5. You represent the plaintiff in *Burris v. Warner* (Case K). Draft requests for production directed to the defendant.

6. You represent the defendant in *Burris v. Warner* (Case K). Draft requests for production directed to the plaintiff.

7. You represent the plaintiff in *Vasquez v. Hot Dog Enterprises* (Case F). Direct requests for production directed to the defendant.

§ 8.32

1. *Hardy v. Riser,* 309 F.Supp. 1234 (N.D.Miss.1970).

8. You represent the defendant in *Vasquez v. Hot Dog Enterprises* (Case F). Draft requests for production directed to the plaintiff.

9. You represent a party in a case assigned by the instructor. Respond to the requests for production prepared by the student attorney representing the opposing party by:

(a) Indicating which documents or things or other requests you would provide.

(b) Noting your objections to other requests and explaining the basis for the objections.

10. You represent the plaintiff in *Burris v. Warner* (Case K). Draft a request for production and inspection of the Dodge Omni owned by the defendant.

11. You represent the defendant in *Burris v. Warner* (Case K)

(a) Through an interrogatory answer you discover that the manufacturer of the helmet (Stirling Helmets) failed to have that model helmet certified to meet the Department of Transportation's safety standards. You want to inspect the helmet's post-accident condition to judge its conformity with DOT impact-resistance standards. The plaintiff's lawyer has told you that they also wish the helmet to be inspected by an expert. Your expert advises you that the only accurate test is a procedure that impacts the helmet into a flat anvil, which might crush and destroy the helmet.

(1) Draft a request for production and destructive testing of the helmet.

(2) Draft a proposed court order anticipating plaintiff's objection to a destructive testing procedure.

(b) You want to substantiate the evidence that the motorcycle headlight might not have been working while the plaintiff was riding north on Oak Avenue. Your expert advises you that inspection and testing of the filament in the headlight could determine if the light was on at the time it shattered on impact. Draft a request for production, inspection, and testing of that part of the motorcycle.

12. Draft a combined set of interrogatories and requests for production in *Northern Motor Homes v. Danforth* (Case J).

(a) For the plaintiff, directed to the defendants.

(b) For the defendants, directed to the plaintiff.

13. This case is a federal civil rights case in which the plaintiffs have sued to recover damages for the death of their husband and father, Broderick Hauser, who was shot and killed by police in a factory in the Uptown section of Mitchell on June

1, 198X. The complaint alleges that the police officers and their superiors unjustifiably and without provocation shot Mr. Hauser during the course of a chase. The defendants have answered claiming that they had probable cause to arrest Mr. Hauser, that he appeared to be armed, also that the police heard shots, and that the police reasonably believed they were in danger of being seriously injured. The police department conducted an extensive investigation of the shooting. The following documents and products stem from that investigation:

A. Police radio tapes of the incident.

B. Physical evidence from the scene of the shooting.

C. Physical evidence from the home of the decedent seized following his death.

D. Reports of the analysis of the physical evidence made by the police.

E. Autopsy Report.

F. Photographs of the scene of death.

G. Written unsigned statements from the eyewitnesses to the shooting.

H. Written signed statements by eyewitnesses to the shooting.

I. Police report written by the officers on the scene.

J. Results of polygraph examinations conducted by the police of the police officers involved.

K. Police internal affairs investigation report regarding the shooting.

L. Police reports of prior incidents involving Hauser.

M. The clothes Hauser wore when he was shot.

N. The gun that was used to shoot him.

O. Ballistics reports by the police.

The plaintiffs have served requests for production which request the disclosure of all these documents and products. You represent the defendants. Which information do you believe to be discoverable? Would you disclose any information you believe non-discoverable for tactical reasons? Under what circumstances?

Reconsidering and Redrafting Requests

14. You represent the Defendant Summit Insurance Company in *Pozdak v. Summit Insurance Company* (Case B). Fran Pozdak has sued for breach of contract seeking to recover $250,000 for the fire loss to his building and $1,000,000 for the loss of its contents. You defend claiming Pozdak committed arson

which bars recovery under the contract. An associate in your firm prepares the following draft:

Defendant requests that the Plaintiff provide the Defendant with the following documents:

1. A Purchase Agreement, Contract for Deed, mortgage, tax assessments, and other property documents that relate to the value of the Plaintiff's real property at 560 Wesley Avenue.

2. Bills, invoices, receipts, and other documents containing information relating to the value of the contents of the property destroyed in the fire at 560 Wesley Avenue.

3. All documents that contain information concerning the liabilities and assets of the Plaintiff as of July 3.

4. Copies of all insurance documents providing coverage to the real property and personal property at 560 Wesley on July 3.

Defendant also requests that Plaintiff permit Defendant to:

1. Visit the remnants of the fire located at 560 Wesley Avenue.

2. Photograph the car Plaintiff owned on July 3.

(a) Which of these requests would you not submit, and why?

(b) Redraft those you would submit.

(c) What other requests would you submit, and why? Draft those requests.

(d) If you represented the Plaintiff Pozdak and received this set of requests, how would you respond to each of the requests. Identify specific objections you would make.

15. You represent Mike LaBelle in *Miyamoto v. Snow Cat* (Case C). You have sued the Snow Cat Company for negligence, product liability, and breach of warranty. Snow Cat denies all allegations. An associate in your firm prepares the following draft:

Plaintiff Mike LaBelle pursuant to the rules of civil procedure submits the following requests on Defendant Snow Cat. These requests are continuing in nature. You must provide the opportunity to Plaintiff permitting the inspection and copying of the following materials:

1. All written statements, notes, and memoranda that include statements provided by any and all witnesses to this case.

2. The sales contract and all documents provided Mariko Miyamoto when she bought the snowmobile from Defendant.

3. All photographs, film, movies, videotapes, and other graphic representations taken by the Defendant of the scene of the accident and the snowmobile involved in the accident.

4. All tests, reports, and documents prepared by an expert, by an employee of the Defendant, or in the possession of the Defendant relating to the throttle mechanism of the Snow Cat snowmobile.

Plaintiff further demands that the Defendant make available to the Plaintiff the following opportunity as soon as possible:

1. A visit to the factory in which the Snow Cat snowmobile was manufactured.

2. An inspection of the offices of Snow Cat Company to review files containing engineering, manufacturing, and marketing information and customer complaints about the Snow Cat snowmobile.

(a) Which of these requests would you not submit, and why?

(b) Redraft those you would submit.

(c) What other requests might you submit, and why? Draft those requests.

(d) If you represent Defendant Snow Cat, how would you respond to each of the requests? Identify specific objections you would make.

16. You represent Hot Dog Enterprises in *Hot Dog Enterprises v. Tri–Chem* (Chapter 1). Draft a Rule 45 subpoena directed to:

a) Joseph Piranha, the general contractor on the Kansas restaurant project,

b) Margaret Pei, the architect who designed the restaurant building in Kansas

Rule 45 Subpoena

17. You represent the defendants in *Northern Motor Homes v. Danforth* (Case J).

(a) Draft a Rule 45 subpoena directed to the Mitchell National Bank to obtain documents from the bank.

(b) What discovery advantages do you gain if you were to make the Mitchell National Bank a party to the lawsuit with Northern Motor Homes?

Physical Examinations

18. Draft a motion for an adverse physical examination of the opposing party in *Burris v. Warner* (Case K) by a physician of your choice:

(a) You represent the plaintiff.

(b) You represent the defendant.

19. Draft a proposed order for an adverse physical examination in *Burris v. Warner* (Case K).

(a) You represent the plaintiff.

(b) You represent the defendant.

20. You represent the defendant in *Vasquez v. Hot Dog Enterprises* (Case F). The plaintiff seeks damages for emotional distress. Draft a motion for an independent psychological evaluation of Juanita Vasquez.

(a) You represent the plaintiff. What arguments would you make to oppose the taking of an independent examination?

CHAPTER 9
REQUESTS FOR ADMISSIONS

Your request for admission to our law school has been received and we are pleased to inform you. . . .

Your First Admission

§ 9.1 INTRODUCTION

Requests for admissions are the least used of the discovery devices.[1] Though most lawyers have at one time or another drafted requests and responses, few make frequent use of requests for admissions. To some extent, admission requests have been a victim of the overall success of the discovery rules.

Use of the other discovery devices (particularly depositions and document production requests) permits the inquiring party to establish information in a manner that leaves the responding party little room for later denial. After all, depositions are taken under oath and key documents are often generated by the opposition. Consequently, admission requests have become something of the forgotten stepchild of discovery.

This tendency to overlook admission requests also stems in part from the adversary system and the mutual distrust harbored by litigation opponents. Many lawyers and parties simply believe a discovery device premised on receiving straight, truthful, yes-or-no answers from the other side is doomed to failure. These skeptics overlook that interrogatories, document requests, and depositions depend to a large

§ 9.1

1. *See* Paul R. Connolly, et al., Judicial Controls and the Civil Litigative Process: Discovery 28 (1978).

extent upon the basic honesty of opposing counsel. But the skeptics are not entirely misguided or paranoid. The more commonly employed discovery devices are useful even where the opposition lies, cheats, and steals because these devices will still illuminate the issues in the case. The admission request, if denied, provides significantly less information. To a large extent, in fact, requests for admission are not so much a discovery device as a mechanism for streamlining proof at trial or determining exactly which matters will be contested at trial. Admissions requests are thus not inherently inferior to the more popular discovery mechanisms—just different.

§ 9.2 PURPOSES

Rule 36 is not a pure discovery device in that it does not require a party to disclose information. Rather, Rule 36 is limited to coercing concession from a party by way of admissions, denials, or simple statements. Admissions cannot be sought from a non-party. Although admission requests can be phrased like interrogatories or deposition questions, Rule 36 serves different purposes, which can make it more useful under certain conditions. For example, an interrogatory answer or deposition response may be phrased in a self-serving or equivocal manner. However, responses to admission requests permit less flexibility.

Rule 36 requires that the responding party "specifically deny the matter or set forth in detail the reasons why the answering party cannot truthfully admit or deny the matter." Rule 36 further requires that a "denial shall fairly meet the substance of the requested admission." When good faith requires that a party qualify an answer or deny part of the admission request, the responding party must specify the portion of the admission that is true and qualify or deny the remainder. An answering party may not give lack of information or knowledge as a reason for failure to admit or deny unless it represents that it made reasonable inquiry and that it can not admit or deny based on known or readily obtainable information. A party can not object to an admission request merely because it views the request as touching upon a genuine issue for trial.

In short, interrogatories, document requests, and depositions usually seek information whereas admission requests seek commitments. Responses to the other discovery devices, although often persuasive, are not conclusive proof as is an admission, which is conclusive evidence that cannot be contradicted at trial unless withdrawn (which requires the permission of the court). To be sure, the line between seeking information and seeking a commitment can become blurred. Top lawyers, for example, frequently use depositions to "score points" by obtaining an admission to an adverse fact or locking the deponent into an unflattering characterization of events. Similarly, an opponent's responses to admission requests helps the lawyer "discover" the opponents likely points of contention at trial. Nonetheless, Rule 36 is more of an adjunct to trial practice than a discovery procedure. Admissions expedite trials and relieve the parties of expenses involved in proving facts.

Despite its link to trial, the scope of Rule 36 is as broad as that of the other discovery devices. It explicitly incorporates the scope of Rule 26(b). Admission requests can address any matter or thing relevant to the subject matter of a case as well as touching upon information "reasonably calculated to lead to the discovery of admissible evidence. Of course, Rule 36 presupposes that some information has been discovered and is known. The admission request shapes the information into statements designed primarily for evidentiary purposes for trial, helping the discovering party to obtain an early determination of the facts and issues that will be relevant and admissible at trial.

Considerations involved in drafting requests parallel those for drafting interrogatories or similar deposition questions. In short, the Rule 36 request looks like the pointed discovery request. It is also subject to the same alternative responses such as requests for a protective order, extensions of time, etc. as well as being a proper subject of a motion to compel discovery. Use of an admission request does not preclude use of interrogatories or depositions regarding the same topic (or vice versa) as discovery procedures are cumulative and complementary.

§ 9.3 REQUESTS

The timing of requests for admissions depends upon the applicable rules of the jurisdiction. Federal Rule 36(a) permits requests for admissions to be served only after the time specified in Rule 26(d), which rule requires that the parties meet and confer in accord with Rule 26(f). This meeting typically takes place early in the litigation. Rules 36(a) and 29 also expressly permit the parties by written stipulation to vary this time unless the time extensions interfere with scheduling deadlines imposed by a court. These rules also allow any party to seek leave of court to submit requests at an earlier stage of litigation. The parties when they meet and confer in accord with Rule 26(f) may establish a discovery plan which would include the timing and scope of requests for admissions. If the parties are not able to agree to specific requests or their timing, they may formally serve requests for admissions on a party in accord with Rule 36. In the federal system, parties may no longer unilaterally serve requests for admissions with pleadings.

In federal courts that have opted out of the new disclosure rules and in state court jurisdiction which have not adopted these provisions, requests may usually be served at any time, including with pleadings. A responding party has 30 days to respond, which requires a party to serve requests no less than 30 days before a certain trial date, otherwise, the responding party need not respond. A scheduling order or pretrial order or a judge or local rule may establish different time limits for the service of requests for admissions.

Rule 36 requests must be served upon the respondent party and all other parties to the lawsuit. Rule 36 requires that each admission matter be separately set forth but does not set a limit on the number of requests. However, some local rules do limit the number of admission requests a party may propound.[1] Finding examples of requests is perhaps more difficult than for other discovery devices. Admission requests are less litigated and thus few cases list the actual requests submitted. The 1939 *Walsh* case[2] does detail a number of early American, though still appropriate, requests:

> The defendant, The Connecticut Mutual Life Insurance Company, requests the plaintiff, Mabelle Walsh, to make the following admissions for the purpose of this action only, and subject to all pertinent objections to admissibility, which may be interposed at trial:
>
> That each of the following statements is true:
>
> 1a. In October, 1922, Samuel A. Walsh (plaintiff's deceased husband) sustained a personal injury, to-wit, a fracture of his jaw.
>
> 1b. Said fracture was on the right side of lower jaw.
>
> 1c. Said Samuel A. Walsh consulted Dr. Henry S. Dunning of New York, in October, 1922.
>
> 1d. Said Samuel A. Walsh consulted said Dr. Dunning in October, 1922, for said fracture of the jaw.
>
> 1e. Exhibit A, annexed hereto, is a correct copy of said Dr. Dunning's record of his treatments of said Samuel A. Walsh in October and November, 1922.
>
> 1f. The facts stated in Exhibit A, annexed hereto, are correct.
>
> 1g. In or about October, 1922, or thereafter, said Samuel A. Walsh informed the plaintiff that he had received an injury to the jaw.
>
> . . .
>
> 1i. Said Samuel A. Walsh informed the plaintiff that he sustained said injury to his jaw by being struck by a person's fist.
>
> 1j. Said Samuel A. Walsh informed the plaintiff that he sustained said injury to his jaw while he was intoxicated by the use of alcoholic stimulants.
>
> 1k. Said Samuel A. Walsh informed the plaintiff that he sustained said injury while engaged in a fight or brawl.
>
> 1l. Said Samuel A. Walsh informed the plaintiff that he had been treated by Dr. Dunning for said injury.

Form 20 appended to the Rules of Civil Procedure provides an official illustration:

§ 9.3

1. *See* S.D.Cal.R. 230–1 (25 requests); D.S.C. Order Re Requests for Admission (20 requests); W.D.Tex.R. 26(d)(1) (10 requests).

2. *Walsh v. Connecticut Mutual Life Insurance Co. of Hartford, Conn.*, 26 F.Supp. 566, 569–570 (E.D.N.Y.1939).

Plaintiff *A.B.* requests defendant *C.D.* within ______ days after service of this request to make the following admissions for the purpose of this action only and subject to all pertinent objections to admissibility which may be interposed at the trial:

(1) That each of the following documents, exhibited with this request, is genuine. [*Here list the documents and describe each document.*]

(2) That each of the following statements is true. [*Here list the statements.*]

Despite the blank in form 20, the number of days allowed for the response usually does not vary. Rule 36 allows a party a minimum of 30 days to respond (45 days if served with the summons and complaint). Consequently, the number 30 or 45 would usually appear on that blank line. Rule 29 prohibits the attorneys from extending the time, but Rule 36(a) allows a court to increase or decrease the responding time and, interestingly enough, such allowance may be made upon an *ex parte* application by the requesting party.[3] Such requests are unusual, however, and it would be even more unusual for a judge to grant an order without allowing the responding party an opportunity to oppose any such application.

The use of requests early in a case may avoid the efforts and expenses of further discovery and trial preparation, but it is not possible in many cases to frame Rule 36 requests intelligently until after thorough discovery or during trial preparation.

Strategy and drafting tactics for Rule 36 may require the inclusion of:

- A preface regarding alternative responses to admissions;
- Definitions describing the meaning of certain words or phrases;
- References to the time periods of the requests;
- Other appropriate instructions.

The following guidelines for drafting a request may be useful:

- Draft a precise and direct request, not an interrogatory.

  Ask: Do you admit that: You said "The sky is falling" when you first saw the sky falling?

  Not: Describe in detail what you said about the sky falling when you observed the sky falling from the sky.

- Phrase a request for which a yes or no answer provides you with the admission or denial you seek.

  Ask: Do you admit that: The color of the sky you saw falling was blue?

  Not: Do you admit that: The color of the sky you saw was blue, green, yellow, orange or some other color?

3. 8 Charles A. Wright & Arthur R. Miller, Federal Practice and Procedure § 2257 (1970). *See also* 48 Minn.Stat.Ann., R.Civ.P. 36.01.

- Eliminate unnecessary adjectives, adverbs, and other characterizations.

  Ask: Do you admit that: A one-foot square piece of sky hit your school desk?

  Not: Do you admit that: A large, segmented portion of the upper, thinner atmosphere landed with a shattering thud upon the relatively small location you occupied in the school room?

- Draft requests as simple, singular requests in separately-numbered paragraphs.

  Do not ask: Do you admit that: The sky that fell from the sky, which you observed fall on August 20, 1980, hit the top of your head on August 21, 1980, causing you hospital emergency-room expenses of three bushels of corn?

  Rather ask: Do you admit that: (1) you saw a piece of the sky fall on August 20, 1985? (2) a piece of the sky fell on August 21, 1985, and hit the top of your head? (3) you were treated at the Roost Hospital Emergency Room on August 21, 1985? (4) you paid a Roost Hospital bill of three bushels of corn on August 21, 1985?

- Avoid incorporations by reference.[4] Compose each request as a complete admission by itself.

  Do not ask: Do you admit: Paragraph 3 of the cross-complaint?

  Rather, ask: Do you admit: Plaintiff hit Robert Fall on his jaw with her fist on June 1?

Some complex cases involving wholesale information and documents may require the use of admissions incorporating some of the information or documents by reference. If so, indicate what is incorporated as precisely as possible. Incorporation by reference is especially practical if the documents, such as attachments to the pleadings or numbered deposition exhibits, are formally identified.

There is no numerical limit on the number of requests or the number of sets of requests, but requests cannot be harassing, unduly burdensome, or excessive in number. The Federal Advisory Committee recognizes that "requests to admit may be so voluminous and so framed that the answering party [will find] the task of identifying what is in dispute and what is not unduly burdensome," and the committee suggests that the responding party take some responsive action, such as in these situations seeking a protective order under Rule 26(c) or other judicial relief from an oppressive request.[5]

4. The court in *SEC v. Micro-Moisture Controls, Inc.* articulated a rationale: "Such incorporation by reference is improper since it unjustly casts upon the defendants the burden of determining at their peril what portions of the incorporated material contain relevant matters of fact which must be either admitted or denied." 21 F.R.D. 164, 166 (S.D.N.Y.1957).

5. Fed.R.Civ.P. 36(a), Notes of Advisory Comm.—1970 Amendments.

§ 9.4 OPINIONS AND CONCLUSIONS

There used to be some doubt whether admission requests could seek responses to opinions and conclusions. But Rule 36(a) now provides that requests may "relate to statements or opinions of fact or the application of law to fact." It is now clear that one party can demand that another party respond to factual statements, opinions, and conclusions and to legal statements, opinions, and conclusions. The Federal Advisory Committee Notes supply an explanation and illustration:

> [T]he subdivision provides that a request may be made to admit any matters within the scope of Rule 26(b) that relate to statements or opinions of fact or of the application of law to fact. It thereby eliminates the requirement that the matters be "of fact." This change resolves conflicts in the court decisions as to whether a request to admit matters of "opinion" and matters involving "mixed law and fact" is proper under the rule....
>
> Not only is it difficult as a practical matter to separate "fact" from "opinion," ... but an admission of a matter of opinion may facilitate proof or narrow the issues or both. An admission of a matter involving the application of law to fact may, in a given case, even more clearly narrow the issues. For example, an admission that an employee acted in the scope of his employment may remove a major issue from the trial. In *McSparran v. Hanigan,* plaintiff admitted that "the premises on which said accident occurred, were occupied under the control" of one of the defendants.[1] This admission, involving law as well as fact, removed one of the issues from the lawsuit and thereby reduced the proof required at trial. The amended provision does not authorize requests for admissions of law unrelated to the facts of the case.[2]

An example of a factual request would be: "Do you admit that: A piece of the sky, which fell on August 21, 1980, hit your head?" An opinion or conclusion would be: "Do you admit that: The individual who first advised you that the sky was falling on August 21, 1980, appeared to be upset?" An application of law to fact response would be: "Do you admit that: The corporation who manufactured the sky was licensed to do business in Minnesota?"

§ 9.5 DOCUMENTS

Rule 36 specifically allows requests regarding the genuineness of documents, and it requires that copies of documents be served with the request, unless the documents have been otherwise made available or furnished to the responding party. However, many other sorts of admission requests can be made concerning documents: their authenticity, their status as originals or copies, the identity of the author who drafted them, or any Rule 26 relevant matter.

§ 9.4

1. 225 F.Supp. 628, 636 (E.D.Pa.1963), *judgment affirmed* 356 F.2d 983 (3d Cir. 1966).

2. Fed.R.Civ.P. 36(a), Notes of Advisory Comm.—1970 Amendments.

The original of the document need not be attached to a request; a copy will suffice. The responding party seldom wants to admit something about a copy without first having reviewed the original. But the responding party who has the original or who copied the original during a Rule 34 inspection can conveniently compare the Rule 36 copy with the original copy.

The Rule 36 request for admission regarding a document usually seeks the admission of some familiar matter. Should that not be the case, however, the respondent will either deny the sought-for admission because of the lack of familiarity or demand that the requesting party make the original available for review.

A Rule 36 document description need only be detailed enough to identify the document sufficiently for the respondent. A description such as "Exhibit 1 is a copy of the original August 1, 1990, Employment Agreement between the plaintiff and defendant" is more than sufficient to apprise the respondent of the identity of an attached exhibit.[1] In many cases, the circumstances make it clear that the attached is a copy of an original and such a notation may not be necessary. A more detailed description might be necessary if the respondent did not have the original access to the document.

Rule 36 permits the admission of other things besides documents. The rule specifically allows a request to be submitted regarding the truth of "any matter." That includes statements and documents, tangible things and property, and anything admissible at trial. "Anything" includes demonstrative trial exhibits, like a diagram or other visual aid, as well as real evidence.

§ 9.6 RESPONSES

The party receiving Rule 36 requests must respond in one or more ways appropriate to the particular requests. There are seven alternatives. A responding party may:

1. Do nothing,
2. Admit;
3. Deny;
4. Qualify the answer;
5. Object to the request;
6. Move for a protective order; or
7. Request or seek an extension of time.

A party must respond to each individual request by specifying which of these alternative responses apply.

§ 9.5

1. 4A Moore's Federal Practice ¶ 36.-03[4] (2d ed. 1991).

A party can not respond in the alternative to a singular request.[1] A party must choose one and only one of the seven responses for each request and cannot respond alternatively as in a pleading. The response should be a single writing, listing the various requests, followed by the corresponding responses in order, and signed by the party or his or her attorney. The response must be served upon all parties to the action.

Rule 36 is self-executing and quite clear: if you say nothing and send nothing, you have admitted the requests. What is a timely response? One that is made in time: 45 days if the admission requests are served with the summons and complaint. Otherwise, 30 days, unless a court orders a different time.

Courts can enforce these time limits, depending in part upon the reaction of the opposition. If the opposing party accepts a late response, the response is effective. If the opposing party refuses to accept the late response, the court, in its discretion, determines whether to waive the rule's automatic deadline effect. The court's discretion turns on the degree of prejudice suffered by the party relying upon the automatic-effect rule.[2] One court has refused to permit a late reply when the discovering party relied upon the rule and dismissed some witnesses whose relocation would seriously inconvenience and prejudice that party.[3]

An admission seeking something beyond the scope of Rules 26 or 36 will probably be ineffective. For example, a request seeking an admission of a law not applicable to the facts exceeds the scope of Rule 36, so failure to respond to such a request does not constitute an automatic admission.[4] However, one court did establish jurisdiction by an unanswered admission.[5]

If 30 days have passed and no response has been submitted to requests for admissions. Counsel should ordinarily file responses and argue that the late responses constitute "amendments,"[6] or seek a court order, arguing that the delinquent responses have not prejudiced the opposition.

A party who claims not to have received the requests must persuade a judge of that fact. The persuaded judge applying common sense would most correctly conclude that the request was never served and thus there has been no failure to respond.

Where a party went into hiding to avoid admitting something, the court found that the respondent had not taken adequate steps to inform

§ 9.6

1. *Havenfield Corp. v. H & R Block, Inc.*, 67 F.R.D. 93, 97 (W.D.Mo.1973).

2. *Pleasant Hill Bank v. United States*, 60 F.R.D. 1, 3 (W.D.Mo.1973).

3. *Brennan v. Varrasso Brothers, Inc.*, 17 Fed.R.Serv.2d 718, 718 (D.Mass.1973).

4. *Williams v. Krieger*, 61 F.R.D. 142, 144 (S.D.N.Y.1973).

5. *Oroco Marine, Inc. v. National Marine Service, Inc.*, 71 F.R.D. 220 (S.D.Tex. 1976).

6. *United States v. Cannon*, 363 F.Supp. 1045, 1049 (D.Del.1973).

the other party of its address, reasoned that the non-receipt excuse may encourage parties to hide rather than respond, and held that the failure to respond constituted an admission even though the respondent claimed it never received the requests.[7]

A party must respond to the request in a truthful, specific, straightforward, and unconditional manner.[8] Honesty determines how to respond. A party admits something by responding yes or in some other specific affirmative or appropriate fashion. A party bases an admission on whatever knowledge and information has been obtained during discovery. Where a party has no personal knowledge of a fact but only information obtained from a third person, if the party believes the information to be accurate, the party must admit it, regardless of the source of the information.[9]

If a party has some doubt about the information, the party need not admit the fact.[10] For example, supposing a witness to an accident told a party that she thought the traffic light was red, a party need not admit requests querying whether the light was red, if that party has a reasonable doubt about the accuracy of the statement or the credibility of that witness. The decision to admit a fact provided by a witness may depend, then, on the assessment a party makes of that witness's credibility? Sure. Requests for admission may delve into the attorney's mental impressions of a witness made during investigation and so they need not be admitted if they fall under the protections provided such lawyer's mental process under Rule 26.[11]

§ 9.7 DENIALS

Rule 36 states that a denial must be specific about what is being denied and must "fairly meet the substance of the requested admission." This means that a party must review and ask: "Can I specifically, in good faith, honestly, and unconditionally deny all or part of this request?" The rule also requires a party to specify which part of a request is true and which untrue.

To be effective, a denial must deny the truth of the matter. An absolute denial, that is, the use of the word *denied,* unqualified by any other statement, constitutes a sufficient denial.[1] Parties who state that they "refuse" to admit something have not properly denied the request.[2]

7. *Freed v. Plastic Packaging Materials, Inc.,* 66 F.R.D. 550, 552 (E.D.Pa.1975).

8. *See Dulansky v. Iowa–Illinois Gas & Electric Co.,* 92 F.Supp. 118, 124 (S.D.Iowa 1950).

9. *See* Ted Finman, The Request for Admissions in Federal Civil Procedure, 71 Yale L.J. 371, 406 (1962).

10. *See* David L. Shapiro, Some Problems of Discovery in an Adversary System, 63 Minn.L.Rev. 1055, 1087 (1979).

11. These provisions are discussed in § 1.7.3 of this text.

§ 9.7

1. *See generally* Annot., 36 A.L.R.2d 1192 (1954).

2. *Fuhr v. Newfoundland–St. Lawrence Shipping Limited, Panama,* 24 F.R.D. 9, 13 (S.D.N.Y.1959).

And parties who deny the "accuracy" of a request have likewise not properly denied a statement.[3]

A party may not admit and deny something at the same time, but that does not mean lawyers have not tried. For example, one request for admission asked the plaintiff to admit that the plaintiff had released the defendant's corporation from responsibility "for all indebtedness." The response was "Admitted, except that it is denied that the said corporation was released of all indebtedness." [4]

The court held, apparently with a straight face, that the reply constituted an admission. Some authorities construe Rule 36 to require an explanation of the sources for the information and belief for it to be an effective denial.[5] An information-and-belief denial without some explanatory sources may well be ineffective.

§ 9.8 QUALIFYING RESPONSES

A party has to respond in whatever direction the facts, opinions, and conclusions lead. The rule requires a party to "set forth in detail the reasons why the answering party cannot truthfully admit or deny the matter." A general statement that does not include detailed reasons is insufficient.[1]

A party cannot attempt to be evasive or to avoid direct responses by using qualifying answers. Courts do not countenance such conduct.[2] Someone once said, very perceptively, "It is the genius of Rule 36 that responses that do not advance the cause of clarifying and simplifying the issues must be explained." [3]

Rule 36 explicitly envisions limits to qualifying responses. The rule states that "an answering party may not give lack of information or knowledge as a reason for failure to admit or deny unless he states that he has made reasonable inquiry and that the information known or readily obtainable by him is insufficient to enable him to admit or deny."

What constitutes a reasonable inquiry usually depends upon the nature of the request and the extent of the potential inquiry. The Federal Advisory Committee Notes explain that the rule imposes upon the responding party a "reasonable burden" to obtain the information. The notes say that the extent of such investigation should mimic the investigation necessary to the preparation of a case or should include an investigation of all information "close enough at hand to be 'readily

3. *Southern Railway Co. v. Crosby,* 201 F.2d 878, 880 (4th Cir.1953).

4. *Riordan v. Ferguson,* 147 F.2d 983, 986 n. 1 (2d Cir.1945).

5. *See* 23 Am.Jur.2d, *Depositions and Discovery* § 304 (1965).

§ 9.8

1. *Villarosa v. Massachusetts Trustees of Eastern Gas & Fuel Associates,* 39 F.R.D. 337, 338–339 (E.D.Pa.1966). Stating that defendant can "neither admit nor deny the truthfulness of the statements" is insufficient as a response.

2. *Dulansky v. Iowa–Illinois Gas & Electric Co.,* 92 F.Supp. 118, 124 (S.D.Iowa 1950).

3. James L. Underwood, A Guide to Federal Discovery Rules 164 (1979).

obtainable.' "[4] Cases have held that a party must make a reasonable effort to discover a date, short of undue hardship[5] or of any substantial reason to the contrary.[6] The guidelines all reduce to one standard: what inquiry would a reasonable attorney advise his or her client to make?

Rule 36 allows a party to plead inability to respond fully by claiming that the requested admission involves a contested issue in the case: "A party who considers that the matter of which an admission has been requested presents a genuine issue for trial may not, on that ground alone, object to the request; he may, subject to the provisions of Rule 37(c), deny the matter or set forth reasons why he cannot admit or deny it."

The sanctions provisions of Rule 37(c) concern the expenses that a party who fails to make an admission may have to bear if that party has no good reason for declining to admit. The general rule and the intent of Rule 36 are to admit any request that is substantially correct by admitting what is correct and denying the part that is incorrect. However, in some requests, one piece of information renders the entire request deniable in good faith. It can often be a difficult and close decision.

A party can add more information to a response than the request seeks. It is an appropriate tactic for an attorney to include helpful information in some responses. The legitimacy of the tactic depends on the precise request and response, but some requests may require a qualified response that includes some narrative information. Usually such a tactic can be used if a request has not been carefully and precisely drafted, leaving room for an interpretive or narrative response.

§ 9.9 OBJECTIONS

Any objection that pinpoints the defects of a request is proper. The types of objections appropriate to requests for admission are the same types applicable to interrogatories and requests for production.[1] Whatever objection is interposed, specific reasons explaining the grounds must be included. Objections based on inaccurate, immaterial, or incompetent grounds may be insufficient.[2] Objections based upon Rule 26(b) irrelevancy and upon claims of privilege may be more common than others, but it is difficult to estimate.

Because Rule 36 is denominated a discovery rule subject to Rule 26's definition of relevance, an irrelevancy objection based upon the more restrictive Federal Rule of Evidence 401 that it should have no effect,

4. Fed.R.Civ.P. 36(a), Notes of Advisory Comm.—1970 Amendments.

5. *E.H. Tate Co. v. Jiffy Enterprises, Inc.*, 16 F.R.D. 571, 574 (E.D.Pa.1954).

6. *See Lumpkin v. Meskill*, 64 F.R.D. 673, 678 (D.Conn.1974).

§ 9.9

1. *See* 4A Moore's Federal Practice ¶ 36.06 (2d ed. 1991); and §§ 3.5 and 4.12 above.

2. *See United States v. Schine Chain Theatres, Inc.*, 4 F.R.D. 109, 112 (W.D.N.Y. 1944).

but it might. The remnants of previous decisions and past rules affect current practice. Some practitioners, judges, and commentators continue to recognize as a legitimate objection a response that the request seeks an admission useful only for informational purposes and not for trial purposes.[3] This practice runs counter to the clear intent of Rules 26 and 36. However, the split personality of Rule 36, as both a discovery device and a trial expedient supports such practice.

However, an objection based upon privilege is not defined by the discovery rules. The law of evidence exclusively determines the propriety of a privilege-based objection to a request. A legitimate privilege objection can arise in a number of settings.

An objection may be based on "defective drafting." For example, an objection may be more properly phrased as "vague" or "ambiguous" or "compound" or with some other word specifying the nature of the defect. These may also be fairly common objections.

An objection based on a ground sufficient to obtain a protective order, like a confidential trade secret, is also conceivable and realistic.[4] Consider its advantage: such an objection relieves counsel of the need to seek a Rule 26 protective order and places the burden on the opposition to obtain a Rule 37 order. The objection must contain the specific grounds on which it is based.

Rule 36 has eliminated a number of formerly valid objections, including: the request presents an issue for trial; the request includes disputable matter; the request seeks a factual opinion or a mixed question of law and fact. Case law also has declared a number of objections improper, including: the requesting party already knows the answer,[5] or the request relates to matters on which the requesting party has the burden of proof.[6] "The very purpose of the request is to ascertain [what] ... is a genuine issue for trial."[7] Matters in dispute are usually fair game for the requesting party.

§ 9.10 RESPONSE STRATEGIES

In responding to requests, an attorney must consider the impact of the responses upon the case. The more harmful the impact an admission may have upon a case, the more scrutiny an attorney should devote to uncovering objections or drafting good-faith qualifying answers or denials. This scrutiny must also weigh the risk that the responding party may challenge the sufficiency of a response that is not an admission. A non-admission may increase costs, expenses, and time disproportionately to its impact on a case. Moreover, admissions usually foreclose

3. 4A Moore's Federal Practice ¶ 36.-04[2] (2d ed. 1991).

4. Kent Sinclair, Federal Civil Practice 739 (1980).

5. *Electric Furnace Co. v. Fire Association of Philadelphia,* 9 F.R.D. 741, 743 (N.D.Ohio 1949).

6. *Adventures in Good Eating, Inc. v. Best Places to Eat, Inc.,* 131 F.2d 809, 812 (7th Cir.1942) (burp).

7. Fed.R.Civ.P. 36(a), Notes of Advisory Comm.—1970 Amendments.

an area to discovery, whereas denials may prompt the other attorney to use discovery devices to ferret out information.

An admission constitutes proof of a matter and eliminates any need for discoverable information to support or rebut the admission—any subsequent request is irrelevant. A party may, however obtain more time to respond to requests by court order. Rule 29 makes it clear that "stipulations extending the time provided in Rule . . . 36 may be made only with the approval of the court." You can't get much clearer than that. However, some attorneys overlook the technical enforcement of this rule and accept a response after more than 30 days.

Requests to which response is not timely become admitted. However, a court has the power to convert an untimely response into a timely response by retroactively extending the time limit.[1] Rule 36 also allows untimely answers as "amendments" to admissions: Rule 36(b) allows a party to "withdraw" admissions and "amend" answers. A party who files an untimely response could seek to withdraw the admissions and substitute the late responses as amendments. The rule allows this unless it adversely affects the presentation of a case or otherwise prejudices the requesting party.[2]

Rule 36 allows a requesting party to dispute an objection through a motion and court hearing. If the court determines that the objection is justified, it will stand. If not, the court must order an answer.

The objecting party has the burden of showing the validity of the objection.[3] That makes sense. If the objection does not make sense, the court may order the objecting party to pay cents to the requesting party who had to seek the hearing.

§ 9.11 CHALLENGING RESPONSES

Rule 36 allows a requesting party to challenge the sufficiency of any response through a motion and court hearing. If the court determines that a response did not comply with Rule 36, the court has three options: (1) to declare the request admitted,[1] (2) to order an amended answer,[2] or (3) to postpone the "final disposition" of the request until a pretrial conference.

A court will most likely choose the third alternative when the request either seeks a factual response that requires detailed investigation or seeks a mixed question of law and fact. The judge may recognize that the responding party simply needs more time to formulate a response.

§ 9.10

1. *French v. United States,* 416 F.2d 1149, 1152 (9th Cir.1968).

2. *Pleasant Hill Bank v. United States,* 60 F.R.D. 1, 3 (W.D.Mo.1973).

3. *See* Kent Sinclair, Federal Civil Practice 741 (1980).

§ 9.11

1. *Weva Oil Corp. v. Belco Petroleum Corp.,* 68 F.R.D. 663 (N.D.W.Va.1975); *Jackson v. Riley Stoker Corp.,* 57 F.R.D. 120 (E.D.Pa.1972); *United States v. Heichman,* 45 F.R.D. 122 (N.D.Ill.1968).

2. *Alexander v. Rizzo,* 52 F.R.D. 235, 236 (E.D.Pa.1971).

A non-response or an improper response to a request automatically becomes an admission after the appropriate time passes. An improper response must be challenged by the requesting party and may lead to an admission if the judge so orders. The Advisory Committee Notes explain that it is usually more effective and fair to decide the fate of a response within a reasonable time before trial. This avoids an untimely or an unfair surprise at trial for one of the parties.

Any and all discovery devices can be employed to supplement requests for admissions. For instance, an attorney can submit interrogatories to the responding party asking that the party explain the "whys" of or facts supporting the denial or qualification of a response.

§ 9.12 CHANGING ADMISSIONS

Rule 36 permits a party to seek a court order allowing the withdrawal of the previous admission and substitution of an amended response. The rule spells out the considerations the court must employ:

> Subject to the provisions of Rule 16 governing amendment of a pre-trial order, the court may permit withdrawal or amendment when the presentation of the merits of the action will be subserved thereby and the party who obtained the admission fails to satisfy the court that withdrawal or amendment will prejudice him in maintaining his action or defense on the merits.

One reason might be that the admission was a genuine mistake, should not have been made, and distorts the merits. Another reason might be that the circumstances have changed, so the admission is no longer true.[1]

Non-requesting parties must persuade a court that a withdrawal or amendment will "prejudice" a case by indicating that they relied upon the admission to their detriment. They may be able to show that some investigation was deferred, some discovery curtailed, or some bit of evidence deteriorated as a result of reliance on the admission.

The requesting party may have great difficulty countering these prejudice claims. A factor significantly influencing the degree of prejudice is the timing of the request for the withdrawal or amendment. The sooner the change is sought after submission of the admissions, the more likely the court will grant it. The closer in time to trial the change is sought, the more likely the court will deny it. This provision of Rule 36 does not include amendments to other responses besides admissions, like denials, objections, or qualifications.

Why would a responding party want to amend a favorable response like a denial or an objection? A party might want to amend a qualification, but the provision specifically limits the procedure to "admissions." Only the portion of a qualified response that was an admission would be included within the provisions. A party has an obligation under Rule

§ 9.12

1. James L. Underwood, A Guide to Federal Discovery Rules 156 (1979).

26(e) to supplement responses to admission. Those provisions do not square with the Rule 36 provisions regarding amendments. Rule 26 requires a party unilaterally to amend an admission. A reconciling interpretation of the two rules would seem to be that a party has a duty to supplement admissions under Rule 26, but that the supplementation cannot be done unilaterally. It requires a court order under Rule 36.[2]

§ 9.13 EFFECTS OF ADMISSIONS

Rule 36(b) declares admissions to be conclusive proof of the matter asserted for purposes of the pending action only, unless a court allows a withdrawal or an amendment. The Federal Advisory Committee explains that an admission has the same effect as a pleading admission or as a stipulation of facts executed by the attorneys.[1] The factfinder (the judge or jury) must accept the admissions as accurate and proven and cannot disbelieve them. The party that made the admissions cannot contradict or rebut the admissions at trial.

Admissions are automatically admissible at the trial. A party need only offer them to the court. Another party can, however, object to their being offered. They remain subject to any appropriate evidentiary objections brought by any party. For example, even though a party has admitted a request, the court could sustain that party's irrelevancy objection to that request and thereby exclude an admission from the trial.

The effect of an admission that has been withdrawn and amended is not certain. The courts have apparently not resolved the question. A requesting party could introduce a withdrawn admission as a prior inconsistent statement at the trial and the responding party could explain or rebut it.[2]

A denial of an admission does have an effect at trial. Itcan be used for impeachment purposes or to preclude the denying party from introducing contrary evidence. An unjustified denial, which causes the requesting party to prove the matter at trial, results in the responding party's paying for the costs of proof.[3]

2. 8 Charles A. Wright & Arthur R. Miller, Federal Practice and Procedure § 2264 (1970 and Supp.1994).

§ 9.13

1. 4A Moore's Federal Practice ¶ 36.08 (2d ed. 1991).

2. 8 Charles A. Wright & Arthur R. Miller, Federal Practice and Procedure § 2264 (1970, Supp.1994).

3. Fed.R.Civ.P. 37(c). *See Popeil Brothers, Inc. v. Schick Electric, Inc.*, 516 F.2d 772, 777 (7th Cir.1975); *Leas v. General Motors Corp.*, 50 F.R.D. 366, 368 (E.D.Wis. 1970).

PRACTICE PROBLEMS

Requests for Admissions

Draft a variety of Rule 36 requests for admissions in the following problems, including statements involving facts, opinion, genuineness of documents, and application of law to fact. Form requests may be useful as guides in composing requests but may not be copied. The Summit Discovery Rules place no limit on the specific number of requests but do require the requests to be reasonable in number. Your instructor may specify limits.

1. You represent Hot Dog Enterprises in *Hot Dog Enterprises v. Tri–Chem* (Chapter 1). Draft requests for admissions directed to the defendant.

2. You represent Tri–Chem in *Hot Dog Enterprises v. Tri–Chem* (Chapter 1). Draft requests for admissions directed to the plaintiff.

3. You represent the plaintiff in *Northern Motor Homes v. Danforth* (Case J). Draft requests for admissions directed to the defendants.

4. You represent the defendants in *Northern Motor Homes v. Danforth* (Case J). Draft requests for admissions directed to the plaintiff.

5. You represent the plaintiff in *Burris v. Warner* (Case K).

6. You represent the defendant in *Burris v. Warner* (Case K).

7. You represent the plaintiff in *Vasquez v. Hot Dog Enterprises* (Case F). Draft requests for admissions directed to the defendant.

8. You represent the defendant Hot Dog Enterprises in *Vasquez v. Hot Dog Enterprises* (Case F). Draft requests for admissions directed to the plaintiff.

Reconsidering and Redrafting for Admissions

9. You represent the Defendant Summit Insurance Company in *Pozdak v. Summit Insurance Company* (Case B). Casey Pozdak has sued for breach of contract seeking to recover $250,000 for the fire loss to his building and $1,000,000 for the loss of its contents. You defend claiming Pozdak committed arson which bars recovery under the contract. An associate in your firm prepares a draft of the following requests for admissions:

Defendant demands that the Plaintiff admit:

1. That Casey Pozdak increased the value of his fire insurance contract with the Defendant to $250,000 for real property coverage and $1,000,000 for personal property coverage four months before the fire of July 3.

2. That Casey Pozdak had been accused of insurance fraud while in college.

3. That Casey Pozdak could have driven from Stacy Lindberg's cabin to Mitchell the evening of July 3.

4. That Casey Pozdak owes Stacy Lindberg $50,000.

5. That Casey Pozdak owns a 19XX BMW Turbo and owes $15,000 on it.

6. That the fire insurance policy between the Plaintiff and Defendant in force on July 3 states that: "Payment shall not be made under the terms of this policy for the fire destruction of the insured building and contents if the insured fire was caused by arson and if the insurer caused or participated in the arson."

(a) Which of these requests would you not submit, and why?

(b) Redraft those you would submit.

(c) What other requests would you submit, and why? Draft those requests.

(d) If you represented the Plaintiff Pozdak and received this set of requests, how would you respond to each of these requests.

10. You represent the plaintiff in *Northern Motor Homes v. Danforth* (Case J). The defendants have submitted the following requests for admissions to you. Draft responses to these requests.

Do you admit that each of the following statements is true?

(a) Sara Duncan was an agent and employee of Plaintiff and was at all times acting within the scope of her employment in dealing with Defendants on May 25 and 26, 19XX.

(b) Plaintiff provided Defendants with a "Limited Warranty," an exact copy of which appears as Exhibit A in the Answer.

(c) Between June 11 and June 22, Plaintiff did not check nor test the gas mileage of the Voyageur Camper.

(d) On June 25, 19XX, John Danforth telephoned and talked to Bill Burke.

(e) The Voyageur Motor Home was in the possession of Plaintiff for repairs from July 1 through July 8.

(f) The law of the State of Summit permits Defendants to revoke acceptance in this case if defects in the Voyageur Motor Home substantially impair its value to Defendants.

11. You represent the defendants in *Northern Motor Homes v. Danforth* (Case J). The plaintiff has submitted the following requests for admissions to you. Draft responses to these requests.

Do you admit that each of the following statements is true?

(a) John and Joan Danforth failed to pay the July 24, 19XX installment of $229.02.

(b) John and Joan Danforth signed a Retail Installment Contract, an exact copy of which appears as Exhibit A in the Complaint.

(c) John and Joan Danforth accepted the Voyageur Camper on May 26, 19XX.

(d) John and Joan Danforth drove and used the Voyageur Camper from May 28 to July 30, 19XX.

(e) The failure to pay the July 24, 19XX, installment payment of $229.02 constituted a default of the retail installment contract.

(f) Paragraph 4 of the Retail Installment Contract permits Northern Motor Homes to accelerate all payments if a default occurs.

12. You represent the plaintiff in *Burris v. Warner* (Case K). Respond to the requests for admissions prepared by the student attorney representing the defendant.

13. You represent the defendant in *Burris v. Warner* (Case K). Respond to the requests for admissions prepared by the student attorney representing the plaintiff.

14. You represent the plaintiff in *Vasquez v. Hot Dog Enterprises* (Case F). Respond to the requests for admissions prepared by the student attorney representing the defendant.

15. You represent the defendant in *Vasquez v. Hot Dog Enterprises* (Case F). Respond to the requests for admission prepared by the student attorney representing the plaintiff.

*

CHAPTER 10

ENFORCING DISCOVERY RIGHTS

I can't get no satisfaction.

I can't get no satisfaction!

Cause I try and I try ...

I can't get no, I can't get no satisfaction, no satisfaction.

Mick Jagger and Keith Richards

§ 10.1 INTRODUCTION

Discovery is designed to take place primarily with satisfaction and without court involvement. Interrogatories, depositions, document production, and requests for admissions are all normally used without a judge's ever ordering or barring them. Discovery does not, however, always follow this design.

Parties may have real disagreements about what is discoverable, leading to unresolved disputes. Legitimate attempts to discover information may be met not with satisfactory responses, but rather with silence, objections, insults, threats, or worse. Parties sometimes also initiate discovery for improper purposes or serve overly broad or unduly burdensome discovery requests. Rule 37 provides a judicial remedy; other devices provide informal approaches to obtain information from your opponent. You can increase your chances of discovery success by exhausting informal methods of enforcing your discovery rights. Local rules or practice may even require you to employ these informal cooperative devices before seeking judicial relief.

§ 10.2 INFORMAL ENFORCEMENT

If your initial discovery request is ignored, receives inadequate response, or is met by objection, a Rule 37 motion is frequently not the best first step. A telephone call or a letter reminding opposing counsel of the discovery obligation and asking for a definite response will occasionally bring an adequate response, especially if noncompliance is due to simple inadvertence by opposing counsel. A letter is probably preferable to a telephone call since it documents the request for voluntary compliance should a motion to compel discovery become necessary. Even if noncompliance is not inadvertent, however, such a letter can bring results. And if the letter is met only with objections or inadequate response, you are in a better position to obtain judicial assistance because your opponent will have told you the basis for the non-response. If the letter does not bring a response, your case for a court order compelling discovery or penalizing your opponent for noncompliance is strengthened.

Negotiation is another important tool for enforcing discovery rights. Documenting the negotiation offers also bolsters your position if you should have to seek an order from a judge. If you can demonstrate that, despite your willingness to accommodate the reasonable objections of your opponent, discovery has still not been forthcoming, a court will be more inclined to order discovery and to award you the expenses incurred in having to seek the order. For example, demands for interrogatory answers and production of documents may be objected to on the grounds that the information sought constitutes trade secrets and other confidential information. Rule 26(c)(7) specifically provides that this is a proper subject for a protective order to limit the use of this information. Offering to stipulate to only limited use may obviate having to bring a motion to achieve the same result. The broad provisions of Rule 29 would support stipulations to overcome objections to discovery even if there is no specific ground for objecting or for obtaining a protective order.

In addition to being informal and efficient, an attempt to resolve discovery disputes between counsel may be required by rule. The federal rules of civil procedure and some state rules require counsel to meet and confer in an attempt to resolve a discovery dispute without the necessity of court involvement. These "meet and confer" rules generally require an attorney to discuss the discovery dispute with opposing counsel and to certify to the court that such a conference has been held prior to the filing of any motion to compel discovery.

§ 10.3 THE DISCOVERY PLAN

Litigants may have to meet early in a case, before discovery disputes arise, to develop a discovery plan. Fed. R. Civ. P. 26(f) directs that litigants must meet in person and create a discovery plan in all cases not exempted by local rule or special order of the court. The attorneys may meet in person, or develop a plan through telephone and letter communications. Following this meeting, the litigants must submit their discovery plan to the court and can then begin formal discovery.

Former Federal Rule 26(f) require the court to become involved in this discovery process by conducting a discovery conference and issuing an order. Present Federal Rule 26(f) no longer provides the court with this authority. Federal Rule 16 now provides the court with the power to issue a scheduling order which would include a discovery plan. This order may be necessary in situations where the parties are unable to agree on a discovery plan pursuant to Rule 26(f), or if the court wanted to impose restrictions different than the provisions of the discovery plan agreed on by the parties. Some federal district courts by local rule or standing order will continue to schedule a discovery conference and provide for the issuance of an order regarding discovery schedules.

The purpose of the meeting between litigants to discuss discovery, and the availability of court intervention, is to encourage the parties to mutually agree on discovery issues. The thinking is that the parties will agree to discovery issues reducing the likelihood of discovery disputes and eliminating the need for Rule 37 motions. This may well be the result among thinking lawyers. Sections 5.3 & 5.11 explains the timing and other aspects of discovery plans.

§ 10.4 FORMAL ENFORCEMENT

Rule 37 provides methods for obtaining judicial assistance in enforcing discovery rights. It is also the exclusive source of authority under the rules for the imposition of discovery sanctions.[1] The rule foresees a two-step process: first, an order compelling discovery must be obtained, if needed, under Rule 37(a); then sanctions may be imposed if the order is not obeyed. This two-step process is not required in every instance (what is?), but it is the usual procedure.

§ 10.4.1 Seeking Disclosure or Discovery

The federal rules of civil procedure now provide for disclosure and discovery. The sanctions available for the failure to comply with these rules include sanctions covering both disclosure and discovery violations. Some of the federal sanctions apply exclusively to disclosure violations; other provisions apply exclusively to discovery violations; and some sanctions apply to either violation.

Rules of procedure for state courts generally provide for discovery between parties, and do not require affirmatively disclosures by parties.

§ 10.4

1. Courts occasionally relied on Rule 41, governing dismissals, or on some consideration of "inherent power," in imposing discovery sanctions. The United States Supreme Court rejected this practice, stating that use of these devices "can only obscure analysis of the problem before us." *Societe Internationale Pour Participations Industrielles et Commerciales, S.A. v. Rogers,* 357 U.S. 197, 207, 78 S.Ct. 1087, 1093, 2 L.Ed.2d 1255 (1958). The Supreme Court relied heavily upon the analysis of this problem by Professor Rosenberg. *See* Maurice Rosenberg, Sanctions to Effectuate Pretrial Discovery, 58 Colum.L.Rev. 480, 484 (1958).

Sanctions available under these state courts rules will be limited to discovery sanctions. Some state court rules require disclosure and, in these situations, sanctions will be available both for violations of disclosure as well as discovery provisions.

§ 10.4.2 The Order Compelling Disclosure or Discovery

A court order is a condition precedent[2] to imposing sanctions.[3] An order compelling disclosure or discovery is required only in those types of discovery normally made without any order. For example, a second order for a physical examination is not required before sanctions can be imposed for failure to comply with an initial Rule 35 order; Rule 37(b)(2) allows imposition of sanctions directly in this case. Neither is an order compelling discovery needed under Rule 37(d) for complete failure to appear for a deposition, to serve answers or objections to interrogatories, or to provide a written response to a request for production or inspection under Rule 34.[4] In order for this subdivision to be applicable, however, there must be a total failure to make discovery. Rule 37(d) does not provide relief for partial response or arguably inadequate responses.[5] Willfulness may be of importance in determining which, if any, sanction should be imposed for failure to comply with the order, but it is not intended to be of significance in determining whether the order itself should be granted.

If a motion to compel disclosure or discovery is granted, the rules encourage the award of attorney's fees and other expenses to the party seeking the order.[6] The intent of the rule is to make the award of expenses presumptively appropriate without limiting the power of the court to exercise its discretion in this area.

By presenting an accommodating, reasonable posture to a discovery request, you can greatly enhance your chances of convincing the court that expenses should be awarded in your case. (You might also, for

2. Consult your contracts course notes.

3. *See, e.g., National Hockey League v. Metropolitan Hockey Club, Inc.,* 427 U.S. 639, 643, 96 S.Ct. 2778, 2781, 49 L.Ed.2d 747 (1976), *rehearing denied* 429 U.S. 874, 97 S.Ct. 197, 50 L.Ed.2d 158 (1976); *Schleper v. Ford Motor Co., Automotive Div.,* 585 F.2d 1367, 1371 (8th Cir.1978); *Wembley, Inc. v. Diplomat Tie Co.,* 216 F.Supp. 565, 573 (D.Md.1963).

4. *See* William Danforth, The 1975 Amendments to the Minnesota Rules of Discovery, 3 Wm. Mitchell L.Rev. 39 (1977). *See generally,* Note, The Emerging Deterrence Orientation in the Imposition of Discovery Sanctions, 91 Harv.L.Rev. 1033 (1978). *See* § 6.7 of this text for a more detailed discussion of sanctions in these cases.

5. *See, e.g., Israel Aircraft Industries, Limited v. Standard Precision,* 559 F.2d 203, 208 (2d Cir.1977).

An order compelling discovery is available for a failure to answer. Rule 37(a)(3) states that "an evasive or incomplete answer is to be treated as a failure to answer." The rule was most recently amended to remove any requirement of showing the failure to be willful.

6. *See, e.g., Societe Internationale Pour Participations Industrielles Et Commerciales, S.A. v. Rogers,* 357 U.S. 197, 212, 78 S.Ct. 1087, 1095, 2 L.Ed.2d 1255 (1958); *Fox v. Studebaker–Worthington, Inc.,* 516 F.2d 989, 993 (8th Cir.1975).

added effect, hold a plastic Bic instead of a Cross pen during the hearing.) If you are opposing a portion of a discovery request, the prompt and complete response to those portions not meriting objection helps establish your good faith in objecting to the other portion. The award of attorney's fees is sometimes, by terms of the order, expressly made the obligation of the attorney and not of the client. This is a variation of the "deep-pocket" theory, but also reflects the extreme reluctance of courts to allow a case to suffer on the merits at the expense of inappropriate or unethical practice on the part of a party's attorneys.[7]

A request for an order compelling disclosure or discovery is made upon motion, with notice to all parties and to any other affected persons (*e.g.*, a non-party deponent).[8] Local rules may place a time limit on filing this motion in certain instances. The motion may be brought in either of two courts: the court where the action is pending or the court where a deposition is being taken. The latter court is appropriate only when a deponent fails to answer questions at either an oral or a written-question deposition. The party then has the option to bring the motion in either court, unless the deponent is a non-party. (In the latter event, the motion may be brought only in the court where the deposition is being taken.) The provision is designed to minimize the burden on a deponent who is not otherwise involved in the litigation. Any motion for an order compelling discovery other than for failure to answer deposition questions may be brought only in the court where the action is pending. Even if there is a choice of courts, one court may determine that the other is a more appropriate court, and have the motion heard there.

§ 10.4.3 Imposition of Disclosure Sanctions

Federal Rule 37(a) provides that parties may bring a motion seeking an order compelling disclosure. Rule 37(a)(3) states that evasive or incomplete disclosures, answers, or responses are to be treated as a failure to disclose. Further, Rule 37(c) authorizes a specific sanction applicable for failures to disclose. This rule states that a party who without substantial justification fails to disclose information required by Rule 26 shall not be permitted to use as evidence any information not disclosed, unless the failure is harmless. This sanction recognizes that a party who fails to properly disclose information shall not be able to benefit from this non-disclosure by subsequently relying on this information at trial or at a hearing or in support of or opposition to a motion, unless a party has a substantial reason for such failure to disclose or unless the failure does not prejudice any other party. See § 10.5.4. In addition to this sanction, other sanctions of Rule 37 will be available for failing to disclose information.

7. For a discussion of the reluctance of courts to impose sanctions that penalize a party's case on the merits for the actions of that party's attorneys, *see* Charles B. Renfrew, Discovery Sanctions: A Judicial Perspective, 6 Litigation (Winter 1980), at 5.

8. Notice is required to these parties and non-parties by Fed.R.Civ.P. 6(d). The procedural requirements of discovery motion practice are discussed in § 6.8.2 of this text.

§ 10.4.4 Imposition of Discovery Sanctions

Federal Rule 37(b) offers the court a wide range of sanctions that may be imposed for failure to comply with an order for discovery. The rule allows the imposition of contempt only for violation of an order in the court where a deposition is being taken. But in all other cases the court is granted authority to enter "such orders in regard to the failure as are just." Rule 37(b)(2) lists the major sanctions that are specifically authorized:

- Facts may be deemed established;
- Evidence may be barred;
- Pleadings may be stricken or a dismissal or default judgment entered;
- A party may be found in contempt; or
- The six-way power seat may be removed from the attorney's Mercedes.

Local rules may provide supplementary sanctions for noncompliance and may also provide sanctions for misuse or abuse of the discovery process.

An order compelling discovery results in immediate compliance in the vast majority of cases. The objecting party may feel that the information sought is not discoverable, or that producing it will be unduly burdensome, or may have some other good-faith objection, but in virtually all cases a decision by a court on the merits of the objection will end the dispute—and the party will comply with the court's order.

If the order does not result in compliance, a second motion for an order imposing sanctions must be made, with notice and hearing given. The choice of sanction to be imposed is left to the discretion of the court, however, so the party seeking a severe sanction must literally move the court to impose it. Courts traditionally stated that the more severe sanctions of contempt, default, and dismissal would be imposed only as last-ditch efforts to punish a party who willfully abuses the discovery process or who flagrantly flouts the court's authority.[9] Until recently, the imposition of severe sanctions was frequently reversed by appellate courts, which found that the severe sanctions amounted to an abuse of discretion.[10] Now, however, courts have recognized that the more severe sanctions of contempt, default, and dismissal may be imposed as a deterrent to disobedience of discovery orders as well as to provide a

9. *See, e.g., Wilson v. Volkswagen of America, Inc.,* 561 F.2d 494, 503 (4th Cir. 1977), *cert. denied* 434 U.S. 1020, 98 S.Ct. 744, 54 L.Ed.2d 768 (1978); *Kropp v. Ziebarth,* 557 F.2d 142, 146 (8th Cir.1977), *appeal after remand* 601 F.2d 1348 (1979); *In re Professional Hockey Antitrust Litigation,* 531 F.2d 1188, 1193–1195 (3d Cir. 1976), *judgment reversed* 427 U.S. 639, 96 S.Ct. 2778, 49 L.Ed.2d 747 (1976), *rehearing denied* 429 U.S. 874, 97 S.Ct. 197, 50 L.Ed.2d 158 (1976).

10. *See, e.g., Sapiro v. Hartford Fire Insurance Co.,* 452 F.2d 215, 217 (7th Cir. 1971) (per curiam); *B.F. Goodrich Tire Co. v. Lyster,* 328 F.2d 411, 415 (5th Cir.1964); *Gill v. Stolow,* 240 F.2d 669, 670 (2d Cir. 1957).

penalty to the party who has disobeyed such an order.[11] The United States Supreme Court gave its clear approval to the use of discovery sanctions to deter abuse of the discovery process in *National Hockey League v. Metropolitan Hockey Club, Inc.*[12] The trial court had, as a discovery sanction, dismissed the plaintiffs' antitrust suit. The court of appeals reversed the dismissal, finding that "extenuating factors" existed, including a lack of bad faith on the part of the plaintiffs' attorneys. The Supreme Court reversed the court of appeals and reinstated the dismissal, stating:

> [T]he most severe in the spectrum of sanctions provided by statute or rule must be available to the district court in appropriate cases, not merely to penalize those whose conduct may be deemed to warrant such a sanction, but to deter those who might be tempted to such conduct in the absence of such a deterrent.[13]

The more drastic sanctions still are not imposed by most courts unless the noncompliance with the order is flagrant.[14] If you feel that dismissal or default is warranted, you must make a strong showing of the opponent's notice of the order, understanding of what was required, repeated violations, any expressions of intent not to comply, and the degree to which your position has been prejudiced. The presence of prejudice may be a key factor, on appeal, in determining whether dismissal or default is properly within the discretion of the trial court.[15]

If less severe sanctions are possibly adequate, you should expect that they will be relied on by the court. The exclusion of evidence on a certain claim or defense or the establishment of facts supporting your claim or defense are powerful sanctions and may adequately remedy the noncompliance with the court's order. The recalcitrant party is denied a trial only to the extent that he or she has been uncooperative. These orders are seldom reversed on appeal (what is?) and may therefore be even more desirable if otherwise adequate.

§ 10.5 SELECTION OF A SANCTION

§ 10.5.1 Introduction

Since the range of sanctions available is great, and substantial policy reasons support the imposition of either severe or mild sanctions, it is

11. *See, e.g., Robison v. Transamerica Insurance Co.,* 368 F.2d 37, 39 (10th Cir. 1966) ("The office of 37(d) is to secure compliance with the discovery rules, not to punish erring parties.").

12. 427 U.S. 639, 96 S.Ct. 2778, 49 L.Ed.2d 747 (1976), *rehearing denied* 429 U.S. 874, 97 S.Ct. 197, 50 L.Ed.2d 158 (1976) (per curiam).

13. 427 U.S. at 643, 96 S.Ct. at 2781.

14. *See, e.g., Societe Internationale Pour Participations Industrielles Et Commerciales, S.A. v. Rogers,* 357 U.S. 197, 212, 78 S.Ct. 1087, 2 L.Ed.2d 1255 (1958); *Fox v. Studebaker–Worthington, Inc.,* 516 F.2d 989, 993 (8th Cir.1975). The sanctions actually imposed vary widely. Recent decisions on the imposition of various sanctions are discussed in § 6.5 of this text.

15. *Wilson v. Volkswagen of America, Inc.,* 561 F.2d 494, 504–505 (4th Cir.1977), *cert. denied* 434 U.S. 1020, 98 S.Ct. 744, 54 L.Ed.2d 768 (1978). *See also Thomas v. United States,* 531 F.2d 746, 749 (5th Cir. 1976) ("Consideration must be given to such factors as good faith, willful disobedience, gross indifference to the rights of the adverse party, deliberate callousness or gross negligence.").

frequently difficult to determine which sanctions a court might reasonably be expected to impose in a particular case. The following discussion analyzes some of the major factors courts consider.

§ *10.5.2 Default and Dismissal*

Courts are willing to impose the severe sanctions of default or dismissal when the conduct giving rise to the sanction is repeated and clearly taken with knowledge of the court's order compelling discovery. In one case, a default judgment for $142,500 was entered against a defendant for failure to respond to interrogatories and produce documents after repeated requests and an order of the court.[1] Another court ordered a default judgment of $285,000, with interest and expenses, for willful failure to appear for a deposition and to produce documents pursuant to request.[2] The courts have held that attempts to comply with discovery orders after a history of noncompliance do not necessarily exonerate a party. Courts have continued the imposition of the most extreme sanctions of default and dismissal notwithstanding such eleventh-hour actions.[3]

Making inaccurate or misleading statements to an opponent or the court regarding discovery may also be the basis for imposition of severe sanctions. If a party acts pursuant to a plan to deceive counsel and the court regarding discovery matters, a court will dismiss a complaint.[4]

§ *10.5.3 Contempt*

A contempt sanction is a severe sanction available against both a party and an attorney,[5] but it is not favored by the courts. If the factual circumstances surrounding the discovery conduct justify the finding of contempt, the dismissal or default sanction would probably also be available. Since a contempt sanction may require an additional evidentiary hearing, while default or dismissal requires no further hearing and actually removes a case from the court's calendar, these latter sanctions tend to be preferred in situations involving a party's noncompliance.[6]

§ 10.5

1. *See Affanato v. Merrill Brothers*, 547 F.2d 138, 141 (1st Cir.1977).

2. *See Paine, Webber, Jackson & Curtis, Inc. v. Inmobiliaria Melia de Puerto Rico, Inc.*, 543 F.2d 3 (2d Cir.1976), *cert. denied* 430 U.S. 907, 97 S.Ct. 1178, 57 L.Ed.2d 583 (1977). *See also Brown v. McCormick,* 608 F.2d 410, 414 (10th Cir.1979).

3. *See Factory Air Conditioning Corp. v. Westside Toyota, Inc.*, 579 F.2d 334, 337–38 (5th Cir.1978) (per curiam); *State of Ohio v. Arthur Andersen & Co.*, 570 F.2d 1370, 1374 (10th Cir.1978), *cert. denied* 439 U.S. 833, 99 S.Ct. 114, 58 L.Ed.2d 129 (1978).

4. *Independent Investor Protective League v. Touche Ross & Co.*, 607 F.2d 530, 533 (2d Cir.1978), *cert. denied* 439 U.S. 895, 99 S.Ct. 254, 58 L.Ed.2d 241 (1978), *rehearing denied* 439 U.S. 998, 99 S.Ct. 604, 58 L.Ed.2d 673 (1978). *See also G–K Properties v. Redevelopment Agency of City of San Jose*, 577 F.2d 645, 647 (9th Cir.1978).

5. *See Schleper v. Ford Motor Co., Automotive Division,* 585 F.2d 1367, 1372 (8th Cir.1978).

6. An evidentiary hearing is required by the courts, to determine if a factual issue exists, in determining whether or not a valid order had been violated. No such hearing is required if the party found in contempt opposes contempt merely on legal grounds. *See I.B.M. Corp. v. United States,* 493 F.2d 112, 119–120 (2d Cir.1973), *cert. denied* 416 U.S. 995, 94 S.Ct. 2409, 40 L.Ed.2d 774 (1974).

The contempt sanction takes two forms: civil contempt and criminal contempt. The distinction between them has been the subject of much discussion. Generally, however, civil contempt is imposed to compel compliance with a court order, while criminal contempt is imposed to punish an affront to the court's authority.[7] Civil contempt is thus resorted to when other sanctions would be either less effective or more difficult for the court to impose or administer. Civil contempt is an appropriate sanction for use to compel a non-party's compliance with a discovery order since other sanctions, such as default, dismissal, and preclusion of evidence, may have little, if any, impact on the non-party.

Litigants have sometimes taken the position that contempt is inappropriate when the litigant acted upon the advice of counsel. But it is generally held that reliance upon counsel's advice is not a *defense* to the contempt sanction, although it may properly be considered by a trial court in determining whether or not to find contempt.[8] Raising such a defense may also waive any privilege relating to the advice given.

§ 10.5.4 Preclusion Orders for Disclosure Violations

A court may issue a preclusion order prohibiting a party from introducing evidence at a trial or hearing or in support of a motion if a party violates a disclosure requirement. Federal Rule 37(c) explicitly provides the court with this authority. It makes sense that if a party fails to disclose information the party should not be able to benefit from its non-disclosure. There are two restrictions placed upon the imposition of this sanction. First, if a party has "substantial justification" for failing to disclose, the sanction may not be imposed. A reasonable reason for failing to disclose may include a justifiable interpretation of Rule 26 which a party believed did not require disclosure, or a party's negligent failure to include all pages of a copied document provided the other side. The other limitation to the imposition of a preclusion order is if the failure to disclose is harmless. A harmful result occurs if an opposing party is prejudiced by the failure to receive the information. Prejudice occurs when a party is placed at a significant disadvantage because of the lack of information.

§ 10.5.5 Preclusion Orders for Discovery Violations

A preclusion order prohibiting a party from introducing evidence is generally considered a less severe sanction than dismissal or default. Courts have been willing to enter preclusion orders for simple failure to identify documents or witnesses, regardless of whether that conduct

7. *See, e.g., Ramos Colon v. United States Attorney for District of Puerto Rico,* 576 F.2d 1, 4–5 (1st Cir.1978).

8. *Compare United States v. I.B.M. Corp.,* 60 F.R.D. 658, 666 (S.D.N.Y.), *appeal dismissed* 493 F.2d 112 (2d Cir.1973), *cert. denied* 416 U.S. 995, 94 S.Ct. 2409, 40 L.Ed.2d 774 (1974), *direct appeal dismissed* 416 U.S. 976, 94 S.Ct. 2378, 40 L.Ed.2d 756 (1974), *with Colorado Mill & Elevator Co. v. American Cyanamid Co.,* 11 F.R.D. 306, 307 (W.D.Mo.1951).

constitutes flagrant or repeated violation of court orders.[9] A preclusion order may be a serious sanction, however. If the evidence or witness precluded (or issue determined) is of crucial importance, and if no other evidence exists on that issue, it is possible for the preclusion order to be determinative. Summary judgment may be issued after the entry of a preclusion order.[10]

§ 10.5.6 Restriction of Further Discovery

Another sanction frequently imposed by courts, whether explicitly or not, is the restriction of the recalcitrant party's discovery rights. Experienced litigation attorneys have long known that failure of a party to comply with valid discovery requests essentially negates any rights that party may have to enforce its own discovery requests. Thus, at least during the period of a party's noncompliance, discovery may be delayed or unavailable. Rule 37(d) specifically permits the court to stay further proceedings. This is a sanction that, though not frequently used in the form of an absolute stay, is occasionally relied upon by courts to enforce discovery.[11]

§ 10.5.7 Imposition of Costs

The rule favors the award of expenses, including attorney's fees, to the party bringing a meritorious motion for imposition of sanctions, and courts have been willing to enter appropriate orders compelling payment of substantial costs.[12] Attorneys frequently forget that the award of expenses is primarily compensatory and not punitive and that eleventh-hour compliance with the motion or prior order does not erase the liability for expenses of bringing the motion. Courts are increasingly willing to award expenses, even if the underlying motion has been "mooted" by an eleventh-hour disgorging of information. The seeking of such an award may be wise tactically, since it may prompt a more timely response to future discovery requests. This holds equally true for motions for orders compelling discovery and for motions to impose sanctions.

§ 10.5.8 Failure to Make Admissions

Failure to make admissions under Rule 36 may result in an order requiring the party failing to admit to bear the cost of proving items not

9. *See, e.g., Admiral Theatre Corp. v. Douglas Theater Co.,* 585 F.2d 877, 897 (8th Cir.1978).

10. *Riverside Memorial Mausoleum, Inc. v. Sonneblick–Goldman Corp.,* 80 F.R.D. 433, 437 (E.D.Pa.1978). *See also State of Ohio v. Arthur Andersen & Co.,* 570 F.2d 1370 (10th Cir.1978), *cert. denied* 439 U.S. 833, 99 S.Ct. 114, 58 L.Ed.2d 129 (1978).

11. *See, e.g., Griffin v. Aluminum Co. of America,* 564 F.2d 1171, 1173 (5th Cir. 1977) (the court suggested that barring further proceedings by recalcitrant *pro se* plaintiff would be an appropriate means of sanctioning his refusal to appear for a deposition).

12. *Marquis v. Chrysler Corp.,* 577 F.2d 624, 641–642 (9th Cir.1978); *Goodsons & Co., Inc. v. National American Corp.,* 78 F.R.D. 721, 723 (S.D.N.Y.1978).

admitted. This order is to be granted under Rule 37(c) unless the court finds that:

> (1) The request was held objectionable pursuant to Rule 36(a), or (2) the admission sought was of no substantial importance, or (3) the party failing to admit had reasonable grounds to believe that he might prevail on the matter, or (4) there was other good reason for the failure to admit.

The Federal Advisory Committee Notes indicate that the award of expenses is "intended to provide post-trial relief," and the courts generally follow the clear indication of the rule.[13] The courts have generally given narrow interpretation to the four exceptions to imposition of costs under Rule 37(c). Having reasonable grounds to believe that a party might prevail is probably the most likely basis for defeating a claim for costs.[14] A party generally has a difficult time establishing that the admission sought was of no substantial importance [15] or that there was other good reason for failure to admit.[16] As with every other discovery request, poor drafting may make the request objectionable even if a properly drawn request might not be so.

§ 10.5.9 Sanctions Against Attorneys

It is important to remember that sanctions may be imposed against parties and also against their attorneys. Now do we have your full attention? Rule 37(b) of the Federal Rules of Civil Procedure specifically provides that the award of expenses may be made against "the party failing to obey the order *or the attorney advising him or both.*" Courts have been willing to impose sanctions directly against the attorney if the record clearly establishes that the attorney's conduct is responsible for the discovery violation.[17] The imposition of costs against the attorney, and not against the client, is more likely if the circumstances make it appear that the client was reasonably diligent in responding to the discovery request.[18] In one case, the court exonerated both parties to an action but found that counsel for both sides had so frustrated the discovery process that it ordered each attorney to pay the attorney's fees of the other party, with an express provision that the parties were not to

13. *Ogletree v. Keebler Co.,* 78 F.R.D. 661, 662 (N.D.Ga.1978).

14. *See, e.g., Security–First National Bank of Los Angeles v. Lutz,* 297 F.2d 159, 166 (9th Cir.1961).

15. *See* 8 Charles A. Wright & Alan R. Miller, Federal Practice and Procedure § 2290, at 804 (1970 and Supp.1994).

16. *See, e.g., David v. Hooker, Limited,* 560 F.2d 412, 419 (9th Cir.1977).

17. *See Edgar v. Slaughter,* 548 F.2d 770, 773 (8th Cir.1977). *See also* Comment, Sanctions Imposed by Courts on Attorneys Who Abuse the Judicial Process, 44 U.Chi.L.Rev. 619 (1977). *In Roadway Express, Inc. v. Piper,* 447 U.S. 752, 766–767, 100 S.Ct. 2455, 2464, 65 L.Ed.2d 488 (1980), the Supreme Court affirmed the imposition of sanctions on attorneys who unreasonably extend court proceedings.

18. *See Independent Investor Protective League v. Touche Ross & Co.,* 607 F.2d 530, 534 (2d Cir.1978), *cert. denied* 439 U.S. 895, 99 S.Ct. 254, 58 L.Ed.2d 241 (1978), *rehearing denied* 439 U.S. 998, 99 S.Ct. 604, 58 L.Ed.2d 673 (1978); *Stanziale v. First National City Bank,* 74 F.R.D. 557, 560 (S.D.N.Y.1977) (ignorance of the date upon which the interrogatory answers were due); *Szilvassy v. United States,* 71 F.R.D. 589 (S.D.N.Y.1976) (it was not clear to what extent, if any, plaintiff was at fault).

reimburse the attorneys for these expenses.[19] The award of attorney's fees under Rule 37 is for the benefit of the party injured by the conduct of the dilatory party or attorney, not for the benefit of that party's attorneys.[20] Monetary sanctions against attorneys have also been imposed under the authority of federal statute that provides:

> Any attorney or other person admitted to conduct cases in any court of the United States or any Territory thereof who so multiplies the proceedings in any case as to increase costs unreasonably and vexatiously may be required by the court to satisfy personally such excess costs.[21]

This statute was adopted early in this century, but it has been used only rarely.

§ 10.5.10 Sanctions Against Pro Se Parties

Appellate courts have been willing to establish more lenient standards for imposition of sanctions against parties appearing without trained lawyers. Although the *pro se* party is not excused from compliance with the discovery rules, the party is generally not subjected to severe sanctions unless it appears affirmatively that the party was aware of the obligations imposed by the rules and willfully disregarded them. One court reversed the dismissal of a complaint by a *pro se* plaintiff who had failed to appear at his deposition and failed to produce documents upon request. The court found that the party did not adequately understand his obligations under the discovery rules and concluded that dismissal was inappropriate. The court also found the imposition of monetary sanctions inappropriate and concluded that an order staying further proceedings would have been appropriate under the circumstances. Finally, the court noted that, although an order compelling attendance at a deposition is not required prior to the imposition of sanctions, it would be appropriate in a case involving a *pro se* litigant.[22]

The courts do not, however, permit the *pro se* plaintiff to take advantage of a lack of representation. In one case in which the *pro se* plaintiff made misrepresentations to the court, the court permitted dismissal of the action for failure to appear for a deposition.[23] It is thus prudent for counsel involved in litigation with unrepresented parties to ensure that the parties are specifically aware of the obligations under the rules, that they are provided copies of all pertinent documents, and that

19. *Associated Radio Service Co. v. Page Airways, Inc.*, 73 F.R.D. 633, 636–637 (D.Tex.1977).

20. *Hamilton v. Econo–Car International, Inc.*, 636 F.2d 745 (D.C.Cir.1980), reversing *Hamilton v. Motorola, Inc.*, 85 F.R.D. 549, 551–552 (D.D.C.1979).

21. 28 U.S.C.A. § 1927. Sanctions may be imposed under this statute only against attorneys, not against parties or clients. *Chrysler Corp. v. Lakeshore Commercial Finance Corp.*, 389 F.Supp. 1216, 1224 (E.D.Wis.1975), *motion dismissed* 66 F.R.D. 607 (1975).

22. *Griffin v. Aluminum Co. of America*, 564 F.2d 1171, 1173 (5th Cir.1977). *See also United Artists Corp. v. Freeman*, 605 F.2d 854, 856 (5th Cir.1979).

23. *Roberts v. Norden Division, United Aircraft Corp.*, 76 F.R.D. 75, 81 (E.D.N.Y. 1977). *See also Hines v. S.J. Enterprises, Inc.*, 25 Fed.R.Serv.2d 227, 228–229 (E.D.Mo.1978).

they are advised of dates, deadlines, and the nature of their obligations. It is probably prudent to obtain an order compelling discovery against any *pro se* party, even if the discovery involved is one of those types that does not require an order compelling discovery as a condition precedent to the imposition of sanctions.

§ 10.6 STREAMLINING THE TWO-STEP PROCESS

Rather than holding two hearings on two separate motions, as discussed previously, courts frequently indicate in the order compelling discovery what sanction will be imposed for failure to comply with the order. The court may specifically order that no further hearing will be necessary or available in the event of noncompliance. The sanction may then be imposed upon motion and affidavits demonstrating noncompliance with the order. A second hearing may not be required. The use of this streamlined procedure has been upheld,[1] and there are tactical advantages to attaining a sanction within the order to compel discovery. In addition to saving time and expense, an order that specifically outlines what will happen if it is not followed may result in a stronger likelihood of compliance. Judges may be more inclined to impose harsh sanctions conditionally, in the hope of obtaining compliance, and less inclined to impose a harsh sanction after the fact.

In a different situation the two-step process does not function meaningfully. If a party provides answers that appear to be complete, but that do not disclose claims, defenses, witnesses, or documents upon which the answering party plans to rely at trial, there is clear potential prejudice. But a motion compelling discovery is of no use; the party seeking discovery has no means either of knowing that the answers are incomplete or of convincing a court to enter an order compelling discovery. Rule 37(d) allows the imposition of certain Rule 37(b) sanctions without any preceding order compelling discovery. It provides the strongest tool to combat the undisclosed claim, defense, witness, or piece of evidence: barring the use of that witness or evidence or the introduction of proof on a claim or defense that is not timely disclosed.[2]

§ 10.7 NARROWER ENFORCEMENT PROVISIONS

Rule 37(d) applies to three types of failure to make discovery: failure to appear for a properly noticed deposition, failure to serve any answers or objections to interrogatories, and failure to serve a written response to a request for a Rule 34 inspection. This rule, like Rule 37(b), authorizes the court to impose sanctions as it deems appropriate and lists specific sanctions. The only sanction not repeated from Rule 37(b) is the contempt sanction. Since no court order is in force in a

§ 10.6

1. *Johann Maria Farina Gegenuber Dem Neumarkt v. Roger & Gallet,* 296 F.2d 119, 120 (2d Cir.1961) (court found conditional order not appealable); *O'Neil v. Corrick,* 307 Minn. 497, 239 N.W.2d 230 (1976) (per curiam).

2. Rule 37(d) is especially useful to prevent the testimony of an undisclosed expert witness.

situation calling for Rule 37(d) sanctions, contempt is considered to be an inappropriate sanction.[1]

The rule gives a trial judge the power to remove any tactical advantage gained by playing a fast and loose game of discovery and allows this conduct to be penalized. Striking pleadings, entering judgment by default or dismissal, barring evidence, and deeming facts established are all available. The most frequently imposed sanctions are to bar testimony from the undisclosed witness, to bar receipt in evidence of the unproduced document, or to deem facts established when the recalcitrant party has control of the proof.[2] Monetary sanctions, also available under Rule 37(d), may apply in addition to or in lieu of any other sanctions. The award of attorney's fees and expenses is presumptively appropriate under this rule.[3]

§ 10.8 MOTION PRACTICE

The most obvious reason for bringing a motion is to compel certain relief. To have an order compelling discovery entered, you must serve a motion on all opposing or otherwise interested parties and, in federal court, you will also have to discuss the discovery dispute with the opposing party in an effort to avoid court intervention. A formal motion can be an expensive way to achieve what a phone call to the opposing attorney will sometimes accomplish.

But if your opponent is being particularly stubborn, you may feel it simpler to convince a judge, rather than your hard-headed opponent, of your right to the information sought. There may be an advantage to bringing a motion: it will reveal to the court, and establish in the record, your opponent's attitude. Depending on you and your opponent, it may also make the motion docket more interesting for the other attorneys present.

A discovery motion can also give you an opportunity to see and evaluate your opponent: to learn how well prepared, how familiar with court procedures, and how convincing opposing counsel is. Motions may also serve the less laudable, not to mention potentially unethical, purpose of delaying the process or increasing the burdens of litigation for a financially weaker opponent.

Discovery motions have disadvantages as well. If you are asserting any objections to your opponent's discovery requests, a court is quite likely to treat both parties the same way, by granting discovery to both or denying it to both. A motion taken under advisement, even if followed by a favorable order, may not yield discovery for months, while less favorable terms arrived at by agreement may result in immediate

§ 10.7

1. *Schleper v. Ford Motor Co., Automotive Div.*, 585 F.2d 1367, 1371 (8th Cir. 1978).

2. Charles B. Renfrew, Discovery Sanctions: A Judicial Perspective, 67 Calif.L.Rev. 264 (1979).

3. Fed.R.Civ.P. 37(d), Notes of Advisory Comm.—1970 Amendments, reprinted in 28 U.S.C.A. § 66.

discovery. Although the rules clearly favor the award of expenses, including attorney's fees, to the prevailing party in a discovery motion, judges have often not shown the same enthusiasm in awarding them. Except in flagrant cases of obstreperousness, courts frequently follow the general American rule and require each party to bear the costs incurred by that party.

§ 10.9 ENFORCING SUBPOENAS AND NON-PARTY DISCOVERY

Motions to compel discovery most frequently relate to discovery disputes between parties to a pending action. Occasionally, however, non-parties are drawn into discovery disputes through use of the subpoena power. When this occurs, special discovery considerations come into play.

Fed.R.Civ.P. 45(d) permits the issuance of a subpoena to compel a non-party's attendance at a deposition. Such a subpoena may also compel the witness to produce and permit inspection and copying of documents and tangible things. Neither Rule 45 nor Rule 34 relating to inspection authorize an order requiring a non-party to permit entry onto land.[1] As you recall, or will recall, Rule 45 permits the issuance of a subpoena duces tecum to obtain documents from a non-party without scheduling a deposition.

Motions relating to non-party discovery fall into two classes: motions by parties and motions by the non-party. If a party seeks to object to discovery directed to a non-party, the motion will be handled as any other motion for a protective order or as a motion to quash the subpoena.[2] If a non-party objects to the discovery, or the party requesting discovery needs to compel discovery, different considerations are involved.

A non-party's objections to complying with a subpoena are usually asserted in a motion to quash the subpoena. Although there is no specific reference in the rules of civil procedure to motions to quash subpoenas, these motions are routinely considered by the courts. Because the rules do not provide for these motions, there is also no specific standard for considering the motions. Courts routinely apply a liberal standard to considering motions of non-party witness for protection from the burdens of litigation. This judicial approach is frequently justified by the relative lack of interest the non-parties have in the litigation, and by the recognition of the broad scope of discovery intended to permit parties to discover information known to their adversaries.

Although "quashing" a subpoena relieves a non-party from any obligation to comply with it, the relief available to non-parties should not

§ 10.9

1. *See Pollitt v. Mobay Chemical Corp.*, 95 F.R.D. 101 (S.D.Ohio 1982); Note, Peter Feuerle, Rule 34(c) and Discovery of Nonparty Land, 85 Yale L.J. 112 (1975).

2. *See Shepherd v. Castle*, 20 F.R.D. 184, 188 (W.D.Mo.1957).

be considered so limited. Courts have essentially granted non-parties the right to seek, and obtain in appropriate cases, any relief a party could obtain in a motion for a protective order under Fed.R.Civ.P. 26(c).[3] Most frequently the courts will limit the scope of discovery from the non-party, place conditions on the use of the information discovered, limit further dissemination of the information, or require the non-party to be compensated for the burdens placed on it by the subpoena. Courts are becoming increasingly receptive to claims of great burden from non-parties who are drawn into a discovery morass. These awards have been substantial in amount, and have at least once been made after the non-party complied with the subpoena without objecting to the burden imposed.[4]

Courts will also be inclined to require a party to exhaust the possibilities of obtaining the requested information from one of the parties to the litigation before seeking to impose the production requirement on a non-party.[5] In addition to the financial burdens of litigation, courts are willing to consider seriously the privacy rights and interests of non-parties.[6]

A party seeking to enforce discovery from a non-party usually brings a motion for imposition of sanctions, normally contempt. Fed.R.Civ.P. 45(f) authorizes the court issuing a subpoena to treat as a contempt any failure to obey it. In addition, the entire range of sanctions permitted under Fed.R.Civ.P. 37 are permitted against non-parties to the extent they are logically applicable. (A non-party cannot very well be sanctioned by a preclusion order, or by dismissal or default).

Fed.R.Civ.P. 37(a)(1) requires that a motion to compel discovery from a non-party be made in the court where the deposition is being taken. Because the subpoena power under Rule 45 is limited to compel attendance at a deposition within the district where the deponent works or resides, motions for enforcement or relief from subpoenas are also required to be brought in this district.

Since the failure to obey a subpoena may be treated as a contempt, why would you need to bring a motion compelling discovery against a non-party who had been properly subpoenaed? First, courts are reluctant to impose severe sanctions upon a non-party who is either uninformed on his or her obligations or has valid objections to a subpoena. Even though the party should seek an order quashing the subpoena in advance of the time directed for compliance, courts will frequently overlook a non-party's noncompliance. Second, and more important, the

3. *See* § 4.10, *supra.*

4. *Compare United States v. Columbia Broadcasting System, Inc.,* 666 F.2d 364, (9th Cir.1982), *cert. denied* 457 U.S. 1118, 102 S.Ct. 2929, 73 L.Ed.2d 1329 (1982), *on remand* 103 F.R.D. 365 (D.Cal.1984) (court reversed denial of approximately $2.3 million to non-party retroactively) *with Florida v. Kerr–McGee Corp. (In re Coordinated Pretrial Proceedings in Petroleum Products Antitrust Litigation*), 669 F.2d 620 (10th Cir.1982) (court conditioned enforcement of subpoena on payment to non-party of $9,000).

5. *See Bada Co. v. Montgomery Ward & Co.,* 32 F.R.D. 208, 210 (E.D.Tenn.1963).

6. *Premium Service Corp. v. Sperry & Hutchinson Co.,* 511 F.2d 225, 229 (9th Cir.1975).

subpoena only requires the party to attend the deposition and produce any documents requested in the subpoena. It does not require the witness to answer any particular questions; it simply requires attendance and submission to some questioning.[7] Thus, a motion to compel discovery or production of subpoenaed documents or things is necessary if the non-party refuses to comply in all respects with the subpoena.

In considering the special consideration or deference non-parties may receive in discovery matters, non-parties should be considered in two separate classes: non-parties who have had no contact with the litigation or the parties and those persons who are non-parties but have some personal, business, or professional relationship with a party. Thus, the courts are going to be much less deferential to the objections of a party's former auditor then to the objections of an accounting firm who happens to have information about practices within a particular industry but has no relationship with a party. The courts have been particularly protective of independent scientists and experts who may have scientific information relevant to the litigation but have not been retained as experts by any party. These individuals will not be required to give testimony since they have not voluntarily submitted to being brought into the litigation.[8]

§ 10.10 DISCOVERY MALPRACTICE

The increased willingness of courts to impose severe discovery sanctions may give rise to increased claims of malpractice against attorneys. The orders entered by courts, directing attorneys and not their clients to bear the costs of discovery motions, clearly impose a penalty upon counsel who abuse the discovery process. The findings of the court may be pertinent in subsequent claims brought by a party against the attorney. Courts frequently impose monetary sanctions directly against the attorneys, when they perceive the attorney to be at fault in obstructing discovery, although they are increasingly willing to visit the attorney's negligence or willfulness upon the client. It is clear, then, that the possibility of imposition of severe sanctions exists and should cause attorneys to be especially careful to ensure compliance by their client, as well as by themselves, with any court orders regarding discovery. Recognizing this problem, some have even suggested that counsel should seriously consider withdrawing from representation of clients who refuse to fulfill their discovery obligations.[1]

A leading case exhibiting the willingness of the courts to punish a party for the failure by its attorney to act is *Affanato v. Merrill Bros.*,[2] in which the court affirmed an award of default judgment for $142,500

7. *Fremont Energy Corp. v. Seattle Post Intelligencer*, 688 F.2d 1285 (9th Cir.1982).

8. *Buchanan v. American Motors Corp.*, 697 F.2d 151 (6th Cir.1983); *Andrews v. Eli Lilly & Co.*, 97 F.R.D. 494 (N.D.Ill.1983).

§ 10.10

1. *See, e.g.*, Edna S. Epstein, et al., An Up–Date on Rule 37 Sanctions after *National Hockey League v. Metropolitan Hockey Clubs, Inc.*, 84 F.R.D. 145, 172–173 (1980).

2. 547 F.2d 138 (1st Cir.1977).

upon defendant's failure to answer interrogatories despite repeated orders that they be answered. The court, saying the sanction was being imposed for the acts of defendant's attorney, stated:

> What is important is that the conduct of counsel with which defendant is chargeable consisted of a series of episodes of nonfeasance which amounted, in sum, to a near total dereliction of professional responsibility by the associate in the law firm defendant had obtained. Granting that isolated oversights should not be penalized by a default judgment, the court was entitled to conclude that the conduct here went well beyond ordinary negligence, and that the final default was appropriate.[3]

Obviously, this judicial finding of conduct "well beyond ordinary negligence" will be of substantial value to the defendant in pursuing contribution or indemnity from the law firm or the individual attorney involved.

A more novel claim of malpractice might be grounded upon a client's complaint that his or her own attorney conducted inadequate discovery. Economic factors impinge upon every decision either to conduct or refrain from additional discovery. If the attorney and client consider these factors and together decide not to pursue further discovery, it appears unlikely that a malpractice claim could be perfected.

§ 10.11 CONCLUSION

The disclosure and discovery rules are not self-enforcing. Although attorneys frequently modify disclosure and discovery rights and attempt to resolve disputes without court involvement, it is important that sanctions available under the rules of civil procedure be understood. It is also important to recognize the fundamental purpose of discovery, because courts impose sanctions in order to secure that very purpose: the just, speedy, and inexpensive determination of litigation.[1] Courts exercise wide discretion in determining how this end may best be achieved. It is important for attorneys to approach disputes from both a practical and legal standpoint.

PRACTICE PROBLEMS

1. You represent the defendant in *Hot Dog Enterprises vs. Tri–Chem.* The plaintiff has submitted interrogatories and requests for production and has asked questions during depositions of managing agents from Tri–Chem seeking the disclosure of information and discovery of documents relating to trade secret data concerning Bond–Mor. Your client is concerned, obviously,

3. 547 F.2d at 141.

§ 10.11

1. *See* Fed.R.Civ.P. 1.

that the public disclosure of this information would provide competitors with extremely valuable data.

(a) Draft a motion seeking a protective order to protect this information.

(b) What would you say to opposing counsel when you meet and confer in an effort to resolve discovery disputes without court intervention?

(c) What arguments would you advance in support of this motion?

(d) Draft a proposed protective order for submission to the court.

2. You represent the plaintiff in *Hot Dog Enterprises vs. Tri–Chem.* You seek the disclosure of essential information regarding the chemical composition of Bond–Mor. You have submitted interrogatories, requests for production, and deposition questions to Tri–Chem seeking the disclosure of this information, all of which requests have been denied.

(a) Draft a Rule 37 motion seeking the disclosure of this information.

(b) What would you say to opposing counsel when you meet and confer in an effort to resolve discovery disputes without court intervention?

(c) What arguments would you advance that this information be disclosed to specific representatives of your party, experts retained in the case, and yourself?

(d) Draft a proposed Rule 37 order compelling production of this information.

3. You represent the defendant in *Hot Dog Enterprises vs. Tri–Chem.* Assume that the trial judge has ordered the disclosure of information you deem to be protected by a trade secret and by an attorney-client privilege. What options do you have in response to the court's order? What would you do?

4. You represent the plaintiff in *Hot Dog Enterprises vs. Tri–Chem.* You obtain pursuant to a proper protective order information from Tri–Chem relating to the chemical composition of Bond–Mor. In addition to Hot Dog Enterprises, other clients retain you to represent them in prospective litigation against Tri–Chem. How, if at all, may you use the protective information obtained in your lawsuit representing Hot Dog Enterprises on behalf of your other clients? What if attorneys representing other plaintiffs in litigation with Tri–Chem regarding Bond–Mor or prospective plaintiffs who may have claims against Bond–Mor contact you requesting information about Bond–Mor? How may you respond to them?

5. You represent the defendants in *Northern Motor Homes v. Danforth* (Case J). In October Joan Danforth developed respiratory problems. A medical expert who examined her has advised you that inhalation of fumes from the propane stove (the fumes were released because of the fire on June 29) may have caused damage to her lungs. The court has allowed you to amend the counterclaim by adding a product liability claim.

You have submitted a request for production, Number 17, for documents that contain the names and addresses of all customers of the plaintiff who have purchased Voyageur Motor Homes with propane stoves. You intend to contact these individuals and discover whether they have had any problems with the stove. The plaintiff has refused to disclose these names, contending that: (1) such information is confidential; (2) the documents that contain such names also contain private business data that is irrelevant to the claim; and (3) the privacy of these customers will be unnecessarily breached by the defendants.

Your investigation has revealed that the plaintiff designed and manufactured the propane stove installed in the Voyageur. You have submitted a request for production, Number 18, seeking documents detailing the design and manufacturing processes involved in the production of the propane stove. The plaintiff has refused to comply with this request, explaining that: (1) Northern Motor Homes has a patent on the Saf–T–Lok valve on the stove; (2) such documents contain trade secrets; and (3) the disclosure of the information would put Northern Motor Homes at a significant disadvantage with its competitors.

(a) Draft a motion seeking a protective order to obtain the information sought in request Numbers 17 and 18.

(b) Draft a protective order that provides you with the information you need and which meets the legitimate concerns of the plaintiff.

6. You represent the plaintiff in *Northern Motor Homes v. Danforth* (Case J). The defendant has failed to respond within 30 days to the interrogatories that you drafted. Subsequently, you wrote a letter to the defendant's attorney demanding answers. You never received a response to that letter. Draft a Rule 37 motion and proposed order seeking appropriate sanctions for the defendant's failure to respond.

7. You represent the defendants in *Northern Motor Homes v. Danforth* (Case J). The plaintiff has failed to respond within 30 days to the interrogatories that you drafted. You subsequently wrote a letter to the plaintiff's attorney demanding answers. You never received a response to that letter. Draft a Rule 37 motion and proposed order compelling answers and seeking appropriate sanctions for the plaintiff's failure to respond.

8. You represent the plaintiff in *Northern Motor Homes v. Danforth* (Case J). The defendants have responded to your interrogatories (see Ch. 7, Problem 12) by completely and satisfactorily responding to interrogatories (a) and (c) and by answering the remaining questions as follows:

(b) The plaintiff was present and knows this information.

(d) It would be difficult and burdensome to respond. Ask this question during the defendants' depositions.

(e) Improperly drafted question.

(f) We object on the grounds that this question seeks legal information.

Draft a Rule 37 motion and proposed order compelling answers and seeking appropriate sanctions.

9. You represent the defendants in *Northern Motor Homes v. Danforth* (Case J). The plaintiff has responded to your interrogatories (see Ch. 7, Problem 12) by providing complete and satisfactory answers to interrogatories (c) and (d) and by answering the remaining questions as follows:

(a) This information is available from the defendants.

(b) Burdensome. A deposition is a more appropriate discovery device to use to obtain these facts.

(c) Objection. Requires a legal conclusion.

Draft a Rule 37 motion and proposed court order compelling answers and seeking appropriate sanctions.

10. You represent Summit Insurance Company in *Pozdak v. Summit Insurance Company* (Case B). You know that Pozdak has severe financial problems and no longer has a home, workplace, or gallery. You figure that his lawyer is being paid an hourly rate. Melissa Tandy, a Vice President with Summit Insurance, suggests that because of Pozdak's need for money that you as the lawyer engage in a discovery program that will delay the case from going to trial for as long as possible. She also points out to you that it is in the best interests of Summit Insurance to prolong the litigation because the Company will earn interest by investing the money instead of paying it to Pozdak. Do you initiate a prolonged discovery program? Why or why not? What factors influence your judgment?

11. You represent the City of Mitchell in *Giacone v. City of Mitchell* (Case D). Kay Olsheski advises you that the City does not have the money or resources to provide notice or hearings to water customers who want to challenge the City's right to terminate their services during this budget year. Olsheski suggests that you defend the lawsuit to permit the City another 12 to 18 months to consider changing the termination procedures.

Martha Giacone is represented by the Mitchell Legal Services Office, and you know that the limited resources of that office make it very difficult for them to prosecute the lawsuit. Would you plan a discovery program to provide the City with the additional time and to take advantage of the problems of the Legal Services Office? Why or why not? What factors influence your judgment?

12. You represent Rainbow Computer in *Mitchell Computer Club v. Rainbow Computer* (Case E). The attorney for the Computer Club is a recent law school graduate and began practice one month ago. Your initial conversations with this attorney lead you to conclude that this lawyer is woefully inexperienced to conduct a major class action lawsuit. You have a well established reputation with the local judges in the Mitchell courts. You know that the practice of most Mitchell defense lawyers is to routinely delay providing discovery responses until the last possible moment, usually the day that the opposing lawyer has scheduled a hearing to enforce a discovery request. You also know that the judges when faced with a request for attorney's fees from the moving lawyer seeking to enforce discovery requests will seldom grant such a request, and only if especially egregious circumstances exist. Would you take advantage of your opponent's inexperience, your reputations, and the local practice that tolerates late discovery responses? Why or why not? What factors influence your judgment?

13. You represent Juanita Vasquez in *Vasquez v. Hot Dog Enterprises* (Case F). You know that HDE is very sensitive to publicity surrounding the sexual harassment lawsuit. Would you plan a discovery program to take advantage of this sensitivity by disclosing information the press would publicly broadcast or print?

14. You represent Hot Dog Enterprises in *Vasquez v. Hot Dog Enterprises* (Case F). You figure that you could make things very difficult for Juanita Vasquez by probing during her deposition very sensitive areas of her life, including her sexual experiences. This aggressive deposition approach may make her more willing to settle the case for less money. What would you do? Why? What factors influence your judgment?

PART FOUR

PRETRIAL MOTION PRACTICE

*

CHAPTER 11
PRETRIAL MOTION PRACTICE

If you are going to play the game properly, you'd better know every rule.

Barbara Jordan

§ 11.1 SCOPE OF MOTION PRACTICE

§ 11.1.1 Introduction

Motions play a very important role in civil litigation before trial. Motions may result in the termination of a case without trial or may cause the parties to agree on a settlement. It is important for civil litigators to be adept at both the mechanical or procedural aspects of motion practice as well as the strategic uses of motions.

A motion is any request to a court for an order.[1] This definition has support in Fed.R.Civ.P. 7(b) and various state rules, which apply to all such requests. Motions include requests made to a clerk as well as those made to the judge. Motions are also defined to include "all motions, applications, petitions or other requests for judicial action."[2] The term does not include requests which do not call for entry of any order or ruling by the court.

This chapter addresses some of the strategic and tactical uses of pretrial motions. Many motions that might appropriately be brought are not specifically considered simply because it is impossible to define motion practice by exhaustive cataloging. If a particular case calls out

§ 11.1

1. *See, e.g., Reed & Martin, Inc. v. Westinghouse Elec. Corp.*, 439 F.2d 1268 (2d Cir.1971).

2. C.D.Cal.R. 1.2(p). *See also* E.D.Cal.R. 1(c)(11).

for the entry of an order which no court has ever in history entered, the appropriate motion is a request for that order.

§ 11.1.2 Procedure

Although some motions have additional requirements, almost all pretrial motions require this procedural package: written notice of motion, motion, memorandum of law, affidavit (unless no facts need be established in order for the motion to be granted), and exhibits. Depending upon local practice, even varying according to each judge, the movant may need a hearing date prior to filing and serving the motion. In other courts, the motion will ordinarily be decided without hearing.

Many courts hold regular motion days and set motions on for hearing at the next available time on one of these days. Some judges attempt to bring some efficiency to these days by scheduling these motion day hearings at set intervals. More often, courts schedule all motion hearings for the same time, resulting in the half-day "cattle call", an egregious waste of legal resources but a great way to write a letter home to your parents and still bill the time. Other courts schedule motions on an ad hoc basis. As in so many areas of practice, a litigator needs to learn the local and individual convention before beginning to draft the papers.

Motions that determine the merits of the case ("dispositive motions") are generally final orders and immediately appealable. Motions that determine procedural issues but not the merits of the case ("nondispositive motions") are generally interlocutory and cannot be reviewed on appeal until the merits of the case are decided. On appeal, the standard of review varies according to the nature of the motion, particularly whether it decides "purely" legal issues or was based in part upon facts found by the court. Trial decisions in between such extremes are decided within the court's discretion and reviewed according to the "abuse of discretion" standard.

§ 11.1.3 Approaching Pretrial Motions

At the commencement of litigation, counsel should seek, like Woody Allen's parents,[3] to take the long view by generalizing about the case, trying to sum it up, planning it out, anticipating likely maneuvers and those of opposing counsel, and then attempting to plan the likely motions of both sides. After all this the litigator needs to select which ones are really necessary to make and when and how. Undoubtedly, this master plan drawn from a lofty perch will change throughout the course of the litigation, but it is wise to have it.

The decision to bring a motion should be made after at least some initial cost-benefit analysis. If the potential benefits of the motion sufficiently outweigh its certain costs, the motion should be made and made well or not at all. In the federal courts and in states with block

3. *See* Woody Allen, Side Effects at 65 (1980).

calendar systems, a single judge oversees pretrial and trial of a case. The initial pretrial motion is the court's first substantive look at counsel and the parties. A near-frivolous motion or a poorly presented motion is not the desirable first impression to give the court. In this area of procedure, knowing when to refrain can be as valuable as knowing when to go forward.

The wide-open nature of motion practice requires both creativity and restraint on the part of attorneys. Although a motion will never be inappropriate simply because it is unprecedented, many motions are simply frivolous and unnecessary. The spirit of federal and state rules of civil procedure display a strong policy against dilatory motion practice. Restraint is necessary to prevent overuse of motions and wasted judicial time. Motion practice should be a positive and productive part of the trial lawyer's tools, but should seldom be the primary tool for either slaying or wearing down the opposition. In addition to improperly imposing on the courts, frivolous motions raise serious questions of professional ethics.

The precise scope of motion practice depends upon the facts and law applicable to a case and effective strategic and tactical determinations. Only by reviewing these facets of motion practice and considering the resources of the client can an attorney make an informed judgment concerning the proper scope and use of motion practice.

§ 11.2 MECHANICS OF MOTION PRACTICE

§ 11.2.1 Form of Motion

Unlike the mechanics of law firm profit sharing, the mechanics of motion practice are not difficult to master. Indeed, very little is formally required to bring a motion. This procedural simplicity is deceiving, however, for there are frequently additional requirements which must be met in order for the motion to be effective.

This section focuses on the requirements of motion practice contained in the Federal Rules of Civil Procedure. A party contemplating either bringing or defending a motion should consult the local rules of the court in which the action is pending. Many, many aspects of the mechanics of motion practice are governed by local rules that vary significantly from court to court. These rules may affect the time limits for bringing motions, the supporting documents either required or permitted, the right to present oral argument, and a myriad of other details.

Most motions must be made in writing. This is a specific requirement of Fed.R.Civ.P. 7(b)(1), and also a requirement of many state court rules. This form of documentation provides:

- The other side clear notice of the motion
- The judge and the opposing lawyer with information about the grounds for the motion, reasons why it should be granted, and the specific relief sought

- The facts and the law that support the motion
- The opposing lawyer with an opportunity to prepare a response to the motion
- A record of the motion for subsequent use in the trial court and if appellate review is sought

The rule presumes the opposing lawyer can, and does, read the mail.

The form of motions is generally the same for pleadings and other papers filed in a case in both state and federal courts. A motion is not, however, a pleading.[1] Fed.R.Civ.P. 7(b)(1) states that an application to a court for an order shall state with particularity supporting grounds and the order sought. Fed.R.Civ.P. 7(b)(2) requires motions to comply with the requirements of the rules for captions, signing, and all other matters of form. Fed.R.Civ.P. 10(a) requires a motion to be headed by a caption setting forth the name of the court, the title of the action, the court file number, and a designation of the type of document it is (such as "Motion" or "Motion to Compel Arbitration.") Alternative examples of motion forms include:

Alternative Form A

[Caption]

Plaintiff/Defendant [Name of party] moves this Court pursuant to Fed.R.Civ.P. ______ to [describe relief sought].

The grounds for this motion include: [describe with particularity].

This motion is based upon the files, records, proceedings, affidavit of [party/witness/attorney], the [any other sources], the attached memorandum of law (if necessary or appropriate), and oral and documentary evidence to be presented at the hearing on the motion (if anticipated).

____
[Signature]

Alternative Form B

[Caption]

The [Name of party] respectfully moves this Court as follows:

1. (Describe the motion, state the relief sought, and describe the grounds with particularity and any additional reasons.)
2. (Additional motions.)

____
[Signature]

Fed.R.Civ.P. 11 and similar state rules require a motion to be signed by an attorney of record, or, if a party is not represented by an attorney, by the party. The signature should be accompanied by the signer's

§ 11.2

1. *See, e.g., In re Zweibon,* 565 F.2d 742, 747 (D.C.Cir.1977).

address and phone number. This requirement of signature is a formal requirement, and many clerks of court do not accept an unsigned motion for filing. More importantly, the requirement of a signature is a requirement that the signer certify that the motion is made in good faith and with sufficient grounds.

Fed.R.Civ.P. 10(c) permits adoption by reference of any statements made in other pleadings or of documents attached to a motion or any other pleading. The rule specifically applies to motions, and is intended to streamline court documents to the extent feasible. Although repetition of documents is permitted, it is generally preferable to incorporate any long portions or entire documents by reference. Even where material is incorporated by reference in the formal pleadings and motions of a case, counsel frequently provide copies of that material as attachments to briefs or memoranda. This is a matter of convenience to the court and other parties.

The only important requirement for the content of motions is the provision of Fed.R.Civ.P. 7(b)(1) which requires that motions "state with particularity the grounds therefor, and shall set forth the relief or order sought." Although the language of the rule is clear, the degree of specificity of "grounds" for a motion has never been clearly articulated by the courts. One court has suggested that the requirement that grounds be stated with particularity may be met by "reasonable specification of such grounds." [2] Right! That hardly sheds much light on what must be included. The courts have compounded the problem by suggesting that a more stringent standard will be imposed in situations where the party opposing the motion alerts the moving party as to the insufficiency of the state of the grounds.[3] These rulings are probably consistent with the general view that the requirement for specific statement of grounds may be waived by the opposing party's failure to object.

In one instructive case on the adequacy of the statement of grounds in a motion, the court was confronted with a motion for a new trial. The motion stated as grounds the following, and the court found that the motion was deficient for not stating the grounds sufficiently:

> The verdict was inadequate.
>
> The learned trial judge erred on the law.
>
> The learned trial judge erred in rulings on the evidence.
>
> The learned trial judge erred in his charge to the jury.
>
> The charge of the learned trial judge to the jury was prejudicial to the plaintiffs.[4]

2. *United States v. 64.88 Acres of Land, More or Less, Situate in Allegheny County, Pa.*, 25 F.R.D. 88 (W.D.Pa.1960).

3. *See, e.g., Bartholomew v. Port*, 309 F.Supp. 1340 (E.D.Wis.1970); *Steingut v. National City Bank of N.Y.*, 36 F.Supp. 486 (E.D.N.Y.1941).

4. *Lynn v. Smith*, 193 F.Supp. 887, 888 (W.D.Pa.1961).

The movant apparently confused the need to be concise with saying nothing. Although the court did not state sufficiently what would have been minimally sufficient, it is clear that a more appropriate statement of the motion would have been as follows:

1. The verdict was insufficient as a matter of law, and reflects passion and prejudice on the part of the jury.

2. The trial judge erred on the law in the following separate actions:

   a. in dismissing plaintiff's claim, contained in Count I of his complaint, for strict liability in tort,

   b. in refusing to submit the issue of punitive damages to the jury, and

   c. in permitting defendant's counsel to argue lack of insurance to the jury

3. The court erred in ruling on the evidence by

   a. permitting defendant to offer evidence of plaintiff's driving record,

   b. refusing to receive plaintiff's proffered evidence of defendant's drinking problems, and

   c. admitting defendant's testimony that defendant was not insured.

4. The court erred in its charge to the jury by stating that the plaintiff had the burden of proving his absence of negligence, and further, in refusing to give plaintiff's requested instructions numbered 1–15.

One means of requesting a court to take action is a letter to the court. This is, however, not accepted as a motion. Obviously, a letter should never be sent to the court unless all other attorneys in the case are simultaneously provided copies.[5] Even if the ethical concern for *ex parte* communication is met by mailing copies to all counsel, letters should not be used to request relief. In one case, a court considered such a letter request and entered an order highly critical of the counsel sending the letter.[6] Sending the judge a "Thank you" note after a motion is decided is similarly *verboten*.

§ 11.2.2 Notice of Motion

Every written motion must be accompanied by a written notice of motion. Fed.R.Civ.P. 6 requires that such written notice be served and filed with a motion. The notice of a motion always gives the opposing parties notice of the fact that a motion is being submitted to the court. Most often, the notice also contains the hearing date for the motion. In

5. *See* Model Code of Professional Responsibility DR 7–110(B)(2).

6. *See* *Tate v. International Business Machines Corp.*, 94 F.R.D. 324 (N.D.Ga. 1982).

some courts, however, the notice is to be served by the parties notifying them of a date upon which a response is due, and notice of the hearing on the motion is given by the court. A typical notice of motion states:

NOTICE OF MOTION

[Caption]

To: [Name and address of attorney], Attorney for ______

PLEASE TAKE NOTICE that Plaintiff/Defendant ______ will bring the attached/following motion on for hearing before this court at [Courthouse address] in Room ______ on ______, 19__, at __ o'clock __.m., or as soon thereafter as counsel may be heard.

____

[Signature]

The notice of motion may be combined with the motion in a single document bearing a single caption. In that case, the document is, logically enough, called a "Notice of Motion and Motion."

NOTICE OF MOTION AND MOTION

[Caption]

To: [Name and address of attorney], Attorney for [Party]

PLEASE TAKE NOTICE that the undersigned will move this Court in Room ______ at [Courthouse address] on the ______ day of ______, 19__, at ______ __.m., or as soon thereafter as counsel can be heard, for [state the relief sought] on the ground [state with particularity].

____

[Signature]

Did you notice that we said "most" motions must be written? We did because most state rules and Fed.R.Civ.P. 7 permit oral or "speaking" motions in two situations: if a particular rule specifically provides that a motion may be made *ex parte* or if made "during a hearing or trial."

The first situation is easy to understand and apply. Courts have specifically recognized that the type of "hearing" at which a non-written, or "speaking" motion may be presented is one at which a verbatim recording is made.[7] The exception for a "hearing" contemplates an evidentiary hearing where objections or motions to exclude evidence, for limiting instructions, for a mistrial, or for similar relief are necessary. A court session for argument of a motion, though commonly called a hearing, is not a hearing for the purpose of not requiring a written motion. If there is no need for a spontaneous motion, or if the event precipitating a motion is one which has been known for some period of time, the court will not permit the motion to be made orally or intravenously.

7. *See Alger v. Hayes,* 452 F.2d 841 (8th Cir.1972).

§ 11.2.3 Service of Motion

All motions must be served on all parties to an action. Fed.R.Civ.P. 5 requires service of all motions except those that may be heard *ex parte.* The only exception to this rule is applied to some parties who, though named in the action, are in default for failing to appear in the action. *See* Fed.R.Civ.P. 55. This exception applies only to parties who have never appeared in the action, not to a party who does not appear at some particular proceeding or who does not respond to an individual motion or notice. Although the burden of service upon all parties is on the moving party, actual, timely service by the clerk of court or another party may satisfy the rule. Good practice requires, however, that the moving party serve all other parties. Fed.R.Civ.P. 5(b) requires that the motion be served upon the attorney once a party has appeared through an attorney. Service upon the party, once an appearance has been made on behalf of that party by an attorney, is not proper and is ineffectual.

Although the rule literally requires service only of the motion, good practice requires service of all supporting papers as well. Indeed, this may be required by local rule. Counsel should faithfully follow the general rule that if they provide something to the court, they should provide copies to all other parties.

Service of a motion must be made in accordance with the applicable rule. In federal court actions, Rule 5 applies. Normally service will be made upon the attorney who has appeared for a party. If the party has not appeared through an attorney, but is not yet in default, or if the party has appeared *pro se,* the party should be served in accordance with the rules for service of the initial summons and complaint. If the party has not appeared, and it is nonetheless desired that a motion be served upon that party, the motion should be served in accordance by one of the methods used to serve the summons and complaint to commence an action.

Service upon an attorney or party following appearance is normally made either by delivery to the attorney's or party's address of record, or by mailing to that address. Service by mail is effected at the time of mailing under Fed.R.Civ.P. 5(b) and hand delivery is complete upon delivery to the proper address. If an opposing party is served by mail, an extra three days is added to the time to respond to the motion by operation of Fed.R.Civ.P. 6(e). Delivery may be required in order that the opposing party be allowed sufficient time before a scheduled hearing.

A motion is made when it is served, not when it is filed. Thus, it is necessary that service take place sufficiently before the hearing that the parties have the period of time permitted by the rules to respond. The rules of the jurisdiction determine the minimum notice requirements, which may be as long as 30 days or as short as 5 days.

§ 11.2.4 Supporting Documents

In addition to a written motion and notice of hearing, motions usually are usually accompanied by other documents, including affidavits, a proposed order, and a memorandum of law or brief.

Affidavits. Affidavits perform a simple role in motion practice: they establish an evidentiary basis for facts necessary for the consideration of a motion. Some motions inherently require the submission of affidavits, while other motions either do not require affidavits or do not even permit affidavits. For example, a motion to dismiss for failure to state a claim under Fed.R.Civ.P. 12(b)(6) looks only to the legal sufficiency of the pleadings, and affidavits have no role in deciding the motion. If affidavits are considered, the motion is converted to a motion for summary judgment, and the other party will be given an opportunity to gather and present evidence as well.

Affidavits may be from a party, a witness, a third person, an expert, or even an attorney. All that is normally necessary is that the affiant (witness) be competent to testify under the applicable rules of evidence. Affidavits of attorneys should be used sparingly, to provide facts unavailable from other sources. If the attorney is the only or the best witness, then the attorney should make the affidavit. If an attorney's affidavit is the only factual basis for a claim or defense, the filing of the affidavit may result in the opponent filing a motion to disqualify the attorney from representation.

Statements in an affidavit may be based on personal knowledge or hearsay, or may be statements of opinion. To the extent that some of the statements do not constitute admissible evidence under the rules of evidence, an opposing party may interpose objections. For this reason, it is frequently prudent for the affidavit to include foundation information so that the affiant's testimony is both admissible and credible.

A form of an affidavit looks like this:

[Caption]

STATE OF ____________)
) ss.
COUNTY OF ___________)

Affiant, having been duly sworn on oath (or having duly affirmed) states as follows:

1. I am [describe status].
2. [Explain reasons supporting motion in separately numbered paragraphs].

____

[Signature of Affiant]

Subscribed and sworn to before me this ______ day of ______, 199_.

____

Notary Public

Proposed Order. Some courts require the submission of a proposed order. Even if not required, it may be very helpful to the court to submit a proposed order. Most importantly, such an order permits the relief to be phrased in a way that is acceptable (and presumably advantageous) to the prevailing party. Courts have a natural willingness, once they have decided how to rule, to permit the order to issue in the language of the prevailing party. Some courts feel that such an order will be vigorously defended on appeal, and that the prevailing party has determined that the phrasing used in the order is most conducive to affirmance on appeal.

In only a few courts is there any reason not to submit a proposed order. Some courts view the routine submission of a proposed order as inappropriate and discourage their submission. If there is doubt about the preferences of a particular judge, that judge's clerk can be consulted prior to the hearing.

An alternative to filing a proposed order with the motion papers is to prepare a proposed order and bring it to the hearing so that it can be offered to the judge. In some cases this method should be used so that multiple alternative orders may be made available depending on the court's rulings. This method is especially useful in conjunction with motions seeking alternative relief.

An order may also be submitted for entry by the court after the court has announced a decision orally. An attorney may volunteer to prepare such an order or the judge may direct an attorney to do so. A written record of a ruling may be useful for communicating the decision to third parties, and may permit the court to perfect the language of a decision.

Examples of orders appear in Appendix B. Sample forms for orders granting or denying motions are:

ORDER GRANTING MOTION

[Caption]

This court heard the motion of [plaintiff/defendant] for [description of motion] on ______, 199__. [Name] appeared as attorney for plaintiff; [Name] appeared as attorney for defendant.

Based upon the notice, pleadings, records, and files in this action, upon the memoranda of counsel, and upon the oral and documentary evidence and arguments presented at the hearing in this matter,

IT IS ORDERED [describe relief].

Date: ______________________

____
Judge

ORDER DENYING MOTION

[Caption]

This Court has reviewed a motion for [purpose of motion] brought by [plaintiff/defendant]. [Name] appeared on behalf of the plaintiff, and [name]

appeared on behalf of the defendant. After hearing arguments by counsel, this Court denies the motion.

Date: ____________________

____

Judge

Memoranda and Briefs. Few motions should be submitted without a written brief, memorandum, or statement of points and authorities. These documents are distinctly titled, but the differences in name are not normally significant. Regardless of title, few such documents are sufficiently "brief." The important purpose of such documents is to provide the court with the legal and factual arguments favoring the party's position with respect to the motion. Most jurisdictions either require or strongly favor their submission. Chapter 13 describes the submission of memoranda and briefs in detail.

Opposing Documents. Many jurisdictions require the submission of documents opposing a motion, particularly if the motion is to be decided on the written submissions and not on oral arguments. Other jurisdictions require opposing documents even if there will be a motion hearing. Still other jurisdictions do not expect opposing documents to be submitted because the hearing provides an opportunity for opposing to object to the motion.

Even if a written response is not required, one should nearly always be provided. Even a two-page response outlining a party's arguments or reason for opposing a motion will let the court know that the motion is opposed and give the court some understanding of the basis of the opposition.

§ 11.2.5 Local Rules

An important source of additional requirements for handling motions is the local rules adopted by many state courts and every federal district court. These latter rules are authorized by Fed.R.Civ.P. 83 to the extent they do not conflict with the Rules of Civil Procedure. Many of the local rules govern the details of the mechanics of motion practice. For example, local rules may set limits on the timing of filing and service of the motion and supporting documents or add a requirement that the papers be received, rather than merely mailed, on or before the required date. Many courts limit the page length of memoranda or briefs.

Many local rules add an important, substantive condition precedent to the filing of any motion, requiring the attorney seeking to file a motion to meet and confer with opposing counsel concerning the subject matter of the motion, and to certify in the motion papers that such a conference was held.[8] Yes, its true. Opposing lawyers must actually

8. For a complete listing of these rules, *see Crown Cork & Seal Co. v. Chemed Corp.,* 101 F.R.D. 105, 106 n. 1 (E.D.Pa. 1984).

talk to each other. These "meet and confer" rules are becoming increasingly common, and it is important for counsel to comply with both the meeting and the certification aspects of the rule. Courts can refuse to hear a motion that does not comply with the rule, and many have done so.[9] The "meet and confer" rule should not impose a significant burden on counsel because few attorneys would subject their clients to the expense of the preparation, briefing, service, filing, and hearing of a motion to which no serious opposition existed. Many attorneys routinely propose that a stipulated order be signed either before the motion is served or at the same time the motion is served. This practice gives an additional opportunity for the parties to agree on the motion.

Another common local rule requires that any opposition to a motion be made in writing within a specified period of time, anywhere from 1 to 20 days before the hearing. If a brief in opposition to the motion is not filed within the required time, the motion may be treated as uncontested and may be granted by default. In practice, counsel may normally gain extensions of time to respond from either opposing counsel or the court.

§ 11.2.6 Withdrawing Motions

Because motions are usually optional, they may be withdrawn at any time prior to a hearing. Once submitted to the court, however, the motion may usually only be withdrawn if the court consents. There are few occasions when the court would not permit the withdrawal of a motion, but they can occur. For example, if it is apparent that a motion for summary judgment is being withdrawn because of the likelihood that judgment would be entered against the moving party, the court may refuse to permit withdrawal of the motion.

§ 11.2.7 Timing of Motions

In federal courts, Fed.R.Civ.P. 5 governs the general timing for advance service of motions. Unless a specific rule concerning a particular motion states otherwise, motions and supporting papers must be served upon opposing counsel at least five days before the hearing on the motion. By operation of Fed.R.Civ.P. 6, weekends and legal holidays are not counted in computing this five-day period. Where any other rule requires service more than seven days in advance of the hearing, weekends and holidays are counted in determining the time periods. Most state court rules contain comparable provisions for timing generally and for specific motions. Many federal judges and state court district judges also establish a general motion timing rule through either a local rule or standing order. Time periods established for advance service usually range from five to thirty days. In many of these same jurisdic-

9. *See In re Folding Carton Antitrust Litigation,* 83 F.R.D. 132, 134 (N.D.Ill. 1979).

tions, the respondent is required to serve opposition papers a specified time before the hearing, usually one to fourteen days.

§ 11.2.8 Extensions of Time

As Linus has been telling us for years, no problem is so big or complicated that it can't be run away from. If Linus were an attorney instead of a comic strip character, he would (a) be less well-liked and (b) have said "one can generally escape through avoidance any difficulty, no matter how big or complex." Of course, he would be wrong in part. You can defer the inevitable but not avoid it. Thus, counsel unable to meet a pleading deadline should ordinarily be able to get at least one reasonable extension of time from opposing counsel or the court. The key words here are "reasonable" and "one." Eventually, the pleading will be due.

Rule 6(b) authorizes extensions of time by the court whenever the rules require something to be done within a certain time (*e.g.*, file and serve an answer, produce documents). Most states have similar rules, statutes, or customary practice that permits enlargement of time limits. Rule 6(b) specifically states that the court may not extend time for post-trial motions and motions for relief from defaults.

Rule 6(b) provides that the court may extend time in its discretion upon a "request" made before the time to act set forth in the rules has expired. Most courts have construed this to require a written motion, but under appropriate circumstances, a telephone call to the judge, even *ex parte,* might be appropriate to preserve the discretionary standard of Rule 6, even if a formal written motion, opposition response, hearing, and decision comes later. Under such circumstances, a flexible approach should be undertaken by both counsel and the courts.

If a motion to enlarge time is made after expiration of the deadline for which enlargement is sought, the court, according to the terms of Rule 6, may grant the extension only where the failure to make the motion in time resulted from "excusable neglect" and is otherwise considered grantable in the court's discretion. Although courts have occasionally employed an elastic definition of excusable neglect [10] or found "unique circumstances" [11] to support an untimely extension request, the leading cases of such generosity are older. The Supreme Court has more recently shown a preference for strict (some would say harsh) construction of the time deadlines of the civil, criminal and appellate rules as well as those of certain statutes. In particular, the

10. *See, e.g., Hargreaves v. Roxy Theatre, Inc.,* 1 F.R.D. 537 (S.D.N.Y.1940). *But see Driver v. Gindy Manufacturing Corp.,* 24 F.R.D. 473 (E.D.Pa.1959) (oversight or unfamiliarity with federal rules not excusable neglect).

11. *See, e.g., Harris Truck Lines, Inc. v. Cherry Meat Packers, Inc.,* 371 U.S. 215, 83 S.Ct. 283, 9 L.Ed.2d 261 (1962), *on remand* 313 F.2d 864 (7th Cir.1963), *cert. denied* 375 U.S. 821, 84 S.Ct. 59, 11 L.Ed.2d 55 (1963) (unique circumstances justify extension of seemingly inflexible time for taking appeal); *Eady v. Foerder,* 381 F.2d 980 (7th Cir.1967) (unique circumstances of reliance on erroneous district court ruling permit extension of time to move for new trial).

Court has read literally the rules regarding or affecting deadlines.[12] The high court viewpoint undoubtedly influences many lower courts despite the remote possibility that an enlargement decision would reach the Supreme Court. Counsel should err on the side of caution.

As a practical matter, counsel should seldom need to persuade the court to grant an extension. Attorneys usually agree to reasonable extensions of time. When they do, they should execute a written stipulation of their agreement, leave a signature line for the judge, and submit the stipulation to the court for approval, technically within the time period for which enlargement is sought. It is hard to imagine a court disapproving the stipulation, even if slightly late, unless counsel appear to be conspiring to act in dilatory fashion.

Agreements to extend time are generally thought to be a matter of courtesy among counsel. Sanctions may be imposed against an attorney for failing to agree to an extension of time in which to file a brief.[13] This decision underscores the responsibility that all attorneys have to cooperate to make the legal system operate to permit the goals of Fed.R.Civ.P. 1 (just, speedy, inexpensive resolution of disputes) to be achieved.

Under the rules, the mere agreement of counsel is not sufficient to create an extension.[14] Only the court can legally extend time to act. Most attorneys ignore this, preferring to reach telephone agreements with opposing counsel and confirm them by letter. This practice may create problems. The agreement may estop opposing counsel from seeking discovery sanctions or seeking default judgment without notice but it does not limit the authority of the court to hold untimely any response received late, even if under an informal lawyers' agreement. Any sanctions imposed by the court needs to be in proportion to the offense but the imposition of attorneys' fees, a refusal to consider some matter, and even dismissal or default could result. Even where the court abuses its discretion, it takes time and money to appeal and win. Why not just do it properly, as the extension rule says it should be done?

Where counsel cannot agree, the party needing an extension must move for it. The format and procedure set forth generally in this chapter govern, as do the strategic and advocacy considerations set forth in chapter 13. Perhaps most important in a contested motion for enlargement of time is an affidavit of counsel or client testifying as to

12. *See, e.g., Griggs v. Provident Consumer Discount Co.,* 459 U.S. 56, 103 S.Ct. 400, 74 L.Ed.2d 225 (1982), *on remand* 699 F.2d 642 (3d Cir.1982) (strict construction of language of Fed.R.App.P. 4(a)(4)); *Mohasco Corp. v. Silver,* 447 U.S. 807, 100 S.Ct. 2486, 65 L.Ed.2d 532 (1980), *on remand* 103 F.R.D. 614 (N.D.N.Y.1984) (strict construction of time limits for commencing Title VII actions, dictum praises "strict adherence to all procedural requirements").

13. *Regional Transportation Authority v. Grumman Flxible Corp.,* 532 F.Supp. 665 (N.D.Ill.1982).

14. *Orange Theatre Corp. v. Rayherstz Amusement Corp.,* 130 F.2d 185 (3d Cir. 1942). Fed.R.Civ.P. 6(b) specifically states that "the court" may enlarge time; the rule does not mention stipulation of the parties. Rule 29 permits the parties to stipulate to most everything about discovery except the time limits for answering interrogatories, producing documents or responding to requests to admit. Where counsel stipulate to an extension of these deadlines, the written agreement should be submitted to the court for approval.

the reasons for enlargement. If extension is justified and the amount of additional time requested is reasonable, extension should be granted almost as a matter of course on the first application. Second applications for extension of the same initial deadline or a pattern and practice of seeking extension may wear out counsel's welcome with the court. However, the court can grant such repeated requests if timely made and absolutely necessary. Where the motion is occasioned by the opposition's failure to agree to modest and justified extensions, repeated Rule 6(b) motions may convince the court of the opposing lawyer's needless contentiousness.

Decisions on extensions of time are interlocutory and will seldom if ever satisfy an exception to the final order rule, which permits appeal only of final judgments.[15] When the movant loses a motion to enlarge time, review of even the most unreasonable decision must await final adjudication, unless the consequences of a denial of enlargement (*e.g.*, dismissal) make appeal available.

§ 11.2.9 In Forma Pauperis

A party who is financially unable to prepay costs or provide security for costs in an action may be able to obtain an order permitting the party to proceed *in forma pauperis*. The order permits the indigent party to proceed in the action without paying expenses. Because most clerks will not accept for filing any motion until the filing fee is paid, it is frequently necessary to obtain leave to proceed *in forma pauperis* at the very early stages of the action. Leave is usually obtained by order, and is sought *ex parte*. The exact procedure an applicant must follow varies from jurisdiction to jurisdiction. Some jurisdictions require a written motion, affidavit of indigency, and submission of proposed pleadings to the judge. The judge then determines the propriety of the request. Other jurisdictions only require the submission of the affidavit of indigency, which is then reviewed by the clerk or court administrator. Under federal law, the applicant must submit an affidavit that states the facts of indigency, the nature of the action or defense to be taken in the action, and the affiant's good faith belief that relief is available.

In forma pauperis applications may be heard *ex parte* because there is no need for notice to the other parties. Potential opposing parties in the action would not generally have any standing to object to an indigent person proceeding *in forma pauperis*.

If it appears that a request for leave to proceed *in forma pauperis* was improperly granted, the court may modify its earlier order. If the court initially determines that the statements of poverty are untrue the court can deny or dismiss the application. In most instances, *in forma pauperis* applications are routinely granted. Usually the court accepts the statements of the affiant and conducts no independent investigation.

15. 28 U.S.C.A. § 1291.

An order permitting a party to proceed *in forma pauperis* commonly provides that the indigent will not have to pay filing fees, service costs, and related expenses. Other types of expenses may or may not be covered. Discovery costs, deposition expenses, expert costs, witness fees and transcript costs are usually not included in the original order. These expenses, unlike filing and service fees, cannot be absorbed in the judicial administration budget, but require the court to pay money to third persons. In an unusual case these expenses will be covered by the order or by a supplemental order. If these expenses, or any other expenses incurred by the indigent, are recovered as costs, they will be reimbursed to the court.

§ 11.3 STRATEGIC USE OF MOTIONS

Motions may be used for a wide variety of strategic purposes. This section explores some of the tactical uses of motions, and examines how motions fit into an overall strategic plan.

Generally, motions may be used to control the timing of various events in litigation, to shape the issues to be decided by the court, to dispose of claims and defenses that are not meritorious and to seek specific relief. Motion practice is an important part of the arsenal of both plaintiffs' and defendants' attorneys, although they may use motions differently.

Motions may also be used as a vehicle to educate the court on the nature and merits of a party's case. This use of motions is especially important if a case is assigned to the trial judge early in the litigation, since that judge will naturally retain some of the information gained during the hearing and consideration of motions.

A final strategic purpose of motions, and perhaps the most important, is to preserve procedural rights. For example, a motion showing good cause is required under Fed.R.Civ.P. 35 to obtain a physical examination of a party. In the absence of an appropriate motion, the right to conduct such an examination is lost.

Timing. One of the arts of effective motion practice relates to the timing of the motion. Motions may be brought for specific strategic purposes for which timing is crucial. For example, motions may have a significant impact on the settlement posture of a case. If such a motion is brought and won prematurely, this potential value may not be realized. Conversely, if a motion has value in forcing the action and limiting the scope of discovery, it should be brought promptly.

In addition to strategic value, timing may affect the merits of a motion. Many motions are lost because they are brought at an inopportune time. Motions for summary judgment are routinely denied if brought before the opponent has an opportunity to conduct discovery. Motions for injunctive relief may be denied simply because the passage of time has made the effectiveness of an injunction limited or the administration of it a burden upon the court.

Timing is also a part of motion practice because the use of motions can affect the timing of other events in the litigation. Although the use of motions solely to delay litigation is not proper, motions can postpone consideration of other matters. For example, the filing of a motion to dismiss under Fed.R.Civ.P. 12 postpones the due date of an answer on the merits until after the motion is decided. This result may be advantageous, and it is proper to consider this strategic purpose before filing a motion to dismiss. It would be improper to file a motion for this purpose without regard to the merits of the motion, but if the motion has merit, it is not improper to use it to tactical or strategic advantage.

Use With Other Motions. Many motions gain great strategic value when used in conjunction with other motions. The filing of a set of motions may improve the motions' strategic effectiveness. Several motions serve as prerequisites for others. Other motions are logically linked, and attain greater effectiveness if used together. An example of such motions would be a motion to compel discovery, a motion to impose sanctions, and a motion for expedited hearing. Those motions might well achieve a better result in the face of urgent need for discovery information if filed together than if filed and heard separately. Similarly, a party may seek an injunction against an opponent's attempts to seek extra-judicial relief and at the same time seek to amend the pleadings to allege a cause of action for permanent injunctive relief and damages caused by the conduct. This situation also shows how two motions might be combined but with reduced, rather that increased, effectiveness. The filing of a motion to amend the pleading to seek damages while at the same time seeking injunctive relief may result in the court denying injunctive relief for the reason that the damage action provides an adequate remedy at law.

Multiple motions may also be useful in educating the court, even if the single motions would be of minimal value. For example, if there are three or four valid bases for dismissing an action, the court will undoubtedly be more inclined to grant a dismissal if the motions are presented simultaneously. Filing multiple motions may permit bringing a wider range of facts to the court's attention, and may make the court more aware of the overall context of the individual motions.

There is no general requirement that all motions a party may wish to bring be filed or heard together. In fact, the rules only require that multiple motions be filed together in one circumstance. Fed.R.Civ.P. 12(g) requires that if a party elects to file any motion under Rule 12, then all motions which can be made under Rule 12 must be included.

Although the rules do not prohibit filing motions separately, common sense should guide counsel contemplating bringing a series of motions. Courts do not warmly receive any motions which are used merely to harass or impose a burden on an opponent. The use of multiple motions for these purposes taxes the patience of most courts. There is also a risk that the single possibly meritorious motion will not be given a credible hearing if it follows a handful of non-meritorious or frivolous motions.

Order of Filing. There is no single correct or magical order in which any given motions should be heard, and there is little that can be said on the proper order of bringing motions as an absolute rule. In forming a strategic plan for litigation of individual cases, however, a party may enhance the value of motions by considering the order in which they are to be submitted to the court.

The order of bringing a summary judgment motion, a motion to compel discovery, and a motion *in limine* may be of great strategic importance despite the fact that the motions can theoretically be brought in any order. There are six different combinations of how these motions might be separately brought, and any one of these combinations may be the best in an individual case. The summary judgment motion may be brought first, in order to educate the court about the weakness of the opponent's case in order that a subsequent motion to compel discovery will benefit from an expansive view of the scope of discovery. Similarly, the motion *in limine* might be brought last in order that the court realize that the trial is at hand, and that an early evidence ruling is not, in fact, much earlier than it would otherwise be made. If discovery is needed in order to support the motion for summary judgment, the best order for bringing those motions should be apparent even to the nonlawyer.

The order of bringing motions should also be considered in a defensive context. For example, if the adversary has announced its intention to bring a motion for summary judgment on a particular issue, a motion to compel discovery relevant to that issue may be appropriate. In fact, the bringing of such a motion should either postpone the summary judgment motion or blunt its force by making it appear as a mere defensive response to the motion to compel discovery. If, however, the summary judgment motion is brought first, then the discovery motion may appear simply to be a defensive tactic relating to that motion. In these circumstances, the order of bringing the motions may make a difference in the ultimate outcome.

Alternative Motions. Just as a party may plead claims or legal theories in the alternative (even if they are inconsistent or hypothetical), a party may present motions in the alternative. For example, a party seeking summary judgment may also move the court for an order compelling further discovery in the event the court denies summary judgment on the basis of the existence of a factual dispute.

As a practical matter, alternative pleading is useful in avoiding procedural traps and premature closure of defenses. However, presentation of alternative motions frequently dilutes the strength of all the motions. In the example above, the party seeking summary judgment should probably do only that, for seeking discovery in the alternative is a near-admission the case either lacks sufficient factual repose to make summary judgment appropriate or that the party considers the motion unlikely to be granted.

Use of Motions to Educate Court. Motions have a tremendous value in introducing the court to the facts and issues of a case. This value is present only if the motion will be heard before the judge who will try the case, but many courts have assignment systems in which cases are assigned to the trial judge for pretrial motions. If the trial judge will hear the motion, it may be extremely advantageous to bring certain pretrial motions on for a hearing so that the judge will be exposed to the issues of the case and the strengths of a particular party's position. Indeed, many judges have expressed appreciation of motions for summary judgment as a means of introducing them to cases they are managing and will ultimately try.

Parties frequently use Rule 12 motions, particularly motions to dismiss for failure to state a claim under Rule 12(b)(6), to educate the court. These motions serve to alert the court at an early stage of the proceedings what the legal issues are, and can be useful to draw attention to a bizarre or novel theory of recovery relied on by a defendant. Similarly, a plaintiff may make good use of a motion to strike a frivolous defense in order to show the court that the defendant's position is either tenuous or untenable. Even if these motions are not granted, they may have served a purpose that will yield returns later in the case.

A corollary of using a motion to educate the court is using the motion to test the court. This use of the motion first seeks to expose the judge to a critical issue in the case and then obtain some useful information on how the judge may rule. Parties will hang on desperately to the language of a judge denying a motion, and may seek to use this information in settlement. More importantly, however, the party may use the information gleaned from the decision on the motion to plan further steps in the case. For example, if the court expresses doubt about some particular factual issue, the proof might be bolstered on that issue.

If a motion can be useful in educating the court in an action which will be tried to a jury, it can be more persuasive in an action which will be tried to the court. In a bench trial case, the information which may properly be passed to the factfinder long before the trial takes place may be very influential.

Motions as a Condition Precedent to Further Review. The rules occasionally make the bringing of a certain motion not only strategically wise, but procedurally necessary. For example, it is necessary to bring a motion for an order compelling discovery as a condition precedent to obtaining sanctions for failure to make discovery in most situations. Thus, the party facing inadequate or nonexistent discovery responses should seek an order compelling responses from the recalcitrant party.

Motions for Reconsideration. The term "Motion for Reconsideration" appears nowhere in the Federal Rules of Civil Procedure. Nonetheless, the motion is a frequent and occasionally important part of the motions arsenal. Because the motion to reconsider is not linked to a rule and because many decisions concerning reconsideration go unreported, there is little case law and less appellate precedent concerning the motion. More than in any other procedural areas, each jurisdiction will have its own practices regarding motions to reconsider, and many federal district courts have local rules regarding them. Some general considerations are applicable, however, and some inherent limitations apply to use of these motions.

Motions to reconsider can seek to accomplish different ends. Most frequently, however, the motion will seek one or more of the following:

- A statement of specific bases or grounds for an earlier decision;
- To present a new argument or one better tuned to the court's now apparent predisposition to rule; or
- To request the court to consider intervening decisional or case law developments, or intervening factual developments.

The first type of motion for reconsideration is generally made following a somewhat cryptic ruling from the court on some other motion. Courts often rule on motions by simple order or by oral decision from the bench. In these cases, the basis for the ruling may be far from clear, especially where one or both parties argued several theories on the issue. When one loses such a motion with a terse ruling, counsel may wish to seek reconsideration simply to determine the court's specific reasoning (if any) to better approach the judge in the future. This use of a motion for reconsideration may also permit a more successful attack on appeal. Thus, where possible, the losing party will attempt to obtain a written decision on its motion for reconsideration. However, moving to reconsider at the moment of an unfavorable bench ruling should at least force the court to expound on its thinking in the presence of the court reporter.

A motion to reconsider may also be used where intervening developments, either of a factual or legal nature, have cast doubt on the correctness of the initial ruling. A change in precedential law will not support a motion for relief from a judgment under Rule 60, but it may well persuade the court to change its view of a summary judgment ruling, a protective order, or a pretrial evidentiary ruling. Certainly, reversal of cases given res judicata or collateral estoppel effect in the first ruling provides powerful support for a reconsideration motion. The mere passage of time may show that assumptions underlying the earlier decision proved incorrect or that the initial ruling failed to accomplish the result expected by the court. This form of reconsideration motion is especially appropriate in the context of discovery rulings.

As a practical matter, only motions for reconsideration involving intervening factual and legal developments are well-received. Other motions will seldom change the judicial mind. They can, however, build a record for appeal and, where the trial court has obviously erred twice, may provide some basis for reaching settlement pending a trial sure to be reversed.

Some courts which are unpersuaded by a motion for reconsideration simply "deny" the motion. Other courts grant the motion for reconsideration, but then affirm their previous decision. Although either method makes clear the court's view, the latter approach probably more accurately reflects the court's decisional process. Many motions for reconsideration are disposed of by one-sentence orders, although detailed decisions are sometimes issued.

§ 11.4 APPEALABILITY OF DECISIONS ON PRETRIAL MOTIONS

The general rule in federal courts and nearly all state courts is that only final orders are immediately appealable. Appeals courts ultimately do review interlocutory (non-final) orders eventually, after the passage of time and events brings the case to a final decision. Occasionally, however, interlocutory orders become moot due to later developments and never can be reviewed, adding an item to the list of life's little injustices.

Everyone agrees that only final orders are appealable, but just what is a final order? A final order can be defined as one that conclusively determines the rights of the parties.[1] The Supreme Court has characterized a final judgment as one that ends the litigation on the merits and leaves nothing for the court to do but execute the judgment.[2]

If one can roughly identify the eventual case winner because of a decision on a motion, the order is probably final and appealable. A minority of states have significantly more liberal definitions of finality. Some expressly permit interlocutory appeals. Legislatures frequently make certain orders appealable for public policy reasons, just as specific statutes may confer federal jurisdiction on particular classes of cases.

Even federal law, which enunciates the final order rule in one section of the Judicial Code, modifies it in the next. Interlocutory orders granting, continuing, or modifying, refusing or dissolving injunctions are usually appealable.[3] So are orders appointing or winding up receiverships as well as admiralty orders determining the rights and liabilities of parties. This portion of federal law recognizes that in many cases the decision on a preliminary matter effectively determines the winner although the trial itself is months away or may never be had. Most states treat the appealability of equitable remedies in similar fashion, either by statute or through case law.

Dispositive motions are more likely to result in final, appealable orders. In the overwhelming proportion of the cases, this occurs when

§ 11.4

1. *Bendix Aviation Corp. v. Glass,* 195 F.2d 267 (3d Cir.1952).

2. *Catlin v. United States,* 324 U.S. 229, 65 S.Ct. 631, 89 L.Ed. 911 (1945).

3. *See* 28 U.S.C.A. § 1292(a).

the dispositive motion is granted. Examples of frequently made dispositive motions are the Rule 12(b) motions to dismiss, particularly Rule 12(b)(6) motions for failure to state a claim, Rule 12(c) motions for judgment on the pleadings, Rule 55 motions for default judgment (the mere entry of default without entry of judgment is not appealable); Rule 56 motions for summary judgment; Rule 50 motions for a directed verdict; Rule 59 motions for a new trial, and Rule 60 motions for relief from judgment, the last three lying outside the scope of this book. If any of these motions, except the new trial motion,[4] is granted, a final, appealable order usually results. If denied, the motions create only interlocutory orders that must await review.

Non-dispositive motions are those tending to deal with the procedure of the case rather than its substantive outcome. Both grants and denials of such motions fail to conclusively determine the judgment winner, although decisions on key procedural motions may be the handwriting on the wall, creating a procedural framework far more favorable to one side than the other. However, non-dispositive motion decisions tend to be like temper tantrums. They are forgotten and forgiven if victory ultimately results. Examples of frequently made non-dispositive motions are motions to amend the pleadings, to join parties, to assert additional claims, to exclude or admit evidence, to affect case management (*e.g.*, bifurcation, transfer, consolidation, separate trials, severance, continuances, appointments of special masters), and to determine the trier of fact (judge or jury).

Interlocutory Appeals. Almost all discovery motions and resulting orders are non-dispositive and hence interlocutory.[5] Orders independently affecting a claim of privilege or dismissing cases or claims as a sanction for failure to follow the discovery rules constitute the only real exceptions to this rule of thumb. Motions for protective orders of all varieties and most motions for sanctions, even if successful, do not result in dispositive final orders. There exist some circumstances where courts may find discovery orders not interlocutory.

Statutory Appeals. As with any general rule, exceptions exist. In federal courts, one statutory exception, embodied in 28 U.S.C. 1292(b), permits the trial court to certify an order for immediate appellate review if the trial judge finds that the order involves a controlling question of law as to which there is substantial ground for difference of opinion and that an immediate appeal from the order may materially advance the ultimate termination of the litigation. The appeals court is not bound to accept the certification but may refuse and remand the case to the trial court. Comparatively few state courts have such a certification procedure, accomplishing the necessary "escape hatches" from a strict finality rule through other means.

4. The new trial motion is only partially dispositive in that it would, if granted, end the old trial but not the case. The denial of the motion, but not the grant of it, concludes the case.

5. *See* Roger S. Haydock & David F. Herr, Discovery Practice § 8.9 (2d ed. 1988, Supp. 1994).

Collateral Order Appeals. Another key federal exception to the final order rule has evolved through case law. The exception, known as the collateral order doctrine, permits interlocutory review of decisions that (1) conclusively resolve the issue in question where (2) the issue is completely separate and distinct from the merits of the litigation, and where (3) the order will be effectively unreviewable after final judgment.[6] The collateral order doctrine justifies the interlocutory review accorded the non-party discovery decisions discussed above. Other examples of appealable collateral orders include orders disqualifying counsel, holding a party in contempt,[7] or granting or rejecting a defense of official immunity.[8] As one might discern from these examples, there appears to be an unspoken fourth component to collateral order review. Where denial of interlocutory review creates an unacceptable risk that the entire case must be tried and retried because of initial error or where the interlocutory order implicates an important policy concern, courts are more likely to fit the order within the collateral order doctrine. State courts are split regarding the doctrine, with most having it but few using the same terminology and analysis found in the federal courts.

Rule Appeals. Federal Rule 54(b) and many similar state rules provide that a court may, in multiple claim or multiple party actions, direct the entry of final judgment when its orders conclusively adjudicate the dispute as to that claim or party where the court expressly determines that there is no just reason for delay in finality or appealability. A Rule 54(b) determination, like a Section 1292(b) certification, need not be accepted by the appeals court if the appellate court rejects the trial judges express determinations. Like the collateral doctrine, Rule 54(b) questions are occasionally complex. Fortunately, help is available.[9]

Writ Appeals. Interlocutory review may also be available through the extraordinary writs, primarily mandamus and prohibition. A writ of mandamus directs a court to perform some clear and essentially ministerial duty. A writ of prohibition restrains the trial court from issuing and enforcing an order exceeding its powers (*i.e.*, an order the appellate court finds to be egregiously in error and causing immediate and virtually irreparable harm). Although both are authorized in federal courts by the All Writs Act,[10] counsel seldom successfully obtain either writ in federal court. However, petitions for these writs as a means of interlocutory review and issuance of the writs is more common in state courts, suggesting that in many states these writs perform the function of the collateral order doctrine widely used in federal court. Examples of situations justifying the writs are discovery orders imperiling privileged

6. *See Cox Broadcasting Corp. v. Cohn,* 420 U.S. 469, 95 S.Ct. 1029, 43 L.Ed.2d 328 (1975), *on remand* 234 Ga. 67, 214 S.E.2d 530 (1975); *Cohen v. Beneficial Industrial Loan Corp.,* 337 U.S. 541, 69 S.Ct. 1221, 93 L.Ed. 1528 (1949).

7. *See, e.g., United States v. Ryan,* 402 U.S. 530, 91 S.Ct. 1580, 29 L.Ed.2d 85 (1971).

8. *See,* e.g., Mitchell v. Forsyth, 472 U.S. 511, 105 S.Ct. 2806, 86 L.Ed.2d 411 (1985), *on remand* 772 F.2d 894 (3d Cir. 1985).

9. *See* 10 Charles A. Wright, et al., Federal Practice and Procedure §§ 2653–57 (1983).

10. 28 U.S.C.A. § 1651.

materials such as documents subject to the attorney-client and trial preparation privileges [11] or requiring disclosure of trade secrets.[12]

Contempt Appeals. The least preferred method of obtaining interlocutory review involves going into contempt of court by refusing to comply with the offending order and thus invoking the collateral order doctrine. For the daring (and often foolhardy) party or attorney, this tactic can provide both immediate appellate review and notoriety, perhaps even martyrdom. If the court holds the recalcitrant attorney in criminal contempt, immediate review is assured. Civil contempt orders directed toward parties are not immediately appealable unless linked with an otherwise appealable order.[13] In civil contempt, the party "holds the keys to his own cell" and may unlock the door merely by complying with the initial trial court order. Because of the seriousness of the sanctions available, attorneys should exhaust all other means of obtaining interlocutory review before using contempt. As Thurman Arnold once said, if someone has to go to jail, make sure its the client rather than the lawyer.

§ 11.5 ETHICAL USES OF MOTIONS

§ 11.5.1 Ethics of Motion Practice

Motion practice is no different from all other aspects of practice with respect to the obligations an attorney has to a client. The preparation and submission of motions does not present any particularly difficult ethical problems relating to the lawyer's duties to the client. Motion practice may, however, involve situations which require the lawyer to be aware of ethical responsibilities to the court. Because the client's interests do not always coincide with the court's, these situations may present difficult ethical dilemmas to the lawyer.

In motion practice, the most important instance of this facet of a lawyer's responsibility arises when the lawyer becomes aware of legal authority contrary to the position being advanced to the court in a motion. At trial, the conflict between the duty to preserve client confidences and the duty not to defraud the court may become more important. The Code of Professional Responsibility provides that an attorney shall disclose controlling decisional or statutory law which is adverse to his or her client's position. Disciplinary Rule 7–106(B)(1)

11. *See, e.g., Harper & Row Publishers, Inc. v. Decker,* 423 F.2d 487 (7th Cir.1970), *affirmed* 400 U.S. 348, 91 S.Ct. 479, 27 L.Ed.2d 433 (1971), *rehearing denied* 401 U.S. 950, 91 S.Ct. 917, 27 L.Ed.2d 234 (1971). *But see La Buy v. Howes Leather Co.,* 352 U.S. 249, 77 S.Ct. 309, 1 L.Ed.2d 290 (1957) (mandamus review granted where judge erroneously referred case to special master due to crowded docket.)

12. *See, e.g., Hartley Pen Co. v. United States District Court,* 287 F.2d 324 (9th Cir.1961).

13. *See Halderman v. Pennhurst State School & Hospital,* 673 F.2d 628 (3d Cir. 1982) *cert. denied* 465 U.S. 1038, 104 S.Ct. 1315, 79 L.Ed.2d 712 (1984) (civil contempt orders appealable under *Cohen*); *IBM Corp. v. United States,* 493 F.2d 112 (2d Cir.1973), *cert. denied* 416 U.S. 995, 94 S.Ct. 2409, 40 L.Ed.2d 774 (1974) (civil contempt not appealable).

requires such a disclosure when opposing counsel fails to reveal the controlling authority. This is an important obligation of lawyers which is directly contrary to the instincts developed in the adversary system.

Although the scope of DR 7–106(B)(1) initially appears quite limited, an ABA Opinion has construed the rule to require disclosure of more than "controlling" authorities. Formal Opinion 280 articulated the following three-part test to guide attorneys in determining whether disclosure of adverse law is required:

> Is the decision which opposing counsel has overlooked one which the court should clearly consider in deciding the case? Would a reasonable judge properly feel that a lawyer who advanced, as the law, a proposition adverse to the undisclosed decision, was lacking in candor and fairness to him? Might the judge consider himself misled by an implied representation that the lawyer knew no adverse authority? [1]

Consequently, DR 7–106(B)(1) may require disclosure of all adverse authority significantly affecting the outcome of an issue.

Equally important as the ethical responsibility to disclose adverse authority is the potential tactical mistake of failing to do so. Dealing fast and loose with the law or facts before the court may have devastating effects on the immediate motion and on future proceedings in that case. This practice may also give rise to the imposition of sanctions against the attorney, including the payment of attorneys' fees incurred by the opponent.[2] Many lawyers fail to realize the importance that judges place upon the reliability of lawyers and the statements and representations they make to the court. Failure to disclose adverse authority may cast a pall over all the statements and arguments on a given motion, and create long-lasting problems in other aspects of the case as well.

When presenting a motion to the court, lawyers also have an ethical duty not to make certain types of arguments. Since an attorney's role is to advance the client's position, the attorney must refrain from interjecting personal opinion into courtroom presentations. The disciplinary rules prohibit lawyers from asserting their personal knowledge of facts in issue and their personal opinion as to the justness of a cause, the credibility of a witness, or the culpability of a civil litigant.[3] However, an attorney may argue "for any position or conclusion with respect to the[se] matters" which is based upon an "analysis of the evidence."[4]

§ 11.5

1. ABA Comm. on Professional Ethics and Grievances, Formal Op. 280 (1949).

2. *See Knorr Brake Corp. v. Harbil, Inc.*, 556 F.Supp. 484, 487 (N.D.Ill.1983) *judgment reversed* 738 F.2d 223 (7th Cir.1984) (court concluded attorney "played fast and loose with precedents" and imposed sanctions).

3. *See* Model Code of Professional Responsibility, DR 7–106(c)(3)–(4) (1979).

4. Model Code of Professional Responsibility, DR 7–106(c)(4) (1979). The Code also prohibits a lawyer from "stat[ing] or allud[ing] to any matter that he has no reasonable basis to believe is relevant to the case or that will not be supported by admissable evidence." *Id.* at DR7–106(C)(1).

One of the major ethical concerns relating to motion practice centers on misuse, or rather, overuse, of motions for improper purposes. Although no "bright line" rules may be drawn to determine what motions are permissible and which are not, some standards do exist.

The ABA Code of Professional Responsibility DR 7–102 provides in part:

> (A) In his representation of a client, a lawyer shall not:
>
> (1) File a suit, assert a position, conduct a defense, delay a trial, or take other action on behalf of his client when he knows or when it is obvious that such action would serve merely to harass or maliciously injure another.[5]

This ethical constraint is also embodied in Fed.R.Civ.P. 11 which applies directly to motions. By signing a motion, the attorney for the party certifies that, among other things, it is not interposed for delay. An example of improper and unethical motion practice is a motion for change of venue made solely to cause inconvenience and delay.[6]

§ 11.5.2 Attacking Unethical Counsel (and Even Judges)

Motions to Disqualify Counsel. One tool which is being increasingly relied on to protect against unethical practices in litigation is the motion to disqualify opposing counsel. Unfortunately, the motion is also used to obtain a tactical advantage over opponents.

Motions to disqualify opposing counsel have become an all-too-prevalent part of many litigators' arsenals. Although the motion is occasionally a necessary tool to permit a party a fair trial, it is frequently used to prevent a fair trial from taking place. The motion to disqualify counsel had its heyday some years ago, when courts would permit the mere making of the motion to act as stay of proceedings while the motion was made, argued, and an appeal taken as a matter of right. The United States Supreme Court has decided that motions refusing to disqualify counsel are not appealable,[7] however, and the courts have become increasingly hostile to frivolous motions to disqualify.[8] If a motion to disqualify is brought solely for tactical reasons, the courts readily award costs and attorneys' fees.[9]

Disqualification of counsel is most frequently sought on the grounds of conflict of interest. This conflict may arise from the prior representation of a client or from the simultaneous representation of a party in

5. Code of Professional Responsibility, DR 7–102 (1979).

6. *See* ABA Comm. on Professional Ethics, Informal Op. 557 (1963).

7. *Firestone Tire & Rubber Co. v. Risjord,* 449 U.S. 368, 101 S.Ct. 669, 66 L.Ed.2d 571 (1981), *on remand* 718 F.2d 1106 (8th Cir.1983), *appeal after remand* 756 F.2d 1322 (8th Cir.1985).

8. *See, e.g., Freeman v. Chicago Musical Instrument Co.,* 689 F.2d 715, 721–722 (7th Cir.1982) (can be "misused as techniques of harassment"); *Comden v. Superior Court of Los Angeles County,* 20 Cal.3d 906, 145 Cal.Rptr. 9, 576 P.2d 971 (1978), *cert. denied* 439 U.S. 981, 99 S.Ct. 568, 58 L.Ed.2d 652 (1978).

9. *Minerals Engineering Co. v. Wold,* 38 Fed.R.Serv.2d 598 (D.Colo.1983) (costs awarded against attorneys, not clients).

more than one action. The other, less common, ground for disqualification motions is the situation where a lawyer is, or should be, a witness.

In the situation of current representation of a party whose interest is adverse to that of a former client, courts increasingly use the "substantial relationship" test to determine if disqualification is necessary.[10] This test requires disqualification if the two matters are substantially related, and presumes that the prior representation involved disclosure of client confidences. That presumption may, however, be rebutted in most cases.[11] The courts have required, however, that the relationship of the issues in the two cases be very clear or identical.

In cases of simultaneous representation, the courts apply a less stringent test if disqualification is necessary. No substantial relationship has to be proved, and the courts are ready to order disqualification if it appears that the lawyer's ability to provide independent advice and undivided loyalty to the clients is affected.[12]

The problem of the testifying advocate has been the most difficult for the courts. The Code of Professional Responsibility prohibits an attorney from accepting representation in a matter when it is clear that the attorney is going to be, or ought to be, a witness in the proceeding.[13] The Code also requires an attorney in such a position to withdraw from future representation. The Code allows four exceptions to the rule requiring withdrawal, and these exceptions provide much of the grist for the mill of litigation of these motions. Withdrawal is not required if the testimony will relate solely to uncontested matters, to matters of formality, or to the nature and value of the attorney's services, nor when withdrawal would "work a substantial hardship on the client." This last exception becomes increasingly important as the litigation proceeds, and the courts are notably reluctant to order disqualification at the later stages of the proceedings. Although the Code of Professional Responsibility clearly requires disqualification of an entire firm if one member is disqualified,[14] courts have not stringently imposed that requirement in the situation of the testifying advocate.[15]

A condition precedent to bringing a motion for disqualification, even if not expressly stated by the court, is a demand that the attorney involved withdraw voluntarily. Courts are especially likely to view the

10. This test was given life in *T.C. Theatre Corp. v. Warner Brothers Pictures,* 113 F.Supp. 265 (S.D.N.Y.1953), *reargument denied* 125 F.Supp. 233 (1953). It has now been widely followed. *See, e.g., Silver Chrysler Plymouth, Inc. v. Chrysler Motors Corp.,* 518 F.2d 751, 754 (2d Cir.1975), *overruled on other grounds, Armstrong v. McAlpin,* 625 F.2d 433 (2d Cir.1980) (en banc), *vacated* 449 U.S. 1106, 101 S.Ct. 911, 66 L.Ed.2d 835 (1981).

11. *See Gas–A–Tron of Arizona v. Union Oil Co. of California,* 534 F.2d 1322 (9th Cir.1976), *cert. denied sub nom. Shell Oil Co. v. Gas–A–Tron of Ariz.,* 429 U.S. 861, 97 S.Ct. 164, 50 L.Ed.2d 139 (1976). *But see In re Corrugated Container Antitrust Litigation,* 659 F.2d 1341 (5th Cir.1981) (no rebuttal allowed as to long-standing attorney-client relationship).

12. *See, e.g., Cinema 5, Limited v. Cinerama, Inc.,* 528 F.2d 1384 (2d Cir.1976).

13. Model Code of Professional Responsibility, DR 5–102(A) (1979).

14. Model Code of Professional Responsibility, DR 5–102(A) (1979).

15. *See, e.g., Bottaro v. Hatton Associates,* 680 F.2d 895 (2d Cir.1982).

motion as a procedural ploy if it comes without warning, and without giving the attorney a chance to consider the propriety of continuing in the representation. In all other respects, the motion should be approached in the same way as any other motion. It is important, however, that court be given the facts upon which to make a decision. Affidavits should clearly establish the grounds for the motion and the likelihood that the harm intended to be prevented by the applicable ethical rule is likely to occur if the motion is not granted.

Motions to Disqualify the Court. Motions to disqualify the court from hearing a matter are relatively rare. For obvious reasons, the party seeking such relief will want to attempt to have the judge recuse himself or herself voluntarily. Nonetheless, a motion to recuse is occasionally necessary.

The foundation for a motion to disqualify a judge is a provision of the Code of Judicial Conduct which directs the court to be disqualified. A motion for disqualification of a judge, like that for disqualification of an attorney, usually asks the court to order that the substantive provisions of the appropriate disciplinary rules be enforced prophylactically through a court order of disqualification. In addition to the Code of Judicial Conduct, specific statutes may facilitate the disqualification of a judge.

Canon 3 of the Code of Judicial Conduct requires a judge to disqualify himself or herself if the judge:

> (a) has personal bias or prejudice concerning a party, or personal knowledge of disputed evidentiary facts concerning the proceeding;
>
> (b) served as a lawyer in the matter in controversy, or a lawyer with whom he previously practiced law served during such association as a lawyer concerning the matter, or the judge or such lawyer has been a material witness concerning it;
>
> (c) knows that he, individually or as a fiduciary, or his spouse or minor child residing in his household, has a financial interest in the subject matter in controversy or is a party to the proceeding, or any other interest that court be substantially affected by the outcome of the proceeding; or
>
> (d) his spouse, or a person within the third degree of relationship to either of them, or the spouse of such a person:
>
> > (1) is a party to the proceeding, or an officer, director, or trustee of a party;
> >
> > (2) is acting as a lawyer in the proceeding;
> >
> > (3) is known by the judge to have an interest that court be substantially affected by the proceeding; or
> >
> > (4) is to the judge's knowledge likely to be a material witness in the proceeding....

These grounds requiring judicial disqualification restate what we all expect from judges: impartiality. Title 28 of the United States Code 455 requires that a judge "shall disqualify himself in any proceeding in which his impartiality might reasonably be questioned." Judges are also required not to hear appeals of cases decided by them.[16]

These rules and statutes are directed to the judges, not the parties, and are intended to set the standards to permit the judges to determine whether it is proper that they sit on a particular case. The motion for disqualification asks the court specifically to consider the propriety of his or her sitting on a case, and establishes the record for an appeal if appropriate action is not taken by the court. It is important to remember, however, that the motion to recuse a federal judge is decided in the first instance by that judge. For that reason, it is probably tactically unwise to bring motions for recusal casually.

An alternative method for obtaining recusal or disqualification of a judge is to file an affidavit of bias or prejudice. Title 28 of the United States Code 144 permits a party to disqualify a judge by filing an affidavit stating facts from which the inference of actual bias or prejudice can be inferred. The affidavit must be signed by the party, but the attorney of record for that party must also sign it to certify that it is made in good faith. The statute specifically requires that the affidavit be timely filed, and provides that it must be filed within 10 days of the beginning of the term of court.

In addition to permitting disqualification upon a factual showing of actual bias or prejudice, many state courts permit the disqualification of a judge without a showing of cause.[17] These jurisdictions essentially permit the peremptory challenge of any judge by a party. Proposals have been made to create such a system in the federal courts, but no such legislation has passed Congress.

For the same reason that motions for disqualification of counsel have been criticized by the courts, motions to disqualify judges have not been warmly received.[18] The motion has received an appropriately cold reception where it is filed after the judge has heard motions in the matter for a period of years.[19] It is inherently inequitable for a party to be able to disqualify a judge after having an opportunity to review preliminary rulings in an attempt to determine the judge's likely final decisions in the case.

§ 11.5.3 Withdrawal and Substitution of Counsel

A party may desire to change counsel, or to terminate representation by present counsel without naming additional counsel. Both situa-

16. 23 U.S.C.A. § 47.

17. *See, e.g.,* Minn.Stat.Ann. 542.16; 48 Minn.S.A., R.Civ.P. 63.03 (notice of removal may be filed, no grounds necessary).

18. *See, e.g., Delesdernier v. Porterie,* 666 F.2d 116, 121 (5th Cir.1982), *cert. denied* 459 U.S. 839, 103 S.Ct. 86, 74 L.Ed.2d 81 (1982) (lack of timeliness requirement makes the motion "a mere litigation strategem").

19. *In re International Business Machines Corp.,* 618 F.2d 923 (2d Cir.1980).

tions frequently arise, and may give rise to motions which either must or should be brought.

Substitution of counsel is normally effectuated without a motion. The new attorney should prepare a document signed as any pleading indicating that the party is now represented by the new attorney. That document, normally termed a "substitution" constitutes that attorney's appearance in the case. The party seeking substitution should also obtain the written consent of the former attorney. The substitution and consent are frequently combined in a single document. That document should then be served on all parties, and filed with the court. The clerk will then note the new appearance on the docket.[20] Upon substitution the former attorney will not be provided notices by the court, and need not be served with pleadings or notices by the other parties. A motion is required for substitution only in rare circumstances. The court in a class action will be interested in any change in counsel for the class representatives. If court approval of a substitution is not obtained, it is possible that the court would decertify a class for the reason that the class representatives would be deemed not able adequately to represent the class with the new attorney.

Withdrawal of counsel frequently requires a motion. The rules of civil procedure do not require such a motion. Many federal courts do require a motion to withdraw an appearance. Even if the court does not require a motion to withdraw, it is frequently desirable to make a motion and obtain court approval to withdraw.

Before an attorney considers withdrawing as counsel for a party, the attorney must determine if withdrawal is ethically permissible. Disciplinary Rule 2–110 of the Code of Professional Responsibility governs withdrawal and creates an elaborate set of requirements for withdrawal. The rule defines when an attorney may withdraw, and sets forth those circumstances which require the attorney to withdraw. In either case the attorney must, before withdrawing, take "reasonable steps to avoid foreseeable prejudice to the rights" of the client.[21] The rules require that the attorney give the client notice of the withdrawal, adequate time to retain substitute counsel, and provide the client with all file materials. The applicable ethical rules should be consulted before seeking withdrawal to determine if withdrawal is permissible.

§ 11.5.4 Motion Malpractice

Motion practice is not likely to be a source of legal malpractice liability in its own right. There is little unique to motion practice which results in unusual exposure to malpractice claims. Many of the same errors which result in malpractice liability throughout the litigation process may, however, occur in connection with the filing or defense of motions.

20. Fed.R.Civ.P. 79(a).

21. Model Code of Professional Responsibility DR 2–110(A)(2) (1979).

Probably the most important area of malpractice exposure in civil litigation relates to the failure to meet deadlines. Missing a statute of limitations creates clear malpractice liability. Other deadlines may be equally important. For example, the failure to take some required action regarding a motion in a timely manner may equally prejudice the client's rights. It is important that some reliable system be used by lawyers to insure that applicable deadlines are identified and then noted so they do not pass without the appropriate action being taken.

One situation which arises only in motion practice and which is an important source of malpractice exposure relates to motions for any form of relief on the grounds of excusable neglect. Many of the requirements of the rules of civil procedure will be waived or extended in situations of excusable neglect.[22] In making a plea for relief based on excusable neglect, the attorney may be required to make statements which amount to admissions of malpractice. Although professional responsibility to the client requires that all efforts be made to obtain relief from a rule or statute (or an order or judgment entered based upon them) if neglect has occurred and if such relief is justified, the attorney should be aware that the client's interest and the lawyer's may diverge at this point. Usually, an attorney will be energetic in pleading neglect as a basis for obtaining relief from the court because the relief, if granted, will prevent any claim of malpractice by the client by removing any damages. The attorney is not under any obligation, however, to make statements which are not factually accurate, and is under an affirmative obligation not to make any inaccurate statements for the purposes of obtaining relief from the court.[23]

Attorneys may be held liable for damages for failing to defend against motions. In one case an attorney did not present factual information in response to a motion for summary judgment despite the existence of facts which would establish a sufficient factual dispute to render summary judgment inappropriate. The court concluded that those facts, if proven by the client, would permit a judgment for legal malpractice.[24] Here, liability exists in the motion context even though there is little likelihood of liability for failing to present evidence or call a witness at a trial.[25] The stringent procedural requirements of Rule 56, and the fact that a summary judgment will dispose of a case on the merits, result in a clear obligation to present facts to the court in a proper manner so that a summary judgment is not ordered precipitously.

Similarly, an attorney may be liable for failing to pursue relief which might be available by motion. Although the client would have to prove that the failure to obtain the relief by motion resulted in ultimate harm,

22. Among the rules which permit some relief on the grounds of excusable neglect are Rule 6 (extension of time); Rule 13(f) (omitted counterclaims); and Rule 60 (relief from judgments or orders).

23. Model Code of Professional Responsibility DR 7–106(c) (1979).

24. *Partin v. Olney,* 121 Ariz. 448, 591 P.2d 74 (App.1978).

25. *See, e.g., Outboard Marine Corp. v. Liberty Mutual Insurance Co.,* 536 F.2d 730 (7th Cir.1976).

it is possible to be liable for damages. In one case, the attorney failed to pursue a motion for consolidation, and the court permitted the client to pursue a claim for damages.[26] In that case, the failure to consolidate resulted in the entry of two separate judgments against an insurer for the same damages in a fire loss. Although the court found that sufficient factual disputes existed to make the entry of summary judgment against the attorney inappropriate, the court permitted the action to proceed. Analogous claims for liability may be imagined for many other types of motion.

An attorney may also be exposed in motion practice to liability arising from errors of law. In particular, there may be liability for failure to conduct research or investigation into legal authority.[27] This potential area of liability exists as to every procedural and substantive facet of the case, and requires consideration in every contemplated motion and in defending every motion brought against one's client. The duty to research does not require exhaustive research of every issue, and the courts impose some "rule of reason" approach to the duty. The possibility of malpractice liability for the failure to conduct legal research requires the exercise of some judgment, however, and it may be prudent to involve the client in deciding how much time and effort should properly be expended in research. The financial resources of the client will determine in many situations the extent of research and appropriate response. This inherent conflict between what should be done and what is economical raises many difficult ethical dilemmas. In practice, however, few clients will be disposed to blame an attorney or assert any claim for a bad result when the client helped map the strategy and make the decision to limit research expenditures.

PRACTICE PROBLEMS

Drafting

1. Draft a notice of motion, motion, proposed order, and necessary supporting documents (excluding a memorandum) in the case assigned by your instructor.

Redrafting Exercise

2. You represent Lawn Turf in *Lawn Turf v. National Seed*. You have decided to move for a summary judgment. An associate in your law firm drafts the following documents. Redraft them. Do not draft the caption or signature provisions.

---

26. *Adams, George & Wood v. Travelers Insurance Co.,* 359 So.2d 457 (Fla.App. 1978).

27. *See Smith v. Lewis,* 13 Cal.3d 349, 118 Cal.Rptr. 621, 530 P.2d 589 (1975). *See generally* Note, Lawyer Malpractice—The Duty to Perform Legal Research, 32 Fed.Ins.Couns.Q. 199 (1982).

FACTS

On September 23, National Seed Company sent a mailing of sample clover seed to potential customers with the note appearing in Note A. On September 30, the Lawn Turf Company sent the defendant a telegram which appears in Wire A. On October 1, National Seed sent Lawn Turf a reply note, which appears in Note B and which Lawn Turf received on October 3. On October 5, Lawn Turf sent a wire which appears in Wire B and which National Seed received on October 6.

Beginning on October 7, a three-day rainstorm destroyed the National Seed clover seed crop. On October 11, the National Seed manager, Geraldine O'Hara, telephoned the president of Lawn Turf, Solomon Baritz, and said she could not deliver the seed. Because of the time of the year, Lawn Turf could not obtain any replacement red clover seed and lost $12,200 in profits it would have earned by selling the seed to retailers.

The term "f.o.b." means the place delivery will occur. F.O.B. Mitchell means the seller will deliver without charge to the buyer at Mitchell.

Note A:

Red Clover, 50,000 lbs. like sample. I am asking 24 per, f.o.b. Mitchell, Summit.

National Seed

Wire A:

National Seed: Sample received. Your price too high. Wire another offer, naming absolutely lowest f.o.b.

Lawn Turf

Note B:

Lawn Turf: I am asking 23per pound for the car of red clover seed from which your sample was taken. No. 1 seed. Have an offer of 22per pound, f.o.b. Mitchell.

National Seed

P.S. All quotations subject to contingencies beyond our control.

Wire B:

National Seed: Note received. Accept your offer. Ship at least 50,000 lbs., and 60,000 lbs., if available, promptly, route care of Comtrak Railroad to Mitchell, Summit.

Lawn Turf

MOTION DOCUMENTS

Motion for Summary Judgment

Plaintiff by its lawyers file this motion for a summary judgment pursuant to the rules of civil procedure of the District Court of Mitchell. Plaintiff has a right to a summary judgment as a matter of law because between the parties there exist no genuine issues of material fact. The Plaintiff bases this motion on the attached documents.

Affidavit

Solomon Baritz, being sworn under oath, states as follows:

1. That affiant is Solomon Baritz, the President of Lawn Turf.

2. That Lawn Turf is the Plaintiff in the above entitled action.

3. That on or about October 11 affiant received a phone call from Geraldine O'Hara.

4. That Geraldine O'Hara is the manager of National Seed Co.

5. That affiant was told by O'Hara that she would breach her contract with Lawn Turf.

6. That Lawn Turf never received the Red Clover seed contracted with National Seed.

7. That Lawn Turf suffered a loss of $12,200 because Lawn Turf could not replace the non-delivered seed and lost the profits it would have earned by selling such seed to its retail distributors.

8. That there exists no genuine issue of material fact in this case.

Further affiant sayeth not.

Proposed Order

Upon all the files, records, motions, and arguments submitted by counsel in this case, IT IS ORDERED:

Summary Judgment be entered in the favor of the Plaintiff in an amount of $12,200.

____

Judge

Motion Problems

3. You represent the defendant Terrell Poser in *On Broadway v. Off Broadway.*

On March 17, 198X, Shelly Fridley opened a dinner theater named "On Broadway" at 680 East Fifth Street in Mitchell. Stage productions are conducted during dinner. On October 15 of the same year, Terrell Poser opened a similar dinner theater named "Off Broadway" at 420 East Fifth Street in Mitchell. Stage productions are conducted during dinner.

Summit has an Unfair Competition Statute which provides in Section 64.1 that:

> Any person performing an act of unfair competition within this state may be enjoined. Unfair competition means deceptive or fraudulent business practices.

Money damages are not recoverable under this statute.

The Summit Supreme Court has held in *Givens, Inc. v. Muhammad Productions, Inc.*, 346 Sum.2d 674 (1983) that:

> To state a cause of action for unfair competition, a plaintiff need allege that its name has acquired a secondary meaning,

> that the defendant's name was later adopted and used, that defendant's name is likely to deceive or confuse the public, and the plaintiff has been or is likely to be damaged by the defendant's conduct.

Id. at 678.

Assume the Court has denied the Plaintiff's request for injunctive relief until after discovery has been completed. Discovery is near completion now, and Poser tells you that he wants to delay the trial of the case as long as possible and to prolong proceedings by submitting some motions. Poser explains that he anticipates he will lose the case but wants to make as much money as possible from the dinner theater under the lease terms of its present location. Poser, also a lawyer, suggests you file a motion for judgment on the pleadings or a motion for summary judgment motion or any other applicable motion. What would you do? What factors influence your decision?

4. You represent HDE in *Vasquez v. Hot Dog Enterprises* (Case F). The President of HDE agrees that Wankle did sexually harass Vasquez but that Vasquez is asking for far too much money in damages. The President wants to disassociate HDE from Wankle. You advise the President that HDE could claim that Wankle was not an employee of HDE who was acting within the scope of his employment, perhaps relieving HDE of liability. You also advise the President that the scope of employment issue is a factual matter that can only be resolved at trial. The President suggests that you bring a summary judgment motion to resolve the claim before trial to avoid unnecessary publicity. The President also notes that the motion, even if unsuccessful, may help negotiate a reasonable settlement because of the extra fees and costs Plaintiff will incur in defending the motion. You advise the President that you have serious problems with bringing such a summary judgment motion. The President replies that HDE has retained your law firm for all of its legal business and that this is part of that legal business. Would you bring the summary judgment motion? Why or why not? What factors influence your judgment?

*

CHAPTER 12

PRETRIAL MOTIONS DIRECTED TO THE MERITS AND TRIAL

Lawyers spend a great deal of their time shoveling smoke.

Oliver Wendell Holmes, Jr.

§ 12.1 MOTIONS AFFECTING THE SCOPE OF THE LITIGATION

§ 12.1.1 Introduction

Many motions may be available to control the scope of litigation. These motions may be used by the parties and the courts to achieve the fair and efficient handling of cases. Motions may be available to permit two or more cases to be handled as one action for the purposes of pretrial matters, or to combine the cases of a single trial. Similarly, it may be necessary or desirable to have certain issues tried separately, either to prevent an unduly complex or confusing trial or to prevent unfair delay or similar prejudice.

Courts have great discretion in dealing with motions to control the scope of the litigation. Generally they require a balancing of competing interests. Because of the wide discretion involved, arguments on these motions are particularly focused on the facts rather than on the law.

§ 12.1.2 Consolidation

Federal civil practice provides for essentially two types of consolidation—(1) consolidation of pretrial proceedings and (2) consolidation for trial. Rule 42(a) and 28 U.S.C.A. § 1407, the multidistrict litigation

(MDL) statute, provide for both varieties of consolidation. As a practical matter, pretrial consolidation is more common because it is usually more readily available and convenient. Both types of consolidation require that there be a common factual question and most courts additionally will exercise discretion to consolidate only when it will provide speed, efficiency, cost savings, or convenience. These standards are more likely to be met in pretrial than in trial consolidation.

Far-flung actions involving the same parties or transactions are often consolidated for pretrial proceedings in order to provide efficiency and conserve resources. Most courts will consolidate for trial only when at least substantial portions of the related cases can be tried at once before the fact finder. This standard is ordinarily more difficult to meet than the common parties, common issues, convenience, and distance standards applicable to pretrial consolidation. Under the federal rules, different actions can not be merged into one,[1] but different actions can be tried together and decided by the same jury or judge. Thus, in the typical situation, the cases of *A* v. *D, B* v. *D,* and *C* v. *D* become, by appearance at trial, *A* and *B* and *C* v. *D.*

Courts probably have inherent power to consolidate the pretrial proceedings and trial of cases pursuant to inherent docket control authority. However, Rule 42(a) has codified this authority by providing that the judge may order a joint hearing or trial "of any or all the matters in issue in the actions" whenever the actions involve a common question of law or fact. The rule further authorizes the judge to order all such actions consolidated and to make all appropriate procedural order "as may tend to avoid unnecessary costs or delay."

In effect, the rule establishes a necessary but not sufficient condition for consolidation—existence of common legal or factual issues. If the requisite commonality exists, the court has discretion to consolidate, to whatever extent is appropriate.

The multidistrict litigation (MDL) statute, 28 U.S.C.A. § 1407, sets forth nearly the same requirement that the actions to be consolidated or coordinated have a common question of fact but, in contrast to Rule 42(a) is not concerned with common legal issues. For consolidation, section 1407 specifically requires that the MDL panel find that transfer and consolidation or coordination "will be for the convenience of the parties and witnesses and will promote the just and efficient conduct of such actions." MDL consolidation is discussed in sections 12.1 and 12.3.3. Rule 42(b) does not authorize consolidation of cases pending in different districts.[2] Such consolidation can occur only pursuant to the MDL statute.

In either Rule 42 or MDL consolidation, the court may consolidate only so much of the actions as is prudent, severing the non-related or

§ 12.1

1. *Johnson v. Manhattan Railway Co.,* 289 U.S. 479, 496–497, 53 S.Ct. 721, 726, 727, 77 L.Ed. 1331 (1933).

2. *Swindell–Dressler Corp. v. Dumbauld,* 308 F.2d 267 (3d Cir.1962).

non-economical portions of the matters, and in MDL actions, remanding the severed portions to the districts where they were originally filed. Refusal to consolidate will seldom be an abuse of discretion, unless some litigant actually suffers undue prejudice from separate trials. Consolidation rulings are likewise seldom reversed as an abuse of discretion unless the consolidation brings confusion, increased expense, or unduly prejudices some litigants because of joinder with others. These negative aspects more often occur in trial consolidation. In ordering consolidation of trial, the judge must consider the seventh amendment and ensure that all litigants have the same right to jury trial that they possessed when the actions were separate. However, the mere trial of multiple issues involving multiple parties by one jury does not violate the seventh amendment, just as trial by different juries of separated issues does not violate the seventh amendment.[3]

Consolidation of some actions may be automatic under the local rules of the applicable federal court.[4] Many state statutes or rules provide for either mandatory or discretionary consolidation.[5] Most federal district courts require litigants to designate cases as related to prior pending actions in the district where they address the same transaction or occurrence or involve some of the same parties. Even where counsel does not so designate, the clerk may automatically consolidate upon review or judges may consolidate cases *sua sponte* if the requirements of the local rule appear satisfied.

Rule 42(a) sets no time limit for seeking consolidation. However, motions to consolidate for trial are generally deemed untimely if made after the final pretrial conference or the filing of the final pretrial order.

Neither the grant or denial of a consolidation motion is a final order appealable as of right. Although the collateral order doctrine and special certification under 28 U.S.C.A. § 1292(b) have been used to permit interlocutory appeal of such orders, this is rare. Even rarer is appellate review of a consolidation decision via mandamus.

§ 12.1.3 Consolidation in MDL Litigation

As previously noted, 28 U.S.C.A. § 1407 permits transfer and consolidation or coordination of actions filed in different jurisdictions. Rule 42(a), by its terms, is limited to consolidation of actions in the same federal district. The MDL statute and the rule both establish common issues of fact as a prerequisite for consolidation. However, Rule 42(b) may justify consolidation based on common legal issues. Section 1407 does not. The MDL law sets a more stringent standard than the rule and requires, as a condition for transfer and consolidation, that the MDL

3. *Cecil v. Missouri Public Service Corp.*, 28 F.Supp. 649, 650 (W.D.Mo.1939). *See also* section 14.3, *infra*.

4. *See, e.g.,* E.D.Pa.R. 3(c) (automatic assignment of related cases to same judge).

5. *See, e.g.,* Ark.Stat.Ann. § 27-1305, *superseded by* Ark.R.Civ.P. 42; West's Ann. Cal.Civ.Proc.Code § 1048; 48 Minn.S.A., R.Civ.P. 42.01.

panel find consolidation to be more convenient for parties and witnesses and that it promote the just and efficient conduct of the action.

A party seeking consolidation files a motion with the MDL clerk in Washington, D.C., and then files the pleading in the district where its case currently pends. The Panel may also transfer and consolidate on its own motion. The MDL panel, consisting of seven circuit and district judges whose membership changes from time to time (appointments to the panel are by the Chief Justice of the United States), holds monthly hearings on the motions. Notice is given to all parties of possibly affected actions. If a minimum of four Panel members are persuaded to consolidate, the Panel orders all of the common actions transferred to one judge and jurisdiction for pretrial purposes only.

After pretrial proceedings are complete, the transferee judge may exercise discretion and retain the cases for trial, consolidating the trials as thought prudent. In many cases, the transferee judge will have become so familiar with the intricacies of these complex cases that he or she is best suited to preside at the trials. The MDL panel may separate some portions of the cases involved and transfer only the common or convenient portions to one district judge for pretrial coordination, remanding the separated claims and issues to the original districts in which each was filed. Where the movant can show sufficient need for a sudden decision on the transfer motion, the MDL panel may hold an expedited hearing. Review of MDL orders is available only by writ of mandamus as provided by 28 U.S.C.A. § 1651.

The MDL Panel has established its own rules of procedure which govern practice before the Panel. The rules include numerous requirements for the content of documents served and filed in MDL proceedings, and set stringent time limits for the proceedings. The rules also contain substantive requirements not found elsewhere, such as provision for consolidation of later "tag-along" actions as well as severance and remand of consolidated cases. The Panel rules can be found in U.S.C.A. directly following 28 U.S.C.A. § 1407.

§ 12.1.4 Severance

Unfortunately, many judges and lawyers have used the term severance to refer to a decision to conduct separate hearings or trials. When an action is severed, multiple actions are created and each of the newly-made cases usually proceeds to a final judgment independent of the other, severed claims that once comprised but one action. When separate trials are ordered, the claims or issues are tried separately, but one judgment entered for the action as a whole.[6]

Severance concerns the parties to a lawsuit. Severance is governed by Rule 21, not Rule 42(b). Fed.R.Civ.P. 21 severance can be a cousin to

6. *See Thomas/Van Dyken Joint Venture v. Van Dyken,* 90 Wis.2d 236, 279 N.W.2d 459 (1979).

severance under Fed.R.Crim.P. 14 concerning prejudicial joinder. Pursuant to Fed.R.Crim.P. 14, the trials of criminal defendants may be severed so that Defendant *A*, Chauncey Frontman, is not unduly prejudiced by trial before the same jury with defendant *B*, Rocco Fingerbuster. In civil actions, severance is most frequently used to correct jurisdictional or pleading defects.

Separate trial ("separation") concerns issues as well as claims and occurs when the court conducts different proceedings limited to particular issues of the case. It is governed by Rule 42(b). The most common form of separate trial is bifurcation of the liability and damages phases of trial, which is discussed in section 12.1.6. Separation is used to promote convenience and judicial economy and to divide and decide first the issue or issues that may make further proceedings unnecessary. Civil lawyers (no oxymoron intended) will have relatively few occasions for seeking severance but will seek or oppose separation many times in a career.

Rule 21 provides (welcome back, active voice) that parties may be added or dropped by court order on motion or *sua sponte* and that any claim against a party may be severed and proceeded with separately. The Rule provides authorization but not a specific standard for granting or denying motions to sever a party or claim from an action; case law controls the field.

A claim may be severed in order to provide for efficient disposition of the case where multiple unrelated claims might cause confusion. Severance of this type resembles separation, as does severance to accommodate party or witness convenience. Claims have also been severed for venue transfer to a more convenient forum. Severance can also be used to correct a procedural defect of the case. For example, claims have been severed to cure improper venue by severing the claims against those raising winning venue defenses. The severed claims may then be either transferred or dismissed. Individual claims have been severed when class action certification is denied. Separate trials have been ordered to prevent prejudice. Logically, severance would similarly be available. As with consolidation and separate trials, the trial court is vested with broad discretion. However, severance is the exception, and not the rule.

The federal rules enunciate no time limit concerning severance. A severance motion made at or before the final pretrial conference will usually be timely. Neither a grant nor a denial of severance constitutes a final, appealable order. Like orders concerning consolidation or separate trials, severance orders may occasionally meet the requirements of the collateral order doctrine or may merit trial court certification for appeal pursuant to 28 U.S.C.A. 1292(b). But don't bet the farm on it.

§ 12.1.5 Separate Trials

Separating the trials or hearings of different issues presented in a case has proven an effective management tool for judges. Separation (not to be confused with severance) can be used to decide a jurisdiction or venue issue by hearing early in the case, even (or especially) if it involves fewer than all claims or parties in the case. Section 12.3.6, discusses separation's most used form, bifurcation of liability and damages portions of a trial.

Although separate trials on other matters are not yet common, separation is widely used in pretrial proceedings though not always so recognized. As previously discussed, courts frequently hold pretrial hearings to determine jurisdiction, venue, joinder, sufficiency of service and other matters. Although these proceedings are seldom considered separation by the court, most likely because they result in response to a Rule 12(b) or other motion, the functional impact of these typical pretrial activities is to separate and determine the issues.

Rule 42(b) provides that the court, for reasons of convenience, economy, or avoiding prejudice, may order a separate trial of any claim, including counter, cross, and third party claims. Rule 42(b) also authorizes the court to hold separate trials of "any separate issue." The only specific constraint contained in the rule requires that the court must, in ordering separation, preserve the parties' right to a jury trial as required by the seventh amendment or federal statute. Many states now have separate trial rules patterned after federal rule 42; [7] most states provide for separation of some sort by civil rule, local rule, or statute. Even if not so stated, courts of any jurisdiction probably have inherent authority to separate issues and claims under the appropriate circumstances.

The federal rule granting judges broad discretion to separate seems a necessary adjunct to the liberal federal rules regarding joinder of claims and parties. Rule 13(i) specifically authorizes entry of judgment on counterclaims and cross-claims separated under Rule 42(b). These judgments may also be certified final and appealable pursuant to Rule 54(b). Rule 20(b) provides that the court may order separate trials to prevent delay or prejudice when an existing party to an action has no dispute with new parties added by other litigants. Rule 42(b) subsumes Rule 20(b), and the standards and procedure for separation under the rules are the same. Rule 20 merely permits the court to order separate trials where there has been joinder of a party having no dispute with an existing party. Rule 42 permits this and other separation whenever it will promote economy or justice.

Here, as with consolidation and severance, judicial discretion is the order of the day. As previously noted, the general spirit of the federal rules favors consolidated adjudication of disputes between the parties and resists piecemeal litigation absent a good reason. A defendant facing one claim in a multi-party and multi-claim suit can often present a compelling case for separation where that claim can be tried and resolved simply much earlier than trial on the whole could occur. After decision, the separated claim nevertheless remains interlocutory until the entire action is adjudicated unless certified by the court pursuant to

7. *See Weeks v. Bareco Oil Co.,* 125 F.2d 84 (7th Cir.1941).

Rule 54(d).[8] In the case posited above, a motion for 54(b) certification by the trial court should probably be granted by the trial court and accepted by the appeals court. But, under the facts of the hypothetical, a Rule 21 motion to sever the lone claim against Defendant *X* would also probably succeed, resulting in a new separate action upon which adjudication of the claim would automatically be a final judgment.

Separate trials or hearings, particularly bifurcation, are most frequently used in personal injury cases, but have also been ordered in bankruptcy, contract, trust, and insurance actions. Separate trials are used with some frequency in admiralty and maritime cases, not only in bifurcation of liability and damages but also to try issues of insurance coverage, arbitrability, and jurisdiction. Patent validity may be tried separately from patent infringement. Where patent issues are a subpart of a commercial dispute, they will often be separated (and tried later if at all possible, by most judges). Where counterclaims, cross-claims, or third-party claims raise issues unrelated to the complaint, these claims may be tried separately.

As previously noted, a separate trial or hearing can be particularly apt for resolving questions of jurisdiction, venue, joinder, or sufficiency of service. Separate trials have also been used to adjudicate affirmative defenses such as res judicata, statute of limitations, laches, estoppel, waiver, release, and accord and satisfaction.

Courts can grant separate trials on their own motion and often do so by making bifurcated trials their standard practice. Where a party desires a less common form of separation, a motion is required. Where the motion is denied, the movant may always renew it if unfolding events strengthen the case for separation. The motion for separate trials has no time limits set in the rules. It will usually be timely if made at the final pretrial conference, the time of filing the final pretrial order, or before.

Both the grant and the denial of motions for separate hearings or trials are interlocutory and neither is a final, appealable order. Like other scope motions discussed in this section, separation motions do not frequently satisfy the criteria for collateral order review, trial court certification pursuant to 28 U.S.C.A. 1292(b), or mandamus pursuant to 28 U.S.C.A. 1651. The trial court decision will be upheld unless it was an abuse of discretion.

§ 12.1.6 Bifurcation

Bifurcation of liability and damage issues is the leading use of Rule 42(b). The procedure for moving for and opposing bifurcation is identical to that for all Rule 42(b) motions. Some federal districts make bifurcation the norm in tort actions by local rule.[9] Many judges do this by standing order or personal practice. The trend appears to continue

8. *See* 48 Minn.Stat.Ann., R.Civ.P. 42.02.

9. *See Mitzel v. Schatz,* 167 N.W.2d 519 (N.D.1968).

despite statements that bifurcation is to be the exception and not the rule.[10]

Separation of liability and damages in personal injury cases is thought to provide great efficiency and economy since a defense verdict on liability will eliminate the need for a damages trial, cutting total trial time by as much as 50 percent, perhaps more in cases where damages evidence exceeds liability evidence. In addition, some argue that bifurcation promotes clearer jury understanding by reducing the information that the jury must assimilate at any one time and by making possible shorter, less complex jury instructions. Bifurcation is most appropriate where the liability and damages issues are wholly unrelated. The court has broad discretion in deciding whether to bifurcate. On appeal, the decision will be reversed only for an abuse of discretion.

Some, principally the plaintiff's bar, have criticized bifurcation as standard practice,[11] noting that defendants are statistically nearly twice as likely to win bifurcated cases.[12] Pro-plaintiff lawyers see this as at least unfair and perhaps a violation of the seventh amendment right to jury trial. Without waxing academic, we note that there appears to have been no equivalent of bifurcation in England or America in 1789, the year the amendment became law. Most authorities including the Supreme Court, accept the historical test for analyzing seventh amendment issues arising in common-law actions.[13] Defense attorneys counter that the statistical evidence of differing results merely illustrates how, in most unbifurcated actions, the plaintiff benefits from sympathy linked to evidence of the severity of the injury rather than to the issues of liability.[14] Furthermore, they note that these same studies show an overall 20 percent time saving from bifurcation.[15] Although, according to the committee notes of Rule 42(b), bifurcation is not supposed to be the rule, the practice continues to grow. It is undeniably at least somewhat pro-defendant but on rare occasion may be preferred by the plaintiff.

Another jury trial issue in bifurcation concerns whether the same jury must hear both the liability and the damages evidence. Courts have held that use of different juries does not violate the seventh amendment.[16] Most courts, however, prefer use of a single jury to hear both

10. *See, e.g.,* N.D.Ill.R. 21.

11. For an example of opposition to regular bifurcation, see Jack B.Weinstein, Routine Bifurcation of Jury Negligence Trials: An Example of the Questionable Use of Rule Making Power, 14 Vand.L.Rev. 831 (1961).

12. Rosenberg, Court Congestion: Status, Causes, and Proposed Remedies, *in* The Courts, The Public, and the Law Explosion 29, 149 (Harry L. Jones, ed. 1965).

13. *See, e.g., Dairy Queen, Inc. v. Wood,* 369 U.S. 469, 82 S.Ct. 894, 8 L.Ed.2d 44 (1962).

14. For an example of views favoring bifurcation, see Warren F. Schwartz, Severance—A Means of Minimizing the Rule of Burden and Expense in Determining the Outcome of Litigation, 20 Vand.L.Rev. 1197 (1967).

15. *See* Hans Zeisel & Thomas Callahan, Split Trials and Time Saving: A Statistical Analysis, 76 Harv.L.Rev. 1606, 1619 (1963).

16. *See, e.g., Moss v. Associated Transport, Inc.,* 344 F.2d 23 (6th Cir.1965).

liability and damages, reasoning that the jury knowing precisely how the injury occurred and why is best able to adjudicate less liquidated elements of damage such as pain and suffering and loss of consortium.

§ 12.2 DISMISSALS

§ 12.2.1 Voluntary Dismissals

At first blush, the concept of a voluntary dismissal seems something of a contradiction in terms for litigation premised on an adversary system. But voluntary dismissals are frequently sought. For example, a plaintiff acting in good faith may conduct discovery and conclude it has no case. Continued prosecution could result in court-imposed penalties for bad faith litigation. More frequently, plaintiff commences litigation in the wrong jurisdiction or where venue is improper. In such cases, defense counsel may even alert plaintiff to this and request voluntary dismissal as an alternative to the more time-consuming and expensive process of proceeding by motion to dismiss. Where the instant litigation arises from an event producing several lawsuits, plaintiff may wish to voluntarily dismiss the case in order to reinstate the action in another forum where it may be more easily consolidated with similar actions.

Voluntary dismissals are not limited to plaintiffs but may be taken by defendants asserting counter, cross, or third-party claims as well. Thus, defendants may wish to dismiss the counterclaim filed on a hunch unsupported by the evidence produced in discovery, or defendant may seek to dismiss the permissive counterclaim or third party complaint in the interest of starting a separate action in a more favorable or convenient forum. Any and all parties may seek voluntary dismissal, usually with prejudice, as a condition of settlement.

Voluntary Dismissal as of Right. There are essentially two varieties of the motion for voluntary dismissal—voluntary dismissal as a matter of right and voluntary dismissal upon such terms and conditions as the court deems proper. Under Rule 41(a)(1), plaintiff may file a notice of voluntary dismissal and have the action dismissed at any time before service by the adverse party of an answer or a motion for summary judgment. Some states also have a version of Rule 41 which requires plaintiff to file the notice of dismissal within a specified time period regardless of the nonexistence of an answer or summary judgment motion. In federal court, Rule 41 applies, even in diversity cases, since voluntary dismissal is a question of federal procedure rather than state substantive law.

Rule 41(a)(1) specifically provides that a party's right of voluntary dismissal is cut off by service of an answer or summary judgment motion. A motion by the adverse party to dismiss the action because of lack of jurisdiction, improper venue, defective process, or defective service of process does not act to cut off plaintiff's right to file a notice of voluntary dismissal. Neither does a motion to dismiss for failure to state a claim. The presence of substantial court proceeding prior to a motion to dismiss may cut off a Rule 41(a)(1) voluntary dismissal.[1]

A plaintiff may also automatically obtain dismissal by filing a stipulation of dismissal signed by all parties to the litigation who have appeared in the action.

Voluntary Dismissal by Motion. Where a defendant who refuses to stipulate to dismissal has answered or moved for summary judgment, the plaintiff must then make a motion for voluntary dismissal to the court. The court has discretion to deny the motion entirely or condition an order of voluntary dismissal upon the terms and conditions which the court believes just under the circumstances of the case. The court's decision is reviewable on appeal according to the "abuse of discretion" standard. Usually, the court will grant a voluntary dismissal motion made in the early or middle stages of the cases and condition dismissal on plaintiff's payment of all or part of defendant's costs, attorney's fees, or expenses.[2]

Rule 41(a)(2) provides that all dismissals granted by the court are without prejudice unless otherwise specified in the court's order. Where the motion to dismiss is made late in the case or is made on the basis of an obviously meritless claim, the court may make the dismissal with prejudice as a condition for granting the motion.[3] Where the plaintiff seeking dismissal would be subject to some other sanction were the case adjudicated on the merits, the court may make this additional sanction a condition for granting a motion for voluntary dismissal.

In determining whether to grant a motion for voluntary dismissal, the court will generally consider whether the defendant will suffer real prejudice. The mere fact that plaintiff will gain a tactical advantage from voluntary dismissal is generally not sufficient ground for denying the motion. The court, if it finds significant prejudice, then examines whether the prejudice can be cured by imposition of costs, expenses, fees, or specific orders (*e.g.*, excluding testimony of witness unavailable in subsequent action if first action is dismissed, etc.).

In certain litigation, voluntary dismissal requires court approval even where the parties have agreed or where no answer or summary judgment motion has been interposed. Examples are class actions, cases where a receiver has been appointed, where the action alleges violation of the immigration laws, or false claims against the United States, or any other action where court approval is statutorily required for dismissal.[4]

The court's discretion to grant a motion for voluntary dismissal is limited where defendant has filed a counterclaim. In these cases, absent

§ 12.2

1. *Harvey Aluminum, Inc. v. American Cyanamid Co.*, 203 F.2d 105 (2d Cir.1953), *cert. denied* 345 U.S. 964, 73 S.Ct. 949, 97 L.Ed. 1383 (1953).

2. *American Cyanamid Co. v. McGhee*, 317 F.2d 295 (5th Cir.1963).

3. *See, e.g., Scallen v. Minnesota Vikings Football Club, Inc.*, 574 F.Supp. 278 (D.Minn.1983).

4. Rule 41(a)(1) expressly provides that such federal statutes, Rule 23(e), and Rule 66 override Rule 41's normal applicability.

stipulation of the parties, dismissal is permitted only if the counterclaim can stand on its own and remain pending for adjudication. If the counterclaim was compulsory, the court has ancillary jurisdiction to let it remain as a separate lawsuit. Where the counterclaim is permissive, there must be an independent basis for jurisdiction. Thus, the presence of a counterclaim is not usually a significant bar to voluntary dismissal except in cases where the counterclaim is in the nature of an affirmative defense or claim for set-off, or where the permissive counterclaim is premised on state law and the parties are non-diverse.

Procedure. As previously noted, dismissal of right by notice or signed stipulation is generally without prejudice. However, where the plaintiff takes voluntary dismissal of right after having previously taken voluntary dismissal of right in any action which involved the same claim, the plaintiff's second voluntary dismissal of right is with prejudice and acts as an adjudication on the merits of the claim. If the plaintiff voluntarily dismisses an action and then reinstitutes the action or a new action that involves the same claim against the same defendant, the court may enter an order providing that plaintiff pay the costs of the action previously dismissed and may stay the proceedings in the second action until plaintiff complies with the order to pay costs. A party that has taken a voluntary dismissal of right through filing a notice of dismissal may turn around and withdraw the dismissal provided that there has not been undue delay in the change of heart and that the other parties to the action will not be unduly prejudiced by the reinstigation of the claim.[5]

Where plaintiff seeks voluntary dismissal by the court and the court sets terms and conditions on the dismissal, the plaintiff has two options—(1) comply with the terms and conditions set by the court and obtain the order of dismissal; or (2) continue to prosecute the claim and withdraw the motion for voluntary dismissal. The claimant is under no obligation to accept the court's conditions and may continue to press forward with the case it once sought to dismiss.

§ 12.2.2 Dismissal for Failure to Prosecute

Rule 41(b) authorizes dismissal of any action or claim for "failure of the plaintiff to prosecute or to comply with these rules or any order of court". The rule also authorizes dismissal in a bench trial where the plaintiff has presented evidence but shown no right to relief. Rule 41(b) has been held to simply codify this inherent power of the court.[6] In addition, many federal courts have local rules setting specific standards for dismissal for want of prosecution.

Rule 41(b) also authorizes dismissal for failure to obey a court order. Rule 37 also provides this as a possible sanction for failure to comply

5. *Robinson v. Worthington,* 544 F.Supp. 956 (M.D.Ala.1982).

6. *Link v. Wabash Railroad Co.,* 370 U.S. 626, 82 S.Ct. 1386, 8 L.Ed.2d 734 (1962), *rehearing denied* 371 U.S. 873, 83 S.Ct. 115, 9 L.Ed.2d 112 (1962).

with discovery orders and procedures. Since most pretrial orders are discovery orders and because courts have been increasingly willing to impose dismissal as a Rule 37 sanction, this Rule has tended to dwarf this provision of Rule 41(b).

In a sense, the Rule 41(b) motion is a motion seeking termination of the action due to claimant's post-complaint laches. Where the claimant has permitted the case to stagnate and grow stale, involuntary dismissal is justified. The court's focus is upon the state of the case at the time the motion is made. A claimant cannot launch into a flurry of activity after years of inertness and thereby avoid dismissal.[7] However, the mere passage of time will not automatically eliminate a case. Once properly commenced, a case is either adjudicated or dismissed. Until then, it remains pending. Dismissal requires an order.

The primary basis for dismissal for failure to prosecute is the passage of time without any activity in the case. As previously noted, some local rules provide that whenever there is an absence of any docketed materials in a case for a certain length of time (*e.g.,* 1 year), the matter is dismissed under Rule 41(b), or placed in the suspense file for another specified period of time, and then dismissed. Many of these local rules provide that, upon the absence of activity for the requisite time, the action may be dismissed unless there is activity within a relatively short period of time (*e.g.,* 30 to 90 days after announcement of the change in case status).[8]

The period of time necessary to justify dismissal for inactivity varies according to jurisdiction, with reported cases dismissing actions for as little as four months inactivity and others dismissing cases for nine years of non-prosecution. Courts should also consider whether the plaintiff has been warned about dismissal. If so and the problem is not corrected, dismissal within a comparatively short period after the warning has been sustained. An additional consideration is the plaintiff's excuse for delay.

An action can also be dismissed under Rule 41(b) where plaintiff is not ready for trial or refuses to proceed at trial and fails to produce a satisfactory explanation. Failure to appear at a court proceeding such as a hearing or pretrial conference can result in sufficient nonprosecution to warrant dismissal if it is without adequate excuse or part of a pattern of long-standing delay. However, in these situations, plaintiff has also presumably failed to comply with a court order. Courts dismissing in such cases have not always clearly distinguished which section of Rule 41 is the basis for the ruling. Both grounds are seemingly simultaneously applicable in these cases.

7. *See Alexander v. Pacific Maritime Association,* 434 F.2d 281 (9th Cir.1970), *cert. denied* 401 U.S. 1009, 91 S.Ct. 1254, 28 L.Ed.2d 545 (1971).

8. For a dated but valuable list of local rules governing dismissal for non-prosecution, see *Link v. Wabash Railroad Co.,* 370 U.S. 626, 631 n. 7, 82 S.Ct. 1386, 1389, n. 7, 8 L.Ed.2d 734 (1962), *rehearing denied* 371 U.S. 873, 83 S.Ct. 115, 9 L.Ed.2d 112 (1962).

A grant of dismissal, with or without prejudice, is a final, appealable order. A denial of dismissal is not, absent application of the collateral order doctrine. Trial court certification pursuant to 28 U.S.C.A. § 1292(b) may also be available. On appeal, the court will apply the abuse of discretion standard to the trial court decision,[9] but with less deference than usual because procedural dismissals are disfavored while trial on the merits is favored. Dismissal for failure to prosecute is procedural law under the *Erie* doctrine and thus determined according to federal common law in federal court.

§ 12.2.3 Dismissal on Other Grounds

Introduction. Rule 12(b) provides a comprehensive but not an exhaustive list of grounds for dismissal. Only the limits of the legal mind limit the full range of reasons to dismiss an action or claim. Although 2,000 years of Anglo–American jurisprudence (aided by borrowing from 3,000 years of civil law) have probably enunciated all possible dismissal grounds available today, the list may expand or contract according to changes in substantive law, the civil rules, social views, and human creative evolution.

We have already discussed dismissal due to pleading deficiencies (sections 4.1–4.3), dismissal because of jurisdiction and venue defects (sections 4.5 and 4.7), non-joinder of parties (section 4.8), failure to obey a discovery order (section 10.5.2) and absence of legal claim in cases of undisputed material fact (section 4.4).

Rule 41(b) authorizes federal courts to dismiss a claim or case for failure to comply with the civil rules or any court order. Although other sections of the federal rules (*e.g.,* Rule 37's sanctions for disobeying a discovery order) have made Rule 41(b) something of a judicial backstop for punishing the renegade litigant, the rule forms an important backstop.[10] The rule has been applied where litigants refused to produce a witness, clients failed to attend a settlement conference when ordered by the court, a party did not amend a pleading or correct a procedural defect within the time provided by the court, and where counsel has repeatedly violated orders concerning permissible trial conduct.[11] Either counsel or client may be subject to contempt depending on who actually violates the court order in question.

§ 12.3 SUMMARY JUDGMENT MOTIONS

§ 12.3.1 Summary Judgment Generally

Frequently made, and often bulging from the girth of exhibits and appendices, motions for summary judgment are at once popular and

9. *Provenza v. H & W Wrecking Co.,* 424 F.2d 629 (5th Cir.1970).

10. Where dismissal is sought because of failure to obey a discovery order, Rule 37 provides the exclusive means for seeking dismissal. Rule 41(b) is not applicable. *Societe Internationale pour Participations Industrielles et Commerciales, S.A. v. Rogers,* 357 U.S. 197, 78 S.Ct. 1087, 2 L.Ed.2d 1255 (1958).

11. *See, e.g., Syracuse Broadcasting Corp. v. Newhouse,* 271 F.2d 910, 914 & n. 1 (2d Cir.1959).

unpopular with judges obligated to read even the nonmeritorious ones. Where successful, the motion shortens proceedings and saves time. Where unsuccessful, it takes time [1] and, at best, educates the court (and opposition). One prominent judge has described the motion as "plagued by confusion and uncertainty." [2]

Unless the motion is granted, clients may be similarly disenchanted because of the cost of making the motion, which ordinarily requires substantial attorney time. But the motion, despite its misuse, abuse, and length, appears frequently and remains popular for a reason: when it works, it works very well, eliminating the time, expense, and uncertainty of trial. Even when summary judgment is denied, some well-heeled parties seeking delay will nevertheless find favor with the motion. It may also be useful to narrow the issues for trial and to "flush out" the adversary's case even when not otherwise successful.

Summary judgment can be particularly effective for the nontarget defendant in multiparty litigation, for the party mistakenly named in an action, for the party whose liability hinges on resolution of only a legal question, or for a party facing a claim or defense that clearly lacks any factual support. For these parties, the burden of a trial, even if it involves merely sending an attorney to monitor the proceedings, will usually outweigh the burden of presenting a summary judgment motion.

Essentially, a summary judgment motion is an effort to prevail in litigation, or a portion of litigation, where the material facts of the controversy are not in dispute. The motion is therefore available wherever this situation exists. A motion for summary judgment can be made as to any "claim" in the case, including third-party complaints, counterclaims, cross-claims, intervention, and interpleader.[3] Whether to employ the motion depends on the strategic and tactical considerations discussed below.

Although defendants move for summary judgment more frequently than plaintiffs,[4] the motion is equally available to all parties. In most cases, however, plaintiffs must prove at trial the set of facts entitling them to relief. Because plaintiff must shoulder the burden of persuasion, a plaintiff-movant must, in order to prevail, create a record in support of summary judgment that establishes without factual dispute that plaintiff has carried that burden. Ordinarily, this will be difficult if the defendant-nonmovant introduces even a smattering of barely proba-

§ 12.3

1. *See, e.g., Sewell Plastics, Inc. v. Coca-Cola Co.,* 119 F.R.D. 24 (W.D.N.C.1988) (denying summary judgment motion despite stack of supporting and opposing documents more than three feet high and noting that much of the material was merely argumentative assertion by counsel).

2. William F. Schwarzer, Summary Judgment under the Federal Rules: Defining Genuine Issues of Material Fact, 99 F.R.D. 465, 465 (1983).

3. 10 Charles A. Wright, et al., Federal Practice and Procedure § 2717 (1983 & Supp.1991). *See, e.g.,* Lundeen v. Cordner, 354 F.2d 401 (8th Cir.1966), *motion denied* 356 F.2d 169 (8th Cir.1966); Haynes v. Felder, 239 F.2d 868 (5th Cir.1957).

4. *See* Joe S. Cecil & C.R. Douglas, Summary Judgment Practice in Three District Courts (1987); Paul R.J. Connolly & Patricia A. Lombard, Judicial Controls and the Civil Litigative Process: Motions 69–76 (1980).

tive opposition matter since the defendant may hide behind the burden of proof as well as its material in opposing the motion. Nonetheless, plaintiffs may obtain summary judgment where the defendant fails to contravene plaintiff's prima facie proof of its case or where the nature of the dispute admits of unquestionable proof from a credible source.[5]

When granted, the motion results in a final judgment on the merits of the claim, subject to the general rules of claim and issue preclusion and appealability.[6] When denied, the motion does not result in any prejudice to a litigant's legal or factual position at trial. It does, however, bar a second summary judgment motion on the same legal theory in the absence of new factual matter.[7] However, the movant may make a second summary judgment motion on a different legal theory.[8]

§ 12.3.2 Factual Disputes: Knowing Them When You See Them

The notion that there can be an absence of disputed fact after commencement of a lawsuit seems initially contradictory to both lawyers and laypersons—but it happens. Notwithstanding Rule 11's admonition that all claims have evidentiary support (*see* § 3.5), a plaintiff may file suit on a hunch, hoping to confirm an inkling as to the reasons for some adverse event. When the facts developed in discovery show the hunch to be incorrect, the defendant finds a factual setting appropriate for summary judgment. Often, the heated relations of the parties may lead to litigation, with both sides essentially assuming the correctness of their view of reality. After discovery, uncontested material facts may emerge despite the different stories that led to the lawsuit. Litigation also may occur where, from the beginning, there existed little factual disagreement between the parties but a major dispute as to the legal relief available. In this type of case, the litigation seeks resolution of legal questions rather than factual questions. Summary judgment is available and appropriate even at the early stages of such cases. Because the court, in deciding a summary judgment motion, ordinarily does not resolve factual issues but merely determines whether there exist disputed issues of material fact, a grant of summary judgment does not violate the litigants' right to jury trial under the Seventh Amendment or Fed.R.Civ.P. 38.[9]

5. *See, e.g.,* Lundeen v. Cordner, 354 F.2d 401 (8th Cir.1966), *motion denied* 356 F.2d 169 (1966) (affidavit of neutral nonparty witness conclusive on issue of whether decedent intended to change life insurance beneficiary). Although the more narrow basis of the *Lundeen* opinion rests on the nonmovant's failure to contravene this affidavit, the opinion can be read as suggesting that this particular evidence was not subject to meaningful contravention.

6. *See, e.g., Jackson v. Hayakawa,* 605 F.2d 1121 (9th Cir.1979), *cert. denied* 445 U.S. 952, 100 S.Ct. 1601, 63 L.Ed.2d 787 (1980).

7. *See, e.g., Lindsey v. Dayton–Hudson Corp.,* 592 F.2d 1118 (10th Cir.1979), *cert. denied* 444 U.S. 856, 100 S.Ct. 116, 62 L.Ed.2d 75 (1979).

8. *Mayer v. Distel Tool & Mach. Co.,* 556 F.2d 798 (6th Cir.1977).

9. 10 Charles A. Wright, et al., Federal Practice and Procedure § 2714 (1983 & Supp.1994); United States v. Burket, 402 F.2d 426 (5th Cir.1968).

Courts have had some difficulty defining precisely what constitutes a genuine factual dispute within the meaning of Rule 56. The U.S. Supreme Court has stated a dispute is genuine "if the evidence is such that a reasonable jury could return a verdict for the nonmoving party." [10] This language and other statements by the Supreme Court in three important 1986 cases dealing with summary judgment [11] suggest that where the claimant raises a dispute but does not produce supporting evidence sufficient to withstand a motion for a directed verdict or j.n.o.v., the court may nevertheless grant summary judgment pursuant to the "genuine dispute" language of Rule 56 without contravening the right to a jury trial.[12] Although there is contradictory and confusing language in these opinions, the Court essentially said that a factual dispute is not "genuine" under Rule 56 where the trial judge finds one side's supporting evidence so weak as to be insubstantial. Despite the pronouncements in favor of summary judgment, the Court cautioned that summary judgment not become a trial by affidavit and that "[c]redibility determinations, the weighing of evidence, and the drawing of legitimate inferences from the facts are jury functions, not those of a judge.... The evidence of the non-movant is to be believed, and all justifiable inferences are to be drawn in his favor." [13]

At this point, the intrepid litigator has a right to ask: "what exactly are judges allowed to do in deciding a summary judgment motion?" Although some language and the results of the Supreme Court cases can be read as suggesting that judges may dismiss claims where they see the defense case as stronger,[14] our informal assessment and a preliminary

10. *Anderson v. Liberty Lobby, Inc.,* 477 U.S. 242, 251, 106 S.Ct. 2505, 2511, 91 L.Ed.2d 202 (1986).

11. *See Matsushita Elec. Indus. Co. v. Zenith Radio Corp.,* 475 U.S. 574, 106 S.Ct. 1348, 89 L.Ed.2d 538 (1986), *on remand* 807 F.2d 44 (3d Cir.1986), *cert. denied* 481 U.S. 1029, 107 S.Ct. 1955, 95 L.Ed.2d 527 (1987); *Celotex Corp. v. Catrett,* 477 U.S. 317, 106 S.Ct. 2548, 91 L.Ed.2d 265 (1986), *on remand* 826 F.2d 33 (D.C.Cir.1987), *cert. denied* 484 U.S. 1066, 108 S.Ct. 1028, 98 L.Ed.2d 992 (1988); *Anderson v. Liberty Lobby, Inc.,* 477 U.S. 242, 106 S.Ct. 2505, 91 L.Ed.2d 202 (1986).

12. A court may grant a directed verdict when it finds the nonmovant's evidence insufficiently "substantial" to merit jury deliberation (*see Galloway v. United States,* 319 U.S. 372, 63 S.Ct. 1077, 87 L.Ed. 1458 (1943), *rehearing denied* 320 U.S. 214, 63 S.Ct. 1443, 87 L.Ed. 1851 (1943)) even though this places the judge in the position of doing some weighing of the evidence in order to determine whether nonmovant's evidence is substantial or merely a "scintilla" (*see Galloway,* 319 U.S. at 404, 63 S.Ct. at 1094 (Black, J., dissenting)). Although one can still debate whether this limited judicial fact assessment is prudent, Justice Black and other strong advocates of jury autonomy have lost this battle: some court evaluation of facts and screening of nonmeritorious claims at trial or after verdict does not violate the Seventh Amendment. Open to question, though, is whether (1) allowing such fact assessment during the pretrial stage of litigation gives inadequate "preservation" to the Seventh Amendment, and (2) the language and intent of Rule 56 permit fact weighing as part of this screening. The Supreme Court's 1986 trilogy suggests the answer to both questions is "yes," a departure from the traditional view that prevailed from 1938 until 1986. *See* Allen R. Kamp, Federal Adjudication of Facts: The New Regime, 12 Am.J.Trial Ad. 437 (1989). *See also* William F. Schwarzer, Summary Judgment under the Federal Rules: Defining Genuine Issues of Material Fact, 99 F.R.D. 465 (1983).

13. *Anderson v. Liberty Lobby, Inc.,* 477 U.S. 242, 255, 106 S.Ct. 2505, 2513, 91 L.Ed.2d 202 (1986).

14. *See* Jeffrey W. Stempel, A Distorted Mirror: The Supreme Court's Shimmering View of Summary Judgment, Directed Verdict, and the Adjudication Process, 49 Ohio St.L.J. 96 (1988).

study by the Federal Judicial Center suggest that lower courts have not hurried to take up the mantle of a more aggressive summary judgment suggested by the Court's cases. To be sure, the trilogy is oft-cited, particularly the "reasonable jury" language of *Liberty Lobby.*[15] However, courts appear to have applied the "substantial evidence by the nonmovant" and "reasonable jury" tests gingerly and have found a genuine factual dispute to exist whenever the nonmovant has created a record of controverted fact questions except in a small class of cases where either the veracity of the controverting matter is highly suspect or where the evidence, even where credited, is so weak as to prompt widespread judicial agreement that the nonmovant's support is but an insubstantial scintilla.[16] Where trial courts granted summary judgment because they apparently doubted the veracity of nonmovant's evidence, particularly witness testimony, appellate courts have tended to remember the admonition that assessments of credibility are for the jury and have denied or reversed summary judgment.[17] Courts have also tended to find the substantial evidence standard met where the dispute involves the range of permissible inferences drawn from essentially agreed-upon conduct or contract language.[18]

This change in the summary judgment standard, whether deemed mere fine-tuning or a significant alteration, probably devolves to one major change in attorney behavior surrounding summary judgment motions. Before the trilogy, lawyers opposing summary judgment argued that their submitted affidavits or other material created contested issues of fact and automatically precluded summary judgment. Now, just to be safe, these same attorneys argue that they have submitted substantial evidence that would support a reasonable jury verdict in favor of their clients. Prior to the trilogy, counsel seeking summary judgment sought (and often strained) to characterize the opposition's papers as failing to raise any conflicting facts. Since the trilogy, summary judgment proponents have the luxury of arguing that the nonmovant's submissions, although creating a fact dispute, are insufficient to sustain a favorable jury verdict, particularly where the nonmovant bears the burden of persuasion.

15. *See, e.g., Waters v. Thornburgh,* 888 F.2d 870, 873 (D.C.Cir.1989); Peppers v. Coates, 887 F.2d 1493, 1498 n. 9 (11th Cir.1989).

16. *See, e.g., Sorlucco v. New York City Police Dept.,* 888 F.2d 4, 6 (2d Cir.1989) (reversing trial court grant of summary judgment on issue of unlawful discharge where despite absence of direct proof of liability; reasonable jury might infer intent to discriminate from defendants' conduct); *In re Phillips Petroleum Securities Litigation,* 881 F.2d 1236 (3d Cir.1989), *on remand* 738 F.Supp. 825 (D.Del.1990) (denying summary judgment in securities fraud claim where plaintiff had introduced some circumstantial evidence upon which jury might infer wrongdoing but granting summary judgment on fraud-based RICO claim where plaintiffs "produced no probative evidence of reliance" on defendants' statements).

17. *See, e.g., DiMartini v. Ferrin,* 889 F.2d 922 (9th Cir.1989), *opinion amended* 906 F.2d 465 (9th Cir.1990); *Sorlucco v. New York City Police Dept.,* 888 F.2d 4 (2d Cir.1989).

18. *See, e.g., Gulden v. Crown Zellerbach Corp.,* 890 F.2d 195 (9th Cir.1989) (whether conduct was intentional attempt to injure); *Dardaganis v. Grace Capital, Inc.,* 889 F.2d 1237 (2d Cir.1989), (whether preferred stock was "equity investment" under terms of agreement).

One useful approach for counsel focuses on whether any factual conflicts are truly material to the case. A material fact is one whose resolution will affect the outcome of the case, one that is central to an element of a claim or defense. Tangential disputes do not preclude summary judgment.[19] For example, two automobile accident litigants may argue over a vehicle's speed. However, where the liability claim rests on defendant's admitted running of a red light, at least a partial summary judgment on negligence is available. Notwithstanding this, a court may deny summary judgment if it believes trial resolution of the speed issue is required for apportionment of negligence, determination of causation, or damages calculation so long as the court finds the determinations better and more efficiently done through trial of all issues together.

A related issue concerns the nature of the evidence. Where the evidentiary and factual conflict is direct, summary judgment must be denied absent the rare instance where the court may disbelieve a witness or source. For example, where the plaintiff in an automobile accident case swears the stoplight was green in his favor while the defendant claims it was green in her favor, they have presented conflicting direct evidence. Summary judgment is unavailable. Many cases, of course, are fought through circumstantial evidence—evidence that allows a factfinder to draw two or more conclusions and does not compel a particular conclusion. Recent cases have suggested that courts might have more freedom to find a nonmovant's evidence insufficiently substantial where it is exclusively circumstantial.[20] The theory behind this reasoning posits that a judge may find some inferences from weak circumstantial evidence too implausible to sustain a reasonable jury's verdict. Under this view, judges have more freedom to reject inferences at odds with presumptions imbedded in the substantive law. Although the distinction between circumstantial and direct evidence has not been well developed by the courts, it is tangible enough to be used by counsel.

Proponents of summary judgment may argue for greater judicial freedom to enter summary judgment where the nonmovant's evidence is circumstantial. Opponents can characterize any cases disfavoring circumstantial evidence as an aberration and cite the traditional rule that the court should not infer when ruling on a summary judgment motion.[21] Nonmovants may also read the cases disparaging the probative value of circumstantial evidence as nonetheless granting only a modicum of freedom for courts to draw or bar inferences, freedom that is bounded

19. *Church of Scientology of Cal. v. Cazares,* 638 F.2d 1272 (5th Cir.1981); *Nabhani v. Coglianese,* 552 F.Supp. 657 (N.D.Ill.1982).

20. *See, e.g., Matsushita Elec. Indus. Co. v. Zenith Radio Corp.,* 475 U.S. 574, 106 S.Ct. 1348, 89 L.Ed.2d 538 (1986), *on remand* 807 F.2d 44 (3d Cir.1986), *cert. denied* 481 U.S. 1029, 107 S.Ct. 1955, 95 L.Ed.2d 527 (1987) (granting summary judgment to defendant where plaintiff's evidence of antitrust conspiracy was circumstantial and Court found conspiracy unlikely according to economic theory); *see* Collins, Summary Judgment and Circumstantial Evidence, 40 Stan.L.Rev. 491 (1988).

21. *See Bragen v. Hudson County News Co.,* 278 F.2d 615 (3d Cir.1960), and cases cited in note 19, *supra.*

according to the substantive law of the case. In addition, opponents of summary judgment can argue that their submissions, although circumstantial, are far more probative than those of losing claimants in the case reports.

§ 12.3.3 Strategy and Tactics

There is no absolute formula for determining whether to move for summary judgment. However, the attorney considering the motion should at least ask the following questions:

- Do the uncontested facts favor my client?
- By how much?
- Are they as uncontested as I think?
- If they are contested, can the court be convinced to view the contravening matter as merely a scintilla of evidence?
- Even if the opposing matter likely to be offered by the nonmovant is substantial, can it be characterized as sufficiently off-point to be deemed "immaterial" under Rule 56?
- Will trial make the facts more favorable to my client?
- By how much?
- Does the law favor me?
- By how much?
- Is it well-settled law or debatable law?
- Who is the judge?
- Is this a jury case?
- Am I in a good or bad strategic situation at present?
- Will passing time improve or detract from our position?
- What is the likely result of the motion?
- What effect will this likely result have on the case?

In determining whether to make a motion for summary judgment, the attorney should first consider the client's position in the case. If the client is the likely winner at trial or the clear favorite in the early going, summary judgment is more attractive. If the client is the underdog, a motion may only hasten defeat. Attorneys must also consider the nature of the issues of the case. Summary judgment is most useful where the dispute is legal rather than factual. Also consider the current overall positions of the parties. Whether ultimately the favorite or underdog, the party currently occupying the better position (e.g., holding the funds at issue in an interest-bearing account) may have little or nothing to gain from an earlier final judgment (such as removing a cloud over its reputation, prospectus, etc.) and may find it more efficient to appear for a short, victorious trial rather than move for summary judgment. In jurisdictions where motions languish, making the motion may actually delay the ultimate decision. The party in a poor position will want to move the litigation along. Depending on the case and the court, this may or may not argue for making a summary judgment motion.[22]

Attorneys should also consider whether a judge or a jury will be the factfinder. Summary judgment motions can be effective in educating the court about the case, especially in a bench trial. However, a motion made and lost before the court may only prejudice the judge against your asserted facts and legal arguments at trial. In jury cases, many lawyers continue to see summary judgment as a useful means of educating the court in hopes of getting more favorable (or at least better reasoned) rulings on other pretrial matters such as joinder of claims and parties, discovery disputes, and evidence rulings. Although this conventional wisdom may well be correct, we have significant reservations about the "educational" summary judgment motion. Where the motion is only educational and the movant does not have a realistic chance of success, making the motion probably violates Rule 11 and ethical standards of motion practice. Where the motion is not frivolous but is sufficiently unlikely to succeed, counsel should seriously consider whether the costs of the motion (counsel fees and distraction, transaction costs in assembling information, possible delay, revelation of trial argument tactics) outweigh the benefits of a more educated judge. A well-done pretrial order or trial brief may be a better tool for educating the court. In addition, counsel may use summary judgment in jury cases to remove at least some inflammatory or embarrassing aspect of the case from the jury's consideration. Where the client benefits from the jury's consideration of all the facts, it makes sense to keep these issues in the case through trial, even where one could prevail on these points in a partial summary judgment motion (discussed in § 12.3.14).

If the bulk of legal authority weighs in your favor, you will more likely want to move for summary judgment. Where you are advancing a novel legal theory, one with little case support or based on the minority, but arguably better, rule, you will probably want to refrain from seeking summary judgment unless the time and expense of trial make an early loss preferable to a later loss. Those pushing the bounds of the law will ordinarily have better success where the underlying facts prompt sympathy from the court, providing a reason to go the extra doctrinal mile in their favor. Unless these facts are both undisputed and overwhelmingly in your favor, the cold summary judgment record will not help as much as the Technicolor trial. There are exceptions to this conventional wisdom. If assigned a judge who is likely to be receptive to unsettled

22. Some judges routinely set motions for oral argument and hearing as soon as permitted by the rules and decide motions from the bench or shortly after hearing. Other judges defer decision on summary judgment motions to concentrate on other court business. If the presiding judge gives summary judgment high priority, the party seeking expedition should make a summary judgment motion. Where the judge attaches low priority to summary judgment motions, filing the motion will seldom speed resolution of the case and may in fact delay final judgment as trial scheduling is deferred during the pendency of the summary judgment motion.

legal arguments, or where the legal position is more sympathetic in the abstract than are the underlying facts, a summary judgment motion may actually be the better path for the legal trailblazer.

§ 12.3.4 Timing

Fed.R.Civ.P. 56(a) permits a claimant (either the plaintiff or any other party claiming a right to relief in any other pleading) to move for summary judgment twenty days after commencement of the action. If another party serves a summary judgment motion, a claimant may immediately seek summary judgment. Fed.R.Civ.P. 56(b) permits any party defending a claim to move for summary judgment at any time. However, a party aiming for summary judgment ordinarily waits until at least the initial discovery is completed.

Although the rules appear to permit claimants the right to move for summary judgment as soon as twenty days after commencement of the action, courts in multiparty cases frequently require all parties interested in a fund to have appeared before the claimant may move for summary judgment against any party.[23] The apparent rationale for these holdings is the prudence of having all parties "report in" before the court determines the existence or nonexistence of a material factual dispute.

If the motion is made early, it will have to be good! If the legal position is that good, a motion to dismiss under Rule 12(b)(6) for failure to state a claim may be available. If it is, it should be made before conducting discovery. Where, however, an affidavit from a party or witness resolves a factual matter, counsel prefer the early summary judgment over the motion to dismiss. Some attorneys have the bad habit of moving to dismiss when they should be patient, gather facts, and then seek summary judgment. Others are apt to bring a motion for summary judgment, guns and affidavits (and supporting discovery) blazing, when their prime argument attacks the opponent's legal claim. Both extremes should be avoided. No judge grants early summary judgment where it appears that the movant seeks to stampede the opposing party. The competent opponent of the early summary judgment motion will either seek time for discovery, as allowed by Fed. R.Civ.P. 56(f), or will have a client or witness file affidavits establishing fact issues precluding summary judgment. Bringing the motion prematurely may result in both denial of the motion and also cooler reception to subsequent motions and at the trial. As previously noted, denial of a summary judgment motion will foreclose a second summary judgment motion on the same legal theory.

Those wishing to interpose an affidavit precluding summary judgment are less able to employ clever phrasing and half-truths when faced

23. *See, e.g., United States v. McFaddin Express, Inc.,* 197 F.Supp. 289 (D.Conn. 1961).

with carefully drafted interrogatories, requests to admit, or a transcript of a well-conducted deposition.[24] Thus, as a general rule, even the most rabid lawyer should conduct some discovery before moving for summary judgment. Thereafter, the timing of the summary judgment motion becomes subject to the complicated matrix of factors that affect the decision of whether to make the motion. When seeking summary judgment, do so far enough in advance of trial that the court may fully consider the motion without being tempted to deny the motion because of a nearby trial date. Summary judgment motions made on the eve of trial without good reason for the delay are sure to be denied and serve only to increase the cost of the litigation. Although initial discovery should be completed before the motion is made, the movant need not permit protracted discovery once there is enough information to support the motion.

§ 12.3.5 Procedure

A court's consideration of a summary judgment motion, including the court's determination as to the existence of a material factual dispute, is procedural rather than substantive under the *Erie* doctrine.[25] The process by which the court considers and decides summary judgment motions is a matter of federal law. The definition of what constitutes a material fact, however, is a question of state substantive law.[26] In some states, summary judgment is automatically a two-edged sword permitting the entry of judgment against the moving party even if no cross-motion for summary judgment is filed.[27]

Despite decisions to the contrary, it is generally recognized that the better rule is that the filing of a summary judgment motion, like the filing of a Rule 12 motion to dismiss, tolls the time for answering.[28] Both claimants and those defending claims must serve their summary judgment motions at least ten days prior to any hearing or oral argument held on the motion. Where a hearing is scheduled, a party opposing summary judgment has until the day before the hearing to serve any opposing affidavits.[29] In many federal district courts, local rules require that a party opposing a summary judgment motion, or any motion, serve a responsive brief and affidavits within a specified period of time (usually ten to twenty days) or the motion is treated as uncon-

24. For detailed guidance on the means of conducting effective and useful discovery, *see* Roger S. Haydock & David F. Herr, Discovery Practice §§ 3.5–3.6 (depositions), 4.4 (interrogatories), and 7.3–7.5 (requests for admissions) (2d ed. 1988, Supp. 1994).

25. *See Erie R. Co. v. Tompkins,* 304 U.S. 64, 58 S.Ct. 817, 82 L.Ed. 1188 (1938), *mandate conformed to* 98 F.2d 49 (2d Cir. 1938), *cert. denied* 305 U.S. 637, 59 S.Ct. 108, 83 L.Ed. 410 (1938), *rehearing denied* 305 U.S. 673, 59 S.Ct. 229, 83 L.Ed. 436 (1938).

26. *See, e.g., Fitzsimmons v. Best,* 528 F.2d 692 (7th Cir.1976).

27. *See, e.g.,* 48 Minn. Stat.Ann., R.Civ.P. 56.03; N.Y.—McKinney's CPLR 3212(b).

28. *See* 10 Charles A. Wright, et al., Federal Practice and Procedure § 2718 (1983 & Supp.1991).

29. Fed.R.Civ.P. 56(c).

tested.[30] Local rules or standing orders also frequently require a party to serve its memorandum in opposition a specified time (usually three to eight days) before the hearing. Another local rule of some popularity treats all material facts set forth by the moving party as admitted unless controverted with specificity by the opponent, usually in a specific listing of contested facts.[31] Where the nonmovant fails to satisfy this type of local rule, the court may more readily conclude that summary judgment is warranted.[32]

There is some question as to the need for a "hearing" on summary judgment motions. The weight of authority suggests that federal courts may, pursuant to Fed.R.Civ.P. 78, decide motions without a hearing where the court determines that an oral hearing will not be helpful to the court.[33] The general rule is that federal courts hold a hearing as envisioned by Fed.R.Civ.P. 56(c) prior to deciding the motion.[34] In practice, the hearing is usually an oral argument regarding the nature of the disputed facts, if any, and the applicable law. Testimony is rarely presented.

Oral testimony may be heard to resolve a particular factual dispute where all other material facts are agreed upon.[35] In state court proceedings, hearings are almost always held. Standard practice has the movant pick a hearing date corresponding with the local court's permissible motion calendar and serve the motion on opposing counsel a bare minimum ten days before the hearing. Where the motion raises complex issues, the opposing party should request an extension of the hearing.

Rule 12 provides that a motion to dismiss accompanied by affidavits or other evidentiary supporting papers must be treated as a motion for summary judgment. If the court converts the Rule 12 motion to a summary judgment motion, it must give the parties notice and an opportunity to be heard.[36] Notice is required by due process considerations because a grant of summary judgment is an adjudication on the merits.

30. E.D.Pa.R. 20 (twenty days); D.N.D.R. 10 (ten days).

31. *See, e.g.,* D.Me. Local Rules 19(b)(2); E.D.N.Y. Local Rule 3(g); S.D.N.Y. Local Rules 3(g); D.P.R. Local Rules 311.12.

32. *See, e.g., United States v. Pilot Petroleum Associates, Inc.,* 122 F.R.D. 422 (E.D.N.Y.1988) (court reveals exasperation with nonmovant but grants twenty additional days for complying with local rule). Even where the court treats the uncontroverted or improperly controverted facts as admitted, it may not grant summary judgment unless the movant also demonstrates entitlement to judgment as a matter of law. *See* § 12.3.11, *infra.* Any other view of local rules on summary judgment, or local rules regarding uncontested motions, would be inconsistent with Rule 56. *See Jaroma v. Massey,* 873 F.2d 17, 20–21 (1st Cir. 1989).

33. *Hamman v. Southwestern Gas Pipeline, Inc.,* 721 F.2d 140, 38 Fed.R.Serv.2d 179 (5th Cir.1983), *appeal after remand* 821 F.2d 299 (5th Cir.1987), *vacated in part on rehearing* 832 F.2d 55 (1987); *Benson v. Matthews,* 554 F.2d 860 (8th Cir.1977).

34. *Season–All Industries, Inc. v. Turkiye Sise Ve Cam Fabrikalari, A.S.,* 425 F.2d 34 (3d Cir.1970).

35. *Walters v. City of Ocean Springs,* 626 F.2d 1317, 1321 (5th Cir.1980).

36. *See* Fed.R.Civ.P. 12(b); *Beacon Enterprises v. Menzies,* 715 F.2d 757 (2d Cir. 1983); *Georgia S. & F. Ry. v. Atlantic Coast Line R. Co.,* 373 F.2d 493 (5th Cir.1967), *cert. denied* 389 U.S. 851, 88 S.Ct. 69, 19 L.Ed.2d 120 (1967).

§ 12.3.6 Supporting Papers

The motion need not be accompanied by supporting papers. Fed. R.Civ.P. 56(a) and (b) specifically state that a party may seek summary judgment "with or without supporting affidavits." Of course, if the movant is to prevail, the record must show absence of a genuine, material, fact dispute. Counsel may show this by referring to the pleadings and depositions without actually attaching them to the motion. However, the better procedure is to attach as appendices to the motion those portions of the record on which the movant relies.

Fed.R.Civ.P. 56(c) states that the pleadings, depositions, answers to interrogatories, admissions on file, and affidavits may be used by the court in deciding a summary judgment motion. The admissions need not be denominated as responses to requests for admissions but may be contained in any document filed with the court (e.g., pleading, motion, memorandum of law, or letter to the court).[37] If, however, the moving party seeks to rely on a document that is not currently part of the record, the document must be referred to in an affidavit and attached to the affidavit as an exhibit.[38] The affidavit must actually lay a foundation for the exhibit and establish its evidentiary admissibility. However, the court may consider inadmissible documents if the opponent makes no objection.[39] The movant may ask the court to take judicial notice of a fact not contained in the record, just as the court may take judicial notice at trial pursuant to Fed.R.Evid. 202.[40]

Attorneys frequently fail to pay sufficient attention to the proper use and presentation of supporting papers despite their importance. As a general rule, relying on an affidavit is less effective than relying on a pleading, answer, admission, or deposition. Because these documents may be used at trial, they receive greater trust. An affidavit, although rebuttable, is not subject to challenge by cross-examination. Unlike judicial admissions or helpful deposition testimony from an opponent or nonparty, affidavits have an air of suspect self-servingness about them. An affidavit laying the foundation for documentary evidence may be very persuasive, however. Certainly, an uncontroverted affidavit is of significant persuasive force, especially if the affiant is a disinterested witness.

Counsel frequently find it useful to append relevant portions of the record to a summary judgment motion. This makes the motion easier

37. *United States v. White Motor Co.,* 194 F.Supp. 562, 571 (N.D.Ohio 1961), *reversed in part* 372 U.S. 253, 83 S.Ct. 696, 9 L.Ed.2d 738 (1963). No matter what the context, attorneys should expect to be treated like criminal defendants in at least one respect: anything they say—at oral argument, in chambers, in a letter, in memoranda of law, in a pretrial order, or even in a phone conversation with opposing counsel—may potentially be used against him or her. *See, e.g., Ashland Oil, Inc. v. Arnett,* 875 F.2d 1271, 1283 (7th Cir.1989) (trial brief; listing factors courts consider in determining whether to bind party to pretrial representations); *Sadowski v. Bombardier Ltd.,* 539 F.2d 615 (7th Cir.1976) (pretrial order).

38. *Federal Deposit Ins. Co. v. Lauterbach,* 626 F.2d 1327 (7th Cir.1980).

39. *Davis v. Howard,* 561 F.2d 565, 570 (5th Cir.1977).

40. *See* 10A Charles A. Wright, et al., Federal Practice and Procedure § 2723 (1983 & Supp.1994).

for the court to consider, and courts always enjoy having their existence made easier. The added convenience will not prompt the judge to grant a summary judgment motion despite adverse law but may encourage decision of your motion in advance of others that require the judge (or law clerk) to visit the file room to locate and review the entire record. However, attach only those materials the court needs to consider. When counsel includes the entire record as part of the motion, the court faces the same voluminous record contained in the file room, only now it clutters the chambers.[41]

The Supreme Court decision in *Celotex Corp. v. Catrett* [42] confirmed that a party seeking summary judgment need not file supporting materials if it can demonstrate that the nonmovant claimant bearing the burden of proof has failed to proffer sufficient evidence supporting each element of its claim. In these circumstances, the movant's showing of an absence of proof supporting claimant triggers the burden set forth in Rule 56(e) that the claimant introduce specific facts showing that there is a genuine issue for trial. The Court was less clear, however, as to what constitutes a sufficient demonstration of claimant's failure to introduce evidence supporting the claim.

Justice White's concurring opinion (which provided the swing vote on the outcome) stated that "the movant must discharge the burden the rules place upon him: It is not enough to move for summary judgment ... with a conclusory assertion that the plaintiff has no evidence to prove his case." [43] A reading of this concurrence, the plurality opinion, and the dissent suggests a relatively wide zone of acceptable summary judgment practice. The movant should articulate for the court the elements that claimant must prove to prevail and then point out the absence in appropriate portions of the record of any material supporting claimant. Similarly, the movant can trigger the Rule 56(e) burden by pointing to the existence of evidence tending to contradict necessary elements of the claim. For example, if a plaintiff must prove permanent physical injury, defendant satisfies its summary judgment production burden by noting that plaintiff's deposition either fails to claim such injury under apt questioning or in fact disavows permanent injury. Where the deposition is merely silent, the nonmovant plaintiff would presumably place this fact in sufficient dispute by submitting an affidavit claiming such injury, so long as the affidavit does not expressly contradict her deposition testimony.[44]

41. For a scathing judicial reaction to attachments run amok, *see Sewell Plastics, Inc. v. Coca-Cola Co.,* 119 F.R.D. 24 (W.D.N.C.1988) (court declined to consider three-foot stack of supporting papers and ordered parties to submit ten-page statements of undisputed facts).

42. 477 U.S. 317, 106 S.Ct. 2548, 91 L.Ed.2d 265 (1986), *on remand* 826 F.2d 33 (D.C.Cir.1987), *cert. denied* 484 U.S. 1066, 108 S.Ct. 1028, 98 L.Ed.2d 922 (1988).

43. 477 U.S. at 328, 106 S.Ct. at 2555.

44. *See Camfield Tires, Inc. v. Michelin Tire Corp.,* 719 F.2d 1361 (8th Cir.1983) (affidavits in opposition to summary judgment may explain deposition testimony but court permitted to accord no weight to affidavit attempting to contradict or rewrite deposition testimony).

Justice Brennan's *Celotex* dissent (joined by two others) would also under some circumstances require the summary judgment movant to depose the nonmovant's witnesses to "affirmatively show the absence of evidence" in support of the nonmovant's claim in order to discharge the movant's production burden. Although Justice Brennan did not see this as inconsistent with Chief Justice Rehnquist's plurality opinion, we think that the plurality (Justices Rehnquist, O'Connor, and the since-retired Justices Burger and Powell) and concurring Justice White as well as many trial judges might not require this much effort by movants, at least not in the ordinary case. One prominent summary judgment scholar has suggested that plaintiffs must, under *Celotex,* present prima facie proof of each element of their claims in order to defeat summary judgment.[45]

Determining when a movant has discharged the burden of production is relatively easy in the average case but ultimately presents a delicate question of balancing the legitimate interests of claimants and respondents. If the court makes it too easy for a summary judgment movant to discharge the burden of requiring the claimant to respond with specific facts as required by Rule 56(e), the movant can at low cost require the nonmovant to expend substantial pretrial time, expense, and energy proving up its case on paper through compilation of affidavits and additional depositions. On the other hand, requiring the defendant to depose what are rightfully plaintiff's witnesses in order to discharge the burden will in most cases make it too easy for plaintiffs to file suit and exert significant coercive settlement pressure on defendants because of the cost of making a summary judgment motion that still may be negated by plaintiff's counter-submissions.

Since *Celotex,* both the Supreme Court and lower courts have failed to articulate clear general rules on this point. Trial courts and litigators are probably best guided by a common sense of fairness. Where the defendant notes absence of evidence supporting an essential element of plaintiff's case, plaintiff should ordinarily be required to produce evidence that is available to it without undue hardship or expense in order to avoid summary judgment. Where, however, the defendant has ready access to information concerning an element of the claim, it is not unreasonable to require a defendant to offer this evidence in order to discharge its initial summary judgment burden.

§ 12.3.7 Affidavits

Fed.R.Civ.P. 56(e) requires that affidavits be made on personal knowledge and set forth facts "as would be admissible in evidence." The affidavits must also establish the testimonial competence of the affiant and must be based on personal knowledge. Thus, an affidavit

45. *See* Martin B. Louis, Intercepting and Discouraging Doubtful Litigation: A Golden Anniversary View of Pleading, Summary Judgment, and Rule 11 Sanctions under the Federal Rules of Civil Procedure, 67 N.C.L.Rev. 1023 (1989). *See also* Martin B. Louis, Federal Summary Judgment Doctrine: A Critical Analysis, 83 Yale L.J. 745 (1974).

will not be sufficient, either for supporting summary judgment or opposing it, if the affidavit is conclusory or merely restates the party's pleadings. Although an overly strict view of what constitutes admissible evidence in an affidavit or other document before the court on a summary judgment motion may be error,[46] the affidavits cannot establish a case through inadmissible hearsay, speculation, or the party's "common-sense" explanation of what happened.[47] In rare cases a deficient affidavit may be ignored by the court and will be ineffective to put facts at issue. The U.S. Supreme Court has stated that affidavits must possess at least some probative value.[48] In addition, affidavits may not be used to contradict the affiant's deposition testimony in order to create an issue of material fact.[49]

Frequently, the party preparing affidavits assumes facts to be uncontested and therefore proven. Even if some unstated facts in the affidavits but necessary for judgment are uncontested, the court cannot, absent the applicability of judicial notice, consider these facts until they are proven. Affidavits must therefore set forth all facts necessary to support the factual conclusions contained in them. Frequently, an affidavit implicitly relies on an admitted or unrebutted averment in the pleadings as proof of that fact. A better procedure is to refer explicitly to this portion of the pleadings and to attach a copy of the pleadings to the affidavit as an exhibit. Parties frequently seek to rely on documents affixed to the summary judgment motion as appendices. Unfortunately, such documents, unless already part of the record, cannot be considered by the court unless incorporated by reference in an affidavit and attached to the affidavit as exhibits. Attorneys often overlook this important rule and refer to documents but neglect to make them admissible by attaching them to a foundation-laying affidavit.

Where the nonmovant fails to set forth by affidavit or otherwise the "specific facts showing that there is a genuine issue for trial," the party may seek leave of the court to move for a stay of decision on the

46. *See In re Japanese Electronic Products Antitrust Litigation,* 723 F.2d 238 (3d Cir.1983), *reversed on other grounds* 475 U.S. 574, 106 S.Ct. 1348, 89 L.Ed.2d 538, *on remand* 807 F.2d 44 (3d Cir.1986), *cert. denied* 481 U.S. 1029, 107 S.Ct. 1955, 95 L.Ed.2d 527 (1987). *See, e.g., Catrett v. Johns–Manville Sales Corp.,* 826 F.2d 33 (D.C.Cir.1987), *cert. denied* 484 U.S. 1066, 108 S.Ct. 1028, 98 L.Ed.2d 992 (1988) (the remand of the Supreme Court's *Celotex* decision), where the Court arguably permitted hearsay testimony to defeat a summary judgment motion where the declarant was available by subpoena for trial but not necessarily willing to make an affidavit.

47. In some cases, hearsay in affidavits may be considered. *See Catrett, supra* note 47; *DiMartini v. Ferrin,* 889 F.2d 922 (9th Cir.1989), *opinion amended* 906 F.2d 465 (9th Cir.1990) (in response to summary judgment motion invoking qualified immunity defense, which prevents discovery, nonmovant may use hearsay via affidavit to oppose the motion).

48. *First Nat. Bank of Ariz. v. Cities Service Co.,* 391 U.S. 253, 289, 88 S.Ct. 1575, 1593, 20 L.Ed.2d 569 (1968), *rehearing denied* 393 U.S. 901, 89 S.Ct. 63, 21 L.Ed.2d 188 (1968).

49. *See Camfield Tires, Inc. v. Michelin Tire Corp.,* 719 F.2d 1361, 1364 (8th Cir. 1983) (citing cases). *Accord, Martin v. Merrell Dow Pharmaceuticals, Inc.,* 851 F.2d 703 (3d Cir.1988). However, an affidavit may be considered and may create a factual issue where it "explains" an internally inconsistent deposition of the affiant. *Camfield Tires, supra,* 719 F.2d at 1364–1365; *Kennett–Murray Corp. v. Bone,* 622 F.2d 887, 893 (5th Cir.1980).

summary judgment motion in order to permit discovery or additional time for taking affidavits in opposition to the motion. Nonmovants in this position should seek a stay as soon as possible and act quickly to obtain the necessary materials to oppose the motion as required by Fed.R.Civ.P. 56(e) so that the court will not suspect an attempt to merely delay the inevitable. The party seeking this stay must specifically allege the additional information to be discovered that will create disputed issues of material facts.[50] It is not enough for the party merely to allege there might be some facts "out there someplace" that may create a dispute.

Where it appears to the court that affidavits have been made in bad faith or solely for the purpose of delay, the court may, pursuant to Fed.R.Civ.P. 56(g), require the party presenting such affidavits to pay the other side's reasonable expenses, including attorney's fees, incurred as a result of the bad faith or delay-causing affidavits. Normally, this requires the offending party to pay the costs and legal fees associated with the summary judgment motion. The court may also assess incidental and consequential damages resulting from the improper affidavits or may also hold the offending party or attorney in contempt.[51] In practice, courts have traditionally been reluctant to impose the sanctions of this rule and have, when faced with dishonest affidavits, disregarded them and decided the summary judgment motion in favor of the opposing party. Only in egregious cases have the courts invoked Fed.R.Civ.P. 56(g) to impose sanctions.[52]

§ 12.3.8 Opposing Summary Judgment

After being served with a summary judgment motion and supporting papers establishing facts entitling the moving party to judgment, the nonmovant cannot merely deny the contents of the moving party's affidavits, properly incorporated documents, pleadings, or other materials. Fed.R.Civ.P. 56(e) requires the opposing party to set forth specific facts showing that there is a genuine issue for trial. This showing must be made under the rule "by affidavits or as otherwise provided." Rule 56(e) requires the party opposing summary judgment to produce some admissible evidence that, even if unlikely or unpersuasive, shows a dispute requiring resolution by trial and is not so weak or unpersuasive that it would not withstand a motion for directed verdict or j.n.o.v. Even an affidavit by a party, an obviously self-interested person who might gladly stretch the truth, is sufficient if it meets the requirements of Rule 56 (*i.e.,* is based on personal knowledge and is not in sham contradiction of a deposition).

50. *See Shavrnoch v. Clark Oil & Refining Corp.,* 726 F.2d 291 (6th Cir.1984).

51. *See Clark v. Hancock,* 45 F.R.D. 512 (S.D.Ga.1968); Fed.R.Civ.P. 56(g).

52. *See* Robert E. Rodes, Jr., et al., Sanctions Imposable for Violations of the Federal Rules of Civil Procedure 23 (1981). Professors Wright, Miller, and Kane observe that "[t]here appear to be few situations in which the courts have resorted to Rule 56(g)." 10A Charles A. Wright, et al., Federal Practice and Procedure § 2742 (1983 & Supp.1994).

The court does not consider credibility in deciding a motion for summary judgment. If the affidavits would require the court to weigh the facts on any issue properly raised in the motion papers, a genuine issue of fact exists. If that fact is material under the applicable law, the court will deny summary judgment. Regarding the sometimes thorny question of what constitutes a genuine factual dispute, *see* § 12.3.2.

Courts disregard a party's sworn testimony by affidavit only where the facts are unbelievable to any reasonable person. Usually this requires that the affidavit's statement be refuted by undeniable objective evidence. For example, an affiant who adamantly swore that he could see the late afternoon accident to the east of his house while he watched the sunset could be disbelieved by the judge despite the volumes of case reports stressing that credibility issues are for the jury (although better practice would support giving the witness a chance to explain the sunset problem, particularly if the rest of the testimony were not suspect). In the somewhat rare cases where the court finds that the affidavit contains false testimony, the court is entitled, as is any factfinder, to disregard the entire evidence of that witness (Fed.R.Civ.P. 56(g)).

§ 12.3.9 Continuance

A party opposing summary judgment may ask the court to defer ruling on the motion for a reasonable time so that the party may conduct discovery or obtain opposing affidavits. Fed.R.Civ.P. 56(f) permits such a continuance where the opposing party can articulate reasons for the absence of the essential materials. On occasion, key potential affiants may be temporarily unavailable. Where the summary judgment motion has been made early in the case, supported most commonly by affidavits of the moving party, the opposing party should be accorded a reasonable opportunity to conduct discovery.[53]

§ 12.3.10 Cross-Motions for Summary Judgment

Frequently, the party opposing a summary judgment motion agrees with the opponent regarding the absence of any disputed material facts but opposes the motion on legal grounds. A party in this situation may make a cross-motion for summary judgment. This motion agrees that no genuine issue of material fact exists but argues that the applicable law requires entry of judgment against, rather than in favor of, the initial movant. Although there is inherent court authority to enter summary judgment against the moving party, federal courts generally grant summary judgment only after a party expressly seeks it.

§ 12.3.11 Standard for and Availability of Summary Judgment

Fed.R.Civ.P. 56(c) establishes the standard for granting or denying summary judgment, providing that summary judgment

53. *See Black Panther Party v. Smith*, 661 F.2d 1243 (D.D.C.1981), *cert. granted and judgment vacated* 458 U.S. 1118, 102 S.Ct. 3505, 73 L.Ed.2d 1381 (1982).

shall be rendered forthwith if the pleadings, depositions, answers to interrogatories, and admissions on file, together with the affidavits, if any, show that there is no genuine issue as to any material fact and that the moving party is entitled to judgment as a matter of law.

Despite this simple two-prong test—(1) does the record show the absence of any genuine material factual dispute and (2) on the basis of the uncontested facts does the law entitle the moving party to relief? — some courts have spoken as if summary judgment were an extraordinary event. As Professors Wright, Miller, and Kane have noted, the correct standard set forth in the rule "is often lost amid the precedents [purporting to be] applying it." [54] Over the years, some courts have addressed summary judgment in terms usually reserved for Halley's Comet and similarly rare events, stating that summary judgment is granted in the clearest of cases, that summary judgment is a drastic measure, that summary judgment is denied where there is the "slightest doubt," and such other erroneous interpretations of the clear wording of the rule.[55] As commentators have noted, the evolution of this line of cases is unfortunate but is also becoming steadily less important as courts faced with teeming dockets apply the literal language of the rule to spare themselves needless trials.[56] The beyond-a-shadow-of-a-doubt line of cases runs counter to both the standard set forth in Fed.R.Civ.P. 56(c) and the requirement of Rule 56(e) that a party do more to respond to the motion than rest on the averments of the pleadings. Even naked allegations raise more than "the slightest doubt" about a set of facts.

Not every disputed fact is a material fact sufficient to prevent a summary judgment.[57] A fact is material if it is "outcome determinative" under the applicable law, that is, if its existence in a case will have some impact in deciding the facts of the case.[58] Inferences that may be drawn from a set of facts will be sufficient to create disputed material facts.[59] All inferences to be drawn from the underlying facts must be viewed in a light most favorable to the party opposing the motion and the record must reveal that the opposing party would not prevail under any discernible circumstances.[60] Conclusive assertions of ultimate facts will usually be insufficient to create material facts; the disputed facts must

54. 10 Charles A. Wright, et al., Federal Practice and Procedure § 2712 (1983 & Supp.1994).

55. Statistics in the Ninth Circuit indicate that summary judgments are affirmed or denied in the same proportion as are all other types of decisions. *See* William F. Schwarzer, Summary Judgment under the Federal Rules: Defining Genuine Issues of Material Fact, 99 F.R.D. 465 (1983).

56. 10 & 10A Charles A Wright, et al., Federal Practice and Procedure §§ 2712, 2719 (1983 & Supp.1991).

57. Oakland County v. City of Berkeley, 742 F.2d 289 (6th Cir.1984).

58. *See United States v. Gilbert,* 920 F.2d 878, 882–83 (11th Cir.1991); *Big O Tire Dealers, Inc. v. Big O Warehouse,* 741 F.2d 160 (7th Cir.1984).

59. *Taylor v. Gallagher,* 737 F.2d 134 (1st Cir.1984).

60. *Kreuzer v. American Academy of Periodontology,* 735 F.2d 1479 (D.C.Cir. 1984).

be specifically established.[61]

As discussed more completely in § 12.3.12, one can argue since the Supreme Court's summary judgment trilogy that Rule 56(c)'s meaning has implicitly shifted; the words "no genuine issue as to any material fact" now mean "the nonmovant has failed to present substantial evidence that would support a favorable verdict by a reasonable jury." Although this argument is not without force, courts since 1986 appear not to be significantly more aggressive in granting summary judgment. Although in some cases courts will grant summary judgment where material facts conflict on the ground that the nonmovant's facts are so woefully nonprobative as to constitute merely a scintilla of evidentiary support, most courts will find the existence of a sufficiently genuine dispute of material fact whenever the nonmovant has offered any probative evidence on the point. Most significantly, the 1986 trilogy focuses judicial attention on the burden of proof by reminding trial courts that the party bearing the burden has a significant obligation under Rule 56(e) to submit evidentiary matter that tends to prove its claim.[62] Since most summary judgment motions are made by defendants against plaintiffs (who bear the burden of persuasion), the emphasis is useful to those seeking summary disposition.

The language of Rule 56(c) appears mandatory. Where the standard is met, the "judgment sought shall be rendered forthwith." This command is less overpowering than the language would suggest. Although a court would ordinarily abuse its discretion in denying a summary judgment motion that clearly satisfied the rule, trial courts have significant discretion to deny the motion "even if the movant otherwise successfully carries its burden of proof if the judge has doubt as to the wisdom of terminating the case before a full trial."[63] Of course, many, if not most, motions fall between the clearly justified and the baseless. In most cases, the bulk of facts are undisputed, but some are hotly contested. Whether the disputed facts are material and whether the dispute is "genuine" lie within the eye of the beholding court. Consequently, courts as a practical matter have broad discretion in determining the contested nature of facts[64] and may almost always

61. *Miller v. Solem,* 728 F.2d 1020 (8th Cir.1984), *cert. denied* 469 U.S. 841, 105 S.Ct. 145, 83 L.Ed.2d 84 (1984).

62. Although this material must ordinarily itself constitute admissible evidence, this is not always required so long as the nonmovant can demonstrate the capacity to produce admissible evidence on the point at trial. *See Catrett v. Johns–Manville Sales Corp.,* 826 F.2d 33 (D.C.Cir.1987), *cert. denied* 484 U.S. 1066, 108 S.Ct. 1028, 98 L.Ed.2d 992 (1988).

63. *Veillon v. Exploration Services, Inc.,* 876 F.2d 1197, 1200 (5th Cir.1989).

64. *Compare* the district court's disdain for the "conspiracy evidence" of the plaintiffs in *In re Japanese Electronic Products Antitrust Litigation,* 513 F.Supp. 1334, 1366 (E.D.Pa.1981) with the benefit of the doubt accorded this evidence by the court of appeals in the same case, 723 F.2d 238 (3d Cir.1983). A 5–4 Supreme Court decision in 1986 appeared to view the evidence more from the vantage of the district court, reversing the Third Circuit. *Matsushita Electronic Indus. Co., Ltd. v. Zenith Radio Corp.,* 475 U.S. 574, 106 S.Ct. 1348, 89 L.Ed.2d 538 (1986), *on remand* 807 F.2d 44 (3d Cir.1986), *cert. denied* 481 U.S. 1029, 107 S.Ct. 1955, 95 L.Ed.2d 527 (1987).

justify denying summary judgment to permit those facts to be more clearly established at trial.

Similarly, a court is presumably able to determine the law in every case. That is, after all, the court's job. Consequently, a court may not deny summary judgment merely because the legal issues are complex. However, the court may deny summary judgment where further factual development may make some legal determinations unnecessary.[65] Thus, despite the "shall" language of Fed.R.Civ.P. 56(c), the real inquiry by the court more likely asks:

1. Can I grant the motion?
2. Do I want to? Or would waiting for trial be worthwhile?

Many courts, taking comfort in jury determinations or the likelihood of settlement prior to trial, find denying summary judgment the safer and therefore wiser course. Court congestion and new prevailing schools of judicial thought are changing this attitude but have not eradicated it. The party seeking summary judgment should therefore emphasize the relative irreversibility of the judgment it seeks.

As a practical matter, summary judgment is relatively rare in certain types of cases. For example, in negligence, fraud, civil rights, and antitrust cases, summary judgment will be rare because the issues are often inherently factual in nature and require examination of motive, intent, and care. These issues do not usually come undisputed.[66] Summary judgment can be fairly common in cases involving disputed contracts or property where facts are uncontested and the dispute centers around the legal construction of the facts.[67] Although summary judgment on the merits in negligence, civil rights, and antitrust cases is rare, summary judgment on their jurisdictional issues is more common (*e.g.*, are the wrongful acts of Boola–Boola College "state action"?).

For many years, the traditional view held summary judgment rarely available in large, complex cases. This view, an ideological relative of the view that summary judgment cannot be granted where any doubt exists, has fallen from favor. Nevertheless, the complexity of "big" cases and their abundant factual records make summary judgment still difficult to obtain, although not for any different standard.[68]

§ 12.3.12 Summary Judgment and the Burden of Persuasion

The Supreme Court has resolved a lingering controversy and held that a court, in ruling on a summary judgment motion, should consider

65. *See Kennedy v. Silas Mason Co.,* 334 U.S. 249, 68 S.Ct. 1031, 92 L.Ed. 1347 (1948).

66. *See, e.g., Ammons v. Franklin Life Ins. Co.,* 348 F.2d 414 (5th Cir.1965).

67. 10A Charles A. Wright, et al., Federal Practice and Procedure § 2728 (1983 & Supp.1994).

68. *See Kennedy v. Silas Mason Co.,* 334 U.S. 249, 68 S.Ct. 1031, 92 L.Ed. 1347 (1948). *Cf. Carroll v. United Steelworkers of America, AFL–CIO–CLC,* 498 F.Supp. 976 (D.Md.1980), *affirmed* 639 F.2d 778 (4th Cir.1980) (summary judgment available even in complex cases).

the substantive burden of persuasion that would be in effect at trial.[69] Although the Court acknowledged that this could not be done with great precision, it suggested that rulings on a summary judgment be "filtered through the prism" of the substantive burden of persuasion at trial. For example, if (as in *Liberty Lobby*) a public figure plaintiff seeks to recover for defamation, he must prove actual malice (knowing falsity or reckless disregard of the truth) by the defendant with clear and convincing evidence. Therefore, if the defendant moves for summary judgment, the plaintiff must under Rule 56(e) not only introduce some specific facts tending to satisfy each element of a defamation claim but also must submit sufficiently weighty evidence to enable a reasonable factfinder to conclude that plaintiff has shown defamation by clear and convincing evidence rather than by a mere preponderance of evidence.

This new charge to trial courts is admittedly slippery. What constitutes clear and convincing proof is itself idiosyncratic.[70] When a judge seeks to determine what a factfinder in another context might deem to be sufficient to shoulder the clear and convincing burden, the process is a step or two further attenuated. At a minimum, judges seeking to import the substantive trial burden of proof into the pretrial summary judgment standard must do at least a modicum of assessment of the persuasive impact of the nonmovant's evidence. In such cases, then, the Supreme Court's summary judgment trilogy decisions would appear to have most definitely accorded more latitude to judges in rendering summary judgment.[71] Fortunately, most civil actions are subject to a preponderance of the evidence standard. Consequently, our recent reading of the cases suggests that in a typical case the court will examine the plaintiff-nonmovant's submissions to determine whether there is a significant quantum of material evidence in its favor. If so, summary judgment will be denied. Occasionally, a more aggressive district court may hold that a discernible amount of evidence is nonetheless too small to support a reasonable jury's verdict. In that small class of cases where plaintiff must demonstrate its right to relief by clear and convincing evidence—defamation, fraud, punitive damages claims—courts have more discretion to treat nonmovant's submissions as too insubstantial to resist summary judgment. Since these claims are also disfavored by the law, we expect courts to exhibit more frequent grants of summary judgment for these defendants, although no clear pattern has yet emerged.

69. *Anderson v. Liberty Lobby, Inc.,* 477 U.S. 242, 106 S.Ct. 2505, 91 L.Ed.2d 202 (1986).

70. *See United States v. Fatico,* 458 F.Supp. 388 (E.D.N.Y.1978), *judgment affirmed* 603 F.2d 1053 (2d Cir.1979), *cert. denied* 444 U.S. 1073, 100 S.Ct. 1018, 62 L.Ed.2d 755 (1980) (survey of federal district judges shows that when asked to equate "clear and convincing" proof to a percentage of certainty, responses ranged between 60 and 75 percent; proof "beyond a reasonable doubt" responses ranged from 76 to 95 percent).

71. It was for that reason that then-Judge (now Justice) Scalia, in writing the circuit court *Liberty Lobby* opinion, declined to consider the burden of clear and convincing evidence, finding that this would then involve the court too heavily in pretrial fact assessment. *See Liberty Lobby, Inc. v. Anderson,* 746 F.2d 1563, 1570–1571 (D.C.Cir.1984), *decision vacated* 477 U.S. 242, 106 S.Ct. 2505, 91 L.Ed.2d 202 (1986).

§ 12.3.13 Appealability and Review

A grant of summary judgment results in entry of a final judgment on the merits. Accordingly, a grant is immediately appealable as a final order under 28 U.S.C.A. § 1291(a) if it terminates the litigation. Denial of a motion for summary judgment is not a final order and can be appealed only where it fits an exception to the final order rule or is certified for immediate appeal by the court pursuant to 28 U.S.C.A. § 1292(b). A summary judgment decision denying an injunction is not ordinarily appealable under 28 U.S.C.A. § 1292(a)(1), which permits appeal for interlocutory orders denying injunctions.[72] The rationale for these decisions appears to be that an evidentiary hearing with factfinding in an injunction proceeding is a prerequisite to immediate appeal, and these elements are usually absent in a denial of summary judgment.

Although Rule 56 is available for seeking of summary judgment as to all "claims" in an action and may therefore be used in connections with third-party claims, cross-claims, and similar proceedings, summary judgment is final only when it completely resolves the litigation. Where summary judgment is granted as to some claims or parties in multiclaim or multiparty litigation, the order will not be appealable. If the court determines that there is no just reason for delay and directs the immediate entry of judgment, the order will be viewed as a final order under Fed.R.Civ.P. 54(b), provided the appellate court accepts the trial court's certification.[73]

On appeal, the court's review of a grant of summary judgment is "plenary" or de novo as to legal questions.[74] All reasonable factual inferences will be made in favor of the nonmoving party.[75] The procedures imposed on the parties by the trial court are subject to an abuse of discretion standard. The appellate court's review of the trial court's determination of the existence of factual disputes, being a legal question or a mixed question of law and fact, is subject to de novo review. However, as a practical matter, the reviewing court will usually grant more deference to the trial judge in this area than it will regarding the legal question of whether the moving party is entitled to judgment. The reviewing court may also affirm the grant or denial of summary judgment on grounds different from those of the district court.[76]

§ 12.3.14 Partial Summary Judgment Motions

Rule 56 provides that both claimants and those defending claims may move for summary judgment in their favor on all or part of any

72. *Goldstein v. Cox,* 396 U.S. 471, 90 S.Ct. 671, 24 L.Ed.2d 663 (1970).

73. *See, e.g., Baca Land & Cattle Co. v. New Mexico Timber, Inc.,* 384 F.2d 701 (10th Cir.1967); *Gabbard v. Rose,* 330 F.2d 705 (6th Cir.1964).

74. *See Goodman v. Mead Johnson & Co.,* 534 F.2d 566 (3d Cir.1976), *cert. denied* 429 U.S. 1038, 97 S.Ct. 732, 50 L.Ed.2d 748 (1977).

75. *Poller v. Columbia Broadcasting System, Inc.,* 368 U.S. 464, 82 S.Ct. 486, 7 L.Ed.2d 458 (1962).

76. *See Reynolds v. United States,* 643 F.2d 707, 710 (10th Cir.1981), *cert. denied* 454 U.S. 817, 102 S.Ct. 94, 70 L.Ed.2d 85 (1981).

claim, counterclaim, or cross-claim affecting them in an action. Rule 56(c) permits summary judgment to be entered on liability alone even where there remains a genuine dispute as to the amount of damages. The broad authorization of the rule thus provides the possibility of summary judgment on either all or only a part of any issue in the case, and for or against some or all of the parties.

Fed.R.Civ.P. 56(d) specifically grants the court authority to determine, on the basis of summary judgment motions and proceedings, the material facts that are not in dispute and to enter an order establishing these facts, thereby removing them from the trial. In this way, the court may, by determining the overlap in the parties' factual positions, eliminate uncontested issues and restrict trial to only the contested matters. The parties may also move the court to take this action, although it is more often a matter for court initiation. Counsel often achieve the same result closer to trial by stipulating to uncontested facts in the pretrial order.

Partial summary judgment as to claims and liability is a powerful weapon and one that is probably underutilized. In all but the most hotly contested matters, at least part of some of the claims would involve undisputed facts capable of legal resolution without trial. However, counsel may have tactical reasons for refraining from seeking partial summary judgment. A party may be entitled to summary judgment on the strongest part of a case but may wish to keep those issues before the factfinder that will determine other, less clear-cut issues. The costs of a partial summary judgment motion that fails, even if granted, to resolve the litigation completely may not warrant the motion. Nevertheless, the motion is probably underused. One of the litigants should usually attempt a partial summary judgment motion where:

- important material facts are uncontested
- hotly contested or emotional facts are not material
- one party is entitled to judgment as a matter of law on at least one claim in the action

Advance rulings may assist the court as well by conserving the court's time and resources. The motion ordinarily creates little increased expense to the parties and may facilitate settlement of the litigation.

Partial summary judgment motions are subject to the same procedural requirements as any other summary judgment motion. Orders granting partial summary judgment are ordinarily not final or appealable under 28 U.S.C.A. § 1291. An order disposing of some, but not all, of the claims or issues between two or more parties is interlocutory in nature and not appealable except by certification or some exception to the final order rule. An order that resolves all of the claims for one or more parties is final in nature and may be appealable if a judgment is actually entered. Fed.R.Civ.P. 54(b) permits the entry of partial judgment on the express direction of the court and a determination that no just reason exists for delay in entry of judgment. Because a partial summary judgment grant is interlocutory in nature, it is subject to review by the trial court at any time before final judgment. Courts do not welcome constant requests to reopen matters previously resolved by summary judgment, but consider it in unusual cases.

Section 11.3 discusses the use of partial summary judgment as part of an overall case strategy. Counsel can use the motion in conjunction with motions in limine. By focusing the court's attention on the factual disputes in the context of impending evidentiary rulings, counsel may convince the court of inevitable rejection of an opponent's claims or defenses. Partial summary judgment rulings may also make certain evidence inadmissible by removing issues from the case and thus change the overall settlement posture of the case. Courts, increasingly attuned to the effect their decisions may have on settlement, may consequently also be increasingly receptive to partial summary judgment.

§ 12.4 MOTIONS AFFECTING TRIAL CALENDAR AND CASE MANAGEMENT

§ 12.4.1 Introduction

Trial courts are generally accorded great deference by appellate courts in the management of trial court calendars. The court has great discretion in these matters, and a party seeking appellate review of decisions relating to the trial calendar must show actual and substantial prejudice.[1] The trial court's discretion with respect to some decisions is nearly absolute, and will not even be subject to appellate review.

Motions which affect the trial calendar are specially treated by trial judges because these motions, more than any other group, present issues which affect the interests of the court and the litigants in other actions as well as the parties to the action in which the motion is made. By their very nature, motions to advance one cause on a trial calendar will have potential impacts on all the other cases on that calendar.

Motion practice on issues concerning the trial calendar will differ considerably depending on the type of calendar used by the court. Courts generally use either a master calendar system, individual calendar system, or some combination of the two.

The master calendar system relies on the pooling of all cases before a multi-judge court. The trial judge will not be assigned to the case until it is called for trial, and that judge will probably not have heard prior motions in the case. This system promotes the maximum utilization of judges, but also encourages postponement of decision of difficult issues and requires a new judge to become familiar with the case each time a motion is heard.

The individual assignment, or "block", system provides for the assignment of cases to individual judges as the cases are filed, and for

§ 12.4

1. *See, e.g., Galella v. Onassis,* 487 F.2d 986 (2d Cir.1973).

the assigned judge to handle all proceedings in cases assigned to him or her. The initial assignment is usually made on some random or quasi-random basis, and random reassignment occurs if the assigned judge recuses him or herself. This system is thought to encourage earlier rulings on pretrial matters, since the judge realizes that it is the judge who will ultimately have to make the ruling. Although cases may be assigned to judges randomly on a basis of numerical equality, the resulting workloads invariably will not be equal because of the different burdens presented by various cases.

Some courts use a hybrid system which incorporates aspects of both the master calendar and individual calendar systems. One variation of the master calendar or pooled system calls for the cases to be assigned to an individual judge at some time before trial, but after the case has been handled on a pooled basis for some period of time. Courts using the individual assignment system may convert to a block system temporarily to deal with designated older cases and to equalize the inevitable variations in calendar backlogs. The block system may also be used to deal with a large number of similar actions pending on various individual calendars.

In courts using the master calendar system, it is necessary for decisions affecting the calendar to be made at a single source. Local rules will normally require motions affecting the trial calendar to be heard by the chief judge or by a designated calendar judge. In courts using the individual calendar system, motions concerning the calendar will be heard by the judge to whom the case is assigned.

§ 12.4.2 Motions for Continuance

A motion for continuance asks the court to postpone the setting of a case on the trial calendar. Normally, a continuance will not affect other aspects of the case's status (although discovery and motion cutoff dates may restrict other activity). A continuance should be distinguished from a stay in this regard. A stay of proceedings normally holds all activities in abeyance, and may be ordered before the action ever appears on a trial calendar. Stays of proceedings are frequently entered to permit a similar suit to proceed in another court, or to permit arbitration proceedings to take place. Courts are rarely reversed for denying a continuance, and virtually never reversed for allowing one.[2]

The grounds for which a continuance may be sought are myriad. The fundamental basis for allowing such a motion, however, is prejudice which would occur if a party is required to go to trial at the date initially established. Incapacitating illness of trial counsel or a necessary witness may require granting a motion for continuance. Similarly, courts will

2. *See Aghnides v. Marmon Group, Inc.,* 463 F.2d 384 (4th Cir.1972), *affirming* 344 F.Supp. 829 (S.D.W.Va.1971) (continuances for illness affirmed).

deny a motion for a continuance if it is apparent that the party has had ample opportunity to prepare the case and has failed to do so.[3]

§ 12.4.3 Motions for Jury or Bench Trial

The jury trial is a central part of the court system in the United States, and the right to a jury trial is a valuable, important right. In federal court cases, the right to a jury trial is guaranteed by the seventh amendment to the United States Constitution in all actions triable to a jury at common law. Many state constitutions have similar provisions, and a multitude of federal and state statutes have extended the right to a jury trial to actions which did not exist at common law. Fed.R.Civ.P. 38(a) makes it clear that the rules of civil procedure preserve the rights of parties to trial by jury. In general, however, a jury will not be available in actions which seek relief which is equitable in nature, such as injunctions, specific performance, or an accounting.

Because a jury trial is a fundamental right, a motion is not normally necessary to secure a jury trial. Most jury trials are held without any motions relating to the right to a jury. In some cases, however, a party may inadvertently waive a jury, or may belatedly demand a jury trial. A party may also demand a jury in a situation where it is clearly not entitled to a jury trial, and the opposing party may seek to have the jury demand stricken and the action removed from the jury calendar. Even if the parties are not entitled to a jury trial, the courts are given unlimited latitude to permit an advisory jury to consider the issues, and a party may desire to seek an advisory jury by motion.

A motion for a jury trial is one of the more unfortunately necessary motions in the litigator's arsenal. A party may secure a jury trial simply by demanding one in a timely manner, so a motion should not be required. Nonetheless, the motion for a jury trial is frequently brought, often by parties with experienced counsel who have neglected to make a demand.

Most motions for a jury trial arise as a result of the operation of Fed.R.Civ.P. 38(d), which deems the failure to make a jury demand a waiver of the right to trial by jury. This provision, though clear in the rules, has proven to be a trap for unwary counsel, and many motions are submitted to the courts asking that the parties be relieved of the burdens imposed by the rule. One reason for the frequency of these motions is that some states have practices which require an affirmative act before waiver will be found.

If a party makes a demand for a jury, the action is treated as a jury case and will be placed on the jury calendar. Once a jury demand is made, the case must be tried to a jury unless the parties agree to have it tried to the court alone or there is a motion to strike the jury demand and have the action tried to the court. Under Fed.R.Civ.P. 39(a) this motion can be made by any party or upon the court's own motion.

3. *See, e.g., Jackson v. Sentry Indemnity Co.,* 76 F.R.D. 600 (E.D.Tenn.1977).

Even in actions which are not triable to a jury, the court may empanel a jury to hear testimony and render a verdict. Fed.R.Civ.P. 39(c) authorizes the use of an advisory jury, and specifically allows a party to seek an advisory jury by motion. Usually, a motion for an advisory jury will be made to the trial judge shortly before the beginning of trial, although there is no limitation on the time during which the motion may be brought.

An advisory jury is used whenever the trial court feels it will be of value in finding the facts. In practice, advisory juries are relatively rarely used. Some courts have suggested that the advisory jury should be used only in very unusual circumstances,[4] although the decision of the trial court to use or not use an advisory jury will not be overturned, nor even reviewed by some courts.[5]

One reason for the vast discretion allowed the trial courts in deciding whether to use an advisory jury is the limited effect its use will have on the review of the action. If an advisory jury is used, the court simply considers the jury's verdict or answers to special interrogatories in framing the court's own findings of fact. The jury's verdict does not have any separate vitality, and is not binding in any way on the trial court. The trial court is free to reject the jury's findings, or may adopt the findings as the court's own.

Because the court can use an advisory jury without any motion from the parties, a motion must persuade the trial court that an advisory jury would be useful under the facts of the case. There is no right to an advisory jury. Courts may be particularly inclined to use an advisory jury in cases where the principal dispute centers around the credibility of witnesses. An advisory jury is unlikely to be used in cases presenting complex technical issues or complicated issues of mixed law and fact.

§ 12.4.4 Managing Large, Complex, and Multi-District Cases

Courts have increasingly recognized that special problems exist in the management of complex, protracted, and geographically far-flung litigation and litigation involving numerous parties. Efforts to adapt the Federal Rules of Civil Procedure to control the course of complicated cases have resulted in the Manual for Complex Litigation (Manual) for federal court actions. Similar rules and procedures similar to those set forth in the Manual are applied by state court judges, either through use of local rules or by entry of appropriate orders in individual cases.

The Manual has no authority or binding role on the decisions made for the management of complex cases. Rather, the Manual establishes recommended procedures to be used to handle complex cases efficiently. The procedures created by the Manual call for active and aggressive involvement of the court in the management of complex cases from the

4. *See, e.g., Moss v. Lane Co.*, 471 F.2d 853 (4th Cir.1973).

5. *Delman v. Federal Products Corp.*, 251 F.2d 123 (1st Cir.1958).

day the complaint is filed. The Manual provides for four pretrial conferences, and suggests specific areas and problems that are appropriate for discussion and resolution at each stage in the litigation.

The Manual is a useful tool to the courts, and can be a useful tool to lawyers seeking to structure and control a large case. Although the Manual recommends procedures which may be implemented by the court without any motion of counsel, it is permissible to move the court to take any desired action in a complex case. The Manual suggests many tools which may be of value to one party or to all the parties in a complex case, and should be consulted by all counsel involved in these cases.[6]

Masters are widely used to expedite the handling of large and complex cases. Fed.R.Civ.P. 53 provides for the appointment and compensation of masters, and permits the courts to delegate substantial powers to a master. Masters are appointed by the trial judge, and are directed to make reports to the court on matters assigned to them. Although masters are frequently appointed upon the court's own motion, there is no reason that a party cannot initiate the appointment of a master by motion. Masters are not routinely used, but may be of value in particularly complex or intractable cases. Fed.R.Civ.P. 53(b) states that reference to a master is to be the exception rather than the rule, and the courts have generally followed that mandate. Appellate courts have readily criticized the reference of matters to masters,[7] and have issued writs of mandamus to compel the trial court to decide matters within their jurisdiction rather than refer those matters to masters.[8] Courts have also expressed concern about the expense the appointment of a master would impose on the litigants.[9] Masters are compensated by the litigants in a manner and amount determined by the court.

§ 12.5 MOTIONS FOR PROVISIONAL RELIEF

§ 12.5.1 Types of Preliminary Substantive Relief

There are occasions in which it is possible to obtain substantive relief from the court without going through the entire trial process. These situations are limited because one side's early obtaining of substantive relief without a trial is the opponent's denial of its right to trial.

The most common form of preliminary relief is injunctive relief, which is available to maintain the status quo in the relationship of the parties until the court can determine an appropriate final remedy. Other forms of provisional remedies include pre-judgment garnishment,

6. The Manual and its advantages to various parties are discussed in Forde, Use of the Manual for Complex Litigation—The Plaintiff's Viewpoint, 15 Forum 137 (1979) and Wyllie, The Use of the Manual for Complex Litigation—The Defendant's Viewpoint, 15 Forum 163 (1979).

7. *See, e.g., La Buy v. Howes Leather Co.,* 352 U.S. 249, 253, 77 S.Ct. 309, 311, 312, 1 L.Ed.2d 290 (1957), *rehearing denied* 352 U.S. 1019, 77 S.Ct. 553, 1 L.Ed.2d 560 (1957); *Adventures in Good Eating, Inc. v. Best Places to Eat, Inc.,* 131 F.2d 809, 815 (7th Cir.1942) (burp!).

8. *See, e.g., In re Watkins,* 271 F.2d 771 (5th Cir.1959).

9. *Fraver v. Studebaker Corp.,* 11 F.R.D. 94 (W.D.Pa.1950).

attachment, sequestration, and receivership. These remedies are similar to tools available to enforce a judgment of a court, and will be available without a judgment in limited circumstances.

§ 12.5.2 Temporary Injunctive Relief

Courts provide three types of injunctive relief: a temporary restraining order (TRO), a preliminary or temporary injunction, and a permanent injunction. These injunctions seek: (1) to prevent or prohibit adverse conduct or behavior by a defendant and (2) to protect and restore rights and remedies of a plaintiff. All three types of the injunctive orders require a party either to refrain from doing something or to do something. A permanent injunction may be granted after a trial on the merits if justified by the facts and circumstances of the case. A preliminary or temporary injunction may be issued to preserve the status quo pending a final decision reached at the trial. A TRO may be issued on an *ex parte* or emergency hearing basis to prevent immediate irreparable injury until a hearing can be held for a preliminary or temporary injunction. Both TRO's and preliminary injunctions are of limited duration, and will be discussed collectively as "temporary injunctive relief." A party can obtain injunctive relief, an extraordinary remedy, only when the situation is clear and compelling.[1]

Courts have granted temporary injunctive relief in a wide range of circumstances. Judges have granted temporary restraining orders and preliminary injunctions to preserve constitutional rights, to protect the economic security of a business, to protect good will or reputation, to protect a copyright or patent infringement, to protect a personal services contract, to prevent harm to the environment, and to censor attempts at humor in this book.

The procedures for obtaining temporary injunctive relief are technical, complicated, and exacting. This extraordinary remedy should be reserved for extraordinary situations. Judges are reluctant to exercise their power and enjoin or restrain defendants unless an emergency or crisis exists. Temporary injunction proceedings are prepared, presented, and determined in an extremely short period of time providing little opportunity for reflection. Intense pressure affects the parties and the judges. Difficult judgments are often made in an emotionally charged and physically exhausting atmosphere. This environment tests the mind and mettle of the lawyers and the judges and should be avoided unless the interests of a client demand emergency action.

The plaintiff should seek such injunctive relief only after all other remedies have failed or would clearly be inadequate. Reasonable, good faith efforts should be made to contact the adverse party and to seek voluntary compliance with a request or a temporary negotiated result until a regular lawsuit can be commenced and adjudicated. A plaintiff

§ 12.5

1. *See, e.g., Illinois v. City of Milwaukee,* 599 F.2d 151 (7th Cir.1979), *vacated on other grounds* 451 U.S. 304, 101 S.Ct. 1784, 68 L.Ed.2d 114 (1981), *cert. denied* 451 U.S. 982, 101 S.Ct. 2313, 68 L.Ed.2d 839 (1981).

should also avoid seeking a temporary restraining order at the very last moment. Eleventh hour TRO applications leave literally no time for the other party to appear at an emergency hearing or for the judge to consider optional remedies. However, some situations force a plaintiff to seek an unanticipated TRO. The defendant may create an emergency, leaving a plaintiff with no alternative. In these situations the plaintiff should inform the judge that defendant's conduct requires an emergency proceeding.

The defendant who receives notice and has an opportunity to defend a TRO request may be well advised not to oppose but to voluntarily agree to do something or not do something, rendering moot the need for such an order. This tactic will provide the defendant with more time to prepare a defense at a hearing for a temporary injunction. A defendant client may balk at such voluntary action thinking it a sign of weakness or an admission of liability. However, the judge, who will ultimately decide the issue will appreciate the extra time provided by defense counsel. Often the plaintiff will be satisfied with the word of defense counsel that the status quo will not be changed. Some plaintiffs may insist on a written agreement. Care should be taken in drafting such a voluntary restraint, with particular attention paid to the scope of the conduct and the duration of the compliance.

§ 12.5.3 Grounds for Injunctive Relief

Three major aspects are involved in the consideration of temporary injunctive relief:

1. Jurisdictional matters, including control over persons or subject matter as well as the power of the court to grant the relief.

Various sources of the law regulate jurisdiction. Numerous state and federal statutes and constitutional provisions provide the court with jurisdiction over the persons and property involved in an injunctive proceeding. The applicable state or federal law will determine whether or not a party has a right to request injunctive relief.[2]

2. The grounds supporting the issuance of an injunction.

The propriety of granting or denying injunctive relief depends upon the facts and circumstances of a case. The following sections discuss the criteria developed by case law, rules, and statutes for determining whether or not grounds exist for equitable relief.

3. Procedural matters controlling the mechanics of issuing an injunctive order.

Procedural matters have been codified in rules such as Fed.R.Civ.P. 65 and corresponding state rules. Later sections in this chapter detail the procedures involved in seeking a temporary restraining order and a preliminary injunction. Specific federal and state statutes in certain cases will preempt or supplement the general procedures established by

2. *See Lemon v. Kurtzman,* 411 U.S. 192, 93 S.Ct. 1463, 36 L.Ed.2d 151 (1973).

rules. The general rules of civil procedure establish a detailed framework for obtaining temporary injunctive relief but do not usually establish a comprehensive framework. For example, Federal Rule 65 describes the type of notice required for a motion hearing and the form of a restraining order but does not prescribe the type of hearing required nor provisions for the enforcement of an injunction. Traditional common law equitable procedures and doctrines will govern matters not expressly covered by civil procedure rules.

The party who seeks temporary injunctive relief has the burden to show that sufficient grounds exist to grant the remedy.[3] The discretion the trial judge exercises in determining whether to grant or deny injunctive relief will rest upon an analysis of several factors that case law has developed to determine the propriety of temporary injunctive relief. These criteria include:[4]

1. The existence of threat of irreparable harm to the plaintiff if the injunction is denied.

2. The balancing of this harm with the injury suffered by the defendant if the injunction is granted.

3. The reasonable probability that the plaintiff will prevail on the merits.

4. The extent of the public interest.

Irreparable Harm. Fed.R.Civ.P. 65 states that immediate and irreparable injury, loss, or damage constitute the grounds for the issuance of temporary injunctive relief. This factor may represent the most important prerequisite for the issuance of a temporary injunction. Temporary injunctive relief will only be justified if the threatened irreparable harm may render the relief sought by the plaintiff ineffectual or impossible to grant at a later time.[5] The irreparable injury must be likely to occur. An adequate remedy at law, such as money damages, may provide sufficient compensation for an injury, rendering injunctive relief unnecessary.[6] In actual application, the irreparable harm standard is not as draconian as it first sounds. Most courts will find the requisite harm if the movant will be substantially hurt absent the injunctive relief and if movant's loss is difficult to calculate in monetary terms or involves particularly dear though technically compensable consequences (*e.g.*, injury or great risk to a loved one), or would result in waste if allowed to occur only to be recompensed by money damages. One respected commentator argues that any stringent form of the irreparable injury rule

3. *See, e.g., Robert W. Stark, Jr., Inc. v. New York Stock Exchange, Inc.,* 466 F.2d 743 (2d Cir.1972); *United States v. Veon,* 538 F.Supp. 237 (E.D.Cal.1982).

4. *See, e.g., Massachusetts Coalition of Citizens with Disabilities v. Civil Defense Agency & Office of Emergency Preparedness of Com. of Massachusetts,* 649 F.2d 71 (1st Cir.1981); *Allison v. Froehlke,* 470 F.2d 1123 (5th Cir.1972).

5. *Friendship Materials, Inc. v. Michigan Brick, Inc.,* 679 F.2d 100 (6th Cir. 1982); *National Tank Truck Carriers, Inc. v. Burke,* 608 F.2d 819 (1st Cir.1979).

6. *Nuclear–Chicago Corp. v. Nuclear Data, Inc.,* 465 F.2d 428 (7th Cir.1972); *Local Union 499 of International Brotherhood of Electrical Workers, AFL–CIO v. Iowa Light and Power Co.,* 224 F.Supp. 731 (S.D.Iowa 1964).

(*e.g.*, "what's a few deaths, we can put a value on them later") is itself "dead." [7]

Balancing of Hardships. The balance of hardships factor requires a court to weigh the hardship occurring to the plaintiff if the injunction is denied with the severity of the impact on the defendant, if the injunction is granted.[8] It makes sense that a temporary injunction should only be granted if it appears that more harm would result from its denial rather than from its being granted. If an injunctive order would create a significant burden for the defendant, which outweighs the relief provided the plaintiff, the injunction will be refused. Courts will grant temporary injunctive relief even if there is damage to the defendant if the injury is inconsiderable or may be adequately indemnified by bond.

Likelihood of Success. Courts require that plaintiff show some likelihood of success on their merits. The degree of success may vary depending on the jurisdiction and the circumstances of a case. The federal courts have created a bewildering number of phrases in an attempt to define "likelihood." Courts have described this degree of success as "reasonable certainty," "strong probability," "substantial probability," "clear showing of probable success," "high probability," "probability," "probable cause for success," "substantial likelihood," "reasonable likelihood," "probable chance," "reasonably good chance," "reasonable possibility," "possibility." [9] The most commonly acceptable phrase may be "a reasonable probability of success." It is clear that a plaintiff need not prove success to a certainty, but must establish a prima facie case.[10]

Public Interest. The nature of the public interest in a case is a final factor that bears upon the court's discretion in granting or denying the temporary injunction. The degree to which the grant or denial of the requested injunctive relief furthers or inhibits the public interest and the policy considerations that underlie the positions of either party influences the judge in determining which party should prevail. Public interest issues may arise in cases involving governmental agencies as well as rights between private parties. In cases involving private interests and not public interests, the court need not significantly rely on the impact the granting or denying of injunctive relief may have upon broad principles of public policy.

Equitable Defenses. The granting or denying of temporary injunctive relief depends on the trial court's exercise of equitable discretion. Traditional equitable defenses may influence the decision of the judge. Bad faith conduct, the absence of "clean hands," and laches constitute

7. *See* Douglas Laycock, The Death of the Irreparable Injury Rule, 103 Harv. L.Rev. 688 (1990).

8. *Omega Satellite Products Co. v. City of Indianapolis*, 694 F.2d 119 (7th Cir. 1982); *Blackwelder Furniture Co. v. Seilig Manufacturing Co.*, 550 F.2d 189 (4th Cir. 1977).

9. *See* 11 Charles A. Wright & Arthur R. Miller, Federal Practice and Procedure § 2948 (1973 and Supp.1994).

10. *Automated Marketing System, Inc. v. Martin*, 467 F.2d 1181 (10th Cir.1972); *Blackwelder Furniture Co. v. Seilig Manufacturing Co.*, 550 F.2d 189 (4th Cir.1977).

grounds that may bar the granting of injunctive relief. The notion that a plaintiff must "do equity" to receive equitable relief affects the thinking of the judge. In those cases where both the plaintiff and defendant have been involved in some misconduct, the party that has been involved in the more egregious behavior usually is barred from equitable relief.

Two general prerequisites for binding a person to an injunction are that: (1) the court have in personam jurisdiction over the person and (2) the defendant have notice of the injunctive order. Fed.R.Civ.R. 65(d) provides that an injunctive order is "binding only upon the parties to the action, their officers, their agents, their servants, employees, and attorneys. . . ." Persons who are not parties to the injunction or at privity with parties are not bound by a decree. The "privity" concept described in case law decisions appears to be synonymous with the individuals listed in Fed.R.Civ.P. 65(d) and corresponding state rules. A non-party cannot be bound to an order unless there exists sufficient connection between the non-party and the party to protect the rights and interests of the non-party.[11]

§ 12.5.4 Temporary Restraining Orders

A party may obtain a temporary restraining order under Fed. R.Civ.P. 65(b) to preserve the status quo until the hearing for a preliminary injunction can be conducted. The moving party must show that immediate and irreparable injury, loss, or damage will result before the adverse party or the party's attorney can be heard in opposition. The nature of the irreparable injury to a party will depend on the facts of a case. The three additional factors considered in granting temporary relief (balance of hardships, likelihood of success, and public interest) may or may not be required depending upon the jurisdiction. Fed. R.Civ.P. 65(d) explicitly provides for the granting of a temporary restraining order if the ground of immediate and irreparable harm has been established.

A temporary restraining order may be granted with or without notice. A party seeking an *ex parte* order must state to the court "the efforts, if any, which have been made to give notice of the reason supporting" the claim that notice should not be required.[12] Notice to the opposing party of an application for a temporary restraining order may be done formally through writing or informally through oral communication. The purpose for the notice is to provide the opposing party with an opportunity to be heard in opposition to the motion for a temporary restraining order at a specified time and place. Informal notice will usually be sufficient because time is a critical factor in seeking a restraining order. A telephone call made to the opposing party or lawyer will commonly suffice. Some form of notice will usually be required, except in extraordinary circumstances, to comply with the

11. *Regal Knitwear Co. v. N.L.R.B.*, 324 U.S. 9, 65 S.Ct. 478, 89 L.Ed. 661 (1945).

12. Fed.R.Civ.P. 65(b).

requisites for a fair hearing and with the spirit and letter of the applicable civil procedure rule or statute.

Temporary restraining orders may be granted without notice in emergency circumstances. These emergency situations are rare and unusual. An emergency situation justifying issuance of an *ex parte* restraining order exists if the order provides the sole method to preserve the rights of the moving party.[13] Another situation justifying a TRO without notice occurs when notice to the opposing party would exacerbate a situation and result in the adverse party acting in a manner that renders moot the need for the restraining order. Examples include an opposing party's threat to destroy disputed property or to remove property beyond the jurisdiction of the court. Other situations may require that notice be provided to the opposing party. A court may be unable to issue an *ex parte* order restraining a party's constitutional rights.

A party seeking a temporary restraining order will usually need to provide the court with the following documents:

1. A motion for a temporary restraining order.

2. An affidavit or verified complaint showing specific facts which establish immediate and irreparable injury, loss, or damage.

3. A written certification by the applicant's attorney explaining the notice provided the other side or the efforts, if any, which have been made to provide notice and a reason supporting a claim that notice should not be required.

4. A motion for a temporary or preliminary injunction.

5. A notice of motion or order to show cause for a temporary or preliminary injunction.

6. A summons and complaint commencing the litigation and detailing the injunctive claims.

7. Other documents. Local rules may require the submission of additional documents, such as an affidavit indicating whether any previous application has been made for a temporary restraining order. This information advises the judge whether a previous application has been made, the court or judge before whom it was made, the determination made at that time, and what new facts, if any, justify another request.

8. Security. Typically a bond or surety document will be required.

9. A proposed temporary restraining order.

The nature of information contained in an affidavit or verified complaint must persuade a court that reasons exist for issuing a tempo-

13. *Granny Goose Foods, Inc. v. Brotherhood of Teamsters & Auto Truck Drivers Local No. 70 of Alameda County,* 415 U.S. 423, 94 S.Ct. 1113, 39 L.Ed.2d 435 (1974).

rary restraining order.[14] The statements must be based on reliable information, factual in nature, to convince the judge to grant an order. Affidavits need not, however, meet the standards established by evidentiary rules regarding admissibility of information.

Fed.R.Civ.P. 65(d) requires that every restraining order be specific in terms, set forth the reasons for its issuance, and describe in reasonable detail the acts sought to be restrained. This rule also specifically provides that the description in the order not be made by reference to the complaint or other documents and that such incorporation by reference cannot satisfy the requirement that the restrained acts be described in sufficient detail. A restraining order should be drafted concisely and clearly, and should state the reason supporting its issuance. The restraining order must specifically describe in reasonable detail the acts prohibited or mandated. A non-specific restraining order may be necessary in situations in which the information needed to obtain details is known only to the party restrained or when the inclusion of specific information in the order would cause injury to the applicant.

The duration of a restraining order depends upon the law of the jurisdiction and the circumstances of the case. Procedural rules or statutes often prescribe a limited number of days for an order to remain in effect. Fed.R.Civ.P. 65(b) specifies that a restraining order expires at a time and date established by the judge in the order which time may not exceed ten days unless a party shows good cause for an extension for an additional ten days, or unless the restrained party consents to an extension for a longer period of time. The limited duration of a temporary restraining order reduces the possible harm caused by an order granted without a hearing and ensures an immediate injunction hearing.

Typically a TRO will continue until the judge makes a ruling after a hearing for the temporary injunction. If the terms of a TRO in federal court do not specify the duration, the order will automatically expire after ten days unless a party establishes good cause or the restrained party consents to a continuation. The party seeking an extension may need to obtain an extension during the life of the order. Fed.R.Civ.P. 65(b) requires a party to obtain an extension before the original TRO expires.

§ 12.5.5 Preliminary Injunctions

The purpose of a preliminary injunction is to protect the plaintiff from irreparable harm and to preserve the status quo until a trial on the merits so that the impact of any judgment shall not be adversely affected by the conduct of the parties during litigation. This need to preserve the court's power and the judicial process from being rendered futile by a party's action or inaction may be the most compelling reason to grant a

14. *See Fuentes v. Shevin*, 407 U.S. 67, 92 S.Ct. 1983, 32 L.Ed.2d 556 (1972), *rehearing denied* 409 U.S. 902, 93 S.Ct. 177, 34 L.Ed.2d 165 (1972).

preliminary injunction. Various jurisdictions refer to a preliminary injunction by different labels. Some jurisdictions describe this form of injunctive relief as a temporary injunction, an interlocutory injunction, a provisional injunction, an interim injunction, an impermanent injunction, an injunction *pendente lite,* and other synonymous phrases. A preliminary injunction differs from a temporary restraining order in that it may not be issued *ex parte* and may remain in effect for a longer time. A preliminary injunction has all the force and effect of a permanent injunction and may be granted only after an evidentiary hearing.

A rule or statute will typically outline the process that must be followed to obtain a preliminary injunction. Fed.R.Civ.P. 65(a)(1) states that no preliminary injunction shall be issued without notice to the adverse party. Sufficient notice may be provided by a written notice of motion or by an order to show cause directed to the adverse party. Fed.R.Civ.P. 65(a)(2) also requires that a hearing be held on the application for a preliminary injunction.

A party has a right to a hearing before a preliminary injunction may be granted against that party.[15] The federal rules do not dictate the requirements for the notice nor the details of the hearing for a preliminary injunction. In situations where no specific rule or statute prescribes the mechanics of a preliminary injunction procedure the general provisions from that jurisdiction which regulate notice and hearings will apply. "Notice" implies that a party will be provided with sufficient notification and a fair opportunity to oppose the application for a preliminary injunction.[16] "Hearing" requires the trial of an issue or issues that include an opportunity to present evidence and arguments.[17] Fed.R.Civ.P. 6(d) requires a minimum of five days notice before a hearing may be held. Shorter notice may breach due process requirements. If a party wants a hearing scheduled with less than five days notice, either a court order must be obtained reducing the time or consent must be obtained from the adverse party stipulating to the earlier date.

Preliminary Injunction Documents. The documents necessary to obtain a preliminary injunction resemble the documents needed to obtain a temporary restraining order. They include:

1. A notice of motion or order to show cause and a motion for a temporary injunction. The motion should specify the grounds for the preliminary injunction and the parties and specific acts sought to be enjoined.

15. *See Granny Goose Foods, Inc. v. Brotherhood of Teamsters & Auto Truck Drivers Local No. 70 of Alameda County,* 415 U.S. 423, 94 S.Ct. 1113, 39 L.Ed.2d 435 (1974).

16. *Marshall Durbin Farms, Inc. v. National Farmers Organization, Inc.,* 446 F.2d 353 (5th Cir.1971); *Carter–Wallace Inc. v. Davis–Edwards Pharmacal Corp.,* 443 F.2d 867 (2d Cir.1971), *on remand* 341 F.Supp. 1303 (E.D.N.Y.1972), *judgment affirmed* 474 F.2d 529 (2d Cir.1972), *cert. denied* 412 U.S. 929, 93 S.Ct. 2753, 37 L.Ed.2d 156 (1973).

17. *Sims v. Greene,* 161 F.2d 87, 88–89 (3d Cir.1947).

2. A proposed preliminary injunction order detailing the specific relief requested.

3. A summons and complaint which describe the claims for injunctive relief.

4. Affidavits or a verified complaint to provide the information supporting the need for the injunction. A court may grant a preliminary injunction on the basis of written sworn statements. Fed.R.Civ.P. 6 and similar state rules require that written statements be served no later than one day before a hearing. Considerations regarding the evidentiary value and impact of affidavits and verified information discussed in section 12.5.4 regarding applications for temporary restraining orders apply with equal force to preliminary injunction hearings.

5. Security in the form of a bond or surety.

6. A memorandum of law explaining the legal basis for the relief sought.

7. Proposed findings of fact and conclusions of law granting of the temporary injunction.

The party opposing a motion for a preliminary injunction may also submit affidavits and a memorandum of law in opposition to the motion.

Preliminary Injunction Procedures. A preliminary injunction hearing may involve oral testimony in court or deposition testimony obtained through discovery. Testimonial evidence may be preferred if there exists a factual controversy which may more easily be resolved by the judge after hearing and observing the demeanor of witnesses. Some situations do not permit live testimony because of time deadlines. Some judges discourage oral testimony to avoid having to hear the same testimony again at the trial. Depositions provide another means to present the judge with essential information through direct and cross-examination. Preliminary injunction hearings may include a combination of evidence submitted by affidavit, verified pleadings, discovery responses, deposition testimony, and oral testimony during the hearing.

A conference convened to consider a motion for a temporary restraining order or a hearing scheduled pursuant to a motion by a restrained party to modify or dissolve an injunction may be converted into a preliminary injunction hearing. If the parties can offer evidence to the same degree as at a properly scheduled preliminary injunction hearing, a temporary restraining order conference or a modification/dissolution hearing may be properly declared to be a preliminary injunction hearing. This conversion should only occur if parties have sufficiently prepared and if they have a full opportunity to present evidence and arguments.

Usually the court in granting or denying a preliminary injunction must prepare findings of fact and conclusions of law regarding the grounds for its decision. Fed.R.Civ.P. 52(a) and similar state rules require the judge to file such written findings and conclusions to support the decision. Either party may submit proposed findings and conclusions to assist the judge.

A party to a preliminary injunction hearing may request that the trial of the action on the merits be advanced and consolidated with the hearing on the motion. Fed.R.Civ.P. 65(a)(2) provides that before or after the commencement of the preliminary injunction hearing the court may order the trial to be advanced and consolidated. Ordinarily such a consolidation is not appropriate because the parties lack sufficient time for trial preparation and discovery. Consolidation is inappropriate if the facts and issues raised at the preliminary injunction hearing will differ from those raised at the main action.

This provision is included in Fed.R.Civ.P. 65 and similar state rules intended to encourage the practice of accelerating the trial and eliminating the situation of basing preliminary injunction on partial evidence. A valid objection raised by one party may be sufficient to preclude an accelerated proceeding. A court on its own motion may transform a preliminary injunction proceeding into a consolidated hearing at any time provided the parties receive fair notice and an opportunity for a full hearing.[18] Limited circumstances may justify a court in issuing a final adjudication in a case on its own motion, such as a frivolous complaint or motion.

Fed.R.Civ.P. 65(a)(2) further attempts to achieve judicial economy by automatically rendering admissible at the trial all evidence received at the preliminary injunction hearing. This provision makes it unnecessary for a party to repeat testimony at the trial although such duplication will be necessary to provide the finder of fact with the essential information, to allow a factfinder to observe the credibility of witnesses, to add details to the facts, and to permit a different judge to hear the facts first hand.

A party's right to a jury trial is preserved if trial is consolidated with the preliminary injunction hearing. If a case involving injunctive relief includes issues triable by a jury as of right, any consolidated trial must preserve these rights. Fed.R.Civ.P. 65(a)(2) recognizes this principle by expressly stating that the rule relating to consolidation must be construed and applied in a way that protects a party's right to a jury trial. This provision does not restrict the trial court's power to grant a preliminary injunction based on issues that ultimately will be determined by a jury. A judge may properly decide a jury issue in granting or denying a preliminary injunction, although that issue must be decided by a jury at the trial on the merits.[19]

The court's preliminary injunction decision does not bind subsequent judges. The findings of fact and conclusions of law made by a judge after the preliminary injunction hearing become part of the record

18. *See University of Texas v. Camenisch,* 451 U.S. 390, 101 S.Ct. 1830, 68 L.Ed.2d 175 (1981).

19. *Beacon Theatres, Inc. v. Westover,* 359 U.S. 500, 79 S.Ct. 948, 3 L.Ed.2d 988 (1959).

but are not binding at the time of trial. A preliminary decision by a judge does not adjudicate the merits of the issues because a preliminary injunction hearing is only a hearing and not a trial.

§ 12.6 MOTION FOR PRETRIAL EVIDENCE RULINGS

Motions for pretrial evidentiary rulings are usually made to prevent the opposing side in the action from even offering objectionable material in evidence because of the prejudicial effect the mere disclosure of the evidence or its foundation would have. These motions are commonly called "motions *in limine*," which literally translated from Latin means "at the very beginning," or "at the threshold." The name is somewhat apt, for these motions are typically brought shortly before the beginning of trial, at the final pretrial conference, with the filing of the final pretrial order, or at the commencement of voir dire.

Generally, a motion *in limine* will seek two related rulings: first, a ruling on the admissibility of the questioned evidence, and second, an order directing counsel not to refer to the evidence and to instruct all witnesses not to mention the evidence once it is ruled inadmissible. The second ruling is what justifies an *in limine* ruling. Unless there is some danger of prejudice if the second ruling is not entered, there is no compelling reason for making the evidentiary ruling prematurely.

The motion *in limine* is most frequently used to bar inquiry that poses a substantial danger of eliciting evidence that is clearly prejudicial and inadmissible, or evidence whose probative value is far surpassed by its potential prejudicial effect.[1] Such an exclusionary motion seeks to forbid the asking of a prejudicial question or the use of innuendo to allude to the prejudicial information. Typical examples would be motions to forbid questioning of a party concerning previous arrests, or extramarital affairs. Most of the evidence sought to be excluded at trial is somewhat less inflammatory and generally falls under the headings of: references casting doubt upon a party's character; collateral source payments; liability insurance coverage; subsequent remedial measures; settlement discussions; and the existence of other litigation. *In limine* motions to exclude evidence on these grounds are equally available to plaintiffs and defendants.

The rules of civil procedure do not specifically provide for such motions. Most courts have now found sufficient authority for motions *in limine* in the inherent power of the courts to supervise trial and pretrial proceedings.[2] In the federal system, that inherent power is codified by Fed.R.Evid. 103(d) & 403 and Fed.R.Civ.P. 16.

§ 12.6

1. *See New Jersey v. Portash,* 440 U.S. 450, 99 S.Ct. 1292, 59 L.Ed.2d 501 (1979) (error for trial court to permit use of immunized grand jury testimony for impeachment); *United States v. Cook,* 608 F.2d 1175, 1186 (9th Cir.1979), *cert. denied* 444 U.S. 1034, 100 S.Ct. 706, 62 L.Ed.2d 670 (1980) (although Rule 403 exclusion is a proper subject for *in limine* motion, defendant's previous robbery convictions were admissible for impeachment).

2. *See, e.g., Burrus v. Silhavy,* 155 Ind. App. 558, 293 N.E.2d 794 (1973); *Sperberg*

Whether to use a motion *in limine* and the means of employing it will vary from case to case. Commentators are nearly unanimous in describing the motion as underused. As cases become more complex, and as the judiciary takes a firmer hand in controlling court dockets, motions *in limine* have become increasingly useful. The motion gives an opportunity to have important evidentiary questions resolved with adequate forewarning, sufficient legal analysis and research, and an opportunity for the court to reflect upon the competing interests.

§ 12.7 MOTIONS TO VACATE DEFAULTS

Motions to vacate default judgments frequently become involved in pretrial procedures. A client may permit a default judgment to be entered before consulting and retaining an attorney and—presto—something immediately must be done about that judgment. All is not necessarily lost if a default is obtained, and the litigation is not over. Relief may be more than possible in certain circumstances.

Defaults and default judgments frequently cause motions for relief from orders and judgments. By definition, these final orders usually occur when a party has failed to defend an action. Consequently, once the order is entered the only recourse available to the defaulted party is a motion for relief from the default or default judgment pursuant to Fed.R.Civ.P. 55(c) and 60(b) or similar state rules. Although appeal is another available option, assuming the party learns of the judgment while it is appealable, appeal is not entirely satisfactory. Since the defaulted party was not a part of the trial court proceedings, the record on appeal is unlikely to urge reversal. Appellate courts are generally not receptive to appeals raising issues which have not been presented to the trial court. Thus, relief should usually be sought from the default in the trial court.

Fed.R.Civ.P. 55(c) provides that the trial court may, for good cause shown, set aside an entry of default and, if a default judgment has been entered, set aside the judgment pursuant to Rule 60(b). The distinction between default and default judgment is important, and is frequently either overlooked or confused by courts and lawyers. Default occurs when, pursuant to Rule 55, a party obtains an adjudication that an opposing party has failed to appear in the action. A default is obtained by submitting proof to the clerk that the opposing party has "failed to plead or otherwise defend." Upon such a showing, the clerk must enter default in favor of the moving party.[1] This default settles the liability issues of the case on the merits, but is not a judgment. The default is not an adjudication of the damage issues, and a judgment cannot be rendered until damages are proved.

v. Goodyear Tire & Rubber Co., 519 F.2d 708 (6th Cir.1975), *cert. denied* 423 U.S. 987, 96 S.Ct. 395, 46 L.Ed.2d 303 (1975).

§ 12.7

1. Fed.R.Civ.P. 55(a).

Once a default is entered, a default judgment may be obtained in either of two ways. Where the claim sought is for a "sum certain for or a sum which can be by computation made certain," the clerk may enter a default judgment.[2] Typically the lawyer will submit a fact affidavit from the client explaining the sum certain and may attach as exhibits supporting documents authenticated in the affidavit. Default judgment may also be entered by the court in cases where the amount at issue is certain and must be entered by the court. Where the sum is uncertain, a hearing or other fact-finding process is required.[3] If the party against whom default is sought has appeared in the action, the moving party must give written notice of the application for default judgment.[4] The court may conduct any hearing necessary to determine the amount of damages or any other matter in the litigation. Typically the hearing will be scheduled as a motion hearing with the client and other witnesses testifying and bills introduced to prove damages. Unlike the ministerial entry of default or sum certain default judgment by the clerk, the court has discretion to grant default judgment and determine the amount. In effect, the default judgment proceedings before the court become a trial on the issue of damages, even though the defaulted party is absent. It is difficult—but not impossible for some—to lose any proceeding where there is no opposition, and a default judgment hearing is no exception. Unless bizarre or erroneous theories of damage are pursued, reasonable damages will be recovered.

Attack on a default judgment may be made in two ways. First, the substance of the default may be challenged, showing that it was not properly granted. Second, the order or judgment can be attacked using the grounds contained in Fed.R.Civ.P. 60(a) and (b). The first option will not normally be available because it is not often that the opposing party will fail to follow the rules concerning defaults (the rules are not complex and even private practitioners earning less than $2,000 gross a year can comply with them). If a claimant fails to give the 3–day notice required by Fed.R.Civ.P. 55(c) when the defendant has appeared, the motion for relief will be granted. Although "appearance" normally contemplates an answer or motion, courts will also require the 3–day notice to be given to parties who have written to the claimant or had other contact with the claimant, considering this contact to constitute a constructive appearance.[5] A direct attack on the default is also appropriate to challenge inherent error in the judgment itself. This may arise if the damages are awarded without adequate evidentiary support, if a legally erroneous theory of recovery is allowed, or if the judge was never properly sworn in.

If the default judgment is properly entered, the movant must show the applicability of Fed.R.Civ.P. 60(a) or (b) to obtain relief from the

2. Fed.R.Civ.P. 55(b)(1).

3. Fed.R.Civ.P. 55(b)(2).

4. Fed.R.Civ.P. 55(b)(2).

5. *See Kinnear Corp. v. Crawford Door Sales Co.*, 49 F.R.D. 3 (D.S.C.1970); *Dalminter, Inc. v. Jessie Edwards, Inc.*, 27 F.R.D. 491 (S.D.Tex.1961).

judgment. Grounds for obtaining relief under Federal Rule 60 and similar state rules include: clerical mistakes, other mistakes of inadvertence or surprise, excusable neglect, newly discovered evidence, fraud, misrepresentation or misconduct of opposing party, a void judgment, a satisfied judgment, or any other reason justifying relief. The most common ground is usually excusable neglect, which covers client misunderstanding of the nature of a summons and complaint or their failure to timely contact an attorney. Typically there are time limits regarding when a party may assert one or more of these grounds. The time may be stated in the rule as a reasonable time or a one year period.

Where applicability of Rule 60 is shown, the court retains discretion to deny the motion. As a practical matter, however, defaults are disfavored, and a trial on the merits is strongly preferred by the courts. Thus, denial of a motion to set aside a default after the movant has established one of the grounds of Rule 60 is likely to be viewed as an abuse of discretion.[6]

In addition to establishing that Rule 60 applies, the party seeking to set aside a default or default judgment must establish that there is a valid defense on the merits and that the claimant will not be substantially prejudiced by vacation of the default.[7] The requirement of establishing a meritorious defense is obvious, and may be accomplished by submitting a proposed answer with the motion. Some courts require that a proposed answer be submitted as one of the motion papers. The courts have little interest in permitting a party to avoid and delay the inevitable. The requirement of showing an absence of prejudice to the claimant is not as onerous as it may sound. The courts require "substantial" prejudice to exist.[8] The fact that the claimant will have to try the case on the merits, a burden inherent in vacating any default, is clearly insufficient prejudice to prevent vacating the default. Additionally, if there are means to ameliorate the prejudice, the court will consider using them. For example, if the claimant incurred significant expense in obtaining the default, the court can require the payment of those expenses as a condition of vacating the default.

The most frequent bases for finding substantial prejudice are the death or absence of key witnesses, the loss of other evidence, or a judge who has been misplaced. If these factors are not present, it is unlikely that substantial prejudice will be found.[9] Even if witnesses have disappeared, courts have refused to find substantial prejudice, and have insisted on trial on the merits.

6. *Gill v. Stolow,* 240 F.2d 669, 670 (2d Cir.1957) (non-willful default should ordinarily be set aside on timely, supported motion.)

7. *Medunic v. Lederer,* 533 F.2d 891 (3d Cir.1976); *Hengel v. Hyatt,* 312 Minn. 317, 252 N.W.2d 105 (Minn.1977).

8. *Tozer v. Charles A. Krause Milling Co.,* 189 F.2d 242 (3d Cir.1951).

9. *See generally* 10 Charles A. Wright & Arthur R. Miller, Federal Practice and Procedure § 2699 (2d ed. 1983 and Supp.1994).

PRACTICE PROBLEMS

1. Hot Dog Enterprises sues Tri–Chem, as well as the general contractor who constructed the building in Kansas and the architect who designed the building in Kansas.

(a) You represent the general contractor. Plan a motion for a separate trial. Outline a memorandum in support of the motion. Draft a motion. Draft a proposed order.

(b) You represent the architect. Plan a motion for a separate trial. Outline the memorandum in support of the motion. Draft a motion. Draft a proposed order.

(c) Will these motions for a separate trial be granted? Explain.

2. Assume in *Luger v. Shade* (Case H), that Luger sues Shade and Develco but not Gotbucks. Gotbucks then starts a separate suit for declaratory judgment declaring him to be the true owner of the townhouse. The Luger suit is filed in federal district court in Beachstate while the Gotbucks suit is filed in federal district court in Gothamstate, where Gotbucks resides.

(a) As counsel for Luger, plan a motion to consolidate the actions. Since the Gotbucks suit is in Gothamstate, what must first be done? What if Gotbucks also moves for consolidation in Gothamstate? With competing motions, who wins?

(b) Draft such a motion.

(c) Outline Gotbucks' response to Luger's motion to consolidate.

3. You represent Shop Format, a defendant in *Rheinwald v. Whirling Dervish Lathes* (Case I).

(a) Plan a motion for a separate trial and outline the memorandum in support.

(b) Draft such a motion.

4. You represent Develco in *Luger v. Shade* (Case H).

(a) Plan a motion for separate trials.

(b) Draft such a motion and outline a memorandum in support.

(c) Will the motion be granted?

5. Hot Dog Enterprises sues Tri–Chem. You represent Tri–Chem.

(a) Plan a motion to bifurcate the issues of liability and damages.

(b) Outline the memorandum in support.

(c) Draft such a motion.

(d) Draft a protective order.

(e) Will the motion be granted? Explain.

6. In *Miyamoto v. Snow Cat* (Case B).

(a) As counsel for defendant Snow Cat, plan a motion to bifurcate the issue of liability and damages. Outline the memorandum in support.

(b) Draft such a motion.

(c) As plaintiff's lawyer, outline a memorandum in opposition to bifurcation.

7. Hot Dog Enterprise sues Tri–Chem properly in federal district court. Several days after serving and filing the federal lawsuit, you, as the attorney for HDE, decide you made a mistake and should have brought the lawsuit in an appropriate state court. Tri–Chem has not answered or served any motion. What can you do?

8. Hot Dog Enterprises sues Tri–Chem in federal district court. Tri–Chem serves an answer on HDE. You represent Tri–Chem. The attorney for HDE telephones you and tells you that HDE plans to dismiss the federal district court action and prefers to file a lawsuit in state court in Kansas. How would you respond to the attorney's request for a stipulation? Why?

9. Hot Dog Enterprises sue Tri–Chem, and Tri–Chem answers. You, as the attorney for Tri–Chem, refuse to stipulate to a voluntary dismissal by HDE of the lawsuit. HDE brings a motion asking the court to dismiss the action. The judge asks you why you oppose the motion? How do you respond? Why?

10. Hot Dog Enterprises sues Tri–Chem, and Tri–Chem answers. Hot Dog Enterprises appears at a conference scheduled by the federal district court to discuss settlement and discovery, but refuses to discuss settlement. The court imposes a discovery schedule. HDE responds to some but not all of the discovery requests by Tri–Chem. Tri–Chem brings a summary judgment motion. HDE opposes the motion on the grounds that the summary judgment motion is premature because discovery has not been completed. The judge denies the motion and orders HDE to complete discovery. HDE continues to refuse to respond to all proper discovery requests by Tri–Chem. You represent Tri–Chem. What can you do? Why?

11. In *Vasquez v. Hot Dog Enterprises*, the plaintiff Juanita Vasquez submits interrogatories and requests for production on defendant HDE and schedules depositions after the discovery cut-off date established by the court. Plaintiff Vasquez also serves defendant HDE affidavits in opposition to its motion for summary judgment two weeks after the deadline established by

local court rule. Plaintiff Vasquez further fails to appear at the pretrial conference. You represent HDE. What can you do? Why?

12. Juanita Vasquez first sues Hot Dog Enterprises in state court with claims based upon violation of state laws and breach of contract. The plaintiff dismisses this case voluntarily and without prejudice. Juanita Vasquez then sues Hot Dog Enterprises again, this time in federal district court alleging violations of federal statutory law, state law, and breach of contract. You represent Hot Dog Enterprises. How may you respond to the second complaint? Why?

13. Hot Dog Enterprises sues Tri–Chem.

(a) You represent Hot Dog Enterprises. Do you prefer a trial before a judge or a jury? Why?

(b) You represent Tri–Chem. Do you prefer a trial before a judge or a jury? Why?

14. Juanita Vasquez sues Hot Dog Enterprises.

(a) You represent Juanita Vasquez. Do you prefer a trial before a judge or a jury? Why?

(b) You represent Hot Dog Enterprises. Do you prefer a trial before a judge or a jury? Why?

15. Briefly review the following case files:

Hot Dog Enterprises vs. Tri–Chem (Case A)

Pozdak vs. Summit Insurance Company (Case B)

Vasquez vs. Hot Dog Enterprises (Case F)

Which of these cases will most likely involve successful summary judgment motions brought by either party to obtain a judgment? Why?

16. Hot Dog Enterprises sues Tri–Chem for violation of federal and state laws, negligence, and products liability. You represent Tri–Chem. General counsel for Tri–Chem asks you how you plan to defend a case and whether you will attempt to bring a summary judgment motion seeking to dispose of any of the causes of action or claims for relief. What do you say to general counsel? Explain.

(a) Assume you represent Hot Dog Enterprises, and the general counsel for Hot Dog Enterprises asks you the same question. What do you say? Explain.

17. Juanita Vasquez sues Hot Dog Enterprises. The complaint includes the following causes of action and claims for relief:

(1) Violation of the federal anti-discrimination acts, 42 U.S.C.A. § 2000e,

(2) Violation of the State Human Rights Act,

(3) Breach of written employment contract,

(4) Breach of oral employment contract,

(5) Breach of contract based upon personnel handbook,

(6) Breach of contract based upon good faith and fair dealing, and

(7) Punitive damages for willful and malicious conduct by defendant.

You represent Hot Dog Enterprises.

(a) Prepare a discovery and motion plan seeking to dismiss as many causes of action as possible through summary judgment.

(b) Assume the facts are established through discovery in an affidavit as stated in the case file. Which causes of action and claims would you seek to dispose of by motion? Why?

18. Plan a summary judgment motion based on a case provided by your instructor.

(a) Outline a memorandum in support of a summary judgment motion assigned by your instructor.

(b) Draft a motion for summary judgment and all supporting documents based on the case provided by your instructor.

19. *State Farm Fire & Casualty Co. v. Tashire,* 386 U.S. 523, 87 S.Ct. 1199, 18 L.Ed.2d 270 (1967). Early one September morning in 1964, a Greyhound bus proceeding northward through Shasta County, California, collided with a southbound pickup truck. Two of the passengers aboard the bus were killed. Thirty-three others were injured, as were the bus driver, the driver of the truck and its lone passenger. One of the dead and ten of the injured passengers were Canadians; the rest of the individuals involved were citizens of five American States. The ensuing litigation led to the present case, which raises important questions concerning administration of the interpleader remedy in the federal courts.

The litigation began when four of the injured passengers filed suit in California state courts, seeking damages in excess of $1,000,000. Named as defendants were Greyhound Lines, Inc., a California corporation; Theron Nauta, the bus driver; Ellis Clark, who drove the truck; and Kenneth Glasgow, the passenger in the truck who was apparently its owner as well. Each of the individual defendants was a citizen and resident of Oregon. Before these cases could come to trial and before other suits were filed in California or elsewhere, petitioner, State Farm Fire &

Casualty Company, an Illinois corporation, brought this action in the nature of interpleader in the United States District Court for the District of Oregon.

In its complaint State Farm asserted that at the time of the Shasta County collision it had in force an insurance policy with respect to Ellis Clark, driver of the truck, providing for bodily injury liability up to $10,000 per person and $20,000 per occurrence and for legal representation of Clark in actions covered by the policy. It asserted that actions already filed in California and others which it anticipated would be filed far exceeded in aggregate damages sought the amount of its maximum liability under the policy. Accordingly, it paid into court the sum of $20,000 and asked the court (1) to require all claimants to establish their claims against Clark and his insurer in this single proceeding and in no other, and (2) to discharge State Farm from all further obligations under its policy—including its duty to defend Clark in lawsuits arising from the accident. Alternatively, State Farm expressed its conviction that the policy issued to Clark excluded from coverage accidents resulting from his operation of a truck which belonged to another and was being used in the business of another. The complaint, therefore, requested that the court decree that the insurer owed no duty to Clark and was not liable on the policy, and it asked the court to refund the $20,000 deposit.

Joined as defendants were Clark, Glasgow, Nauta, Greyhound Lines, and each of the prospective claimants. Jurisdiction was predicated upon 28 U.S.C.A. § 1335, the federal interpleader statute, and upon general diversity of citizenship, there being diversity between two or more of the claimants to the fund and between State Farm and all of the named defendants.

(a) You represent Petitioner State Farm Fire & Casualty Co. Plan the interpleader action.

(b) Draft all necessary interpleader documents.

(c) As judge, decide whether the interpleader action is proper. Do you agree with the Supreme Court?

20. *LASA Per L' Industria Del Marmo Societa Per Azioni of Lasa, Italy v. Southern Builders, Inc. of Tenn.*, 45 F.R.D. 435 (W.D.Tenn.1967), *reversed* 414 F.2d 143 (6th Cir.1969). Southern Builders, Inc. of Tennessee, City of Memphis and Continental Casualty Co. have moved to dismiss a cross-claim filed against them by Alexander Marble and Tile Co., a partnership. A.L. Aydelott and A.L. Aydelott and Associates, Inc. have filed a motion to dismiss a third party complaint filed against them by this same partnership. The contentions are that the cross-claim and third party complaint are not authorized by the Federal Rules of Civil Procedure....

The original complaint was filed by an Italian corporation, referred to herein, for brevity, as "LASA." This complaint, twice amended and supplemented, alleges in substance as follows. Southern Builders, a Tennessee corporation, as principal contractor, entered into a contract in 1962 with the City to build a city hall and under the contract obligated itself to the City to pay for all labor and materials. Southern Builders procured and furnished to the City a statutory performance and payment bond, with Continental Casualty as surety, under which Southern Builders obligated itself to the City to perform the contract and to pay for all labor and materials. Alexander Marble and Tile Co., a partnership, whose partners are Tennessee residents, together with Marble International, Inc., a Texas corporation, as joint venturers, entered into a subcontract with Southern Builders under which they were to supply all marble and anchoring devices and install the marble. Alexander then contracted with LASA to supply to it all of the marble for a contract price of $468,641.26. The marble was supplied as agreed, and there was a balance due of $127,240.80.... The City improperly released retainages to the principal contractor, Southern Builders. LASA therefore sues Alexander ... Marble International, Southern Builders, Continental Casualty and the City for the alleged balance due.

To this original complaint Alexander (partnership and corporation) filed an answer and counterclaim ... [in which] they contend that the actual net contract price for the marble was only $265,050.00; that, after LASA had failed to ship marble as agreed and had threatened to cease shipments, the price was then under duress increased, first to $336,030.00 and then to $370,686.90; that a total of $406,967.74 has actually been paid to LASA; that much of the marble that was shipped arrived late, was broken, or was of the wrong type; and that LASA had failed to ship all the marble it was obligated to ship. Alexander by this counterclaim sues LASA for overpayment of the contract price and for unliquidated damages for failure to ship marble as agreed.

To this original complaint, Continental Casualty and Southern Builders have filed answers and Southern Builders has filed a counterclaim. They aver that Southern Builders is obligated to pay only "just and valid" claims for labor and materials and that LASA has no such claim; aver that nothing is owed LASA for marble delivered and installed on this job; deny that the City improperly released any retainages; and aver that LASA failed to ship marble as agreed. Southern Builders by its counterclaim sues LASA for all damages to it because of LASA's failure to ship marble as agreed to Alexander.

Alexander (partnership) has filed a cross-claim against Southern Builders, Continental Casualty and the City ... for a balance alleged to be due under its subcontract with Southern Builders.

In the same cross-claim, it further averred that Southern Builders, under the insistence of the architect, A.L. Aydelott, hindered Alexander in the performance of the subcontract.... It is further averred that Southern Builders, under the insistence of Aydelott, wrongfully terminated the subcontract, forced Alexander off the job, and brought in another subcontractor which was allowed to finish the job not in accordance with the original specifications (as Alexander had sought) and at an inflated price. It is further averred that Southern Builders and Aydelott injured the business reputation of Alexander by publicly blaming Alexander for many ills not its fault and which were the fault of Southern Builders and Aydelott. Alexander, in this cross-claim, accordingly also sues only Southern Builders for unliquidated damages, actual and punitive.

Southern Builders and Continental Casualty have filed answers to Alexander's cross-claim against them, and Southern Builders has filed ... cross-claims against Alexander for any amount it is held to be liable to LASA in the original action. Southern Builders further cross-claims against Alexander for unliquidated damages for not maintaining progress schedules, for faulty materials and workmanship, for overdrawing money pursuant to false project information, and failing generally to follow the specifications, the subcontract, and the general contract.

Alexander has also filed a third-party complaint, which has been once amended, against A.L. Aydelott and Associates, Inc. and against Aydelott, individually, who is its principal officer (hereinafter collectively referred to as "Aydelott") alleging that they had the architectural contract with the city.... It is alleged that Aydelott negligently provided improper specifications and insisted they be followed; negligently failed to require Southern Builders to properly perform its work; wrongfully required Alexander to install marble in inclement weather; willfully refused to approve Alexander's estimates for work done; wrongfully directed Southern Builders to terminate the subcontract, allowed the new subcontractor at an inflated price; wrongfully misinterpreted the specifications and the subcontract; and wrongfully and maliciously injured Alexander's business reputation. Alexander sues in this amended third-party complaint for unliquidated actual and punitive damages under the general law and, under a Tennessee statute, for treble damages for inducing Southern Builders to breach the subcontract.

(a) Diagram the parties, pleadings, and motions in this case. (And you thought first year exam questions were unrealistic.)

(b) As counsel for A.L. Aydelott and A.L. Aydelott and Associates, plan the motion to dismiss the third-party complaint.

(c) Draft such a motion and a proposed order, and outline a supporting memorandum.

(d) As judge, decide whether what all has happened is proper (you cannot disqualify yourself).

21. *Parker v. Twentieth Century–Fox Film Corp.*, 3 Cal.3d 176, 89 Cal.Rptr. 737, 474 P.2d 689 (1970). Plaintiff is well known as an actress, and in the contract between plaintiff and defendant is sometimes referred to as the "Artist." Under the contract, dated August 6, 1965, plaintiff was to play the female lead in defendant's contemplated production of a motion picture entitled "Bloomer Girl." The contract provided that defendant would pay plaintiff a minimum "guaranteed compensation" of $53,571.42 per week for 14 weeks commencing May 23, 1966, for a total of $750,000. Prior to May 1966 defendant decided not to produce the picture and by a letter dated April 4, 1966, it notified plaintiff of that decision and that it would not "comply with our obligations to you under" the written contract.

By the same letter and with the professed purpose "to avoid any damage to you," defendant instead offered to employ plaintiff as the leading actress in another film tentatively entitled "Big Country, Big Man" (hereinafter, "Big Country"). The compensation offered was identical, as were 31 of the 34 numbered provisions or articles of the original contract. Unlike "Bloomer Girl," however, which was to have been a musical production, "Big Country" was a dramatic "western type" movie. "Bloomer Girl" was to have been filmed in California; "Big Country" was to be produced in Australia. Also, certain terms in the proffered contract varied from those of the original. Plaintiff was given one week within which to accept; she did not and the offer lapsed. Plaintiff then commenced this action seeking recovery of the agreed guaranteed compensation.

The complaint sets forth two causes of action. The first is for money due under the contract; the second, based upon the same allegations as the first, is for damages resulting from defendant's breach of contract. Defendant in its answer admits the existence and validity of the contract, that plaintiff complied with all the conditions, covenants, and promises and stood ready to complete the performance, and that defendant breached and "anticipatorily repudiated" the contract. It denies, however, that any money is due to plaintiff either under the contract or as a result of its breach, and pleads as an affirmative defense to both causes of action plaintiff's allegedly deliberate failure to mitigate damages, asserting that she unreasonably refused to accept its offer of the leading role in "Big Country."

(a) As Plaintiff Parker's attorney, plan a motion for summary judgment.

(b) Draft such a motion and include all necessary supporting papers, a proposed order, and outline the legal memorandum in support.

(c) Representing the defendant movie company, outline your memorandum in opposition to summary judgment. What actions can you take to keep material facts in dispute (without breaching legal ethics, of course).

(d) As judge, decide.

22. *Alderman v. Baltimore & Ohio R. Co.*, 113 F.Supp. 881 (S.D.W.Va.1953). Plaintiff ... brings this action against defendant ... to recover for personal injuries sustained by her as a result of the derailment of one of defendant's trains near Adrian, West Virginia, on February 14, 1952.

Plaintiff was not a fare-paying passenger. She was traveling on a trip pass, which afforded her free transportation.... The following conditions were printed on the pass: "In consideration of the issuance of this free pass, I hereby assume all risk of personal injury and loss of or of damage to property from whatever causes arising, and release the company from liability therefor, and I hereby declare that I am not prohibited by law from receiving free transportation and that this pass will be lawfully used."

Plaintiff in her original complaint charged defendant with negligence in the maintenance of its tracks and the operation of its train. After a pre-trial conference, at which the legal effect of the release from liability contained in the pass was discussed, plaintiff filed an amended complaint charging defendant with willful or wanton conduct.

On the basis of the amended pleadings and supporting affidavits filed by defendant, defendant moved for summary judgment under Rule 56 ....

It is undisputed that the derailment was caused by a break in one of the rails as the train was passing over the track. It is also shown by defendant's affidavits, and not denied, that the break in the rail was due to a transverse fissure inside the cap of the rail, which broke vertically under the weight of the train; that such a fissure is not visible upon inspection; that such defects occur in both new and old rails; and that a visual inspection was in fact made of this particular rail the day preceding the accident and the defect was not discovered.

(a) What information can plaintiff introduce by affidavit to avoid summary judgment?

(b) Draft the affidavit.

(c) If plaintiff's knowledge is not sufficient to refute defendant's affidavits, what can plaintiff do to avoid summary judgment? Outline the memorandum and draft any necessary motions or supporting papers to do it.

23. You represent the plaintiff in *Luger v. Shade* (Case H). You hear through your investigator that Shade is thinking of emulating other noted big-time white collar criminals and skipping off to a foreign dictatorship that lacks an extradition treaty with the United States. However, Shade reputedly has large assets in Pine Island and his soon-to-be ex-woman friend will execute an affidavit confirming the rumor.

(a) Plan a motion for a temporary restraining order, a motion for emergency attachment, proposed order, the necessary affidavits, and outline the supporting memorandum.

(b) Draft such documents.

24. As counsel for plaintiff in *Giacone v. City of Mitchell* (Case D):

(a) Determine what equitable relief, if any, should be sought for plaintiff.

(b) Draft the appropriate motion for temporary injunctive relief, including the proposed order and any additional supporting papers.

(c) Outline the arguments for the memorandum supporting plaintiff's motion.

(d) Outline the arguments for the memorandum opposing defendant's motion.

(e) As judge, decide.

25. You are counsel for Shelly Fridley in *On Broadway v. Off Broadway* (Problem 3, Chapter 11).

(a) Plan an appropriate motion for temporary injunctive relief, including the proposed order and any additional supporting papers.

(b) Draft these documents.

CHAPTER 13

EFFECTIVE PRESENTATION OF MOTIONS

The speaker who does not strike oil in ten minutes should stop boring.

Mark Twain

If you want to win a case, paint the Judge a picture and keep it simple.

John W. Davis

§ 13.1 MOTION PRACTICE GENERALLY

How a judge decides a motion often depends upon how the attorneys present their positions through written briefs and oral arguments. Initially, an attorney needs to plan how to provide motion information to the judge. Many lawyers leave these matters to piecemeal, spontaneous decisions. An attorney can significantly improve the persuasive value of motion advocacy through complete and thorough planning. This preparation need not be done in a solitary way. Discussions with colleagues, clients, support staff, and others familiar with the case or issues should begin at an early stage.

Rules of procedure, local rule requirements, the preferences of judges, custom, and tradition all affect the manner in which information may be presented. But the attorney still faces many tactical decisions regarding how specific factual and legal information should best be communicated to the other attorney and the judge.

The two fundamental benchmarks of an effective motion presentation are brevity and clarity. This standard is not absolute but flexible. Presentation should vary in relation to the complexity of a motion. All written and oral presentations must be clear, which requires that the information communicated be understood with a minimum of effort.

The manner of presentation is also influenced by allocation of the burden of persuasion. The movant has the burden to convince the court that the motion should be granted. The opposing party has the burden to rebut such arguments. The degree of the burden of persuasion and rebuttal depends upon the specific motion. The fact that the opposing party does not have as significant a burden as the movant lulls some opposing lawyers into believing they need not be overly concerned with presentation—an often inaccurate perception.

The movant may provide the judge with enough information to meet the burden of persuasion and the judge may expect the opposing party to present an equally compelling argument in rebuttal. The failure to present an effective opposition prompts many judges into ruling for the movant. Opposing attorneys need to design a written and oral presentation that meets their clients' interests in opposing the motion.

The party whose conduct necessitated the motion being brought (*i.e.*, often the obstinate, obstreperous party) may have a greater burden than the moving party. For example, a party who seeks an order under Rule 37 to enforce a discovery request may have been forced to bring the motion because of the refusal of the other side to cooperate during discovery. Some motions result because of the tactical maneuvering, questionable conduct, or intransigent behavior of an opposing party.

The type of motion involved further affects the presentation. Whether the motion is routine or unusual or whether it is commonly granted or often denied will affect how both attorneys approach memo writing and oral argument. The party bringing an unusual motion or one that is seldom granted will have a more difficult task in obtaining relief. However, it is important not to present too detailed and lengthy an argument.

The primary obligation of the attorney is to promote and preserve the best interests of his or her client (*i.e.*, win). But counsel must balance this dominant role with the attorney's important role as an officer of the court. This role requires the lawyer to be candid and honest and to avoid unprofessional and discourteous behavior. An attorney should be necessarily assertive and persistent while also being respectful and restrained.

An advocate must also adopt a professional belief and interest in the case, believing in the motion, the client, and the relief sought. Further, the lawyer needs to perceive the case as interesting and significant to approach it with a degree of enthusiasm. Affirmative perceptions of belief and interest must also be communicated to the judge.

Written and oral presentation should include reasons to grant or deny the motion. The advocate needs to review these reasons and develop an overall theme that reflects these reasons. Every motion presentation needs a central and unifying theme around which the argument revolves. Many motions lend themselves to more than one theme, or to a main theme with subthemes. Counsel should limit the number of themes and subthemes so that the argument does not become confusing.

Themes vary from case to case and from motion to motion. A theme may reflect the primary issues, factors contained in a procedure rule, criteria established by case law, equitable facts which require some relief, or other facets of the motion. The theme or themes should be emphasized at strategic times throughout the motion presentation. Phrases or words that capture the meaning of the themes need to be selected and consistently used to highlight the reasons why the motion should be granted or denied.

The issues that need resolution are usually contained in the rule, case, statute, or other source that underlies the motion. The attorney needs to identify these issues and fashion an argument which resolves the issues in a favorable way. An effective practice is to write out these issues employing the language of the rule, case, statute, or other source. Some lawyers use their own language and paraphrase the issues. The judge usually is more interested in what the legal source of the issue states rather than what the attorney believes the source to state. Sections 13.3 and 13.4 explain more about issues in written briefs and oral argument.

§ 13.2 MOTION ADVOCACY

§ 13.2.1 Selecting Issues to Present

A motion argument consists of a series of points that an attorney asserts and explains. These include both factual and legal contentions. A point is an affirmative and positive statement of an issue that reflects how the lawyer believes the issue should be resolved. The design of a motion presentation initially involves the determination of which points need to be argued. Points should advance the goals of obtaining the relief sought. Include points that discuss dispositive issues, explain essential information, and contain persuasive arguments. Collateral, marginal, and tangential arguments should be excluded. Deciding what to exclude is as important as the decision of what to include.

After the appropriate points are selected, the lawyer should consider whether a point should be made in a written document, during the oral argument, or in both. Some points are more effectively made in writing, and vice versa. Some points are critical and require an explanation during both opportunities.

The order in which the points are presented affects their persuasive impact upon a judge. Several considerations determine the order or disorder in which the points should be presented:

Which point is the most important? The factors established by a rule, decision, or statute elevate the importance of some points.

Which points are the strongest? The strongest point may deserve the most time.

Which point should be made first? The typical goals for the beginning of a written or oral presentation are:

- To capture the attention of the reader or listener.
- To create an impression that the merits of the position support the relief sought.
- To establish a framework for a persuasive argument.
- To prevent the reader or listener from becoming ill.

How should the remaining points be ordered and which point should be made last? Points are often presented in a chronological or logical order. An inductive approach, from the specific to the general, or a deductive approach, from the general to the specific, may provide a logical structure. Ask Aristotle. Focus on the most persuasive point and ignore other points. In an oral argument anticipate the judge interrupting and asking questions. The final point in a memo or oral argument should be designed to leave the judge with the conclusion that the relief sought should be granted.

§ 13.2.2 ***Presenting the Facts***

Several levels of facts may need explanation. There are those facts that gave rise to the litigation, those facts that specifically relate to the motion, those facts that have not been discovered or developed, and those facts no one cares about. The precise facts the judge needs to know to determine a motion depend upon the motion and the case. Facts may also be distinguished by their dispute status: some facts will be undisputed; some stipulated and admitted; and others disputed.

Facts may be categorized on the basis of their content. There are facts, inferences, opinions, conclusions, and other shades of factual information, (including surmises, guesses, and gossip). An attorney in presenting information usually mixes these various categories. Not all information that falls within these categories may be appropriate for a motion hearing. True facts, reasonable inferences, opinions based on rational perspectives, and realistic conclusions, are examples of proper information. Exaggeration or fabrication is inappropriate.

Facts may be presented in either of two primary ways. The beginning of a written brief or oral argument may include an explanation of the facts. Or the facts may be intermittently explained in the body of the brief or argument. The nature of the facts and their importance to the motion affect their placement. If the facts are simple, a concise chronological explanation at the beginning of the presentation will suffice. If the facts are complex, an outline of the basic facts may be initially explained followed with a more detailed description during the presentation. If the motion presents a legal issue for which the facts are not critical, their explanation may be minimal. If the motion presents mixed issues of fact and law, the relevant facts need to appear throughout the presentation. The description of facts should be done selectively and thoughtfully to avoid unnecessary repetition and to provide the court with all essential factual information.

Facts are presented at a motion hearing usually by the submission of affidavits or taking live testimony. Affidavits provide an efficient and inexpensive means of affording the judge with necessary information. Written affidavits should either accompany the moving papers or be submitted a reasonable time before the motion hearing. The presentation of live testimony through the direct and cross-examination of witnesses and the introduction of exhibits also provides relevant facts. Other modes of factual presentation include stipulations of facts, deposition transcripts, interrogatory answers, and responses to requests for admission. A party relying upon these sources needs either to affirmatively offer this information during the motion hearing or refer the judge to the file during oral argument. The judge may also accept facts through judicial notice of information that is generally known or is capable of accurate and ready determination by accurate sources. A court may also consider general factual information consisting of statistical data. The type of motion brought determines the required or preferred manner of presentation.

The movant typically has the responsibility to initially explain the factual basis of the motion to the judge. The opposing party may also need to address the facts. If the movant's explanation is inaccurate, distorted, incomplete, or otherwise defective then the opposing party will need to correct or add facts in a memo or during oral argument.

Factual descriptions should be objective, accurate, organized, narrative, selective, material and descriptive. If you can describe facts like that, move to the head of the firm.

1. *Objective.* The facts should be presented in a way that reflects an objective and historical explanation of what happened and that excludes subjective characterizations or interpretations of events. A judge is more likely believe and trust an attorney who explains facts in an objective manner rather than in a slanted, biased fashion. Conclusions and judgments concerning the meaning of facts should be reserved for the argument portion of the oral presentation.

2. *Accurate.* It is obviously impermissible for an attorney to misrepresent facts. All facts, good and bad, supportive or harmful, strong or weak, must be presented in a straightforward manner. Misstating the facts is unethical, unprofessional, and a poor tactic.

3. *Organized.* The most common methods to structure the explanation of facts include the chronological and topical structures. Simple facts may be more readily explained in a chronological sequence; complex facts may be better described in a topical order.

4. *Narrative.* Whichever structure is employed, the facts should be explained in a narrative manner that portrays a story in an interesting and informative way.

5. *Selective.* Facts should be selected that emphasize the strengths of a party's position.

6. *Material.* Only those facts that are material to the motion should be explained.

7. *Descriptive.* The facts should be presented in a way so that the reader or listener sees the event through the eyes of the reader or speaker and feels, to the extent possible, the events occurring.

A major problem with factual explanations occurs when an attorney improperly provides the court with facts that do not appear in an affidavit, in testimony or an exhibit, in the file, or on the record. The other attorney should resist the use of such information by pointing out to the judge the inappropriate source of the information.

A blurred line exists in some motions in trying to determine where the facts must be formally introduced as if the hearing was a trial or whether the attorney can informally introduce the facts by describing them during oral argument. An attorney cannot properly testify concerning information (although many try), but an attorney can explain what facts support the position asserted in a motion.

§ 13.2.3 Presenting the Law

Many motions revolve around issues of law, and the bulk of an argument may involve legal explanations. Legal arguments can be divided into several categories. The movant may request the judge to grant the motion because:

- Direct, established legal precedent exists.
- Precedent from other jurisdictions supports a favorable ruling.
- Precedent from another area of the law in the motion jurisdiction may be applied by analogy.
- No precedent exists and the case represents a matter of first impression.
- Legislative history dictates a certain result.
- Recognized rules of statutory construction support a specific interpretation.
- Agency rulings support a position.
- The judge can do anything he or she wants.

Legal arguments may also be intertwined with factual arguments in which the movant asks the judge for relief because:

- The facts match previous cases in which identical or similar relief was provided.

- The facts can be distinguished from previous cases in which relief was denied.
- Statistical data or analysis support the movant's conclusion.

A motion presentation should include an explanation of supporting cases, statutes, rules, regulations, constitutional provisions, secondary authorities and other persuasive legal sources such as Mad magazine. The judge will be influenced by precise legal authorities and analyses and not by the personal or professional opinion of the lawyer. Legal authorities should be selected that have the most precedential value in the jurisdiction. Court decisions from appellate courts within the same jurisdiction as the motion court are obviously most applicable and persuasive. State judges are most responsive to decisions from their appellate courts. Federal district court judges are most persuaded by appellate decisions from their circuit. Some judicial decisions from outside the jurisdiction of the motion court may also be persuasive. The following factors dictate the degree of persuasiveness:

- *The Status of the Court.* A state court judge will be influenced more by a Supreme Court decision of another state than a state intermediate appellate court decision. A federal court judge will be influenced more by a federal circuit court opinion than a district court judge's decision. State court judges will be more persuaded by a United States Supreme Court decision rather than another state supreme court. Federal judges will be more persuaded by state supreme court decisions more than federal court decisions on matters that relate to state law issues. Justices of the Peace will be more influenced by attorneys who contributed to their campaigns.
- *The Similarities Between the Issues.* If the motion involves the identical law, rules, or procedures adopted in another jurisdiction then how the courts of that jurisdiction interpreted and applied such provisions will usually be influential.
- *The Age of the Precedent.* An older decision may be influential in a case dealing with common law matters. A newer decision may be more influential in a case which deals with modern issues.
- *The Basis for the Precedent.* Precedent from other jurisdictions will be persuasive if the reasoning of the courts in adopting the precedent matches similar public policy or other concerns in the jurisdiction of the motion.
- *The Location of the Court.* Decisions from neighboring courts will often be more influential than decisions from distant courts, except in Alaska and Hawaii.
- *The Reputation of the Judge.* The greater the reputation of the judge who issued the decision the greater its impact.
- *The Type of Case That Led to the Decision.* The impact of a decision is influenced by whether it is a leading case in the area, a

case of first impression, an unusual case, a case that represents a moderate position, or another type of case.

- *The Philosophy of the Court and Judge.* The closer the philosophy of a court or a judge with the courts in the motion jurisdiction the more weight that precedent will have. For example, Midwestern judges may view with logical skepticism decisions from the coasts, particularly if the opinion was written in a hot tub.

Some of these considerations also apply to the impact that legislative enactments from outside the motion court's jurisdiction may have upon a hearing.

The manner of presenting legal explanations will be critical to the judge's understanding and acceptance of the legal arguments. Common problems that reduce the effectiveness of legal explanations include:

- *Inaccurate Descriptions.* Arguments do not accurately describe the status of the law. The failure of lawyers to thoroughly prepare for a hearing often account for this problem. Ethical prohibitions forbid lawyers from intentionally portraying the law inaccurately.
- *Vague Explanations.* Some lawyers present a vague or ambiguous explanation or fail to clarify the status of the law.
- *Incomplete Descriptions.* Some arguments contain correct and clear but incomplete statements of the law. Ethical regulations require lawyers to disclose controlling legal precedent that resolves an issue.
- *Rambling Dissertations.* The judge usually knows some or most aspects of the applicable law and general treatise-like dissertations are inappropriate.
- *Unnecessary Explanations.* A memorandum or brief may be more effective and efficient to explain a legal position. Matters adequately addressed in a memo need not be repeated orally.
- *Long Quotes.* Arguments that contain lengthy case quotations usually are ineffective. Judges usually are more interested in an analysis of the case quotes rather than the reading of them.
- *Specific Citations.* The reading of case citations, the spelling of names, and the repeating of numbers and pages, only unduly lengthen the argument. It is more efficient for the attorney to provide such citations to the judge in an outline of authorities.
- *Sounding Like a Law Professor.* Some lawyers remain enamored with their law school experience and retain questionable traits. Fortunately, most of these lawyers seek and obtain counseling.

§ 13.2.4 Effective Use of Facts and Law

The nature of the motion will determine whether the law or the facts will predominate as controlling factors. The most effective arguments will often be a mixture of factual and legal contentions. The usefulness of a fact will often depend upon its relationship with the controlling law. The effectiveness of precedent will depend upon the underlying facts that support the legal contentions.

The advocate must present to the court in a brief and during oral argument reasoned analysis why the position of the attorney should be accepted by the judge. Many other motions will present matters that have no direct authority. In these situations the task of the advocate is to explain what reasons support a ruling by the judge in favor of the advocate even though no authority exists.

Equity and Emotion. Additional factors beyond the law and facts also affect the manner of presentation of the oral argument. Equity and emotion also influence the decision making process. Judges will rest their decision not only on matters in the head but also on matters of the heart.

Choice of Language. Language should be assertive and expressive but not biased and excessive in tone. Words and phrases that overstate a position, exaggerate a fact, or stretch the law undermine the persuasiveness of a point. The use of such language creates an impression that the attorney's written and oral statements are unreliable, causing a judge to view the entire presentation with skepticism.

It is not easy for advocates to recognize the hyperbole of their statements, particularly after they read their advertising copy. An attorney may employ words and phrases that the attorney perceives to be correct and deserving but that the opposing lawyers may view as insulting and demeaning and the judge may view as unfair and unnecessary. Unrestrained statements occur most often with the use of adjectives and adverbs. Words such as obvious, clear, ridiculous, inane and similar words constitute common excessive language.

Rhetorical Questions. A traditional argument technique is the rhetorical question. An attorney may ask questions the answers to which the attorney believes to be obvious and supportive of the position asserted. This technique may be ineffective because the answers may not be obvious, or because the answers may be so obvious there is no need to ask a question, or because it is the role of the judge and not the attorney to ask questions. Rhetorical questions can be used effectively if asked sparingly, at the appropriate time, and without making the attorney sound like a Jeopardy contestant.

Candor. It is critical for an attorney during the presentation of an argument to be candid with the court. Not all the facts in a case may support the moving party's position; a movant should not inappropriately castigate the facts that weaken a position. The law may not clearly support the position of the moving party; a movant should not pretend precedent to be clear unless it is so supportive. Where the court has discretion to grant or deny a motion; a movant should not argue that the court has only one possible option. Ethical concerns also restrict the content of written and oral presentations. Section 10.5 explores the impact of these various ethical limitations.

Opposition Weaknesses. A motion argument needs to refer to the weaknesses in the other side's position. The movant may need to anticipate the positions of the other side and expose their weaknesses during the main argument; the movant will have to counter points made by the other side during rebuttal. Defensive comments about the other side's position should be avoided. An argument appears weak if it primarily attacks the other side.

Personalization of an Argument. An attorney should avoid making an argument containing personal views. The judge is not interested in not the lawyer's personal opinion, unless, of course, the lawyer is right. It may be appropriate in some cases for the attorney to mention his or her professional opinion. In arguments involving issues the resolution of which are unclear a judge may be influenced by the professional opinion of an attorney. If a judge recognizes that the attorney understands the law in the area and has offered a reasonable explanation of it as it applies to the case or if the judge has faith in the integrity of the lawyer and accepts the facts as explained by the lawyer, professional opinions may have an impact.

An attorney should always avoid interjecting personal comments about the opposing party, counsel, or the judge. Characterizations critical of the integrity, behavior, and intelligence of individuals are usually unprofessional, discourteous, and ineffective, even if done only in retaliation. Such outbursts may seem appropriate and feel good at the time but they will only make the violator the brunt of the judge's luncheon conversation the following day.

Collateral Considerations. Most motions do not resolve the litigation but only resolve one facet of the case. This reality may prompt some judges to consciously or unconsciously resolve a motion in favor of a party for reasons beyond the merits of the motion. Some judges will be inclined to use their ruling to steer the case in a certain direction or to place the losing party at a disadvantage forcing that party to react in a certain way. These judges usually do not publicize their thinking but use appropriate law to support a result they intend. The judges justify their rulings based on pragmatic considerations.

Economic Factors. The manner of presentation is affected by the resources of the client. Whether the client can afford to pay for the attorney's fees and costs to pursue or oppose a motion often dictates how an attorney proceeds. A moving lawyer has an obligation in bringing a motion to have available sufficient client resources to support the granting of the motion. An opposing attorney may not be able to fully resist a motion because a client cannot afford to pay for such resistance. These situations present difficult issues of client representation, ethical concerns, and motion practice. The influence of economic considerations cannot be ignored and needs to be addressed with a client before a motion is brought and before the manner of presentation has been designed.

Pragmatic Concerns. Motion advocacy is only effective if attorneys take into consideration the realities of motion practice. Many approaches that appear to be persuasive in the abstract will have little impact when applied to real situations. Many lawyers misconstrue the usefulness of certain strategies and tactics. These lawyers fail to consider the time judges have available, incorrectly believe judges will not be distracted, improperly assume that judges will afford their cases special attention, inaccurately believe that their motions present interesting questions, and ignore the human perspective of judges. These attorneys practice as if motions were conducted in Never–Never land.

§ 13.2.5 Differences From Appellate Advocacy

Many of the same considerations that apply to effective appellate advocacy also apply to persuasive motion advocacy. But not all. Motion advocacy differs from appellate advocacy in several respects:

- Usually only one judge decides a motion instead of a panel or an entire court.
- Issues on appeal typically involve more vital matters than many motions.
- The impact of a ruling on a nondispositive motion is usually much less significant than a decision on an appeal.
- The trial record and transcript of a case establishes the set facts for an appeal. A motion often has several alternative ways for facts to be introduced and considered.
- A motion memorandum is often substantially shorter than an appellate brief.
- Detailed court rules establish strict requirements for the format and structure of an appellate brief.
- Issues briefed and argued on appeal are limited by the record.
- Many motion oral arguments occur in an informal atmosphere or in chambers.
- Some appellate arguments appear in the media, whereas notable motion arguments only appear in dreams.

These differences, and the existence of similarities, determine whether or not an approach effective on the appellate level is likewise useful in a motion setting.

§ 13.3 BRIEFS AND MEMORANDA

§ 13.3.1 Memorandum Contents

A motion memorandum may contain various types of information. The most common types include fact and legal argument. Some courts describe a motion memorandum as a legal memorandum but that labelling is misleading because a memorandum invariably includes descriptions of the facts of the case intermingled with the applicable law.

Some judges and lawyers differentiate between a brief and a memorandum, defining a brief as a lengthy memorandum and a memo a shorter, less inclusive document. This book will use the two terms interchangeably. A brief is a memo is a memorandum.

Should you use one? A memorandum may be voluntarily submitted by a lawyer, may be requested by the judge, or may be required by court rule. It is advisable for an attorney in seeking a ruling from a judge to provide some written legal documentation supporting the relief sought, as long as the attorney knows how to write. Attorneys who oppose motions should almost always submit memoranda.

Memoranda take several forms. A motion memorandum may be:

- A lengthy brief consisting of several separate sections.
- A moderate length memo.
- A short outline of points and authorities.
- Copies of relevant rules, cases, and statutes.

There is no set or established format for all memoranda. A motion brief should be structured in a way that most effectively addresses the issues and meets the needs of the judge. A short memo may not need any elaborate structure. The longer the memo the more important the structure becomes to ensure the clarity and persuasive value of the written argument. The length of a brief may be dictated by local court rule or customary practice.

Many motions can be adequately supported with an outline listing the major points and a summary of the citations of cases, statutes, and rules that support the points. The format for an outline can be as varied and flexible as the needs of the judge to receive the necessary information. This format is appropriate for simple motions and for situations which do not justify the expenses, time, and effort necessary for a memorandum. Another efficient way to provide a judge with the relevant law is to copy all or part of a rule, decision, or statute.

A motion memorandum may consist of some or all of the following parts:

1. Caption and title.
2. Introductory explanation.
3. A description of the facts.
4. A statement of the issues.
5. Legal analysis and argument.
6. A conclusion explaining the relief sought.
7. Footnotes.
8. Appendices.

Additional sections for a brief may also include a Table of Contents and a Table of Authorities. The parts and their sequence may vary depending upon the scope and length of a memo and the practice in a jurisdiction.

The length of a memo depends upon what needs to be written and the verbosity of the attorney. Maximum page limits commonly imposed on appellate briefs may not exist for motion memos. The primary reason court rules do not specify precise page limits is because the practice is such that attorneys typically submit short memos without having to be told, just like law school assignments. The expenses and time necessary to produce a substantial memo is not justified unless a motion involves significant issues similar to appellate issues. Some jurisdictions not only impose format and page limits but also specify page size, paper quality, type size and other details. No judge has ever complained of a brief's undue brevity.

Caption and Title. The first or cover page of the memo should contain the caption (title of court, identification of parties, docket number) in the upper part of the page along with a title of the memo in support of or in opposition to the motion. Preliminary information may also include the names and addresses of counsel, a statement indicating whether oral argument is requested, and the date of the memo or the phase of the moon.

Introductory Explanation. The prefatory statements of a brief may include a variety of information. The opening statement may:

- Describe the parties.
- Concisely explain the case.
- Briefly describe the status of the litigation.
- Explain the nature of the motion.
- State the jurisdictional basis for the court.
- Summarize the reasons supportive of the motion.
- Explain the relief sought.
- Unintentionally convince the judge the *other* side should clearly prevail.

An introductory statement should be concise, a paragraph or a page in length. Its purpose is to provide the judge with an overview of the legal situation and an understanding of generally what is requested, why it is requested, and what relief is sought. It may be advisable for a lengthy brief to include a summary of the issues, the points that will be made, or an outline of the positions that will be asserted. The introduction should not become overly lengthy or repetitive of other parts of the memo.

Presentation of the Facts. The presentation of facts is important in all briefs. The presentation of facts is part of the advocacy role of a brief, and should be addressed with care. Notwithstanding their importance, attorneys frequently give the facts short shift, or make other errors in presenting the facts. The goal of the advocate is to avoid these mistakes and present the facts in the most effective manner possible.

The attorney in drafting a recitation of the facts in a memo may need to indicate the source of the facts, that is, what document, witness, affidavit, discovery response, or testimony supplies the facts. An explanation of facts in an appellate brief routinely includes a reference to the page number of the record. This easy reference may not be available in a motion presentation, but it may be critical for the judge to know what support there is for the factual statements presented.

The placement of the facts in the beginning of a brief provides an opportunity to grab the attention of the judge. Explain facts in an interesting style which highlights the human dynamics of the motion. Usually a narrative explanation employing descriptive and impact words is effective.

Statements of Issues. A statement of an issue is a question the answer to which resolves all or part of a ruling on the motion. Dispositive issues in a motion brief serve several purposes: they present the questions raised by the motion; they provide the judge with a concise explanation of what has to be decided; and they provide an opportunity to subtly influence the judge.

The following guidelines are useful in composing effective statements of issues:

1. A limited number of issues should be selected. These questions should be distilled to major, critical issues. Usually this results in a few or, at the most, several issues. Complex motions may involve more issues. The statement of issues can be structured to include both major issues and minor subissues to distinguish between critical and less important issues.

2. An issue should not present a self-evident proposition. No information is conveyed and little persuasive impact is made by stating an issue the answer to which is obvious. A question such as "Should the complaint be dismissed because the plaintiff failed to comply with the proper rules?" says nothing and requires an affirmative answer regardless of the facts of the case.

3. An issue should combine a legal proposition with factual information. A question that contains a general abstract proposition without reference to the specifics of a case serves little purpose.

4. An issue should be informative. It should not merely state a conclusion but should include some information that focuses on the subject matter of the motion.

5. A question should be concise and not unnecessarily lengthy. A question should not be so concise that it omits important concepts.

6. The question should comprise a complete sentence. The use of the common preface "whether" will create a phrase but not a grammatically correct question.

7. The question should be readily understandable on the first reading. Some issues will not make sense until after they have been read a few times.

8. The issue should be acceptable to the opposing lawyer. The question should not be designed to be self-serving but should objectively reflect what a judge must decide.

9. The issue should be drafted in a persuasive way. The lawyer as advocate should attempt to phrase a question that places an issue in as favorable a position as possible. A judge after reading the issue should perceive some justification for answering the question in favor of the drafter.

10. The issue should not cause the judge to erupt with an uncontrollable fit of laughter.

It may not be necessary to include a separate statement of issues section in a brief. The questions may be initially presented in the body of the argument immediately followed by a legal explanation. A memorandum may not need any separation between a question and the written answer provided by the lawyer. It may be more effective to use the "argument" section of the memo to employ points which explain conclusions in an affirmative manner rather than as questions.

The appropriate composition of an issue can be achieved through drafting and redrafting. An attorney needs to edit drafts to create a favorable issue. The following examples have been redrafted to obtain a more effective description of an issue:

Instead of: Whether the defendant failed to respond to discovery requests by the plaintiff justifying a Rule 37 sanction.

Rather: When a Defendant fails to respond to the Plaintiff's Interrogatories and Requests for Production of Documents should a Court dismiss the Defendant's Counterclaim under the authority of Rule 37?

Instead of: Is it appropriate for this Court to permit Plaintiff to file an amended complaint at this stage of the proceeding pursuant to Rule 15.

Rather: Should this Court under Rule 15 permit the Plaintiff to amend paragraph 3 of the Complaint to conform the pleadings to the evidence?

Argument. The argument constitutes the main portion of the brief. Its ultimate purpose is to demonstrate that favorable legal precedent and the facts support the asserted position. The overall approach to be taken in a legal argument is to argue the propriety of the relief sought. Section 13.12 has discussed in general the manner of effectively presenting this information. This section will consider additional factors applicable to a written brief.

The legal argument is usually organized according to the points that need to be made. A typical organizational structure asserts a point and follows it with a narrative explanation and analysis. The points selected for a brief usually reflect the issues presented by the motion. Points are typically phrased as affirmative statements of the questions and are placed as headings for the parts of the legal argument.

A written memo can be made easier to understand if it visually looks organized. Headings and subheadings which reflect the points and subpoints assist in creating a well organized structure. Sections of a memo should be separated into divisions or subdivisions. Numbers, letters, spacing, capitals, underlinings, italics, boldface, and other devices may also be used to provide a visual structure.

The points and argument should be sequenced in an orderly and personal manner. The rules, decisions, or statutes may detail the order of the points to be argued. For example, Rule 23 establishes four initial factors that need to be addressed in determining the propriety of a class action. Another effective sequence is to order the points from most significant to least significant.

Transitions should be employed to connect the separate parts of the argument. These transitions demonstrate the relationships between points and strengthen the cumulative effect of the entire brief. The type of transition depends upon the sequence of the argument. A short paragraph transition may be necessary to bridge two major arguments. A sentence transition may be sufficient to connect some points.

It may be desirable for lengthy briefs to draft the initial paragraph of a section as an introductory paragraph which summarizes the assertions made in that section. A prefatory paragraph may make that section of the legal argument more comprehensible. Some appellate courts require the inclusion of a "Summary of Argument" prior to the argument. A summary paragraph should not be lengthy nor repetitive of the argument. The following examples demonstrate the difference between poorly drafted points and edited improved drafts:

Instead of: An order declaring that the applicant be deemed an appropriate intervenor in this action should be issued by the Court.

Rather: Applicant has a right to intervene under Rule 24(a) because applicant has an interest in the subject matter of this case.

Instead of: This Court must vacate the previous judgment entered in this case.

Rather: The method of service in this case constitutes a clerical error under Rule 60(a) permitting the default judgment entered against the defendant to be vacated.

The legal argument needs to include those facts applicable to the law presented. These facts may need to be interpreted as well as described. The advocate may draw reasonable inferences, comment on the meaning of specific information, and argue the effect the facts have upon the law.

Legal Sources. The most direct legal source should be used as a source and citation. Direct sources such as cases, statutes, rules, regulations, and opinions by the judge should be the primary sources and citations contained in a memo. The weight afforded secondary sources, such as treatises, encyclopedias, articles, canned briefs, and horoscopes will vary. If a jurisdiction has adopted the analysis or conclusions of a secondary source, the weight may be persuasive. The preference, though, should be to include a direct cite which supports the proposition in the secondary source. Some non-direct sources are very useful in providing a historical explanation of a law, in summarizing a legal development, or in providing a survey of an area of the law.

Legal Descriptions. The court decisions contained in the written argument may be described in several alternative ways including:

- A detailed explanation of both the facts and the holding of the case.
- A summary explanation of the holding of the case.
- The inclusion of quotations from the case.
- A historical description of the decisions preceding the case.
- An analysis of the public policy and other reasons underlying the decision.
- A reference to the judge or court who decided the case.
- A summary of commentaries about the case from legal articles or other cases.
- The citation of a case following a statement of law it supports.
- A photograph of the judge who wrote the opinion.

These alternatives also reflect, with some modifications, ways to describe statutory and regulatory law. The extent of a description of legal precedent depends upon the importance of the source of law to the argument. The attorney should provide the judge with sufficient information about a source of law to permit the judge to appreciate and evaluate the significance and effect of the case, statute, or rule. The more important the precedent the more detailed and elaborate the explanation is appropriate.

The use of quotations from a case or other legal source are effective if properly presented, and if not fabricated. A quotation must be accompanied by an exact cite to its source. A quote without any reference to the facts or holding of a case is usually ineffective. A quote will usually need to be accompanied by information about the source that places the quote in perspective. Some major cases, statutes, or rules may be well enough known that such an explanation is unnecessary.

Exact language from a court decision or other legal source can be very persuasive and should be used in many situations instead of paraphrasing a decision. Attorneys should never rely on headnote summaries, since they are tools for locating law and not the law itself. Lengthy quotations should be limited. A judge will usually be more interested (or amused) in a lawyer's analysis and less interested in reading a long quote. A case, statute, or rule that is critical and that deserves a lengthy quotation should probably be read by the judge in its entirety. The careful selection of quotations provides a proper balance of precise information. Numerous quotations should also be limited.

The source of law relied upon in a brief must contain a proper citation. A uniform system for citation of legal authorities and publications exists and is widely accepted and extensively used. Citations should usually conform to this preferred method contained in the Uniform System of Citation.

There may be reasons why a prescribed form should not be used. The local practice or custom of a jurisdiction should take precedence over the standard form. The use of an alternative citation form should also be employed if that alternative is a more understandable way to communicate the source of the law to the judge.

Some signals or abbreviations should not be used in a motion brief. "*Supra*" refers to previous citations; "*infra*" refers the reader to a subsequent source or point. These signals should be avoided because they interrupt the train of thought of the reader and require the reader to take extra time to locate the other cite. "*See generally,*" "*see also,*" and "C note" refer to general background material or music which is usually not useful or persuasive information for a motion. Some signals are designed to designate the type of authority contained in a citation. "*See*" refers to basic source materials that support the proposition. "*But see*" or "*contra*" refers to contradictory authority. "*Oops*" refers to a mistake. Some signals will be unfamiliar to the reader of a memo. The exact meaning of signals may be clear to a law review editor or a legal publisher but may not be clear to a judge or opposing lawyer. An explanation of the holding of a case may be more useful than a standard signal. Citations will be most informative if they are used consistently throughout a memo, if their abbreviated description is understandable, and if they are accurately cited including a reference to the page of the legal proposition.

Citations should be made in the least intrusive manner possible. The placement of citations may disrupt the information intended to be conveyed. A full case name and complete citation when placed in the middle of a sentence or paragraph may cause some confusion. It may be more effective to place citations at the beginning or ending of a topical discussion or to include a case name in a sentence and the case citation after the sentence or in a footnote.

Citation of multiple authorities to support a proposition of law should usually be avoided. Legal sources that reflect the most recent and authoritative source will be more persuasive than a series of miscellaneous citations. Some lawyers include a list of "string" citations to bolster a legal proposition. A judge will usually prefer to be advised of the controlling case in a jurisdiction, not a list of cases. A listing may be appropriate in certain situations to show the historical nature of a proposition or its acceptance by many jurisdictions.

The order of citations, when more than one is legitimately used, depends upon the status of the court and the date of the decision. The highest court decision that establishes the proposition must go first. That is, federal decisions should be placed in a sequence with the United States Supreme Court cases followed by Court of Appeals decisions followed by District Court opinions. And state court cases should be placed in a sequence with Supreme Court opinions followed by Appellate Court cases (if any) followed by lower court decisions. More than one court decision from the same tier of courts or from the same court must be ordered by date with the most recent decisions placed before older decisions.

Conclusion of Memorandum. A conclusion may serve several purposes. It provides an opportunity for counsel to:

- Restate the themes of the motion.
- Clarify the specific relief requested.
- Summarize major issues and points.
- Include a reference to a matter not included in a previous part of the memorandum, such as equitable considerations.
- Beg for victory.

The conclusion should be concise and direct. A conclusion should not repeat what has been stated previously but should highlight some matters in a final attempt to persuade the judge to grant the client the relief sought. A short memo may require nothing more than a one or two sentence conclusion. A paragraph conclusion will be more appropriate for a lengthier brief.

Footnotes. Footnotes can be an effective means to provide information about legal citations, supplemental facts, and supporting material. The use of footnotes permits an attorney to support a position without disrupting the flow of the narrative presentation. Propositions can be analyzed without having to include citations in the text. Footnotes also provide a location for the inclusion of collateral information, lengthy quotations, or the attorney's résumé. Footnotes should be located or begin on the same pages as the textual statement. It is inconvenient and awkward for a reader to check footnotes located at the end of the brief.

Some limitations should be followed in employing footnotes. Substantive information should not be placed in a footnote if it provides direct or significant support for a statement. Footnotes should be reserved for secondary information. Footnotes should also not be overdone because many judges will not thoroughly read comments in a footnote. They reason that important comments should be in the text.

Some information may be effectively disclosed in an appendix to a brief. Information may be placed in an appendix because it is too lengthy to be included in the text or because it is of secondary significance. Relevant statements, rules, regulations, and other materials and documents may need to be reproduced in whole or in part if the determination of some issues requires their review and study. Examples of information that may be included in an appendix are:

- Copies of entire or partial cases, statutes, or rules.
- Affidavits that contain factual information, although these usually will be attached to a motion or submitted separately.
- Copies of pleadings, discovery requests, discovery responses, or other file documents.
- Certified legal cartoons.

These materials will be included for the convenience of the judge and opposing lawyer and for their persuasive value. Attaching these documents to the memorandum makes the task of the judge that much easier, creates an impression that the submitting party is knowledgeable, and increases the chance that the judge will review all relevant information.

§ 13.3.2 Opposition Memoranda

A written response to the facts, issues, and arguments asserted by the opposing lawyer may be critical in obtaining relief or preventing the court from issuing a premature order. A written brief may create an impression with the judge that the other side's position is accurate and convincing unless countered with an equally effective reply memo. Failure to respond to a brief may also suggest to the judge that the opposing attorney believes that the positions asserted by the other side are proper and appropriate or that the attorney cannot read. An opposing memo or reply brief should not be automatically prepared. Some positions deserve no rebuttal; others may be rebutted adequately during oral argument.

An effective responsive brief contains an offensive approach describing affirmative reasons which supports the position of the opposing party and arguments directly responding to the positions asserted by the other side. An attorney planning a responsive memo must initially analyze the other side's brief to determine which arguments need to be rebutted in writing. This review of the other's side statements should focus on revealing weaknesses and mistakes including the following errors:

- Factual misstatements or omissions.
- Legal errors, such as incorrect descriptions or inaccurate citations.
- Inadequately supported factual or legal conclusions.
- Excessive or inaccurate language.
- Improper analysis of the facts or the law.
- Inappropriate issues or points.
- Illogical arguments.
- Inconsistent positions.
- Concessions.
- Dropped fly balls.

The order in which the responsive arguments should be made will depend upon which order appears to be the most effective. An obvious order is the sequence in which the arguments appear in the other side's memo. Another order is to list the rebuttal points from the strongest to the weakest. Still another order is to weave the rebuttal points in with the arguments advanced by the drafting attorney. Whatever order is employed and whether the rebuttal arguments should appear in a separate section of the brief or mixed with other arguments depends upon the favorable impact the order will have upon the judge.

§ 13.3.3 Effective Brief Writing

Preparing an effective brief requires careful blending of law, facts, and other ingredients. The following suggestions will be helpful in drafting a clear and understandable brief.

- *Be specific and concrete.* Avoid being vague and gravel.
- *Use simple sentences.* Write in a straightforward manner.
- *Untangle complex or run-on sentences.* Divide a long sentence into two or more sentences; subdivide separate ideas into independent sentences; avoid the use of lengthy clauses; do not write like this.
- *Use simple and common words.* Unusual or unknown words may confuse and slow down the reader, although they will increase dictionary sales in the jurisdiction.
- *Employ positive statements.* Affirmative statements make more of an impact than neutral or negative statements.
- *Avoid legalese.* Words that typically appear in certain legal documents should be excluded, such as "whereas," "hereafter," and "them dummies."
- *Selectively use foreign language words and phrases.* Some Latin and other foreign terms have commonly understood meanings. Outdated or unusual phrases will only confuse readers unless they have taught classical language.

- *Avoid showing off.* Do not use words merely to impress the judge or opposing lawyer or to unnecessarily require them to ask a law clerk the meaning of a word.
- *Use the active voice (unlike parts of this Chapter).* The subject of a sentence, not the object, should perform the act described by the verb.
- *Use the passive voice occasionally and for variety.* The active voice reflects an advocacy approach while the passive voice presents a less forceful presentation.
- *Use proper verb tenses and number.* Do not mix verb tenses in the same sentence or paragraph. Do not use a plural or married verb with a singular noun clause or phrase.
- *Match the noun with the correct possessive adjective.* A singular noun requires a singular possessive adjective; a plural noun requires a plural possessive adjective. Not "The corporation breached their contract" but "The corporation breached its contract."
- *Sparingly use parentheses (if you can control yourself).* Parenthetical material (if important enough) should be included in the text and (if of secondary importance) can be included in a footnote. Parentheses are useful to designate an abbreviation for a party or citation.
- *Eliminate unnecessary words.* Do not use two words when one will do or one word when none will do.
- *Use the same words to denote the same thing.* Avoid using the same word to mean different things or different words to mean the same thing like our use of "brief" and "memorandum."
- *Eliminate repetitive, unnecessary, and superfluous redundancies.* Do not use pairs of words that have the same effect, like "each and every" and "final and conclusive." Avoid using pairs of words which include each other, such as "necessary or desirable" and "authorized and directed," unless you have stock in a paper company.
- *Use parallelism.* If more than one section, paragraph, sentence, or clause is similar in substance, structure them similarly.
- *Avoid ambiguous sentences.* Do not misplace modifiers: "Plaintiff saw defendant while signing the contract" does not clarify who signed the contract.
- *Avoid indefinite pronouns as references.* Avoid phrases such as: "After a party sues another party, he. . . ."
- *Use shall, will, must, and may appropriately.* "Shall" indicates an obligation to act. "Will" indicates a future act. "Must" indicates a command. "May" indicates a discretion to act or a month.

- *Employ definitions or shortened names where necessary.* These can provide necessary information and reduce repetition but should be used sparingly, *e.g.*, for the identification of parties, citations, or terms.
- *Avoid using the word "such" and "said".* Use the, that, or those instead.
- *Use gender-neutral terminology.* Avoid the use of gender-specific nouns or pronouns when referring to both sexes.
- *Modify dangling participles.* The noun or pronoun modified by a clause should be included in proper relation to the modifier.
- *Correct split infinitives.* An adverb placed between "to" and the verb should be avoided, unless a split infinitive reads better. State: "To think rapidly" instead of "to rapidly think."
- *Do not follow all these rules slavishly.* Even George Bernard Shaw recognized the need to write freely if the result sounds better due to frequent conversational use and acceptance. To make a brief really hum, restrained rebellion is alright.

The writing style of a brief should be varied to avoid a monotonous memorandum. The following guidelines suggest ways to vary writing styles.

- Vary the length and form of sentences.
- Alter the length and format of paragraphs.
- Use different words to begin sentences and paragraphs.
- Use transitional words, phrases, and sentences.

A major technique in producing well written memoranda is redrafting, redrafting, and redrafting. An attorney should plan to edit drafts of memos until they present a clear and precise argument.

Review several considerations in editing a brief:

Is the structure appropriate?

Is the meaning clear?

Is the impact persuasive?

Is the writing style understandable?

Have grammatical mistakes been corrected?

Have typographical errors been eliminated?

Have citations been cite checked?

Will the brief win a Pulitzer?

The practice of many lawyers to extend the deadline for finishing the writing of a brief until the last moment leaves little or no time for written redrafts. Time needs to be taken to make necessary revisions. A second re-draft substantially improves the substance and style of a memo. A third draft should produce a final draft or a near final draft. Some lawyers edit a second draft for substance and a third draft for style. Citations which have been cite checked may also need to be corrected during one of the drafts.

Another technique to improve the quality of a brief is to have another person critique the memorandum. This person should read the brief both from the perspective of the judge and from the perspective of an editor. Portions of the brief that are unclear or incomplete can be marked. Other portions of the brief that need editing can be rewritten by this or another person. The revision should not make substantive changes regarding the facts and the law, but only suggest stylistic and grammatical revisions unless the editor has a comprehension of the case, motion, and the law.

Typografikal or speeling erors substancialy reeduce the impakt of the brief. A memo should not be submitted until all mistakes have been eliminated. An imperfect brief may leave a judge with an impression that the attorney was also sloppy in stating the facts or researching the law.

§ 13.4 ORAL ARGUMENT

§ 13.4.1 Role of Oral Argument

Oral argument is an important part of most motions. Oral argument in support of or in opposition to a motion may serve many purposes:

- Acquainting the judge with the facts of the case and the background of the motion.
- Explaining the law or reasons which support the relief sought.
- Highlighting important issues in the case.
- Narrowing issues to be resolved.
- Clarifying any misconceptions held by the judge.
- Covering matters unresolved by written memorandum.
- Persuading the judge concerning the merits of the attorney's position.
- Answering questions of the judge.
- Convincing an undecided judge.
- Suggesting alternative ways to resolve the problem underlying the motion.
- Fulfilling a lawyer's desire to be a Hepburn or a Newman.

Oral argument can be extremely effective. The written brief may inadequately provide the judge with the information necessary to resolve the matter in the client's favor. A face to face presentation may dispel problems and misconceptions a judge has with a motion. The argument permits an advocate to focus on those aspects of the case critical to a resolution of the motion. The motion argument also reduces the chance that an unfair decision may result because of an erroneous impression of the judge formed prior to the argument.

§ 13.4.2 Preparation

Preparation initially includes the selection of the attorney to make the argument. Proper preparation by an attorney for a motion argument requires the attorney to know the facts of the case, the purpose of the motion, the relief sought, and the supporting law. Counsel should review motion documents and memoranda. It may be necessary with some motion briefs to update the law cited. This updating may reveal recent favorable developments and prevent the embarrassment of relying on unauthoritative law.

Thorough preparation also involves the consideration of the following questions.

How Much Time Will Be Allowed for the Argument? Some courts schedule motion argument for specific and limited periods of time; other courts schedule motions in sequence and permit lawyers an unspecified reasonable time for argument. These limits may be appropriate for most motions. Other motions require additional time. If more time is needed than allocated by the court, the clerk or court deputy may be contacted and additional time requested, or the attorney may set the courtroom clock back.

Counsel should not prepare the presentation to occupy all the time available. Oral argument is not designed to cover each and every issue but rather is designed to focus on important matters. The time should be structured to cover only significant points with time left unstructured to deal with anticipated questions from the judge.

How Familiar Will the Judge Be With the Motion? An attorney must determine the degree of familiarity a judge has with a case and motion. Many judges will not have read the file or moving papers; other judges will have reviewed or skimmed the relevant documents; others may have had their law clerks brief them on the motion; still others will have read all the moving papers. The extent of the judge's familiarity with the motion dramatically affects the content of the oral argument. An attorney must plan a different beginning and explanations depending upon what the judge knows or does not know.

Determining the familiarity a judge has with a motion may or may not be difficult. The general background of a judge is easily obtainable; the specific knowledge a judge has about a motion may not be as obvious. The usual practice or habit of a judge in preparing for motion hearings provides information about the probability of the judge being prepared for a particular motion. More specific information may be obtained by spying or by contacting the clerk or law clerk and inquiring whether the judge had or will have time to read the file and moving papers. Some judges advise the lawyers about the degree of their preparation. It may be necessary or advisable to prepare two arguments: one for the unprepared judge, and the other for the prepared judge. The advocate is then be prepared for both contingencies and be able to sleep better at night.

How Does the Judge Typically Conduct Oral Arguments? Judges differ in their approach to motion argument. Many judges act in a professional and courteous manner; a few judges are hostile or rude. Every jurisdiction seems to have at least one, which helps make the other judges look better. Judges may ask questions in a curious, polite manner or in an aggressive, attacking style. It is critical for the attorney to discover the tendencies of the judge before a motion so the argument can be shaped for the judge and prepared to counter any problems the judge may create. Judges do not always act according to their reputation.

How Will the Sequence of Arguments Proceed? Usually the moving party has the opportunity to open and close the argument. The movant typically argues first followed by opposing counsel who receives an equal opportunity to present an argument. Other parties to the case argue at the appropriate time in support of or in opposition to the motion. The order of the parties listed in the caption or their support or opposition to the motion usually provides an appropriate order.

Rebuttal argument opportunities are usually offered to all parties. Judges typically allow lawyers to continue to argue as long as their statements appear relevant and not cumulative and as long as time permits or until the judge is put to sleep.

Will the Argument Be Held in Chambers or in the Courtroom? Arguments on motions may occur either in the chambers of the judge or in the courtroom. The formality of the argument and the type of presentation made will vary between these settings. A chambers location permits a more informal basis for an argument. A courtroom location requires a more formal presentation.

Some judges have a strong preference regarding the location of the argument, other judges may be neutral. Some judges expect motion discussions to occur in chambers unless some testimony is required; other courts routinely schedule arguments for the courtroom regardless of the nature of the motion. An attorney who believes the location of a presentation may affect a judge's ruling should request that the matter be heard in the most advantageous place, short of Tahiti.

Reasons that support a courtroom location include: (1) the motion hearing is a public hearing and should take place in the courtroom; (2) the judge will better understand the complexities of the motion if a formal presentation is made; (3) the party has a right to argue in a courtroom; (4) evidence including testimony or exhibits will need to be formally, introduced; (5) visual aids will be used as part of the argument; and (6) the wood paneling matches the lawyer's briefcase. Reasons that support a chambers discussion include: (1) an informal atmosphere is more appropriate to decide the motion; (2) the primary issue concerns the law and not facts; (3) matters that are private and confidential will be discussed; (4) a chambers discussion will take less time than a formal courtroom presentation; and (5) the judge does not look good in black.

Will a Record Be Made of the Argument? Jurisdictions vary regarding the recording of motion arguments. Some courts electronically record motion hearings; others have a court stenographer present. These jurisdictions record hearings because the proceeding is a public matter and should be preserved, because factual matters will be presented and such evidence needs to be preserved, or because everything in a courtroom is traditionally recorded.

Some judges request that the lawyers stipulate that no oral record and transcript be made. A lawyer may insist that a record or album be made. A judge may refuse to supply any means to make a record. An attorney who believes that a record is essential should request that a record be made. Should the court deny this request, the attorney may need to provide a court reporter or equipment and initially absorb this expense.

Should a Record Be Made of the Proceeding? A motion hearing that includes the presentation of facts by live testimony should be recorded and a transcript later made if the case proceeds to trial. These facts may be a basis for evidence or impeachment at the trial. A motion hearing that involves legal discussions may need to be recorded in limited situations. A record of legal presentations holds everyone accountable for statements made and restrains everyone from saying inappropriate things, well, almost everyone. Absence of a record affects what some lawyers and judges say and do.

Should the Client or Other Individuals Be Present at the Hearing? The advocate should consider having the client appear at the motion hearing. Appearance is necessary if the client is to testify. An appearance may also be advisable to help remind the judge that the motion does involve real problems. Many clients may not be able to afford the time or expense involved in attending marginal return. The client need not attend just for the sake of being there. The presence of some clients can prevent a tactical problem for the advocate. Clients may expect a lawyer to say or do something, and their presence may unduly influence a lawyer. For example, some clients expect Rambo as their lawyer and too many counsel oblige. However, client attendance in apt situations demonstrates concern, can provide information, and permits impromptu settlement negotiations.

The presence of other individuals also depends upon their need to be present. Those who will testify should be available; and those who may help the lawyer should also be available, including a law partner, an associate, a law clerk, an expert, a seer, or a clergy person. These individuals should not interrupt the advocate during the argument and should not pass notes or try to gain the advocate's attention, unless there exists some critical reason.

§ 13.4.3 Oral Presentation

Structure. An argument must be structured in a way that contains everything an attorney needs to say in readily understandable order. Typically the movant needs initially to explain the motion, the relief sought, and the nature of the case. There is not much flexibility in the initial part of the motion argument because the judge will need to know certain information. Both sides will have substantial flexibility in structuring the substance of the argument. The movant will be able to order the presentation of the remainder of the argument after the introductory phase, and the opposing attorney is able to structure the entire argument.

The preparation of a structured argument should contain some "disposable" matters which may have to be abandoned because of lack of time. The judge may raise issues not considered by the attorney; the other lawyer may raise some matters that need to be addressed. Flexibly structured arguments permit sections to be eliminated when necessary. An attorney should not expect to deliver an entire pre-planned argument. The argument should be designed to serve as a means of developing a conversational dialogue with the judge.

Design oral presentation should be designed to take advantage of techniques appropriate for oral argument. Single words, colloquialisms, common metaphors, informal phrases, timely sneezes, and persuasive coughs may be effective orally although not suitable in written form. The written preparation for motion argument should be reviewed to eliminate statements that are effective in writing but fare poorly when communicated orally.

The ultimate question a motion argument must address is: what can counsel say to influence the judge to accept the position of the lawyer? The facets of motion advocacy discussed in section 13.2 affect the degree of influence. The following sections discuss particular considerations that apply to oral argument.

Opening Remarks. The argument should not begin until the court indicates that counsel may proceed. A few judges still say: "Ready, set, go." The beginning of a motion argument should contain the following information in a few sentences:

1. A self-introduction by the attorney, the identification of the client represented, and the position of the attorney regarding the motion (*i.e.*, movant, respondent, opposing lawyer).

2. An explanation of the motion. Describe the motion and the law that authorizes it. If the motion is a common, recurring procedure this explanation may be very limited. If the motion is unusual, it may require more of an initial explanation.

3. A statement of the relief sought. It is critical to an understanding of the motion for the judge to know exactly what the movant or opposing party seeks. With some motions, the relief is obvious; with others, a clear explanation is required.

4. An outline of the content of the argument. A brief explanation of what will be covered informs the judge about what will be said, the positions asserted, the order of the points, the length of the argument, and whether the judge should pay attention or just pretend.

This overview description should be concise. It should not become overly lengthy or detailed, become a mini-argument, or prompt the judge to begin asking questions.

The judge's knowledge concerning the case and motion and the judge's conduct in the beginning of the motion hearing often dictate how an attorney should begin. If the judge is prepared, the lawyer should present a quick overview of information to refresh the judge's recollection. If the judge has not reviewed the file or motion papers, introductory remarks need to focus on these explanations.

Presenting Facts During Oral Argument. An attorney must prepare to explain the relevant facts to the court. If a motion involves several independent issues it may be more effective to include an explanation of the relevant facts immediately before each legal argument or instead of describing all facts in the beginning. Some judges may instruct the lawyer to bypass the factual explanation and to proceed to the argument because the judge is familiar with the facts.

The presentation of facts during oral argument differs in several respects from the description of facts provided in a written memo. An oral presentation provides the advocate with more flexibility concerning what is included and excluded. By observing the judge and the effect of what the attorney says, the advocate can alter the explanation to meet the needs of the judge. Oral argument also permits the lawyer to interject some emotion and perhaps drama into the factual description. The lawyer should attempt to impress upon the judge the notion that the case involves persons with real life problems and not just problems raising abstract legal issues. It is easier and more effective for the advocate to emote during oral argument rather than in a law library.

Argument. The lawyer should usually plan to concentrate the bulk of an oral argument on the points likely to be dispositive of the motion. In selecting points, counsel should ask: what points must be made in order to obtain or block the motion? The order of the points selected also needs to be determined. The advocate should usually begin with as strong a point as appropriate.

Lawyers exhibit conscious or unconscious tendency to avoid arguing tough issues and instead to focus on easier issues. Unfortunately, the tough issues may involve dispositive matters and, because of that fact, must be addressed even if they are difficult to analyze. The advocate must rise to this challenge and confront the tough as well as the easier issues. Remember your first job?

During oral argument counsel should usually limit an explanation of the law to the essentials. The holding of a case, the language of a statute, the intent of a rule may be sufficient to support a point with legal authority. Oral argument is not, however, designed to provide the judge with a detailed description of the law. That can best be accomplished in a written brief.

Citations to the legal authorities should also be reserved for the brief, unless an authority is not included in the memo. References to cases during argument should include the full name of the case unless the case is well known to the judges by a shortened description. It will often be helpful to the judge to include the date of the case and the court who decided it.

The use of quotations in oral argument presents some additional considerations. Quoted material may be the most effective way to make a point rather than a paraphrase of the information. The general rules concerning reading quotations—keep the quotation short and do not quote often—reflect good advice. The selective use of quotations in oral argument can be balanced by referring to the inclusion of a full quotation in a memo. The danger in editing quoted material is that the meaning of information may become distorted or the judge may perceive that the attorney is inappropriately slanting the quote, which is probably why the quote has been edited.

Quotes should be written out and readily available to the advocate during oral argument to avoid wasting time and interrupting the flow of the argument. Certain quotations, particularly from statutes and rules, may be more effectively analyzed if the judge is asked to read along a copy of the quote provided the judge. Sort of like an adult Sesame Street.

Concluding Statement. Many arguments are more effective if they are short. Some arguments would have been more effective if they ended before they began. A well conceived presentation need not be lengthy.

The argument should close with a statement that states the relief requested, repeats the theme or themes of the motion argument, and contains any other remark that may persuade the judge. Closing remarks should be concise and brief. The attorney should plan the closing statement in advance and reserve the last minute or so for closing remarks. An argument should not end with a verbal whimper, but should conclude with an oral bang that the judge will remember into retirement.

If a judge has not been persuaded by the content of the argument and the manner of its delivery, a few ending remarks will have no impact. If time is limited, it may be better for an attorney to use available time for substantive rebuttal rather than for concluding remarks. A "thank you, your Honor" may be the best possible form of a conclusion.

§ 13.4.4 Styles of Argument

The presentation of a motion argument involves consideration of matters that are similar to other oral argument situations. The specific techniques that should be applied depend upon several factors including the type of motion, the position asserted by the attorney, the familiarity the judge has with the case, and the time available for argument.

The range of presentation approaches extend from the formal, appellate argument approach to the informal, conversational approach. The location of the motion hearing, the preference of the judge, and the type of motion will influence the approach taken by the attorney.

The advocate needs to be both assertive and deferential, and to avoid being overly aggressive and obnoxious, which can be difficult for many of us. One way to decide how to present the argument is to fashion a presentation that avoids pitfalls and deficiencies that weaken an approach. Counsel should generally avoid:

1. *Reading an Argument.* This form of presentation quickly bores the judge, causes the attorney to lose eye contact, destroys flexibility in dealing with questions and openings, and make it difficult for the judge to listen and concentrate.

2. *Memorizing an Argument.* This approach prohibits effective rapport because the attorney is concentrating on what was composed instead of what is being presented, because forgotten information will cause an embarrassing period of silence and stammering, and because the flexibility and credibility of such an approach is inhibited. Further, the last thing anyone who survives law school wants to do is memorize anything except their hourly rate.

3. *Engaging in an Argument With the Other Attorney.* The argument should be directed to the judge. While the positions of the other side need to be challenged and rebutted, the focus of the argument should be directed to the judge, notwithstanding the fun associated with verbally wrestling with the opponent. Judges hate being left out.

4. *Debating a Point for the Sake of Debating.* Do not lose sight of the purpose of the motion—to obtain specific relief for a client. Some attorneys get caught up in the argument and say things to debate a point, that may have little to do with gaining relief for a client.

5. *Sounding Overly Formalistic and Oratorical.* Some lawyers argue motions with a very formal approach, identical to an approach they saw in an old movie or would take toward an appellate argument. Usually a formalistic approach, during either a motion or appellate makes the attorney appear to be too rigid, distant, stiff, detached, rational, cold, and, yes, less effective.

6. *Appearing Too Casual.* Some attorneys, in an attempt to be conversational, take what appears to be an overly casual, unconcerned tact toward the motion. The judge may sense that the attorney is not serious enough, undercutting the impact of the argument.

7. *Interrupting the Opposing Lawyer.* Interruptions should be reserved for situations when the opposing lawyer makes statements that are prejudicial or mischaracterize something that requires immediate correction. These circumstances become obvious when the hair on the

back of the head bristles at a 90–degree angle. It is unprofessional and discourteous to interrupt opposing counsel unnecessarily. It is more effective for the lawyer to take notes and wait until the other attorney is done and then comment on any misstatements or inappropriate remarks.

Several benchmarks typify an effective oral argument approach:

- The attorney in preparing the argument has fixed the general content of the argument in his or her mind.
- Counsel has selected the exact words and phrases to express the argument.
- The attorney extemporaneously delivers the information combining the prepared argument with the spontaneous presentation.
- This flexible approach permits a natural conversational style and the inclusion of instinctive comments that seem appropriate at the moment.
- The argument is geared to the needs and interests of the judge with the attorney directly responding to questions.
- The lawyer does not sound like an advocate on the People's Court.

8. *Responding to Judge's Decision at Oral Argument.* In a growing number of jurisdictions, particularly in the federal system, judges are advising attorneys prior to oral argument of their decision. These judges invite the attorneys during oral argument to argue why the judge should or should not render the decision.

Some judges post a copy of a tentative decision or otherwise provide the attorneys with a copy before the argument. Other judges read to the attorneys at the beginning of oral argument their decision. The purpose of oral argument in these situations is markedly different than situations when the judge makes a decision after oral argument.

The party who loses, of course, has a much more difficult response to make. The attorney must attempt to change the judge's mind. The attorney who has tentatively won may not need to say much of anything. The attorney who has won a partial victory may need to argue for a complete victory.

The approach taken by these judges places a high premium on the quality of the written memorandums submitted by the attorneys prior to the argument. Advising the attorneys ahead of time of the judge's tentative decision does allow the attorneys to focus the argument on the issues the judge deems to be controlling. This approach avoids the wasteful use of time in oral argument discussing issues the judge does not decide. It can be, though, disquieting if not depressing, to be on the losing end before the argument. But, then, what is another small challenge like this compared to finishing law school?

Judges will vary in their general approach to motion hearings and in their specific approach to particular motions. Some judges are active and ask many questions; others are passive; and still others ask at least some questions. The approach an attorney takes during a motion argument may affect what the judge does. An approach that actively involves the judge in the motion hearing may be most effective. The more a judge participates in a motion hearing the better informed the judge will become and the more likely it will be that the questions and concerns that the judge has will be addressed.

An attorney should be pleased when a judge asks a question and should conduct the argument in a way that invites the judge to ask questions. The decision the judge makes will be based in part upon answers to questions the judge receives. In reality, argument is only effective to the degree it addresses the needs of the judge. Responses to questions also clear up any misunderstandings or misperceptions of the judge. Questions provide additional benefits. They usually ensure that the time will be well used and help make the argument presentation more interesting and varied.

Questions can be classified into various categories. The substance of a question can be classified as seeking:

- Facts concerning the motion or case or facts involved in supporting legal authorities.
- Information relating to procedure rules, including their impact on the motion.
- Legal authorities, including cases, statutes, and rules.
- Policy considerations.
- Information about the relief sought.
- Matters the attorney should have but never did consider.

Questions can also be classified according to the manner in which the judge makes a query. Judges may ask:

- Neutral, fair questions that seek information.
- Friendly, helpful questions designed to assist the advocate in making a point.
- Adversarial, hostile questions that display the judge's attitude and opinion toward an issue.
- Difficult, probing questions that force the lawyer to analyze a situation.
- Useless, irrelevant questions that indicate the judge has some problems with the motion.
- Confusing, awkward questions that reveal that the judge has missed a point.

The proper classification of a question assists the lawyer in providing a responsive answer. Categorizing questions during the argument is often difficult but is necessary for the lawyer to determine why the judge may be asking the question and what information the judge needs to know.

The proper response to a question may be a key factor in the effectiveness of the oral argument. The following suggestions will help in phrasing an effective response:

1. *Understand the Question.* The attorney should first make certain that he or she has heard the full question and comprehends it. Too often an attorney does not listen to a question and responds to a query they wished they were asked instead of the actual question, just like law school exams. Some questions may be easily misinterpreted or misunderstood. If this occurs the attorney may need to rephrase the question for clarification purposes or ask the judge to repeat the question.

2. *Do not Interrupt the Judge.* The lawyer should let the judge complete the question. Many judges chide an attorney who interrupts. Lawyers may be inclined to interrupt to show the judge they know the answer and to attempt to rush and save time. The attorney's preconception of the question often backfires because the completed question may be different than the anticipated question.

3. *Promptly Answer the Question.* An attorney should rarely postpone answering a question. The judge has a reason for making an inquiry and expects an immediate response. An unanswered question may cause the judge not to listen to the continuing argument until the answer is given and may be perceived by the judge as an effort to avoid responding to a question. In some situations it may be sufficient to provide a short answer and to explain more later in the argument.

4. *Directly Answer the Question.* It will do the attorney little good to hedge or respond obliquely to add tangential explanations. A direct answer should be immediately made followed by any qualifications or explanations.

5. *Succinctly Answer a Question.* An answer should be given that satisfies the question, just like law school exams. A lengthy answer that goes beyond providing the judge with the necessary information should be avoided.

6. *Candidly Respond to a Question.* All answers must be stated in an honest and straightforward manner. Many questions will focus on a weakpoint and lawyers may attempt to argue a point rather than respond to it. An answer to a question may result in a concession which some lawyers are loath to make. An effective advocate realizes the need to candidly admit a weakness or a concession. The effect of an admission may be reduced by providing additional information and the impact of a concession may be reduced by placing the concession in perspective.

7. *Monitor Non-verbal Reactions.* What an attorney says in answer to a question should match the attorney's delivery of the response. An uncertain look in the eyes, a flushed face, a quiver in the voice, an underconfident expression, an embarrassing silence, a lengthy stammer, falling to the courtroom floor, these and other non-verbal responses may signal the real answer by a lawyer. As much as possible the lawyer

should maintain direct eye contact with the judge and visibly appear to be confident.

8. *Phrase an Answer in as Favorable a Way as Possible.* The lawyer should attempt to respond to an inquiry in a way that advances the client's position.

9. *Do Not Answer the Inappropriate Question Directly.* Rare circumstances may permit the lawyer to attempt to avoid responding to a question. Some questions may require a lawyer to qualify an answer or to explain to the judge legitimate reasons why a question cannot be answered. Some questions properly permit a lawyer to postpone an answer until later in the argument. Still other questions may dictate that no answer be given. These circumstances occur infrequently. Many questions may seem irrelevant or unnecessary to the attorney, but are not to the judge.

10. *Be Candid and Cautious in Answering Certain Questions.* Certain questions will be more difficult than others to field. It may be necessary for the lawyer to candidly state that he or she has not considered the question nor an answer and for the judge to consider the spontaneity of the answer. Some questions seek information the attorney lacks. In these situations, the lawyer must candidly say: "I don't know," just like law school exams.

11. *Use an Answer to a Question as a Transition to Make a Point.* After an answer has been provided, the lawyer should direct the response back to the planned argument. Counsel should blend desired points with responses to judges' questions. An advocate should attempt to maintain control and direction over the argument by shifting the discussion to strong points that support the client's positions.

12. *Do Not Repeat a Response to a Question.* A prepared argument may contain responses to a question in a subsequent part of the argument. A lawyer should not repeat an answer but should flexibly revise the planned argument and continue on to a new point.

13. *Do Not Laugh.* It usually is ineffective for the attorney to double over in laughter or ask the judge for the punch line.

14. *Do Not Engage in a Debate With the Judge.* A line of questioning may prompt an attorney to engage in a sharp debate with the judge. This situation may arise because of intense questioning or because of some hostility by the judge. Persistent questioning by the judge may reflect an effort to test the validity of the advocate's positions. The attorney should rise to the challenge and respond with equal persistency. Hostile questions may reflect a nasty judge who is acting unfairly or is oblivious to the demeanor portrayed. The advocate will need to act with restraint in responding. It will be more effective for an attorney to be tolerant and polite rather than contentious.

This does not mean that there is nothing that an attorney can or should do when facing an unfair judge. The lawyer may politely request that the judge refrain from inappropriate behavior or questioning, or the lawyer may state on the record his or her impression of what is happening in order to protect the client's interests. These tactical decisions are difficult to make because the judge will attempt to rule impartially on the motion and the reaction of the attorney may unconsciously or consciously affect that decision. Section 11.5 explores some of these ethical dilemmas for the lawyer.

§ 13.4.5 Communications Skills

An attorney should have two primary communication goals: first, to emulate persuasive communication skills, and second, to avoid ineffective communication deficiencies.

Effective Skills	Ineffective Skills
Appropriate dress and appearance	Poor grooming and demeanor
Maintaining eye contact with the judge	Avoiding eye contact and looking at papers, walls, or ceilings
Modulating voice tone, pitch, and volume	Speaking in a monotone or talking too loudly or too softly
Avoiding verbal glitches	Repeating verbal glitches such as "uh," "ah," or "you know"
Varying facial expressions	Maintaining constant, same, expressions
Using natural and relaxed gestures	Using no gestures, or employing distracting gestures
Appearing confident and comfortable	Engaging in distracting habits or nervous tics
Using good diction and clear, distinct delivery	Displaying poor diction and delivery
Employing understandable words and phrases	Engaging in unnecessary legalese
Maintaining proper pace and timing and pauses	Talking too fast or too slow and not using transitions
Being respectful of court	Acting disrespectful toward court

The more common distracting mannerisms that occur during argument include swaying or slouching, tugging at clothes or glasses, jingling coins, brushing hair away from the face, holding a pen, drumming fingers on the lectern, shuffling papers, sweating through outer garments, and dry heaving.

Common courtesies that judges expect of lawyers include specific behavior and modes of addressing individuals involved in the motion hearing. The following guidelines reflect typical expectations:

- Attorneys will rise when addressing the court.
- An argument will begin with "Your Honor," or "May it please the court," or "If the court please." "You look marvelous in black" is less acceptable.

- Counsel will preface a comment with the phrase "Your Honor" or "Judge" when appropriate.
- Categorical answers should be stated as "Yes, Your Honor" or "No, Judge."
- Opposing lawyers should be referred to by their last names prefaced with Ms., Miss, Mrs., or Mr.
- Other judges should be referred to by title, not simply their last name or any nickname. (*e.g.*, "Justice Holmes", not "Holmes"; "Judge Smith", not "Hanging Tom.")
- Clients and witnesses should be similarly addressed and referred to by their last names and not first names, during both questioning of witnesses and during oral argument.
- Comments toward all persons in the courtroom should avoid insults or sarcasm.
- Counsel should be appropriately respectful toward all and should neither be rude nor discourteous.
- Compliments or flattering comments to the judge should be avoided to avoid any appearance of impropriety or favors.
- Faces, grimaces, rolling eyes, snickering smiles and other non-verbal reactions made during the other attorney's argument are bad manners.

Notes. Notes usually will be necessary for a motion hearing, and their proper use makes a presentation more effective. Notes provide the advocate with a convenient reference for information during the argument, with a ready listing of points and authorities, with a guide to the structure of the argument, and with answers to questions asked by the judge. The absence of notes may indicate that the attorney has not prepared for the argument and make it difficult to present a complete and accurate argument. Notes should not distract from the presentation and should be employed in a way that increases the persuasive influence of the lawyer. Various ways written notes can be used include:

- An outline of the argument, with key issues, facts, phrases, and words highlighted.
- A set of note cards that contain separate portions of the argument.
- A listing of important facts, citations, and other data that provide the attorney with readily accessible information.
- An index of the motion papers and case documents in situations involving numerous documents.
- Concise summaries or relevant quotations of applicable decisions, rules, or statutes involved in the argument.
- Minute etchings on the retinas of the eyes.

The notes may be written on a legal pad, a limited number of index cards, or in a looseleaf notebook. Whatever format is used should be geared to the needs of the argument. A lengthy or complex argument may require a comprehensive notebook with tabs for quick reference to cases, statutes, affidavits, or memos. A single or short argument may only need a separate sheet of paper.

Lectern. Many courts have a lectern for the attorney to stand behind. Some courtrooms will have counsel tables arranged so that the attorney stands to the side of the table. The availability of a lectern provides a handy place for written notes but may afford insufficient space for supporting documents or books. An attorney needs to remain aware of the appropriate use of the lectern. It should not be leaned upon, clenched with unusual force, pushed around or slept on. Many courts expect an attorney to stand behind it and not move, other judges will permit the attorney to move from side to side.

Situations in courtrooms where attorneys must stand by counsel table cause many attorneys to appear uncomfortable or awkward. It is difficult for some attorneys to stand without something in front of them. They try to lean over on the table, stand in front of a chair, slouch, or place their hands in and out of their pockets. Attorneys need to become comfortable standing alone by practicing standing with their arms comfortably at their sides and by using appropriate gestures.

Visual Aids. Motion hearings that involve the introduction of exhibits provide opportunities for the use of real or demonstrative evidence during a motion argument. Other forms of visual aids may assist an attorney in oral argument presentation. Diagrams, maps, graphs, charts, pictures, overhead transparencies, slides, motion pictures, videotapes, models, physical evidence, and copies of the lawyer's accounts receivable may increase the impact of an argument.

The advocate must learn to use these exhibits effectively and to bring them to the hearing. The size of the exhibits must be large enough for the judge to see. Electronic exhibits need a machine and extension cord, which usually is not available in the courtroom. The attorney should rehearse with the exhibits to avoid making mistakes with them during the argument. It may be sufficient in a motion hearing with only one judge to provide the judge and opposing counsel with document exhibits to avoid having to enlarge or mount them.

These types of visual aids may not be used customarily in a motion hearing, but counsel should consider them if they serve a useful purpose. These devices add another dimension to the way the argument is presented and to the extent a judge understands the argument.

Visual aids are not always useful or helpful. They may confuse an argument or distract from the verbal presentation. They may cost too much or take too much time and effort to set up and explain. The other side may oppose them and require further argument on their propriety. Some judges perceive illustrative aids as gimmicks. These and other problems need to be considered in deciding whether and how visual aids should be employed.

Practice. Practice. Practice. The success of an argument depends upon the thoroughness of the attorney's presentation. It is critical to the effectiveness of a presentation that it be rehearsed. A rehearsal helps with timing, reduces reliance on notes, and builds confidence. The extent of a rehearsal depends upon the complexity or magnitude of the motion and the experience of the lawyer.

There are several types of rehearsals. An attorney can informally prepare by mentally going over the argument, can verbally rehearse by spontaneously practicing out loud, can follow a prepared outline or script, or can combine these formats. Rehearsals may be several in number or ongoing as the attorney uses these opportunities to shape the argument. An attorney may prefer to rehearse an argument in separate parts and refine each part or may prefer to practice an argument from beginning to end and make revisions after completion. A sequence of more than one rehearsal permits adjustments to be made in successive practices. Rehearsals and self-critiques should continue until the presentation is smooth, the attorney feels comfortable and confident, and the time of the argument conforms to the time available before the judge.

Significant oral arguments should be rehearsed in front of someone. An imaginary judge or a mirror may be sufficient for most arguments, but presentations that involve substantial issues or money may deserve a more thorough rehearsal with someone present who can provide a helpful critique. Anyone—a friend (if any) or a non-lawyer (if known)—can comment on the clarity of the argument. A colleague knowledgeable in the area can offer additional suggestions about both the content and presentation of the argument. A colleague may also be able to ask questions typical of the ones a judge may ask. Both the advocate and the colleague can anticipate questions that probably will be asked in order to make the rehearsal as realistic as possible. Rehearsals may also include the use of video equipment with the advocate being able to watch a replay of the argument and to have someone else further critique the performance.

§ 13.5 POST-ARGUMENT BRIEFS

Supplemental briefs may be necessary to provide the judge with some additional legal authorities, analysis, and citations. Post-argument briefs should be limited to new matters that arise during the argument, and not to satisfy the urge to have that wanted last word. The attorney who receives a supplemental memo will be able to submit a post argument reply memo. Typically, a judge establishes deadlines for the brief, for example, ten days for a supplemental brief and another ten days for a reply brief. Perhaps the judge needs the attorney's written comments regarding a recent development and a short letter from both lawyers will be adequate. An attorney should not *ex parte* submit a supplemental written memo or letter to the judge. A copy must be served on opposing counsel.

§ 13.6 WAIVER OF ORAL ARGUMENT

The presentation of a motion usually involves oral argument. Some judges and courts restrict an oral presentation and have lawyers submit motions in writing only. These jurisdictions perceive that an oral argument is unnecessary to the proper determination of a motion and that time and expenses can be saved by not having a motion hearing. Attorneys facing these restrictions usually have an opportunity to submit a request to the court explaining why oral argument should be scheduled.

In all situations, whether or not a jurisdiction imposes restrictions on a motion hearing, an attorney should consider whether oral argument is worth the time, expense, and effort. Usually, the answer to this question will be yes, most often a resounding yes, particularly by the movant who has the burden of persuasion. There are situations when oral argument may be appropriately waived, even by a movant. A motion may be simple and straightforward and need no oral presentation. A motion may be more effectively presented through a written presentation.

There are alternatives to attorneys appearing in court to argue a motion. The most common option is a telephone conference call including the judge and opposing lawyers. Some courts provide a conference call by rule. Even if the local rules are silent on this subject, most courts will consider a request for a conference call. Telephone presentations offer many of the advantages of a live presentation without some of the disadvantages. A teleconference call permits the attorneys to present their positions and to answer questions by the judge and saves the lawyers travel and waiting time. The most difficult factor is deciding who should pay for the call.

PRACTICE PROBLEMS

1. Plan a memorandum in support of or in opposition to a motion assigned by your instructor.
2. Outline a memorandum in support of or in opposition to a motion assigned by your instructor.
3. Draft the memorandum in support of or in opposition to a motion assigned by your instructor.
4. Edit the memorandum drafted by your classmate and provided to you by your instructor.
5. Edit the memorandum provided by your instructor.
6. Plan an oral argument in support of or in opposition to a motion assigned by your instructor.
7. Outline an oral argument in support of or in opposition to a motion assigned by your instructor.

8. Write out an oral argument in support of or in opposition to a motion provided by your instructor.

9. Critique the outline or content of the oral argument provided by your instructor.

10. Critique the following memorandum. What could counsel have done more effectively to present the position?

Memorandum Draft

UNITED STATES DISTRICT COURT DISTRICT OF MITCHELL

First Division

Martha Giacone, et al.,	)	
Plaintiffs,	)	
vs.	)	
City of Mitchell, Mitchell Municipal	)	MEMORANDUM
Water Department, State of Summit, State Public Utility Commission,	)	
Defendants	)	

Defendants State of Summit and Public Utility Commission bring this motion to support their motion that this Court dismiss Plaintiff's pretended Complaint because it fails to state subject matter jurisdiction and a claim upon which relief can be granted pursuant to Federal Rule of Civil Procedure 12.

The Plaintiff's Complaint alleges four causes of action including two Title 42, United States Code, Section 1983 claims, and two pendent state claims. The federal constitutional claims are based on equal protection and due process violations. The state claims are alleged breaches of the Summit Public Utility Act, Summit Statutes 36.1 et seq.

Defendants submit this motion in lieu of an Answer responding to the Complaint.

ARGUMENT

PLAINTIFF'S COMPLAINT SEEKING MONETARY DAMAGES SHOULD BE DISMISSED BECAUSE OF THE ELEVENTH COMMANDMENT.

Plaintiff seeks money damages from the Defendants. Such money claims are barred by the Eleventh Amendment which provides that no State shall be sued without its express permission. *See, e.g., Clark v. Baynard,* 108 U.S. 436 (1883). In *Hans v. Louisiana,* 10 S.Ct. 504 (1890), the Supreme Court reviewed this Amendment and interpreted it broadly, holding that a federal court could not entertain a lawsuit brought by a citizen against his own state.

Obviously, the Defendant State of Summit is a state of the United States and falls within the protective ambit of the Eleventh Amendment. The Public Utility Commission is a creature of the State, having been created by Article XVII, Section 4 of the Constitution of the State of Summit. The Public Utility Commission is an instrumentality of the State. Summit Statute 36.2 states that all immunities reserved to the State are reserved to the Commission making it completely immune from federal litigation. While there has been no holding by the Federal Circuit Court of Appeals in this District, other Circuits have upheld similar state institutions to be immune. *Walstad v. University of Minnesota Hospital,* 442 F.2d 634 (8th Cir.1983). Congress did not enact Section 1983 to override the Eleventh Amendment. *See,* for an extensive discussion, *Fitzpatrick v. Bitzer,* 427 U.S. 445 (1976).

It is clear that States are absolutely immune from 1983 actions. *Quern v. Jordan,* 440 U.S. 332, 342 (1979). The scope of the protection afforded States is well settled. No retroactive monetary relief can be obtained against a state, or even state official or agencies. *Edelman v. Jordan,* 415 U.S. 651 (1974). There is no federal case allowing a plaintiff to recover money damages against a State or its instrumentalities, in a situation anywhere similar to the claims presented by the Plaintiff in this case. Plaintiff alleges no other federal constitutional or statutory claims, and their allegations that this Court has jurisdiction pursuant to 28 U.S.C. Sections 1331 and 1343 are inaccurate and wrong.

THE PENDENT STATE CLAIMS MUST BE DISMISSED BECAUSE NO INDEPENDENT GROUNDS FOR FEDERAL JURISDICTION EXIST.

The two state claims asserted by the Plaintiff must be dismissed by this Court because of the holding of the United States Supreme Court in *Pennhurst v. Halderman,* 104 S.Ct. 900 (1984). In *Pennhurst,* the Court held that state officials who violated state laws in carrying out their official duties are protected by the Eleventh Amendment from relief that seeks money damages as well as declaratory and injunctive remedies. This decision applies with equal force to this case, requiring this Court to dismiss all state claims against the Defendants.

Further, there is no private cause of action specifically provided in Summit Statutes Sections 36.1 et seq., the basis of the pendent state claims. If any utility user has any private remedy under Chapter 36 that decision should first be reviewed by the Summit Supreme Court as a case of first impression. This federal Court should not determine this issue under the doctrine of comity.

NO STATE OFFICIALS WERE INVOLVED IN THIS CASE, REQUIRING THE CLAIMS AGAINST THE STATE TO BE DISMISSED.

Only city employees and officials were involved in this case. No agent of the State of Summit was involved. No agent of the State Public Utility was involved. Paragraph 6 of Plaintiff's Complaint alleges that the State Public Utility Commission reviews and approves the termination procedures adopted and used by the City of Mitchell. The correct facts, explained in the affidavit of Johanas Montague, the State Public Utility Commissioner, is that the state department accepts for filing copies of termination procedures used by municipal and public utilities. Neither the State nor the Public Utility Commission approves the regulations. There is absolutely no control exercised by the State or the Commissioner regarding the individual termination policies of utility companies. In this case no state agent or employee knew the plaintiff, was involved in any decision to terminate her service, or terminated her service. *See* Affidavit of Johanas Montague, attached to this Memorandum. As a matter of law, the city employees and agents are not state officials. State officials may be enjoined in their official capacity from violating the constitutional rights of a Plaintiff and prospective injunctive relief may be obtained against those state officials. *Ex Parte Young,* 28 S.Ct. 441 (1908). But that is not the case here. The law of the forum state, Summit, applies in this case. In *Sams v. Zeliski,* 346 Sum. 272, the Summit Supreme Court held in a tort negligence case that the acts of a municipal employee were not acts attributable to the state. There is nothing in the facts of this case, nor the law, that converts the city employees in this case into state actors.

For all these reasons the Defendants respectfully request that this Court dismiss all claims against them.

____

THOMAS SHAWNBAUER
Office of the Attorney General
State of Summit
State Capitol Building
Mitchell, Summit

(a) Critique this Memorandum. What could defense counsel have done to more effectively present the position of the State?

(b) Redraft this Memorandum. Assume an associate in your firm drafted this memo and submitted it to you, before it was served and filed, for your comments and critique.

11. You represent Martha Giacone and receive the above memorandum.

(a) Plan a response to the memorandum.

(b) Outline a response to the memorandum.

(c) Draft a memorandum in opposition to defendant's motion.

12. Critique the following motion argument. What could defense counsel have done more effectively to represent the position of the college of law? What could counsel for plaintiff have done more effectively to represent the plaintiff's position?

Motion Hearing Transcript

Judge: The next motion is, ah, *Birk v. Summit College of Law.* Appearances?

Wandell: Your honor, I represent the defendant.

Judge: And your name is?

Wandell: Chris Wandell.

Judge: Your honor.

Wandell: Yes, Judge, your honor.

O'Gara: And I am Pat O'Gara, your honor, representing the plaintiff in this case and opposing this motion.

Judge: Very well, proceed counsel.

Wandell: Your Honor, the defendant . . .

Judge: Up here at the lectern, Mr. Wandell.

Wandell: Yes . . . Your Honor, the Defendant in this case is the Summit College of Law. We are bringing a Rule 12 motion to dismiss Plaintiff's complaint for failure to state a viable cause of action before this court, in this jurisdiction. Specifically, the defendant Law School contends that it has no obligation to provide a due process type hearing to the plaintiff in determining whether the plaintiff did or did not deserve tenure and, secondly, that the procedures provided the plaintiff, a hearing by the faculty, was sufficient to provide plaintiff with a full and fair opportunity to contest the allegations against her in her seeking tenure.

To the first point. The defendant institution is not a public university or anything like that. It is a private institution of the highest learning and has unfettered discretion to establish reasonable policies concerning the hiring, retention, and tenure of its faculty. The plaintiff in accepting employment at Summit College of Law agreed to be bound by the procedures and policies of the College. She cannot now claim they are improper or unreasonable because she agreed to abide by those same policies and procedures. The law is quite clear in this area. The cases are legion which support this position. For example, the Supreme Court of Coastland has held in *Formath v. Pigmalion College of Fine Arts* at 376 P.2d 764:

> The claims of the Plaintiff are meritless when directed toward this Defendant. The Plaintiff who seeks reinstatement as a faculty member has no right to pursue such a claim against a private institution. Pigmalion has established regulations which govern reinstatement. The Plaintiff is bound by these regulations. This holding clarifies and reaffirms our decision in *Bjorke v. Rasmussen Business College,* 309 P.2d 352.

And so Your Honor . . . by the way, our brief provides a listing of other decisions which say the same thing.

Judge: Do you cite any case from this jurisdiction?

Wandell: Yes, Your Honor, we do on page . . . 11, no 13 . . . yes, here, actually the citations from this jurisdiction involve cases involving public institutions and not private institutions. There appears to be no case which has required private institutions, that is, has held private institutions to the same standards or requirements that public institutions have been held to. And that lack of authority provides the plaintiff with no cause of action against my client. May I continue, Your Honor?

Judge: Do I understand that the Summit Supreme Court has yet to consider a case involving the facts in this case?

Wandell: Well, basically Judge, the cases that the Supreme Court has considered have involved the denial of tenure of faculty members, but have not involved a private institution like Summit College of Law. It is explained in detail in our brief.

Now, moving on to the second part ... point. Summit College of Law carefully and reasonably determined that plaintiff did not meet the criteria required to receive tenure and provided her with a fair hearing to challenge that decision. The provisions of the College's tenure policy are set forth in the Faculty Manual attached to the affidavit of Dean Groll submitted in support of this motion. Those procedures specify the criteria that a faculty person must meet to receive tenure. A vote of the tenured members of the Summit faculty determined, after detailed consideration, that the Plaintiff did not meet those standards. She then had an opportunity to again present her case to the Dean who agreed with the determination of the tenured faculty.

This case is a relatively straightforward case, Your Honor. It is quite clear that the plaintiff has no valid claim to assert against the defendant and we request that the complaint be dismissed pursuant to Rule 12.

Judge: Counsel, by my consideration of the affidavit of Dean Groll, does not that consideration transform the Rule 12 motion into a Rule 56 motion for summary judgment?

Wandell: I don't think so, Judge. You don't need to even rely on the affidavit. The tenure policy of Summit was mentioned in the plaintiff's complaint and you need go no further than reviewing that pleading to decide this motion.

Judge: Why then did you provide an affidavit?

Wandell: That point is addressed in our brief Your Honor. But, basically, well, it is detailed why in the memorandum. Do you want me to find that part, Your Honor?

Judge: No, that's o.k. for now. Ms. O'Gara, you may proceed.

O'Gara: The plaintiff, Beverly Bink, opposes this motion for several reasons. The complaint does state a claim upon which relief can be granted. Count I of the Complaint states that the defendant has breached its employment contract with the Professor Bink. Paragraph 3 alleges that the College of Law failed to follow the explicit provisions of its contract with Professor Bink in denying her tenure. Count II of the Complaint states that there exists an implied covenant in the employment contract which permits Summit College to deny tenure only for reasonable cause, which covenant the College breached in this case. The defendant admits that this second claim presents an issue of first impression before the courts of Summit. The facts of the complaint read in a light most favorable to the plaintiff clearly and forcefully allege two claims for which injunctive and monetary relief, as requested, can be provided by this Court.

Judge: What implied covenant do you claim was breached in this case?

O'Gara: The implied covenant of good faith and fair dealing. It is the plaintiff's position that the defendant, her employer, cannot arbitrarily or without good reason fire her. They have in this case and that clearly provides her with a claim against them. The Supreme Court of Summit in two cases has implied this covenant in other contractual relationships. In *Furth v. Allied Products,* a consumer sued a retailer for breach of a retail installment contract, among other claims including fraud. The Summit Supreme Court held that the defendant retailer owed a duty of good faith dealings toward the consumer which arose from their contractual relationship. Four years ago in *Ogala Realty v. Ching Enterprises*, the Supreme Court applied the Summit Commercial Code statutory standard of good faith dealings between merchants codified in Summit State's Statutes Section 332–104 to a contract for the sale of commercial equipment. The plaintiff submits that these two cases provide by analogy an obvious viable claim for the plaintiff in this case.

Judge: How do you respond to the Defendant's position that because Summit College of Law is a private and not a public institution it should be dismissed from this case?

O'Gara: First, Your Honor, the defendant's position seems to be based on the premise that the complaint alleges constitutional claims, which it does not. And secondly the status of the College of Law, whether public or private, does not alter its contractual obligations towards the plaintiff.

Judge: Surely you don't suggest that a private institution cannot fire its faculty because of economic reasons. What if enrollment drops and it cannot afford to pay faculty?

O'Gara: Those facts are not before this Court in this case, Your Honor. The plaintiff does not challenge the defendant's right to terminate professors because of dire financial straits. The precise reasons why plaintiff was terminated in this case are unclear at this stage of the litigation. We have noticed a motion for this hearing which we will address after this motion has been argued which seeks a court order requiring the defendant to disclose information about the tenure committee meeting and the votes of individual faculty at that meeting to clarify who voted based on what reasons. Without that information this Court cannot decide the propriety of defendant's motion to dismiss, which should be denied, at least, because it is premature.

Wandell: Your Honor, excuse me, that is a preposterous argument. It is quite clear that in this state that information is privileged and not obtainable.

Judge: Let's consider that motion now. Ms. O'Gara, present your argument.

(a) What questions could the judge have asked to clarify the issues and resolve the motion?

(b) You represent the plaintiff.

(1) Plan an argument in opposition to the motion of the defendant and in support of your motion.

(2) Outline an argument in opposition to the motion of the defendant and in support of your motion.

(3) Write out an argument in opposition to the motion of the defendant and in support of your motion.

(c) You represent the Summit College of Law. How would you have differently planned, outlined, and presented the argument in support of your motion as against the motion of the plaintiff?

*

PART FIVE

SETTLEMENT OF LITIGATION

*

CHAPTER 14

THE SETTLEMENT PROCESS

Discourage litigation. Persuade your neighbors to compromise whenever they can. Point out to them how the nominal winner is often a real loser in fees, expenses, and waste of time. As a peacemaker, the lawyer has a superior opportunity of being a good person. There will be business enough.

—Abraham Lincoln, Law Lecture

§ 14.1 ROLE OF SETTLEMENT IN LITIGATION

Settlement is a very important part of the pretrial litigation process. Although the statistics vary, somewhere between 90 and 97 percent of all civil litigation ends in settlement or dismissal before trial.[1] Many lawyers become experienced "litigators" long before they can legitimately call themselves "trial" lawyers. Settlement is therefore an appropriate topic to discuss at the end of this book. If importance determined where chapters were located, it would be one of the first chapters in the book.

The law favors settlements.[2] Settlement promotes judicial economy, saving valuable court time as well as avoiding delay for the parties, while removing the uncertainty inherent in trial, particularly jury trial. Settlement also conserves the resources of the parties, and therefore society, that would otherwise be spent on court costs, legal fees, and other

§ 14.1

1. *See, e.g.,* C. Robbins, Attorney's Master Guide to Expediting Top–Dollar Case Settlements 1 (1980) (estimates 98% of all litigation settled).

2. *See United States v. Pfizer Inc.,* 560 F.2d 319 (8th Cir.1977); *Du Puy v. Director, Office of Workers' Compensation Programs, U.S. Dept. of Labor,* 519 F.2d 536 (7th Cir.1975), *cert. denied* 424 U.S. 965, 96 S.Ct. 1459, 47 L.Ed.2d 732 (1976).

expenses.[3] There is also a widely held view that settlements, being by definition satisfactory to the parties, are more effective at removing discord within our social and commercial fabric, and are therefore more desirable from a societal view. There is nearly unanimous agreement of scholars and commentators that settlement is desirable and should be encouraged.[4]

The settlement "process" itself is well nigh impossible to describe. Settlement may be arrived at as a result of a multitude of different processes, and usually occurs only after a number of those processes have been brought to bear on the dispute giving rise to the litigation. The tools of settlement include all of the pretrial procedures discussed in the foregoing chapters of this book. Negotiation also plays a central role in the settlement of most actions. The courts play varying roles in the settlement process, ranging from no involvement to heavy, or even coercive, participation in settlement discussions.

This chapter cannot provide even a complete introduction to litigation settlements and negotiation. Entire books have been written on negotiation,[5] and even those works have difficulty explaining the dynamics and nuances of negotiation skills. Conscious efforts to study one's negotiation skills and to review techniques used by others can, however, be of great value in developing negotiation skills.

§ 14.2 THE ROLE AND PRACTICE OF NEGOTIATION IN PRETRIAL LITIGATION

Litigation seldom settles through the abrupt capitulation of the other side (although if you frequently experience immediate opponent collapse, you are obviously in the right line of work). Even "overnight" successes are the culmination of months of intensive preparation, including earnest (at least on one side) but unsuccessful attempts at a negotiated settlement. Similarly, even where there is a formal settlement mechanism (*e.g.*, a summary jury trial) or active judicial involvement (a/k/a arm-twisting) designed to achieve settlement, resolution by the parties always involves some negotiation by counsel, unless counsel has totally abdicated the role of zealous advocate for the client.

Preparation. In a sense, negotiation, like trial, begins at the outset of the dispute. Before filing a complaint, client and counsel should create a reasonably clear picture of their objective: is it to end the contract, obtain compensation, stop disparaging statements, or something else? Once the general object has been identified, the best lawyers often outline more specific tentative best and worst case analyses such as estimating the realistically acceptable settlement range for a personal

3. *See Autera v. Robinson,* 419 F.2d 1197 (D.C.Cir.1969).

4. For one academic criticism of the propriety and desirability of encouraging, or even permitting, settlement, see Owen M. Fiss, Against Settlement, 93 Yale L.J. 1073 (1984). Professor Fiss's views are not widely shared, however.

5. *See* Roger S. Haydock, Negotiation Practice (1984); G. Williams, Legal Negotiations (1983); Roger Fisher & William Ury, Getting to Yes (1981).

injury claim. Many experienced lawyers use the "get it in writing" theory against themselves, making a settlement memorandum to the file at the outset of the case. Later on in the heat of the case, they refer to such memos to remind themselves of their evaluation of the case during more placid times. Often, tempers cool after the initial bellicose euphoria of filing the complaint as clients become bored with the technicalities of litigation and tired of paying legal bills. Whatever the effect of the litigation experience on attorney and client, early settlement evaluations must be constantly reviewed in light of changing conditions: new facts emerging from discovery, the bankruptcy of one of the parties (or its insurer), a new government assistance program or tax ruling that makes litigation less attractive.

Timing. For most cases, extended negotiation and discussions are most likely to occur after a significant amount of discovery and through the final pretrial conference (where the judge's urging provides an additional push). Settlement is unlikely to precede some significant discovery in a complex or high stakes case. After the final pretrial conference, many lawyers and clients see no turning back from the battle, but this attitude is not unusual. Settlement not only occurs "on the courthouse steps" as counsel tread in to select a jury but also after jury selection (when each side has a chance to make a more specific evaluation of the factfinder), after significant evidence rulings, or after key testimony ("Gee, how'd you find out about my client's conviction for embezzlement 9 years ago? Anyway, here's the settlement check you wanted.") Settlement even occurs during jury deliberations (longer deliberations tend to make everybody more nervous and susceptible to serious negotiation) or after verdict. Rulings by the trial court on post-trial motions and counsel's assessment of the risks on appeal also affect the timing of a settlement.

Competitive Approach. At whatever time is deemed right by at least one lawyer, negotiations can occur. Negotiation styles are as varied (and as warped) as are lawyers' personalities. Some lawyers demand the moon (if they represent a plaintiff) or reject any possible rapprochement (if they represent a defendant) while steaming full speed ahead toward trial. These lawyers may be very aggressive and outspoken or soft-spoken and polite. This does not mean that lawyers who take extreme positions are not interested in settlement. On the contrary, every sane lawyer is interested in settlement where the facts and law suggest it and the other parties are reasonably likely to agree to a settlement that is favorable, or at least fair. "Extremist" lawyers just happen to believe that they will most likely obtain good settlements for their clients by being tough, prepared, and unafraid of trial. Many are even adverse to making the first offer (or even suggestion) of settlement. In essence, they play a litigation variant of the teenage hot-rodders game of "chicken," seeking to unnerve the opponent into first hitting the brakes.

Cooperative Approach. Increasingly, a more cooperative tone for negotiation has gained favor, at least among commentators.[1] Under this approach, lawyers do not play chicken, refrain from issuing ultimatums, and seldom stake out hard and fast "positions." Rather, the facilitative lawyer, when negotiating, stresses the mutual interests of the adversaries and the joint benefits that might be derived from a "custom-made" settlement rather than through pursuit of the less flexible remedies offered by litigation. A perhaps classic illustration of this is a parable of two people fighting over an orange when one wants the fruit to eat while the other wants the rind for baking.[2] If litigated, only one will end up with the orange and will incur substantial litigation costs that may well exceed the value of the fruit (or, alternatively, the rind). However, an intelligently crafted settlement can provide each with what they really want less expensively and without the risk of losing all. Now, while the real world of disputes may not resemble a Disney movie, the cooperative school of negotiation has a powerful point: frank discussion of interests, goals, and objectives can often lead to better results than does mere posturing.

Client Approval. Of course, in being cooperative, lawyers should not be dupes: they should hold paramount their client's needs and interests and should not disclose confidential or privileged information.[3] Similarly, clients must be advised of pertinent facts affecting the settlement posture of the case and must authorize attorney strategy and tactics regarding negotiations, especially the deals offered or counter-offered and the specific range of settlement authority vested in counsel. Unfortunately, some clients have short memories; others are fair weather friends; others are easily confused. When conferring with clients and crafting a negotiation strategy, it is usually wise to confirm these matters in writing. This is impossible in the heat of battle but memorialization in a later file memo is often wise.

Strategy Selection. Which negotiation strategy is best? As with so many other issues in law, the answer is a resounding "it depends." Certainly, the list of tough and cooperative negotiation styles is not exhaustive. Rather, they are perhaps best viewed as poles of a continuum, with many lawyers in between the two "extremes" or varying their approaches with particular issues in the case or in response to particular stimulae. Lawyers are generally better doing what comes naturally (so long as this natural instinct is within the acceptable range of social behavior) rather than trying to imitate someone else. Similarly, you will typically enjoy more success by being yourself. If the cooperative style

§ 14.2

1. This approach is perhaps best captured in the national best seller, Getting to Yes by R. Fisher and W. Ury (1981). R. Haydock, Negotiation Practice (1984), also essentially advocates more cooperative and less contentious negotiation styles.

2. Fisher and Ury popularized it. *See* Getting to Yes 59, 76 (1981). For an expansion of the cooperative possibilities of the "battle of the orange" *see* Stephen P. Doyle & Roger S. Haydock, Without the Punches: Resolving Disputes Without Litigation 7–8 (1991).

3. However, the legal system often provides extra "breathing room" for settlement. For example, Fed.R.Evid. 408 provides that nothing said at a settlement meeting may be used as evidence if the dispute proceeds to trial.

suits you, by all means engage it in, subject to the caveat of preventing the less scrupulous from taking unfair advantage of you. If you feel more comfortable with the aggressive persona and waiting for your opponent to make the first conciliatory move, this will probably work best for you. Often a combination of approaches or a variance of approaches brings good results. Lawyers with different instinctive styles often make a good negotiating team. We've all seen enough prime time TV to know how to play "good cop/bad cop." It may be unoriginal, but many lawyering teams swear by it.

Evaluation. In coming to a negotiation strategy and evaluation of the worth of a case, many lawyers attempt to use a rough mathematical formula of sorts. It is best illustrated by a typical claim for personal injury. If, for example, plaintiff asserts negligence by defendant in causing an auto accident, the calculus might proceed something like this:

- Plaintiff and counsel see the case on liability as strong since defendant hit the rear of plaintiff's car while it was stopped at a traffic light. Plaintiff and a bystander pedestrian will testify the light was red but defendant will testify that the light had been green for several seconds. A "fix-it" ticket issued to plaintiff a week prior to the accident shows that at least one tail light was burned out and plaintiff admits that this was not corrected before the accident. Plaintiff's counsel estimates a 70 percent chance that a jury will find for plaintiff on liability.
- Plaintiff incurred $10,000 in medical expenses and spent $12,000 for a used car to replace his, which was totaled in the accident. Plaintiff missed a year of work from his $40,000 per year job as a suburban school teacher and continues to have back pain, especially after a long day of classes. Plaintiff's expert witness doctor and treating physician will testify the condition is permanent while the defendant's expert doctor will testify that the back will be as good as new within two-to-three years (plaintiff is 42 years old). Plaintiff has been forced to quit coaching the junior varsity ice hockey team, which was a source of real joy to him. Plaintiff's counsel views the accident as having caused plaintiff $62,000 in provable out-of-pocket or economic loss damages. As to the pain-and-suffering damages, counsel's estimate is $200,000 but he also sees a 25 percent chance that the jury will believe the defendant's doctor that the injury is not permanent.
- Plaintiff's counsel multiplies the amount of "realistically" calculated damages by the probability of recovery.

.70 times $ 62,000 = $ 43,400
.75 times $200,000 = $150,000 times .70 = $105,000 [4]
Total Estimated Settlement Value = $148,400

4. This calculation is oversimplified in that a jury might believe the injury to be non-permanent but award more in pain-and-suffering damages for the past and future temporary injury. Conversely, a jury

- Plaintiff's counsel mutes the valuation by remembering that the medical expenses and part of the replacement car purchase price were covered by plaintiff's insurance and that plaintiff also collected unemployment benefits and some disability insurance for his year away from work. Although these funds cannot be mentioned at trial under the evidence rule excluding consideration of collateral sources of compensation, the $33,000 figure is significant and may be subconsciously appreciated by the jurors, many of whom have similar insurance protection.
- Plaintiff's counsel also deducts the costs of trial expenses (*e.g.*, expert fees) saved if the case is settled, estimating this amount at $2,000. The lawyer's one-third contingency is another matter. It encourages plaintiff to hold out for the maximum realistic settlement since plaintiff will at best realize only two-thirds of any settlement amount.
- All told, plaintiff's counsel recommends settling the case for a figure in the $115,000–$135,000 range and with client approval aims her negotiating strategy toward achieving that figure. Through discovery, plaintiff's counsel knows that defendant has $300,000 worth of liability coverage in his auto policy. If defendant had only $100,000 worth of coverage, the settlement objective would be considerably clearer: try to obtain the policy limits.

Illustrations like the above suffer from a misleading appearance of quantitative precision. Picking a percentage likelihood of victory or a damage award (especially for non-economic damages) is more of an intelligent "guesstimate" than an exact science. Nonetheless, experienced trial lawyers routinely amaze new associates with the accuracy of their predictions. It can be done—but not with consistent computer-like precision.[5]

Tactics. Having evaluated the case is but half the battle. After setting settlement objective and parameters, counsel must still negotiate toward the goal, by whatever method preferred. If the attorney's style is to make a settlement demand, the lawyer must pick an opening amount. As with settlement styles as a whole, demand amount styles vary. Some lawyers prefer a big demand that leaves plenty of room to move toward opponents making them think they have "gotten something." Plaintiff's lawyer above might, for example, demand $250,000 from the defendant driver who has thus offered nothing and hope for a result that "splits the difference."

could see the injury as permanent but award less compensation.

5. *See* Fleming James, et al., Civil Procedure §§ 6.3 & 6.4 (4th ed. 1992) (presenting estimate of "true" value of claim and discount for likelihood of success and other factors in different form); Roger S. Haydock, Negotiation Practice § 2.3 at 24 (1984) (attorneys given case to evaluate as part of survey gave widely varying assessments of liability and damages).

Other lawyers prefer to make a demand only slightly above the bottom line goal. This leaves some room to feed the opponent's negotiating ego but is less likely to make the opponent regard the demander as unreasonable, out-of-touch-with-reality and not worth further negotiations. If the plaintiff's attorney above demanded $140,000 and stood pat until the defendant came close, this approach would be the "goal plus cushion" school of demands. In a small legal community where personal habits cum vices become well-known, the more reasonable demander probably fares better: other lawyers come to take a demand seriously and can get down to the fine points of negotiation faster than is possible when trying to filter out puff and blarney of a highball demand.

Techniques. Whatever the negotiator's style, counsel should focus on objective facts and hard-headed analysis of law when assessing the situation and dealing with opponents. A lawyer who overestimates a position due to emotional attachment to the case or desire to placate the client ultimately disserves both case and client.

Counsel should also plan the negotiation environment:

- Telephone vs. in-person meeting;
- Presence or absence of clients;
- Lawyer's office or neutral site;
- General discussion vs. specific analysis of liability or damages documents;
- Preferred timing for negotiations;
- Open vs. closed demeanor;
- Friendly vs. hostile;
- Grave vs. light-hearted.

Counsel must also think through the particulars of the negotiation agenda:

- What to disclose;
- What not to disclose;
- What positions to take;
- What fallback positions are available;
- What items are readily traded for some consideration from the opponent;
- Which items are essentially "non-negotiable" and so on.

Within the broad outlines of a lawyer's overall negotiation style, claim valuation technique, and demand/offer approach lie many personal variants of negotiation "micro-procedure." Whatever the style, attorneys usually fare better in negotiations where they prepare well regarding the factual record of the case and controlling points of law. A poised and prepared negotiator will not only be taken as a serious threat should trial ensue (and thus constitute an independent incentive to settle) but also will often convince opposing counsel of realistic limitations on their position.

Client Needs. All of the above negotiation considerations are subject to the real world constraints of client needs. For example, if the hypothetical automobile plaintiff above has a destitute ne'er-do-well brother in need of funds, the client may be interested in getting paid sooner even at some loss in claim value (besides, his back may get better). An insurance company often is at the other extreme. It has the money third party claimants want and can afford to wait a long time without becoming impatient. However, in most states, unreasonable insurer behavior can lead to extra-contractual damages like punitive damages. Even the deepest pockets may have some incentive to avoid foot-dragging. However, as a general rule, parties with ample resources (in money, market position, patents, friends in high places, whatever) are in a better position to plan and execute patient negotiation in aid of more advantageous settlements.

§ 14.3 SETTLEMENT WITHIN THE LITIGATION PROCESS

Settlement is frequently a direct part of the litigation process. Most often settlement will occur as a direct result of negotiation between attorneys. Settlement negotiations are often prompted by other events in the lawsuit which make settlement appear attractive to the parties. Unfortunately, the event most likely to prompt settlement is an impending trial date or, frequently, a jury sitting in a courtroom ready to hear evidence. All trial lawyers know that the realization that a trial is about to be held may be one of the most effective things to make parties view their cases realistically.

Courts also take an affirmative and active role in the settlement process. Courts are increasingly recognized to be involved in the management of cases and not merely in deciding narrow disputes submitted by motion or for trial.[1]

Informal Involvement. Judges are frequently involved in settlement of actions by informal discussions and suggestions that the parties consider compromise and settlement of their disputes. Judges may initiate these discussions by asking questions about the status of settlement discussions when the attorneys are before the court for other reasons. Judges may also specifically inquire about any attempts to resolve a specific dispute before submitting it to the court for resolution by motion. Many courts have adopted local rules which require counsel to "meet and confer" in an attempt to resolve disputes before filing motions for relief. These rules are discussed in greater detail in section 11.2.5. Enforcement of these rules gives the court an opportunity to

§ 14.3

1. *See* Robert F. Peckham, The Federal Judge as a Case Manager: The New Role In Guiding a Case From Filing to Disposition, 69 Calif.L.Rev. 770 (1981). *But see* Judith Resnik, Managerial Judges, 96 Harv.L.Rev. 374 (1982) (author critical of role of judges as managers and doubts their effectiveness as resolvers of disputes in that capacity).

inquire of counsel about the discussions, and also to point out the overall advantages settlement may have.

Court Approval of Settlements. Judicial approval or consent is not normally required for settlement of civil litigation. The parties are allowed to settle their disputes on whatever terms are agreeable to all concerned. There are two circumstances in which a proposed settlement must regularly be submitted to the court for approval. In addition, there may be additional reasons to ask for the court's approval of a settlement.

First, most states require that actions involving injuries to minors not be settled without court approval. These requirements are intended to insure that the interests of the minor are adequately protected in the settlement process and that the settlement of the litigation appears to be reasonable under the circumstances. The statute, or the court without specific statutory directions, may require that the proceeds of the settlement which are not used to pay for expenses which have already been incurred be placed in a trust account which assures safe investment of the funds. Court approval may be required for any disbursement of the settlement proceeds during the child's minority.[2] A personal representative of a decedent may also be required to obtain approval of settlements involving the decedent's estate, as may the heirs or trustee authorized to pursue a wrongful death action. For the same reasons, a trustee in bankruptcy may need the approval of the court before compromising any claim of or against the debtor's estate.

Second, settlement of class actions also requires court approval. Fed.R.Civ.P. 23(e) and similar state rules require that any settlement of a class action be submitted for the court's approval. The purpose of this rule is to protect the unnamed class members from a settlement which unfairly benefits the class representatives at their expense and to prevent the use of a class action to extort excessive settlements.[3]

In most other cases the parties may enter into any settlement they believe serves their interests. If a settlement may affect others, or is novel in some way, it may be desirable to have the settlement approved by the court. A trustee, personal representative, or other person who is a party to a case in a representative capacity, may want to obtain judicial approval of a settlement for protection against future claims that the settlement was not appropriate. Although courts will not routinely grant advisory opinions which might affect the rights of persons not parties to the matter before them, courts may be persuaded to review and approve a settlement if the parties submit it for approval.

Settlement Conferences. Many courts routinely hold conferences involving counsel and often the parties for the express purpose of exploring settlement. Settlement conferences are the natural outgrowth of pretrial conferences held under Fed.R.Civ.P. 16 and its state court

2. *See, e.g.,* Minn.Stat.Ann. § 540.08.

3. *See generally* Forde, Settlement of the Class Action, 5 Litig. (Fall 1978), at 23.

equivalents. When initially adopted, the federal rule did not make any reference to settlement. Settlement was not identified in the rule as one of the purposes of holding pretrial conferences and settlement was frequently not discussed at them. Many judges did, however, use Rule 16 pretrial conferences to discuss settlement, and the rule was redrafted and settlement was included as one of the specific purposes of holding a pretrial conference.

Judges use widely divergent techniques to encourage settlement of lawsuits. Most judges attempt to structure the pretrial settlement conference to remove certain obstacles to settlement. For example, most judges require that the attorney who will actually try the case attend the pretrial conference in order to prevent the settlement discussions from breaking down due to the lack of knowledge or lack of authority to settle on the part of the attorneys in attendance. Similarly, most courts require that the parties attend, along with any other persons who have authority to settle the case. The purpose of these requirements is to bring all of the persons necessary to resolving the dispute together so that meaningful discussions can take place.

After bringing the necessary players together, courts use differing techniques to encourage discussions to take place. Many judges will ask one of the parties, frequently the plaintiff, to summarize the current status of the settlement discussions that have taken place prior to the pretrial conference. The judge or magistrate may then ask the parties each to outline their current settlement positions and the reasons they feel support their positions. The dynamics of the settlement process then become largely a matter of individual judgment of the participants. The judge or magistrate may directly confront the weakness in one party's position, or may confront the respective weaknesses of each party's case. The judge may dwell on any of the factors which might be used in negotiations between parties and it is impossible to itemize those areas. Frequently, the judge will focus on the experience the judge has had with similar cases. The purpose of the judge's comments may be to insure that the parties understand the difficulties presented in a particular case. Alternatively, the judge may seek to increase the parties' overall perception of the risks of continuing the litigation. Judges will occasionally suggest how crucial rulings may be made on evidentiary questions or speculate on what type of jury instructions might be given. These comments may serve the purpose of preventing either side from having an unrealistic view of what will transpire at trial.

Frequently a judge will become a mediator and separate the various "sides" to the dispute and conduct separate conversations with each attorney. This informal mediation technique may increase the candor with which settlement positions are advanced because it reduces the need for posturing for the opponents. The judge may be able to form a ready opinion of the likelihood that further settlement efforts will bear fruit and may use these separate meetings to devise a strategy for conducting the balance of the pretrial conference.

Another technique occasionally used by judges is to speak directly with the parties rather than to the attorneys. This may be especially useful where the party, not the attorney, is unwilling to compromise in order to achieve a settlement. The judge may be able to convince the party that some compromise is appropriate and that the case is not an appropriate one for an intractable settlement posture. Although the judge will want to speak directly with the party or person with settlement authority, the attorney should always be allowed to be present. The attorney can assist the party in responding to the judge and can insure that the judge's comments are consistent with what the attorney expects is reasonably likely to occur at trial. If an attorney announces a certain settlement proposal has been communicated and recommended to a party but that the party nonetheless does not want to accept it, the judge may very well want to address the party's concerns about settling directly.

Alternative Settlement Techniques. Courts have recently begun using other innovative techniques to encourage settlement of litigation. These methods include:

1. Mandatory, non-binding arbitration;
2. Mediation;
3. Summary jury trials; and
4. Use of court-appointed experts.

All of these devices are designed to encourage the parties to take a realistic view of the litigation and to compromise their positions based on the likelihood of success in the litigation after considering the expenses likely to be incurred. There are other devices for helping the parties resolve issues or entire disputes in pending lawsuits which either are not widely used or are simply variations of the normal litigation process or the alternative devices which are discussed separately.

Mandatory Arbitration. Mandatory non-binding arbitration is provided for by rule in some courts for all civil cases and is provided by court option in other jurisdictions. Regardless of whether it is universally required or required only in certain cases, non-binding arbitration may be an effective tool to cause the parties to view their disputes realistically.

When conducted as a mandatory part of the litigation process, non-binding arbitration will normally be held before an arbitrator selected or approved by the court. Some of the courts which provide for non-binding arbitration require the arbitrator's award to be entered as a judgment unless one of the parties objects and demands a trial *de novo.* Other systems simply require the award to be given to the parties for whatever use they may make of it in settlement.

Mediation. Mediation is used to require the parties to identify their differences in an attempt to resolve them. The role of judge in a pretrial conference may be similar to that of mediator. The role of mediator is limited to bringing the parties together, however, and a mediator does not normally decide any issues. The judge, magistrate, court administrative employee, or neutral lawyer or third person may be a mediator.

Some courts have instituted mandatory mediation or conciliation programs in certain types of cases. In certain family court matters, for example, mediation may be required by the court and may be useful. Additionally, even if mediation is not routinely required by the court, there are many situations in which the court may require mediation on an ad hoc basis. Parties may play a role in instituting this mediation, or may agree on mediation under the court's auspices which would not be agreeable outside the court process. Because mediation does not proceed to any sort of "decision" other than an agreed-upon settlement, it is inherently non-binding.

Summary Jury Trial. The summary jury trial is an innovative judicial tool for resolving disputes which has had some significant success. The procedure for the trial is simple: the parties present summaries of their cases, in the nature of arguments and summaries of testimony and exhibits, to a jury drawn from the regular jury pool. The "evidence" portion of the case is presented solely by the attorneys and no witnesses are called. Each side is limited to a one-hour presentation and the court then instructs the jury on the law using a dramatically streamlined charge. The jury then deliberates and returns either a unanimous verdict or separate signed "verdicts" of each jury member. The summary trial result has no binding effect and is not admissible in another trial for any purpose. Courts using the device normally require the parties to attend the summary trial and have reported significant success in settling cases using it.[4]

This procedure is particularly useful in cases where the attorneys and parties understand the facts and governing law, but have widely divergent views of the likely results of a trial. It is, for example, useful in helping the parties evaluate the unique "value" of a personal injury case since it permits the parties to present the facts of the case to a factfinder. The fact that the parties are present at the proceedings may also help in convincing them that the other side of the case has merit which may be considered by a jury. This tool will only be of value if the attorneys have a sincere desire to have the case settled fairly. The attorneys are responsible for presenting the "evidence" in such a way that the summary trial jury hears evidence analogous to what the jury in a full trial would hear. To the extent the summary trial does not present a realistic view of both sides of the case to the jury, its value as a settlement device is diminished.

The summary jury trial is clearly a settlement device which is part of the judicial system. The fact-finder is drawn from the regular jury pool and is intended to reflect the makeup of an actual petit jury. This device also works well only where the parties have engaged in discovery

4. *See generally* Lambros & Shunk, The Summary Jury Trial, 29 Cleve.St.L.Rev. 43 (1980).

and have prepared their cases for trial. It is a means of removing disagreement about what will happen in a trial and is therefore useful to settle pending civil cases which appear impossible to settle. Unlike mediation, it is not directed to resolving the underlying dispute, but rather, is a means of providing better information to the parties to allow them to compromise and settle the pending action.

Use of Court–Appointed Experts. Federal courts and most state courts permit the appointment of neutral experts by the courts. Fed. R.Evid. 706 specifically authorizes the use of court-appointed experts and similar state rules and the inherent power of the courts also permits the court to appoint such experts. Court-appointed experts may be very useful in resolving disputes, although they are not widely used. Some judges have, however, begun to appoint neutral experts in certain cases, and are using them more frequently. Neutral experts are not popular with lawyers since they are viewed as preempting the proper role of the lawyers and litigants. In cases where the court anticipates a "battle of the experts," however, the court-appointed expert may be of value not only to the fact-finder, but also the court and the parties in permitting a reasoned approach to evaluating the likely result of a trial. Cases which may lend themselves to the successful use of this device tend to be large cases headed for lengthy and expensive trials.

§ 14.4 EXTRA–JUDICIAL TOOLS FOR SETTLEMENT

Many of the tools which are used for resolving disputes in litigation may be used outside of the litigation process. Additionally, there are many methods for resolving disputes which make no use of the litigation process and bear little similarity to it. These tools include:

- Settlement Without Suit;
- Mediation;
- Arbitration;
- Mini–Trials;
- Fact–Finding;
- Private Judging; and
- Combination or Hybrid Processes.

Section 1.8 explained the first three of these methods: settlement, mediation, and arbitration. Each of these may be modified to meet the specific needs of parties to a dispute.

Arbitration can be designed to provide relief to parties during settlement. The arbitrator may be required to select between the last offers made by each party ("last best offer" arbitration). This has effects of encouraging the parties to make the most reasonable settlement offer and preventing the arbitrator from compromising the dispute or "splitting the baby." The parties may also submit a dispute for arbitration within fixed bounds. This type of arbitration is similar to trial under a "High–Low" agreement as discussed in § 14.5.3.

Mini–Trials. One extra-judicial device for settling large lawsuits which has received recent attention is the "mini-trial." There is no single formula for a mini-trial because it is a procedure which the parties must agree on. Its use in one large patent dispute (*Telecredit v. TRW*) has been widely described in the legal literature, however, and that case is a useful model for understanding how the mini-trial can be used.[1] The essential features of the mini-trial are a limited period for expedited discovery of a limited nature, the exchange of position papers and exhibits, a one- or two-day trial of the dispute to the top management of the corporate parties, and the meeting of corporate management representatives who attended the trial in an attempt to resolve the dispute. Counsel for the parties would not be present during the "deliberations."

A neutral advisor or moderator can be used to structure the mini-trial proceedings and help keep the proceedings directed to the effective resolution of the dispute. The advisor would not normally participate in the initial evaluation of the positions of the parties or the soundness of their respective settlement postures. The advisor would be available to provide input into the likely result of a trial. In the *Telecredit/TRW* case the parties agreed that all statements and positions made or taken during the mini-trial proceedings would be inadmissible at trial for any purpose, that the advisor could not be called as a witness at trial, that his predictions of trial results could not be used in any way, and that the parties could not go to the court for any reason during the mini-trial proceeding. The parties implemented these agreements by stipulating that breach of those ground rules would prejudice the opposing party and would be prima facie grounds for a mistrial, disqualification of counsel, and recovery of any costs incurred.

The mini-trial in the *Telecredit/TRW* case involved the presentation of a case-in-chief for four hours, rebuttal for an hour and a half, and an hour of questions and answers. On the second day of the mini-trial the defendant put on its case-in-chief in the same way. After the mini-trial itself was concluded, top management met to "deliberate", and arrived at a settlement agreement in principle within 30 minutes.[2]

Fact–Finding. Fact-finding is a tool for resolving disputes in which an independent third person is brought into a dispute to identify facts which are in dispute and those that are not in dispute. This process may assist the parties in reaching agreement on some issues, narrowing their dispute, or may permit the parties to compromise their positions on matters on which there is no agreement but also no serious dispute. A fact-finder does not normally make any decisions. It is possible for a fact-finder to step into the role of mediator or conciliator upon conclusion of the fact-finding in order to suggest a means of resolving the remaining disputes.

§ 14.4

1. *See* Ronald L. Olson, Dispute Resolution: An Alternative for Large Case Litigation, 6 Litig. (Winter 1980), at 22.

2. *Id.* at 23.

Private Judging. Another extra-judicial method for resolving disputes is the use of a private judge. The device permits parties to submit their dispute to a private (usually former or retired) judge for resolution. Some states have recognized the procedure by statute,[3] although it is available to any parties who can agree on a judge to act as referee. If there is a mechanism for private judging recognized by the courts it may be possible to have the referee's decision enforced like a judgment. A private judge may be assigned as a special master by the court if there is a lawsuit pending and the parties want to have the court retain jurisdiction.

Private judging has been criticized as an alternative means of dispute resolution because it will normally be available to wealthier litigants and because its widespread use would remove incentives for improving the court system.[4] Private judging may be desirable because the parties may select a judge who has experience in resolving the type of dispute involved. Private judging is also of value when one or more of the parties feels that the rules of procedure, evidence, and appeal provided in the civil litigation process are preferable to those of arbitration or other means dispute resolution since the private judge essentially presides over a civil action, although it is conducted outside the courthouse. There is no reason that a private judge can not convene a private jury and hold a jury trial.

Combination or Hybrid Methods. It is possible for the various distinctive tools for dispute resolution to be combined to suit the needs of particular parties. Mediation and arbitration can be combined in a process called "Med–Arb." The parties may engage in a mediation process with the understanding that the mediator can make a binding decision which may be enforced under the arbitration statutes if the mediation reaches an impasse. Conciliation and arbitration can be combined in a similar manner. A mini-trial can be conducted with the provision for a binding result by the neutral advisor if the parties cannot agree on a settlement. A summary jury trial can be used with a stipulation that the jury will not disclose its verdict or the verdict will be sealed for a fixed period of time while the parties attempt to settle the case and that the verdict will be a final, binding verdict if it is disclosed to the parties.

The parties have great latitude in designing a means for resolution of a dispute which is satisfactory to them. Even if the parties do not agree on a binding means of resolving the dispute, they may agree to submit to a non-binding process with the further agreement that if a party does not abide by the result that party will bear the costs of any further litigation if that litigation does not result in a more favorable result. Imagination and the willingness to permit a dispute to be

3. *See* West's Ann.Cal.Civ.Code Proc. § 638.

4. *See generally* Robert Gnaizda, Secret Justice for the Privileged Few, 66 Judicature 6 (1982); Robert Coulson, Private Settlement for the Public Good, 66 Judicature 7 (1982).

resolved define the ultimate limits on the dispute resolution process. Creative lawyers and parties who desire to live their lives or run their businesses rather than litigate can frequently settle seemingly intractable disputes.

§ 14.5 DOCUMENTATION OF SETTLEMENTS

§ 14.5.1 Settlement Agreements

Settlement agreements should almost always be reduced to writing. Even if an oral agreement would be legally adequate, a written agreement is less likely to be the subject of further disputes.

If the subject of the agreement is within the statute of frauds, the settlement agreement may be required to be in writing. The statute of frauds looks to the settlement agreement itself and not to the underlying claims. Thus, if an action claiming damages for fraud in the sale of securities is settled by an agreement to convey certain real estate to the plaintiffs, the settlement agreement would be within the statute. Local court rules may also require settlements to be reduced to writing. This section considers some of the types of agreements which may be used to preserve and give effect to a settlement.

Settlement agreements are governed by contract law and should therefore be drafted with contract law principles in mind. Most importantly, the settlement document should make it clear that valuable consideration is being given by all parties. The consideration requirement is almost always met in compromise settlements, but it is useful to recite the consideration in order to remove any doubt about its presence in the transaction.

One reason that more than one document is normally used to effect a settlement is the desire to keep the terms of a settlement confidential. There is no requirement in most jurisdictions that a settlement agreement be filed with the court or that its contents be made public in any way. Thus, the parties may preserve the confidential nature of the terms of the settlement agreement itself by having it specify any documents necessary to be filed with the court. Those documents would not contain the terms of the settlement.

§ 14.5.2 Documents Implementing the Settlement

In addition to a settlement agreement, most settlements require some document to implement the agreement. For example, if a lawsuit has been commenced, a dismissal is necessary. This section examines some of the documents which are used to put a settlement into effect. The variety of potential settlement documents makes it impossible to catalog all possible useful forms. Indeed, just as innovative negotiation strategies may permit the settlement of actions which could not otherwise be settled, creative use of agreements and various legal forms may permit a settlement to be effectuated which gives valuable benefits to all parties.

Dismissals. By far the most common device executed as part of a settlement of litigation is a dismissal. There is not, however, a single standard form of dismissal which is appropriate in all cases. In preparing a dismissal, and in preparing a settlement agreement which requires a dismissal, it is important to distinguish between dismissals with prejudice and dismissals without prejudice. If a dismissal is entered with prejudice, then the resulting judgment of dismissal will have full *res judicata* effect. A dismissal without prejudice does not have any *res judicata* effect, and the plaintiff may recommence the action at any time (before, of course, the statute of limitations would bar it).[1] Under Fed.R.Civ.P. 42(a) a dismissal, whether voluntary or by order of the court, that does not state whether it is with or without prejudice, will be deemed to be without prejudice. Not all state courts have the same rules. In any event, it is prudent to provide specifically in the settlement agreement for the language of the dismissal, and the dismissal should clearly be made either "with prejudice" or "without prejudice."

Upon completion of a settlement or as a condition of the settlement, the parties may seek to vacate any prior judgments or orders in the matter. Usually, this is desired by the losing party in order to erase the preclusive effect, the adverse precedent, or the public relations embarrassment of the judgment or order. Courts vary in their willingness to vacate a prior judgment upon the request of settling parties. Some courts do so routinely. Others refuse. Still others weigh competing policy considerations and decide accordingly.[2]

A dismissal should also address the question of whether costs may be taxed by the prevailing party.[3] If a judgment of dismissal is entered, the defendants will normally be deemed prevailing parties, and will be entitled to tax costs. In fact, most settlements never contemplate that costs will be taxed, however, so the agreement should not leave the question open. The dismissal should normally state all parties should bear their own costs and disbursements or that no party shall be entitled to tax costs or disbursements. Silence on this subject is just a potential basis for further litigation. If the parties intend costs to be taxed, it may be desirable for the parties to agree as part of the settlement on exactly what items and what amounts are properly taxable. Again, a specific agreement is likely to obviate further litigation.

§ 14.5

1. Many jurisdictions have statutes which toll the running of any statute of limitations during the pendency of an action on the claim. Thus, if the first action is brought a month before the statute of limitations would run, a dismissal of the action without prejudice even after it has been pending for five years would not prevent the case from being refiled. These statutes and relevant case decisions are collected in Annot., 13 A.L.R.3d 979 (1967 & Supp.1984).

2. For representative cases regarding the different approaches, *see Kaisha v. U.S. Philips Corp.*, ___ U.S. ___, ___ n. 2, 114 S.Ct. 425, 426 n. 2, 126 L.Ed.2d 396 (1993), *rehearing denied* ___ U.S. ___, 114 S.Ct. 904, 127 L.Ed.2d 95 (1994).

3. The procedures for and right to taxation of costs are discussed David F. Herr, Roger S. Haydock & Jeffrey W. Stempel, Motion Practice § 23.2 (2d ed. 1991, Supp. 1994).

If the parties agree to the dismissal of an action without prejudice it may be desirable for the plaintiff to obtain a specific agreement tolling the running of the statute of limitations. This means of settlement may be useful in an action where the plaintiff has a number of different claims against more than one party. A defendant the plaintiff views as a secondary defendant for any reason may be able to convince the plaintiff to pursue other parties if the plaintiff can be assured that any potential claims will not be lost.

"Standstill" Agreements. In some cases the parties do not want to have the pending litigation dismissed, yet agree that nothing should transpire in the case unless the settlement agreement is not discharged by full performance. This may be a more desirable way to resolve a case which has been pending for a long period of time or is pending in a jurisdiction with an unusual trial calendar backlog.

The settlement agreement in such a case should contain appropriate provisions to memorialize the intentions of the parties. It may be desirable to supplement the agreement itself with a stipulated order removing the case from the trial calendar but preserving its priority for trial if the settlement is not effectuated or if some future contingency either does or does not arise. It may be especially appropriate to submit such an order to the court for approval in order to prevent the court from unilaterally dismissing the case or striking it from the calendar upon learning that a "settlement" has been reached.

Release. A release is one of the most frequently-encountered settlement documents. The parties may execute a separate document entitled "Release" or "Release of All Claims," or may include language of release in a settlement agreement. Unless there is some particular reason for execution of a separate document it is probably better to include the release language in a comprehensive settlement agreement.

The most important thing to consider in preparing a release is the finality of the document. Although there are grounds for setting aside a release, such as fraud and mutual mistake, releases are intended to be final and permanent and courts routinely construe them as such. It is also important to remember the time-encrusted, if not time-honored, rule of tort law that "Release of one joint tortfeasor is a release of all." That rule will operate to release persons not even mentioned in the release nor intended by any party to the agreement to be benefited by it. If the case is one involving multiple tortfeasors it is imperative that the attorneys, especially the attorney for any claimant, to be sure that the settlement does not unwittingly result in the loss of rights not intended by the parties. Special considerations of releases in multi-party situations is discussed in section 14.5.3.

It is not difficult to prepare an adequate release. The word "release" is not necessary. Any writing which reflects an intention to release will be sufficient to release. In practice, however, elaborate language is used. Indeed, it is harder to limit the effectiveness of a release than it is to expand it. An example of language from an expansive release for a simple personal injury is:

> The undersigned ______, for herself and her heirs, successors, and assigns, hereby releases, forgives, and acquits ______, and its officers, directors, employees, agents, servants, independent contractors, attorneys, insurers, sureties and the heirs, successors, and assigns of any of them, from any claims, demands, causes of action, and actions, whether in tort, contract, or otherwise, whether now existing or hereafter arising, for any injury, known or unknown, real or imaginary, presently existing or which may arise at any time in the future, for any act, omission, or failure to act at any time from the beginning of history to the end of time.

In practice such a device is neither necessary nor particularly effective. It is certainly possible to prepare equally effective releases with a fraction of the verbiage.

Covenant Not to Sue. A covenant not to sue is simply a contractual undertaking not to sue or otherwise pursue rights in the future. It is generally a part of any settlement agreement intended to resolve all pending disputes and may be contained in a release document. A covenant not to sue is not, however, a release in itself. The enforcement of a covenant not to sue is effected not by the doctrine of bar by release, but rather, by estoppel. This form of settlement document may have special value in effectuating a settlement of some, but not all, claims against a party or in settling claims against some, but not all, parties. As discussed in section 14.5.3, it may be a useful tool to avoid the "release of one is release of all" rule in tort cases.

Loan Receipts. Loan receipts represent one of the classic legal fictions recognized by the courts. Loan receipts are widely used in insurance settlements, particularly in property insurance cases. A loan receipt is a written agreement that permits one party to pay another a sum of money, usually an insurer paying an insured, and to have the payment considered a loan rather than an outright payment. Usually, however, the loan receipt will provide that the "loan" need only be repaid out of the proceeds and to the extent of some future litigation or claim. Thus, the "loan" is never intended to be repaid directly.

The courts have recognized this fiction, however, and have upheld the arrangement as a loan and not a payment. This device has seen widespread use in property insurance subrogation actions to permit an action to be brought in the name of the insured rather than insurer by allowing the insured to remain the real party in interest.[4]

A loan receipt may also be used for other purposes. It may permit the parties to control the tax treatment of the settlement or may be advantageous for other accounting reasons. It is another tool which may be used to effect a partial settlement.

4. The use of a loan receipt in this context and its treatment by the courts of the various states is discussed in a useful annotation, Annot., 13 A.L.R.3d 42 (1967 & Supp.1984).

Final Accounting. One important settlement document frequently overlooked by attorneys is a final accounting of the settlement to the client. It is usually prudent to explain to the client in writing just what was paid or received in a settlement and how the settlement proceeds were applied. If a plaintiff settles a case and pays a contingent attorney's fee based on a percentage of the settlement, a *pro forma* billing should be submitted to the client showing how the fee was calculated, what deductions were made for disbursements or expenses, and what other adjustments, if any, were made. This is an important way to insure that no confusion exists as to the distribution of the settlement proceeds.

§ 14.5.3 Settlement of Multiple-Party Lawsuits

Settlement of actions involving multiple parties may present special problems which require careful consideration by all counsel. The central focus of these problems is the rule that release on one tortfeasor releases all and the rules of contribution and indemnity among the parties. Because contribution and indemnity law varies widely from jurisdiction to jurisdiction, it is impossible to identify all means of settling various types of multi-party lawsuits. The introduction of comparative negligence, comparative fault, and refinement of questions of contribution and indemnity in cases involving both fault-based and non-fault liability have made these questions virtually unique to each jurisdiction. Creative attorneys have been able to achieve good results for their clients but analyzing settlement problems and preparing documents which are consistent with the interests of the parties and which comply with the applicable law.

One good example of a partial settlement of multiple claims is the Pierringer release, named after a Wisconsin case approving its use.[5] This release releases the plaintiff's claims against the settling defendant, satisfies any claim for that defendant's portion of the negligence, and indemnifies that defendant from any contribution claim. The settlement specifically reserves the plaintiff's claims against the non-settling defendants. The plaintiff agrees to reimburse the settling defendant for any additional sums which may be awarded or imposed against that defendant. Settlement on this basis is disclosed to all the other parties in the case and can be disclosed to the jury. The Pierringer release has been recognized in other jurisdictions and is well-suited to most states with comparative negligence laws.[6] The Pierringer release is effective because it permits the settling defendant to be completely extricated from the litigation, without fear of further cross-claims.

A markedly different settlement device is the Mary Carter Agreement, named after the Florida case of *Booth v. Mary Carter Paint Co.*[7]

5. *Pierringer v. Hoger,* 21 Wis.2d 182, 124 N.W.2d 106 (1963).

6. *See, e.g., Frey v. Snelgrove,* 269 N.W.2d 918 (Minn.1978).

7. 182 So.2d 292 (Fla.App.1966), *affirmed* 202 So.2d 2 (Fla.1967). An essentially similar settlement device is the Gallagher covenant, named after the Arizona

Mary Carter agreements are secret agreements between the plaintiff and one defendant whereby the defendant continues to defend the lawsuit with the understanding that its maximum liability will be diminished by increasing the liability of the other defendants in the case.[8] Mary Carter agreements are widely criticized, and are unenforceable in some states, because they tend to continue, rather than end litigation, and because they are collusive and secret.[9] They also raise significant ethical problems for the attorneys.[10]

Mary Carter agreements are not normally releases. They may be embodied in various forms of settlement agreements, including covenants not to sue and loan receipts. Because of the serious questions about the judicial effectiveness and ethical propriety of Mary Carter agreements attorneys probably should not enter into the agreements unless the courts of the jurisdiction have approved their use. Some state courts have ruled that they are illegal *per se.*[11]

Another innovative settlement device is the High–Low agreement. This device essentially removes some of the risk of litigation for both settling parties by establishing a highest amount the defendant be required to pay and also the lowest amount the plaintiff can recover. In a personal injury case with hotly contested questions of damages, the parties might agree that plaintiff will recover the amount of a verdict within the range of $40,000 to $120,000. If the verdict is less than $40,000, including $0, the plaintiff would still recover $40,000. Similarly, even if the jury returned a verdict of $500,000 the defendant would only have to pay $120,000.

High–Low settlements are neither automatically acceptable nor illegal *per se.* In a simple one-plaintiff/one-defendant case they are not particularly problematical. Indeed, many cases of this nature have fully settled after a preliminary high-low agreement was reached. These settlements offer some of the advantages of settlements, but also have some of the offensive features of Mary Carter agreements. The high-low settlement does contemplate that the case will proceed to trial, so the agreements do not save judicial resources except as an incentive to further settlement. In multi-party cases, more difficult questions arise. If a high-low agreement between the plaintiff and one of several defendants is kept secret from the other parties the arrangement is quite similar to the Mary Carter agreement. One important difference is that the parties in a high-low situation do not have the full reversal of interests. A high-low agreement does not cause the settling defendant to be trying at trial to have the plaintiff recover a larger, rather than

case of *City of Tucson v. Gallagher,* 108 Ariz. 140, 493 P.2d 1197 (1972).

8. *See Ward v. Ochoa,* 284 So.2d 385, 387 (Fla.1973).

9. *See Bedford School District v. Caron Construction Co.,* 116 N.H. 800, 367 A.2d 1051 (1976) (continue litigation).

10. *See* Abigail Carson, Are Gallagher Covenants Unethical?: An Analysis Under the Code of Professional Responsibility, 19 Ariz.L.Rev. 863 (1977).

11. *See Lum v. Stinnett,* 87 Nev. 402, 409, 411, 488 P.2d 347, 351, 352 (1971) (agreements "contrary to law and public policy" and "inimical to true adversary process.").

smaller, judgment. The high-low settlement does not require secrecy, and it is probably the best practice to disclose any such agreement to the court and other parties. Since the high-low agreement does not provide the settling defendant any certainty regarding exposure to claims to contribution or indemnity as in a Pierringer settlement it may not be particularly appealing to the defendant.

§ 14.5.4 Structured Settlements

A form of settlement which is used increasingly in personal injury and other litigation is the structured settlement. The term "structured settlement" refers to any of a wide variety of settlements in which a claimant who is injured is compensated, at least in part, by a string of payments over a period of time rather than in a lump sum payment at the time of settlement. Structured settlements generally address the cash flow needs of the parties as well as the tax ramifications of the settlement to both the party receiving funds and the party paying them.

Deferred payment has always been a tool used to facilitate the settlement of certain disputes. In commercial cases, it may be impossible for one party to make a single large payment. Indeed, the structured settlement was borne as a result of attorneys who took the cash flow needs of their clients into consideration in arriving at settlements. In this sense, structuring payment terms should be considered as a part of any settlement.

"Structured settlement" has special implications, however, in personal injury litigation. Due to favorable tax treatment of personal injury settlements paid over time, it is frequently possible to arrange a stream of future payments to an injured person resulting in tax-free cash flow to pay for future medical expenses, loss of income, and other expenses. Payments received for personal injuries are normally not considered "income" for income tax purposes.[12] Once the payments are received, however, any earnings (*e.g.*, interest, dividends or capital gains) on the money received would be considered income. A series of IRS rulings determined that, under certain circumstances, an annuity paid in settlement of a personal injury claim would be deemed non-income despite the fact that a portion of the value of the annuity reflects the time value of money over the life of the annuity. These rulings were a tremendous incentive for parties settling large personal injury cases to use a structured settlement calling for deferred payments. Because an annuity paying 20 annual payments of $50,000 can be obtained by a defendant for considerably less than $1,000,000, it provides an incentive for the parties to structure any settlement. Payment of settlement proceeds over time may also suit the needs of an injured person who anticipates

12. This view was consistently upheld by the Internal Revenue Service in various rulings prior to 1982. The Periodic Payment Settlement Act of 1982, Pub.L. No. 97–473 amended section 104(a)(2) of the Internal Revenue Code specifically to exclude damages from personal injuries or sickness from income, whether received as a lump sum or periodically.

life-long need for medical services and care. Structured settlements are now specifically recognized in the Internal Revenue Code.[13]

A structured settlement may, however, place increased burdens on an attorney. Some of these risks may be reduced by careful attention by the attorneys. Other risks inhere in structured settlements. These risks must be understood by the attorneys and must to explained to the parties. Most important, it is necessary to insure that the promise to make payments into the future is not an empty promise. This is a risk even with substantial defendants where injuries to a young plaintiff are involved, since no one can accurately predict the financial soundness of any company far into the future. This risk is normally handled by requiring the defendant to obtain an annuity issued by a first-rate insurance company to fund any payments under the structured settlement.

It is also important for the plaintiff's attorney to attempt to minimize the risk that agreed-upon future payments will be inadequate to pay for future expenses. This risk exists in any settlement of claims for future losses. A structured settlement may present an opportunity to reduce this risk or pass the risk to the settling defendant by requiring the defendant to pay directly future medical expenses or other expenses the cost of which cannot be accurately predicted. A structured settlement may require the payment of such expenses as incurred without regard to the amount. Structured settlements may also attempt to anticipate the effect of future price inflation by providing for a graduated schedule of future payments. This may be accomplished by tying the future payments to an economic price index such as the Consumer Price Index or by defining for increases every year either in absolute dollars or as a percentage.

The structured settlement may create difficult problems of determining the appropriate attorneys' fee for the plaintiff. If the case is handled on a contingent basis it may be difficult to assess the fee. A "million-dollar" settlement may cost the defendant and have an actuarial present value of only $200,000. Determining the appropriate fee in such a case may not be readily accomplished. Many structured settlements provide three tiers of payments: a lump-sum payment at the time of the settlement, a guaranteed series of future payments which will be paid to the plaintiff or the plaintiff's personal representative regardless of the plaintiff's longevity, and additional future payments during the life of the plaintiff after the period of guaranteed payments. Thus, the plaintiff might recover $100,000 upon settlement, 15 certain annual payments of $50,000 on each succeeding year, and annual payments thereafter of $50,000 during the plaintiff's life. The actual recovery under that agreement will not be determined until the plaintiff dies, and the cash to pay a 25% contingent attorney's fee in addition to accrued bills will in any event not be on hand at the time of settlement. The

13. I.R.C. §§ 104(a)(2) & 130, 26 U.S.C.A. §§ 104(a)(2) & 130.

plaintiff's attorney may be placed in a difficult position of having to negotiate for a larger lump-sum payment to pay an attorney's fee.

Some states require mandatory "structuring" of certain judgments. A number of states have adopted the statutes similar to the Uniform Law Commissioners' Model Periodic Payment of Judgments Act.[14] These laws require periodic rather than lump-sum payments of judgments in certain circumstances. Although these laws do not apply directly to most settlements, they do have a significant impact on settlements since they determine what would happen if actions are tried. These laws are generally considered to be favorable to defendants and their insurers since they require the payment of judgments in a way the parties could always agree on in the absence of legislation.[15] It is important to know of the increasing legislative interest in settlements and the impact the laws have on settlement practices.

§ 14.6 ENFORCEMENT OF SETTLEMENTS

§ 14.6.1 The Need to Enforce Settlements

When settlement is reached between the parties to an action, the matter is usually concluded. Most often the parties, satisfied if not enthralled with their bargain, comply with the terms of the settlement and retreat from the battle to their tents, carrying on their lives.

Occasionally, however, one party fails to fulfill part of the bargain. One party may belatedly recognize a bad bargain, and balk at consummating the settlement. Another party may be unable to comply with agreed upon settlement terms because of lack of money. Occasionally, outside circumstances may change after the settlement is reached, adversely affecting the value or cost of settlement for a party. For example, the 3,000 shares of XYZ Oil Co. stock accepted in settlement plummet in value upon expropriation of the company's Persian Gulf assets. Sometimes, the breaching party is simply unscrupulous.

Three available remedies include:

1. Amendment or supplementation of the pleadings to allege the settlement agreement as an executory accord;

2. Initiation of a separate action for breach of the settlement agreement; and

3. A motion to enforce settlement.

The third remedy is the most common and is usually the most cost-effective. Amending the pleadings and commencing a separate action both require significant delay, and require the parties to expend additional resources. A motion to enforce the settlement may be an effective tool to accomplish the intended result of the settlement agreement.

14. For a text of the model act and information on versions adopted by the various states, *see* 14 Uniform Laws Annotated 20 (Supp.1984).

15. *See generally* Choulos, Structured Settlements: Curse or Cure?, 16 Trial 73 (1980).

§ 14.6.2 *Motions to Enforce Settlement*

Judges frequently show greater disdain for motions to enforce settlement than for other disdainful types of motions. In reviewing the enforceability of a written settlement agreement the judge may have to find or imply that one party is dishonest. In reviewing oral settlement agreements between counsel, a judge may have to determine whether an attorney had authority of the client to settle, whether an attorney properly represented and counseled a client, whether an attorney exceeded the authority of the client, or whether one party deceived the other party or is attempting to deceive the court. Despite the unpleasantness of airing the breach of settlement, the court will probably be favorably disposed to the party who can establish that a settlement occurred and was breached. Consequently, the reported cases enforce settlement far more often than they find an absence of settlement. One surmises that the judicial pain of implying dishonesty of a party or ultra vires action by counsel is outweighed by the joy of removing a case from the docket.

A motion to enforce settlement should be made before the court that had jurisdiction over the original claim. Amendment of the pleadings to seek enforcement of a settlement is unnecessary and superfluous because a motion will accomplish the same result. The commencement of a new action may only be necessary in a situation in which the original court no longer has personal or subject matter jurisdiction over the underlying action and settlement. The new action would begin with a short complaint alleging the existence of the settlement agreement and a cause of action for breach. The requested relief may be either specific performance or reinstatement of the original claim. The latter would subsequently require reinitiating the original claim in the new forum if the complaint for breach of settlement is granted.

The movant's best tactic will be a simple motion to enforce directed to the original judge, a judge who thought the case had settled some time ago. This judge, who may have even entered an order of dismissal because of the settlement and instructed the calendar clerk to close the file, will want to resolve the matter expeditiously. The original court also knows the procedural background of the case, and may even have been involved in the settlement discussions upon which the settlement was based.

Because the court may have entered an order dismissing the case or placing it in the inactive file, the movant seeking to enforce settlement may need first to make a motion to vacate the earlier action removing the case from the calendar and to reinstate the action on the court's calendar. This can be accomplished either through a short motion filed in advance of the motion to enforce or in a request for reinstatement made as part of the underlying motion to enforce. Where the movant makes a separate and preceding motion to vacate and reinstate, the movant should file a notice of motion, motion, proposed order, memorandum, and affidavit setting forth the facts which justify reinstatement. Because the same supporting documents will be required for a motion to enforce settlement and because even the contents of the documents will be identical in part, it is easier and probably a better practice to submit a combined motion to reinstate and enforce settlement. If this is done, a single notice of motion, motion, affidavit or affidavits and memorandum need be filed. It is probably desirable to submit separate proposed orders even if a combined motion is filed. One advantage of specifically seeking both reinstatement of the action and enforcement of the settlement is the flexibility it allows the court. In the event the court denies the motion to enforce, the movant will nonetheless want to reopen the original action as soon as possible to avoid problems with the statute of limitations, res judicata, collateral estoppel, and similar doctrines. A separate proposed order of reinstatement makes this possible.

Often, an order dismissing the action or placing it in the "suspense" file will be entered upon the court's learning of the settlement. These orders are routinely entered by some judges without the request of the parties, or even despite requests that they not be entered. Such an order will normally specifically reserve to the court the possibility of reopening the matter if the settlement is not achieved or if other good cause is shown. If the order mentions the possible vacation of dismissal or suspense and of reinstatement, it should not be difficult to establish entitlement to relief if the settlement is breached. The memorandum supporting reinstatement in this case may be terse, and the factual support in the affidavits may be brief.

If the order dismissing the action or placing it in the suspense file is silent about reinstatement, some discussion about the court's inherent power to reopen the matter on the basis of its inherent authority, the authority granted by Fed.R.Civ.P. 60(b), and the interests of justice is in order. Failure to comply with the terms of a settlement agreement constitutes misconduct of an adverse party within the meaning of Fed.R.Civ.P. 60(b)(3).[1] That rule permits the court to relieve a party of the effect of an order or judgment upon a showing of fraud, misrepresentation, or other misconduct. It would appear that the breach of settlement also qualifies as "any other reason justifying relief" from the order under Fed.R.Civ.P. 60(b)(6).[2] By its terms, Rule 60(b) applies only where a party seeks relief from a judgment or final order. Depending upon the wording of the order in question, the movant seeking to enforce settlement may be able to argue that the order of dismissal or suspense is not final within the meaning of Rule 60, especially where the order was conditioned upon a settlement which has not been performed. Rule 60 applies only to final orders because of the court's clear authority to change, modify, reverse, or vacate any interlocutory order. In the case of an interlocutory order, no further authority from the rules is required.

§ 14.6

1. 11 Charles A. Wright & Arthur R. Miller, Federal Practice and Procedure § 2860 (1973 and Supp.1994).

2. 11 Charles A. Wright & Arthur R. Miller, Federal Practice and Procedure § 2864 (1973, Supp.1994).

§ 14.6.3 Procedure

The movant should normally schedule a hearing on the motion to enforce. Preferably, the movant obtains the hearing date and time from the court prior to serving the motion. Where the court does not regularly conduct a motion day, the court may be reluctant to schedule a hearing prior to service and filing of the motion. In that event, the movant should press for a hearing immediately after the motion is made.

At the hearing, the movant should arrive with the witnesses and exhibits necessary to prove the case if the motion is contested. In effect, the hearing on the motion is a mini-trial on a breach of contract claim, the contract being the settlement agreement. In some instances it will be obvious that the opposing party has few or no factual contentions in opposition to the enforcement motion. In these situations, the opposing party will either interpose a legal argument based on the relatively uncontested facts (*e.g.*, lack of actual or implied authority of counsel) or will not contest the motion and will chalk one up to delay and anticipated judgment dodging.

The prudent movant will view these situations on a sliding scale. Where the facts are in hot dispute, the moving lawyer should come to the enforcement hearing as if to a trial or hearing on a motion for a preliminary injunction. This level of preparation should be limited only by the constraints of the availability of probative evidence. Where the facts at issue are relatively minor, where the opposition to the motion is essentially legal, or where the delaying breaching party is not likely to contest the motion vigorously, the client's resources should be preserved. But, as always, erring on the side of caution and over-preparation is advisable.

Depending on the nature of the alleged settlement, either affidavits, witnesses, documents, or exhibits should accompany the motion for enforcement. For example, where the settlement provided that the opposing party would pay attorney's fees, at least a portion of one affidavit should aver this fact and set forth the amount of fees requested. The request for fees should be explained, including dates, description of services rendered, time expended, and extension at a normal billing rate. The billing rate should be established to be reasonable under the prevailing standards of the legal community. This approach is consistent with the "lodestar" approach to determining fees to be awarded in actions under certain statutes and in class actions.[3] Where specific performance or a confession of judgment is part of the settlement, these too should be set forth in the relief requested in the motion and should be supported with affidavits and proof at a hearing. If the successful movant expects the opposing party to take irreparably harmful action to avoid an order enforcing the settlement, the movant should request appropriate injunctive relief and be prepared to prove up the case for the

3. *See, e.g., Hensley v. Eckerhart,* 461 U.S. 424, 103 S.Ct. 1933, 76 L.Ed.2d 40 (1983) (outlining method for calculation fees in civil rights class actions).

injunction at the main hearing. Consequently, the law of settlement has established relatively low barriers to proving settlement.

Although settlement is essentially a contract between the parties and proof of the settlement resembles proof of contract (*e.g.*, offer, acceptance, consideration), most courts have held that the proper contract law to be applied varies with the case. In determining the applicable law in construing settlements, the court will usually examine the underlying causes of action. Where the underlying claim is federal or "implicates the operation of a network of federal statutes," the court should apply the federal common law of contracts.[4] Thus, federal law would apply to settlements of disputed claims in civil rights, patent, trademark, copyright, and antitrust actions.[5]

Where the underlying cause of action is based on state law, the court will apply the contract law of the state with the closest nexus to the settlement.[6] This will usually be the state whose law would supply the rule of decision in the underlying cause of action.[7] However, in certain cases, choice of law principles would support the application of the law of a nonforum state. Usually, however, the forum state will be the location where settlement is negotiated, reached, and memorialized. In such cases, forum state contract law should usually be applied even if it would not have been applied to the original underlying claim.

A Fourth Circuit case, *Gamewell Manufacturing, Inc. v. HVAC Supply, Inc.*,[8] stated that federal courts should apply a federal common law of contracts in construing settlement disputes with respect to federal litigation already in progress because such disputes "implicate federal procedural interests distinct from the underlying substantive interests of the parties."[9] The Fourth Circuit essentially views settlement law as purely procedural and not within the substantive law arm of the *Erie* doctrine.[10] Although this approach would presumably be more consistent than other choice of law methods, the *Gamewell* decision is a trailblazer, and it is not yet clear whether it will be followed.

Showing breach of the settlement, once settlement has been established, should be relatively straightforward. The major controversy in a motion to enforce usually concerns the authority of counsel (or some other agent of a party) to agree to the settlement terms and bind the

4. *See Bergstrom v. Sears, Roebuck & Co.,* 532 F.Supp. 923, 931 (D.Minn.1982). *See generally* Note, Displacement of State Rules of Decision in Construing Releases of Federal Claims, 63 Cornell L.Rev. 339 (1978).

5. *See Fulgence v. J. Ray McDermott & Co.,* 662 F.2d 1207, 1209 (5th Cir.1981).

6. *See Roberts v. Browning,* 610 F.2d 528, 533 (8th Cir.1979); *Okonko v. Union Oil Co. of California,* 519 F.Supp. 372 (C.D.Cal.1981).

7. *Id.*

8. 715 F.2d 112 (4th Cir.1983).

9. 715 F.2d at 115.

10. *See Erie Railroad Co. v. Tompkins,* 304 U.S. 64, 58 S.Ct. 817, 82 L.Ed. 1188 (1938), *mandate conformed* 98 F.2d 49 (2d Cir.1938), *cert. denied* 305 U.S. 637, 59 S.Ct. 108, 83 L.Ed. 410 (1938), *rehearing denied* 305 U.S. 673, 59 S.Ct. 229, 83 L.Ed. 436 (1938).

party. A party in breach of a settlement seldom questions the terms of the settlement, at least not if the settlement terms have been memorialized in some writing. More commonly, the party breaching the settlement argues that the attorney made the agreement without the party's authority. Usually that ultra vires agent is the attorney for the party, or was formerly attorney for the party.

§ 14.6.4 Authority to Settle

Most jurisdictions require that attorneys compromise and settle claims only with the actual authority of their clients.[11] The Code of Professional Responsibility and the Model Rules of Professional Conduct mandate that an attorney obtain the approval of a client before agreeing to a settlement.[12] This authority may be *express* because of the words of the party to counsel or implied because of the actions of the party and counsel.[13] Apparent authority, however, is not enough in most jurisdictions, even though apparent authority is binding the most contexts other than settlement.[14] In some states, an exception to this rule arises when the settlement is reached by counsel in the presence of the court.[15] The party's behavior after settlement may prove the existence of implied actual authority of counsel to effect a binding settlement or may establish ratification of the settlement by the party.[16] Similarly, a representative sent to a pre-trial conference before a judge requiring such persons to be persons clothed with full settlement authority may be found, despite his or her actual authority, to have sufficient authority to bind the party.

The party opposing a motion to enforce settlement has a relatively simple objective—to show that no settlement was ever reached or agreed to. That party can show this by refuting the moving party's proof of settlement or by showing that counsel or another agent who agreed to the settlement lacked authority to settle.

Once settlement is established, the court will force the party to elect a remedy, and either seek specific performance of the terms of the settlement or reinstate the original claim.[17] The preferred route will vary according to the terms of the settlement, the likelihood of success in the underlying action, the time and expense required for trial, and the resources of the parties.

11. *See, e.g., Aetna Life & Casualty, Cas. & Sur. Div. v. Anderson,* 310 N.W.2d 91, 95 (Minn.1981).

12. *Compare* ABA Code of Professional Responsibility EC 7–7, EC 7–8 & DR 7–101(A)(3) *with* ABA Model Rules of Professional Conduct 1.2.

13. *See Carroll v. Pratt,* 247 Minn. 198, 76 N.W.2d 693, 698 (1956).

14. *See Ghostley v. Hetland,* 295 Minn. 376, 204 N.W.2d 821, 823 (1973).

15. *See, e.g.,* Minn.Stat.Ann. § 481.08.

16. *See Aetna Life & Casualty, Cas. & Sur. Div. v. Anderson,* 310 N.W.2d 91, 95 (Minn.1981); *Fingerhut Manufacturing Co. v. Mack Trucks, Inc.,* 267 Minn. 201, 125 N.W.2d 734 (1964).

17. *See Dankese v. Defense Logistics Agency,* 693 F.2d 13 (1st Cir.1982); *Village of Kaktovik v. Watt,* 689 F.2d 222, 223 (D.C.Cir.1982).

PRACTICE PROBLEMS

1. Hot Dog Enterprise sues Tri–Chem for violation of federal and state statutes, for negligence, and for products liability seeking actual and punitive damages.

(a) You represent HDE. General counsel for HDE asks for advice regarding optional methods to resolve the dispute. Do so.

(b) You represent HDE. General counsel tells you to settle the lawsuit.

(1) Plan appropriate settlement documents.

(2) Outline appropriate settlement documents.

(3) Draft appropriate settlement documents.

(c) You represent Tri–Chem. General counsel for Tri–Chem asks you to advise Tri–Chem on alternative ways the lawsuit can be resolved. Do so.

(d) You represent Tri–Chem. General counsel has instructed you to settle the case.

(1) Plan appropriate settlement documents.

(2) Outline appropriate settlement documents.

(3) Draft appropriate settlement documents.

2. In *Pozdak v. Summit Insurance* (Case B), prior to a lawsuit being commenced the potential parties agree that Pozdak will accept $100,000. You represent Summit Insurance. Draft a release or any other appropriate settlement documents.

3. In *Miyamoto v. Snow Cat* (Case C), the plaintiff only sues Snow Cat. After discovery has been completed, Snow Cat proposes a structured settlement offer to Miyamoto of $300,000 payable over ten years.

(a) You represent Mike LaBelle, advise him whether he should accept a structured settlement or whether he should demand a cash settlement.

(b) You represent Snow Cat. Draft the structured settlement documents. Create any additional facts you need to draft the documents.

4. In *Giacone v. City of Mitchell* (Case D), the City agrees to establish procedures which provide water customers with notice and an opportunity to contest a decision to terminate their water service.

(a) Assume the lawsuit is not a class action and there has been no damage to her house. You represent the Plaintiff. She does not want any money and you approve the procedures established by the City. Draft the appropriate settlement document(s).

(b) Assume the lawsuit is a class action for declaratory and injunctive relief only. The judge will only approve a settlement if it contains an order agreed to by the City consenting to implement the established procedures. Draft the appropriate documents to resolve the case.

5. In *LaBelle v. Mitchell Arts Council* (Case G), assume the Defendant agrees to reinstate the Plaintiff and to pay all back pay, and that is all.

(a) Draft the appropriate settlement document(s).

(b) Assume that 16 weeks after LaBelle is rehired pursuant to the settlement Mitchell Arts Council fires LaBelle again because of lack of money. What relief is available to LaBelle?

(c) Draft a motion and proposed order to enforce the settlement, including any necessary affidavits and other supporting papers and exhibits. Outline a supporting memorandum.

6. In *Luger v. Shade* (Case H), assume that defendant Develco offers to settle with Luger one-on-one for $50,000, cutting Shade loose to defend the rest of the suit on his own.

(a) You represent Develco. Draft a Pierringer-type release or any other appropriate settlement document for Develco and a memorandum of settlement.

(b) As the Lugers' lawyer, should you recommend acceptance? What else do you need to know? What should your counteroffer be?

(c) You represent Shade. Is there anything you can do about this side agreement? What?

7. In *Luger v. Shade* (Case H), assume that Develco in settlement offered Luger a less desirable townhouse condo in Fire Island plus $15,000 in cash and payment of Luger's legal fees, but paid by installment over two years. The Lugers accept. When they arrive at the condo, it is rife with structural problems. Then, Develco's second installment check bounces.

(a) What relief is available to the Lugers? What relief do they want?

(b) Draft a motion and proposed order to enforce the settlement, including any necessary affidavits and other supporting papers and exhibits. Outline a supporting memorandum.

(c) Now, draft the civil commitment papers for the Lugers citing as proof of their diminished mental capacities their acceptance of a second Develco townhouse (just kidding).

8. In *Vasquez v. Hot Dog Enterprises* (Case F), assume that plaintiff and HDE reach settlement, one provision of which is the rehiring of plaintiff and protection for her against further sexual harassment. Two months after Vasquez begins round two at Sunray, Don Winkle, a cousin of Wankle's, begins consistently making lewd remarks to Vasquez and brushing against her at the time card line. The rest of the crew finds this hilarious.

(a) As counsel for Vasquez, what can you do? What should you do?

(b) As counsel for HDE, outline your reaction to any action plaintiff is likely to take. What is the most likely scenario?

(c) As the judge, what, if anything, should you do to resolve this case? Suggest a preferred tactic? What will you want to know before making any decision?

CHAPTER 15
PRETRIAL CONFERENCES AND PRETRIAL ORDERS

Life is just one damned thing after another.
—Frank Ward O'Malley

§ 15.1 PRETRIAL CONFERENCES AND ORDERS GENERALLY

One facet of civil litigation must, if only by its name, be included in a book on pretrial litigation: the pretrial conference. An innovation of the Federal Rules of Civil Procedure adopted in 1938, the pretrial conference has had an important, although at times somewhat ill-defined, role in federal civil litigation since then. The pretrial conference has now become a standard part of state-court litigation as well.

An adjunct to the pretrial conference is the pretrial order. Most pretrial conferences are either preceded or followed, or both, by a pretrial order. These orders serve widely differing roles; in some courts merely notifying the parties of the scheduling of an upcoming pretrial conference and in others creating onerous burdens of preparation and submission of all materials for trial. Other pretrial orders merely record the events at a pretrial conference, while others follow the conference and create additional burdens.

One reason for placing this chapter at the end of the book is that the subject seems a logical seque to the study of trial practice. Pretrial orders and preparation for pretrial conferences involve activities that are essentially trial activities, such as identifying and marking trial exhibits, stipulating to facts, identifying and listing witnesses (sometimes in the order in which they will be called), and submitting proposed jury instructions or findings of fact. These activities are normally part of trial, but pretrial orders may require that they be done prior to trial.

Pretrial conferences also present the same opportunities for advocacy presented both by the various pretrial proceedings discussed above and by trial. Even in courts that do not routinely hold pretrial conferences, a party may be able to have the court hold a conference by requesting it. That request may be an effective means to permit meaningful settlement discussions to take place. If an opposing attorney has indicated that he or she agrees with a settlement proposal but that the client will not accept it, a pretrial settlement conference may be especially useful. A judge may be in a unique position to give the parties a perspective on the proposed settlement needed to make the party realize settlement is appropriate.

§ 15.2 THE PRETRIAL CONFERENCE

Rule 16 of the Federal Rules of Civil Procedure establishes the boundaries of the courts' power to hold pretrial conferences. One of the major purposes of pretrial conferences, settlement, is discussed in the previous chapter. Other purposes may be more important, and preparation for the other aspects of pretrial conferences can certainly be more time-consuming.

The federal rules initially intended the pretrial conference to provide the court with an effective means of exercising control over civil actions. The rule was viewed as necessary in part because of the relaxation of pleading requirements, liberalization of joinder of claims and parties, and the broadening of discovery under rule practice. Pretrial conferences seek to return some focus to the proceedings.

The variety in what can and does transpire at different pretrial conferences is literally impossible to describe. Notwithstanding that disclaimer, here goes. First, differences exist in the agendas for pretrial conferences based on the stage of the litigation. Many courts have traditionally held initial pretrial conferences early in an action, often shortly after the pleadings have closed. These early pretrial conferences are also sometimes called "status" or "scheduling" conferences. These conferences differ considerably from pretrial conferences held later in the action. The "status" pretrial conference frequently establishes various deadlines for completing discovery, submitting motions, and marking the case as "ready for trial." Settlement may be discussed, although it is rarely the focus of the early conference.

Fed.R.Civ.P. 16(b) now requires the court to hold a preliminary scheduling conference and requires the court to enter a scheduling order that limits the time

(1) to join other parties and to amend the pleadings;

(2) to file and hear motions; and

(3) to complete discovery.

The rule also permits the court to schedule further conferences and to consider "any other matters appropriate in the circumstances of the case."

Pretrial conferences held later in the lawsuit usually have much broader agendas. Fed.R.Civ.P. 16(c) provides a nonexclusive list of subjects which may be covered. The rule states:

> The participants at any conference under this rule may consider and take action with respect to
>
> (1) the formulation and simplification of the issues, including the elimination of frivolous claims or defenses;
>
> (2) the necessity or desirability of amendments to the pleadings;
>
> (3) the possibility of obtaining admissions of fact and of documents which will avoid unnecessary proof, stipulations regarding the authenticity of documents, and advance rulings from the court on the admissibility of evidence;
>
> (4) the avoidance of unnecessary proof and of cumulative evidence;
>
> (5) the identification of witnesses and documents, the need and schedule for filing and exchanging pretrial briefs, and the date or dates for further conferences and for trial;
>
> (6) the advisability of referring matters to a magistrate or master;
>
> (7) the possibility of settlement or the use of extrajudicial procedures to resolve the dispute;
>
> (8) the form and substance of the pretrial order;
>
> (9) the disposition of pending motions; [1]
>
> (10) the need for adopting special procedures for managing potentially difficult or protracted actions that may involve complex issues, multiple parties, difficult legal questions, or unusual proof problems; and
>
> (11) such other matters as may aid in the disposition of the action.

Among the specific subjects which may be covered at a pretrial conference but are not directly mentioned in the rule are the following:

1. The necessity or desirability of a further conference of the parties prior to a formal pretrial conference.

§ 15.2

1. The fact that the court is authorized to rule on pending motions at a pretrial conference does not mean that motions should be noticed to be heard at the time a pretrial conference is scheduled. Many courts will not permit motions to be heard at a pretrial conference; others will hear motions only in unusual circumstances. In many cases, the time for bringing motions on for hearing will have passed before a pretrial conference is scheduled. In any court it is prudent either to have the motion heard before the pretrial conference or to obtain specific permission from the court to schedule the motion to be heard at the pretrial conference.

2. Method of jury selection and number of peremptory challenges by individual parties in multi-party cases.

3. Proposed voir dire questions.

4. Requested preliminary instructions to the jury.

5. Specification of theories of claims or defenses.

6. Specification of special damages.

7. Identification of any statutes, regulations, or ordinances applicable to the claims or defenses or relied upon by any party.

8. Specific acts of negligence claimed by any party.

9. Identification of all expert witnesses and exchange of reports.

10. Limitation on the number of expert witnesses.

11. Disclosure of interested parties or insurers.

12. Disclosure and review of any demonstrative evidence for the trial (*e.g.*, charts, models, films).

13. Requested jury instructions.

Between what the rule specifically provides for and what may be considered under the broad language of the rule, there is little that cannot be considered at a pretrial conference. Most of the matters to be considered will be disclosed in the pretrial order setting the conference. Prudent counsel will also check with other attorneys to determine how the particular judge handles pretrial conferences.

The courts in pretrial conferences wield great power. The court may enter orders at pretrial conferences even in the absence of a motion by the parties. For example, if a court has the power to dismiss an action for failure to comply with the rules under Fed.R.Civ.P. 41(b), it may exercise that power by dismissing the case at a pretrial conference.[2] Similarly, the court may be able to grant a directed verdict at a pretrial conference if the evidence adduced during discovery is patently insufficient to survive a motion for directed verdict at trial,[3] although these results represent extreme pretrial conference outcomes.

Obviously, it is a good idea to attend a pretrial conference if the court schedules one. The United States Supreme Court has recognized that an action can be dismissed for failure to attend a pretrial conference, and courts ordering pretrial conferences tend to take them seriously.[4]

Some pretrial conferences are more "pre" than others. Although pretrial conferences are generally thought of as separate proceedings

2. *See Buss v. Western Airlines, Inc.*, 738 F.2d 1053 (9th Cir.1984), *cert. denied* 469 U.S. 1192, 105 S.Ct. 968, 83 L.Ed.2d 972 (1985).

3. *See Fidelity & Deposit Co. v. Southern Utilities*, 555 F.Supp. 206 (M.D.Ga. 1983), *judgment reversed* 726 F.2d 692 (11th Cir.1984).

4. *Link v. Wabash Railroad Co.*, 370 U.S. 626, 82 S.Ct. 1386, 8 L.Ed.2d 734 (1962), *rehearing denied* 371 U.S. 873, 83 S.Ct. 115, 9 L.Ed.2d 112 (1962).

held some weeks or months before trial, pretrial conferences can, and frequently are, held on the day of trial. This timing is particularly appropriate in courts using a master calendar system of assigning cases for trial, since the morning of trial will be the first time the trial judge is known. A pretrial conference at the time of trial is used for the same purposes as one held months before trial. In addition, this last-minute conference may be useful for resolving issues the attorneys or court did not think of at the earlier stages of the litigation.

The variety in format of pretrial conferences extends as well to the mechanics and formality of the conference. Some judges hold the conferences in open court, others prefer to hold pretrial conferences in chambers. Even in chambers some judges approach the matter very formally, allowing each attorney to make a "presentation" in turn, while other judges turn immediately to discussion between the parties of various particular matters. For example, the judge may immediately ask each attorney why more than one expert witness is necessary, rule after hearing from the attorneys that only one such witness per side will be allowed to testify at trial, and then move on to the next issue. Settlement may be the first thing brought up by the judge, or it may be the last. Some judges will not bring up settlement until they have heard from the parties, but will not decide anything until settlement has either been or talks have proven fruitless or even hopeless. This practice increases each party's uncertainty about the litigation, and presumably may make them more receptive to compromise.

Decorum at a pretrial conference must be suitable to the circumstances. The attorney's behavior must always be respectful and cooperative, but a conference held in chambers may lend itself to a more practical, informal presentation than is appropriate in open court.

§ 15.3 PRETRIAL ORDERS

Pretrial orders are orders entered as part of the pretrial conference procedures. Pretrial orders include orders entered prior to a pretrial conference that establish the conference agenda or mandate certain preparation by the parties. Other pretrial orders are entered during or following the conference. Some pretrial orders direct the parties to prepare a joint, or agreed, pretrial order to be entered subsequently by the court. Some judges have forms used solely for memorializing pretrial conference discussions; other judges summarize the discussions at the pretrial conference in an "order" made on the record rather than in a written order. Regardless of its form, a pretrial order may be very important to later handling of the case.

Generally, the burdens imposed by a pretrial order are commensurate with the complexity of the litigation. In simple, two-party litigation the court may not even enter a pretrial order. If a pretrial order is entered in such cases, it is usually limited in scope. In complex, multi-district or multi-party litigation, the court may enter a series of complex pretrial orders.[1] We have included below a sample pretrial order which fits somewhere in the middle of the spectrum. It is less burdensome than some of the orders issued in complex litigation, but imposes significant burdens on the parties. Most of this burden is simply the acceleration of various aspects of trial preparation. The order does not require counsel to prepare things that they would not otherwise do, but requires them to prepare such things as witness lists, exhibit lists, requested instructions and trial briefs long before trial.

The most important aspect of pretrial orders, however, is their binding nature. Unless the court permits an order to be modified, the order controls the conduct of all further proceedings in the litigation. Thus, the pretrial order's statement of the issues to be litigated becomes a binding statement of what will be the scope of the trial. If other issues are litigated without objection, the order will be deemed modified by consent just as pleadings will be deemed amended by consent.[2] In most cases, however, the order does fix the scope of the litigation and controls the later proceedings, so it is important to insure that the order is acceptable.

Sample Pretrial Order

IN THE UNITED STATES DISTRICT COURT FOR THE EASTERN DISTRICT OF PENNSYLVANIA

STANDING ORDER RE PRETRIAL ORDER

(The Pretrial Memorandum described in Rule 21(c) of the Local Rules of Civil Procedure is NOT required.)

Item One: If after a settlement conference it appears that the case will not settle, the Final Pretrial Conference shall be held as scheduled by the Court. Counsel are hereby directed to confer in advance of such pretrial conference for the purpose of preparing a *Pretrial Order,* which Order shall be delivered to the Judge's chambers, in duplicate, prior to the date of the pretrial conference unless otherwise directed.

The aforesaid Pretrial Order shall consist of *one* document, shall be *signed by all* counsel, and shall reflect the efforts of *all* counsel. It is the obligation of plaintiff's counsel to initiate the procedure for preparation and completion of this Final Pretrial Order.

The Final Pretrial Order, as filed, shall govern the conduct of the trial of the case. Amendments to this Order shall be allowed only in exceptional circumstances to prevent manifest injustice.

Item Two: After the Final Pretrial Conference, the Pretrial Order shall be signed by the judge. The case shall then be ready for trial.

Item Three: The Pretrial Order shall be prepared on the attached form with addenda as required (an original and one copy for the Court, one copy for each counsel).

§ 15.3

1. The Manual for Complex Litigation provides suggested procedures for holding pretrial conferences and using pretrial orders in complex litigation. The *Manual* includes sample orders, as does United States District Judge William Schwarzer in William Schwarzer, Managing Antitrust and Other Complex Litigation (1982).

2. *See, e.g., Gorby v. Schneider Tank Lines, Inc.,* 741 F.2d 1015 (7th Cir.1984).

IN THE UNITED STATES DISTRICT COURT FOR THE EASTERN DISTRICT OF PENNSYLVANIA

) CIVIL ACTION
) NO. ______

FINAL PRETRIAL ORDER

This matter having come before the Court at a pretrial conference held pursuant to Rule 16 of the Federal Rules of Civil Procedure, and ______ having appeared as counsel for the plaintiff(s) and ______ having appeared as counsel for the defendant(s), the following Order is hereby entered:

PART I: WITNESSES, DEPOSITIONS, ANSWERS TO INTERROGATORIES AND PLEADINGS

(Only the witnesses listed herein will be permitted to testify at the trial. Any objections to a witness must be noted by opposing counsel. Only those depositions, answers to interrogatories and pleadings listed herein will be admitted into evidence; any objections of opposing counsel to such use will be deemed waived if not set forth herein.)

A. *Plaintiff's Witnesses*

1. The plaintiff intends to call the following witnesses in regard to liability:

2. The plaintiff intends to call the following witnesses in regard to damages:

3. The plaintiff intends to offer into evidence the following portion(s) of the deposition, pleadings and/or answers to interrogatories:

4. The defendant waives all objections to the receipt into evidence of the above deposition, pleadings and/or answers to interrogatories except as follows:

B. *Defendant's Witnesses*

1. The defendant intends to call the following witnesses in regard to liability:

2. The defendant intends to call the following witnesses in regard to damages:

3. The defendant intends to offer into evidence the following portion(s) of the deposition, pleadings and/or answers to interrogatories:

4. The plaintiff waives all objections to the receipt into evidence of the above deposition, pleadings and/or answers to interrogatories except as follows:

C. *Expert Witnesses*

(No expert shall be permitted to testify unless listed below. No expert shall be permitted to testify unless a summary of his qualifications is attached hereto. Said summary shall be read into the record at the time he takes the stand, and no opposing counsel shall be permitted to question his qualifications as an expert unless the basis of objection is set forth herein. No expert witness will be permitted to testify unless all opposing counsel, prior to the date of this Order, have been informed in writing as to the substance of said expert's testimony.)

1. Plaintiff's expert witnesses and identification of writing containing substance of testimony:

2. Defendant's objection to the qualifications of plaintiff's expert is:

3. Defendant's expert witnesses and identification of writing containing substance of testimony:

4. Plaintiff's objection to the qualifications of defendant's expert is:

PART II: EXHIBITS

(Only the exhibits listed below shall be introduced at the trial. Any objection to an exhibit, and the reason for said objection, must be set forth herein or it shall be deemed waived. All parties hereby agree that it will not be necessary to bring in the custodian of any exhibit unless an objection to this procedure is set forth below.)

A. *Plaintiff's Exhibits*

1. Plaintiff intends to introduce the following exhibits into evidence (list by numbers with a description of each exhibit):

2. Defendant objects to the introduction of plaintiff's exhibit (set forth number of exhibit and grounds for objection):

B. *Defendant's Exhibits*

1. Defendant intends to introduce the following exhibits into evidence (list by numbers with description of each exhibit):

2. Plaintiff objects to the introduction of defendant's exhibit (set forth number of exhibit and grounds for objection):

PART III: FACTS

A. *Stipulation of Facts*

(Set forth a comprehensive stipulation of all uncontested facts in narrative form. Said stipulation shall include all answers to interrogatories and admissions which facts are agreed to by all parties. Said stipulation shall be read into the record as the first evidence at trial.)

B. *Plaintiff's Contested Facts*

1. Plaintiff intends to prove the following contested facts in regard to liability:

2. Plaintiff intends to prove the following contested facts in regard to damages:

C. *Defendant's Contested Facts*

1. Defendant intends to prove the following contested facts in regard to liability:

2. Defendant intends to prove the following contested facts in regard to damages:

PART IV: LAW

A. *Plaintiff*

1. Plaintiff's statement of the legal issues in this case:

2. Plaintiff's statement of the law applicable to the aforesaid legal issues:

B. *Defendant*

1. Defendant's statement of the legal issues in this case:

2. Defendant's statement of the law applicable to the aforesaid legal issues:

PART V: MISCELLANEOUS

(Set forth any additional stipulations of counsel and/or orders concerning the trial of this case.)

PART VI: JURY/NON–JURY TRIALS

A. *Jury Trials*

1. Unless stated to the contrary herein, the issues relating to liability shall be severed and tried to verdict. Thereafter, all issues relating to damages will be tried before the same jury. The decision concerning bifurcation of the trial will be made by the Court at the pretrial conference as a result of an informed exercise of discretion on the merits of the case.

2. Requests for instructions to the jury shall be submitted, in duplicate, to the Court prior to the commencement of a jury trial. There is reserved to counsel the right to submit additional requests for instructions during the course of the trial on those matters that cannot reasonably be anticipated.

B. *Non–Jury Trials*

1. Unless stated to the contrary herein, the issues relating to liability shall be severed and tried to verdict. Thereafter, all issues relating to damages will be tried. The decision concerning bifurcation of the trial will be made by the Court at the pretrial conference as a result of an informed exercise of discretion on the merits of the case.

2. Requests for Findings of Fact and Conclusions of Law shall be submitted, in duplicate, to the Court prior to commencement of the trial. There is reserved to counsel the right to submit additional requests during the course of the trial on those matters that cannot reasonably be anticipated.

Amendments to this Pretrial Order will not be permitted except where the Court determines that manifest injustice would result if the amendment is not allowed.

____
Attorney for Plaintiff

____
Attorney for Defendant

Date: _________________________ ______________________________
Judge

The local rule referred to in this pretrial order contains an exhaustive list of items which the attorneys must discuss and attempt to agree on at the conference required by the order. The combined effect of these requirements is to create an onerous set of pretrial requirements.

*

APPENDIX A *

CLIENT DEPOSITION INSTRUCTIONS

Your deposition will soon be taken. It is a normal, regular procedure in a case such as yours. These instructions are meant to explain to you what a deposition is, acquaint you with procedures, answer most of your questions about depositions, and advise you how to conduct yourself during the deposition. Please read these guidelines thoroughly and carefully. We have already met or will meet before the deposition to review the facts and to prepare you fully for the depositions.

This booklet will assist you with that preparation by presenting general guidelines applicable to all depositions. However, individual depositions vary because of different people, different lawyers, and different facts. There may well be some differences between depositions, as discussed here, and what we have already discussed or will later discuss about your deposition. You should always follow my specific advice. Should you have any questions after you read these guidelines, ask me them the next time we meet or before the deposition.

Your deposition has been scheduled for [*time*], at [*place*]. Please meet me before the deposition at [*time*], at [*place*]. Please meet me at my office to prepare for the deposition at [*time*]. Should the above dates and time conflict with your schedule, please telephone ______ immediately at ______.

* Some ideas appearing in this appendix are adapted with permission from the copyrighted publication, About Your Deposition: 95 Questions and Answers. The booklet contains an excellent explanation of personal injury depositions, and it may be obtained from The Lawyers and Judges Publishing Co., P.O. Box 42050, Tucson, AZ., 85733.

Contents

I. GENERAL INFORMATION

A. *Definitions and Background Information*

Q: What is a deposition?

A: A deposition is one of a number of procedural "discovery" methods used by an opposing attorney to "discover" information about your case. It is part of the other side's investigation of the case. The opposing attorney will ask you a series of questions. You will take an oath to tell the truth in answering all questions.

Q: What is a deponent?

A: A deponent is a person who gives information to the lawyer in a conference-type setting. This whole process in which the lawyer questions the deponent and the deponent gives information is called a deposition. The "deponent" is the same as the "witness."

Q: Why is my deposition being taken?

A: So that the opposing lawyer can determine what you know about the facts and details of the case. A deposition enables a lawyer to form an impression and to make an appraisal about you, about what you know, and about how you say it.

Q: What rules govern the deposition?

A: The rules that regulate what happens during a lawsuit. These rules allow the lawyers to obtain information through discovery before the trial to better prepare for the trial. These rules also increase the chances of settling the case so that you may not have to testify again at trial.

Q: How is this information going to be used?

A: The information tells the other side what you know. Your deposition gives the other lawyer an opportunity to determine how good a witness you are going to be. The information also helps settle cases because both sides know the various versions of what happened and they can more easily agree on a settlement before trial.

Q: What if this case goes to trial? How is the deposition transcript used in court?

A: Statements that you make during a deposition may be evidence for court. If you admit or deny certain things or give certain information, this information may be used as evidence in court. It may also be used as "impeachment" evidence; that is, evidence that will be used to show that you have said something inconsistent. If your testimony differs at trial from your testimony during the deposition, the other attorney may be able to read from, or have you read from, the deposition transcript, and point out the inconsistency to the judge and jury. The deposition transcript could also be used instead of your live testimony, should you be unavailable at the time of the trial.

B. *Logistics*

Q: Do I have to attend the deposition?

A: Yes. Your lawyer has been served with a written notice of your deposition and you must attend. It may be possible for the time and date of your deposition to be changed, and you should discuss this with your attorney if you have any questions.

Q: How long does a deposition take?

A: That depends on the particular case and the lawyer asking the questions. Your lawyer may be able to estimate the time for your deposition. Your schedule should be arranged so that you will not be hurried or rushed for time when you testify.

Q: Will there be any breaks during the deposition?

A: Yes. There will be breaks periodically throughout the deposition, depending on its length. You should be as comfortable as possible at all times. Tell your lawyer about any physical conditions or problems that you have which require special attention. Your lawyer will arrange for any breaks you need during the deposition.

Q: Will I be allowed to drink coffee or water or smoke during the deposition?

A: You will usually be allowed to drink water or coffee or some other refreshment. You may or may not be allowed to smoke. No eating is permitted. If you need a break, let your lawyer know.

Q: Will I get reimbursed for lost wages or transportation expenses?

A: No. You will have to bear those costs as part of your involvement in this lawsuit.

Q: What should I wear to the deposition?

A: You should present your best appearance. Dress as if you were going to appear in court and wear neat, moderate, and comfortable clothing. Your attorney may want you to dress differently; and will so advise you.

Q: Will the deposition take place in a courtroom?

A: No. It takes place in an informal setting, frequently in the examining attorney's office, often in the court reporter's office, occasionally in the courthouse, sometimes in the opposing attorney's office, and at times in the deponent's office so that certain documents will be accessible. Your lawyer will advise you as to the exact location of the deposition.

Q: Will there be a "deposition room"?

A: The room will usually be a conference room or library office. There will be a table and several chairs around the table. You will sit in one of the chairs next to your lawyer, and the other people will sit on the other chairs.

Q: Who will be present during my deposition?

A: Your lawyer will be there with you. The lawyer or lawyers representing the party or parties in the case will also be there, as will a court reporter-stenographer, who will record what happens.

Q: Will there be anyone else present during my deposition?

A: Ordinarily not. If there will be, your attorney will advise you. Sometimes parties to an action will exercise their right to sit in during depositions.

Q: Can I bring anyone with me to the deposition?

A: Ask your lawyer in advance to tell you who may or may not sit in with you at the deposition.

Q: Can I object to the presence of someone at the deposition?

A: Probably not. The parties can be there, as can their lawyers. If you expect that someone you do not want to attend will be there, contact your lawyer.

Q: Is the deposition conducted like a trial?

A: Not exactly. There will be no judge or jury present, but otherwise you will be answering questions in somewhat the same manner as you would during a trial. Although a deposition seems less formal than a court hearing, it is important to remember that the deposition testimony can be used in court. So don't let the informal setting make you less careful in answering the questions.

Q: Will my answers be recorded?

A: Yes. Everything said during the formal part of the deposition will be recorded. A court reporter-stenographer will record everything you and everyone else says on a "stenographic machine" or by shorthand, or by tape recorder or videotape. There may be times when somebody says, "Let's go off the record," and if you see the reporter stop or take his or her hands up off the machine, then that means no real record is being made. This testimony may later be "transcribed" (typed up in a booklet form) by the reporter-stenographer, with copies made available to the court and to the attorneys. Also, the lawyers will be taking notes.

Q: Will my deposition be videotaped?

A: Some courts encourage the use of tape recorders or videotape equipment. If your deposition will be videotaped, your attorney will discuss this aspect with you.

II. THE DEPOSITION ITSELF

A. *The Deposition Begins*

Q: How does the deposition begin?

A: The reporter-stenographer will ask you to raise your right hand and take an oath to tell the truth. After the oath has been administered or after you have affirmed to tell the truth, the other attorney will ask you questions or may explain some deposition procedures and then begin the questioning.

Q: How should I conduct myself during the deposition?

A: Remain polite and calm at all times. Do not become angry or upset. Be courteous, but do not become overly friendly with, or tell jokes to, the opposing lawyer or the reporter-stenographer. Do not talk at the same time someone else is talking. The reporter will not be able to transcribe two people talking at the same time.

Q: What if I am nervous?

A: You probably will be a little nervous. That's normal, but control it so that you will testify accurately and clearly. The information you give is important, but of almost equal importance is the impression you make on opposing counsel.

Q: Whom should I look at when I give my answers?

A: The other attorney will be asking you the questions, and you should ordinarily look and talk to that attorney. You want to make certain that you speak clearly and loudly enough so that the reporter-stenographer can accurately record what to say. Do not nod your head or use facial expressions or gestures to answer questions. Be certain that you verbalize whatever you do so the reporter-stenographer can record that.

Q: What should I do if I do not understand something that has happened during the deposition?

A: Ask your attorney to explain to you what happened.

Q: May I ask my attorney questions in private during the deposition?

A: Yes. If at some point you're confused, ask to speak to your lawyer. But you should avoid overdoing this. It may look like you and your attorney are planning or changing your answers.

Q: Is it permissible for me to talk to my lawyer during a break in the deposition or when there is a lull in the questioning?

A: If you have some questions or concerns about the deposition, you should discuss them with your lawyer. But be careful not to talk too loudly, or other people will overhear you.

Q: Will I be told anything about the lawyer who will ask me the questions?

A: Yes. Your lawyer will discuss with you the type of questioning usually conducted by an opposing attorney. Your attorney may even tell you something about the attorney's personality, approach, pace, and other factors.

Q: Should I answer differently if the other attorney is friendly or hostile towards me?

A: No. Don't be disarmed by friendliness or intimidated by hostility. Tell the truth, regardless of the disposition of the attorney. Whether friendly or hostile, the attorney will not have your best interests in mind.

B. Types of Questions

Q: What kind of questions will the other attorney ask me?

A: The other attorney will generally ask you questions about what you know and what happened and may also ask you questions about your personal history and background.

Q: Must I answer every question the opposing lawyer asks?

A: Yes, unless your lawyer objects, or unless you do not know the answer or do not remember the details. Do not make up answers.

Q: What if I consider questions about my personal history and background to be confidential and private?

A: The law usually allows the other attorney to ask you questions about your personal history and background because such information often has a direct or indirect significance to the case or is of importance or interest to the other attorney. If such information is protected by the law, then your attorney will object and advise you not to answer. If your attorney does not object, then you should answer the questions. Your lawyer will protect you.

Q: Do I have to answer hypothetical or "possibility" questions the other attorney asks me?

A: The other attorney may ask you "if" questions, or "assume" questions: "What if this happened?" or "Assume that happened?" You do not have to answer such hypothetical or possibility questions and you should not guess at answers. Simply tell the attorney you can't answer and do not want to guess.

Q: What if the other lawyer does not ask me certain questions which I think are important?

A: Do not volunteer facts or answers to questions you have not been asked. For example:

Q: Where do you live?

A: I live at 1934 Suburban Avenue. My spouse and I live there and we have three children. I work at 3M. My spouse works at Mounds Park Hospital.

Since you were only asked where you live, you should simply give the address and not the other information. If the other attorney wants the other information, he or she will ask for it. If you continue giving details that you have not been asked about, the deposition will become unduly long and disorganized.

Q: What if the other attorney asks me a question that will hurt my case if I answer it?

A: You must tell the truth, regardless of whether your answer will hurt or help your case.

Q: Will the other lawyer ask questions in order, or skip around from subject to subject?

A: Different lawyers ask questions differently. Some follow a pattern, others skip from subject to subject. If you pay close attention, you should be able to answer the questions easily. Remember that you have the right to have a question repeated or clarified if you did not understand or did not hear it. If you tell the truth and stick to the facts as you know them, no amount of skipping around should confuse you.

Q: Will the other attorney ask me any trick questions?

A: You have watched Perry Mason too often. If an opposing lawyer tries to trick you, your attorney will be aware of the situation and will take steps necessary to protect you. Do remain alert, though; otherwise you could become confused.

Q: Will more than one lawyer be asking me questions?

A: That depends on how many parties there are in the case. If each of the parties is represented by a different lawyer, each may ask you some questions.

Q: Will my attorney ask me questions during the deposition?

A: Your attorney may or may not ask you questions after the other attorney has finished asking you questions. Your attorney may ask you questions to clarify some of your answers or to have you give some additional information. This is why you need not volunteer testimony, because your attorney may add information by questioning you later.

C. Specific Questions to Expect

Q: If I am asked, "Did you talk to your lawyer before coming to this deposition?" what should I say?

A: The truth: Yes. There is absolutely no reason for you to hide the fact that you talked to your lawyer before coming to the deposition.

Q: What if the other lawyer asks, "Did your lawyer tell you what to say at this deposition?"

A: Your lawyer will not tell you what to say. Your lawyer will tell you to testify truthfully and to the best of your ability and knowledge. Your lawyer will prepare you for your deposition by referring to reports, notes, and other documents in the file and will review facts in order to refresh your recollection.

Q: What if the other attorney asks, "Do you realize you are testifying under oath?" or "Is that really your sworn testimony?"

A: Some attorneys, by asking such questions, may try to intimidate you or try to insinuate that you are lying. These are usually scare tactics. If you have answered your question honestly, according to the best of your ability, while these tactics may bother you, they should not concern you. Your attorney will protect you if these questions and tactics get out of hand.

Q: Will I be asked if anyone ever sued me or if I was ever a party in a lawsuit?

A: Probably. Answer the questions truthfully.

D. Responses

Q: How should I answer the questions the other attorney asks?

A: Listen to the question. Be sure you understand it before you respond. Take a moment to think about it and make sure that you understand it. Proceed at your own pace. Answer the question asked; don't ramble and don't volunteer any information. Be brief and concise. You are only obligated to answer the question directly. Give only information as to what you saw or heard. Don't speculate as to what other people were doing or what they were thinking. Do not ask questions in answer to questions.

Q: Should I be animated or speak in a monotone?

A: Speak as you normally do. Speak clearly, slowly, distinctly, and audibly. Remember also that the reporter will be taking down everything that is said during the deposition. The reporter can only take down verbal responses and cannot take down a nod of the head or a gesture.

Q: What should I do if I did not hear a question?

A: Simply say that you did not hear the question asked. The opposing lawyer will then either repeat the question or ask the reporter to read the question to you.

Q: What happens if I do not understand the question the other attorney asks me?

A: Speak right up and tell the attorney that you do not understand the question and that you cannot answer it. Before you answer a question, make certain you understand it. You should not and do not have to answer any question you do not understand. Also, if the opposing attorney uses a word that you don't know, don't hesitate to say so. It's important that you not act as if you understood the word and not try to bluff your way through.

Q: Would it be a good idea for me to memorize much of my testimony so I won't forget what to say?

A: Do not memorize your testimony. A deposition is not a memory contest. Your lawyer will prepare you and suggest ways to help you remember answers during the deposition.

Q: Should I conceal any information?

A: No. The lawyer questioning you has a right to certain information. Answer each question as truthfully and honestly as you can. Give a full and complete answer; do not withhold any information. However, do not volunteer additional information.

Q: Can I explain my answers?

A: The attorney will ask you some questions that will require a yes, no, or I-don't-know response. You should answer such questions accordingly. If you cannot answer a question with a simple yes, no, or "I don't know," then explain your answer. The other attorney may nonetheless insist that you answer with a yes, no, or "I don't know." If so, tell the other attorney that you cannot answer the question that way, but only in your own way. Your attorney will protect you if you have difficulty in answering the question.

Q: What if the opposing lawyer interrupts my answer to a question before I'm done?

A: Your attorney will recognize that you have not been permitted to complete your answer. It is possible that your lawyer may not be interested in having you complete your answer and may then do nothing. Your lawyer may ask you if you care to complete your answer or may decide that your interrupted answer is all that opposing counsel is entitled to receive under the circumstances. If your completed answer is vital to your case, your lawyer will make it possible for you to complete your answer. Listen carefully to your lawyer and be guided by these instructions to you and any remarks to the stenographer or the opposing lawyer.

Q: What if I do not remember for certain or I am not sure about an answer?

A: There is nothing wrong with an answer that says, "I don't know" or "I don't remember." You will not be expected to remember everything. You should explain what you remember. If you do not remember something for certain or something completely, then you should say so. If you can give a reasonable approximation of something, then you may do so. For example, if you are asked questions about what someone said, and you do not remember exactly what was said, you should respond: "I don't remember the exact words, but he said something to the effect that...." If you are asked about time, speed, or distance, and you are not certain but can make a reasonable estimate, then you may respond: "About one hour," or "Around 30 miles per hour," or "I am not sure, but I would estimate...." If you cannot make a reasonable approximation or a reliable estimate, or you do not recall the particular facts, say so. Use your best judgment. Do not guess or speculate about something. Give only information you have. If the other attorney insists on an answer or on your best judgment, and you can only guess or speculate, tell the attorney that you cannot answer the question.

Q: Should I give my opinion about something?

A: If the other attorney asks you for your opinion, then give it. If you are not asked for it, then do not volunteer your opinion unless you need to in order to explain an answer fully.

Q: What if the other attorney is dissatisfied with my answer?

A: You are there to tell the truth, not to adapt your answers to satisfy the other attorney. Most often, because the other attorney will be representing the other side, your information will not be favorable to that attorney's position. You should not be concerned whether you satisfy or dissatisfy the other attorney.

Q: What if I realize during the deposition that I have given an incorrect or inaccurate or incomplete answer to a previous question?

A: You may ask that that particular question and answer be asked or read again. Then you should think carefully about any change you wish to make in your testimony. The other lawyer may ask questions about the change in your testimony in an attempt to discredit your corrected answer. But it is usually more important for you to correct an answer than it is for you to leave an incorrect answer on the transcript. If you have a doubt about what to do, then you should speak to your attorney about the matter.

Q: What if I feel during the deposition that things are not going well or that the other attorney is taking advantage of me, what should I do?

A: Your attorney is there to protect you, and while you may not think things are going well, your attorney may be satisfied with what is happening. If you feel strongly that something is wrong, then speak to your attorney.

E. Objections

Q: What is an objection?

A: If the other attorney asks you a question and your lawyer considers that question improper, your lawyer will say "Objection," or words to that effect. That word is a signal to you not to answer the question. Do not volunteer to give an answer when your lawyer makes an objection. Your lawyer will make the objection because the question or the expected answer may be improper or confusing or ambiguous. An objection is not a signal for you to explain something. You should remain silent until your attorney no longer objects or gives you permission to answer that question.

Q: Why do attorneys object?

A: Because the attorney thinks the question is something that really shouldn't be answered. The objection is the only way your attorney can speak to you as well as speak to the other attorney to disagree with the nature and type of question. Sometimes an attorney may object just for the record, so that later on, when the transcript is read, the objection acts as a reminder of a possible error.

Q: Will there be many objections during the deposition?

A: Usually not. The other lawyer can ask you many questions that will be proper for the deposition. These same questions may not be proper for the trial. If those questions were later asked at the trial, your attorney might object. But during a deposition, your attorney probably will not object to such questions because the law allows the other attorney to ask them during the deposition.

Q: Why should I answer if my attorney objects?

A: Your lawyer may object, state a reason, and then tell you to answer the question. The rules may require this. Do listen very carefully to the objection because it may give you a clue. It may let you know that you're being led into something. Or an objection that the question calls for "speculation" would be a tip to ask yourself, "Am I speculating or do I really know that?"

Q: What if I think a question should not be answered but my lawyer does not make an objection?

A: Answer the question. Your lawyer is there to protect your interests and to know when to make objections. You may not understand why the other side has asked the question, but you should answer the question unless your attorney objects. If you believe there is no reason at all to answer a question and your attorney does not object, then you might consider conferring with your attorney.

Q: Are there other kinds of objections my lawyer may make?

A: Yes, your lawyer may instruct you not to answer a particular question. Refuse to answer it. If the other attorney asks you whether you will or will not answer the question, say that on the advice of your attorney you will not answer the question.

F. Exhibits and Documents

Q: Will I have to examine any papers?

A: Maybe. It depends on your case. When an exhibit is handed to you, don't start to answer the question until you have taken time to become familiar with it (*i.e.,* read it, examine it, study it). Take your time.

Q: Will the other attorney ask me to identify certain documents or photographs or objects during the deposition?

A: Perhaps. Before answering questions about a document, make certain that you read the entire segment you are asked about. Even though some documents may contain information or appear to have been signed, read, dated, mailed, or handled by you, do not admit such facts unless you have actual knowledge. If you cannot identify all or part of a document, tell the attorney that.

Q: May I look at documents or papers before I answer a question?

A: If the other attorney asks you a question about a document or a thing, then you should first ask to see that document or thing before you answer. If you do not know an answer, but do know that a document or thing contains the answer, then you can tell the other attorney that. Your attorney may prepare some notes with you to refresh your memory during the deposition. If you need to, you can ask your attorney for these notes.

Q: Should I bring any documents with me?

A: Your attorney will advise you whether or not you need to bring with you any documents or objects or things or papers or materials. You can suggest to your attorney certain documents or materials that may help you in preparation for the deposition or during the deposition. But do not bring anything with you or use any materials without first obtaining your attorney's permission.

Q: May I bring documents with me?

A: No. Do not bring anything to the deposition with you unless told to do so by your attorney. If you bring anything into the deposition room, the opposing counsel may want to look at it.

Q: Can I get the documents back?

A: Yes. Speak to your lawyer about this.

Q: What should I do if the other attorney asks me if I will provide copies of certain documents or look up some facts?

A: Do not agree. Turn to your attorney for advice.

Q: Will the other attorney ask me to make a drawing or diagram during the deposition?

A: Perhaps. You should prepare for this by making some rough sketches for the deposition. You will not be expected to prepare an artist's drawing or draw something to scale. When you discuss preparation with your lawyer, you may do a rough sketch at that time.

III. NOW THAT IT'S OVER

Q: Is that all?

A: One deposition is usually adequate, but a second one may be scheduled.

Q: What happens to the record of the testimony after the deposition?

A: The reporter-stenographer will type a transcript of the testimony in booklet form if one of the attorneys requests.

Q: What if the reporter-stenographer makes a mistake in recording the testimony?

A: You will have an opportunity if your lawyer thinks it advisable after the deposition to read the transcript and check it for errors. Your lawyer will know what to do if the deposition is inaccurate. You can make things easier for the stenographer by not talking when someone else is talking, by speaking loudly and clearly, and by spelling difficult words or names. In some instances you will be asked to read and sign the transcript to confirm its accuracy.

Q: Will a deposition be taken from anyone else connected with this case?

A: Probably. Your lawyer may take depositions of other parties or witnesses in the case if those depositions are necessary.

Q: Does the taking of my deposition at this time mean my case is going to trial soon?

A: Not necessarily. Your lawyer will advise you about your expected trial date or the chances of settling the case.

Q: That wasn't so bad. I almost enjoyed it.

A: It is normal to be anxious before and during the deposition, but most people overcome this tension as the deposition proceeds and they become more relaxed. If you perform your role by listening carefully to the questions and by telling the truth and disclosing what you know, you will have done your best. Some things may happen or may be said which bother or confuse you. Your attorney is there to protect and advise you. You will probably find your deposition to be an interesting and challenging experience.

*

APPENDIX B
CASE FILES

The events of these cases occur in mythical jurisdictions which have adopted the Federal Rules of Civil Procedure and Evidence. Unless otherwise indicated, the events take place in the City of Mitchell which is in the State of Summit. Other states include: Coastland, Peakland, Grassland, Gothamland, Heartland, Forestland, and Gulfland.

Case A

Hot Dog Enterprises v. Tri–Chem

DOCUMENTS

The following documents comprise this case file.

Additional Bond–Mor information.

Information on the architect: Eileen Robin

Information on the masonry contractor: Kelly Devitt

Information on the structural engineer: Julie Kouri.

Information on a witness: Donelle Lakemoore.

Research memorandum from Clyde Irfram, Tri–Chem researcher, April 3, 1985.

Confidential memorandum from Tri–Chem research facilities, July 23, 1985.

Research memorandum from Tri–Chem research facilities, June 21, 1986.

Confidential memorandum from Sonja Belacorte, Tri–Chem manager, August 6, 1986.

Letter from Lucinda Ijima, Tri–Chem marketing manager, May 7, 1987.

Letter from Wes Wojcik, Tri–Chem architect liaison, September 7, 1987.

Memorandum from Carl Blackfoot, Tri–Chem research manager, February 15, 1988.

Tri–Chem sales brochure, 1988.

Tri–Chem bulletin, January 1989.

Letter from B. J. Wojcik, Tri–Chem products manager, December 17, 1989.

Letter from M. M. Hughes, consulting engineer, January 12, 1990.

Letter from Ngnon Nashwa, Tri–Chem customer services, November 30, 1990.

TRI-CHEM

Additional Bond–Mor Information

Ordinary cement mortar lacks sufficient adhesive strength to permit construction of a single width brick wall without reinforcement. Tri–Chem developed a family of Zetes Latex products which provides mortar with the strength and adhesion to allow Tri–Chem to sell prefabricated brick panels and walls and to allow their use without reinforcement. Zetes Latex is described as a polymer or copolymer with vinylidene chloride as the primary non-aqueous component. Bond–Mor contains approximately 70% by weight of vinylidene chloride and 30% vinyl chloride.

Chloride is highly corrosive to steel. Steel embedded in cement mortar is normally resistant to or passified against corrosion because the mortar itself is highly alkaline. Alkalines effectively neutralize ordinary rust and corrosion. Zetes Latex additives, Bond–Mor in particular, contain chlorides, including a small amount of free chloride ions in hydrochloric acid that is highly corrosive to steel. The highly alkaline cement in mortar and concrete continuously reacts with the Bond–Mor additive to strip additional chloride ions from the vinyldene chloride component of Bond–Mor. Water and heat, among other things, will cause and accelerate the stripping process resulting in excessive corrosion.

Prestressed mortar is susceptible to corrosion problems when very low levels of chlorides are present. The American Concrete Institute (ACI) has established a 0.06% limit for chloride by weight of cement. Bond–Mor and other Zetes Latex additives typically release 36 to 50 times the 0.06% chloride standard when mixed with concrete or mortar.

The American Bonding Institute (ABI) and the Structural Products Institute (SPI) recommended against the use of calcium chloride. Under standard masonry practices significantly less of the disruptive chloride ions were emitted than were found in Bond–Mor systems containing metals. For example, SPI, in its suggested practices for construction, recommended that "calcium chloride or admixtures containing it shall not be used in mortar or grout in which reinforcement, metal ties or anchors are to be embedded."

The presence of the chloride ions work to corrode steel. The free chloride ions initially present in Bond–Mor, plus those continuously coming into being due to stripping, corrode steel embedded in or adjacent to the Bond–Mor mortar, including steel coated with zinc (i.e. galvanized) or cadmium. Rust generated from the corrosion of steel and the by-products related to the corrosion of zinc occupy more space than is occupied by the metal itself prior to corrosion. This creates expansive forces on the surrounding mortar and brick. The result is cracking, which causes the masonry to crack and deteriorate.

Bond–Mor was test-marketed in the 1980's. From that time to the present it has been marketed nationally to the construction, masonry, and architectural industries.

In 1989, Bricks fell from HDE's Ohio restaurant building. After the bricks fell, HDE was told to cordon off the area beneath and to post warning signs so that customers would not walk near nor touch the bricks. Tri–Chem investigated this problem, made repairs to the walls, and removed the fallen bricks.

ARCHITECT

Eileen Robin

Eileen Robin is a licensed architect who has been practicing in various states since the 1960's. Robin learned of the Bond–Mor product through telephone calls, personal visits, and promotional literature. In addition to being familiar with the product, she was introduced by Tri–Chem to Julie Kouri, a structural engineer, to acquaint Kouri with the Bond–Mor product.

Since her introduction to Tri–Chem and the Bond–Mor product in the mid–1980's, Robin has served as an architectural consultant for Tri–Chem on a variety of projects. In 1986, when HDE came to Tri–Chem to begin work on its Ohio building, Tri–Chem recommended that HDE consult with Robin. Ultimately, HDE retained her as a consultant on the Ohio building.

As a result of her retention by HDE and other companies as a Tri–Chem consultant, Tri–Chem has promoted Robin throughout the United States as an authority and spokesperson for certain aspects of Bond–Mor use. Robin has made considerable fees as a consultant and continues to work with Tri–Chem today.

MASONRY CONTRACTOR

Kelly Devitt

Kelly Devitt is a masonry contractor engaged in the construction of brick buildings throughout the country and operates under the name of Kelly Devitt Company, Inc. Tri–Chem approached Devitt to solicit Devitt's bid on various projects throughout the United States with work done on each project to be done with Bond–Mor. Devitt submitted a bid pursuant to Tri–Chem's solicitations and received various masonry contracts and completed work on these projects with the assistance and oversight of Tri–Chem. Numerous telephone calls, letters, and memos exist establishing this relationship between Devitt and Tri–Chem through the 1980's.

Devitt, through continuing consultation with Tri–Chem, established a company to sell franchises for design and construction of buildings using Bond–Mor prefabricated brick panels. Devitt with the encouragement and active support of Tri–Chem, founded Bonding Systems Incorporated. BSI sold and licensed others to fabricate masonry panels using Bond–Mor.

Tri–Chem promoted Devitt throughout the United States as an authority and spokesperson on certain aspects of Bond–Mor application. Tri–Chem provided Devitt with favorable tests, films, slides, and other promotional material to encourage the sale of BSI franchises throughout the United States thereby increasing the sales of Bond–Mor.

Tri–Chem also utilized Devitt to repair certain structures that had rusted and cracked due to Bond–Mor. In addition, Devitt constructed, with Bond–Mor, the prefabricated brick panels which formed the exterior of the two restaurant buildings of HDE in Kansas.

STRUCTURAL ENGINEER

Julie Kouri

Julie Kouri is a licensed consulting structural engineer engaged in this activity since the mid 1970's. Tri–Chem introduced Kouri to Bond–Mor through oral presentations, telephone conversations, and promotional literature. Tri–Chem also introduced Kouri to architect Eilene Robin to further acquaint Kouri with the capabilities of Bond–Mor.

Kouri was employed as a structural engineer on the building projects of both of HDE's buildings in Kansas. Kouri consulted with a representative of Tri–Chem regarding the design and construction techniques for the buildings made of Bond–Mor prefabricated brick panels.

Tri–Chem's contacts with Kouri extended beyond the Kansas project. Tri–Chem promoted Kouri throughout the United States as an authority and spokesperson for certain aspects of Bond–Mor application. Tri–Chem included Kouri as a co-author, in its literature entitled "Project History: High-bond Mortar Applications," which was distributed nationally. Tri–Chem also promoted Kouri as an outside structural engineer in its literature to encourage the use of Bond–Mor throughout the construction industry.

WITNESS

Donelle Lakemoore

Donelle Lakemoore, a Masonry Engineer and Regional Director for the Structural Products Institute had assisted Tri–Chem in test marketing Bond–Mor. Lakemoore brought to the attention of Tri–Chem evidence that dehydrochlorination causes and accelerates corrosion of steel in contact with Bond–Mor. Lakemoore told representatives from Tri–Chem in early 1988 that recent investigations and field exposures make it necessary to protect steel in or adjacent to masonry from corrosion. Lakemoore showed Tri–Chem officials steel "pencil rods" that were heavily corroded and had been taken from relatively new buildings constructed using Bond–Mor.

RESEARCH MEMORANDUM

TO: Bond–Mor File
FROM: Clyde Irfram, Tri–Chem Researcher
RE: The effects of the proposed mechanism for the basic degradation of Zetes Latex.
DATE: April 3, 1985

After researching the differences between basic mortar and the proposed Zetes Latex product, my conclusions regarding the product are as follows:

The devastating effect in basic mortar of vinylidene chloride polymers is well known. These reactions are rapid and result in a dehydrohalogenation enhance in colored or even black products. The mechanism proposed for the basic degradation of Zetes consists of an attack by the basic component of the acidic hydrogen, accompanied by simultaneous elimination of the chloride atom. In this manner, Zetes differs markedly from basic mortar.

CONFIDENTIAL

Memorandum

TO: Division Managers
FROM: Tri-Chem Research Facilities
RE: The research findings of Dr. W.U. Sun, addressing the Zetes Latex product contained in prestressed concrete.
DATE: July 23, 1985

We recently retained Dr. W.U. Sun to complete a research report entitled: Corrosion of Steel in Prestressed Concrete. During the course of his research, Dr. W.U. Sun discovered and concluded that "Zetes latex should not be used in connection with prestressed concrete." Dr. Sun based this conclusion on the fact that potential dangers of corrosion due to the presence of chloride are greatest in prestressed concrete. Dr. Sun suggested as an alternative product a new latex system that would not release free chloride, and thus deter the corrosion of steel placed in contact with Zetes latex products.

RESEARCH MEMORANDUM

TO: Internal Memorandum
FROM: Tri–Chem Research Facilities
RE: Results of tests designed to measure the durability of latex modified concrete.
DATE: June 21, 1986

We have constructed a test facility to determine the durability of latex modified concrete. We constructed four panels of concrete, each made of different concrete mixture: Panel A contained no Zetes latex; Panel B contained only trace amounts of chloride, the corrosive element found in Zetes latex; Panel C contained 100% Zetes latex; and Panel D contained 50% Zetes latex. The panels were then tested one year later. The metal in Panels A and B, which had not contained any Zetes latex, were found to be clean of rust corrosion. However, Panels C and D, which contained the Zetes latex, were rusted throughout their entire length with deeper corrosion in heavy scale build up.

After observing the effects of corrosion in Panels C and D, we have come to the conclusion that Zetes latex must be the cause of such corrosion. The concrete test lab was not subject to an outside influence, as far as the corrosion of steel is concerned. Consequently, the observed corrosion must have been generated by the conditions within the panels. Since the steel within Panels A and B were clear of rust, and Panels C and D were rusted, we must conclude by process of elimination that the rust was generated internally in the panels and as a result of the Zetes latex product Bond–Mor.

CONFIDENTIAL

Memorandum

TO: Bond–Mor Project Managers Only
FROM: Sonja Belacorte
RE: Research results addressing rust and rust-inhibition in the Bond–Mor product.
DATE: August 6, 1986

It has recently come to my attention that one of our researchers found that steel, placed in contact with mortar containing Bond–Mor, developed rust after just 180 days. In addition, the researcher discovered that corrosion of steel was worse in Bond–Mor mortar than in normal cement mortar.

The researcher also experimented with numerous rust-inhibitors and protective metal coating, most of which worked against Bond–Mor. Over the years, we have experimented with products for sale, many of which are Zetes latex products, including Bond–Mor. Those experiments with Bond–Mor have resulted in the conclusion that when the product is brought into contact with steel it has consistently resulted in corrosion.

TRI–CHEM

May 7, 1987

Dear Masonry Sales Specialists:

In response to inquiries regarding the quality of Bond–Mor, we provide this letter. During the course of extensive experiments, we have discovered that the rates of corrosion of Bond–Mor in and out of mortar are approximately the same for other types of mortar that do not possess the Bond–Mor additive.

We conclude that it is reasonable to say that under a variety of conditions, the corrosion of steel in the two mortars will be about equal. Please do not hesitate to contact us with any further information requests.

Sincerely,

Lucinda Ijima
Marketing Manager

Bond More With Bond–Mor

TRI–CHEM

September 7, 1987

RE: This provides you with up-to-date data regarding the Bond–Mor additive and the corrosion of steel embedded in Bond–Mor mortar.

Dear Architects:

The corrosion of iron is caused by oxygen and water. The Bond–Mor mortar additive contains small amounts of chloride ion which, under certain selective circumstances, can enhance the tendency of mild steel or iron to corrode if oxygen and water are also present.

While chloride ions, which can be leached from Bond–Mor under favorable circumstances, could enhance the corrosion of iron or mild steel, this should have no effect on properly protected metals, such as galvanized materials. If you have further questions regarding the Bond–Mor additive in relation to steel-embedded corrosion, please do not hesitate to contact us.

Sincerely,

Wes Wojcik
Architect Liaison
Tri–Chem

Bond More With Bond–Mor

CONFIDENTIAL

Memorandum

TO: All Tri-Chem Employees
FROM: Carl Blackfoot
RE: Recent research of Bond-Mor product and its corrosive properties.
DATE: February 15, 1988

The Tri-Chem research department conducted a recent study of Bond-Mor and its corrosive properties. The researcher concluded that mortar formulated with Bond-Mor additive was considerably more corrosive to steel than steel embedded in normal mortar. Chlorides released by the degradation of Zetes latex causes depassivation of steel, thus allowing corrosion to proceed.

We have recommended the use of metallic protective coatings, if the structure is frequently in contact with water. Considerably more chloride is being released by Bond-Mor than was expected and protective coatings may be used to ameliorate the corrosion.

TRI–CHEM SALES BROCHURE

1988

After safely testing the effects of adding steel reinforcements to assemblages, Tri–Chem researchers have concluded that:

* Bond–Mor is unique in maintaining greatly improved strains when the cured composition is subject to wet environments.
* With Bond–Mor the performance of structural elements incorporating the system may be completely and confidently predicted.
* Bond–Mor has been safely and sufficiently tested by an extensive and experienced Tri–Chem researcher in state-of-the-art research facilities.

Bond More With Bond–Mor

TRI–CHEM BULLETIN

January 1989

RE: Amendment to Section 9.3 of Bond–Mor use specifications. Distributed as a flyer to be inserted in promotional literature throughout the United States.

All metal anchors, ties, pencil rods, angles, and reinforcing bars for other steels embedded in mortar additives shall be coated with a corrosion resistant metal such as cadmium or zinc, or other such metals having equivalent or better corrosion resistant qualities. Stainless steel shall not be included as having equivalent or better corrosion resistant qualities and therefore should be excluded as an alternative metal.

TRI–CHEM

December 17, 1989

Dear Hot Dog Enterprises:

Re: Response to inquiries regarding Bond–Mor's potential for rust related damage in HDE's Ohio restaurant buildings

In response to your inquiry whether Bond–Mor would rust steel, we wish to provide you with the assurances that from the chemistry of Bond–Mor, cement, and iron, we would expect no contribution by Bond–Mor toward rust related damages. Instead, these properties should inhibit the rust process. Removal of masonry from projects 4 to 7 years old showed no signs of rust. Attempts to force the rusting of steel, under accelerated conditions in the laboratory, have been without success.

We took the time for a thorough study of the problem and are satisfied that Bond–Mor does not contribute to the deterioration of iron reinforcements embedded in Bond–Mor additive mortar. If you wish to make additional inquiries, please do not hesitate to contact us.

Sincerely,

B.J. Wojcik

Tri–Chem Products Manager

Bond More With Bond–Mor

January 12, 1990

Dear Tri–Chem:

I have received a recent letter from the Chairperson to the ACI Committee 531 regarding the concrete masonry structures. The Chairperson stated that it had come to the attention of the Committee that the use of Bond–Mor mortars was causing considerable trouble in the form of steel rusting away in reinforced masonry used in concert with Bond–Mor.

As a member of the Committee, I would appreciate the company's comment of the question thus raised. Please contact me as soon as possible so I might assess the question with all the relevant information. Thank you.

Sincerely,

M.M. Hughes
Consulting Engineer, HDE

TRI–CHEM

November 30, 1990

Dear Casey Pozdak:

Thank you for your letter of October 31, regarding your buildings. It is difficult to comment on the problem at this time, since the report does not give any data addressing potential causes for cracking in the masonry. If you feel there is a "probable product failure, specifically, Bond–Mor," it would be helpful to have some evidence on which this conclusion is based.

As you are aware, there are many different issues involved in what might cause cracking in masonry buildings. The performance of Bond–Mor can be easily checked by removing small pieces of masonry from the areas in question and testing them to determine whether the material is performing as well as it did when the building was constructed. If there is a deterioration in Bond–Mor, we will take prompt action to find the cause of the problem and to rectify it. If the Bond–Mor mortar is performing as it was originally intended, in terms of the strength of the masonry, then I suggest you look for alternative causes to the problem.

Sincerely,

Ngnon Nashwa
Customer Services
Tri–Chem

Bond More With Bond–Mor

Case B

Pozdak v. Summit Insurance Company

Fran Pozdak originally insured his building on 560 Wesley Avenue with Summit Insurance five years ago for $125,000, the fair market value of the building, and the contents of the building (including art works, materials, equipment, and personal property) for a maximum value of $250,000, a high estimate. He made his annual premium payments on time for each of the past five years. Four months ago, two months after he paid this year's annual premium, he increased the coverage on his building to $250,000 and the maximum value of its contents to $1,000,000, a very high estimate. The increased coverage also provided for replacement cost, so that the items would be valued at what it would cost to replace them if they were new, even though they may have only been worth a fraction of their new price.

Five years ago, the Summit Insurance Co. had some concerns about issuing a policy to Pozdak because he had been accused of insurance fraud while in college. Pozdak had claimed that his college apartment had been robbed, and that valuable art work and personal items had been stolen. There were no signs of a break-in at his college apartment, and police never found the allegedly stolen items. He sued his insurance company and settled out of court for about one-third of what he had claimed. Summit Insurance decided to insure though, because the building on Wesley Avenue was relatively new and the college incident was the only suspicious activity at that time discovered about Pozdak.

The following memo was prepared by Brooks Farrell, an investigator with Summit Insurance.

To: Insured File 465Hft46353
Fran Pozdak
From: Brooks Farrell

On Friday, July 3, a fire destroyed the insured's building at 560 Wesley Avenue in Mitchell. The building was owned by the insured, Fran Pozdak, age 32, and used both as a residence and as a business. Pozdak lived in four rooms on the second floor. The first floor included a work area where he sculpted and a gallery where he displayed his work. He bought the building five years ago and has been a sculptor for about ten years.

Pozdak claims that he has acquired a national reputation which substantially increases the value of his art work. This claim does not appear to be supported by reliable sources.

The fire began at approximately 1:30 a.m. Pozdak was not home. No one was injured. The fire completely destroyed the entire building and all its contents. Nothing was salvageable. The Mitchell Fire Department responded to the first call made at 1:45 a.m. by a bar owner in the neighborhood. Five trucks arrived about five minutes later. It took about one hour to control the fire and another few hours to completely put it out. An investigator, Deputy Chief Marcus Tschida, of the Mitchell Fire Department, investigated the site of the fire the morning following the fire.

I contacted him that afternoon and he told me that the origins of the fire were suspicious and that he thought the fire may have been started by an arsonist. He explained that several factors made him suspicious: (1) the "hot spot" (where the fire started) was extensive in nature and the charred remains had evidence of flammable solvents that appeared to be spread over a several hundred square foot area; (2) the fire appeared to have spread very rapidly throughout the building, much more rapidly than usual in a building that was only ten years old; and (3) that Pozdak is in extreme financial difficulties and apparently in need of money.

Deputy Chief Tschida cautioned me that the fire may have been accidental, because Pozdak stored a fair quantity of solvents for his work, the wooden structure would burn down fairly rapidly, and there was no evidence of an "accelerant" in the hot spot (a source of fire such as a torch or a match). I visited the scene of the fire the afternoon of the fire and my observations matched those of Deputy Chief Tschida. Further investigation needs to be done to eliminate other possible causes of the fire (such as electrical circuits).

I also began to investigate the financial status of Pozdak, and I learned that he has difficulty in placing his sculptures in galleries and museums, that he has a drug problem and had eight weeks of treatment six months before the fire which prevented him from sculpting, that he was behind in his mortgage payments on the building, and that he allegedly had back tax problems with both the federal and state governments.

Pozdak told Deputy Chief Tschida when he was interviewed several days after the fire that he was not home that night because he was spending a Fourth of July holiday weekend at a friend's cabin about 100 miles from Mitchell. Pozdak said they had been hiking outdoors that day and that he went to bed early that evening and was asleep when Tschida called him early in the morning about the fire.

I contacted four people during this preliminary investigation:

Stacy Lindberg, the friend whose cabin Pozdak claimed he visited. Lindberg is a very close friend of Pozdak, having gone to high school with him. Lindberg was supposed to have lent Pozdak over $50,000 for sculpting materials which Pozdak still owes him. Lindberg refused to talk to me except to say that we were stuck and would have to pay royally. Lindberg has had financial problems over the years. A commercial credit report indicates that Lindberg has gone bankrupt twice over the past decade with two different corporations and that Lindberg's current financial base is built on an aerobic exercise franchise.

Jan McCulrone, a former employee of Pozdak. Pozdak fired McCulrone several months ago, and she has little regard for Pozdak. She freely talked to me. She told me that Pozdak was in deep financial trouble, that he owed Lindberg and others besides the bank a lot of money, and that his business had fallen off while he was in drug treatment. When he returned he accused her of cheating him by telling him she sold his artwork for less than she actually received and pocketing the difference. The truth was, she said, that Pozdak could not accept the notion that his reputation had been tarnished and he was no longer a regionally recognized artist. She added he never did establish a national reputation for himself. She also told me that she had one conversation with him before she left when he told her that he knew of a way to make money with his building.

John Dodge, a college roommate of Pozdak. He and Pozdak had lived together in the apartment that Pozdak claimed had been burglarized. Dodge said Pozdak only infrequently had left items of art around the apartment during the time they lived together. He said he doubted that a theft had occurred, but he was out of town on the weekend it allegedly occurred. He also said that Pozdak was heavily involved in dealing drugs, and that Pozdak owed a lot of people money all the time. He hasn't heard much from Pozdak since they graduated.

Robin Abercrombie, a bartender at the Wesley Bar, whose owner first noticed the fire. Abercrombie left the bar around 1:30 a.m. and noticed a man getting into a car in the alley which bordered Pozdak's building. Abercrombie generally described the man as about six feet and 200 pounds (which fits Pozdak), dressed in dark clothes. Abercrombie thought he recognized the man as Pozdak because Pozdak frequented the Wesley Bar. Abercrombie described the car as a sports car, probably a new BMW, which Abercrombie noticed because of his interest in buying such a car. Pozdak bought a new BMW last year and owes $15,000 on it.

Pozdak has filed a claim for $250,000 for the building and $1,000,000 for the contents. We initially estimate the replacement cost of the building to be around $200,000. Pozdak has filed a list of sculptures allegedly worth more than $1,000,000. Our insurance policy with Pozdak states:

Payment shall not be made under the terms of this policy for the fire destruction of the insured building and contents if the insured fire was caused by arson and if the insured caused or participated in the arson.

Case C

Miyamoto v. Snow Cat

Mariko Miyamoto was an avid outdoors person. Mariko especially enjoyed winter recreation sports such as skiing and snowmobiling. Mike LaBelle, her husband, did not share her outdoor interests and preferred warm indoor leisure activities. Mariko worked full time as a law school librarian.

On November 8, 198X, Mariko purchased a new Snow Cat snowmobile for $2,380 cash from Sports Enterprises, an authorized Snow Cat retail store in Mitchell. The Snow Cat Company manufactures all its snowmobiles in the state of Coastland. Later that month, after the season's first snowfall, Mariko and her friend, Jill Somerset, who owned a two-year-old Snow Cat, drove to the state of Peakland to snowmobile. Neither of them had obtained a $20 permit to use the trails.

The snow cover varied between a few inches and a foot, although there were sporadic windblown bare patches of ground. Both Mariko and Jill began to snowmobile on marked public land trails. After snowmobiling for about two hours they took a break. Mariko mentioned to Jill how well her new machine ran.

After the break, they decided to veer off the forested land and look for some open land. They raced toward a large open expanse of snow covered pasture at speeds over 60 m.p.h. and approached the crest of a small hill and a barbed wire fence which was the boundary between public land and farmland. The farmer had posted signs about 100 yards apart along the boundary the previous year. Jill claims they never saw any signs.

Jill started to slow down and looked behind to see Mariko continuing straight ahead, past her, at high speeds. Jill yelled a warning, and Mariko shouted back: "The throttle is stuck. I can't slow down." Mariko reached the crest, slammed into the barbed wire, and skidded across some bare earth. She lay there unconscious, her snowmobile destroyed.

Jill straightened out her body and covered her with an extra jacket. Jill then rode to the farmhouse in the distance, had the farmer, J. D. Ojala, call for help, and returned with the farmer to the scene. They loaded Mariko's body on a trailer and left the snowmobile in the field. An emergency helicopter flew to the farm and transported Mariko to the neighboring state of Grassland where she died a few hours later.

Peakland statute prohibits barbed wire fences bordering public lands. No one else except Mariko ever rode her snowmobile. Mike LaBelle retains you the day after the accident.

Statement of Alma Weymuth 10/20/8X
RE: Mariko Miyamoto Page 1 of 1

My name is Alma Weymuth. I worked at Sports Enterprises in Mitchell, Summit, from August 15 through December 15, 198X. I worked there when Mariko Miyamoto bought her Snow Cat snowmobile from Sports Enterprises. I was a mechanic and worked on the snowmobiles. I previously worked for three years at Butte, Peakland as a snowmobile mechanic for Crestridge Winter Sports and repaired Arctic snowmobiles. Before that I spent two years at Peakland Vocational Institute and completed a course in Recreational Vehicle Maintenance.

In the fall of 198X, business was extremely busy for Sports Enterprises. Beginning in October I was working 6 days a week, 10 to 12 hours a day. There was one other mechanic. We could not keep up with the work. We received new snowmobiles in crates and completed assembling them and prepped them when they were sold. We also repaired used snowmobiles.

On several occasions I told Sam Khoulsky, the owner of Sports Enterprises, that we could not complete all the work. He told me sometime in late October to do the best we could, and if we could not do everything, to simply assemble the new snowmobiles and spend less time checking them out. He told us his customers wanted them as soon as possible and he told them he would do his best. Regardless of what he told me I always completed the safety checks on all the new snowmobiles I worked on. I think the other mechanic, Aziz Akan, did what Khoulsky said.

In early November, I overheard a conversation between Sam Khoulsky and Shana Hauser, the factory representative from Snow Cat who was visiting Sports Enterprises. Shana told Sam that some of the Snow Cats may have a problem with the throttle and to make sure they were doubled checked or something. I could not hear everything that was said because Sam closed his office door midway through the conversation. I never heard anything more about it. Sam never said anything to me about any throttle problems.

I do not specifically recall working on Mariko Miyamoto's snowmobile. I made sure that every snowmobile I assembled was safe.

I quit working at Snow Enterprises because I couldn't take the long hours anymore. I now work at Grant's Auto Repairs in Mitchell.

/s/ ______________________
Alma Weymuth
1721 Hopkins Avenue
Mitchell, Summit

Case D

Giacone v. City of Mitchell

Martha Giacone lives in her single family home at 765 Portland in Mitchell. She is 68 years old, receives social security and a small pension from her deceased husband's former employer and owns the home free of any mortgage. She, like all other residents of Mitchell, obtains water from the Mitchell Municipal Water Department. The Department is a municipal corporation organized under the laws of Summit to provide utility services, in this case, water. The corporation is a department of the City of Mitchell. An executive director, Kay Olsheski, oversees the operations of the Department and is appointed by the mayor of Mitchell.

The Water Department has established rules and regulations issued by order of the Executive Director, after public hearing, which detail its billing and collection procedures. Section 5.4 of the Water Department Regulations provides that:

> Water services will be terminated to any subscriber if that subscriber fails to pay a water bill within 30 days after the billing date.

The Water Department bills quarterly. Twice a year Water Department employees visit residences to read water meters. The other two quarterly bills are estimates.

On April 1, Giacone received an $185 water bill based on an estimate of water used. The last time a meter reader read her meter was the previous September. Giacone averaged a bill of about $35 a quarter and this April 1 bill shocked her. She telephoned the Water Department and asked that her meter be read because the estimate was way off. The Water Department employee who answered the phone said a meter reader would be sent out.

Giacone heard nothing until May 10 when she received a postcard from the Water Department stating: "Your water will be turned off in 48 hours unless your bill of $185 is paid by May 12." Giacone again called the water department and this time was told that a meter reader went to her home on April 20, but could not get in and that she had to pay $185 by May 12 or her water would be turned off.

Giacone then suggested that maybe the extremely cold winter caused some pipe to burst underground but was told nothing could be done unless the $185 bill was paid and only then could a meter reader or repair person go to her home. Giacone finally said that she could only pay $35 of the bill and did not have the other $150 but was told that the Water Department had to enforce its policy of terminating for nonpayment.

On the morning of May 13, the Water Department turned Giacone's water off by shutting off a main valve located outside her house. In the afternoon of May 13, Giacone retained you. You telephoned Kay Olsheski who told you that the water would only be turned on if the bill was paid in full plus a $25 service charge, that he had no discretion to suspend the regulations, and that 24 other customers had their water turned off yesterday. The Mayor's office and everyone else refuses to do anything.

Case E

Mitchell Computer Club v. Rainbow Computer

You have been retained by all 27 members of the Mitchell Computer Club. The club was informally organized by purchasers of Rainbow computers, including Ellyn Sutcliffe, Christopher Trout, and Willie Eckersley. Each club member is a resident of Mitchell and has purchased a computer and software manufactured by the Rainbow Computer Company and sold through the Rainbow Computer Company retail store at 2467 Snelling in Mitchell within a three-month period from October to December, 198X.

Each individual paid $750 for the Rainbow Prism Computer and signed a retail installment contract obligating that member to purchase four Rainbow software packages yearly for three years at $125 a program. Rainbow sales personnel told each of the individuals (1) that Rainbow has currently available 20 to 25 varieties of software for business, education, and home use; (2) that Rainbow had plans to produce "hundreds" of software applications over the next three years; and (3) that the Rainbow Prism Computer was "99%" compatible with the IBM PC computer. Pat Palmeter is the sales manager.

After they purchased the computers and at the time of each purchase, all computer club members received the Prism computer (monitor, keyboard, and CPU unit) and one software of their choice from a selection of three. After their purchases, they all learned that Rainbow had developed only ten software game programs, and that the Prism computer is not compatible with the IBM PC because the Prism employs an incompatible operation system, and no manufacturer, not even Rainbow, offers software that works both on the Prism and the IBM PC. Twelve of the individuals have purchased three other software applications from Rainbow during the past year, eight have purchased two, and seven have purchased one.

Case F

Vasquez v. Hot Dog Enterprises

Juanita Vasquez worked as a technical specialist for Hot Dog Enterprises. She earned $8.25 and worked an eight-hour shift from 2:30 p.m. to 11:00 p.m. along with her supervisor, Dan Wankle, and usually eight other nonunion co-workers. She had and has a good work record. She has never received any oral or written reprimands and has not missed any work days, although she has occasionally been late. She is 21 years old and unmarried. She liked her job, but believes she has been sexually harassed and also discriminated against. She recalls several specific instances.

When she first started 12 months ago in September, she complained to Wankle about calendars of nude women posted in the work area. Wankle told her the photos were good for the morale of the male workers and that if she didn't like it, she could buy some calendars of nude men and put those photos up in the women's restroom. The calendars of nude women remain posted through the year.

During this same time period Wankle and other male employees would tell off color jokes about "wetbacks" and "spics." She asked a group of men if they would stop such jokes, and Wankle responded by telling another such joke. The jokes continued over the year.

Sometime during January, Wankle brought to work at HDE a video machine and some "porno" movies for his birthday party. Wankle told Vasquez she had to attend the party in the employee lounge after work or she would be working for some other employer. She went but could not stomach watching the video. She told Wankle she was sick, and as she started to leave he grabbed her by the shoulders, pressed his body against hers, and told her that someday they would be doing what she saw on the videos. Vasquez said, "Never," and Wankle responded by saying then she would "never" get a raise or a promotion. Vasquez does not know whether anyone overheard this conversation.

Over the next few months Wankle seldom talked to Vasquez except to give work orders. A few times she tried to ask him some questions about work hours and vacation time, and he said he could do nothing to schedule her until she was willing to "go all the way." One evening in April after work, Wankle approached Vasquez from behind as she was unlocking her car door in the parking lot. He turned her around grabbed her and tried to kiss her. She pushed him away but he persisted until another employee, Tom, walked by. Vasquez is not sure of Tom's last name, and he is no longer working at HDE. Wankle then walked away saying he preferred white women anyway.

A few days after this episode Wankle met with Vasquez for her first and only written work evaluation. Wankle had a file and some papers but never referred to the documents. He said that Vasquez could get a really good evaluation if only she would change her attitude and loosen up. She asked what he meant, and he said, "You know what you have to do," and ended the meeting.

Vasquez then decided to complain about what Wankle was doing. She went to Robert Clune, Wankle's supervisor, and told him about the birthday party and the April incident in the parking lot. Clune responded by saying the company was not responsible for what happened after work hours between employees and that he would talk to Wankle. Vasquez started to ask about her evaluation when Clune's telephone rang. He said he would ask Wankle about the evaluation and get back to her. He never did so, and Vasquez did not ask him again because she thought Clune sided with Wankle.

Since that incident, Vasquez was the only employee in her department not to work any overtime, and she still has not had any vacation time approved by Wankle. She never received any salary increase since she began working. The five men who worked with her and did the same work all received more money, at least $10 an hour, and one of them had been there only six months. Two other women, Anne Godfrey and Pam Obuten, who also did the same work have been working there about four years and each earned $9.00 an hour.

The last incident Vasquez recalls involved a newly hired woman employee, Nancy Smith, in her department. After a month on the job Smith told Vasquez that Smith had just gotten a salary increase to $8.50 an hour. When Vasquez asked how she managed that, Smith replied that she had gone all the way with Wankle. She said she did so because she needed the money for her two kids.

Vasquez put up with all this because she thought it would be the same any place she worked and because she was working to earn enough money for college. She decided to do something further in August and again told Robert Clune everything that happened to her. He then investigated her complaints and fired Wankle on the basis of the information from Vasquez. Vasquez is still working at HDE in a different department at the same salary.

Subsequently, Vasquez told her story to a newspaper reporter who printed her story in the Mitchell *Chronicle*. She also told the personnel manager of Maplewood Technics who contacted her and then decided not to hire Wankle for a $30,000 a year supervisor job for which Wankle was otherwise qualified and had applied.

Dan Wankle denies harassing or discriminating against Vasquez. He admits hanging up a calendar of women dressed in bathing suits over his desk but denies there were any nude photos or that he ever told Vasquez to post calendars of nude men anywhere. He recalls on a few occasions that when he was in a group of men he would tell ethnic jokes. He told jokes about all races, including his own nationality; he said he used jokes to help make the work atmosphere more comfortable. He was careful never to tell such jokes in the presence of women because he did not feel it was the proper thing to do. If Vasquez heard these jokes it was because she eavesdropped.

He remembers his birthday party. It was another employee and not he who brought an X-rated videotape. The tape was shown after hours, and anyone who wanted to leave did not have to attend. In fact, two of the employees in the department did not stay. He admits he might have tried to dance with Vasquez to some radio music but denies ever suggesting anything sexual to her. He also recalls an incident in the parking lot when Vasquez yelled for help because some guy was trying to grab her. He ran over to help her but by that time the guy had run off. He did not know who it was, and Vasquez thanked him for trying to help.

During his evaluation conference with her, Wankle says he pointed out some problems she was having with her job. She made more errors than any other employee and did not seem to care about her work. He told her he was not going to write anything negative down because he wanted to give her another chance to improve. He had not said anything negative to her previously because it was only in the last few weeks before the meeting that her work really began to deteriorate. She asked for a raise and to work overtime. He said, "Only if your work improves." She then told him that she would go out with him and go to bed if he gave her a raise and overtime. He said no and ended the conference. He told no one what she had said because it embarrassed him. He did not schedule her for overtime because her work did not improve. He had no control over vacations or salary increases.

Wankle is a deeply religious man, a deacon in his church, married with six children, and has never had anyone file any complaints against him before. Wankle has not found a job since he was fired. He would have been hired by Maplewood Technics if Vasquez had not told her story to the personnel manager (and the newspaper reporter).

Case G

LaBelle v. Mitchell Arts Council

On February 15, Terry LaBelle was offered a 30–week, full-time position for $400 a week at Mitchell Arts Council, Inc., a non-profit Summit Corporation, to review the operations of the Council's departments and to make written recommendations to improve the efficiency and effectiveness of the Council's administration. LaBelle accepted and began employment on March 1 and received her paychecks every two weeks for the first ten weeks.

At the end of May, she was informed by Fran Barnoff, the Director of the Arts Council, that he would unfortunately have to discharge her immediately because the funding for her position had been terminated in the Council's new budget. She left immediately but did not receive any paycheck for the 11th and 12th weeks of work.

On June 15, she contacted Wilma Quigley, President of the Board of Directors for the Arts Council, and asked her to intervene. Quigley refused. Also on June 15, LaBelle called Barnoff and asked him for two weeks' pay plus the balance of her 30–week contract. Barnoff told her that there were no funds to pay her.

LaBelle made reasonable attempts to obtain employment from June through October but was unsuccessful. She was not eligible for unemployment compensation and had no other source of income during this time.

She retains you in November. Attached is a copy of Summit Statute § 181.13.

181.13 PENALTY FOR FAILURE TO PAY WAGES PROMPTLY

When any person, firm, company, association, or corporation employing labor within this state discharges a servant or employee from his employment, the wages or commissions actually earned and unpaid at the time of such discharge shall become immediately due and payable upon demand of such employee, at the usual place of payment, and if not paid within 24 hours after such demand, whether such employment was by the day, hour, week, month, or piece or by commissions, such discharged employee may charge and collect the amount of his average daily earnings at the rate agreed upon in the contract of employment, for such period, not exceeding 15 days, after the expiration of the 24 hours, as the employer is in default, until full payment or other settlement, satisfactory to the discharged employee, is made.

Case H

Luger v. Shade

Mack and Meg Luger, farmers from Wheatfield, Summit, have begun to think about retiring to a warmer climate, enjoying life, and letting their son take over the farm and share the joys and tribulations of earning a living from the earth. The Lugers fly to Pine Island, Beachstate in response to an enticing ad placed in the Wheatfield Chronicle by Develco, a resort condominium developer well known for its planned sunbelt retirement and recreational home communities.

Seeing Pine Island is love at first sight for the Lugers. They are particularly charmed by suave and debonair Sam Shade, Develco's top agent over the past five years, someone who makes other sales persons look shy and retiring. Swept away by the beauty of Pine Island, the townhouses, the tennis courts, the pool, the rec center, and the lack of farm implements on the horizon, the Lugers instantly make an offer on a $90,000 condo townhouse shown to them by Shade. Shade seems to have run out of preprinted purchase agreement forms, but closes the sale on a handshake accompanied by his receipt of the Lugers' check for $4,500. Shade promises to fill out the forms that week and ship them to the Lugers for their signatures.

The Lugers return home Monday morning ready to change life overnight. Shade has assured them that the house, virtually complete upon their visit, will be ready in two weeks. The Lugers formally sell most of their land to son George, who has steadfastly helped Dad and Mom on the farm while son Brant became a city slicker lawyer and a great disappointment to Mom and Dad. Luger leases one-fourth of the land to a neighbor for ten years, knowing that George alone can not farm all of the family spread of 1600 acres. George sells his home in town to the town's new bank loan officer and moves into his parents' home, which he has agreed to purchase on a contract for deed.

During this time, Meg begins to wonder about Shade's delay in delivering the townhouse documents. She calls Shade, who apologizes, but assures her that the papers are all but mailed. Meg advises him to hold the papers while the Lugers drive to Pine Island, where they will stay in a hotel for a day or two until the townhouse is finished. Shade agrees and confirms the date of the townhome's availability.

At this time, Shade has already been approached by Gary Gotbucks, an investment banker about to retire at age 45. Gotbucks and his wife are equally taken with the townhouse

Haydock,Fund.Pretrial Lit.3E -24

sought by the Lugers, and Gotbucks offers Shade $100,000 for it. Shade replies that the property is tentatively sold. Gotbucks increases his offer to $130,000, plus $5,000 for Shade under the table, and Shade accepts. They sign a standard Develco purchase agreement. Shade tears up the Luger agreement he had started to type.

When the Lugers arrive, Shade tells them that a terrible mixup resulted in the sale of their townhouse by another Develco agent before Shade could draw up the papers. He gives the Lugers $3,000 of their earnest money with interest and offers to pay their traveling expenses to and from Pine Island. Mack Luger flattens Shade with one punch and then stalks to the townhouse to take it by adverse possession only to find Gotbucks throwing a lavish housewarming party. The Lugers have a couple drinks and call their lawyer.

Case I

Rheinwald v. Whirling Dervish Lathes

Gunnar Rheinwald is a woodworker in Grove, Forestland. He makes custom-made cabinets and furniture and does good, but not outstanding, original work. He runs his own shop out of the back room of his home. In 1981, he bought a new lathe from Whirling Dervish Lathes (WDL) for $6,400. Gunnar ordered the lathe from the WDL mail order catalogue that he picked up at a trade show in Gotham, Gothamland. WDL sends the catalogues directly to potential customers in some states but not Forestland. WDL is headquartered in Peakland, with plants there and in Gulfland. Its sales force travels throughout the United States, with occasional stops in Forestland.

One day at work in early 1982, Gunnar's sleeve got caught in the lathe and his arm was badly mangled. Muscles, ligaments, and tendons were torn but no bones were broken. He was taken immediately to the local hospital emergency room. The injury required surgery, six weeks in a cast, and more than a year of supervised physical and rehabilitative vocational therapy. He was unable to work for ten months and even today has only an 85 percent recovery of use of the arm. However, after 15 months, he was able to do his woodworking with the same skill as before the accident.

The lathe, although ordered directly from WDL, was actually installed by Shop Format, a jobber located in Gotham, which is 140 miles from Forestland. Shop Format failed to install the safety cover designed for the lathe. WDL did not provide the safety cover with the lathe delivered to Rheinwald. The Shop Format installer failed to send the instructions provided by WDL which described the safety cover.

Gunnar's home shop would have flunked an Occupational Safety and Health Act (OSHA) inspection, but his one-man operation is not subject to OSHA regulations.

The WDL lathe was designed by Craftwerker Engineering of Mitchell. Craftwerker regularly mails flyers and other promotional mailings into Forestland but has never performed services there and has never sent any of its employees into the state. It does, however, belong to an engineering promotional group headquartered in Forestland's largest city. Gunnar paid WDL $1,400 but has not paid the $5,000 balance.

Case J

Northern Motor Homes v. Danforth

CASE SUMMARY

Northern Motor Homes, the plaintiff, sold a motor home to Joan and John Danforth, the defendants, on a retail installment contract. They received a written warranty from Northern covering the motor home.

The defendants subsequently experienced problems with the camper and failed to make their installment payments. The plaintiff declared default, accelerated the payments, and brought this action for breach of contract. The Danforths counterclaimed, alleging breach of warranty. The complaint seeks $9,510 and attorney's fees; the counterclaim seeks $15,000 plus additional damages.

The case file includes:

1. Factual Summary
2. Complaint
3. Retail Installment Contract
4. Answer and Counterclaim
5. Exhibit A, Limited Warranty
6. Reply to Counterclaim
7. Legal Memorandum

FACTUAL SUMMARY

Joan and John Danforth had long wanted to own a camper motor home. On May 24, 19XX, they read an advertisement in the Mitchell Sunday Press by Northern Motor Homes advertising a new 20–foot motor home on sale for $17,300. They drove the ten miles from their home to Northern Motor Homes on the next day with their two young children. Sara Duncan, a salesperson, showed them the Voyageur camper and gave them a descriptive brochure. The Danforths looked over the camper and brochure and then asked to take a test drive. During the ten-minute drive, they recall that Duncan explained that the motor home would get "16 miles a gallon on the highway," that financing could be readily arranged, and that Northern Motor Homes had an "experienced" service department and an "extensive" parts department. Duncan recalls explaining that the camper would get "6 to 8 miles per gallon on the average," that financing was available, and that Northern had an "experienced" service and parts department.

The Danforths agreed to buy the motor home, paying $8,000 down and financing the balance. Duncan obtained approval of the financial terms from Mitchell National Bank, and the contract was executed on May 25. Duncan told the Danforths that the camper would be checked, serviced, and ready the next day. On May 26, the Danforths picked up their new camper and drove home. A written limited warranty and an owner's manual were provided, but the Danforths received no oral instructions on how to operate the motor home.

On the way home, the Danforths noticed that the automatic transmission slipped a bit when shifted, but because of their unfamiliarity with the camper, they did not become concerned. On the weekend of June 1–3, they took a 240–mile camping trip. They checked their gas mileage and found they only got 8 miles to the gallon. They paid an average of $1.20 a gallon. They also noticed that the transmission continued to skip and developed a jerk. John called Duncan, who explained that the gas mileage was always lower during the initial break-in period and that as long as the transmission was not leaking oil it could be checked at the 1000–mile maintenance inspection.

The next Friday, June 8, they drove 100 miles to a campground. That night, all the interior lights and electrical outlets in the camper went dead. The Danforths stayed at a $41 motel that night and drove home on Saturday. The transmission problems persisted, and the gas mileage did not improve. About 20 miles from home, the engine temperature gauge indicated "hot" and the camper stalled. Joan turned off the engine and checked the coolant level, which appeared to be sufficient. Joan then tried to restart the engine but failed, and after several minutes the battery gradually lost its power. It cost the Danforths $30 to have the motor home towed to Northern Motor Homes. They had a friend drive them home. Bill Burke, the service manager, called the Danforths on June 13 and told John that the electrical parts needed to repair the camper were not available, so it would not be ready until June 22. On June 15, the Danforths received a letter and payment book from Mitchell National Bank.

Joan picked the camper up on June 22 with no charge for repairs. Burke had not determined the cause of the electrical problem, but he thought that the Danforths overloaded the electrical circuits. Burke discovered that the temperature light was defective and supposed that Joan had flooded the engine while trying to restart it and so had drained the battery. When Burke test-drove the camper, he did not notice any transmission problems. Burke does not recall the Danforths mentioning any gas-mileage problems. The cost of the warranty repairs was $376.

The Danforths left on June 22 for a weekend camping trip 150 miles away. The engine and electrical system worked, but the transmission still slipped and jerked, and the gas mileage did not improve. While camping on Saturday, the water system failed to drain completely. While driving home Sunday, the front brakes developed a squeal. That Monday, June 25, John telephoned Burke, who said the service department was very busy until after the July 4th holiday, but they could bring the camper in for repairs if they wanted. Burke recalls that the service department was busy, but he does not recall that telephone conversation with John. The Danforths, who wanted to use the camper for another planned weekend camping trip, decided to wait until the 1000–mile inspection and reluctantly sent their June $229.02 payment to the bank.

On June 29, they began a 130–mile camping trip. On that Friday drive, the windshield wipers broke. On Saturday while preparing dinner, the propane stove burst into flames. John used a fire extinguisher to douse the fire, but not before the stove and refrigerator units were extensively damaged. No one was injured. The Danforths stayed in a $43 motel that night and returned home Sunday. They took the camper in Monday and complained to Burke.

Burke called the Danforths on July 10. He informed them that the camper had been repaired and inspected at no charge. It was his opinion that Joan's and John's unfamiliarity with the camper had caused the problems. He considered charging them for these repairs ($743), which he believed were not covered by the warranty, but, to preserve good customer relations, he decided against doing so. He did advise them to read carefully and follow the owner's manual. The Danforths told him that their vacation began on July 20, that they planned to drive through rough country roads, and that the camper must be working properly for this one-week trip.

They picked the camper up on July 10 and drove it 90 miles around town for ten days; everything seemed to operate well, though the gas mileage was still low. On July 20, they left for their vacation campgrounds 150 miles away. After driving 70 miles on paved roads and another 80 miles on unpaved roads, the transmission problems reappeared. On Saturday morning, Joan started the engine, but the oil warning light remained on. John checked the oil level and found none measured on the dipstick. They refilled the engine with six quarts of oil at $1.30 a quart. By adding another four quarts, they managed to drive the camper back home. On Monday, they had it towed to Northern Motor Homes and called Duncan to cancel the contract and to complain about their lost vacation. They spent the remainder of their vacation at home.

One week later, on July 30, they received a letter from Northern Motor Homes refusing to cancel the contract, asserting that the oil leak was due to their misuse of the camper on rough roads that had damaged the crankcase, and offering to make the needed engine repairs for an estimated $620 at their expense. The Danforths wrote back, demanding the return of their down payment, their June payment, and reimbursement for $340 of camping accessories usable only with that camper. Two weeks later, on August 13, they received a letter from Mitchell National Bank demanding the July payment. John wrote to the bank explaining their refusal to pay. On August 25, he received a telephone call from Duncan, who said the bank had returned the contract to Northern, and she demanded the July and August payments. The Danforths refused to pay and were served with a summons and complaint on August 31.

Northern Motor Homes sued for the balance of the retail installment contract and did not repossess the motor home. The camper remains unrepaired in the Northern service lot. Northern Motor Homes claims the Danforths own the camper; the Danforths claim they have revoked acceptance.

COMPLAINT

State of Summit
County of West

District Court
First Judicial District

Northern Motor Homes, Incorporated,
Plaintiff,

vs.

John and Joan Danforth,
Defendants.

COMPLAINT
File No. 338217

Plaintiff for its Complaint states and alleges that:

1. On May 25, 19XX, Plaintiff and Defendants entered into a retail installment contract for the purchase of a new 19XX Voyageur camper, a copy of which contract is attached to this Complaint.

2. Defendants failed to make the July and subsequent installment payments and have defaulted on the contract.

WHEREFORE, Plaintiff requests that this Court enter judgment against Defendants in the amount of $9,510.33, plus reasonable attorney's fees, interest, and costs and disbursements.

Dated: August 29, 19XX

DOTEN AND KRAUSE

By: ________________

Lee Krause

Attorneys for Plaintiff

1000 First State Bank

Mitchell, Summit

789–1234

RETAIL INSTALLMENT CONTRACT

RETAIL INSTALLMENT CONTRACT Date: *May 25, 19XX*
Number: *JC505*

John and Joan Danforth
1479 Laurel
Mitchell, Summit

Northern Motor Homes, Inc.
875 Grand Avenue
Mitchell, Summit

New	Year	Make	Model	Motor Home	Vehicle No.
Yes	19XX	Voyageur	20 foot	Camper	BN 481BB569

2. Down Payment		
A. Cash	$8,000.00	
B. Trade-in	$	
C. Sub–Total		$ 8,000.00
3. Unpaid Balance of Cash Price		$ 9,300.00
4. Other Charges:		
A. Tax	$ 418.50	
B. License & Title Fees	$ 80.30	
C. Credit Life	$	
D. Credit Disability	$	
E. Credit Life & Disability	$	
F. Property Insurance	$	
G. Document Filing Fees	$ 16.50	
H. Sub–Total		$ 515.30
5. Unpaid Balance (3 + 4H) AMOUNT FINANCED		$ 9,815.30
6. Finance Charge		$ 3,925.90
7. Total of Payments (5 + 6)		$13,741.20
8. Total Sale Price (1 + 4H + 6)		$21,741.20
9. ANNUAL PERCENTAGE RATE		14.13

REPAYMENT SCHEDULE: Buyer promises to pay the Total of Payments to Seller in *60* installments of *$229.02* each, commencing on *June 25, 19XX* and continuing on the same day of each following month until paid.

Seller: Buyer(s):

CONTRACT TERMS

1. DELINQUENCY CHARGES: Seller may collect from the Buyer in the event any installment shall not have been paid within 10 days after it becomes due, delinquency charges in the amount of 5% of the delinquent installment or $5, whichever is less.

2. SECURITY INTEREST: Seller shall have a Security Interest, as the term is defined in the Uniform Commercial Code of the state in which this contract is executed, in the property until all amounts due under this contract are paid in full.

3. REBATE: Upon default or prepayment by Buyer, a refund credit will be computed in accordance with the Rule of 78's and the laws of the State of Summit.

4. DEFAULT AND ACCELERATION: If Buyer defaults in any payment, or fails to comply with the terms of this contract, or if Seller deems Buyer insecure, Seller shall have the right, at its election, to declare the unpaid portion of the Total of Payments of this contract to be immediately due and payable.

5. ATTORNEY'S FEES: Seller shall be entitled to reasonable attorney's fees from Buyer in an amount equal to the fees and costs incurred by Seller in collecting from Buyer under this contract.

6. ASSIGNMENT: This contract may be assigned by Seller at its option without the approval or consent of Buyer. The assignee assumes all rights and obligations under this contract pursuant to the laws of the state of Summit. After notification of an assignment, Buyer shall make all payments directly to the assignee.

ANSWER AND COUNTERCLAIM

State of Summit
County of West

District Court
First Judicial District

Northern Motor Homes, Incorporated,
Plaintiff,

vs.

ANSWER AND COUNTERCLAIM
File No. 338217

John and Joan Danforth,
Defendants.

Defendants for an Answer to Plaintiff's Complaint state and allege:

1. Defendants admit paragraph 1.

2. Defendants deny paragraph 2 and all other claims of the Complaint.

AFFIRMATIVE DEFENSE AND COUNTERCLAIM

3. Plaintiff by statements, representations, conduct, advertisements, brochures, descriptions, and a written warranty provided Defendants with express and implied warranties covering the 19XX Voyageur Motor Home. A copy of the written warranty is attached as Exhibit A.

4. Plaintiff breached such warranties.

5. Defendants subsequently revoked acceptance of the Voyageur.

6. The remedies provided by Plaintiff have failed in their essential purposes.

7. Defendants have incurred actual, incidental, and consequential damages approximating $15,000 and have suffered additional damages for lost vacation and leisure time in an amount to be determined at trial.

WHEREFORE, Defendants demand that Plaintiff's Complaint be dismissed and that Defendants be awarded a judgment in an amount to be determined at the trial of this case plus reasonable attorney's fees, interest, and costs and disbursements.

Dated: September 22, 19XX

LANO AND FISKE

Terry Fiske
2000 Federal Bank Building
Mitchell, Summit
345–9876

EXHIBIT A
LIMITED WARRANTY

Limited Warranty — Voyageur Motor Home

Northern Motor Homes, 875 Grand Avenue, Mitchell, Summit, warrants each new camper according to the following terms:

1. TIME. This warranty extends for 12 months from the date of purchase or 12,000 miles, whichever occurs first.
2. SERVICE. Northern Motor Homes will repair or replace, at its option, any part defective in material or workmanship.
3. NO CHARGE. Warranty repairs will be made without charge for parts or labor.
4. LOCATION. Warranty service will be provided by Northern Motor Homes at any authorized Northern Motor Homes dealer during normal business hours.
5. EXCLUSIONS. This warranty does not cover:
   (a) Normal maintenance, services, and parts used in connection with such services.
   (b) Repairs necessitated by accident, misuse, negligence, unsuitable alterations, or use not intended for the camper.

NORTHERN MOTOR HOMES DISCLAIMS ANY RESPONSIBILITY FOR ANY INCIDENTAL OR CONSEQUENTIAL OR OTHER DAMAGES OR REMEDIES EXCEPT THOSE PROVIDED FOR IN THIS WARRANTY. ANY IMPLIED WARRANTIES ARE LIMITED TO THE DURATION OF THIS WARRANTY.

Some states do not allow limitations on how long an implied warranty lasts or do not permit exclusion of limitations of incidental or consequential damages, so the above limitations or exclusions may not apply to you.

This warranty gives you specific legal rights, and you may also have other rights which vary from state to state.

NORTHERN MOTOR HOMES, INCORPORATED
APRIL 19XX

REPLY TO COUNTERCLAIM

State of Summit District Court

County of West First Judicial District

Northern Motor Homes, Incorporated,
Plaintiff,

vs.

REPLY TO COUNTERCLAIM
File No. 338217

John and Joan Danforth,
Defendants.

Plaintiff for its Reply to Defendant's Counterclaim states and alleges that:

1. Plaintiff admits that it provided Defendants with the written limited warranty attached as Exhibit A to the Answer but denies providing any other warranties.

2. Plaintiff denies all allegations contained in paragraphs 3, 4, 5, 6, and 7 of the Counterclaim.

WHEREFORE, Plaintiff requests that the Counterclaim be dismissed.

Dated: October 2, 19XX

DOTEN AND KRAUSE

By: __________
Lee Krause
Attorneys for Plaintiff
1000 First State Bank
Mitchell, Summit
789–1234

LEGAL MEMORANDUM

This memo summarizes some of the case law, statutes, and consumer-transaction practice in the State of Summit relevant to the litigation in Northern Motor Homes v. Danforth. Your instructor may prefer to have the law of another state apply and will advise you accordingly.

1. The State of Summit does not have a statutory retail installment sales contract act. The state does have an interest-rate statute that permits the assessment of the 14.3% annual rate contained in the Summers contract.
2. Summit has adopted the Uniform Commercial Code.

(a) Article 2 involving warranties and remedies was adopted verbatim. Implied warranties may be limited to the duration of an express written warranty. Remedies for incidental and consequential damages may be limited if they do not fail in their essential purpose.

(b) Article 9 involving security interests was modified to require a secured party (Northern Motor Homes) to elect a remedy: either the party must repossess the secured property (the camper) or sue for the unpaid balance. The statutory amendment eliminated deficiency judgments.

(c) Summit statutory law prohibits the use of waiver-of-defense clauses in retail installment contracts. An assignee assumes the identical rights and obligations of the assignor, except that the assignee becomes liable to the Buyer only in an amount equal to the contract balance at the time of the agreement.

3. The agreement between Northern Motor Homes and Mitchell National Bank allowed the bank to cancel the assignment and return the contract to Northern if the consumer defaulted on contract payments.

4. The $9,510.33 amount included in the complaint is the unpaid balance of the contract plus delinquency charges, less a refund credit computed as explained in Contract Term 3.

5. The attorney for the Danforths has determined that:

(a) The Limited Warranty conforms to the Federal Warranty Act.

(b) The credit disclosures comply with the provisions of the Federal Truth in Lending Act.

Case K

Burris v. Warner

CASE SUMMARY

Lynn Burris, the plaintiff, was riding a motorcycle on Oak Avenue and collided with a car driven by the defendant, Abby Warner, at the intersection with Elm Street. The plaintiff, a law student, suffered head and shoulder injuries. The defendant, a security officer, suffered facial and back injuries. There were two witnesses to the accident. The plaintiff sued the defendant based on negligence, and the defendant counterclaimed on the same basis. Both the complaint and the counterclaim seek damages in excess of $50,000.

This case file includes:

1. Complaint
2. Answer and Counterclaim
3. Reply to Counterclaim
4. Traffic Accident Report
5. Medical Records of Lynn Burris from Midway Hospital
6. Medical Records of Lynn Burris from Samaritan Clinic
7. Medical Records of Abby Warner from Mitchell Clinic
8. Legal Memorandum

The lawyers for Burris and for Warner obtained a copy of the Traffic Accident Report from the police and voluntarily exchanged medical reports without resort to any formal discovery device.

The Supplement contains additional, confidential facts for each party.

COMPLAINT

State of Summit
County of West

District Court
First Judicial District

Lynn Burris,
Plaintiff,
vs.
Abby Warner,
Defendant.

COMPLAINT
File No. 338417

1. On March 31, 19XX, at the intersection of Elm and Oak in Mitchell, Summit, Defendant, while driving an automobile, negligently collided with Plaintiff, who was riding a motorcycle.

2. As a result, Plaintiff was injured, was unable to attend law school, suffered severe and continuing pain, was unable to lead a normal life, and incurred expenses for medical attention and the damaged motorcycle.

WHEREFORE, Plaintiff demands judgment against Defendant in an amount in excess of $50,000 plus costs and interest.

Dated: June 1, 19XX

NOVACK & McCONNELL

Kay McConnell
100 First State Bank
Mitchell, Summit
789–4321

ANSWER AND COUNTERCLAIM

State of Summit
County of West

District Court
First Judicial District

Lynn Burris,
Plaintiff,
vs.
Abby Warner
Defendant.

ANSWER AND COUNTERCLAIM
File No. 338417

1. Defendant denies the allegations of paragraphs 1 and 2 of the Complaint and all other claims of the Plaintiff.

AFFIRMATIVE DEFENSE AND COUNTERCLAIM

2. On March 31, 19XX, at the intersection of Oak Avenue and Elm Street in Mitchell, Summit, Plaintiff, while riding a motorcycle, negligently collided with Defendant, who was driving an automobile.

3. Defendant suffered physical injuries and continuing pain, was unable to work and perform normal activities, and incurred damages for medical and automobile expenses.

WHEREFORE, Defendant requests that Plaintiff receive nothing and that judgment be entered against Plaintiff in an amount in excess of $50,000 plus costs and interest.

Dated: June 20, 19XX

LA RUE AND SINCLAIR

Kyle Sinclair
200 Federal Bank Building
Mitchell, Summit
340–6789

REPLY TO COUNTERCLAIM

State of Summit District Court
County of West First Judicial District

Lynn Burris,
Plaintiff,
vs.
Abby Warner,
Defendant.

REPLY TO COUNTERCLAIM
File No. 338417

1. Plaintiff denies all allegations of Defendant's Counterclaim.

Dated: June 26, 19XX

NOVACK & McCONNELL

Kay McConnell
100 First State Bank
Mitchell, Summit
789–4321

TRAFFIC ACCIDENT REPORT

MEDICAL RECORDS OF LYNN BURRIS FROM MIDWAY HOSPITAL

MIDWAY HOSPITAL

Pt. Name: Lynn Burris
Pt. No.: 251125

Date	Narrative
3–31–XX	Chief Complaint: Shoulder abrasion and "neck pain."
	History: Patient is a 25-year-old who was just admitted thru receiving with injuries from motorcycle accident. Patient was riding cycle, which struck a car and impacted the pavement with enough force to split open cloth jacket, injuring the shoulder. In addition, the head and neck were "bent back." Current complaint is "my head's throbbing." No loss of consciousness. Patient was wearing a helmet.
	Past Medical History: Usual childhood diseases; no allergies; on no medications.
	Physical Examination: Pulse 96; blood pressure 118/66; respiration: 16; temp. 98.4° (oral).
	Head: Neck appears normal with full range of motion; no masses. Head free of lesions. Eyes, nose & throat normal.
	Chest: Normal.

Date	Narrative
	Heart: Regular at 96. No murmurs.
	Abdomen: Normal.
	Extremities: Deep red weeping 10 × 10 cm. excoriation of right acromion. Lesion is literally packed with sand and asphalt and clothing particles. Full range of motion only with extreme difficulty. Other assorted superficial epidermal abrasions.
	Neurologic: Cranial nerves normal. Reflexes moderate and symmetrical. Mental status: alert & oriented to time, place, & person.
	Impression: Deep dermal abrasion to right shoulder.
	X-rays: (1) right shoulder—negative; no fracture or separation. (2) head and cervical spine—normal; no fractures.
	Plan: Admit for irrigation and dressing of right shoulder abrasion. Observe for possible central nervous system effects. Meds: Codeine 10 mg. every 4 hrs. as needed for pain.
	Took patient to treatment room. Irrigated wound and debrided away (nearly) all of the particulate debris. Patient somewhat uncooperative because of significant discomfort.
4/1 9:00 AM	Redressed patient's wound. Moderate continued serous weeping of the surface with early crust formation. No sign of infection.
	Patient complains of acute headaches and severe neck stiffness and pain. Physical exam confirms this. There is tenderness in the neck area; markedly decreased range of motion as noted yesterday. Cervical musculature very firm to palpation; consistent with spasm and/or ligamentous damage.
	Plan: Discharge home. Codeine 10 mg. every 4–6 hrs. for pain. Robaxin 1 gram 4 times/day for muscle relaxation. Bedrest. Patient to see me in clinic in 3 days. E.B.
4/5	Physical therapy to relieve complaints of cramps in neck. Exam revealed firmness in muscles and limited motion. Treatment consisted of 10 min. massage, 20 min. of hot pads, 10 min. of ultrasound. P.T.
4/7	Treatment repeated. Patient still having cramps and spasm. Marked decrease in muscle firmness after therapy. P.T.
4/9	Treatment repeated. Patient's cramps and spasm receding. Continued decrease of firmness after therapy. P.T.

Date	Narrative
4/11	Treatment repeated. Patient comfortable. Significant decrease in muscle firmness. P.T.
4/13	Final treatment. Patient had no cramps and spasms since last treatment. Exam revealed full motion without pain and no muscle binding. Patient discharged. P.T.

MEDICAL RECORDS OF LYNN BURRIS FROM SAMARITAN CLINIC

SAMARITAN CLINIC

Pt. Name: Lynn Burris Office File: B13–117

Date	Narrative
4/4/XX	Patient returns four days after motorcycle accident with continuing complaint of headache, shoulder abrasion, and neck stiffness. Physical Exam: Shoulder injury healing well with good crusting. No evidence of infection. Redressed. Neck: Fair range of motion; residual but decreased tenderness and firmness. Plan: (1) Physical therapy with heat/massage and ultrasound every other day for 5–7 days. (2) Continue Codeine and Robaxin. (3) Return in 14 days.
4/18/XX	Shoulder healing well. Continues to complain of head and neck pain. Will discontinue meds. Patient to take aspirin 5 grains up to 8/day. Patient discharged from care. Return as needed.
5/1/XX	Patient continues to complain of occasional neck and head pain. Cannot read or watch TV for over 30 minutes without symptoms (unrelieved by aspirin). Shoulder: Looks good. A few particles of debris "tattooing" injury area. Slight loss of pigmentation.
5/15/XX	Still complaining of head and neck ache. Physical exam of area negative. Patient will use heat for muscle spasm. Advised to sleep without a pillow.

MEDICAL RECORDS OF WARNER FROM MITCHELL CLINIC

Patient: Warner
Clinic File: N31F37
Doctor: Harris

MITCHELL CLINIC

Date	Explanation	Initials
3/31/XX	26-year-old involved in minor car accident with motorcycle. Patient driver had 2.5 cm. laceration over left zygomatic arch and complained of lower-back discomfort. Exam: Pulse 98, blood pressure 122/70; no allergies; on no medication. (1) Laceration as above caused by impact with car door. (2) Low back pain without radiation to lower extremities. Reflexes normal. Diagnosis: (1) moderate laceration. (2) low back pain Plan: (1) Close with 1% Xglocaine anesthesia and steri-strips. (2) Tetanus toxoid i.m. (3) Bed rest for back strain. (4) Return in seven days for suture removal or earlier if back pain persists.	E.H.
4/2	Patient returns. Back pain has increased. Unable to sleep or find comfortable position. Exam: Low back tenderness. Reflexes normal. No indication of any organic cause of pain. Patient had no history of back pain. Straight leg raising test indicates decreased range of movement and low back pain. Sore musculature in lumbar region consistent with accident damage to low back. Laceration healing well. Impression: Marked increase in back pain. Plan: (1) Darvon compound 65 for pain. (2) Back exercises. Instructed in low back exercise plan to be done every day. (3) Return for suture removal or as needed.	E.H.

Date	Explanation	Initials
4/6	Patient back for suture removal. Scar prominent but should improve in appearance over time. Patient continues to complain about low back pain. Unable to comply with exercise regimen. Exam reveals continued soreness in lumbar region.	
	Recommend attempting ten-day traction-stretching program with B. Leoni in Physical Therapy.	E.H.
4/7	Patient begins traction program. Hung by upper body in harness for 30 min. at 50° angle. Complained of low back discomfort.	P.T.
4/8	Patient hung for 30 min. at 60° angle. Low back pain continues.	P.T.
4/9	Patient hung for 30 min. at 70° angle followed by five min. of low back stretching exercises. Discomfort present.	P.T.
4/10	Patient hung for 30 min. at 80° followed by ten min. of stretching exercises. Pain decreasing.	P.T.
4/11	Patient hung for 30 min. at 90° followed by 15 min. of stretching exercises. Periodic low back pain remains.	
4/11	Program appears to be working. Soreness and tenderness in low back receding. Back pain subjectively diminishing. Analgesics ended.	E.H.
4/12	Patient hung for 45 min. at 90° followed by 15 minutes of exercises. Pain reducing in intensity.	P.T.
4/13	Patient hung for 45 minutes at 90° and for two one-minute periods at 135° upside down on traction unit. 15 minute exercises continued. Limited pain persists.	P.T.
4/14	Patient hung for 45 min. at 90° and for two 90–second periods upside down at 180°. Exercises continued. Pain gradually lessening.	P.T.
4/15	Patient free of pain since yesterday. Hung 45 min. at 90° and for three 90–second periods at 180°.	
	Exercises completed without pain.	P.T.
4/16	No complaints of pain. 45 minutes of 90° hanging and 5 minutes 180°. Exercises completed without pain.	P.T.
4/17	Exam revealed normal musculature in lumbar region. Reflexes normal. Leg raising tests revealed full motion and only slight pain. Advised patient to continue 15–minute daily exercises for two months. To return at that time.	E.H.

Date	Explanation	Initials
6/25	Patient complains of some low back discomfort and inability to perform strenuous activity. Exam revealed no apparent soreness or tenderness. Musculature, reflexes, and movement normal. Patient will probably continue to suffer subjective pain. Aspirin will relieve discomfort. Recommend continuing exercise program for three more months and return only if condition regresses. Patient discharged.	E.H.

LEGAL MEMORANDUM

This memo summarizes some of the case law and statutes of the State of Summit and other information relevant to the litigation of *Burris v. Warner*. Your instructor may prefer to have the law of another state apply and will advise you accordingly.

1. The State of Summit has a modified Comparative Fault Act, which bars a claimant from recovery if the fault of the claimant is greater than the fault of the person against whom recovery is sought. Therefore, contributory negligence is not an absolute bar to recovery.

2. Summit case law has recognized the doctrine of last clear chance. It is not clear whether that doctrine continues to be recognized after enactment of the Comparative Fault Act.

3. Summit does not place any limits on the type or amount of damages sought by the parties.

4. Summit does not have a "no-fault" act that applies to this case.

5. The Summit Safety Code:

(a) Requires that motorcycle headlights be on whenever a motorcycle is driven on the street.

(b) Does not require motorcyclists to wear helmets.

(c) Does not require automobile drivers or passengers to wear seatbelts.

(d) Provides that the person driving on a through street has the right of way.

6. Evidence of any breach of a safety-code statute, including a speeding violation, is admissible as evidence of negligence but does not constitute negligence per se.

7. Summit law does not require the drivers involved in an accident to file accident reports if the police have done so.

8. The federal Department of Transportation requires all motorcycle helmets manufactured or sold in the United States to comply with published safety standards. The Department does not certify helmets, but it does randomly check helmets to determine if they meet the standards. Failure to comply with the DOT regulations renders the manufacturer subject to a civil lawsuit by the government seeking injunctive relief and a monetary penalty.

9. The stopping distance for a Honda Silverwing from 30 m.p.h. is 33 feet; and from 60 m.p.h. it is 140 feet.

Index

References are to Sections.

†